# REASONING *AND* WRITING WELL

CANADIAN EDITION

A RHETORIC,
RESEARCH GUIDE,
READER AND
HANDBOOK

**Betty Mattix Dietsch**
*Marion Technical College*

**Lara Sauer**
*George Brown College*

**Andrea Lovering**
*Georgian College*

 **McGraw-Hill Ryerson**

Toronto  Montréal  Boston  Burr Ridge, IL  Dubuque, IA  Madison, WI
New York  San Francisco  St. Louis  Bangkok  Bogotá  Caracas
Kuala Lumpur  Lisbon  London  Madrid  Mexico City  Milan
New Delhi  Santiago  Seoul  Singapore  Sydney  Taipei

# McGraw-Hill
# Ryerson

Reasoning & Writing Well
Canadian Edition

ISBN: 0-07-088822-1

1 2 3 4 5 6 7 8 9 10 VH 0 9 8 7 6

Printed and bound in the United States of America

Care has been taken to trace ownership of copyright material contained in this text; however, the publisher will welcome any information that enables them to rectify any reference or credit for subsequent
editions.

Editorial Director: Joanna Cotton
Sponsoring Editor: Karen Ritcey
Marketing Manager: Marc Trudel
Developmental Editor: Christine Gilbert
Editorial Associate: Marina Seguin
Supervising Editor: Jaime Smith
Copy Editor: Jim Zimmerman
Senior Production Coordinator: Paula Brown
Cover Design: Greg Devitt
Cover Image: Gettyone/Roz Woodward
Interior Design: Greg Devitt
Page Layout: Bill Renaud
Printer: Von Hoffman Press Inc.

Library and Archives Canada Cataloguing in Publication

Dietsch, Betty M.
    Reasoning & writing well: a rhetoric, research guide, reader and handbook/Betty Mattix Dietsch,
Lara Sauer, Andrea Lovering.—Canadian ed.

Includes index.
ISBN 0-07-088822-1

    1. English language—Rhetoric—Textbooks. 2. Report writing—Textbooks. 3. Reasoning—Text-
books. 4. College readers. I. Sauer, Lara II. Lovering, Andrea III. Title.

PE1408.D538 2006        808'.042        C2006-901027-7

# Contents in Brief

# Contents

# Preface

Reading, critical thinking, and writing skills are cornerstones of an education—not just for the elite but for everyone who aspires to attain a college diploma or university degree. A fourth cornerstone, oral presentation skills, has been identified recently by many colleges and universities. These skills serve as the foundation of a successful career as well as a solid higher education: to gain credibility in the workplace, employees need to be able to present their ideas cogently and convincingly, both in writing and speaking.

To help students meet and exceed the requirements of their schools and employers, *Reasoning and Writing Well* is a practical and comprehensive process-based rhetoric that demystifies the art of writing well. This book emphasizes not only analytical reading and thinking but also accuracy and ethics. The central goals of *Reasoning and Writing Well* are to enable students to:

- Write with a purpose or an aim that considers the rhetorical situation
- Write clearly, concisely, and accurately
- Use language appropriately and correctly
- Develop an awareness of their voices as writers
- Research a topic using a variety of print and electronic sources, including the Internet
- Document sources correctly
- Read and think critically
- Analyze and evaluate logically and objectively
- Give a presentation before an audience
- Appreciate the value of effective writing and speaking

The philosophy of *Reasoning and Writing Well*, Canadian Edition, is based on the authors' belief that students at all levels of preparedness can be motivated to do their best through encouragement and clear instruction.

# FEATURES OF THE CANADIAN EDITION

As four books in one, *Reasoning and Writing Well* provides exceptionally comprehensive coverage and abundant learning aids. Its features include the following:

## Canadian Content

Canadian content has been added throughout Parts 1-7, including examples, references, and anecdotes. The language throughout the text has been revised and condensed. Chapter summaries have been revised and boxed to be more visually appealing to students. The "Ten Ideas for..." feature at the end of each chapter has been revised and updated to better reflect Canadian culture and values. In Part 3, the "For Your Reference" boxes have been revised and updated to reflect changes in Part 8-The Reader. In Part 4, the Case Study boxes have been revised and updated. The MLA and APA sections in Part 5-Research Writing have been revised and updated to include Canadian examples and sources. Part 8-The Reader has been reduced to 24 readings to make it more accessible to both instructors and students. New exercises and several readings, including an essay by David Suzuki have been added.

## Oral Presentation Chapter

—Separate chapter on public speaking helps students incorporate audiovisual aids into presentations, and guides them in making an effective presentation based on their chosen topic.

## Expansive Research Coverage

—Provides students with detailed coverage on MLA and APA documentation, tips on conducting Internet research, and avoiding plagiarism.

## Critical Thinking and Argumentation

—The four chapters on this topic provide students with comprehensive coverage on critical thinking, evaluation, problem solving, detecting logical fallacies, and shaping effective arguments.

## Revision Workshop

—With five chapters focused on this important skill, *Reasoning and Writing Well*, Canadian Edition, provides the most extensive revision coverage available in a 4-in-1 text. Connects the role of critical thinking to the revision process.

## Workplace Connections

—Throughout the text, examples are drawn from the workplace and everyday life as well as from academic situations in order to increase the material's relevance to students. Offers opportunities for discussion and writing.

## Rhetorical Strategies

—The rhetorical situation is introduced in Chapter 1 and reinforced throughout the book, including related activities. Students are asked to consider elements of the rhetorical context such as the audience, purpose, and occasion. Separate chapters cover each major method of development and progress from prewriting to proofreading, providing step-by-step instruction for each stage of the writing process.

**Reader**—Twenty-four engaging essays, representing diverse authors and points of view, make up the Reader. C. S. Lewis, David Suzuki, Amy Tan, and Robert Sheppard are among the authors included.

**Concise Handbook**—Students can find quick answers to common questions about grammar, punctuation, mechanics, spelling, and usage, and can refer to numerous examples. The Handbook makes reference to related chapters in the text that explain punctuation, sentence structure, and usage.

## Pedagogical Features:

- **Learning Objectives**—outline what students will learn from each chapter

- **Text Boxes**—help students deepen their understanding while strengthening their skills

- **Self-study questions** (with answers at the end of the chapter)—help students strengthen their understanding of concepts and processes, analyze situations, and explore other points of view

- **Practice** (questions, exercises, case studies)—provide a wealth of resources for individual and collaborative learning

- **Ten Ideas for . . .**—provide students with a list of ideas for further writing projects to enhance their understanding of the material.

## Superior Service

Your Integrated Learning Sales Specialist is a McGraw-Hill Ryerson representative who has the experience, product knowledge, training, and support to help you assess and integrate any of the below-noted products, technology, and services into your course for optimum teaching and learning performance. Whether it's helping your students improve their grades or putting your entire course online, your *i*Learning Sales Specialist is there to help you do it. Contact your local *i*Learning Sales Specialist today to learn how to maximize all of McGraw-Hill Ryerson's resources!

McGraw-Hill Ryerson offers a unique *i*Services package designed for Canadian faculty. Our mission is to equip providers of higher education with superior tools and resources required for excellence in teaching. For additional information visit http://www.mcgrawhill.ca/highereducation/iservices.

## Instructor's Resources:

**Instructor's Online Learning Centre**—The Online Learning Centre at www.mc-grawhill.ca/college/dietsch includes a password-protected Web site for Instructors. The site offers a downloadable Instructor's Manual and access to PageOut, the McGraw-Hill Ryerson Web site development Centre.

Visit www.mhhe.com/pageout to create a Web page for your course using our resources. PageOut is the McGraw-Hill Ryerson Web site development centre. This Web page-generation software is free to adopters and is designed to help faculty create an online course, complete with assignments, quizzes, links to relevant Web sites, and more—all in a matter of minutes.

In addition, content cartridges are available for the course management systems **WebCT** and **Blackboard**. These platforms provide instructors with user-friendly, flexible teaching tools. Please contact your local McGraw-Hill Ryerson *i*Learning Sales Specialist for details.

## Student Resources:

**Student Online Learning Centre**—This powerful electronic learning aid, located at www.mcgrawhill.ca/college/dietsch includes interactive student exercises, grammar exercises, Weblinks, tips on avoiding plagiarism, directories for Internet research, study skills, bonus chapter on Employment Writing, and much more.

## Acknowledgements

The Canadian edition would not have been possible without the support of innumerable contributors, including the editorial staff at McGraw-Hill Ryerson and the reviewers of this edition. For their helpful and perceptive feedback, our thanks go to the following colleagues:

Anita Agar, Sheridan College
Cynthia Beech, Georgian College
Sarika Bose, University of British Columbia
Deborah Bridge, Mount Royal College
Crystal Hurdle, Capilano College
Heidi Jacobs, University of Windsor
Moira Langley, Kwantlen University College
Peter Lovrick, George Brown College
Lisa Richardson, Lakehead University
Rhonda Sandberg, George Brown College
Rhonda Schuller, University College of the Fraser Valley
Betti Sheldrick, Mohawk College
Andrea Westcott, Capilano College

Lara would like to thank her students, past and present, who make teaching fun. And finally, for their unfailing support and encouragement, Lara thanks her family: her parents (mom for her on-the-money teaching advice!), her husband Deon, and her son Daniel.

Andrea would like to thank her husband, Cliff, and her daughters, Nadine and Amelia, for their unwavering support in achieving her goals.

Lara Sauer
George Brown College

Andrea Lovering
Georgian College

# THE WRITING SITUATION AND EARLY STAGES OF THE WRITING PROCESS

Part 1

# CHAPTER 1

# Writing in Context

---

**Learning Objectives**

After reading and applying the information in Chapter 1, you'll be able to:

- Identify and analyze the context of your writing (i.e., the rhetorical situation): the occasion, your purpose, topic, audience, and voice
- Identify the four stages of the writing process

---

> *Freedom to be your best means nothing unless you're willing to do your best.*
>
> —Colin Powell, *Priorities*

## WHY LEARN TO REASON AND WRITE WELL?

Various surveys have found that white collar workers spend from 10 to 70 percent of their time writing. For example, a study conducted at California State University at Chico found that technical graduates, "regardless of their job duties, all spend half or more of their career time writing." Skill in writing is crucial for succeeding in college and for advancing a career.

Whether you relish or dread writing or range somewhere in between, *Reasoning and Writing Well* will guide and encourage you to do your best. You'll learn shortcuts to ease the tasks of transferring thoughts from mind to paper and of developing ideas. You'll sharpen both your thinking and writing skills, and refine your ability to reason logically, solve problems, write persuasively, and conduct research. You will learn how to consider a given writing situation and to draft and revise accordingly. You won't be like Calvin who has confused the purpose of writing and misjudged his audience.

## WHAT IS THE RHETORICAL SITUATION?

Every piece of writing has a context or circumstance surrounding it—referred to as the *rhetorical situation*. Basically, this term refers to the way words

CALVIN AND HOBBES © Watterson. Reprinted with permission of Universal Press Syndicate. All rights reserved.

are used in regard to five elements: the *occasion, writer's purpose, topic, audience,* and *writer's voice.* All five elements of the rhetorical situation influence the effec tiveness of writing. (Purpose and audience, in particular, will be emphasized in the chapters to come.) If a writer neglects any of the elements, the writing may ramble, go astray, or miss the mark. The primary goal—to communicate—will not be attained.

## Occasion

The occasion is the event, condition, or need that causes you to write. You may write an apology for hasty words, a thank you for a birthday gift, or an e-mail to a friend to keep in touch. On the job your writing may spring from a client's need, a problem with a supplier, or another complication that requires a written response. Or your job may require regular record keeping and reporting. Different occasions call for different writing strategies. To consider the occasion of your writing, ask yourself: "What is expected?" "What is appropriate?"

## Purpose

Purpose refers to a writer's motive, or reason for writing, which can be stated or implied. Purpose has two aspects: general and specific.

***The General Purpose***    Writing has four general purposes: *to inform, to persuade, to express,* and *to entertain.* More often than not, these general purposes are combined in various ways. For example, most writing is intended to inform, but also has a secondary persuasive element—to convince the reader that it is factual and reliable. Other writing is primarily persuasive, designed to argue a point and secure agreement, yet is also informative. The degree of persuasion varies according to the occasion, purpose, and audience.

Some writing is primarily expressive, allowing the writer to reveal feelings and opinions, usually recalling experience. Expressive writing often takes the form of personal essays, journal writing, diaries, poetry, fiction, or plays. Yet writing may also be expressive to a lesser extent in a business letter, report, or proposal, depending upon the rhetorical situation.

Although some humourous writing seems intended merely to entertain, it may also make a serious point. The clever use of humour can advance a point, as in the writing of Mark Twain or Stephen Leacock. A light-hearted approach captures the attention of readers and makes them more willing to listen. To be successful, humour must not be heavy-handed or derisive—otherwise, it may backfire.

***The Specific Purpose***    To be clear, writing should have a specific purpose. Your instructor may assign a general purpose for a paper, but usually you will choose the topic, the specific purpose, and the audience. Jotting down your specific purpose and audience early will help you select, sort, and shape ideas so that they unite and flow toward a conclusion that is appropriate to the rhetorical situation.

## Topic

In the workplace, as well as in daily life, topics for writing spring from real situations—perhaps late payment of a bill, an incorrect shipment, or a progress report for a contractor. Then you have a specific rhetorical situation to respond to and little, if any, need to narrow the topic. If you have work experience, you may be able to base college papers on topics from those experiences. If not, you might draw from other experience, such as travel, hobbies, or unusual events or people, always remembering to limit a broad topic to one specific purpose.

Whether you draw details from your own experience or research, or seek answers at the library or on the Internet, this book will show you how to proceed.

### SELECTING A TOPIC

The first guideline for successful college writing is to **select a topic you care about**. The second is to **narrow the topic** so that you can focus on one main idea and develop it well for your audience.

## Audience

The writer's *audience* is composed of readers. To accomplish your purpose, you should recognize, respect, and respond to your readers' needs. Knowing characteristics of their backgrounds, interests, and viewpoints will help you to choose a suitable topic and devise an appropriate writing strategy. The more you can learn about the person or group who will be reading your writing, the more effective you can make it. *Writing that is addressed to no one in particular will lack a sense of purpose.*

In the workplace, your readers are probably people you have met or talked to on the telephone or communicated with via email. These readers may be customers, wholesalers, service personnel, or others. In the classroom your instructor may assign an audience or suggest you write for an audience of your classmates. Otherwise, you might visualize a typical reader and write directly to him or her. If puzzled, ask yourself, "Who would be likely to read this writing?"

A helpful strategy for your audience is to deliberately shift your perspective from writer to reader. Try to put yourself into the reader's role—to feel and think as the reader might.

If a writer ignores readers and neglects their needs, they will respond by ignoring the writing. A keen awareness of how readers think and feel will assist you in shaping your writing purpose and in finding an appropriate *voice*.

See Chapter 2.

---

### QUESTIONS TO ASSESS AUDIENCES

1. *To whom am I writing?* What do I know about the age, gender, education, social class, economic status, interests, and attitudes of the readers? How should these characteristics influence my writing?

2. *Why will they read this piece of writing?* How can they benefit? Will they gain information? Be entertained? What else?

3. *How much do they need or want to know?* How much can I assume they already know about the subject? What terms should be defined? How much should I say?

4. *How might they feel about the subject?* How will their feelings affect my word choice and strategy?

5. *How will they react to my point of view?* How should their probable reaction affect my approach to the topic?

---

## The Voice of the Writer

The *writer's voice*, the sound behind the words, is an important part of the rhetorical situation and affects how the audience will respond to a piece of writing. Your written voice is influenced not only by your knowledge, experience, beliefs, and biases, but also by how you feel about the act of writing, the reader, and the topic. For example, your written voice may sound confident or unsure, encouraging or critical, or approving or sarcastic. Actually, a writer has many voices that vary according to the rhetorical situation. To adapt your writing voice to a rhetorical situation, you might begin by asking yourself three questions:

- How much do I know about the topic? Will I need to do research?
- Can I write objectively about the topic?
- What level of formality is appropriate to the audience and occasion?

See page 12.

***How Should a Writer's Voice Sound?***    To be respected by your readers, you need a written voice that not only serves your purpose but also reflects preparation, sincerity, integrity, and (at times) empathy for the audience. Readers expect competence and trustworthiness, and they usually are quick to recognize incompetence, insincerity, arrogance, or dishonesty.

To better understand voice in writing, think about what you do when chatting with a friend face to face: You automatically adapt your voice to the occasion. Your tone is pleasant and friendly. You welcome your friend by your manner *and* your words. When writing informally, you might think of the reader as a friend and use a similar tone. Of course, not all writing carries the mark of a writer's personality.

In between the conversational voice and the academic voice, there are different voices that vary in the degree of formality. For college essays, you will be expected to have a clear, knowledgeable voice, not academic, but not too informal either. For research papers, teachers often expect an *academic voice*.

***Word Choice and Voice***    Seasoned writers select words that are appropriate to the occasion, purpose, and audience. They also listen to the meaning and the music of the words. Precise words specify exactly what you mean. Little surprises in sounds dispel dullness and delight the reader. To evaluate the voice of your writing, read it aloud. How does it sound?

See Chapters 2 and 9.

To help you avoid needless frustration and learn how to start writing easily, here is an overview of the writing process.

## WHAT IS THE WRITING PROCESS?

Although not a set procedure, the writing process has been observed as having five distinct stages. Writers often shuttle back and forth between stages. Rarely is writing a neat linear procedure, even though it may seem so if you have thought long about a subject. In general, every writing process includes prewriting, drafting, revision, and editing/proofreading. Part 1 of this book focuses on the early stages of writing—prewriting and drafting. Part 2 focuses on concerns that arise during revision and editing.

Although there is no one way to write, there are ways to make writing easier and more effective, and you will find them as you traverse through this book. An excellent way to gain confidence is to dispel any myths you may have heard about writing processes. Then you will be less likely to become entangled in the "perfect draft" approach, expecting to perfect each sentence the first time. This method is tedious and exasperating. Those who use it proceed at a snail's pace.

Nor will you be lulled by the false belief that inspiration alone can transform a first draft into a final draft without several revisions. High-quality papers require much more than an hour or two of effort. They require considerable thought and multiple revisions.

## THE FOUR STAGES OF THE WRITING PROCESS

### PREWRITING

This first stage of writing is simply setting forth ideas in whatever shape or form that is handy for you—fragments, lists, or sentences. The purpose of prewriting is to get ideas down on paper (or disk).

### DRAFTING

In the second stage of writing, you transform ideas into sentences in a semi-organized manner. Here the purpose is to let your ideas develop, expand, and form links. Drafting is primarily a stage of discovery and exploration.

See Chapters 5, 6, 7.

### REVISION

Although revision is classified as the third stage of writing, it is ongoing—recurring whenever needed. During revision your goal is to rethink ideas, refine, and develop them. You may drastically reorganize the draft. During this time, you reshape ideas—expanding, deleting, and clarifying.

See Chapters 5, 8, 9.

### EDITING/PROOFREADING

The final stage requires examining ideas, details, words, grammar, and punctuation—attending to matters *within each sentence*. Here the emphasis is not only on accuracy and correctness but also on clarity.

## SUMMARY

- Writing well is a learned skill.
- To write effectively, consider the rhetorical situation, which has five elements: the occasion, purpose, topic, audience, and writer's voice.
- There are four stages of writing: prewriting, drafting, revision, and editing and proofreading. Awareness of these stages can save you time and avoid frustration in the long run.

## *Practice*

**Collaborative Case Problem: Responding to a Rhetorical Situation**

*Directions:* Last night you went to a party off campus. Three students spray-painted parked cars, but you just watched. Soon the police arrived, sirens screaming. The culprits threw down their paint cans and blended into the crowd. One can rolled up to your feet, so you tossed it into the nearest trash can. Police questioned by-standers and noticed an orange smudge on your index finger. They handcuffed you and three guys who had a fine mist of paint spray on their faces (the wind was blow-ing) and took you to the station. The three confessed; you were released. In a letter how would you tell the following persons of the incident?

1. Your guidance counsellor
2. Your best friend, who is doing her student teaching in a nearby town
3. Your parents

## Ten Ideas for Freewriting

*Directions:* Identify and discuss an interesting object, event, pastime, or thought. Perhaps the suggestions below will foster an idea.

1. My ideal job
2. A memorable concert
3. An interesting one-day trip
4. Thoughts of a people watcher
5. A great moment in . . .
6. My closest friend
7. An unusual experience
8. My earliest memory
9. My most thought-provoking experience
10. How to make a mixed CD (or something else)

# Different Voices for Different Occasions and Audiences

---

**Learning Objectives**

After reading and applying the information in Chapter 2, you'll be able to:

- Determine the appropriate voice for a given rhetorical situation
- Identify the three levels of Standard English usage and apply the appropriate level of formality in your writing

---

*True ease in writing comes from art, not chance,*
*As those move easiest who have learn'd to dance.*
*Tis not enough no harshness gives offence—*
*The sound must seem an echo to the sense.*

—Alexander Pope (1688–1744)
*Essay on Criticism*

Alexander Pope knew that for writing to be effective, it should be appropriate to the audience, and the sound should be consistent with the meaning. These two guidelines apply not only to poetry, but also to letters, reports, and college papers. A carelessly worded message may carry a negative tone that could undermine the purpose and antagonize readers.

In the workplace and in college classes, you will be expected to write appropriately according to the occasion, purpose, reader, and topic. To fulfill this expectation, you must observe conventional rules of usage and grammar and use an appropriate voice for the rhetorical situation.

## THE WRITER'S VOICE

Voice is the presence of the writer as perceived by the reader. Behind the words of every piece of writing is the distinctive sound of the writer's voice. This voice—which radiates from word choice, phrasing, and sentence style—reveals an attitude toward the reader and the topic. The writer's voice is like a mirror

9

that reflects not only the writer's authority on a topic but also his or her mindset and personality.

As writers develop proficiency, they listen to the voice of their writing. They consider not only the literal meanings of the words but also the shadowy nuances—the subtle shades of meaning and feeling that accompany words. Some words sound prickly; others crack like a whip. Some are as soft and soothing as a lullaby. A writer's choice of words, level of formality, and attitude greatly influence how the audience perceives the message.

A writer has many voices; for example, let's listen to the three different voices in this series of collection letters.

## WORKPLACE CASE STUDY

### A Series of Collection Letters

Just as the occasion and status of the reader change in each stage of the collection process, so too the writer's voice changes. As the urgency for payment escalates, the concern for the customer's feelings lessens. (Company policies vary.)

#### *Stage 1.* Cheery Reminder
(Assumption: Customer overlooked and will pay.)

Are you enjoying that lovely walnut desk you purchased on April 12? Will you please look around on it for your bill—which seems to have been overlooked.

Your payment is now six weeks overdue. If payment has already been mailed, please disregard this reminder. If not, take a minute to write a cheque for $55.00, the amount of your first month's payment.

#### *Stage 2.* Firm Request for Payment
(Assumption: Pressure needed to collect.)

For many years, you have been one of our preferred customers. We appreciate your patronage and your promptness in sending past payments. You have been fair and responsible; you have kept your credit in mint condition.

But now that A-1 rating has begun to slip away. You are two months behind on the walnut desk, purchased April 12. To protect your credit rating, stop by and pay the $110 (two payments) this week.

#### *Stage 3.* Demand
(Assumption: Warning needed to motivate payment.)

Your credit rating is in serious danger! The payments on the desk, bought April 12, are three months overdue. To clear this obligation and avoid dealing with a collection agency, send payment of $165 today.

If you are unable to clear the entire obligation, we would like to help you. To discuss an alternative payment plan, call us at (800) 555-9891.

> ***Stage 4.* Ultimatum**
> (Assumption: Customer may not pay.)
>
> Unless payment is made within TEN DAYS of the above date, your bill will be turned over to a collection agency. A payment of $220 will clear your obligation for the desk, purchased April 12.
>
> YOU CAN STOP THIS ACTION! Call us now at (800) 555-9891.

## HOW CASUAL CONVERSATION DIFFERS FROM FOCUSED WRITING

Although a speaker uses various voices in casual conversation, the spoken voice tends to be more friendly and less purposeful than the written voice, particularly in focused writing. Casual conversation ambles along at a leisurely pace, often wordy and repetitive at times, perhaps punctuated by witticisms. Often fragmented and abbreviated, it may become sidetracked and never get to the point. The speaker may omit transitions and significant information. When this happens, the listener may frown, raise an eyebrow, or ask a question. Then the speaker has the opportunity to backtrack and explain.

By contrast, even when focused writing is informal, it has a logical order—steadily advancing toward the point to be made. Since few writers have the chance to observe nonverbal feedback or to ask questions of the reader, they must exert more effort than conversationalists to be clear, complete, and diplomatic. To be effective, writing must be more specific, concise, and thorough than casual conversation. The writer must carefully monitor words to avoid causing offence. The writer's voice should sound knowledgeable, kind, and trustworthy.

## STANDARD AND NONSTANDARD USAGE

With each technological advance, new words flow out over the airwaves and into cyberspace. Dictionary publishers scramble to keep up with the flood of new words by bringing out revised editions every few years. To maintain a semblance of order, they classify words in various ways according to usage. All dictionaries have two broad categories of usage—standard and nonstandard.

### Standard Usage

To sound knowledgeable, a writer needs a command of standard usage. Most English words are standard usage, meaning they are widely accepted by educated speakers and writers. These words follow conventional spellings and rules of grammar. Standard usage varies widely, ranging from informal to formal words.

If a word in the dictionary has no usage label, then it is standard. Note that some words have several meanings, both standard and nonstandard. So if you use the word, be sure to apply it in the context you intend. Some dictionaries provide examples showing standard usage. If a word is used primarily in conversation, it will be labelled *colloq.* or *colloquial.*

Sometimes the status of words changes; a word can gain or lose acceptance or acquire new meanings. For example, the word *punk* has several colloquial or slang meanings, but once *punk* was used to refer to a style of dress and music, it became standard English. Often language is a mixture of the informal and formal, technical and nontechnical.

## Nonstandard Usage

Although nonstandard words are sometimes used to lend a sense of realism to poetry and fiction, they are generally inappropriate in college and workplace writing. In fact, Bloomberg, the financial news and data company, filters electronic messages written by anyone who uses the company's desktop terminals. When profanity or ethnic, racial, or gender slurs are typed, a warning appears, and the user must reword the message before it can be sent.

***Dialect and Regionalism***   Words that are limited to a geographic area are identified as *dialect* or *regional.* Dialect is the natural way some folks talk, using colloquialisms such as "hit the road," regionalisms such as "down the road a piece," and fractured grammar such as "didn't never" or "them books." This usage can be difficult to understand; sometimes it is nonstandard. Although dialect is incorporated into some writing to suggest regional or informal speech, it should be avoided in academic papers and business writing.

## Three Vocabularies

A factor that complicates word choice for beginning writers is that most of us have three distinct vocabularies that have varying levels of formality—one for speaking, one for writing, and one for reading. The spoken vocabulary is the smallest and least formal; rough drafts are often written at this level. The vocabulary for writing lies somewhere in between those of speaking and reading. Your final draft, after being revised several times, should contain this middle level, which uses standard words and grammar.

The reading vocabulary is the largest, most specific, and most formal. Sometimes students pull words from this vocabulary or use a word found during research but do not look up the meaning. This practice can result in confusion and error. Awareness of the different levels of formality and your own three distinct vocabularies can help you select an appropriate voice for each rhetorical situation.

## THREE LEVELS OF FORMALITY

In workplace and college writing, three levels of formality—Informal English, Professional English, and Formal English—are used. All three levels follow the conventional rules of grammar. The level a writer selects depends upon the rhetorical situation. The level of formality influences the sound of the writer's voice.

## LEVELS OF FORMALITY

| Nonstandard | | Informal English | Professional English | Formal English |
|---|---|---|---|---|

*Least* _ _ _ _ _ _ _ _ _ |_____ *Most*
*Formal*                                                                        *Formal*
(nonstandard grammar)|              (standard grammar)

## Informal Standard English

Although Informal Standard English may include a well-placed fragment, the verb forms, pronoun agreement, and other grammatical structures are always standard.

Informal Standard English is the language of conversation. You read Informal Standard English in many popular magazines, novels, short stories, poems, comics, ads, newspaper articles, and other writing. A *Wall Street Journal* article entitled "In 24-Hour Workplace, Day Care Is Moving to the Night Shift" uses Informal Standard English in the opening paragraphs:

> There are plenty of places to sleep at the Children's Choice Learning Center here, but nine-year-old Najah Finch isn't napping. Wearing a pink "I am Boy Crazy" T-shirt, she cartwheels around the floor, breaks for juice and popcorn, then settles down at the TV for a Muppet video. Najah's mom isn't due to pick her up for another three hours.
> At 3:30 a.m.
>
> —Barbara Carton

Did you note the conversational voice and the fragment "At 3:30 a.m."? Other clues to informality include the contraction *isn't* and the colloquial use of *mom* (mother). There are different varieties of Informal Standard English; for instance, many business letters and printed materials require all sentences to be complete. The voice may be a bit more formal, as in Stuart M. Berger's *What Your Doctor Didn't Learn in Medical School:*

> The word *hypoglycemia* is the kind of six-syllable medicalese word that my patients hear and tell me: "That's Greek to me, doctor." Well, in the case of this word, it really is Greek! But just in case your ancient Greek is a tad rusty, let's review: *hypo* means "too little"; *gly* is the Greek root for "sugar"; and the suffix *-emia* means "of the blood." String them together, and you have "too little sugar in the blood." (The disease is the polar opposite of diabetes, which creates too much sugar in the blood.)

***Watch the Pronouns***    Did you notice Dr. Berger's use of the first-person (*me*) and second-person (*your*)? This usage is typical of Informal Standard English. Although Professional English and Formal English sometimes include the first

See page H-20 in the Handbook.

person [*I, me, mine, we, our, us*], it is only for a good reason. As a rule, these two levels do not include second person when written. In an oral presentation, second person is desirable since you will be talking directly to an audience—and you will probably mix levels of formality.

## Professional English

Professional English marks a writer as well-educated and knowledgeable. Certain audiences in the professional world (of business, higher education, and literature, for example) expect a more serious, reserved, and authoritative voice than that found at the informal level.

The hallmarks of Professional English are complete sentences, correct grammar, and standard word choice. This level of usage is found in many newspaper articles, textbooks, business reports, annual reports to stockholders, and much academic writing, including research papers. In the article on twenty-four-hour daycare, Barbara Carton's voice changes in the fourth paragraph, where she switches to Professional English. (Note that there are no contractions or informal words.)

> As more single parents and working couples cope with a 24-hour economy, day care is making an uneasy transition to night care. Employers are building round-the-clock centers to attract and keep employees. State and local governments are also supporting extended-hour and night-care initiatives, partly because they feel obliged to help the single mothers they sent to work under welfare reform.

## Formal English

You may be familiar with Formal English. If enrolled in prelaw, paralegal, education, premed, nursing, data processing, engineering, or other such programs, you may read Formal Technical English in your textbooks. Or you may work in a profession where it is spoken and written daily.

| LEVELS OF FORMALITY IN THE WORKPLACE | | |
|---|---|---|
| *Informal Standard* | *Professional English* | *Formal English* |
| memos | memos, email | legal notices, letters |
| customer letters | bulletins | proposals |
| newsletters | newsletters, letters | laws, statutes |
| sales talks | bids, proposals | legal documents |
| letter reports | professional reports | technical reports |
| informal speeches | presentations | formal speeches |
| conversation | policies | policies |
| newspaper articles | contracts, forms | contracts, forms |
| email | manuals | technical documents |

Formal English may include foreign phrases, literary allusions, and specialized or technical terms unknown to the average reader. The sentence structure tends to be long and complex, written in third person. All of these characteristics tend to make the voice of the writer impersonal.

Formal English is primarily written. It is the language of technical manuals, some college textbooks, classical literature, professional journals, formal reports, many insurance policies, and legal and government documents.


## THREE COMMON CONCERNS THAT AFFECT VOICE

Just as the level of formality should be appropriate to each occasion and audience, so too should the writer's voice. Although colloquialisms may give an air of casual friendliness, they are inappropriate for most college writing.


### Out-of-Place Colloquialisms

As you edit your college essays, watch for out-of-place colloquialisms. A sudden, unnecessary downshift to informality is jarring for the unsuspecting reader. Such shifts need to be made carefully and only for a sound reason. To help you avoid some common colloquialisms, consider the following lists:

| *Colloquial* | *Standard* |
|---|---|
| He cleared the *stuff* out of his desk. | He *cleared out* his desk. |
| The client *really wants* to sell. | The client *is eager* to sell. |
| She got a *good deal* on her car. | Her Ford Escort was a *bargain*. |
| Jim is in *a lot* of trouble. | Jim has *many* problems. |
| *I'd hate* to see her do that. | *I would prefer* she not do that. |
| Erin is an *awfully* good doctor. | Erin is a *very* good physician. |
| Jason added his *two cents' worth*. | Jason added his *opinion*. |
| *Alright*, I'll go. | *All right, I will go*. |
| When did Sue *get* married? | When *was* Sue *married*? |
| He takes his *kids* to the office. | He takes his *children* to the office. |

Other colloquial expressions to avoid in expository writing are listed below, along with standard alternatives:

| *Colloquial* | *Standard* |
|---|---|
| looking to | planning to |
| seeing as | since, because |

| | |
|---|---|
| sort of | rather, somewhat |
| headache | problem, concern |
| a couple of | two |
| fight (verbal) | argument, quarrel |
| really good | very good, excellent |
| mad | angry, upset |
| ballpark figure | estimate |
| stuff | items, articles, materials |

Many unsuspecting writers misuse the term *great*, when they mean excellent, elated, or happy: "She's a great dancer." "We were feeling great." The standard meanings of *great* include "very large in size," "large in quantity or number," and "extensive distance or time." Only *informally* does *great* mean "wonderful" or "excellent." If you are unsure of the status of a word, consult a dictionary.

## Switching Pronouns in Mid-Sentence

When students write the way they talk, they may switch from first-person to second-person pronouns unnecessarily. An abrupt shift in person changes the point of view, which is distracting to the reader. Consider this student's rough draft:

> Years ago *I* would start my vegetable plants from seed because it was much cheaper and *you* could get a jump on the season. But as *I* expanded my garden, more and more plants were needed, too many to grow from seed. So *I* would go to garden centres, which is exciting. *You* can select from dozens of kinds and dream of big, red, ripe tomatoes.

These unnecessary shifts in person could be easily remedied by deleting each *you* and replacing it with an *I*. If you have this concern, beware of using *you* in academic writing except in process papers and business letters. Then use *you* correctly for a purpose.

See page H-20.

## Inappropriate Prescriptive Tone

A prescriptive tone lends authority to a statement. Prescriptive language is appropriate when giving directions, establishing rules and laws, and issuing commands. Just as a doctor prescribes medicine, a prescriptive writer offers advice, makes suggestions, or requests the reader to do something. Unnecessary prescription intrudes and irritates. You can usually identify prescriptive language by the words *must*, *should*, *ought*, or *need*. Sometimes appropriate prescription is implied, as in the first two examples that follow:

*Appropriate:*

**Process paper:** First, *detach* all the parts from their plastic frames.

**Persuasive speech:** On the eve of the November election, *set* your alarm clock so that you can cast your ballot and fulfill your civic duty.

**Business etiquette manual:** The boss *should* issue the first invitation to a lunch, dinner, or party.

But prescription can be unnecessary and inappropriate. As you read the two examples below, listen to the difference in tone. [Here the descriptive example is preferable. Prescription is unnecessary.]

*Inappropriate:*

**Prescriptive:** Setting goals *should* be a person's most important objective in life. (The student writer projects her priority onto everyone.)

**Descriptive:** Setting goals is an important part of my life.

In college papers you may be expected to use prescription to explain a process or argue a belief. For a report or other rhetorical situation, you may be expected to write a recommendation. Any prescriptive or descriptive language should be worded appropriately according to the occasion, purpose, audience, and topic.

## THREE CRUCIAL QUESTIONS FOR ACHIEVING AN APPROPRIATE VOICE

In college and on the job, you will be writing for many different audiences via email, letters, reports, papers, and other documents. All of these pieces will require different voices, tailored according to each occasion and audience. To achieve an appropriate voice, you might first consider three important questions:

- **Who will be reading the writing?** What are the primary interests and characteristics of the audience? Adjust your written voice to their culture, occupation, gender, expectations, and educational level.

- **Why will they be reading this writing?** The motivation of the audience will influence how you shape your purpose and voice. Think in terms of advantages: How can they benefit? What words and approach will be effective and appropriate?

- **Can I write objectively about this topic?** Read your writing aloud. Does it sound fair and unbiased? Do the words say what you intend? Is the tone pleasing and suitable to the occasion and the audience?

## SUMMARY

- Voice is the result of all the stylistic decisions a writer makes, including level of formality.
- Use the voice appropriate to the rhetorical situation.
- Focused writing is more orderly, concise, and complete than casual conversation.
- Words are classified as standard or nonstandard. Standard usage is composed of three levels of formality: Informal English, Professional English, and Formal English. Standard English is expected in the workplace.
- Avoid unnecessary colloquialisms, switches in person, and prescription in workplace and college writing.

## Practice

### Identifying the Level of Formality

*Directions:* Identify the level of formality of each example and then check your answers with those at the end of the chapter.

1. "For ten years after finishing college, I made my living running around in short pants in drafty arenas across America, as a professional basketball player. The rhythm of the road—a drive, a flight, a performance, a hotel, a sleep . . . provided a frame through which I saw America and myself. For the past seventeen years, I have crisscrossed America as a politician, a United States senator from New Jersey, following the familiar rhythm— a drive, a flight, a performance. . . ."

    —Bill Bradley, *Time Present, Time Past*

2. Some editors may use the phrase "We can't use it right now" merely to soften the letdown, and many writers take the words as literal truth. However, some editors may mean the phrase literally, so if an editor writes, "We can't use it right now," write back and ask, "When can you use it?" If you receive encouragement from an editor, ask "If I changed the ending (or whatever change the editor suggests), would you be interested in seeing it again?"

    —Kenneth Atchity, "Dealing with Rejection"

3. Linda Ronstadt: "When we were little, we spoke Spanish at home. . . . My Spanish is very rudimentary—child's Spanish, really. But I sing in Spanish, and my new album is all Spanish *canciones* [songs], and I sing two songs in the movie *The Mambo Kings*."

    —James Brady, "In Step with: Linda Ronstadt"

4. "Between eye-wiping and nose-blowing, I told him, 'I don't ever want another dog. It hurts too much. . . .' 'You're right about the hurt, son,' he answered, 'but that's the price of love.'"

—Fred Bauer, "The Price of Love"

5. To every thing there is a season, and a time to every purpose under heaven: A time to be born, and a time to die; a time to plant, and a time to pluck up that which is planted; . . .

—Ecclesiastes 3:1,2 KJV

### Rewriting Colloquialisms and Contractions

*Directions:* When you find colloquialisms or contractions below, rephrase the sentence in Professional English. If the sentence is already Professional English, mark with a C.

1. Tasha is looking to buy a new car.
2. Seeing as Michael has the lead in the senior play, he will be staying after school for the next several weeks.
3. Around 11:30 I'll stop by your office so that we can go to lunch.
4. Tara and Jeanne had a fun time at the flea market.
5. Yesterday Lance had a client who was a big headache.
6. In the employees' lounge are some awfully good cinnamon rolls.
7. That's a ballpark figure.
8. He made a lot of punctuation errors in that letter.
9. I heard Scott and Julie got married last week.
10. Brent bought a really good sound system.

### Groups: Levels of Formality for Different Audiences

*Directions:* Read the case problems below. Then decide which level of formality would be best for each audience.

1. You are a newspaper reporter interviewing Jean Chrétien for a feature in the Sunday paper about his career. Which level of formality will you use?
2. You are a systems analyst, and your boss has assigned a systems project. He has asked for weekly memo reports. What level of formality will you use?
3. You are writing a cover letter to mail with your resume. What level of formality will you use?
4. You are writing a television commercial for antifreeze. You want to appeal to everyone who drives a car, so have decided to feature a mechanic at a local garage. Which level of formality will you use?

5. Imagine you are a physician writing an article that describes a new treatment for cancer. The article will appear in a medical journal that is read primarily by other doctors. What level of formality will you use?

## Answers: Identifying the Level of Formality

1. *Professional:* note the author's profession, and the passage's lack of contractions and colloquilisms.
2. *Informal:* note the use of the first and second person pronouns.
3. *Professional:* note the *occasion* of the passage (i.e., a professional interview), and the use of complete sentences.
4. *Informal:* again, note the use of both the first and second person pronouns.
5. *Formal:* written in the third person, this passage includes parallel sentence structure.

# CHAPTER 3

# Prewriting

## Discovering Ideas

---

**Learning Objectives**

After reading and applying the information in Chapter 3, you'll be able to:

- Generate a topic and ideas for your writing using prewriting techniques such as freewriting, clustering, brainstorming, and questioning

---

*Write down the thoughts of the moment. Those that come unsought for are commonly the most valuable.*

—Sir Francis Bacon

Your experience, observation, and imagination can fuel your writing. You can take amusing, unusual, or perhaps ordinary incidents and transform them—after thoughtful reflection—into essays. Just ask yourself, "How did this experience influence me? What did I learn about life?" Questions such as these start you thinking so that you can draw a conclusion about the incident or event.

Still, some students are reluctant to write because they don't know how to begin. The prewriting techniques explained in this chapter can help anyone start writing quickly. They can also help to divert the flood of anxiety that sometimes overwhelms writers.

## FINDING A TOPIC AND IDEAS BY PREWRITING

Prewriting, the first stage of the writing process, is a time of discovery—you unearth ideas. Prewriting can condense swirling mists of thoughts into words on paper. You uncover raw material to shape and polish later. There is no need to think about order or correctness—*the objective is to produce as many ideas as possible.*

You can prewrite whenever and however you like—on paper, at a keyboard, or with a tape recorder. Many writers keep notepads on their bedside tables to record insights that jolt them awake at 3 a.m. One student keeps a tape recorder in his car to record insights. When ideas are elusive, some writers like to walk along a quiet street or path to let their thoughts settle. Yet it is essential to pin down ideas before they flit away.

The six invention techniques in this chapter are ways to jump-start ideas. By trying all six techniques, you can find out which ones work best for you. All can be done on a computer or with pen and paper, whichever is more comfortable.

## Freewriting

Freewriting is uncensored writing, often in sentence form. Freewriting enables anyone to start writing immediately. It may work well for writers whose thoughts flee at the sight of a fresh sheet of paper, because you can write anything. To freewrite, just empty whatever bits and pieces of ideas are in your mind out onto the paper. Here is an example:

> What to write? There's so much debris in my mind. Clutter. The files are overflowing—it's no wonder I can't find anything to write about. What is significant? Let's see. Life is significant—very, very, very much so. Yet some individuals toss it away so lightly. Just last week in our town, two guys in their twenties carried out a suicide pact. They had been drinking and doing drugs. A bartender overheard them planning the night before. But he didn't tell anyone. Probably thought they were just talking—old saying, you know, that those who talk about it won't. But the truth is they often do. How sad—only one chance and they throw it away. They jump into eternity without a parachute, not knowing where they will land.

This freewriting sample has unearthed three general topics: the value of life, suicide, and the possibility of another life after death. The writer might go on to take one of these three topics as the subject for a second round of freewriting. Freewriting in this way is called *focused freewriting* because, rather than starting with whatever is on his or her mind, the writer has already established a focus for freewriting.

Note that freewriting may not be the best technique for writers who are under time constraints: It may take much longer than other techniques. To avoid a time trap while freewriting, set a timer for ten minutes. Shut off your conscious editor and write quickly. When the timer rings, stop, examine your catch, and develop whatever seems promising.

## Clustering

Clustering, devised by Gabriele Rico, is uncensored brainstorming combined with doodling. Clustering produces an overview of a subject, suggests specific topics,

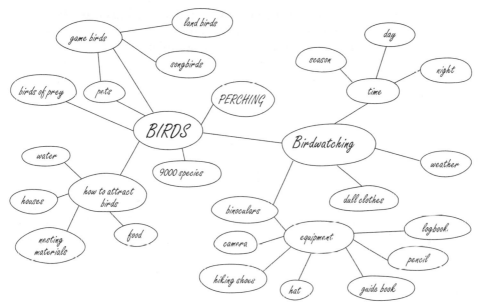

**Figure 3.1** Clustering

and yields related details. To begin, take a fresh sheet of paper and write a general subject in the centre. Then circle the word. As each new thought bursts forth, jot it near the word that prompted it. Circle the new word. Next, draw a line between the two. Repeat the procedure. The sample cluster (Figure 3.1) began with the subject of birds. That central idea branched out, leading to the specific topic of birdwatching.

## Brainstorming

An efficient way to start your mind moving is to brainstorm, either alone or in groups. Brainstorming captures ideas as they flit by, either as words, phrases, or fragments. You can use this technique in a group or alone. *The secret of success in brainstorming is to think fast and forgo criticism.* Remarks such as "That's no good" or "That won't work" dampen enthusiasm and dam the stream of ideas. In brainstorming, all ideas are respected and recorded, no matter how wild.

Brainstorming is often used to create a new product, to improve an existing product, or to solve a problem. You can use this technique to find a topic for a paper, to narrow a topic, and to find supporting details. In a group one person can record responses while others contribute. It is helpful to use a chalkboard because the sight of ideas may trigger others, related but different.

Alone you can talk into a tape recorder without the distraction of making notes. Or you can write a general topic at the top of a sheet of paper and start jotting down possible ways to narrow it, as in this example:

*Water Gardens*

| | | |
|---|---|---|
| half barrels | landscaping a small pond | choosing fish and snails |
| moulded ponds | selecting water plants | preventing algae |
| dig your own | building a waterfall | cost of materials |
| amount of labour | installing a fountain | legal liability |

After you narrow your topic down to one aspect of water gardens, you can start listing possible supporting details.

## Questioning

To use questioning at its best, try projecting yourself into the role of a reporter. What questions could you ask to elicit information from other people? Then try the questions on yourself. Whenever your writing stalls, ask questions to restart the flow of details. The traditional "five W's and an H" (who? what? when? where? why? how?) can be expanded to full-fledged questions:

- Who was involved?
- What happened?
- When did it happen?
- Where did it happen?
- Why did it happen?

- How did it happen?
- What will be its effect?
- What can be learned?
- What is the subject like or unlike?
- How has it changed over time?

## Combining Invention Techniques

As you prewrite, play around with ideas. Many writers find that combining invention techniques is even more productive than using one technique alone. For instance, while clustering, you might try asking yourself brief questions to increase the flow of ideas: What? Where? What next? What else should be said? Who? How? What else? What is interesting? Funny? When? Why? So what? What does the reader need to know?

## GATHERING INFORMATION

All of the discovery techniques mentioned here are useful for gathering ideas from your personal experience. But for most college work, you will need other methods of gathering information.

## Doing Research

Many college classes require research. Chapter 22 explains how to gather information through observation, interviews, and surveys. Chapter 23 explains how to locate sources in the library and on the Internet. Usually, information gained from printed sources is stored on note cards or on a computer using note-taking software. Other data and ideas are often stored in a journal.

## Keeping a Journal

Some instructors require that students keep a journal to store reactions to essays, fiction, and poetry or other ideas for writing. Journals are also useful for recording observations, impressions, and incidents when you conduct first-hand research. For example, a student who worked in a restaurant researched nonverbal communication in her workplace. By smiling and lightly touching patrons as she served them, she found that her tips nearly doubled. The daily notes she kept in her journal provided the material for her report.

In some ways a journal is similar to a diary, but journals often include a wider range of material. A journal can be a private account of conversations, events, perceptions, reactions, or anything else a writer cares to record. Some writers save quotations, funny stories, or poems. Any of these items may prove valuable for later writing.

---

### SUMMARY

- Prewriting, as the first stage of the writing process, is a practical way to manage fear of writing.
- Four common prewriting techniques are prewriting, clustering, brainstorming, and questioning.
- You may also gather information for writing by doing research. Journals and the Internet can help in this regard.

---

*Practice*

### Case Problems: Brainstorming in Small Groups

*Directions:* Choose one of the cases below or devise one of your own. Appoint a recorder to jot down what is said while the others brainstorm possible solutions. Remember to hold off on evaluation.

1. Many personnel in your office pack their lunches. Lately food and beverages have been disappearing from the break room refrigerator. What might be done?

2. Imagine you are a group of citizens concerned about the number of accidents that have occurred in your residential neighborhood because of

speeding and failure to observe stop signs. What alternatives might be tried?

3. A neighbour has become overly friendly. When you moved into the neighbourhood, she offered to babysit your children in her home, which she has done occasionally, refusing a fee. On your birthday, she baked you a cake. Now she has started coming to your front door, entering without knocking, and wandering about your house until she finds you. What can you do?

## Ten Ideas for Freewriting

*Directions:* Freewrite for ten minutes about anything you wish. The suggestions below may be helpful.

1. I wonder . . .
2. Tomorrow . . .
3. I can't . . . but I can . . .
4. Once I . . . but now . . .
5. When I see . . . , I remember . . .
6. Write a short poem.
7. Happiness is . . .
8. Summarize your worst mistake. What have you learned from it?
9. What would you most like to do? How might you do it?
10. Sketch a career plan. What training or education will you need?

# CHAPTER 4

# *Drafting*

## Exploring Ideas

**Learning Objectives**

After reading and applying the information in Chapter 4, you'll be able to:

- Generate a purpose statement
- Develop a thesis statement
- Write effective introductions and conclusions using a variety of methods
- Identify the basic ways to organize a draft

> *Writing and rewriting are a constant search for what it is one is saying.*
>
> — John Updike

Drafting, the second stage of the writing process, is the time to rummage through ideas accumulated during prewriting and unfold them into sentences and paragraphs. It can be exciting—hours may seem like minutes. You may glance at an old idea and suddenly see it in a new light. You may devise a delightful comparison or find a bit of irony or an unusual twist. You may grope for words and settle for temporary substitutes. Regardless, keep writing. The purpose of the draft is to expand ideas on paper as quickly as possible without interruption by an internal censor or other noise.

## Fleshing out Your Prewriting Notes

Before you begin to write, find a secluded spot. Resolve to ignore the telephone or other distractions. Do whatever you can to ensure privacy. To start a first draft, you need a block of uninterrupted time, at least an hour, when your mind is keen. Start wherever you wish—beginning, middle, or end. That way, there is no worry about wording a thesis statement, supplying transitions, or other concerns. There is no need to correct or do anything that will disrupt your concentration. Just glance at your prewriting notes whenever you need more ideas.

Perhaps the best advice is to let ideas go where they will. Don't worry if your first draft wanders into byways. Unnecessary details and mistakes may litter the path of your main idea. That's all right. This draft is for your eyes only. It lets you explore. You can rearrange and clean up later. Sometimes you may think you have little else to say on the topic. To focus and find more material, try asking yourself questions:

- What might readers like to know?
- How might readers feel about the topic?
- How do I feel about the topic? Why?
- What else needs to be said?

Or if you find that you are completely blocked, a break may be the only solution. Before you stop, schedule a specific time to resume writing.

## FOCUSING AN EXPLORATORY DRAFT

Some writers do much of their prewriting and drafting mentally before they ever start to write. They have a distinct sense of purpose and audience and are often able to focus their exploratory draft surprisingly well. A clear central idea unifies the material so that it progresses in a logical way and fulfills the purpose. Other writers know their general topic but circle aimlessly around it, unsure of the central point they will make. Pausing to limit the topic and write a thesis statement, however, can establish a direction for writing.

### Narrowing a Topic

When you narrow a topic, you focus on a segment that you can develop well. You write more about less. If you find yourself rambling or lost while exploring your topic, stop and consider the range you are covering. Is the topic too broad? Can it be covered adequately in the required number of words? To be manageable, a topic should be whittled down to fit the assignment and the rhetorical situation. The pyramid below shows how a very broad topic (top of the pyramid) can be narrowed.

Canada

tourism in the Maritimes

tourism in Newfoundland

benefits of encouraging local tourism

benefits of camping in Gros Morne National Park

### Writing a Purpose Statement

Stating your purpose on paper is a quick, preliminary step to drafting. This way you pin down your main idea. A purpose statement provides the foundation for your thesis statement, which can be written later. First, jot down a brief description of your readers. This step will help to clarify your approach to the topic and the perspective you will take:

## CASE STUDY

### NITA NARROWS HER TOPIC

Nita Jones wishes to research solar energy. Over the years she has read a few articles on the subject, but she wonders what has been discovered recently. She suspects that her general readers are also hazy about the topic. And they may not care one way or the other. She asks several of her classmates and verifies both hypotheses. How can she interest them in the topic? How might they benefit from reading about it? She writes down these questions and starts a list to narrow the topic.

**Question:** How might readers benefit by learning more about solar energy?

**Narrowing:** general-to-specific

solar energy

practical applications for solar energy

solar heating for homes

solar heating during construction of new homes

solar heating for existing homes

As Nita reviews her list, she realizes that every reader is a potential homeowner. At first she considers discussing applications for new home construction, but then she thinks about budget constraints. Few of her readers will be building their first home. Most will buy older homes and repair or remodel them. At this point, she briefly describes her audience and writes a purpose statement.

**Audience:** College students who are potential buyers of existing homes and who are interested in comfort at a reasonable cost.

**Purpose:** To inform the reader of solar heating applications for existing homes and to evaluate practicality.

**Thesis statement:** Solar heating installations can reduce fuel bills and improve the value of an older home.

**Audience for a letter to the editor:** Readers of a Toronto newspaper who have never considered visiting North Bay.

**Audience for a paper on litter control:** Voters who are concerned about the numerous cans and bottles littering city streets, roads, and highways.

Second, start writing the purpose statement. There are just two basic parts: general purpose and specific purpose.

See
Chapter 1
for "Purpose."

**Purpose:** To *inform* readers about *the scenic beauty of North Bay's waterfront, its proximity to hiking trails, and the ease of the drive from Toronto.*

**Purpose:** To *persuade* readers *to vote for a bill requiring deposits on and recycling of all beverage cans and glass bottles.*

## Writing a Thesis Statement

A thesis statement is similar to a topic sentence. Just as a topic sentence states the main idea of a paragraph, so too *the thesis states the main idea of a paper.* Both the topic sentence and the thesis statement act as a contract—a promise the writer makes to the reader. When the writing is effective and complete, the promise is kept.

A thesis can be stated in just one sentence. In some writing, the thesis extends over several sentences. A thesis statement performs four specific tasks:

*Four Tasks of a Thesis Statement*

1. Identify the subject
2. State a claim, an approach, or an attitude
3. Suggest the direction of the writing
4. Set the tone

The following one-sentence thesis, from a paper by student Michele Flahive, contains three parts. Her thesis demonstrates the four tasks:

**Thesis:** For the dedicated player, the challenge, the enjoyment, and the cama-raderie make softball a game worth playing.

**Topic:** Playing softball

**Claim:** For the dedicated player, softball is worth playing.

**Direction:** The focus is on three main points—*challenge, enjoyment,* and *ca-maraderie*—in that order.

**Tone:** Middle level of formality

The sooner you can write a tentative thesis statement, the fewer drafts you are likely to need.

***Where Should the Thesis Statement Go?***    Usually, the thesis statement is placed in the introduction, often in the opening paragraph of short papers. Sometimes it appears at the beginning but more often at the end of the opening paragraph. There it can forge a tight link to later paragraphs. In research or other long papers, the introduction may contain two or more paragraphs. In that case, the thesis sentence generally appears at the end of the introduction.

An easy way to draft a three-part thesis is to make a list and fill in the blanks:

Topic: _____

Main points: _____

_____

_____

Thesis statement: _____

_____

*For Practice:* Choose a topic that can be divided into three parts. For example, "Three reasons I chose _____ College/University." Write the topic in the first blank. Second, think of reasons and list them in the blanks for main points. Third, condense and combine the reasons to make a complete sentence. Even if this tentative thesis doesn't seem quite right, it can still act as a controlling idea and help you organize an exploratory draft. (For more on a three-part thesis, see Chapter 14.)

## DRAFTING AN INTRODUCTION

An effective introduction affords a graceful entry into a topic. Whether you draft your introduction first or last, keep your audience in mind. The opening sentence should arouse interest and induce the reader to continue. The writer's voice sets a suitable tone for the writing, inviting the reader to consider the topic. Although a wide array of introductions appears throughout the book, here is a preview of five common types.

### Begin with an Anecdote That Sets the Scene

An anecdote, or a brief narrative, can capture the reader's attention. You can begin by first setting the scene. To orient readers and forestall puzzlement, state *when* and *where* the experience happened. Sometimes just a few carefully chosen details will give a sense of time and place:

**My Worst Job**

When I was sixteen, my cousin suggested I take a job at a dress factory where she worked. Because she liked the people and the wages, I hired on. For a country girl who had never been inside a factory, the first day was overwhelming. Rows and rows of sewing machines whirred while hundreds of women worked at a furious pace. Finding me an empty chair, the trainer demonstrated how to operate the machine and sew a facing on the bodice of a cotton dress. Since I had made my own clothes for years, the task was simple. Outwardly, the power sewing machines somewhat resembled the old Singer at home. But the piece of technology in front of me was as much like my old machine as a Mercedes is like a Model T. Careening around the curves, I hung onto the cloth and somehow guided it under the presser foot. By lunch time, however, I had mastered the machine and the five-minute task that was my only responsibility. Day after day for an interminable week, I repeated that mind-numbing procedure.

***Overuse of the Pronoun*** **I.**   A successful narrative opening not only provides interest, but also aids in avoiding "I" as the first word in a paper or paragraph. *Using* I *as the first word focuses on the writer, not the needs of the reader.* Usually, there is a more interesting and effective way to open.

In effective business writing, letters should be worded diplomatically to consider the reader's needs. For example, a well-planned application letter for employment focuses on what the writer can do for the company. If, however, most sentences start with *I*, the interviewer may conclude that despite an applicant's skills and experience, a super-size ego is not what the company needs.

To avoid the use of *I* at the beginning, look at the rest of the sentence. Do you see another word or phrase that can be moved up and placed before *I?* Even one word, such as *yesterday, although,* or *when,* will provide a smoother opening than a reference to yourself. To begin a narrative example, briefly tell when and where the action took place. Often just a phrase of three or so words will do. To help you start, here are some ideas.

*Opening Words to Set the Scene*

| References to Time | References to Place |
|---|---|
| Ten years ago | From my window |
| When I was a small child | While working as assistant manager at |
| After I graduated | In the green hills of |
| In 1932 my grandfather | Near Prince Albert National Park |
| Last month my life | On Vancouver Island |

## Begin with a Description

A few words of artful description at the beginning of a paper can explain, illustrate, or provide a bit of background. In the following introduction, Kenny Patrick sets the scene and informs his classmates about fly fishing, using vivid words to explain his fascination with the sport:

### Hooked on a Tradition

Icy water swirls around the wading fly fisherman. With experience gained from thousands of casts, he deposits the tiny brown deer hair fly directly beneath an overhanging branch at the water's edge. His pulse quickens as he gently twitches the tip of the rod. Like a living being, the tiny fly dances across the surface. Suddenly, a bronze torpedo erupts from the depths and snatches the small offering. The fisherman feels the solid pull of a feisty small-mouth bass and sets the hook. With a powerful thrust of its tail, the large fish launches itself into the air. Shaking its head, the bass dislodges the hook. Hands trembling, the fisherman is left with just a memory. Moments like this make fly fishing a frustrating, yet fascinating and educational sport.

## Begin by Stating a Problem

Stating a problem can be a practical way to open. The purpose of Janet Edington's paper was to inform pet owners of ways to enhance the safety of animals when transporting them to the vet.

### Safety First!

Pet owners are frequently faced with the challenge of transporting their animal friends to the veterinarian. This task can be not only nerve-wracking but also hazardous, particularly if they are transporting a nervous cat or a large animal. In an automobile, an even-tempered pet can swiftly turn into a frightened, hostile enemy. The following suggestions are offered to spare anyone the battle scars I carry today.

## Begin with a Surprising Statistic or Striking Bit of History

You may be able to spur a reader's curiosity with a surprising statistic or striking bit of history. The purpose of Kathy Cordle's paper was to inform classmates of a way to kick the tobacco habit that worked for her.

### Kicking the Habit

Concern about the hazards of tobacco is not new. In 1604 King James I of England officially condemned the use of tobacco. An 1859 report about the dangers of tobacco stated that of the sixty-eight persons suffering from cancer of the mouth and throat in a hospital in Montpelier, France, all were tobacco users. In the United States during the early 1900s, admonitions such as "Don't smoke, or it will stunt your growth" and "Now that you are expecting, you'll have to lay off smoking" were common.

## Begin by Disputing a Common Belief or Defying a Stereotype

The writer who surprises readers with a statement that disputes a common belief or an example that defies a stereotype will grab their attention. In the next paragraph, Paul Giacalone's purpose was to entertain his classmates. He begins by expressing a view that runs counter to the commonly held belief that everyone should love the family dog. His offbeat perspective and critically amused tone surprise readers and hook their curiosity.

### The Trials of Tia

Recently my father brought home a very small and very ignorant animal. My parents named it Tia, and they have tried to convince me that it is a dog—I swear it is a rat. Actually, Tia is half rat terrier and half poodle—a strange-looking animal that has not been easy to train. Therein lies the nub of the problem.

---

**THE SEVEN BASIC ORDERS**

1. **Chronology** (time): chronological/reverse chronological
2. **Spatial order** (space): organized by layout, design, direction, or location
3. **Order of importance:** least to most/most to least
4. **Order of generality:** general to specific/specific to general
5. **Order of formation:** whole to parts/parts to whole
6. **Order of complexity:** simple to complex/familiar to unfamiliar
7. **Order of materiality:** concrete to abstract/abstract to concrete

---

## SEVEN BASIC WAYS TO ORGANIZE A DRAFT

To be clear and readable, every completed manuscript should have a logical order. As you sort through your prewriting notes and write your first draft, watch for a dominant order to emerge. Look closely at the transitions you have included. Do they refer to time? To location? To cause and effect? Are some points more important than others? Or does your thesis statement contain a clue to a suitable order? The sooner you can find an order appropriate to the rhetorical situation, the fewer drafts you will need. Seven basic orders are commonly used, and combined, to organize writing. They are:

### 1. Chronology

When dates or events are placed in a natural sequence according to *time*, this arrangement is known as *chronological order*. In process analysis you arrange the steps or stages chronologically. In a research paper, you may combine chronological order with other orders. Narratives usually move forward in chronological order, but not always. A sidewise shift in time may be indicated by transitions such as "meanwhile" or "at the same time."

## 2. Spatial Order

Unlike chronological order, which moves along a time line, *spatial* order locates details according to layout, design, direction, or place. In "Through a Child's Eyes," the writer describes her father, beginning with his head and moving down to his lap (see page 74). Any of the following spatial orders (or their reverse) might be used in description:

| | | |
|---|---|---|
| head to toe | outside to inside | clockwise |
| bottom to top | north to south | circular |
| left to right | up and down | horizontal |

## 3. Order of Importance

Newspaper articles typically use *most- to least-important* order, beginning with the most important information and leaving the least important details until last. Editors know that readers often read only the first few paragraphs of an article or only the front page section. For other writing, *least- to most-important* order is often used. This order places the emphasis on the final point. You might use least- to most-important order in essays of division, classification, illustration, or argument.

## 4. Order of Generality

The order of generality can be used to inform or to convince. An observation, generalization, or basic principle is presented either at the beginning or at the end of the piece of writing. Using the *general-to-specific* order, you begin with the claim, then supply enough specific details to support it. For example, a student wrote, "The magic of a carousel has a way of turning men and women into children again." Then she presented specific details to support her observation. This order can be reversed to *specific to general* with the claim at the end of the writing.

## 5. Order of Formation

The order of formation is convenient to describe and explain a complicated topic or to formulate a balanced argument. This comprehensive order can supply a sense of completeness, conviction, and objectivity. Writers often use the *whole-to-parts* order in problem solving or in an argument. They begin with a summary of a problem or an issue, then move on to look at the individual factors or aspects. This way they present an overview before covering all significant alternatives, angles, or parts.

The whole-to-parts order can also be used to explain less complicated topics. For example, a student described an old rocking chair, starting with the overall appearance of the rocker and then going to its parts. He created an image of the old chair before explaining how it functioned in the life of his family. In some writing situations, this order can be reversed to move from *the parts to the whole*.

## 6. Order of Complexity

Often an effective way to explain an unusual topic is according to its complexity. Going from *the simple to the complex* or *familiar to unfamiliar* will help clarify the topic. By starting with what readers already know and accept, you can orient them and establish rapport. Then they will be more comfortable and willing to explore the complex or the unfamiliar. If you were to begin with a difficult concept or highly technical material, some readers might refuse to read further.

## 7. Order of Materiality

Using an order of materiality, a writer may arrange details by going from *the concrete to the abstract* or from *the abstract to the concrete*. Concrete words refer to actual physical data about a condition, event, experience, object, animal, or person. Through our five senses, we can perceive evidence of these elements. Most of us are able to see, hear, touch, taste, and smell to obtain first-hand proof that concrete items exist. For example, tears are concrete—we can see them, feel them, even taste them. Sometimes tears indicate sadness, but sadness is an abstraction.

See
page 187.
*Abstract* refers to ideas that have no physical referent; nothing material can prove they exist. We can think and talk about abstractions, but we *cannot* see, hear, taste, touch, or smell them. For example, patriotism, love, and integrity are all abstractions. The only way that we can infer that they exist is to look for *concrete* evidence that *implies* their existence. Jeannine Caudill uses this order in "Mother Love."

Writers of description often move from *the concrete to the abstract*, presenting physical details about a subject first. For example, a writer might briefly describe our national flag before describing its symbolic significance. An essay of definition might use the reverse order, *abstract to concrete*, introducing an abstract concept—such as friendship or bravery—then providing concrete instances and examples.

## WRITING AN EFFECTIVE CONCLUSION

Often a first draft does not have a conclusion. The writer may need more time to ponder the meaning of ideas. A few writers, if they have thought long and hard about a topic, may start by writing the conclusion first. The rest of us may have to tug and pull it into shape until it works. An effective conclusion indicates that you have finished what you have to say; it does not rehash opinions or recite the obvious. No new material intrudes. An effective ending flows logically and smoothly from the body, giving a sense of completeness or *closure*. Five basic ways to conclude are described here.

## 1. End with a Reference to a Benefit

Sales letters cite the benefits of a product of a plan. A college paper may conclude by referring to a value, advantage, or benefit. Diane Zachman points out the benefits of a good manicure:

The process of manicuring, when done correctly, gives your nails a vibrant, healthy appearance and keeps them from becoming weak and brittle.

## 2. End by Referring Back to the Thesis

To provide a satisfying ending, writers often refer briefly to the thesis. Notice that this device is an allusion, *not* a repetition of the entire thesis. By reworking an old cliché and repeating key points, Nora Lee Corbett is able to establish closure:

**Thesis:** We raise Leghorn laying hens for their hardiness, longevity, and egg production.

**Conclusion:** On our farm the chicken comes before the egg. And we have learned over the years that the best chicken according to hardiness, longevity, and egg production is the Leghorn.

## 3. End with a Personal Response

Writers sometimes confide their feelings to the reader. Especially at the end of a paper, they may express a sense of sadness, embarrassment, satisfaction, elation, or some other emotion in response to a situation. For example, the student who described her "worst job" concluded with the following:

On Friday I was still doing the same mind-numbing procedure. By then my hands guided the cloth under the pressure foot with ease, but I knew I could not continue unless I underwent a lobotomy. So at quitting time I picked up my paycheque, inhaled the fresh air of freedom, and left with a light heart, knowing I would never go back.

## 4. End on a Note of Optimism

A note of optimism can create a satisfying conclusion. It might be a note of encouragement to yourself or to the reader, or it might be a look toward the future. Sue Taylor concluded "Breaking the Habit" with a congratulatory note to herself:

Since November 7, I have not had one cigarette. Yes, there are times when I still want one, and I am struggling to drop those extra pounds, accumulated from eating all that candy, but I feel really good about myself. I am a winner!

## 5. End with an Unexpected Twist

A conclusion that creeps up on readers, catching them off guard, can surprise and delight. When well done, such an ending seems spontaneous and appropriate. A brief comment or fact can pose an absurdity or profundity that causes the reader to smile or think. Paul Giacalone ended with a twist in his paper about his parents' dog Tia:

I feel the only solution to this problem is either I go or the dog does. After I discussed this with my parents, they went out and bought me a set of luggage for Christmas.

Although a twist may be appropriate for personal writing, it is rarely appropriate for business writing. Customers, employees, and managers need to know what to expect and need to understand the writer's purpose.

## A NOTE OF REASSURANCE AND A BRIEF REVIEW

Drafting should bring a sense of adventure and exploration. Drafting is just the second stage in the writing process, not the last. You don't have to get everything right the first time; you will have chances to go back and revise. So focus on your central idea, follow the suggestions given here, and your work should proceed fairly quickly.

### GUIDELINES: TIPS FOR DRAFTING SUCCESSFULLY

1. *Schedule a block of time for writing an exploratory draft.* Start early so that you will have plenty of time to revise, edit, and proofread.

2. *Study your prewriting notes to determine whether or not the topic is adequate for the assignment.*
   a.   Is the topic significant?
   b.   Has it been narrowed adequately?
   c.   Will it interest the audience?
   d.   Are there enough facts, examples, and details for support?
   e.   How can the topic be presented in an interesting way?

3. *Think about how you want your written voice to sound.* Do you want to sound playful? Serious? Amused? Outraged? Or how? Your attitude toward a topic (and perhaps the assignment) will be reflected in your written voice. (See Chapter 2.)

4. *Begin composing anywhere in the exploratory draft.* Write in a way that is comfortable for you.

5. *Double-space and leave wide margins.* Allow room to mark changes and comments on the draft.

6. *After finishing the first draft, leave it for a day, if possible.* If not, leave it for at least an hour while you have lunch or work on another assignment. You need time to distance yourself intellectually and emotionally before revising.

7. *Save all drafts until you receive the graded paper back.* A paper may go astray. Saving drafts helps avoid losing all your work.

> ### SUMMARY
>
> - Drafting, the second stage of the writing process, is the time to explore ideas uncovered during prewriting. Don't worry about grammar or structure at this stage; revision and editing can come later.
> - Consideration of your audience and purpose will help you focus on the main idea, thus paving the way for a thesis.
> - A thesis statement identifies the subject; states a claim, an approach, or an attitude; suggests the direction; and sets the tone.
> - Try to group your ideas in some logical way, such as chronological order, spatial order, or order of importance.
> - To draft an introduction, you might begin with a narrative, a description, a statement of a problem, an interesting fact, a striking statistic, or a bit of history. You could end by stating a benefit, summarizing your ideas, or providing a twist.

## Ten Ideas for Freewriting

1. I wish . . .
2. The magic of a music box
3. My favourite fragrance is the smell of . . .
4. If I had my way, . . .
5. My job
6. My earliest memory
7. If I could buy a ticket to anywhere, I would . . .
8. My grandfather's _____ _____ was a tool to him, but for me it is a symbol of his . . .
9. Snails (or what else?) are wonderful creatures because . . .
10. If I had more free time, I would . . .

## Practice

### Developing Thesis Statements

Below are groups of supporting sentences on a particular topic. Write an appropriate thesis statement for each group.

1. **topic sentence:**

   _____

   _____

Most of my neighbours also have school-aged children.
There are lots of good schools and parks nearby.
There is very little pollution in Charlottetown.
The community centres offer many after-school programs for preschoolers.

2.   **topic sentence:**

_____

_____

At college, students are responsible for submitting assignments on time.
My college is much bigger than my old high school.
I have to spend much more time doing readings in college.
I'm finding it more difficult to make friends in college.

3.   **topic sentence:**

_____

_____

Many immigrants must leave family, friends, and jobs behind.
Some cannot speak the language of their new country.
Sometimes they may face discrimination.
It is often difficult for new immigrants to find jobs.

# REVISION WORKSHOP: LATER STAGES OF THE WRITING PROCESS

## Part 2

# CHAPTER 5

# Revising, Editing, and Proofreading: An Overview

**Learning Objectives**

After reading and applying the information in Chapter 5, you'll be able to:

- Revise and edit information for logical expression of ideas and clear and accurate order
- Edit for improved word choice and sentence structure
- Proofread for grammar, punctuation, and spelling
- Revise a written draft using peer and self-reviews

*A piece of writing is never finished. It is delivered to a deadline, torn out of the typewriter on demand, sent off with a sense of accomplishment and shame and pride and frustration. If only there were a couple more days, time for just another run at it, perhaps then . . .*

—Donald Murray
"The Maker's Eye:
Revising Your Own Manuscript"

Professional writers rewrite constantly, perhaps reworking one draft dozens of times. How much a writer revises and edits depends on the rhetorical situation and the deadline. Although most instructors do not expect perfection, they do expect several revisions of papers. Yet too many students skip or skimp on revision, editing, and proofreading—turning in rough drafts. A good way to start revision is to assume the role of an editor.

## HOW DO YOU BECOME YOUR OWN EDITOR?

Someone once said that a writer must eventually become his or her own editor. This is even more true today. On the job workers are unlikely to have someone to mark errors and make suggestions—they often work alone at a computer. To start becoming your own editor, evaluate the effectiveness not only of grammar and word choice but also of structure, logic, and development. As you revise, edit, and proofread, ask yourself these two critical questions:

- Is the expression of ideas appropriate to the occasion and the audience?
- Have I fulfilled the purpose?

Revision is concerned with the larger aspects of the draft: the organization and presentation of ideas. The smaller items within the sentence—word choice, grammar, spelling, and punctuation—are treated in the final stages of editing and proofreading. That does not mean you can't jump back and forth between the two stages—work any way you wish. But many writers find it easier and more effective to look at one aspect at a time.

## REVISION: STAGE THREE OF THE WRITING PROCESS

The goal of revision is to rethink and reshape your writing so that it effectively reaches your audience and accomplishes your purpose.

## FIVE MAJOR STEPS OF REVISION

Perhaps you revise in a hit-or-miss fashion that, more or less, works for you. But in this chapter you may find a more efficient way to achieve your purpose. The tools, tips, and options should help you save time and increase the quality of your writing. The secret of revision is this: Just keep repeating the process as often as needed.

### Step 1: Acknowledge the Need for Revision

This first step sounds simple, but some student writers seem to think they have hit the jackpot on their first draft. They refuse to acknowledge the reality that every exploratory draft will need revision. Others think they can merely change a word here and there. But revision is not that quick or easy. No matter how pleased you are with early drafts, keep looking for ways to improve them. After your euphoria wears off, you will find many imperfections.

> ## TOOLS FOR REVISION
>
> - **Outline to corral details.** To check the order of dates, events, steps, or paragraphs, an outline is an excellent tool. It may also uncover a potpourri of items to sort out. To focus a research paper, an outline is essential.
> - **Sketch or diagram the direction of a draft.** You may prefer sketching to making an outline. Just jot down notes, arrows, and pictures to track the path of the main idea. Or you might draw a chain of cause and effect or a time line to chart the chronology of events. Do whatever works for you.
> - **Question.** As you reread a draft, jot brief questions or question marks or ideas in the margins. If you are blocked, bounce ideas off someone face-to-face or by email or telephone. Describing a concern or asking a question will often trigger an answer in your own mind.

See Chapters 17 & 27.

## Step 2: Look at the Big Picture

Print out your draft and read it quickly to ascertain the direction or path of the controlling idea. You cannot do this on-screen, one frame at a time. Ask yourself questions: Is there just one main idea? Does it keep advancing steadily toward the final point? Do you have a final point? Place a check mark wherever the main idea goes astray. If you are unsure about the ending, write "What is my point?" Then select whichever tool you prefer to start work on the draft.

## Step 3: Reread and Mark the Draft

See "Critical Reading," p. 359, Chapter 26.

Reread your printed draft silently and carefully. Mark it as you go but hold off on any drastic action. Just place parentheses around surplus or doubtful material. In the margins, pencil notes, questions, and possible restatements. Or list ideas on another sheet. If your draft has just one or two paragraphs, use brackets to divide logical units of thought into paragraphs. Recheck and number any changes in their order. Next, start revising on screen.

## Step 4: Revise and Refine

Before you start to revise, *rename and copy your draft*—just in case you should change your mind and want to retrieve items you have deleted. Then revise from your marked copy, adding any further ideas onscreen. Keep your eye on clarity. Any passage that seems unclear becomes a candidate for revision. Be prepared to expand, define, cut, splice, summarize, or condense. If you need more information, review your prewriting notes, outline, or diagram or do online research. To evaluate writing, ask questions such as these:

## TIPS FOR REVISING WITH A COMPUTER

Risky shortcuts while using a computer can devour time and elevate blood pressure. The following advice is based on hard-won wisdom.

1. ***Save drafts periodically.*** If your word-processing program has an automatic save feature, you may want to set it for every ten minutes or so. Otherwise, you risk loss of text when a power failure occurs or your computer crashes.

2. ***Save old drafts.*** Save early drafts under different file names, such as *Research 1, Research 2*, and so forth. Place the drafts in *one* file folder to avoid confusion. If you lose your latest draft, then you can go back to the previous one.

3. ***Move text without losing it.*** Copying text and moving it carries risks. If you copy a section and stop to work elsewhere on screen or answer the telephone, instead of pasting in the copied text, you may forget. Then when you copy again or shut down, the passage is lost. To be safe, do not cut the copied portion until you have inserted it into the new spot.

4. ***Take special precautions.*** When moving any text, double-check to be sure you have inserted every line back into the manuscript. When moving entries in the works cited list of a research paper, be especially careful.

5. ***Submit your latest draft.*** It sounds so simple—but one student submitted a six-page formal report with misplaced graphics and omissions. After receiving a C–, he realized he had not submitted the final draft, which had ten pages.

- What else needs to be said?
- What else might the audience like to know?
- Do any parts need to be trimmed?
- Are any details insignificant or irrelevant?

## Step 5: The Final Draft

After the first revision, let your draft cool for half a day or more, if possible. Your thoughts need to settle, so new ideas can sprout. Take a break, but be sure to set a time to return. Then without looking at your paper, jot down your specific purpose and audience. Have they changed? Continue to ask questions to assess your draft: See page 4.

- Is there one clear central idea throughout the paper?
- Are paragraphs arranged in a logical order?

- Does each paragraph relate back to the thesis statement?
- Are paragraphs well developed and interesting?
- Does the conclusion flow logically from the body?

The suggestions that follow are based on common problems encountered by student writers. If they don't apply to you, skip to the next section.

## REFOCUSING A DRAFT

As you revise, you may decide to narrow your topic and refocus it. You might try the pyramid method, shown on page 28, or you might focus the title, revise your outline, or look for a fresh perspective.

### Focusing the Title

A focused title not only sharpens the topic but also suggests the approach the writer will take. A good title specifies and limits the topic whereas an unfocused title gives only a vague idea of what is to come. Let's consider some examples of titles for research papers:

| *Unfocused* | *Focused* |
| --- | --- |
| The Internet and Education | Using the Internet in the Classroom |
| Nutrition of the Elderly | Nutrition for the Elderly Who Live Alone |

The unfocused titles are so broad that the topics could not be covered adequately in a paper. But the focused titles offer a feasible scope. Achieving an appropriate, focused title can be an integral part of revision.

### Outlining

Rather than committing mayhem on a draft, you can save time and effort by testing changes on an outline. Using your scratch outline, refine it into a working outline on screen. Then save and adapt as needed. Print out a copy to keep track of your changes. Some instructors may require a formal outline, particularly with a research paper. You can transform a working outline into a formal outline by following the model on page 47.

If your draft is just not going the way you intend, you might look for a different point of view, a fresh perspective on the topic.

***Finding a Fresh Perspective***   In one episode of P. M. Brady's comic strip "Rose Is Rose," Pasquale, a preschool child, grew tired of his toys and pleaded for a new one. His father listened, then showed him to the door, hinting there was a big toy

## FORMAL OUTLINES

Formal outlines may be written in fragments or sentences. How detailed an outline is depends on the writer and the assignment, but here's a word of warning: Shy away from elaborate outlines. You can invest so much time and energy that you may be reluctant to revise. (For examples of outlines, turn to Chapters 15, 17, and 25.) Both topic outlines and sentence outlines use the following format with numerals and letters to distinguish parts and subparts:

I.
   A.
      1.
         a.
         b.
      2.
         a.
         b.
         c.
   B.
      1.
         a.
         b.
      2.
         a.
         b.

II.  (Repeat as needed)

III.  (Repeat as needed)

## POINTERS FOR MAKING OUTLINES

- Begin with a large roman numeral. Follow with a capital letter, then an arabic number.
- For subtopics, use small letters.
- Use periods after each of the above.
- If you have an A, then you need a B. If you have a 1, then you need a 2. Otherwise, the section does not need a letter or number.

outside. Wading through newly fallen snow, Pasquale looked around and asked where the toy was. His father replied that Pasquale was standing in it.

We are all standing knee-deep in ideas for invigorating our writing. And like Pasquale, we often overlook them. Creativity involves taking everyday experience and transforming it. As writers we can benefit by stepping back to get an off-beat view of our lives. Sometimes an ordinary topic can be enlivened by looking at it from an angle the reader does not expect. John Yeoman decided to give an imaginative spin to an experience by writing from the perspective of his two-year-old self in "Babysitting for Grandfather."

### Babysitting for Grandfather

Everyone except me was getting ready to go somewhere. Being the youngest of the family and a member in good standing of the club known as "the terrible twos," I was used to receiving a lot of attention. But that night my four-year-old sister, dressed in a lacy white dress and black patent leather slippers, was the center of attention. In her hands, she carried a beautiful bouquet of fresh flowers for her role in a wedding.

Of course, so unusual a perspective as John's will not be appropriate for every writing occasion. When a draft seems dull or lifeless, trying out different perspectives can lead to ideas you might not find otherwise.

## CLARIFYING THE DRAFT

After you are satisfied with the focus of the draft and the external order of paragraphs, it is a good idea to check the tone. Read the draft aloud and listen as a reader might. Be critical. How might some readers regard your point of view? How might they perceive your intent? Would they grasp the main point, or might they be distracted or offended by some remark? The following checklist will help you assess your written voice.

*See Chapters 2 and 9.*

---

### CHECKLIST: LISTENING TO YOUR WRITTEN VOICE

1. Is your written voice appropriate for the occasion, purpose, and audience?
2. Does your written voice sound knowledgeable?
3. Might the reader take offense at any of the words?
4. Would a synonym improve the tone without changing the meaning?

## Revising Poor Openings

Have you taken a second look at your thesis statement? Does your first sentence capture the attention of your audience? Or do readers have to stumble through unnecessary words, vague generalities, or other nuisances? One common cause of poor writing is the overuse of the empty expressions *there is, there are,* or *it is.* Try rephrasing the sentence.

To review types of openings, turn to page 31 in Chapter 4. Or you might leaf through Part 3 and look at student papers at the ends of chapters. You will see a variety of techniques for effective openings.

## Revising the Body

As you check the *internal* order of each paragraph, consider that it should be a logical unit with one central idea. Usually, one sentence—the topic sentence—announces the subject of the paragraph and makes a claim. Supporting sentences provide evidence for the claim. They support the topic sentence with explanations, examples, anecdotes, reasons, and facts. If you should find more than one subject to a paragraph, you can either split it into two paragraphs or discard the less important idea.

See Chapter 7.

Skinny paragraphs may need to be fleshed out with more details. Or you may spot gaps in thought. A transitional phrase, sentence, or even paragraph may be needed to bridge ideas. (To find what you need, turn to the index at the back of this book and look up *transition.*)

---

### CHECKLIST: REVISING PARAGRAPHS

1. Is each paragraph organized around *one* central idea?
2. Does each supporting sentence closely relate to the topic sentence?
3. Is each sentence placed in a logical sequence?
4. Is transition needed to connect any sentences?
5. Does any paragraph need more explanation, examples, or details?

---

## Revising the Conclusion

An effective conclusion gives a sense of completeness. You have made your point and left the audience with something to think about. The ending should flow logically and smoothly from the body and be consistent with the opening. An effective ending does not linger to rehash opinions or recite the obvious. No new material intrudes. To see examples of conclusions, turn to page 36 or to student papers in Part 3.

## CASE STUDY

### A *SERIES* OF STUDENT OUTLINES AND DRAFTS

*Roger Moore's final draft, "People Who Flock to Swap Meets," was revised eight times. The four examples show key points of his progress. From a prewriting list, Roger wrote a first draft, revised it, and decided it was still vague. To focus, he listed his audience and purpose, then transformed the list into a scratch outline. He also renamed the categories of customers and rearranged their order.*

### SCRATCH OUTLINE
### (LEAST- TO MOST-IMPORTANT ORDER)

Audience: classmates

Purpose: to inform the class about why I enjoy attending swap meets

*Title: Kinds of People Who Attend Swap Meets*

1. **Sightseers:** arrive in late afternoon and up till closing time. They just look around and complain. Want us to unload but they still do not buy. (It takes all kinds.)
2. **Early Birds:** Are there at 4 a.m. Want to buy cheap parts for resale. Buy very little. Just drink coffee, get in the way, and razz us.
3. **Buyers:** Come promptly at 8:00 a.m. to find parts they need to fix up old cars at their homes. Tell us stories. Visit. Fun to be with.

*From his scratch outline, Roger wrote drafts three and four. Then he tried chronological order, revising his scratch outline into a working outline. To focus the internal order of each paragraph, he used "arrival, purpose, and behaviour" to set up the details.*

*Working Outline (Chronological order)*

1. **Early Birds**
   Arrival: 4 a.m.
   Purpose: Buy cheap for resale
   Behaviour: Buy little; give us a hard time.
2. **Buyers**
   Arrival: 8:00 a.m.
   Purpose: Find parts they need themselves
   Behaviour: Pleasant, polite

3. **Sightseers**
   Arrival: Late afternoon till closing time
   Purpose: Look around
   Behaviour: Complaining

## FIFTH DRAFT

### Swap Meets

Jack, my son, and I have decided there are three types of people who attend swap meets—the early birds, the buyers, and the sightseers. Swap meets are like flea markets, except these swap meets are for car parts only. Set-up times usually start at 4 a.m. This is the time when the early birds try to buy our car parts. They hope to run across a good deal. They don't buy much.

The buyers don't arrive until 8 o'clock or thereafter. They usually look for hard-to-find parts to fix up an old vehicle they are working on. They take their time and hunt carefully through the boxes and piles of parts. They are serious buyers and do not give us a hard time. Some are almost like old friends—we see them regularly.

Sightseers generally come late in the afternoon, often at closing time. They are always complaining about something. Years ago we used to unload parts so they could see them, but then we noticed they would not buy anything anyway.

Swap meets are enjoyable because Jack and I get together, make a little money, and meet some fine people.

*Roger's fifth draft was fairly well developed. Like most early drafts, it needed revision, particularly in the introduction and conclusion. Three more revisions yielded his final draft.*

## FINAL DRAFT

### People Who Flock to Swap Meets

In the summertime my son and I load my panel truck with auto parts every Saturday and head for a swap meet. Swap meets are like flea markets, except these swap meets are for car parts only. At swap meets Jack and I not only make a little money and enjoy the time together but also meet some interesting people. We have found that three types of folks usually attend: the early birds, the buyers, and the sightseers.

The early birds start flocking around the truck as we begin unloading and setting up at 4 a.m., before daybreak. They are usually dealers who are out for a fast buck. They crowd around, getting in the way, hoping to strike a good deal. A few may offer to help unload, but most stand

*continued*

around, drinking coffee and giving us a hard time. Often they make sarcastic remarks in a joking way. They don't buy much.

The buyers don't arrive until 8 o'clock or so. They generally look for difficult-to-find parts to repair an old vehicle they are working on in their spare time. Often they are restoring a classic car in their garage, and they like to tell us about it. We've heard some surprising stories about how much money they made from restoring a junked car. Some of them return regularly; they are almost like old friends. Sometimes they bring their families. They take their time, hunting carefully through boxes and piles of parts. They are serious buyers who ask how much a part costs. If they don't want it, they go on to the next display. Otherwise, they buy.

Sightseers usually come late in the afternoon, often near closing time. It seems they can always find something to complain about. Seldom do they find what they want, and they often become irritated when we are too busy loading the truck to help them. Some even ask us to unload so that they can look over the rest of the parts! Years ago we tried unloading the parts for them to see, but we noticed they would not buy anything anyway. They just wanted to sightsee.

Despite the little irritations, swap meets are still a good place to spend a leisurely Saturday, visiting with my son and meeting interesting people.

# EDITING AND PROOFREADING: STAGE FOUR OF THE WRITING PROCESS

During editing and proofreading, you attend to matters within the sentence. Although editing is a general term meaning to "ready for publication or presentation by amending errors or revising," it is often applied specifically to stage four of the writing process. Proofreading means "discovering small errors and making corrections." Thus the terms overlap somewhat. By delaying editing and proofreading until stage four, writers are free to think about the larger matters of a paragraph. The goal in stage four is to clarify meaning and eliminate grammatical distractions within each sentence so that the writing purpose can be achieved.

## MAJOR TASKS IN EDITING AND PROOFREADING

An essential part of editing is looking closely at the meaning of each sentence as well as its structure. Proofreading requires a scrutiny of grammar and punctuation and typing/keyboarding errors. For more intense concentration, many writers separate editing and proofreading. Others combine the two tasks. Regardless, there is one guideline that is certain to be fruitful: Go through your revised printed draft three or more times. Editing and proofreading just once will not catch all the errors.

## Marking the Revised Draft

After you have added all your revisions onscreen, save them, then run a spelling check. Next print out a clean, double-spaced copy to edit. Off-screen, you will be apt to notice more problems than onscreen. During the first round of editing, do not disrupt your concentration by consulting a thesaurus, dictionary, or handbook—that can come later. Just mark the spot and go on. Your first task is to find and mark concerns that interfere with clarity, completeness, and accuracy.

### *Procedure for Effective Editing and Proofreading*

1. **Read every word.** After your second silent reading, read aloud to spot omissions, errors, and undue repetition. Listen carefully to the sound of the words. Are they pleasing, accurate, and appropriate?
2. **Mark the draft.** Use brackets to set off wordiness. If you notice an error in spelling or grammar, circle it. Place a check mark by any word or sentence you want to return to. Or devise your own system of marking.
3. **Revise sentences and improve wording.** Write changes on your hard copy. In the margins, list possible synonyms for dubious words. To select the best words, look up the meanings.
4. **Add changes onscreen.** After you finish marking your hard copy, make each change onscreen.
5. **Print out a copy.** If your printed draft is quite messy, make a clean copy. Repeat the editing process as needed.

## Making Sentences Clear and Concise

Reading sentences aloud will also help you to evaluate word choice and the placement of ideas. To gain significance, important words should be placed in positions of emphasis—at the beginning or end of a sentence. To edit, underline the important words in your draft, then rearrange the sentence. Simply inverting the sentence and adding a comma will often improve the emphasis, as in this opening of a résumé cover letter:

*Draft:* I have developed a keen eye for detail, line, and colour as an artist.

*Revised:* As an artist, I have developed a keen eye for detail, line, and colour.

If ideas are vague and lightweight, rethink them and restate in more specific words. You might ask yourself, "What do I really intend?" Shorten long rambling sentences by omitting unnecessary phrases, such as *sort of, colour of, kind of, number of, in view of,* and *type of.* Watch, too, for passive voice of verbs, which adds extra words and numbs ideas. Can you rewrite the sentence so that the subject is doing the action? Another way to clear out wordiness is to combine short, related sentences:

***Draft:*** Do you have short, choppy sentences? Are they related? Can they be combined into one sentence?

See
Chapter 8.

***Revised:*** If you find too many short, choppy sentences, try combining related ideas into one sentence.

## Finding Fresh Language

Specific words, fresh language, and comparison enliven humdrum sentences. By choosing precise nouns and perhaps an adjective, you can create visual images: Instead of *flowers*, say *yellow pansies* or *pink iris*. Add power to verbs by refining them. Instead of *went*, say *hurried* or *drove* through a red light, or *fell* through the ice. Don't try to sneak slang or a pet colloquialism such as *mess up* or *stuff* past the reader by wrapping it in a set of quotation marks. Find a better way to say what you mean.

***Create a Simile or Metaphor***   Business and technical writing, as well as literature, employs similes and metaphors. These unusual comparisons use familiar images to lead readers to see or understand less familiar images. A *simile* is an explicit (or stated) comparison of two unlike items or ideas, using *like* or *as*. Let's take a look at these student similes:

- "My tires, *smooth as the soles of worn-out tennis shoes*, have tiny cracks in the sidewalls." (Kim Coffey)
- "Spade, whose pedigree was a mystery, had a tail eighteen inches long that *he could use like a whip.*" (John Spillman)

### PRUNING EXTRA WORDS

Keep sentences clear and vigorous by pruning unnecessary words. Consider these redundancies and their edited counterparts:

| Redundant | Edited |
|---|---|
| absolutely essential | essential |
| actual truth of the matter | truth |
| advance warning | warning |
| cancel out | cancel |
| connected together | connected |
| foreign imports | imports |
| free gifts | gifts |
| past history | history |

## EDITING AND PROOFREADING ON-SCREEN

On-screen editing and proofreading carry the risk of overlooking errors you would normally notice on a printed page. Even after you think your text is error-free, print out a copy and proofread it carefully several times.

1. *As you add each correction on-screen, check it off on the hard copy.* This habit will increase your accuracy.

2. *After you make changes on-screen, read the sentence aloud.* A writer may omit little words or leave extra ones when moving text and revising.

3. *Run a final spelling check right before printing out your last draft.* Last-minute changes can cause errors. If you are not the world's best typist, typos could be lurking in your text.

A *metaphor* is a figure of speech that contains an implicit (or suggested) contrast, such as "His last car *was a lemon.*" Notice that such metaphors contain *is* or *was;* they have no other signal words to announce them. Another type of metaphor is just one word, as in some names: Rocky, Angela, Heather, Ruby, and Forest. Verbs, too, can contain metaphors: the motor *purred;* employees *support* their manager's decisions.

***Experiment with Alliteration and Rhyme***   *Alliteration* is the repetition of the initial (first) consonant sound. In a speech titled "Run-of-the-Mill Miracle," Gary Fenton used *alliteration* in the title (two m's). Later he commented on his daughter's birth: "No doubt about it. Having a baby is not easy. If it were, we would refer to it as leisure, not labor (two l's)."

Note that "doubt about" also rhymes. Alliteration and rhyme can be pleasing and emphatic as long as they are not overdone. Alliteration is easy to use; anyone can use it in titles or phrases.

***Experiment with Old Sayings***   You may be able to revitalize an old saying or cliché by putting a different spin on it. For example, Robin Allen reworked "I never laid a hand on him" to "Sidney was a quiet cat and basically gentle. Even when I gave him a bath, which he hated, *he never laid a paw on me.*" In the paper about "babysitting" for his grandfather, John Yeoman surprises the reader with a revitalized cliché:

> What about me? Why couldn't I go? This is when the plot thickened. Someone had to stay home and watch grandfather, or "Popo" as I called him. It was the classic, though crude, method of reverse psychology. Having a limited amount of reasoning ability at age two, I fell hook, line, and baby bottle.

## PROOFREADING EFFECTIVELY

No significant piece of writing—whether a college paper, a report to a boss, or a business letter—can be considered complete until it has been carefully proofread at least twice for errors. Three times is better. Lapses in grammatical usage, punctuation, and spelling undercut your credibility as a writer and call into question your commitment to your work. In college these errors may result in lower grades; at work they may damage your career prospects. We recommend that you

- *Correct your graded papers soon after their return.* Look up words and errors. (Your instructor may use marks and symbols keyed to the chart in the inside back cover of this book. These pages will guide you to the appropriate page in the handbook.)
- *Keep a list of errors pointed out in your graded papers.* Make a list of common errors you need to work on.
- *Review the word pairs in the Glossary of Usage, H-36.* These words are commonly confused because they look or sound alike. Examples: *effect/affect, ensure/insure, all ready/already.*
- *Learn the rules of standard grammar, punctuation, and spelling.* Don't ask someone else; you may get bad advice. Take responsibility by learning the rules and carefully checking your own work.

## PEER REVIEW: HELPING TO IMPROVE EACH OTHER'S WRITING

Published writers often receive input from writing groups, agents, editors, or reviewers. Peer review in a classroom provides similar help. These reviews enable class members not only to help each other with early drafts but also to sharpen their skill at identifying rough spots in their own writing.

The job of a peer reviewer is to pinpoint problems, not solve them. Revision, editing, and proofreading are the responsibility of the writer. When giving feedback, the reviewer should be tactful. Comments that are overly blunt, unduly critical, or vague can be worse than none at all. Before critiquing, you might ask yourself, "How would I feel if I received this feedback?"

The difference between callousness and tact often lies in the phrasing. Vague reactions such as "I don't like the opening" or "confusing" or "dull" are not very helpful. Responses should be specific so that the writer understands where and what the problem is. Responses can be softened in three ways:

1. *Begin with a positive comment about the draft:*
   - This is an interesting topic.
   - That example is well developed (funny or unusual).
   - The anecdote is delightful (or amusing or charming).
   - The spelling is correct.

## SUGGESTIONS FOR PEER REVIEW

Writers who are prepared to accept constructive criticism can learn much from peer review. Still, peer responses should not be taken as gospel. As you start to revise, evaluate the quality of each response and extract what is useful.

### FOR REVIEWERS

1. Consider one aspect of the writing at a time.
2. Word your comments and suggestions thoughtfully and carefully.
3. Identify concerns tactfully, but don't whitewash.

### FOR REVIEWEES

1. Keep an open mind. Be willing to consider suggestions. Ask about comments that seem unclear.
2. Evaluate each suggestion carefully. If in doubt, make an appointment with your instructor or seek help at the campus writing centre.

2. *Be tentative.* Offer comments as opinion, not a final decree:
   - This sentence *appears* negative. Is that what you intend?
   - This passage *seems* unclear. What do you mean?
   - I *wonder* if this part might work better here? (Not "You ramble.")
3. *Ask polite questions:*
   - Where is the thesis? (Not "You don't have a thesis statement.")
   - Have you thought about the ending yet? (Not "There isn't any conclusion.")

## SUMMARY

- Follow five major steps of revision.
- Revise a written draft by narrowing the title, devising an outline, and developing a clear and fresh perspective.
- Revise the draft for logical order, expression of ideas, and clear and accurate order.
- Edit for improved word choice and sentence structure.
- Proofread for grammar, punctuation, and spelling.
- Revise a written draft using peer and self-reviews.

## *Practice*

### Ideas for Writing

*Directions:* Describe an incident, experience, or tradition, or use one of these options:

1. The job you would like to have in five years
2. Broken promises
3. An anecdote about a family holiday or vacation
4. An incident at summer camp, school, or work
5. The earliest childhood scene or event that you can recall

### Suggestions for Peer Review Practice

1. Reread "Guidelines for Peer Review."
2. Select one of your practice writings to revise and edit.
3. After you finish, find a partner and exchange papers.
4. Write your responses and suggestions on a separate sheet.
5. Return the paper along with the peer review.
6. Question your reviewer about anything you are unsure of.
7. Revise again, using any beneficial suggestions.

# Revision and Accuracy

## Beginning to Think Critically

**Learning Objectives**

After reading and applying the information in Chapter 6, you'll be able to:

- Distinguish fact from opinion
- Eliminate misinformation by not changing expert opinions, and by avoiding generalizations, overstatements, and stereotypes
- Use language accurately

> *Whatever is only almost true is quite false, and among the most dangerous of errors, because being so near truth, it is the more likely to lead astray.*
>
> Henry Ward Beecher (1813–1887)

We live in an era in which propaganda, myth, and other misinformation masquerade as truth. Often inaccuracies come from politicians and reporters. They may confuse, misrepresent, and repeat unverified items so often the misstatements gain widespread acceptance. Studies and polls based on invalid samples also can gain credence. Other misinformation spreads in various ways, including via the Internet. Eventually, some readers may wonder why telling the truth is important. Why bother to be accurate?

## WHY IS ACCURACY IMPORTANT?

Throughout the ages, civilizations have accepted the basic premise that *truth is the cornerstone of trust.* Truth undergirds trust in both social and business relationships.

Accuracy is synonymous with truth; both are an exact rendering of the facts. As writers, we are obligated to check our facts and examine our claims critically in order to provide the most accurate and up-to-date information possible. Expository writing should be factual and accurate.

Concerned with public perception of the media, the *Wall Street Journal* (3 Jan. 2001) printed a letter from the publisher. Reprinted here are the first two points of a section entitled "What We Value":

- **Fairness and accuracy**—There is no substitute in our business for getting the story right, and for putting it in context, for being both accurate and fair.
- **A clear distinction between news and views**—There are places in most any publication, and certainly in every newspaper, for both news and views, for reporting on and analyzing events and trends and for expressing opinions about those events and trends. . . . But we pursue these two missions separately. Our opinions are clearly labeled; our news judgments are arrived at independently.

Whether you write papers, reports, or letters, the two guidelines above can assist you in finding and presenting facts to your audience.


## HOW CAN FACT BE DETERMINED?

Statements and claims that have been rigorously tested and finally accepted by authorities in the field are said to be *established facts*. When you think something is probably true, ask whether or not it is an established fact. Can you find reliable research or other evidence to *prove* it? If not, then it is still in the realm of opinion.

In court, sworn evidence and the risk of perjury should keep witnesses truthful. Yet there can still be problems in accuracy. Two eyewitnesses can disagree about the same event. Perhaps one did not see the entire event, or they interpreted it differently. Then too, recollections fade with time. Expert opinion seems to be reliable most of the time, but even experts disagree. Legally, fact is based on three types of evidence:

1. Eyewitness reports sworn under oath
2. Expert opinion by an authority in the field
3. Material evidence (physical items that can be tested)

Without a doubt, material evidence is the most reliable of all. Hair, body fluids, fingerprints, voice prints, tire casts, and other materials can be carefully analyzed. Usually, the results are accurate, but once in a while human error does intrude. Even electronic devices are not foolproof. Temperature and other factors can hinder the performance of equipment, or someone may tamper with photographs, tapes, or other evidence. Determining what is true can be difficult.

## INFERENCES ARE UNPROVEN

An *inference* is an assumption—an opinion—that is thought to be true but has not yet been proven. For example, on a subzero morning a neighbour's car fails to start. This is the first time the engine has refused to budge. Since the gas gauge registers half full, he *infers* that the battery is weak. He calls the local service station for a quick charge. After that, the motor starts. A battery check reveals a faulty cell. Thus his inference has been proven to be a fact. Some inferences are tested and discredited.

As long as inferences are reasonable and not presented as facts, they seldom cause problems in writing. But sometimes beginning writers confuse inferences and facts, as in the following example:

> When his owner's red pickup truck approaches his pen, Buck realizes raccoon season must be here. During hunting season, his mind is strictly on tracking coon, but at other times his chief pleasure is chasing cats.

What are the problems here? First, dogs cannot understand the concept of "raccoon season" (although they might associate the truck with hunting). Second, the word *strictly* means 100 percent of the time, and it is doubtful that Buck thought only about one thing. Dogs are easily distracted by noises, other animals, and hunger pangs. The final statement—"his chief pleasure is chasing cats"—is not an established fact but a value judgment.

## VALUE JUDGMENTS AND POINT OF VIEW

Lew Wallace's familiar words, "beauty is altogether in the eye of the beholder," point out the elusive nature of value judgments. Too often we regard these opinions as fact. Actually, they are perceptions, which can be illogical and unpredictable. Often we assume other people have (or should have) the same values we cherish. The problem is that value judgments often masquerade as fact.

A *value judgment* is an opinion—an estimate of worth. Frequently, we rate items as bad or good, cheap or expensive, ugly or beautiful. Or we consider actions wrong or right, immoral or moral, according to our own perspective and experience. Yet value judgments are imprecise and variable. They vary from person to person and change with the times. For instance, baseball cards were originally just prizes collected by schoolchildren from packs of bubble gum. Now the cards are valuable and sought by adult collectors. They are regarded from a different point of view.

*Point of view* refers to the way something is perceived—the perspective. We form value judgments based on our differing points of view. Sinclair Lewis, in his early novel *Main Street*, describes two young women who see the town of Gopher Prairie through very different eyes. The impressions of Carol Kennicott, a city girl from Minneapolis, reveal her point of view:

> She glanced through the fly-specked windows of the most pretentious building in sight, the one place which welcomed strangers and determined their opinion of the charm and luxury of Gopher Prairie—the Minniemashie House. It was a tall lean shabby structure, three stories of yellow-streaked wood. . . . In the hotel office she could see a stretch of bare unclean floor, a line of rickety chairs with brass cuspidors. . . . The dining room beyond was a jungle of stained tablecloths and catsup bottles.

At the same time Bea Sorenson, "bored by farm work," walked along the other side of Main Street, thinking about the "excitements of city life" and the Minniemashie House. Her impression reveals very different judgments and a very different point of view:

> A hotel, awful high, higher than Oscar Tollefson's new red barn; three storied, one right on top of another; you had to stick your head back to look clear up to the top. There was a swell traveling man in there—probably been to Chicago lots of times.

Carol and Bea, coming from varying backgrounds, view the town differently. Later they make value judgments about Gopher Prairie, based on their points of view. Carol thinks: "I must be wrong. People do live here. It can't be as ugly as—as I know it is! I must be wrong." But Bea reasoned that even if she didn't receive a salary of six dollars every week, she would work for much less "to be allowed to stay here."

## LISTENING TO THE TONE OF WRITING

A writer's point of view may range from essentially *objective* to highly *subjective* depending on the purpose and the topic. Some writing requires an impersonal voice that presents the facts squarely. The front pages of most Canadian newspapers, for example, carry factual reports in which the writers attempt to relay news stories objectively. The purpose is to report what happened—not to push a particular view. The tone of objective writing is impartial, unslanted, and unbiased; readers seldom get a sense of the writer's opinion or personality.

The purpose of editorial pages is to allow writers to express their individual points of view. In editorials, columns, and letters to the editor, writers interpret facts subjectively, based on their own political, ethical, and economic values. They offer opinions and judgments; they praise and criticize; they urge specific courses of action. Their written voices may convey conviction, indignation, anger, or joy.

A degree of subjectivity is inevitable in almost any writing, but it should be controlled and appropriate to the writing situation. Reading your draft aloud will help you to listen to the tone of your written voice. For help in presenting information fairly, clearly, and accurately, see the box below.

See page 5.

## CHARACTERISTICS OF FACTS, INFERENCES, AND VALUE JUDGMENTS

| *Fact* | *Inference* | *Value Judgment* |
|---|---|---|
| Act, deed, event, state or condition of reality | Assumption, generalization, or decision derived from evidence | Opinion or estimate of worth, an evaluation or rating |
| Objectively proved by observation, experiment, eyewitness, or expert opinion | Has not been proved; has possibility of being proved or discredited | Cannot be proved; will always be an opinion |

## FOUR WAYS MISINFORMATION ARISES

As we grow up, we hear folk wisdom, propaganda, myths, superstitions, and other inaccuracies presented as fact. Steeped in these beliefs, we tend not to question them, and so we accumulate much misinformation without realizing it. Here are four ways misinformation commonly comes to be accepted as fact.

### Expert Opinion Occasionally Changes

We all know that one should not swim for an hour after eating—or do we? This bit of advice was published by the Red Cross over fifty years ago. A lifesaving manual claimed that a swimmer who ate immediately before a dip risked stomach cramps or even death. Now the *Journal of Health, Physical Education, and Recreation* disputes the idea of "stomach cramps." A prominent physical educator was quoted as saying, "I have never seen a case of so-called stomach cramps, although I have observed hundreds of thousands of persons swimming immediately after eating." Medical opinions, as well as other expert opinions, sometimes change over the years.

### A Small Survey Is Inadequate Proof

Sometimes we hear someone generalize after surveying a few friends or considering a few unusual incidents. It's the old story of "everyone else is getting a new prom dress but me." But a small sample is hardly a reliable survey (see Chapter 22).

Overstatement, stereotypic thinking, and generalizing from an unrepresentative sample can lead to the fallacy of hasty generalization. *A hasty generalization is a broad statement, an inference, that lacks sufficient proof.* A hasty generalization can occur when a *trend* or a *tendency* is overstated as if it were true for an entire group or population. Although assumed to be true, a hasty generalization is not an established fact. (This fallacy and others are explained in Chapter 20.)

## Facts Are Overstated

Unintentional overstatement sometimes occurs. We may not recall exactly what we read or heard and may overstate the facts. Or we may paraphrase, using synonyms that give an impression different from the one we intended. And some people exaggerate without being aware of it. For example, the student who wrote the following paragraph was convinced it was absolutely true:

> Lack of participation by people in their government is the number one cause for their loss of control over their own affairs. They say: "I don't care." "My vote doesn't matter." "I didn't have time to vote." These are some of the excuses given for not carrying out one of the most important rights given to the people, the right to vote.

Here a partial truth has been stretched ("number one cause"). This "statistic" is not an established fact. He could have made the statement acceptable by adding one word, *possibly*.

## Stereotyping Shuts out Fact

A writer must be on guard against stereotypes based on gender, race/ethnicity, age, religion, and the like. Stereotyping is classifying someone or something into a tight little box. A stereotypic belief supposedly typifies a group, place, issue, or event. Although the characteristic attributed to the group may be true for some individuals, it is not true for all. Consider the following statements carefully. Then mark each one true or false.

_____ 1. Redheads have quick tempers.

_____ 2. Men are stronger than women.

_____ 3. Politicians can't be trusted.

If you marked all of the statements true, you have probably grown up hearing these stereotypes presented as fact. If you marked some false, you are to be congratulated on your growing skepticism. If you marked all false, you rate an A. Why are all three statements false? None allows for an exception. These statements are *absolute* or all-inclusive: They claim to apply 100 percent of the time. Think about it. Do *all* redheads in the world have quick tempers? Are *all* men stronger than *all* women? Isn't there even one politician who can be trusted? To further complicate matters, item 2 contains an *undefined term*. What kind of strength are we talking about—physical, emotional, intellectual, or spiritual?

Experienced speakers and writers avoid stereotypic thinking, for it is not only unfair and undiplomatic but also inaccurate. Stereotypes shut out new information that conflicts with old, embedded beliefs. Stereotypic thinking is a quagmire that can lead to charges of sexism and discrimination as well as hurt feelings.

## WRITING RESPONSIBLY

Responsible writing presents the truth, and responsible claims are backed by evidence. Readers should not have to grope through a fog of unsupported information to determine the facts. Once you become aware of the slipperiness of fact, you can take three precautions to avoid misstatement: Limit your generalizations, use absolute terms accurately, and identify inferences and opinion.

### Limiting Generalizations

To be accurate and useful in writing, generalizations must be factual. If they are overstated and too broad they undermine your credibility. Thus you need to limit, or "qualify." *Qualifiers are words or phrases that modify meanings and allow for exceptions.* Qualified generalizations often serve as topic sentences and thesis statements. The generalizations below were used successfully as thesis sentences in student essays. (Qualifiers are italicized.)

> *Some* outstanding women have graced history with their heroic feats during battle.
>
> In today's hurried pace, the giving and receiving of love is *often* overlooked.
>
> Crash dieting *seems* to be the surefire approach to coping with obesity.

To limit an overly broad generalization, you may need a word such as *may, might, tend, seem,* or *appear* to make your claim acceptable. Other qualifiers refer to number. To indicate a *majority* (more than 50 percent), you can use terms such as the following:

| | | | | |
|---|---|---|---|---|
| most | largely | overall | chiefly | as a rule |
| usually | primarily | typically | generally | mainly |

To indicate a *minority*, use less specific words. Note, however, that the size of a minority can vary and influence your word choice. If in doubt about the appropriateness of a qualifier, consult two or more good desk dictionaries for fine distinctions in meaning. Terms such as those below can be used to indicate less than 50 percent:

| | | | |
|---|---|---|---|
| many | rarely | often | several |
| few | frequently | irregularly | seldom |
| some | relatively few | sometimes | occasionally |

### Using Absolute Terms Accurately

Absolute terms are inflexible words that state or imply *none* or *all*. These words mean zero or 100 percent. When you revise, examine every statement that

PEANUTS reprinted by permission of United Feature Syndicate, Inc.

contains an absolute term. Be sure you consider what the word means, not just what you intend. If you overstate a case by misusing an absolute, the reader will be apt to take the literal meaning unless you plant a clue that the statement is ironic or joking. The list below will help you recognize absolute terms:

| | | | |
|---|---|---|---|
| all | always | everyone | no one |
| none | never | only | same |
| every | completely | exact | anything |

Can you identify Peppermint Patty's absolute term above?

Other kinds of words can also be all-inclusive. Verbs and adjectives such as the following can also lead to overstatement and misstatement:

| | | | |
|---|---|---|---|
| is | perfect* | greatest | same |
| are | unique* | smallest | best |
| was | worst | opposite | exact |

*Something is either perfect or imperfect; unique or not unique. Phrases such as *very perfect* or *rather unique* are incorrect. If in doubt about such usage, check a dictionary.

## Identifying Inferences and Other Opinions

In workplace writing and college assignments, you may be asked to "draw a conclusion" (inference) from a set of facts, to "write a reaction" (see Chapter 26), or to "interpret facts." To complete such assignments successfully, you need to know how to identify inferences and other types of opinion. Qualifiers such as those below indicate inferences:

| | | | |
|---|---|---|---|
| theory | probably | apparently | seems |
| conjecture | possibly | it appears | imply |
| indicate | evidently | suggests | infer |

As you revise, check to see that no opinions are presented as facts. For example, a widely held belief that is unproved should be identified as opinion. Phrases such as "a common belief" or "the conventional wisdom" indicate the nature of such statements. Other terms that identify opinion include the following:

| | | | |
|---|---|---|---|
| current thinking | viewpoint | reaction | perception |
| appraisal | impression | feeling | folk wisdom |
| point of view | estimate | prediction | view |

## REVISING FOR ACCURACY

Whether you write a report, an essay, a research paper, or some other document, double-check every item to be sure it is logical and accurate. In developing and organizing ideas during prewriting and drafting, it is easy to leave out a word, transpose a number, overstate a generalization, or commit some other blunder. Develop the habit of being thorough, of questioning information that doesn't quite ring true or seems suspicious. The checklist below should be helpful:

### CHECKLIST: REVISING FOR ACCURACY

1. Are all data established facts?
2. Have inferences, value judgments, and other opinions been qualified?
3. Do any generalizations need to be limited?
4. Are all words accurate?
5. Does the tone sound appropriate?
6. Have any significant facts been omitted? Are any more needed?

Only when we learn to think logically and critically, to analyze carefully our own ideas as well as the ideas of other speakers and writers, can we begin to approach "the whole truth." That is what the writing process is all about.

### SUMMARY

- Present only truthful material within your own work.
- Distinguish fact from opinion.
- Eliminate misinformation by not changing expert opinions, and by avoiding generalizations based on a small sample, overstatements, and stereotypes.
- Use language accurately; choose your words carefully.

## Test Yourself

### Fact, Inference, or Value Judgment?

*Directions:* Imagine or examine a Red Delicious apple. Then mark F (fact), I (inference), or VJ (value judgment) below. Check your answers with the key at the end of the chapter.

_____ 1. This apple has four bumps (protrusions) on the bottom.

_____ 2. This apple is attractive to the eye.

_____ 3. This apple has a shiny red skin.

_____ 4. This apple will taste good.

_____ 5. This apple contains dark brown seeds. (The apple is uncut.)

### Opinion or Observable Fact?

*Directions:* Write O for opinion or F for observable fact in the blanks. Then check your answers with the key at the end of the chapter.

_____ 1. The fender was *dented*.

_____ 2. Peggy is *pretty*.

_____ 3. The lighting was *adequate*.

_____ 4. The rock is *moss covered*.

_____ 5. The speech was *boring*.

## Practice

### Collaborative Learning: Fact, Inference, or Value Judgment?

*Directions:* Mark each item as fact (F), inference (I), or value judgment (VJ). If both fact and inference, mark I; if both fact and value judgment, mark VJ. Discuss any disagreement.

_____ 1. Great Britain is an island, not a continent.

_____ 2. Many exquisite bays line Britain's coast.

_____ 3. The beautiful white cliffs of Dover, overlooking the English Channel, are composed of chalk.

_____ 4. The Isle of Man lies in the Irish Sea.

_____ 5. If you mention hunting to a Brit, he or she will immediately think of fox hunting.

_____ 6. Most Canadians are surprised to learn that a subway in London is an underground passageway for pedestrians.

_____ 7. If you want a delicious meal in London, order fish, not steak.

_____ 8. The Tower of London is the most fabulous sight in the city.

_____ 9. In the spring after a rain, Paris has a delicate, shimmering beauty.

_____ 10. The Louvre, the largest art museum and palace in the world, is located on the north bank of the River Seine in Paris.

## Test Yourself Answers

### Fact, Inference, or Value Judgment?

| | |
|---|---|
| *1. F* | *4. VJ* |
| *2. VJ* | *5. I* |
| *3. F* | |

### Opinion or Observable Fact?

*Items 1 and 4 are observable facts. The others are opinions.*

# Revising Paragraphs

After reading and applying the information in Chapter 7, you'll be able to:

- Identify and design basic elements of a paragraph: topic sentence, supporting sentences, and concluding sentence
- Identify five features of effective paragraphs: clarity, interest, unity, coherence, and completeness
- Identify and organize paragraphs according to chronology, importance, complexity, familiarity, emphasis, or some other logical order
- Design paragraphs to suit different writing styles: narrative, description, process analysis, and illustration

*There is a poignancy in all things clear,*
*In the stare of a deer, in the ring of a hammer*
*in the morning. Seeing a bucket of perfectly lucid water*
*we fall to imagining prodigious honesties.*

—Richard Wilbur, "Clearness," *Ceremony*

Clarity is the heart of effective writing, and well-developed paragraphs are essential for clarity. Opening and concluding paragraphs, discussed in Chapter 4, act as a frame for an essay, paper, or report. Body paragraphs focus on making specific points and presenting information in a complete and coherent way. Transitional paragraphs provide connections between different ideas. A single well-developed paragraph by itself may even form a complete brief essay, exam answer, or business communication.

This chapter discusses elements and qualities of successful single paragraphs, as well as body paragraphs within essays, paying special attention to some specific modes of development.

# ELEMENTS OF AN EFFECTIVE PARAGRAPH

To be effective, a paragraph must be centred on one idea, and the sentences must flow in a logical sequence. And regardless of whether the paragraph stands alone or comes in the body of an essay (or other piece of writing), it contains certain elements: topic sentence, support sentences, and concluding sentences.

## The Topic Sentence

The topic sentence contains the main idea of a paragraph. This sentence tells the reader *what* will be covered and *why*. Some topic sentences also tell *where* or *when*. A basic topic sentence has two essential functions:

1. *To limit the subject to one main idea* that can be developed in the paragraph.
2. *To make a claim, assertion, or statement of opinion.* This part of the topic sentence may be a belief, impression, generalization, or recommendation.

Let's consider a topic sentence that performs both these functions:

Uncle Jake, who came uninvited, was a difficult house guest.

The subject of this topic sentence is "Uncle Jake," and the claim is that he was "a difficult house guest." This topic sentence sets up the expectation that the writer will describe Uncle Jake's behaviour. In the body of the paragraph, readers will expect support—examples of what he said and anecdotes of what he did so that they can see for themselves how difficult Uncle Jake was.

## Support Sentences

Support sentences explain the main idea of the topic sentence. They supply *evidence* to convince the reader of the soundness of the claim, assertion, or opinion. You might regard the topic sentence as an argument (view) to be proven. The support sentences supply evidence in the form of facts, definitions, reasons, examples, or illustrations to back up the claim in the topic sentence.

The minimum number of support sentences is generally three or four; often there are more. As you develop support, keep in mind these points:

1. Quality is better than quantity. A few excellent examples are worth more than many mediocre examples.
2. Established facts, definitions, and valid reasons provide credible evidence.
3. Appropriate illustrations and anecdotes increase readers' interest, understanding, and conviction.

## A Concluding Sentence

Besides the two basic parts just discussed—the topic sentence and support sentences—some paragraphs have a third part: a concluding sentence. This final sentence may be a summary of the points made in the support sentences. It can also serve as a *clincher*, providing the paragraph with a sense of completeness by commenting on the subject in an interesting, surprising, or humorous way. In the following student paragraph, the concluding sentence not only alludes to the opening topic sentence but also makes a point.

### Climb Aboard!

The magic of a carousel has a way of turning men and women into children again. As they approach the carousel house, their steps and their hearts suddenly become lighter. Tots tug at adult hands, eager to climb aboard this remnant from a fairy tale. The magnificent carousel stands with hundreds of lights reflected in mirrors on the brightly painted rounding boards. Adventurous riders select mounts from rows of prancing horses or from the menagerie of bears, big cats, goats, ostriches, rabbits, a zebra, a giraffe, or a hippopotamus. The timid and the elderly seem to prefer the sedate pace of the two chariots. When all riders are seated, the calliope signals the ride is about to begin. As the carousel gains speed, whirling faster and faster, the riders' faces are transformed by smiles. Their cares seem to disappear as they are charmed by the magic of the carousel.

—Bonita M. Goings

## QUALITIES OF EFFECTIVE PARAGRAPHS

Effective paragraphs have five distinctive features: clarity, interest, unity, coherence, and completeness. Clarity is of primary importance.

### Clarity

Some writing is like bright sunlight. The main idea shines through the words clearly. For writing to be effective, readers must be able to determine the meaning upon first reading. True, they may need to reread to recall specific details, but the main idea should be apparent the first time.

Clarity is the end result of knowing your purpose, correctly assessing the audience, connecting ideas, selecting appropriate words, and being complete. Important influences on clarity are the level of formality, the voice of verbs, sentence structure, length of sentences and paragraphs, and positions of emphasis (see Chapter 8). Careful revision and editing will help to make your paragraphs clear.

### Interest

An effective paragraph is worth reading. The topic is significant and the development is interesting. A secret of good essay writing is to remember that readers like to be entertained. Try to capture readers' attention and make them eager to continue. Before beginning a draft, consider how you might stimulate interest. Can you approach your topic in an unusual way? What might readers like to know? Then use action verbs and concrete nouns to help the reader share your impression (see Chapter 11).

## Unity

To write effective paragraphs, resist the temptation to create thickets of words. Focus on one major idea (in the topic sentence) to unify the paragraph. *All of the other sentences in the paragraph should link to the major idea.* They may support it with examples, facts, statistics, opinion, or reasons. During the drafting stage, don't worry unduly about unity. At that stage your goal is to expand ideas on paper. But when you start to revise, unity becomes a priority. To check the unity of a paragraph, ask yourself three questions:

- What is the purpose (main idea) of the paragraph?
- Does each support sentence assist in achieving the purpose?
- If not, what needs to be deleted or added?

## Coherence

Think of a paragraph as a jigsaw puzzle—each piece must fit. If not, the paragraph lacks coherence; it does not flow smoothly. If words, phrases, or sentences are in the wrong places, they must be rearranged. If there are gaps between ideas, you need to add transitions to provide connections. Other ways of achieving coherence are by repeating key words and by using parallelism.

***Signpost Transitions***   Like signs on a highway, signpost transitions direct the reader. Usually, these signal words and phrases appear at the beginning of sentences. Just adding a word or phrase to indicate how the material relates to the preceding sentence often makes a paragraph clearer and easier to read.

---

### COMMON SIGNPOST TRANSITIONS

- *To show time:* once, years ago, later, soon, now, today, then, before, when, while, after, meanwhile, as, next, first, second, and so forth
- *To add:* too, also, and, another, besides, in addition, furthermore
- *To show difference:* but, yet, however, still, otherwise, even so, although
- *To show similarity:* like, likewise, similarly, both, resemble, identical
- *To show effects or results:* because, for, therefore, as a result, since, thus
- *To emphasize:* in fact, indeed, above all, again, regardless, nonetheless
- *To point out examples:* for example, for instance

See
Chapter 14.

***Embedded Transition***    Transition that is placed within a sentence is said to be "embedded." *Key words*, *natural relationships*, *synonyms*, and *pronouns* are four types of embedded transition. Repeating key words, substituting synonyms for words, and using pronouns that refer to key words can help you join sentences smoothly into a paragraph. Note how the repetition of key words, natural relationships, synonyms, and pronouns help make the following paragraph coherent:

> *My mother* was the eldest of *her* generation—of nine children—and came from a slightly more elevated social station in Jamaica. *She* had a high school education, which *my father* lacked. . . . Before emigrating, *Mom* had worked as a stenographer in a lawyer's office. *Her* mother, Gram McKoy, was a small, lovely woman whose English wedded *African cadence* to *British inflection*, the sound of which is still music to my soul. The McKoys and the Powells both had *bloodlines* common among *Jamaicans*, including *African, English, Irish, Scotch*, and probably *Arawak Indian*. *My father's side* even added a *Jewish strain* from a Broomfield *ancestor*.
>
> —Colin Powell, ***My American Journey***

***Parallelism***    Parallel structures provide balance in writing and contribute to coherence. Possibly without thinking, you already use parallelism in several ways: for items in a series, coordinate phrases and clauses, compound sentences, and pairs of related sentences (see Chapter 8). You may sense that parallelism smooths sentence structure and gives equal emphasis to coordinate ideas. To check the coherence and parallelism of your paragraphs, read them aloud. The ear is often a better detector of imbalance than the eye. Note the use of parallelism in the following descriptive paragraph by a student:

> **Through a Child's Eyes**
>
> A tall, husky man has long been a very special person in my life. *His hair is the color of bricks in a schoolhouse*, while *his eyes are the color of hickory nut shells. Above his eyes* he wears a permanent frown, but *in his smile* I can see his inner warmth peeking through. *When he speaks*, his voice sounds like a semi-truck going through a tunnel at a high rate of speed. The low, gravelly tones echo like a bouncing tennis ball in an empty room. *When he enters a room*, he resembles a bear just waking from its winter slumber. But *when he sits*, a lap appears that would never turn away a child who wished to crawl upon it. When sitting there, I can detect the faint scent of Old Spice. *His big, muscular arms* make me feel safe from any possible harm. *His huge, powerful hands* are *like vise grips*, but when wiping tears away, they are *like soft cotton*. As rough as this man appears *on the outside, on the inside* he is soft and gentle, just like a newborn kitten. . . . This very dear person is my dad.
>
> —Nancy Smathers

## Completeness

An effective paragraph does not weary readers or waste their time. Details appear for a valid reason: to support the topic sentence. To be complete, a paragraph must supply adequate and appropriate information. But how much is enough? What is suitable? You, the writer, must decide according to each rhetorical situation. Whether your professor assigns a single paragraph or a lengthy paper, you will have to assess the audience and the occasion. You might consider the following points:

- How much are readers likely to know?
- How much more do they need to know?
- Why? How will the information be used?
- Are there enough examples, reasons, or anecdotes to be interesting?
- Is there enough specific support to make my point?

## PREWRITING AND DRAFTING PARAGRAPHS

If you are writing a body paragraph in an essay, the topic sentence introduces one segment of your thesis statement (central idea of the essay). Although this chapter shows some body paragraphs, they are explained in Part 3. This chapter focuses on single student paragraphs.

### Narrowing a Topic Sentence

Beginning writers frequently struggle to limit a general topic. Narrowing a topic requires selecting one significant aspect. The problem may be that you know so much, you can't decide where to start. For example, a first attempt might read "I like horses." But you realize the sentence is boring and too broad. Your mind spinning with ideas, you begin to prewrite. Soon you have a list that yields a suitable topic. Your efforts might look like this:

horses
riding horses
riding horses I have owned
my first riding horse

**Draft topic sentence:** I'll never forget my first horse.
**First revision:** Pinto was my first riding horse; actually, he was a pony.
**Second revision:** My first riding horse was actually a pony, but to my five-year-old eyes, Pinto was the finest of horses.

For most topic sentences, a limit of twenty words or so usually works well. A topic sentence that is too long may overwhelm the reader.

### Positioning the Topic Sentence

Once you have drafted a topic sentence, your next concern is where to place it in the paragraph. Before positioning the topic sentence, consider its function and the effect you want to obtain. Will you place it at the beginning, the middle, or the end?

***The Topic Sentence at the Beginning***   Most expository paragraphs follow the direct approach: The topic sentence is placed at the beginning. There the topic receives more emphasis than in the middle, and the reader knows immediately what the writer will explain.

***The Topic Sentence in the Middle***   Sometimes a writer may wish to take a leisurely path to the main idea. Then the topic sentence may appear in the middle of a paragraph. Placed there, the major idea receives less emphasis than at the beginning or end. In a paragraph of comparison, for instance, a topic sentence might be located midway between the two subjects. There it can identify the purpose and connect the items being compared. Or the topic sentence may be in the middle for other reasons, as in the following paragraph, which describes nonverbal communication:

> Mrs. Clark, who teaches math, is explaining an essential aspect of the subject. She notices that Fred is staring at her with unblinking eyes, his body taut and erect, his feet flat on the floor. She discerns no motion whatever from Fred. Do you think that Fred is listening to the lecture, evaluating what Mrs. Clark is saying? *If you think he is interested, you are wrong.* A young teacher unaccustomed to this posture might fall for it, but a more experienced educator would not. Fred has turned his teacher off and is using a cover-up technique to convince her that he is "all ears."
>
> —Gerard I. Nierenberg and Henry H. Calero
> ***How to Read a Person Like a Book***

Placing a topic sentence in the middle of a paragraph does carry a risk, however. The danger is that if readers are impatient or in a hurry, they may skim over the middle and miss the key idea.

***The Topic Sentence at the End***   At the end of an expository paragraph, the topic sentence acts as a summary, spelling out the controlling idea that is implicit in the sentences that precede it. The following paragraph, for example, builds up to a concluding topic sentence that offers a startling and bleak statistic:

> Many illiterates cannot read the admonition on a pack of cigarettes. Neither the Surgeon General's warning nor its reproduction on the package can alert them to the risks. Although most people learn by word of mouth that smoking is related to a number of grave physical disorders, they do not get the chance to read the detailed stories which can document this danger with the vividness that turns concern into determination to resist. They can see the handsome cowboy or the slim Virginia lady lighting up a filter cigarette; they cannot heed the words that tell them that this product is (not "may be") dangerous to their health. *Sixty million men and women are condemned to be the unalerted, high-risk candidates for cancer.*
>
> —Jonathan Kozol, **"The Human Cost of an Illiterate Society"**

A topic sentence at the end of a paragraph requires the reader to look at the support before the main idea. Since the writer takes time to explain the reasons before making the claim, the readers are less likely to reject the assertion.

## Unifying a Paragraph without a Topic Sentence

Not all paragraphs have a topic sentence. Nonetheless, the main idea must be clear. In narrative writing topic sentences are often lacking, but a general point will still be strongly implied, as in the following paragraph:

> In the spring of 1948, in the first softball game during the afternoon hour of physical education in the dusty schoolyard, the two captains chose teams and, as always, they chose other boys until only two of us remained. I batted last, and first came to the plate with two or three runners on base, and while my teammates urged me to try for a walk, and the players on the field called Easy out, Easy out, I watched the softball coming in waist-high and stepped and swung, and hit it over the right fielder's head for a double. My next time at bat I tripled to center. From then on I brought my glove to school, hanging from a handlebar.
>
> **—Andre Dubus, "Under the Lights"**

The paragraph has no topic sentence, but its point is clearly implied and might be stated as "Without warning, I had become a good softball player."

Diplomacy may be an excellent reason for omitting a topic sentence. Some business letters, such as a credit refusal, may not state the main idea directly. Instead, the refusal is *implied* in a subordinate clause. Unless there is a good reason to omit a topic sentence, however, include one.

## Adjusting Paragraph Length

A paragraph should be long enough to cover the central idea well according to the needs of readers and their purpose in reading.

As a general rule, avoid one- and two-sentence paragraphs as well as a series of short paragraphs. These will give your writing a choppy, careless appearance. (In newspapers and magazines, paragraphs tend to be short because they are crammed into columns and look longer than otherwise.) Introductory paragraphs of short papers (500 words or less) usually range from three to five sentences;

---

### GUIDELINES: DIVIDING LONG PARAGRAPHS

1. ***Divide when a paragraph has more than one main idea.*** Divide where the second idea or a shift to another facet of the major idea begins.

2. ***Divide where there is a lapse in time.*** Time provides a natural break. Tip: Look for transitions of time or a shift in verb tense.

3. ***Divide if there is a shift in person of pronouns.*** First, check to see that the shift is necessary. If it is, that may be an excellent spot to divide.

4. ***In dialogue, start a new paragraph for each speaker.***

introductions for research papers tend to be longer. Body paragraphs often range from five to eight sentences. Conclusions tend to be rather brief, perhaps three to five sentences. A one-paragraph essay may range from seven to twelve or more sentences.

Complexity of the subject also influences length; difficult subjects tend to require more explanation. If a paragraph becomes quite long, consider the needs of the reader, the purpose of the writing, and the coverage required for clarity. If division is needed, look for a shift from one aspect of an idea to another.

## ORGANIZING AND DEVELOPING PARAGRAPHS

You can organize the details in a paragraph according to any strategy that is clear and reasonable. Narrative and process paragraphs are generally in *chronological* (time) order with events and steps presented as they naturally occur. Descriptive paragraphs are generally arranged in *spatial* order according to location or design. For example, in describing objects, animals, or people, you might go from head to toe, left to right, outside to inside, or in another direction. (See "Through a Child's Eyes," earlier in this chapter, for an example of spatial order.) Paragraphs may also be organized in other logical or sequential orders, as explained in Chapter 4. The student paragraphs that follow are organized according to strategies of narration, description, process analysis, illustration, and comparison/contrast.

### Narrative Paragraphs

Narrative paragraphs tell a story or relate an event or anecdote. The writer often sets the scene first, telling *who* or *what*, *when*, and *where*. Description, dialogue, or illustrations may be included to kindle interest and to clarify. Action verbs keep a story moving. Narratives often build suspense and reserve a surprise until the end. They may reveal rather than explain, letting the reader interpret the meaning, or they may direct attention to a social or political concern that has universal relevance (see Chapter 10). The following narrative paragraph by student Suzanne Omaits suggests a fear we all might experience:

**Home Alone**

Quiet holds many sounds. I never knew how many until I found myself alone one Friday night. Was that the wind rubbing a bare branch against the house, I wondered; or was that the front step groaning under someone's weight? I tried not to think about the sound and turned on the television set. But something compelled me to turn in my chair and look over my shoulder at the window. Slowly I turned, dreading what I might see yet afraid not to look. For a moment I froze! Through the fogged glass, I saw a man's face pressed against the window pane, staring at me. Leaping to my feet, I flipped off the lights and TV. Then he began to pound on the window. Realizing he could still see me dimly, I ran to the back room and hid. After a moment I knew I had to get help. Fearfully, I crawled back to the living room to use the telephone. My hands trembled so I could hardly dial. Anxiously, I waited for the familiar voice of my neighbor. Suddenly the pounding stopped. Minutes dragged by until my neighbor arrived. After checking, he assured me the intruder was gone. At that moment a car drove into the driveway. Never was I so glad to hear my parents call, "We're home!"

## Descriptive Paragraphs

An effective description has a specific purpose; details are not just a pleasant filler. *Significant* physical details can capture the essence of a person, place, or object. Concrete words reveal perceptions obtained through the five senses: seeing, hearing, touching, tasting, and smelling. A single dominant impression can unify the details. In the next student paragraph, by Michael Schnitzler, the physical details about a chair and how it has been used down through the years yield a dominant impression of an affectionate family.

See
Chapter 16.

### The Old Rocking Chair

In the corner of our living room sits an old wooden rocking chair. The chair is made of solid maple, varnished and trimmed in gold. The arms are worn smooth, as if someone had used the finest of sandpaper on the wood. On the edges of its arms, I can see indentations in the wood where little tykes did their teething. As I rock back and forth, the old chair squeaks and creaks; but the sounds are soothing. This rocking chair has served several purposes. It has helped to console our three children, countless nieces, nephews, and children of friends. It has rocked babies to sleep for naps and at bedtime. With its soothing rhythm, it has comforted and quieted them when they were restless or sick. Now that the children have grown older, the old chair is seldom used. Yet it sits patiently, awaiting the years when it will hold our grandchildren.

## Process Analysis Paragraphs

Process analysis explains how to do something or how something happens. Chronological order is the clearest way to organize process analysis. Just list steps or actions in sequence as they normally occur. Include enough details for the reader to understand. *If there is a risk during any part of the procedure, give a precaution early.* For conciseness and clarity, use second person (mainly the understood "you"). In the following example, which is directed to someone who has never used a coin-operated car wash, notice how the student writer Kristi Gruber takes an ordinary topic and transforms it into an interesting paragraph:

See
Chapter 12.

### How to Get the Best Shine from a Coin-Operated Car Wash

Whether your car is a prized possession or a necessary nuisance, it deserves an occasional wash. By following five simple steps, you can make your vehicle sparkling clean in just five minutes. First, vacuum the interior with the hose located outside the entrance of the car wash. Be sure the hose inhales every crumb, pebble, and gum wrapper. Second, drive into the wash cage. Third, before you add coins, read the directions for the wand. Then turn the dial to "Prewash." Add the coins and be ready to work fast. Fourth, spray all the exterior once to break up grime. Fifth, switch to "High Pressure Soap" and grip the wand tightly. As you move around the car, spray the top, hood, sides, wheels, and trunk. Sixth, change the mode to "High Pressure Rinse." To prevent streaking, rinse all suds off. Next, switch to "Spot-free Final Rinse." This final step will prevent water spots and ensure a brilliant shine. If you are very dedicated to your four-wheeled friend, take time to wipe her off with the old bath towel you brought along. After that you will probably head down the highway only to be greeted with a gift from a passing bird!

## Illustration Paragraphs

Illustration paragraphs—also called paragraphs of exemplification—present a *series* of examples to support the topic sentence. To maintain unity, every example is closely linked to the controlling idea. As you read the next student paragraph, notice the order of the examples Sharon K. Cleveland used:

### The Fearsome Rabbit

Bathsheba was not the typical Easter bunny. Sheba was a Newfoundland flop-eared rabbit. Soon she grew into a fat fur ball. At maturity, she weighed thirty-five pounds—more than my two-year-old nephew! Our guests loved to watch her hop down the hall, then stand on her hind legs while she washed her face. With her long floppy ears hanging down, she had a sad, gentle look, which was deceiving. One day we came home to find her chewing on a camera bag that belonged to my husband. He yelled, "If I didn't love that rabbit so much, she would be dinner tonight!" Soon electrical cords, woodwork, wooden chairs, books, and other objects also bore the marks of her sharp teeth. As Sheba grew older, she developed a mean streak. One day our son, who was six, went near her litter box and came running—Sheba hopping close behind. As she nipped his bare heel, he screamed, "HELP!" After this incident she would hop toward him, and he would leap onto the couch. He had become afraid of her. Soon we took her to a farm that raised rabbits, where she seems fat and happy.

## Comparison or Contrast Paragraphs

*Comparison* includes both similarities and differences, while *contrast* refers to differences only. The key to writing a good comparison or contrast paragraph is first to select two subjects that might make an interesting pair. Then list specific, significant features of each, matching every detail you list for one subject with a corresponding detail for the other. (See Chapter 15 for outlines.)

### The Eye of the Beholder

This year when the first warm days of April began, I overflowed with energy. I wanted to make our family room as fresh as the spring buds outside. In a frenzy, I started to throw out one piece of junk after another, but each time Jerry would intervene to save a "treasure." First, I discarded a faded, cracked plate; but he rescued his family heirloom. Then I seized the tattered quilt; he returned his comforter for cold nights to its rightful place on the couch. Next I tossed out the stack of old *Time* and *Newsweek* magazines from the coffee table; he retrieved them because he might need a reference for a "current" event. And so it went. Finally, I said, "That sagging old couch we bought at a garage sale simply has to go!" But he objected sharply, "That's my favorite spot to watch football!" Refusing to argue, I stopped. But the first day he goes golfing, I'm calling Goodwill for an immediate pickup. . . . I may keep the plate.

—**Peggy Walker**

## Paragraphs of Definition

Sometimes a paragraph of definition is needed to explain the meaning and context of a word. A technical definition may specify the purpose and the function of a part or appliance. A literary definition may specify the root or origin of the word, the part of speech, and the standard meaning—or several meanings in different contexts. During practice writing, student Mark Jones speculated about the meaning and uses of the word *shaft*.

Words are fun to play with and think about. For example, *shaft* as a noun is a pole or long handle of a spear or other weapon. By that definition, an arrow could be considered a shaft, although it would seem strange to say we shafted a deer. The space shuttle might also be called a shaft. A pretty girl can wear a short dress and show a little shaft. The White House has many shafts; there are pillars at the entrance. *Shaft* is also used as a verb, but only in slang. If Bill shafted Al, then Bill did a wrong or injustice to Al. Bill did not hurl an arrow, spear, or space shuttle at Al, although Al has been hurt by Bill's action. *Shaft* is also the name of an old movie starring a super-cool, super-bad bald man named John Shaft. If violent movies about super-cool, bad, bald men are not appealing, then paying three dollars to rent the film and not liking it would be getting the shaft.

## Transitional Paragraphs

Sometimes a special paragraph of transition is needed to connect two major ideas. In the middle of an essay or paper, you may need a paragraph of transition to bridge a gap or to direct the reader to a shift in thought. For example, Patty Seigneur wrote a brief transitional paragraph for a paper contrasting two good friends:

Sue is a wonderful person and friend, but I found myself wanting a friend more like myself. Then I met June. Quickly, she and I became good friends. We both realized how alike we are and how much we enjoy each other's company.

Notice that only one signpost transition, *then*, is used in this transitional paragraph. But the writer repeats key terms and uses pronouns to establish clear *embedded* transition.

**SUMMARY**

- Basic elements of a paragraph are a topic sentence, supporting sentences, and a concluding sentence.
  - A topic sentence identifies the subject and focuses the paragraph.
  - Support sentences supply proof.
  - A concluding sentence supplies a "clincher" or a sense of completeness.
- Effective paragraphs contain five features: clarity, interest, unity, coherence, and completeness.
- Audience, subject, and purpose determine a paragraph's length.
- Paragraphs are arranged according to chronology, importance, complexity, generality, familiarity, emphasis, or some other logical order.
- Narrative, descriptive, process analysis, illustration, and transition are paragraphs that can be developed within writing.

## *Practice*

### Small Groups: Evaluating Topic Sentences

*Directions:* Check the sentences that would make *good* topic sentences (just four). Discuss why the other sentences would be ineffective.

_____  1. My motto "play before work" received a severe blow this week.

_____  2. The leftover macaroni and cheese in my refrigerator was covered with green mould.

_____  3. Mary Todd married Abe Lincoln.

_____  4. The older I become, the more I appreciate. . . .

_____  5. Overnight the amaryllis opened one large red trumpet.

_____  6. Mr. Inskeep is my favourite teacher.

_____  7. Computers are necessary for most workplaces.

_____  8. A roommate who is a musician can be exasperating.

_____  9. Cutting the Brazilian rain forest is causing weather problems.

_____  10. Every Thursday night I watch my favourite TV program.

### Ideas for Paragraphs

1. How and where to find arrowheads (or lovely shells? what else?)
2. My favourite vacation spot
3. The day I almost drowned
4. Describe a small object you own and its significance
5. Tips for shopping at garage sales (or flea markets or auctions)

6. How to make an unusual salad
7. My first day in school (on the first time I . . .)
8. The raccoons and the water garden (or other animal episode)
9. How to buy a good . . .
10. Why I . . .

# CHAPTER 8

# *Editing*

## Styling Sentences

---

**Learning Objectives**

After reading and applying the information in Chapter 8, you'll be able to:

- Style sentences that fit the rhetorical situation
- Write sentences using action verbs in either the active or passive voice
- Write using three basic sentence types
- Eliminate wordiness

---

*Style is the dress of thoughts; and let them be ever so just. . . .*

—Lord Chesterfield,
*Letter to His Son*

In the workplace, employees are expected to be able to write strong, clear sentences. They may have to dash off email, a memo, a letter to a customer, or a short report. Regardless of time limitations, rereading and revision are imperative. Otherwise, the message may be unclear, inaccurate, ungrammatical, or offensive.

Styling sentences is a challenging task, but it is the mark of a proficient writer. Effective sentences can be plain or ornate, simple or complex, short or long, depending on the purpose. The design and strength of sentences depend on the topic, the needs of the audience, the occasion for writing, and the voice of the writer. The clarity of sentences depends not only on the sentence pattern and word choice but also on correct punctuation, which is discussed briefly in this chapter, along with sentence structure.

As you revise at the sentence level, you will be trying to clarify, to emphasize major ideas, as well as add interest, variety, and style to your writing. Varying sentence patterns to fit particular ideas not only will make your writing clearer but also more interesting. Repeating the same sentence pattern throughout makes for humdrum writing.

There are other ways to spark vitality into lifeless sentences: Replace passive verbs and forms of *be* with action verbs. Create parallel forms for similar ideas. Eliminate awkwardness and unnecessary words. Condense long phrases and clauses. Vary the length of sentences. Position ideas at strategic points within sentences. Vary your choice of words. Revision can make your sentences strong and interesting. (Word choice is discussed in Chapters 2, 6, and 9. See also "Figurative Language" in the index.)

## EFFECTIVE USE OF VERBS

Although sentences can do without some parts of speech, a verb is always required. Even nouns can be omitted—leaving a verb to stand alone as a one-word sentence. For example, "Go!" "Heel!" and "March!" are complete sentences. The verbs you select will influence the strength and clarity of your writing.

### Favouring the Active Voice

Strong action verbs can invigorate writing. Action verbs show movement and help readers to imagine an activity. For example, *ski, swim*, and *skate* show physical activity whereas *think, know*, and *dream* show mental activity. Action verbs can be written in either the active or passive voice. Usually, the active voice is preferred because it is direct and concise. Active voice simply means the subject of the sentence is *performing the action*, as in the example below:

**Active voice:** Johnny *shot* the bear.

However, a verb is in the *passive* voice when the subject *receives the action*. Something or someone else is performing the act or deed. The passive voice consists of a *be* verb and a past participle so that a verb in the passive voice always consists of two (or three) words.

**Passive voice:** The bear *was shot* by Johnny.

Which sentence do you prefer? Why? You probably noticed that the sentence in active voice gives the sharper image of the event. Perhaps you noted that the sentence in active voice has just four words, whereas the one in passive voice contains six words. Although passive voice is useful at times, it lessens the impact of a sentence. To make writing clear and direct, experienced writers prefer the active voice in most situations.

---

**GUIDELINES: WHEN SHOULD YOU USE THE PASSIVE VOICE?**

1. **The person responsible wishes to remain unknown.**
   Example: The new rule was enacted to tighten security.
2. **The one who does the action is unknown.**
   Example: The oriental rug was made in China.
3. **To place emphasis on an important word.** Passive voice allows the important word to become the subject of a sentence.
   Example: The *needs* of the student should be considered.

## Replacing Forms of *Be*

The forms of *be* indicate a state of being or existing here on this planet. They do not show action. Although *be* verbs are sometimes necessary, too many of them tend to make a piece of writing seem wordy and lifeless. The main forms of the verb *be* are *is, am, are, was, were, be, been,* and *being.* To remember them easily, practise saying them in this order:

| | *Say* | | *Remember* | *Say* | *Remember* |
|---|---|---|---|---|---|
| is | (one *i*) | | | be | (three *b*'s) |
| am | (two *a*'s) | | | been | |
| are | | | | being | |
| was | (two *w*'s) | | | | |
| were | | | | | |

With a little thought, you can often replace a *be* verb with an action verb. Such revision not only shortens the sentence but also strengthens it. The following examples illustrate why action verbs are generally preferred:

> **Be verb:** Céline Dion *is* a famous entertainer who entertains millions with her singing. (12 words)
>
> **Action verb:** Céline Dion *entertains* millions with her singing. (7 words)

## SENTENCE VARIETY

Verbs are an essential part of all sentence patterns. The three basic sentence patterns are the simple sentence, the complex sentence, and the compound sentence.

> **Simple:** Interviewers may ask about weaknesses. (independent clause)
>
> **Compound:** Interviewers may ask about weaknesses, but savvy applicants prepare for this question. (two independent clauses)
>
> **Complex:** Since interviewers may ask about weaknesses, savvy applicants prepare for this question. (dependent clause + independent clause)

Using all three structures adds interest to your writing, clarifies relationships among ideas, and emphasizes major points.

## The Simple Sentence

The simple sentence is the workhorse that will pull the load in about 70 percent of your writing. A simple sentence contains a single subject (which may consist of more than one noun) and one or more verbs. The simple sentence is an *indepen-*

*dent* clause—one complete thought that can stand alone. At its simplest, such a sentence may consist of only a subject and verb:

- Eagles soar.

More often though, simple sentences will contain other sentence parts, including objects, prepositional phrases and other modifiers, and perhaps additional verbs:

- Eagles build *large nests*. (subject + verb + direct object)
- Eagles build large nests *in isolated places*. (+ prepositional phrase)
- *Most commonly*, eagles build large nests in isolated places. (+ adverbs)
- Most commonly, eagles build large nests in isolated places and *lay two or three eggs*. (+ second verb and object)

The simple sentence is the primary sentence structure. In a piece of expository writing, as many as two-thirds of the sentences may have this pattern. When only simple sentences are used, however, writing can become boring, and ideas can seem disconnected. As you revise your drafts, look for ways to expand simple sentences into complex sentences or to combine two simple sentences into a compound sentence. With effective revision, you can clarify related ideas.

## The Compound Sentence

Two related simple sentences can be joined to form a *compound* sentence. The compound sentence gives the clauses *equal* rank because both clauses contain important ideas. This means that a compound sentence has two main subjects and two main verbs. If a transition is needed the two clauses are connected by a coordinating conjunction, as italicized in the following examples:

- Geraniums are easy to grow *because* they are quite hardy.
- Minarsi entered the Maine Turnpike at Falmouth, *and* she followed it until Augusta.

**Coordinating Conjunctions**    Coordinating conjunctions link similar elements, such as clauses, phrases, or nouns. There are just seven coordinating conjunctions to learn. An easy way to remember them is to memorize the acronym *banboys:* because, and, nor, but, or, yet, so.

The conjunction you use between clauses in a compound sentence depends on the relationship between the ideas in the two clauses. If the second clause provides additional information, use *and*. If the second clause is in contrast to the first, use *but, or, yet,* or *nor*. If the second clause has a cause-and-effect relationship with the first, use *because* or *so*.

**What Are Comma Splices and Fused Sentences?**    It is incorrect to link independent clauses with only a comma and no coordinating conjunction. The resulting

## PUNCTUATING COMPOUND SENTENCES

If *both* clauses in a compound sentence are four words or less, you may join them without a comma. If one clause or both have five words or more, you have three options—according to the relationship:

1. **Comma and Conjunction.** Connect two related independent clauses with a *coordinate conjunction* preceded by a comma when transition is needed:
   - The hidden job market consists of an estimated 80 percent of available jobs, *but* most job seekers seem unaware that it exists.

2. **Semicolon.** You can use a *semicolon* between two independent clauses when the connection between the ideas is so close no transition is needed:
   - The hidden job market consists of an estimated 80 percent of available jobs; only 20 percent of available jobs are ever advertised.

3. **Colon.** Use a *colon* to indicate that the second clause of the compound sentence will explain the first:
   - The astute job seeker compiles a packet of employment search documents: The packet can contain an up-to-date résumé, cover letter, thank-you letter, and sheet of references.

error is called a *comma splice*. If no punctuation whatever is used between two independent clauses in a compound sentence, the error is called a *fused sentence.*

| | |
|---|---|
| **Comma splice:** | Terrariums are costly at a flower shop, they are inexpensive to make at home. |
| **Correct:** | Terrariums are costly at a flower shop, *but* they are inexpensive to make at home. (comma and conjunction) |
| **Comma splice:** | Weather bulletins warned of ice-glazed roads, however, some drivers ignored the warning. |
| **Correct:** | Weather bulletins warned of ice-glazed roads; however, some drivers ignored the warning. (semicolon) |
| **Fused Sentence:** | The ordinance won wide support it was passed by a two-thirds vote. |
| **Correct:** | The ordinance won wide support; it was passed by a two-thirds vote. (semicolon) |

Although compound sentences are often effective, they should not be overused. Also remember that a compound sentence gives both clauses equal weight. When the idea in one clause is more important, then the two clauses should be combined into a complex sentence.

## The Complex Sentence

A *complex* sentence consists of an independent clause and one or more dependent clauses. The complex sentence ranks a major idea and a minor idea. The major idea appears in the independent clause; the minor idea appears in the dependent clause. To the untrained eye, a dependent clause may look like a complete sentence because both have a subject and a verb. But the dependent clause has a word at the beginning that makes the (minor) idea incomplete. Thus *a dependent clause is always a fragment and cannot stand alone.*

*Fragments (incomplete ideas)*

That has white forepaws

When the doorbell rings

Because McDaniel Motors gives dependable service

*Sentences (complete ideas)*

- The black cat that has white forepaws is Jeff's.
- When the doorbell rings, my dog barks.
- Because McDaniel Motors gives dependable service, Jason has his car serviced there.

**Adjective Clauses**   Adjective clauses are dependent clauses that refer to nouns or pronouns. These clauses are easy to identify because they always start with one of five relative pronouns: *who, whom, whose, which,* or *that.* (Think: four *w*'s and a *t*.)

| | |
|---|---|
| **Essential:** | The car *that he prefers* has bucket seats. |
| | The young woman *who is wearing blue jeans* is Mary's sister. |
| **Nonessential:** | Terry, *who is my brother,* is an avid photographer. |
| | The yellow truck, *which is a Dodge,* represents her life savings. |

Did you notice that the sentences with *essential* clauses need no commas? But *the sentences with nonessential clauses require a pair of commas.* These commas act like tiny parentheses to set off extra material, which could be removed. To test whether or not a clause is essential, try covering it with your hand and reading the rest of the sentence. Does the basic meaning of the sentence change? If so, no commas are needed; the clause is essential. If the meaning does not change, set off the extra material (the nonessential clause) with commas.

**Adverb Clauses**   Adverb clauses, like adverbs, tell *when, where, why, how,* or *under what conditions.* Adverb clauses begin with *subordinating conjunctions.* Some

## DISTINGUISHING *WHO, WHOM, WHICH,* AND *THAT*

1. *That* is always used to indicate essential information. Sometimes *that* is omitted for the sake of conciseness if the meaning is clear. *That* can refer to people, animals, or things.

2. *Who* and *whom* refer only to people. *Which* can refer to animals or things. *Who, whom,* and *which* can introduce essential or nonessential clauses.

introduce reasons or explanations (*because, since, whereas, although*). After you learn to recognize the common subordinating conjunctions, you will be able to identify adverb clauses easily.

*Common Subordinating Conjunctions*

| when | although | if | as | whether |
|------|----------|-----|---------|---------|
| while | even though | until | as long as | before |
| where | so that | unless | as though | than |
| since | because | as if | after | whenever |

The adverb clause may come before or after the independent clause in a complex sentence. Let's look at two versions of a sentence with the dependent clause italicized:

- *When the big Doberman snarled,* I slammed the door.
- I slammed the door *when the big Doberman snarled.*

Which sentence do you prefer? Actually, the first sentence has two advantages: (1) the ideas appear in chronological order; (2) the word *I* appears in the middle of the sentence, where emphasis is minimized.

## PUNCTUATING SENTENCES WITH ADVERB CLAUSES

1. **Introductory adverb clause.** When a long adverb clause (five words or more) appears at the beginning of a sentence, *place a comma after the clause.* If a misreading is possible, use a comma after a short clause.

2. **Concluding adverb clause.** When an adverb clause appears at the end, in a sequence of two events, no comma is needed.

# PARALLELISM: A BALANCING ACT

Grammar rules decree that when two or more parts of a sentence are coordinated, they must be parallel. In other words, you place sentence parts of equal rank in the same grammatical form. Nouns are matched with nouns, active verbs with active verbs, passive verbs with passive verbs, and *be* verbs with *be* verbs. Phrases are matched with phrases, and clauses are matched with clauses. This balance is called *parallelism*.

Undoubtedly, you have used parallelism in your writing without realizing it. You may have chosen parallel forms because they sounded clear or right. Experienced writers use parallelism not only for clarity but also for balance and emphasis.

As you revise, be alert to instances of faulty parallelism. The next few sections discuss situations in which parallelism is required.

## Parallelism with Items in a Series

Items in a series require balance, which is called *parallelism*. Regardless of whether the items are single words, phrases, or clauses, all must be parallel: Every item must be matched according to grammatical form.

***Parallel Adjectives***    In the following example, the three adjectives that follow the pronoun and end the sentence are not only parallel but also alliterative (all start with the same consonant sound of the letter *p*).

> Three factors in the Complainers' view of the world combine to convert useful problem solving into complaining. They find themselves *powerless, prescriptive,* and *perfect.*
>
> —Robert M. Bramson, *Coping with Difficult People*

A writer who was not paying attention to parallelism might have written "without power, prescriptive, and perfect."

***Parallel Prepositional Phrases***    Parallel prepositional phrases can be structured using the same preposition or a different preposition at the beginning of each phrase. When the same preposition applies to all phrases in a series, it may be stated before every item or stated once at the beginning of the first phrase.

- I spend most of my time *at* work, *at* school, or *at* home.
- I spend most of my time *at* work, school, or home.

***Parallel Subordinate Clauses***    As you revise, make sure that all items in a series are parallel. Reading your writing aloud can help you to detect nonparallel structures. The final item in the following series is not parallel. Note how it can be corrected:

> **Not parallel:** I enjoy listening to music, taking long walks, and *also like to work crossword puzzles.*
>
> **Parallel:** I enjoy listening to music, taking long walks, and *working crossword puzzles.*

## Parallelism with Items in Pairs

When a coordinating conjunction is used, the structures on each side should be balanced, although the degree of parallelism can vary. In *Coping with Difficult People*, Bramson often uses pairs of parallel nouns and verbs, as in the following examples:

*Parallel Nouns*    The slight variations in the second example make it less parallel:

- "It pays to follow up any *complaint* or *suggestion* with an inquiry about what's happened."
- "Your coping reply should be to ask, 'Is that a *decision* or just your *opinion* at this stage?'"

*Parallel Verbs*    Notice that to be parallel, verbs *must be the same tense, the same form, and the same voice*. Different tenses should not be mixed. One-word verbs should not be mixed with verb phrases. Passive voice should not be mixed with active voice. The italicized verbs below are parallel:

- The students *are protesting* parking fees and *are requesting* free parking. (Both verbs are present tense and active voice.)
- The students *protested* campus parking fees and *requested* free parking. (Both verbs are past tense, active voice.)

*Parallel Phrases*    Pairs of phrases in the same sentence should be balanced:

- *For richer or for poorer, in sickness* and *in health* (prepositional phrases)
- *To run a company profitably* and *to treat the environment responsibly* need not be conflicting goals. (infinitive phrases)

## Parallelism with Comparisons

Comparisons formed by using *as* or *than* should be parallel: To balance, the two subjects being compared must have the same grammatical form:

- A *spelling check* (noun) is not as accurate as *careful proofreading* (noun).
- For most interviews, *wearing a suit* (gerund phrase) is safer than *wearing casual attire* (gerund phrase).

As you check your comparisons, look for faulty parallelism. Note how the imbalance in the first sentence below can be rectified in two ways:

**Not Parallel:** It is better *to do* (infinitive phrase) school work throughout a semester than *cramming* (gerund) the night before an exam.

**Revised:** It is better *to do* school work throughout a semester than *to cram* the night before an exam. (two infinitive phrases)

## PUNCTUATING SENTENCES WITH PARALLEL STRUCTURES

### SIMPLE SENTENCES

There is *no comma* before the final conjunction in a simple sentence. In the first set of examples, the parallel structures are italicized:

- The talk was both *interesting* and *inspirational*. (two adjectives)
- David has been outstanding not only *in football* but also *in academic work*. (two prepositional phrases)

### COMPOUND SENTENCES

The main subjects and verbs in a compound sentence should be parallel. Note that the final correlative conjunction is preceded by a *comma*.

- *Not* everyone received a bonus, *but* everyone received a raise.
- *Either* he would pay the 96 parking tickets, *or* he would go to jail.

**Revised:** *Doing* school work throughout a semester is better than *cramming* the night before an exam. (two gerunds)

## Parallelism with Correlative Conjunctions

*Correlative conjunctions* work in pairs to link words, phrases, or clauses. These conjunctions add grace and emphasis to a sentence by requiring parallel structure. Common correlative conjunctions include these five pairs:

| | |
|---|---|
| either . . . or | neither . . . nor |
| not . . . but | not only . . . but also |
| both . . . and | |

Correlatives need to be in the right place in a sentence to be logical and balanced. Place the correlative right *before* the word or phrase that it modifies:

**Not parallel:** *Either* you pay the fee for parking *or* a penalty.

**Parallel:** You pay *either* the parking fee *or* a penalty. (Each correlative precedes an article and a noun.)

**Not parallel:** *Not only* was the defendant charged with breaking and entering *but also* with resisting arrest.

**Parallel:** The defendant was charged *not only* with breaking and entering *but also* with resisting arrest. (Both of the correlatives precede a prepositional phrase.)

## ELIMINATING WORDINESS

Even the rough drafts of professional writers ramble and repeat. Although Ernest Hemingway's finished writing is sparse and clean, he worked long and hard to bring it to that state. Once Hemingway was questioned about how often he had revised the ending of his novel *A Farewell to Arms*. He said it had taken thirty-nine revisions for him to be satisfied. Revision is also a necessity for student writers. Some common sources of wordiness are discussed in the following sections.

### References to Self

Self-confident persons sometimes refer to themselves often during conversation. In writing, however, this tendency should be monitored, lest it give the impression of an oversized ego. If *I* appears at the beginning of a sentence, the writer may be able to invert the sentence. Placing *I* in the middle of a sentence makes the reference to self less noticeable. Delete unnecessary words as long as there is no change in meaning:

> **Draft:** I will graduate on June 12 and will be available for employment after that. (14 words)

> **Revised:** After graduating on June 12, I will be available for employment. (11 words)

When a rough draft has two sequential sentences that begin with *I*, try to combine the sentences and delete one of the *I*'s as well as extra words. Then check the revision to be sure it is clear and complete.

> **Draft:** I use Microsoft Word daily to write letters. I also use Quicken for other tasks. (15 words)

> **Revised:** I use Microsoft Word and Quicken daily. (7 words)

Still another way to bypass *I* is to substitute *me* or *my* when a reference to self seems necessary.

> **Draft:** I can type accurately, answer the telephone courteously, and perform basic accounting functions, as you requested in your ad for a receptionist. (22 words)

> **Revised:** My keyboarding skills, telephone etiquette training, and experience with accounts payable/receivable should qualify me for your position of receptionist. (20 words)

Instead of overusing first person singular, some people go to another extreme; they completely avoid *I, me, my,* or *mine.* They may resort to stilted phrases such as "the writer" or "the author of this paper." Experienced writers use *I* sensibly and sparingly.

## Prepositional Phrases

Another source of wordiness may be unnecessary prepositional phrases in a sentence. If you find more than two prepositional phrases in a sentence, check for wordiness. Although using several prepositional phrases may not affect clarity, there may be a clearer, more concise way to make your point. Consider the following sentences before and after revision:

> **Draft:** A new type of compact, the Stallion II by CMG, was rated the safest in recent collision tests of compacts. (19 words)
>
> **Revised:** CMG's new Stallion II was rated safest in recent collision tests of compacts. (12 words)

Common phrases such as "this *type of* car" or "this *kind of* oven" or *"in the amount of $10"* may be shortened to "this car" or "this oven" or "$10."

## Adjective Clauses

Sometimes there is little justification for an adjective clause, and the sentence can be made more effective by trimming the clause down to an appositive. Or you might substitute an adjective for an adjective clause. Consider the following examples:

> **Draft:** Dr. Goldberg, *who has been our physician since I was a child*, is going to retire. (adjective clause)
>
> **Revised:** Dr. Goldberg, *our long-time family physician*, is going to retire. (appositive)
>
> **Draft:** My Appaloosa mare, *which is only two years old*, placed first in the "Best-Trained Horse" trials. (adjective clause)
>
> **Revised:** My *two-year-old* Appaloosa mare placed first in the "Best-Trained Horse" trials. (adjective)

## SENTENCE STYLE

The style of a sentence is influenced by the sentence pattern, the length of the sentence, and the position of the most important idea(s). In addition to the three major sentence patterns discussed earlier, you can use an occasional periodic sentence to provide interest and emphasis.

## Periodic Sentences

A periodic sentence affords an opportunity to combine several related ideas into one grand sentence. This sentence pattern builds anticipation and suspense by presenting less important details before the major idea. This means that the major idea always appears just before the period. Although the subject may be placed early in the sentence, *the verb is always delayed*. Periodic sentences provide not only a refreshing change of pace, but also emphasis. Sometimes they are the ideal structure for a concluding sentence. James Herriot uses a periodic sentence at the end of his story "The Strychnine Episode at Darrowby":

> To me, the outbreak is a sad memory of failure and frustration. Fergus was my only cure. But over the years, when I saw the big dog striding majestically in his harness, leading his master unerringly around the streets of Darrowby, I always had one good feeling.

In the final sentence, Herriot builds to a climax, saying in one sentence what someone else might have said in three. Yet the periodic sentence is not an everyday sentence—it should be used for a significant idea.

## Sentence Length

The length of a sentence is influenced by the kind of idea it houses. Brief sentences emphasize key ideas. Long sentences are like baskets, collecting several less important details. Each type has its place, but neither should be overused. Too many short sentences cause choppiness whereas too many long sentences interfere with clarity. Vary your sentences to produce variety and a change of pace.

## Position of Words within Sentences

Important words should be placed in *positions of emphasis,* either at the beginning or end of a sentence. Likewise, important sentences are usually placed at the beginning or end of a paragraph. The reader may skim over the middle. Ordinarily, the end position of a sentence or a paragraph carries more emphasis than the beginning; the middle carries the least of all. Of the three examples below, which one do you prefer? Why?

- Snatching a field mouse, the spotted owl swooped down, wings outstretched.
- The spotted owl swooped and snatched a field mouse.
- Swooping with outstretched wings, the spotted owl snatched a field mouse.

The first sentence is anticlimactic and the least interesting. The second sentence is an improvement because the events are in chronological order, and the major action is emphasized. In the third sentence, "swooping with outstretched wings" gives a vivid picture of the action.

**SUMMARY**

- Style sentences that fit the rhetorical situation.
- Write sentences using action verbs in either the active or passive voice.
  - Active voice is preferred because it is powerful and concise.
  - Passive voice and *be* verbs lessen the impact of a sentence and contribute to wordiness.
- Write using three basic sentence types: simple (one independent clause), compound (two independent clauses), and complex (an independent clause and at least one dependent clause).
- Trim wordiness during revision.
- Limit references to self, unnecessary prepositions, or unneeded words that slow down the pace of the sentence.
- Place important ideas at the beginning and end of a sentence.
- Highlight important ideas in short sentences and combine less important ideas into longer sentences.

## Test Yourself

### Parallelism

*Directions:* Make the italicized segments parallel. You may have to delete. To check your answers, turn to the end of the chapter

1. Peach orchards dot the south-central shore of Lake Erie in Ohio, but *grapes are grown* along the eastern shore in New York.
2. Ontario's principal crops are corn, soybeans, and *sometimes wheat is also grown.*
3. Raising soybeans is much more profitable than *to raise corn.*
4. To produce a pound of meat on chickens costs much less than *producing* a pound of meat on beef cattle.
5. Canola, which yields an edible oil, is grown more often than ordinary rape, *yielding a similar oil.*

## Practice

### Combining Sentences

*Directions:* Combine the choppy sentences into one well-balanced sentence. Delete any extra words. For help, refer to similar examples in this chapter.

1. Prewriting is the first stage of the writing process. Prewriting is a time of discovery. (*Tip:* Change the first sentence into an appositive and combine with the second.)

2. The subject of a periodic sentence may be placed early in the sentence. The verb is always delayed. (Make a compound sentence.)

3. Engineers and urban planners are designing new highway overpasses. Citizens are urging them to design overpasses that are graceful. They want attractive overpasses.

4. Four concrete bridges in Edmonton, Alberta, were replaced. They were located in the arts district, spanning Sir Winston Churchill Square. They were replaced with arched bridges, outlined in fibre-optic tubing. (*Tip:* Put the two prepositional phrases referring to location first.)

## Test Yourself Answers

### Parallelism

1. *Peach orchards dot the south-central shore of Lake Erie in Ohio, but* vineyards line *the eastern shore in New York. (or another verb)*

2. *Ontario's principal grain crops are soybeans, corn, and* wheat.

3. *Raising soybeans is much more profitable than* raising corn.

4. *To produce a pound of meat on chickens costs much less than* to produce *a pound of meat on beef cattle.*

5. *Canola, which yields an edible oil, is grown more often than ordinary rape,* which yields a similar oil.

# CHAPTER 9

# Editing

## Improving Word Choice

---

**Learning Objectives**

After reading and applying the information in Chapter 9, you'll be able to:

- Improve word choice by understanding denotative and connotative meanings within language
- Use positive language to improve the tone of writing
- Eliminate sexist and racist language
- Tailor technical jargon and scholarly words to the audience
- Replace abstract words with concrete words and examples that clarify abstract concepts

---

> *Words play an enormous part in our lives. . . . Words have power to [mould] . . . thinking. . . . Conduct and character are largely determined by the nature of the words we currently use to discuss ourselves and the world around us.*
>
> —Aldous Huxley

Selecting words is rather like shopping in an enormous supermarket. But instead of roaming the aisles for groceries, a writer thumbs through the pages of a dictionary or thesaurus or goes online to search for the right words. The supply is plentiful, because the English language has more words than any other language. Because there are so many words to choose from, a writer has countless opportunities to be creative, whether writing papers, letters, reports, poetry, or short stories. True, some writing offers more opportunities for creativity than expository writing does, but all rhetorical situations afford leeway in phrasing and sentence structure.

Reading widely and often will help you to become more aware of the nuances and subtle meanings of words. Frequent use of a good thesaurus and dictionary during revision will help you maintain an appropriate tone. Your awareness of the delicate distinctions in words will also increase as you study this chapter. Your skill in detecting inappropriate words and in selecting appropriate words will be honed. With regular practice, your writing will become more precise, positive, and appropriate to the rhetorical situation.

## WORD MEANINGS: DENOTATION AND CONNOTATION

For years you have been looking up *denotations* in dictionaries. Denotations are the specific, literal meanings of words. If you look up the denotation of *horsecar* in *Merriam-Webster's New Collegiate Dictionary*, you will find it is "1: a streetcar drawn by horses [1833] 2: a car fitted for transporting horses."* Denotations seldom cause confusion when writers know a language well and take time to edit carefully. Denotations seldom change. When they do, the changes often take place over a century or more, as in the example above.

Connotative meanings are more difficult to pinpoint. *Connotations* are the hidden meanings beyond the denotation. These subjective meanings are imprecise associations, the emotional overtones attached to words. Our friends may agree with us on some connotations, but may disagree on others. A further complication is that connotations can change gradually or rather suddenly.

Culture, education, occupation, region, generation, and gender influence one's perception of connotative meanings. Individual differences also influence thought and style of expression. Thus connotations contribute not only to meaning but also to the tone of writing. Connotations may be positive or negative, depending on the perception of the audience.

## NEGATIVE AND POSITIVE WORDS

A negative word or an inappropriate word can contaminate an entire message and cause readers to misunderstand. Or they may become so irritated they stop reading and distort the message. As a safeguard, never send an email, note, memo, or letter without rereading and reconsidering your choice of words. When a situation is sensitive, take a day to mull over the best way to phrase the message.

### Focusing on the Positive

During revision, the old adage "Tell them what you can do, not what you can't" is invaluable. Often an idea can be restated indirectly in positive words to soften unpleasant news, as in the examples below:

> **Negative:** We are *out* of the HP Cwi23T tri-color inkjet print cartridges. They will *not* be available for three days.

> **Positive:** The HP Cwi23T tri-color inkjet print cartridges *will* be here in three days.

---

*By permission. From *Merriam-Webster's Collegiate® Dictionary*, Tenth Edition © 1999 by Merriam-Webster, Inc.

**Negative:** I *don't* have my paper finished. I had to work seven days last week.

**Positive:** Professor James, although I worked seven days last week, I *do* have a typed draft. *May* I have another day to *polish?* Or would you *prefer* the rough draft now?

Courtesy words enhance the tone and effectiveness of messages, oral and written. For example, sprinkling courtesy words at the beginning and end of email, memos, and letters helps to create goodwill. Yet we sometimes overlook several positive words that could improve our messages:

| | | | |
|---|---|---|---|
| advantage | courtesy | help | prompt |
| appreciate | encourage | invite | save |
| assistance | enjoy | may | succeed |
| benefit | glad | please | success |
| cooperation | gratitude | pleasure | thank you |

Positive words tend to elicit pleasant responses whereas negative words risk offending. Some common offenders are found in the list below. The words in the "More Favourable" column will improve the tone of your writing.

## IMPROVING YOUR CHOICE OF WORDS

| *Unfavourable* | *More Favourable* |
|---|---|
| wrong | incorrect, inaccurate |
| omitted, forgot | overlooked |
| failed | missed |
| mistake | error |
| advice | suggestion, recommendation |
| complained | reported |
| claimed | stated |
| problem | concern, challenge |
| deal | bargain, offer, opportunity |

If you're struggling to find a positive word, try looking up the negative word in a thesaurus and checking antonyms. Or if you have reason to state a negative idea directly, then you can soften the impact somewhat by using a negative prefix. There are nine common negative prefixes: *non-, un-, im-, in-, dis-, il-, ir-, a-, ab-.* All enable a writer to delete *not.* For example, instead of *not perfect,* you might say *imperfect* or *irregular.*

PEANUTS reprinted by permission of United Feature Syndicate, Inc.

## Do Euphemisms Have a Place?

For the sake of politeness, indirectness and euphemisms are sometimes advisable. Euphemisms are words with overly favourable connotations. Euphemisms are often substituted for unpleasant words, words that might offend or cause pain. For example, the manager who bluntly evaluates work as "poor" or "sloppy" will undermine morale and productivity. But the manager who allows the employee to save face with a euphemism such as "needs to improve" or "can do better" and who encourages with constructive suggestions will have a better chance of motivating. If a euphemism is needed in a touchy situation, that is fine—as long as there is no deception. There is a big difference between tact and deceit.

Over the years, as words lose their favourable connotations, new euphemisms are coined. For example, dealers once sold "used" cars. Later the cars were referred to as "secondhand," but now they are referred to as "pre-owned" or "previously owned." In the 1940s the person who cleaned, maintained the plumbing, and tended the heating system was a "janitor." In the 1960s he or she became a "custodian." In this decade the same job may carry the title of "maintenance engineer."

Connotations of a word can change, becoming either negative or positive. For example, "Dear Madam" was once a polite salutation for a business letter. Now hopelessly outdated, the term is marred by negative connotations. In contrast, the term "Ms." was unpopular in the 1970s, but is now widely accepted as a polite form of direct address. Along with the acceptance of "Ms." has come a new awareness of sexist language.

## INCLUSIVE LANGUAGE

Just as society and culture change, so too does language. One of the biggest changes in North America in the last forty years has been the recognition that women have the same legal rights that men do. With this legislation has come the idea that language should reflect equality by being gender-free or gender-neutral.

## Replacing Sexist Terms with Gender-Free Terms

Some words carry sexist overtones because they contain the root *man: fireman, policeman, mailman.* But these forms are gradually being dropped in favour of gender-free counterparts such as firefighter, police officer, and mail carrier. The following list gives other outmoded words and their updated counterparts.

| REPLACING SEXIST TERMS | |
| --- | --- |
| *Sexist* | *Nonsexist* |
| man, men (if applied to both sexes) | person, people |
| average man | average person |
| chairman | chair, chairperson |
| male nurse | nurse |
| girl, gal, chick | woman (adult) |
| man and wife | husband and wife |

Although masculine nouns and pronouns (*he, his, him*) were used for centuries to include women, this usage is also outmoded. One way to avoid this faux pas is by writing in the plural—for example, "players . . . they." But the plural is not always possible. Then one "he or she" or one "his or her" is relatively unobtrusive. Often the best and simplest way is to use gender-neutral words, omitting any reference to gender.

> **Plural:** The *deans* are to bring *their* projected department budgets.
>
> **Gender-specific:** Every dean should bring *his* projected department budget. (Correct only if all deans are male.)
>
> **Gender-free:** Every dean should bring *a* projected department budget.

## Replacing Offensive Terms with Respectful Terms

Words can discriminate and disrespect on the basis of race/ethnicity, religion, skin colour, or other factors. Although some words may not actually be discriminatory, they may be unwise in terms of politeness and the law. Although the definition of verbal harassment varies, we need to be especially careful when mentioning personal attributes, such as body parts, size, attractiveness, ethnicity, and skin colour.

The purpose here is to alert you to rapidly changing usage. The best advice is to notice the accepted usage in your geographical area.

## TECHNICAL JARGON

*Technical jargon* is the professional or formal language of a trade, profession, or similar group. For example, medical jargon is used daily by pharmacists, physicians, nurses, and technicians. Technical jargon among peers rarely causes problems. But when a message is intended for a layperson, unfamiliar jargon may make the message unclear. At times the resulting confusion could be dangerous.

Perhaps you are wondering when technical jargon is appropriate. The answer seems to hinge upon two questions:

- Can the language be understood by the intended audience?
- Does the language serve a technical purpose?

If the answer to both questions is yes, then use technical jargon, because it does have a valid purpose.

### AVOIDING JARGON

Although a brand of hydrocortisone cream is intended for use by the general public, it carries this warning: "For dermatological use only. Not for ophthalmic use." The message would have been much clearer if it had said: "Apply to the skin only. Do not use near or in the eyes."

## TRITE LANGUAGE AND CLICHÉS

In everyday, casual greetings and small talk, we often hear the same familiar words. Trite, overworked phrases such as the following echo in our ears daily:

| | | |
|---|---|---|
| richly rewarding | last but not least | sooner or later |
| each and every | tip of the iceberg | out on a limb |
| to the tune of | down and out | at first blush |

Other overused and misused words are *a lot* and *get*. Although *a lot* is frequently heard, it is informal. "Alot" is a common misspelling. Instead, you can use a synonym such as *many, much, several, various, some,* or *considerable.* The word *get* has numerous informal meanings that are unsuitable for college writing, for example, "got married." Say "were married."

Why risk boring or antagonizing the reader with repetitive or outworn words and phrases when fresh ones can be located easily? As you search for suitable words, beware of clichés. Like favourite recordings, clichés become worn from overuse. Although they were once original, clichés have become familiar—now they are ingrained in our daily language. Many of William Shakespeare's brilliantly descriptive lines, written four hundred years ago, are now clichés. How many of the following have you used?

| Famous Lines | Source |
| --- | --- |
| The naked truth | *Love's Labour's Lost*, 5.2.715 |
| Out of the jaws of death | *All's Well That Ends Well*, 3.1.396 |
| A dish fit for the gods | *Julius Caesar*, 1.1.173 |
| Parting is such sweet sorrow | *Romeo and Juliet*, 2.2.184 |

Perhaps you are familiar with other clichés such as "fresh as a daisy," "happy as a lark," "solid as a rock," or "his bark is worse than his bite." For most conversations and some informal writing, a cliché now and then may be acceptable. In academic and professional situations, however, clichés do not belong except when used creatively for a reason.

## MAKING THE MESSAGE CLEAR AND APPROPRIATE

As you examine your written words, read them aloud so that you can hear how they sound. Are they clear and appropriate? Consider the occasion. Who is the audience? What sort of language will they expect? How well you fulfill these expectations will influence not only the clarity and success of your message but also your credibility as a writer.

### Making Abstractions Concrete

*Thing* is a shapeless blob of a word, for it is purely abstract. *Thing* can refer to a monster or a gnat, a flask of poison or a glass of buttermilk. *Thing* can mean a condition, quality, vegetable, animal, mineral. In recent years, *stuff* has also been overused. *Stuff* is an elastic word—frequently used as slang to refer to objects, talk, or actions. ("I picked up some stuff"; "Don't give me that stuff about being too busy.") *Thing* and *stuff* often serve as substitutes for thinking. Shrewd speakers and writers tend to shun these words and limit their use of abstractions.

*Abstractions* are general words that identify categories, qualities, or ideas. Some abstractions refer to the intangible—concepts undetectable through the senses, such as *honesty, patriotism, fear,* and *courage.* Certainly, these broad terms have their place, but using unexplained abstractions or too many without concrete examples makes language vague and unclear.

Words that represent tangible qualities, objects, or activities are said to be *concrete.* Concrete words describe details that can be perceived through one or more of the five senses. You can see the delicate perfection of a purple crocus, the luminous rings of a lunar eclipse, and the muted hues of a rainbow. You can hear the whir of a hummingbird's wings or the thump of a human heart. You can smell the fragrance of honeysuckle or the pungent odour of an annoyed skunk. You can touch the fur of a baby rabbit or feel the grit of sandpaper. You can taste the sweetness of raspberry jam or the piquancy of horseradish. Concrete words stimulate the imagination and evoke vivid imagery.

As you revise, look particularly for abstract adjectives (*beautiful, terrible, impressive, delicious, unpleasant,* and the like) that can be replaced by concrete sensory words. Because some topics such as sunsets and love have been so popular, it is difficult to find a fresh way to describe them. In that case, you might choose another topic or devise an unusual comparison that uses concrete imagery.

### *Questions to Find Concrete Words*

1. How did *X* look? Size? Shape? Colour? Length of hair/coat?
2. Does *X* make a sound? Volume? Rate? Pitch?
3. How does *X* feel? Texture?
4. Does *X* have a fragrance or odour? Pungent? Faint? Pleasant?
5. If *X* is edible, how does it taste? Sweet? Sour? Tangy? Acid? How does it feel on the tongue?

## Moving from General to Specific

If your friend tells you she purchased a new car, you have no mental image of the car. To obtain further information, you might ask, "What kind?" She may respond, "A Buick." And so the conversation continues until you learn she has purchased a dark-red, two-door Buick Regal Limited. Although the word *car* is concrete, it is general, lacking descriptive information.

Likewise, other general terms such as *cat, dog,* or *horse* tell very little about a specific animal. For example, do you mean a lion or a domesticated cat? If you mean the latter, is the cat a mixed breed or registered breed? A barn cat or a house pet? Male or female? What age, size, and colour is it? Writers need to be specific so that the reader comprehends quickly. Normally, a specific word or phrase is more appropriate than a general word as long as you don't drench the reader with nonessential details.

In the sentences below, note the differences in the effects of general words and specific words:

**General:** A *dog* went into a *building* and lay down in a *room*.

**Specific:** A *Dalmation* entered the side door of the *brick firehouse* and stretched out in a corner of the *kitchen*.

**General:** *Walking* is a good way to enjoy the *wonder of nature*.

**Specific:** *Hiking* in Algonquin Park is a good way to enjoy the *brilliance of an Ontario autumn*.

## SCHOLARLY OR EVERYDAY WORDS?

A woman went up to Adlai Stevenson after a speech. Enthusiastically, she said, "Oh, Mr. Stevenson, I think your speech was absolutely superfluous!"

He replied, "Thank you. I think I shall have it published—posthumously."

"Fine!" she said. "The sooner, the better."

Leafing through a thesaurus, some students select scholarly or other unfamiliar words without consulting a dictionary. The results may be disastrous or unintentionally amusing. Even if used correctly, words may be inappropriate for a piece of writing.

Lewis Thomas, an editor, physician, and contributor to the *New England Journal of Medicine,* used simple language to explain a complicated process in his book *The Lives of a Cell:*

> Everything in the world dies, but we know about it [only] as a kind of abstraction. If you stand in a meadow, at the edge of a hillside, and look around carefully, almost everything you can catch sight of is in the process of dying, and most things will be dead long before you are. If it were not for the constant renewal and replacement going on before your eyes, the whole place would turn to stone and sand under your feet.
>
> There are some creatures that do not seem to die at all; they simply vanish totally into their own progeny. Single cells do this. The cell becomes two, then four, and so on, and after a while the last trace is gone. It cannot be seen as death; barring mutation, the descendants are simply the first cell, living all over again. . . .

Since Thomas is writing for a lay audience, he is careful to select words they will understand. He begins with a statement about death and relates it to his readers. Then he compares the familiar process of death to that of cell division, which is unfamiliar. Because he supports the abstractions with concrete examples, the result is beautifully clear. For most college writing, don't use a long, obscure word when a short, familiar one will do.

As you examine your word choice for college writing, consider how your audience might perceive the message, then revise accordingly. After any revision, reread each sentence to be sure that it says what you mean. Don't use a long word when a short word will do, but do not sacrifice meaning for conciseness. Clarity should remain top priority.

---

**FOR YOUR REFERENCE:**
**ESSAYS ON LANGUAGE USE IN THE READER**

- "Dawn Watch," John Ciardi, page 424
- "Mother Tongue," Amy Tan, page 462

> **SUMMARY**
>
> - Improve your word choice by understanding denotative and connotative meanings within language.
>   - Denotations are literal, precise meanings that are always defined in the dictionary.
>   - Connotative meanings are hidden meanings that people attach to words.
> - Use positive language to improve the tone of writing.
> - Eliminate sexist and racist language.
> - Tailor technical jargon and scholarly words to the audience.
> - Minimize the use of clichés in your writing.
> - Replace abstract words with concrete words and examples that clarify abstract concepts.

## Test Yourself

### Can You Find the Concrete Terms?

*Directions:* Underline the concrete words in the following excerpt from "Living Like Weasels," by Annie Dillard. Then check your answer against the key at the end of the chapter.

> Weasel! I'd never seen one wild before. He was ten inches long, thin as a curve, a muscled ribbon, brown as fruitwood, soft-furred, alert. His face was fierce, small and pointed as a lizard's; he would have made a good arrowhead. There was just a dot of chin, maybe two brown hair's worth, and the pure white fur began that spread down his underside. He had two black eyes I didn't see, any more than you see a window.

## Practice

### Collaborative Learning: Negative Connotations

*Directions:* Pretend you have had a mild disagreement with a family member. Later you overhear the person describing the exchange. Which terms below would you dislike? Which would be acceptable? Do your group members agree or disagree? If so, why? (Consult a dictionary if you wish.)

| | | | |
|---|---|---|---|
| dispute | quarrel | fracas | brawl |
| bicker | scrap | controversy | altercation |
| squabble | fight | conflict | hassle |
| spat | difficulty | argument | beef |
| tiff | row | disagreement | feud |

**Write a Description Using Concrete Words**

*Directions:* In one paragraph, write a description. Give concrete details and examples. If you wish, describe one of the following topics:

1. The footwear you are wearing
2. A "white elephant" in your home
3. A vehicle you use or have used
4. A favourite hideaway
5. A family heirloom

## *Test Yourself Answer*

> <u>Weasel!</u> I'd never seen one wild before. He was <u>ten inches long, thin as a curve, a muscled ribbon, brown as fruitwood, soft-furred,</u> alert. His <u>face</u> was fierce, <u>small and pointed as a lizard's;</u> he would have made a good <u>arrowhead.</u> There was just <u>a dot of chin,</u> maybe <u>two brown hairs'</u> worth, and the pure <u>white fur</u> began that spread down his <u>underside.</u> He had <u>two black eyes</u> I didn't see, any more than you see a <u>window.</u>

> —Annie Dillard, "Living Like Weasels"

# OPTIONS FOR ORGANIZATION

## Part 3

# *Narration*

## Recounting Events

**Learning Objectives:**

After reading and applying the information in Chapter 10, you'll be able to:

- Identify first and third person narration
- Identify different kinds of narrative openings
- Organize and develop a narrative
- Identify different kinds of narrative conclusions

> *A story has the uncanny ability to raise the spirit out of the flesh like bread rising yeasty in a warm place.*
>
> —Thomas Moore, "Introduction"
> *Best Spiritual Writing 2000*

Narration is used not only in fiction writing but also to relay news of a neighbourhood or news of a nation, to share research data, and to write reports and other documents. Histories, biographies, journals, college papers, magazines, and even advertisements include narratives. Narration is a powerful tool that can captivate an audience—stirring the imagination, eliciting empathy, and lending weight to opinion. This chapter explains techniques of narration, which have a wide range of practical uses.

## PURPOSE OF NARRATION

An effective narrative recounts action for a purpose. If the purpose is to entertain and establish camaraderie, then it may not matter whether the account is fiction or fact. But when the purpose is serious—primarily to reflect, inform, or persuade—then the audience expects facts and should receive them. The writer is obligated to put forth the truth.

## WORKPLACE CASE STUDY

### SPENCER'S LETTER

One afternoon in his office, Spencer leafed through a singles magazine and paused to read the personal ads in the back pages. One, signed "Golden Girl," sounded tantalizing. He typed up a one-page letter on the office computer, placed it in a company envelope with the printed logo. After writing his name above the company name, he addressed the letter to Golden Girl at Box 312. He attached his own stamp. That evening on the way home, he dropped the letter into a mailbox.

Several days later the letter was returned to the company, but not to Spencer. On the outside of the envelope, the post office had stamped: "Moved. Left no forwarding address." As Spencer's supervisor sorted through a newly arrived pile of mail, he noticed the company envelope and the unusual name of the addressee. He opened and read the letter. The vulgar language and sexual content surprised him.

### ACTIVITY

Assume the role of supervisor. You have interviewed Spencer and gained his account of what happened (first paragraph). Write up a brief narrative of the incident in your own words and explain how it affects the company. Make a recommendation for (minor) disciplinary action.

---

Narration may be used as a major or minor writing strategy. If major, then the action is most important. For example, medical personnel write reports of patients' progress. Managers keep brief histories of employees' performance. Law enforcement officers write narratives of events prior to an arrest. Although these records may include description as support, narration is the major strategy.

In this chapter the major mode is narration, but examples of mixed strategies are also provided. In the following case study, narration is the major strategy. The case is based on a real incident; it shows how writing can grow out of an actual situation.

In college you may write narratives not only in English, business, and technical writing classes but also in anthropology, sociology, law enforcement, pre-law, engineering, and other classes.

## ELEMENTS OF NARRATION

Every narrative has six basic elements—the *who, where, when, what, why,* and *how* of the event. The point of view from which the story is told also influences its effect on the audience. Who was involved? Where did the action take place? When?

What happened? How did it happen? Why did it happen? Who is the narrator? The first four questions come early and easily when the writer sets the scene, giving the necessary background. After that the telling becomes more difficult.

## The *Why*

The *why* of a narrative is the cause or reason or motivation that propels the action. This element may not become entirely clear until you are heavily into revision and reexamining the facts. To explore the *why*, you might ask yourself these questions:

- What set off the chain of events? What or who initiated the action?
- How did the central character react?
- What motivated her or him?
- How did relationships and connections influence events?

## Point of View in Narration

Who tells the story and how it is told influences its credibility. Is the writer/narrator giving a firsthand account or describing it secondhand? How reliable is the narrator? How objective? From which attitude or angle does the narrator regard the subject? The point of view shapes a narrative and influences its reception by the audience.

***First-Person Narration***   A writer may tell a story from either a first-person or a third-person point of view, depending on the rhetorical situation and the purpose. Whether or not you choose first person (*I, me, my, mine, we,* or *ours*) will depend upon your role. Is it your story or someone else's? Either way, first-person narration will lend a sense of immediacy, giving the reader a front-row seat on the action.

In first-person narration, an observer or a participant tells the story. This eyewitness account is often written in a conversational tone. First-person point of view works well in journals, autobiographies, and personal essays.

Lindsay Aqui uses first person in her essay.

### Tae Kwon Do Changed My Life

The most important moment of my life was the day I began practising martial arts, specifically the Korean martial art of tae kwon do. Practicing tae kwon do instills in me a sense of pride and confidence. Most importantly, through tae kwon do I have found a very special person who has become my mentor. His name is Chris and he is my coach and my inspiration.

When I first met Chris I was twelve years old and very impressionable. Chris was intimidating and had a presence that demanded respect, but he also exhibited a more gentle side to his personality. Over the years I have spent many hours training with Chris and he has helped me through many difficult situations, always providing support and guidance.

I remember the first time that I truly understood how Chris had impacted my life. We were driving home from a tournament at which I had just won a gold medal. The idle chatter in the car revolved around training, the tournament, and the weather. Suddenly Chris paused and told me that he was very proud of me and knew that I had the inner strength to overcome any obstacle that I would encounter in my life. He told me to always believe in myself and take on the challenges that life presents with enthusiasm. The words that Chris spoke that day have helped me face many challenges and obstacles in my life. The art of tae kwon do has provided me with the inner strength to be the person I know I am.

**Third-Person Narration**   Writers or narrators who are not involved in a story adopt a third-person point of view. They restrict pronouns to words such as *he, she, it, they,* and *them.* Third-person narration puts distance between the reader and the topic, producing a more detached voice than first person provides. A professional response, such as those found in many business and technical reports or research papers, usually requires third-person point of view. There the goal is to focus on facts and results, not on feelings or opinion. Reporters, biographers, and historians use third person in an objective way for various reasons.

The following third-person narrative recounts a disastrous 1981 accident at a Hyatt Regency Hotel. Think how differently a narrative of the accident by a first-person survivor would have sounded.

At 7:05 P.M. on Friday, July 17, 1981, the atrium was filled with more than sixteen hundred people, most of them dancing to the music of a well-known band for a tea dance competition, when suddenly a frightening, sharp sound like a thunderbolt was heard, stopping the dancers in mid-step. Looking up toward the source of the sound, they saw two groups of people on the second- and fourth-floor walkways, observing the festivities and stomping in rhythm with the music. As the two walkways began to fall, the observers were seen holding on to the railing with terrified expressions on their faces. The fourth-floor walkway dropped from the hangers holding it to the roof structure, leaving the hangers dangling like impotent stalactites. Since the second-floor walkway hung from the fourth-floor walkway, the two began to fall together. There was a large roar as the concrete decks of the steel-framed walkways cracked and crashed down, in a billowing cloud of dust, on the crowd gathered around the bar below the second-floor walkway. People were screaming; the west glass wall adjacent to the walkways shattered, sending shards flying over 100 ft. (30 m); pipes broken by the falling walkways sent jets of water spraying the atrium floor. It was a nightmare the survivors would never forget.

—**Matthys Levy and Mario Salvadori**
*Why Buildings Fall Down*

There may be a time when you decide to write in third person about your experience. Perhaps the topic is still hurtful, even heartrending. To gain distance and objectivity, you might write in third-person about yourself, perhaps using a pseudonym. But first consider the nature of the experience. If a recent event has been traumatic, beware. You can become so entangled in emotion that you hit a writing block and lose the point.

## WRITING A NARRATIVE PAPER

You have a treasure trove of stories just waiting to be told, some sad, some happy. Perhaps they are family stories, passed down from generation to generation. Prewriting will help you find them. Mull over the episode and consider:

- How did the experience influence me? Am I happier? Wiser? How so?
- What did I gain or learn? Can I find a lesson or moral?
- How might the narrative affect the audience?

### Prewriting

The simplest way to start prewriting is to list key events in the order they occurred. Leave two inches or so of space between items to insert related details. After listing key events, jot down significant details about each one. Asking questions can guide you:

- What is the purpose of the narrative?
- Who are the readers? How much do they need to know?
- Does the experience remind me of an event in the public eye? How?
- Is the comparison relevant to my purpose?
- What is the source of tension or conflict? (barrier, problem, decision)

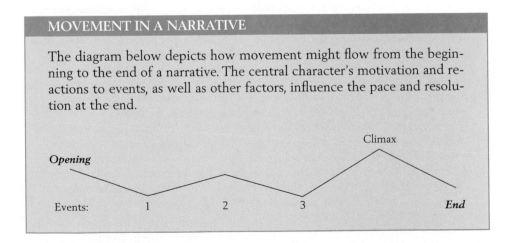

**MOVEMENT IN A NARRATIVE**

The diagram below depicts how movement might flow from the beginning to the end of a narrative. The central character's motivation and reactions to events, as well as other factors, influence the pace and resolution at the end.

### Drafting an Introduction

The purpose of the narrative will guide you in deciding whether to place the thesis at the beginning or end. Does the reader need to know immediately where the main idea is headed? For reasons of clarity and practicality, some rhetorical situations call for an early thesis. Other times the writer may delay the thesis, *laying a foundation to support the point of the narrative* and building to the peak of the action. Then the thesis comes at the end, where it can be stated or implied, depending upon the purpose. To begin a narrative, you may find these questions helpful:

- Where is the best spot to start?
- Should the story be told in first person or third?
- What tone is appropriate?
- What is the source of tension or conflict? (barrier, problem, decision)

The opening usually sets the stage for action. In other words, you identify the central person or character, place, and time. As the action starts rolling, description is usually sparse. Only essential details are shown. Gradually, necessary bits of background appear and conflict or suspense develops.

**Opening with Action**    To create interest, successful writers often open with an action, weaving in brief glimpses of background as the story proceeds. An *action opening* plunges the reader into a story with no unnecessary details or explanations. Right away the main person or character is faced with a decision or immersed in a predicament that must somehow be resolved. (See "Just a Walk" at the end of the chapter.) Other types of openings reveal the action, problem, or conflict gradually.

**Opening with a Quotation**    If you find an appropriate quotation that *specifically* relates to your main idea, then you can easily tie it to the beginning of a narrative. Be sure that any explanation does not delay the action unduly. Do not belabour the point of the quotation lest the reader perceive it as talking down. If you want to use a quotation that relates in a *general* way to your main idea, then you may have to look long and hard to connect it adequately.

See Chapter 16.

**Opening with a Comparison**    An unusual comparison in the title or first paragraph can hook the reader and serve as a unifying thread throughout the narrative. An effective comparison is introduced early and alluded to periodically.

## Organizing a Narrative Paper

Narratives need a clear progression. Each event, detail, and section of dialogue should advance the narrative point and contribute to the unity. If you can limit the focus early, then it will be easier to decide what to include—and what to omit. Or if the white heat of inspiration seizes you, write down everything, then go back and delete extra details, no matter how interesting. Make sure that every detail helps to establish a coherent design.

In most narratives the action is presented in the order that it occurs. Sometimes, however, a writer may disrupt the chronology by a sudden shift to the past, or *flashback*. For example, you might begin a narrative at a dramatic moment near its chronological conclusion, then flash back to events leading up to this point. Keep in mind, though, that flashbacks are tricky to manage effectively because of the special transition and plotting required. As a novice writer of narrative, you may want to stick to chronological order.

## Developing the Narrative Paper

As you develop a narrative, keep in mind the nature of the central character. It is usually advisable to look at people and events from a positive perspective, but be realistic. Human beings are a mix of negative and positive traits, and life is a blend of potholes, porcupines, and poppies. The following questions may be helpful to consider:

- Does the main character have a need or compulsion to reach a goal?
- Does the person have an internal or external conflict? A barrier to face?
- What is the person going to do?
- What is the darkest moment—the crisis? (It usually occurs about halfway.)
- How does the central character react?
- Does the person change or learn?

**Dialogue**    Selected dialogue can enliven a narrative, advance the action, and give clues to the personality of the speaker. It should have the ring of real conversation but move more quickly. Actual conversation often ambles along, backtracks, circles, and pauses. To create realism, copy the way a person talks, perhaps using slang or fragments. Or clip excerpts from actual conversation and shape them into dialogue for your narrative purpose.

When writing dialogue, minimize the use of "he said" and "she said." As long as the identity of the person who is talking is clear, no other identification is needed. Just indent for a new paragraph with each new speaker, no matter how short the exchange is. Set off the dialogue with quotation marks. (See "The Mulberry Tree" on page 120 in this chapter.)

**Concrete Details and Action Verbs**    The trick to writing an effective narrative is to keep it interesting. Include enough *concrete details* of the setting and action to give life to the story, enabling readers to visualize events and feel as if they know the people involved. Use strong action verbs, specific nouns, and modifiers that will appeal to your readers' senses not only of sight but also of hearing, touch, taste, and smell. But beware of including unnecessary description that may be distracting or boring.

**Building Suspense**    Another way to keep readers interested is to build *suspense*. You can do this by hinting at something but withholding crucial details in order to reveal them at a strategic moment. You can also build tension by pacing your narrative so that readers are kept wondering what will happen next. By the end, however, all loose threads should be clearly connected and the conflict or problem resolved. This technique is not applicable to most workplace writing.

## Writing a Conclusion

Although endings of narratives vary widely, every ending should have a sense of completeness. It should leave readers satisfied, convinced, empathetic, hopeful, amused, thoughtful, or wiser. Usually, the complication, problem, or conflict is resolved at the end. To resolve matters successfully, the writer must tell enough but not too much. If an ending is too long and wordy, it may become tiresome or confusing. Underdeveloped endings may leave readers feeling frustrated or cheated. Readers should not be left hanging without a clue to what happened.

***Ending with a Hint or a Hope***   Even if the full story remains untold or the conflict is not resolved, there should be a clue so that readers can draw their own inferences. For example, in *Gone with the Wind*, Rhett is leaving Scarlett, and she is agonizing over his departure. Yet the reader is offered a hint and a hope that life will get better. The novel closes with these words:

> She could get Rhett back. She knew she could. There had never been a man she couldn't get, once she set her mind upon him.
> "I'll think of it all tomorrow, at Tara. I can stand it then. Tomorrow I'll think of some way to get him back. After all, tomorrow is another day."

***Ending with a Surprise***   An unusual incident or twist may bring a story to a satisfying close. The surprise ending contains something the reader does not expect. The surprise may be amusing, embarrassing, enlightening, romantic, or dramatic as long as it is appropriate. To be effective, the unexpected event should grow out of the action, problem, or conflict. For example, Shasta Scharf used a surprise ending that sprang from a key event in "Just a Walk" (at the end of the chapter).

***Ending with a Reaction***   Sometimes a narrative ends with a brief *reaction*, a focused response or thoughtful commentary. The reaction may mention influences, implications, or consequences of the action. There may be an attempt to explain an underlying motive. Columnists, biographers, historians, novelists, and other writers often explore motives that may have precipitated an event. Or the reaction ending may connect a personal experience to one with universal implications, as in "The Mulberry Tree" later in this chapter.

Writing the ending of a narrative may require painstaking effort. In fact, you may attempt more than one conclusion before finally being satisfied. If in doubt about your ending, try asking these questions:

- What is my narrative point?
- Was there an unexpected result?
- Are there any loose ends to resolve?
- Does the voice of the narrator sound appropriate?
- Does the ending seem complete?

See endings in Chapter 4.

Spend time in thought and on revision. The spot where you stop should seem just right, even if it means omitting pet details.

## REVISING A NARRATIVE

When revising a narrative, look at the larger items first. Check the shape of the story. Is the setting clear? Does the action flow well, or should some events be rearranged? Is the direction clear, or are more transitions of time and place needed?

Watch for complicated sentences or cumbersome words that slow the pace unnecessarily. When the action is fast-paced, use short sentences. When movement slows, use longer sentences, combining ideas, to reflect the pace (such as this one). The checklist that follows will also help you revise.

### STUDENT PAPER: NARRATION

In this paper Betty Russell briefly sets the scene before her story starts to unfold. The point of her story appears at the end.

**The Mulberry Tree**

Mr. Grump's mulberries were big, plump, and tempting. At the edge of his yard stood two large trees, loaded with luscious blue-black mulberries. Although I would not have dreamed of stealing, I picked a few off the grass and ate them; the other kids followed. The berries tasted so good.

There were eight of us—me, Alice, Dorothy, and Shirley, my sisters, and our friends, the four Smith sisters. I was ten years old and they were all younger. We often played at a vacant lot near our homes. There we would fill our cans at the "red haw" (hawthorn) tree. We used the red haws to string for necklaces or for pretend food when we played house.

---

### CHECKLIST: REVISING A NARRATIVE

1. Does the narrative begin at a significant spot?
2. Is the complication, conflict, or problem clear?
3. Is the action arranged in the most effective order?
4. Do major details advance the point of the narrative? Do minor details clearly relate?
5. Does the pace of sentences reflect what is happening?
6. Does the ending give a sense of completion?

That afternoon, however, we had taken a different way to the red haw tree, past Mr. Grump's house. When we saw all those big dark berries going to waste underneath the trees, we decide to fill our cans. Then we thanked "Mr. Mulberry Tree" and ran home. Our mother washed the berries and put them in a big bowl for supper. That evening we piled whipped cream on the berries for dessert. We felt so proud because there were enough to treat the whole family.

Two days later all eight girls agreed it was time for more berries and cream. Our parents, thinking the trees were in the empty lot with the red haws, gave permission to go. To our dismay, when we reached the tree, there were no berries on the ground. Even the lower half of the trees were bare of fruit. Lucy Smith and my sister Alice, tomboys of the group, climbed a tree, and started jumping and shaking the branches. Mulberries fell like black rain.

We had started to fill our cans, when suddenly a voice thundered, "What are you kids doing? I'm going to call the police. You are on MY property STEALING my mulberries!"

Within seconds Lucy and Alice slid down from the tree. The other kids were running in different directions. Alice grabbed five-year-old Shirley by the hand, and they ran toward home. I turned to pick up my can and, to my horror, saw Mr. Grump holding my seven-year-old sister, Dorothy, up by the back of her neck. Her feet dangled in the air.

"Let her go!" I shrieked.

"I'm going to hand you both over to the police," he yelled. He held her with one hand and tried to reach me with the other. We circled—he, trying to reach me, and I, trying to reach Dorothy. But I could not get close enough to grab her without his grabbing me. So I ran up and threw the berries, can and all, in his face. He released his grip on Dorothy, and I snatched her hand.

As we cut across yards and down an alley, we could still hear Mr. Grump yelling. When we reached our yard, we slumped against the back of the garage to catch our breath. Our hearts seemed ready to leap out of our chests. How long we leaned there, I don't know.

Then we sneaked in the house. I hid in the closet under the stairs. Dorothy ran upstairs and hid with Alice under their bed. Shirley ran to the kitchen and clung to Mom like a second skin. When dinner was ready, Mom made us come out of our hiding places and demanded to know what we had done. No one said a word.

For two days we stayed in the house, expecting the police to come any moment and take us away. Our fear and guilt stayed with us for a long time. "Thou shalt not steal" was a commandment we never forgot.

## Questions for Discussion

1. What do you learn about the narrator in the first paragraph?
2. What strategy supplements narration?
3. What is the effect of including dialogue?
4. What is the effect of having the commandment in the last line?
5. Does this story remind you of another about a tree with forbidden fruit? What similarities do you see?

## FOR YOUR REFERENCE: NARRATIVE ESSAYS IN THE READER

- "Rosetta Disk Is Foundation's Gift to Future Linguists," David Bank, page 409
- "Home for Christmas," Carson McCullers, page 413

## SUMMARY

- The purpose of a narrative may be to reflect, inform, explain, or persuade.
- A narrative about an experience or fictitious event may not have a thesis statement; the thesis may be implicit. An action opening grabs the reader's attention immediately, whereas an opening that begins with a quotation delays the action.
- A narrative may be told in the first or third person.
- Chronological order is common in narrative, although the chronology is sometimes disrupted by a sudden shift to the past. If a flashback occurs, it should be for a crucial incident.
- Carefully edited dialogue can advance action and heighten interest in your narrative.
- Narrative endings vary; usually, the complication, conflict, or problem is resolved. If not, there should be a clue so that the reader can surmise what will happen.
- When revising, check the larger elements of the narrative first, particularly the order and development. Prune any surplus words or excessively long sentences that slow the pace of the narrative. Check the ending to make sure it is satisfying and complete.

## Practice

### Write a News Story

Assume you are a reporter for your campus or hometown newspaper. Write a news story. You may want to conduct interviews to gain specific details. The following suggestions may stimulate an idea you can use:

1. New construction, new business, or restaurant
2. Historical highlight: A story from the city's history
3. Profile of the president of the university or college
4. Student interviews about campus concerns
5. Plans for an activity such as May Day, a concert, or pig roast

**Write a First-Person Narrative**

Select an incident from your experience that may have caused you to laugh, to cry, to run, to show courage, or to learn. Then do some prewriting about the key events, including your reactions. After that, write a unified paragraph or short narrative. Perhaps one of the suggestions below will help you to find a suitable topic:

1. A learning experience—gulp!
2. Out of the mouth of a toddler . . .
3. Finding a . . .
4. A wonderful day
5. A surprise

## *Ten Ideas for Narrative Papers*

1. An incident on the job (a narrative report)
2. Being stopped for a traffic violation
3. A frightening experience at work
4. I never knew what love was until I met _____ _____
5. The day I realized that my parents knew a lot more than I thought
6. My most embarrassing experience
7. Revenge is not so sweet
8. Sadder, but wiser
9. A strange experience or unusual occurrence
10. My first day on a new job

# Description

## Conveying Impressions

---

**Learning Objectives:**

After reading and applying the information in Chapter 11, you'll be able to:

- Create a dominant impression for a descriptive essay
- Choose between subjective and objective description
- Draft, develop, and revise a descriptive essay

---

> *The background must never swamp the action,*
> *nor must the aura of a place interfere with*
> *the progress of the story.*
>
> —Rosalind Laker
> "Imagination and the Past," *The Writer*

The distant moan of a locomotive may take us back to a railroad siding where we picked and ate wild strawberries long ago. The fragrance of lilacs may remind us of the huge purple bush in grandmother's yard, where we frolicked with small cousins and rested on the lush grass. Descriptions such as these, based on seeing, hearing, touching, tasting, and smelling, allow the reader to visualize and share an experience vicariously.

## WHAT EXACTLY IS DESCRIPTION?

Description has been defined by philosophers as "a mode of perception," a means of knowing. It is a way to impose order upon the confusing complexity of the real world and to understand it, at least partially. It allows the writer to record sensory details, to reflect on an experience and ponder its significance. Description is an excellent way to preserve oral family history and first-hand research.

See pages 105 and 106.

In primary research we *observe, describe, interpret,* and *write* our impressions of concrete details (obtained through the five senses) that we perceive first-hand. This four-stage process enables us to relate the physical parts of what we observe to the whole subject or unit. Then we can contemplate its meaning, whether it be a caterpillar or the earth's crust.

This chapter examines the use of description as a major writing strategy for various rhetorical situations. In much writing, however, description plays a minor role—supporting a major strategy such as narration, process analysis, or comparison.

## PURPOSE OF DESCRIPTION

Whether you write a college paper, grant application, patient or client history, technical report, or other document, suitable descriptive details can strengthen your core idea. Successful description has a purpose: Hand-picked details reinforce the thesis or the point of the description. In research, business, and technical writing, writers use description to help readers understand the material qualities and fundamental structure of physical objects, organisms, and phenomena. Descriptive details can provide concrete evidence to support a thesis.

In expressive writing such as personal essays and narratives, autobiographies, and poems, writers guide the emotional responses of readers by selecting sensory details to create a *dominant impression.*

## CREATING A DOMINANT IMPRESSION

When description is the chief writing strategy, it conveys a dominant impression—a mood—that prevails throughout the piece for a purpose. Then sensory details unite to produce an overall mood, such as delight, fear, or curiosity, adding interest as well as evidence. This mood may be implied or expressed directly. In *Gift from the Sea*, Anne Morrow Lindbergh creates an implicit impression as she describes a shell, found on the beach, and compares the shell to her life:

> The shell in my hand is deserted. It once housed a whelk, a snail-like creature, and then temporarily, after the death of the first occupant, a little hermit crab, who has run away, leaving his tracks behind him like a delicate vine on the sand. . . . Did he hope to find a better home, a better mode of living? I too have run away, I realize, I have shed the shell of my life, for these few weeks of vacation.
>
> But his shell—it is simple; it is bare, it is beautiful. Small, only the size of my thumb, its architecture is perfect, down to the finest detail. Its shape, swelling like a pear in the center, winds in a gentle spiral to the pointed apex. Its color, dull gold, is whitened by a wash of salt from the sea. Each whorl, each faint knob, each crisscross vein in its egg-shell texture, is as clearly defined as on the day of creation. . . .
>
> My shell is not like this, I think. How untidy it has become! Blurred with moss, knobby with barnacles, its shape is hardly recognizable any more. Surely, it had a shape once. It has a shape still in my mind. What is the shape of my life?

As Lindbergh describes the shell, it becomes a symbol of her life. As she reflects, the images establish a thread of continuity, allowing the reader to sense her inner peace amid the problems of life. There is a tranquility, an acceptance of change, as she collects insights along with shells.

## Subjective and Objective Description

Description may be subjective or objective. A *subjective* description, such as Lindbergh's, reveals how the writer feels and thinks about the subject. Subjectivity refers to a personal view, which includes attitude and opinion as well as fact. The purpose of a subjective description is to share thoughts and feelings with the reader. But feeling must be kept within bounds so that it does not get out of control. Too much subjectivity can backfire. An essay with a dominant impression has a subjective slant.

In contrast, the tone of *objective* description is literal, factual, and fair. The tone is impartial and impersonal. In scientific and business writing, much description is based on unbiased, objective observation. Its aim is to reproduce for the reader exactly what the writer observed without reference to the writer's feelings about the subject.

See Chapters 21 and 22.

# WRITING A PAPER OF DESCRIPTION

Whether you have toured Ravenna, Italy, looking at mosaics, or never ventured beyond your city's limits, you have stored numerous sensory impressions. Perhaps you remember a lovely moment, painting, or place that might serve as a topic for a paper. Or perhaps you own an unusual object that has a story behind it. Think about the memory or object and its significance to you.

## Prewriting

After you select a topic, mine your memory by prewriting. You might try asking yourself questions that involve the five senses, as in the example below. Flora Kyle recalls specific details of her grandfather crafting a hope chest.

### Sight: What did I notice?

Grandfather was meticulous. Every joint had to be perfect.
the plane spewing wood curls from chestnut, maple, cedar boards
alternated woods in a chevron pattern on lid with an iron hinge
high luster of the finish
Aunt Lally put a wedding ring quilt she had made in the chest.

*Sound: What did I hear?*

whine of the saw

groan of the plane

scratch of sandpaper

pounding of hammer

Aunt Lally's words when she received chest on her sixteenth birthday

*Smell: What did I smell?*

aroma of cedar

smells of glue and shellac

fresh air when he opened the windows to let out fumes

*Touch: How did the wood feel?*

rough texture of boards

splinter in my finger

crispness of wood curls

satin smoothness of the hand-rubbed finish

*Point of the Description*

Chest is mine. Reminds me of Aunt Lally and my meticulous grandfather.

## Determining the Dominant Impression

A hodgepodge of details without a central point will lack unity. Consider their overall meaning. Why is this topic significant to you? What is the dominant impression, the idea that links the details? The idea need not be dramatic or earthshaking; it need only be important to you for a specific reason.

As you draft, you may uncover the wisp of a story. At first it may appear unimportant, or it may make you uncomfortable. But before tossing it away, take a second look. Paul Allen Dotson, Jr., drafted a description of a dining room light fixture. As he revised, he speculated about its meaning to him and realized it was more than just a beautiful object. There was a memory, an untold story, behind it—one he did not want to tell. But by referring to the story, he enriched the dominant impression.

### The Crystal Chandelier

In the dining room of a house where I once lived hung a crystal chandelier. It was a gorgeous old-fashioned fixture with eight lights and numerous dangling crystals that sparkled with the colors of the rainbow. The chandelier had three settings: High, medium, and low. When it was set on high, my wife and I would entertain friends and relatives, balance our accounts, and write letters. When the chandelier was on medium, I would often lounge in a chair next to the stereo and listen to soft music while staring at the colors emanating from the crystals. Yet my favorite setting was low. There were nights I would arrive home before my wife and would prepare dinner for the two of us. When she would walk into the dining room, the colors from the crystals would shine on her hair; she would smile, and I would see the most beautiful woman in the world. Though we are no longer together, those moments under the crystal chandelier are among my fondest memories.

Although Paul merely hinted at the story in the last line, he enriched the description. Rarely is an entire story told. Someone once said that a story is like an iceberg: Seven-eighths of it stays beneath the surface. The writer must decide how much to reveal. If you think there might be a story lurking in your prewriting notes, ask yourself these questions:

- Why do I have a special fondness for the object or impression?
- Did something happen that cast a shadow on or changed my life?
- How much do I want to say?
- Will that be enough? Will the ending seem complete?

## Selecting a Vantage Point and Transition

You might think of a writer as holding a camera, aiming the lens in a certain direction to record an impression or a story. Wherever the writer is viewing the scene from is the *vantage point*. The writer may remain fixed in one spot or move around. A *fixed observer* describes only what can be seen from one position. A *moving observer* describes from more than one position. With each movement, the writer keeps the reader informed with transitional phrases such as "turning at the first country road," "reaching the summit," or "descending a narrow, crooked stairway."

Imagine in your mind's eye the position from which you will view your topic. Will you remain in one spot or will you move? Will you be close or distant? Will you be observing for a few moments or over a span of time? What would be the most interesting vantage point for the reader? What transitions will you need to keep readers informed of your movements?

See Chapter 4.

## Drafting an Introduction

Some openings take readers directly to a scene. There they observe a specific time and place through the writer's eyes. A short transitional phrase and past tense may set a historical scene. For example. "*In 1890 Central City had* dusty unpaved streets and 132 inhabitants, not counting 56 horses, 63 dogs, and 75 cats." Or a descriptive phrase and present tense may describe a current scene: "*Nestled in a valley in . . . is* a small village that still has a general store and a post office where patrons pick up their mail."

Sometimes a description opens with a specific thesis. More interesting is a vivid comparison. Jennifer Ramey begins her paper, "Maintaining a Marriage," with a simile, followed by a metaphor:

> A good marriage is like a fine-tuned car. Care for it, work on it, and treasure it, and it will run well. Communication is the engine of a marriage. Effective communication goes beyond knowing a partner's favorite foods and activities. Heartfelt communication requires sensitivity—an awareness of the other person's feelings, embarrassments, concerns, and goals. Quality communication requires loyalty and listening with empathy, trying to understand what the other person is experiencing.

## Organizing and Developing a Description

The organization of a description often arises quite naturally from the topic. If you describe an object, a place, an animal, or a person, then spatial order usually works well. In spatial order, details are arranged according to space or location. You can use spatial order to show direction: east to west, north to south, left to right, top to bottom, front to back, inside to outside, or vice versa. For instance, to describe an Irish setter, you might go from the head to the tip of the tail. As a moving observer, you might explore a haunted house, going in through the creaking front door, up the dusty staircase, and through a hall to a narrow stairway. At the top is an attic filled with who-knows-what.

Chronological order, a sequence of time, may be used to describe the changes in a neighbourhood or a person. A street scene might be described from the wee hours of the morning to late at night.

Another possible order for description is from abstract to concrete or from general to specific (or vice versa). For example, to describe the disorder of a pack-rat's nest, you might begin with a general impression of the nest and the shock of finding this mess in your basement. Next might come a description of the items the rat had taken: an old spoon, a shiny silver button, a marble, and other trifles. Or if a topic requires emphasis, you might go from least to most important or from most to least important.

Comparing two views can give a fresh slant to an ordinary topic. For example, late grandfather's old watch might be considered worthless by one cousin, but another might view it as priceless, a family heirloom. People, too, can be described from more than one vantage point, as Lori I. demonstrates.

**My Fiery Grandma**

My grandmother is like a brightly burning fire. She can be warm and welcoming, a "light" ever ready to give aid. However, she can also be cruel and destructive, freely turning emotions into ashes. When controlled, Grandma is a warm, gentle person. She doctors wounds with soft hands and a kindly smile. She can make a person feel safe and protected. She has offered food and shelter to those less fortunate than herself, allowing them to warm themselves at no cost, while still providing all the love her twelve grandchildren could want. She has encouraged hopes and dreams, as if they were dry wood she just needed to spark into life. To enter her presence is like coming into a fire-lit room after being in the cold. The fire is there, warming skin and bones while her welcome fills one with good cheer.

My grandmother is like a fire in less positive ways as well. When she is in one of her fiery moods, her tone and words can blister. The warmth, shelter, and love once freely offered sometimes flare into regret and bitterness, searing what was to an ash. Hopes and dreams she once nurtured can wither under a well-turned phrase. During these times she is like a house fire, destroying and burning everything and everyone in her path. No subject, person, or idea is safe from her at such times. Yet despite these vices, she is still "Gammy," and the entire family would be less joyful without her.

## Writing a Conclusion

Successful endings give a sense of completion and satisfaction. In description, as in narration, the major point often appears at the end. The ending may be a brief summary that explains the point in an interesting way. Or the ending may sound optimistic as it looks to the future. A philosophical ending might relate physical details to an abstract thought. Anne Morrow Lindbergh is both optimistic and philosophical at the close of *Gift from the Sea:*

> The waves echo behind me. Patience—Faith—Openness, is what the sea has to teach. Simplify—Solitude—Intermittency . . . But there are other beaches to explore. There are more shells to find. This is only the beginning.

Sometimes a surprise or twist ending is effective. These endings require preparation. You cannot simply swoop down and attach an ending that is foreign to the description or story. You need to prepare the reader in small ways. Note that Paul mentions his wife early in "The Crystal Chandelier." He does not suddenly introduce her at the end. Effective endings are smooth; they grow out of whatever has preceded them.

## Revising a Description

When revising a description, choose words that convey sharp, clear images—vibrant verbs, specific nouns, and modifiers that crackle with meaning. The audience should be able to visualize the spot, object, or person and savour the other sensory details. The aim is not only to increase interest but also to enhance the dominant impression.

In *The Elements of Style*, E. B. White warns against the use of meaningless modifiers. He calls *very, rather, little,* and *pretty* "the leeches that infest the pond of prose, sucking the blood of words." Beware, too, of stacking adjectives in a series; use one if needed, seldom two, rarely three.

Although the right adjective can convey an idea, an action verb often can convey it better. For example, the two sentences below carry the same idea, but the first slows the pace with a weak (*be*) verb, the adverb *very*, and two vague adjectives. The second version deletes the adverb and adjectives. A strong action verb and a specific noun replace them:

- The tomcat *was* very upset and vocal.
- The tomcat *hissed* his displeasure.

In the previous example, note the repetition of the *s* in the second sentence—the sound echoes the meaning. Such subtle surprises work well in prose when not overdone. As you revise, you may want to consult the following checklist:

---

**CHECKLIST: REVISING A DESCRIPTION**

1. Does the opening line arouse interest for this audience?
2. Is the vantage point suitable? Is any transition needed?
3. Is the written voice appropriate? Should it be more personal or friendly?
4. Is the imagery sharp and clear? Have I involved at least three senses?
5. Are all details effective? Could their order be improved?
6. Are most verbs in the active voice? Are nouns and adjectives specific?
7. Is the dominant impression clear and effective?
8. Does the ending seem complete?

---

TWO STUDENT PAPERS: DESCRIPTION

In the first paper, Jean Ice describes a favourite relative. She uses the concrete-to-abstract strategy, describing appearance before personality.

**Aunt Marzia**

Marzia was an elegant lady. Even as a young girl, she exhibited unusual characteristics for a country lass. Her coal-black hair glistened from regimental brushing and frequent shampooing. Her hair was a halo for a lovely face with arched eyebrows and curling lashes. Her eyes were light green or gray, depending upon the color of her apparel. Her high cheekbones gave her a slight resemblance to a Native American. Her mother was said to be of Indian ancestry.

Marzia was taller than most other women of this generation. She carried her height proudly. Her erect posture and uplifted chin gave her a regal air. Somewhat out of sync with her physical perfection was her quirky little walk. She turned each foot slightly to the side as she strolled the country lanes.

Marzia was different from other members of her family and from her classmates. The other school children wore plain homemade garments, but Marzia used her sewing skill to put tucks in her waists. She also put flounces in her skirts and attached lace or embroidery to her collars. Few people would have guessed her wardrobe was made from feed sacks.

Marzia adored her first name, but she abhorred the way it was pronounced "Marzie" by others. Even her older sisters Clara and Ara did not follow her wishes and mispronounced her name. This elegant lady was a perfectionist in many other ways. She seemed to believe it was her responsibility to reform others to her way of thinking. This was especially true of her nieces. There were only five of us, compared to many more nephews. She expected us girls to speak correctly, dress attractively, and excel in good manners. She tried to accomplish these objectives by correcting us whenever we made an error. Often I, the youngest niece, was overwhelmed by a miscue. Once I pronounced *chic* as "chick," confident that I was right. Consulting a dictionary, after she corrected me, proved how little I knew.

Marzia was well educated for her time and situation. She was graduated from high school when most students were satisfied to complete the eighth grade. She went to normal school and became a teacher in a one-room school. The school was on the outskirts of a very small town, composed mostly of people of color. Marzia prized her students, and they were very fond of her.

When Marzia decided to marry, she was forced to give up teaching; for years ago only single women were allowed to teach. Unlike her sisters, who married for security and a home of their own, Marzia married because of her love for a ne'er-do-well. Although he was short, unattractive, uneducated, and rough of manner and speech, he had a jolly personality, which attracted the young ladies. But even Marzia could not contend with the old demon—liquor. After three years of silent grief, she divorced this man. She was the only member of her family to be divorced.

Marzia lived a long and productive life in spite of the divorce. She was greatly loved by all her younger kin, who were so different from her. When Aunt Marzia died, we all missed her so much. Nobody ever took her place in my life; no one else reminded me that I could do better.

## Questions for Discussion

1. Is Jean's dominant impression implicit or explicit?

2. How is the claim that Marzia is different and "elegant" supported?

3. Were you surprised by the way the nieces accepted her correction? Why or why not?

4. Jean mixes writing strategies. What order is used in her last three paragraphs?

5. What type of ending does she use?

In the second paper, student writer C. J. Banning presents an impressive number of vivid descriptive details. She uses comparison and contrast to explore the topic and to make her thesis more convincing.

### Please, Do Not Forget Me

In England on a barren hillside, stands a long-forgotten castle that has given way to centuries of neglect. Fragments of its once stately gray stone walls litter the courtyard. A spire that once stood tall atop a tower now lies upon a heap of rubble. Windows that once gleamed in the sun are darkened with grime. Winged creatures of the night fly through broken windowpanes. The storeroom is dank and musty;

gone are the fine foods and wines. Gone are the people who danced in the ballroom; gone is the grandeur of former years.

So, too, can be the life of a person suffering from severe depression. Often the person will go into seclusion, letting time and the world pass. Hiding in the dark recesses of the mind, the victim of depression cringes, hoping others will pass on by, paying no heed to the one that dwells within. Little by little, parts of the person are lost in the rubble of distress. Slowly, bit by bit, the self seems to be less and less. No longer does it feel that anyone might want anything it might be able to give. There is no room left for the food of good thoughts or warm feelings. The dark coldness of lost hope and worthlessness permeates the empty storage room. Unkempt thoughts weaken the body as well as the mind.

One summer day someone wonders how the old castle used to be. How had it looked with sturdy walls, clean windows, and polished floors? Had the steeple, standing tall and straight against the blue sky, seemed inviting to all who passed? Was the storeroom full, waiting for the banquets that were to come? Finally, someone decides to do something about the neglect. He picks up a stone and places it back into the wall, then another and another. He washes windows, and the sunlight once again streams through. He sweeps the dusty floor and dreams of the day the castle can be restored.

Despite protests, the victims of depression, too, need help and caring commitment to pick up the pieces of their lives, to wash their eyes and let in the light. They need help to discard the dark thoughts that flit about their minds, help to air the dark musty places that need a caring touch, help to let in a fresh dream of what they might be. Then, one piece at a time, their lives can be restored to become a little better, day after day.

Not all the castle walls and floors that are polished will shine as brightly as before. The storeroom will still have a faint mustiness, and a few stray creatures may venture in. But the castle can be a wonderful, grand place of peace.

### Questions for Discussion

1.  What is the impression in paragraph one? What words contribute heavily?
2.  What specific details in the second paragraph link it to the first?
3.  What do you notice in the third paragraph?
4.  What advice does the writer give in paragraph four?
5.  Does the writer seem to have first-hand or second-hand knowledge of the topic? Why do you think so?

### FOR YOUR REFERENCE: DESCRIPTIVE ESSAYS IN THE READER

- "Caterpillar Afternoon," Sue Hubbell, page 417
- "One Writer's Beginnings," Eudora Welty, page 421
- "Dawn Watch," John Ciardi, page 424

## SUMMARY

- Effective description has a purpose; it is not just a filler. Description often underpins narration, comparison, persuasion, or another major strategy. The tone may be subjective or objective.
- A descriptive paper has a dominant impression. You can select sensory details, referring to sight, sound, smell, touch, or taste to enliven description. Use strong verbs and specific nouns to help description come alive. When planning a description, think about the vantage point or location from which you will observe the subject.
- Sometimes there is a story connected with an object, place, or impression. Depending on the situation, you might merely mention the story or you might develop it. Sometimes a story has a lesson or moral that will give depth to the paper.
- You can organize descriptive details in spatial or chronological order, through comparison, or in another logical way.

## Practice

### Small Groups: *Devising Similes and Metaphors*

*Directions:* In groups of three or four, consider the items below. Select those that appeal to you and devise *unusual* comparisons that are similes and metaphors. Have fun! Appoint a recorder to save the best.

1. Fill in the blanks with a *fresh* comparison:
   a. He walked like a . . .    (Avoid clichés such as *duck.*)
   b. She ate like a . . .      (Avoid *horse.*)
   c. His tongue was as sharp as . . . (Not *knife*)
   d. He dressed like . . .     (Not a *hippie* or *hobo*)
   e. She was as proud as . . .    (Not *peacock*)

2. Comparisons with birds or insects: ladybug, hummingbird, dragonfly, house fly, termite, wasp, blue jay, woodpecker, meadow lark, canary, bobolink, ant, hoot owl, bumble bee, firefly, mosquito, or others. Here are two examples:

   **Simile:** His words bit like the sting of an angry wasp.
   **Metaphor:** His words stung.

### Ideas for Writing a Paragraph

*Directions:* Be specific, using concrete words and vivid verbs. End with a thoughtful comment, perhaps about the function, meaning, or qualities of the object or person, *so that your paragraph has a point.*

1. Describe the vehicle you are driving or riding. What is the dominant impression of you in or on this vehicle?

2. Describe a prized object. Why is it special?

3. Describe the contents of your purse (if you have one). What is the dominant impression to a casual spectator?

4. Describe someone you know. What predominant qualities does he or she have?

5. Describe your favourite piece of old clothing. Why is it special?

## *Ten Ideas for Descriptive Papers*

1. My best boss
2. The atmosphere at an NHL game
3. My first job
4. Life on a prairie farm
5. A moment to remember
6. A favourite hangout
7. The first time I . . .
8. Earliest childhood memory
9. My _____ heritage
10. My neighbourhood

# CHAPTER 12

# Process Analysis

## Explaining How

---

**Learning Objectives:**

After reading and applying the information in Chapter 12, you'll be able to:

- Use transitions appropriate to a process essay
- Draft, develop, and revise a process essay

---

> It is far easier to discuss Hamlet's complexes than to write orders which
> ensure that five working parties from five different units arrive at the
> right time equipped with proper tools for the job.
>
> —G. B. Harrison

Perhaps you have worked with inadequate or nonexistent instructions and know how frustrating that can be. One young man, lacking any instruction, began a welding job only to find the equipment was different from that used on his previous job. He ruined $400 worth of equipment the first night. To write clear directions, you need to analyze the process.

## WHAT IS PROCESS ANALYSIS?

A process is a series of steps, stages, phases, or natural changes that lead to a result. You engage in processes daily, whether brewing coffee, shaving, or driving a car. On the job you may need to write instructions for operating software, explain a process or procedure to a new worker, or show someone how to operate a machine.

*Process analysis* is an explanation or description of sequential actions, operations, or changes that occur for a purpose. A paper of process analysis may explain how to do something, how a condition develops, how an organism grows, or how a phenomenon evolves. Regular occurrences in the natural world—such as digestion, icicles, and hurricanes—involve processes. For clarity, the process is explained in the order that changes/events normally occur. Some processes require one certain order; others can be done in more than one way.

## Directions for Procedures

The simple experiments you conducted in high school science and chemistry labs were procedures. When you assemble shelving or pour a concrete patio, you also perform a procedure. To ensure good results, you follow the instructions carefully. If any steps are omitted or the order is reversed, the deviation may mar the final result. Some procedures, such as operating a chain saw, require warnings that users take precautions. *Include a reason for each precaution so that users take heed.*

Other kinds of processes require multiple sets of directions, all of which have phases, steps, or stages. For instance, the production of steel and the publication of a book involve many processes and people. The *audience* for directions consists of the people who will be performing the procedure.

**Use Second Person for Clarity**    Directions for a procedure should be clear and concise. Therefore they are usually written in second person with the *you* understood. Each step begins with an active verb: "*Insert* the tab . . . ," *Open* the chamber . . . ," "*Lift* the switch. . . ." Most instructions should be more than a brief list—they should explain according to readers' general level of knowledge. On the job, steps of a procedure are often simplified and numbered.

---

### WORKPLACE CASE STUDY

#### ETHAN SOLVES THE OFFICE LOUNGE PROBLEM

The sink of the employee lounge is usually stacked full of dirty dishes. The room smells of stale coffee grounds. Green mould grows on uneaten lunches in the refrigerator. Although employees are assigned weeks to tidy the room, they often forget. Those who remember may wash only the dishes. Ethan has been asked to devise a new system.

After careful thought, Ethan gives each office employee a copy of a quarterly assignment sheet with his or her week marked in red. In a memo he asks the employees to add this date to their calendars. On the refrigerator, he posts a sign that reads: "On Fridays all lunch containers and open soda will be discarded." On a cupboard, he posts this notice:

#### Daily Cleaning Procedure

On your assigned day, please clean between 3 and 5 p.m. Then no one will be using the lounge. The following procedure will save time. (It should take 10–12 minutes.)

1. Close the drain and fill the sink with hot water.

2. Add detergent and let dishes soak.

3. Clear the table and counter of debris. Wash them off.

4. Wipe the microwave inside and out.

5. Wash dishes, rinse, and stack on drainboard.

6. To prevent fire unplug coffeemaker. Dispose of grounds.

7. Wash and rinse coffeemaker.

8. Dry dishes and put in cupboard.

9. FRIDAY: Throw out all lunch containers and open soda cans in the refrigerator. Wipe up crumbs and spills in the refrigerator.

The system has worked surprisingly well. Grumbling about clutter and odour has stopped. The lounge is a much more pleasant place to sit and relax.

## Process Descriptions

The purpose of a process description is to describe a procedure, natural phenomenon, or other process for an audience who would like to know more about it but will not be performing the process. Therefore you supply just enough detail to provide an overview, state the function of each step or stage, and explain how each fits into the process.

Process descriptions are often written in narrative form, using either first- or third-person pronouns. Students in all academic disciplines analyze processes and write narratives. Sometimes the two overlap. For example, you might interview a patient, write a case history, and describe the onset of a health problem. Or you might narrate/explain how a hobby grew into a successful business.

***Using First Person*** Student writer Janice D. uses first person and past tense to begin the story of how her rock garden evolved.

### Gardening with Rocks

Rock gardening wasn't something I gave much thought to until a few years after we bought a house. I can remember the seller pointing out an overgrown bush in the front of the weedy yard, trying to use that as a selling point. Later my husband and I agreed "that will have to be the first thing to go." The first year we were so busy inside we didn't do much outside except to mow the lawn and kill the weeds. But over the next few years, we began to beautify the outside as well. We started small with a tree here, a few flowers and a rock there, which led to our lovely rock garden of today.

See "Caterpillar Afternoon," p. 417

***Using Third Person*** Process descriptions that are not drawn from a writer's personal experience are usually written in the third person. Present tense verbs in *active* voice are used for actions that recur: "The mollusk *opens* its shell . . . ," "Each year the tree *grows* new rings," "The furnace *melts* the glass. . . ."

## TRANSITION IN PROCESS ANALYSIS

A transition is a word, phrase, sentence, or paragraph that connects ideas, informing the reader of what is ahead. Transitions indicate shifts in meaning and relationships of time, location, sequence, similarity or difference, certainty or uncertainty. *Signpost transitions* appear at the beginning of sentences. This method is generally used in procedures. *Embedded transitions* appear at other places in a sentence, as explained in Chapter 14.

For process analysis, use transitions that indicate *chronological* order. For procedures with major and minor steps, distinguish between them. For major steps, use numerical transitions (*first, second, third*, and so forth). For substeps, use other transitions of time, such as *then* or *next*. (Two or three *first's* and *second's* would be confusing.)

| TRANSITIONS TO CLARIFY A PROCESS | | | |
|---|---|---|---|
| *To Emphasize Major Steps or Stages* | | *To Indicate Substeps* | |
| first | (begin) | next | then |
| second | | after that | later |
| third | | while | when |
| fourth | | meanwhile | as soon as |
| fifth | (finally) | during | after one hour |

*An Example of a Process Paragraph Using Transitions*   Student writer JD Rice uses *transitions* in the following paragraph about how to paint a mural.

Have you ever wondered what it would be like to go out and paint a mural on a piece of raw concrete? I will take you through a formula to conduct a proper outline that will be involved in the overall mural. I can honestly say that it does not take a genius or college graduate to operate a spray can. These would be some of the regular procedures that would take place before starting the mural, or murals. *First* you would have the idea of what you were doing on paper. *Next* you would decide on your location and after that select the type and colours of paint you require. *Secondly*, decide what size you are going to go with, and remember size and surface are two very important factors. *Next* you should decide if you're really willing to spend at least five or six hours on the project; also remember painting can be difficult and frustrating. If you are willing to commit yourself, I would *finally* begin by doing an outline of the sketch.

## WRITING A PROCESS PAPER

The purpose of a process paper can be to provide directions for a procedure or to describe a process, according to the assignment. To fulfill either purpose, you first need to estimate how much readers know about the topic and whether they are likely to have performed or witnessed the procedure or process before. This estimate is particularly important for writing directions. It will help you in gauging not only the amount of explanation needed but also the need to include *precautions and a reason* at strategic points:

**Warning:** Perform the steps in the order given. Failure to do so may cause fire.

When writing directions, be specific. Otherwise, some users may decide to take unwise shortcuts. At tricky or risky points, include a reason for the step. For example, "Follow directions carefully *to obtain a smooth finish*. First, prepare surface. . . . Allow each coat of polyurethane to dry overnight. Between coats, sand with the grain of the wood, using 180 or 220 grit sandpaper. Remove dust each time, using a tack cloth or a vacuum cleaner."

### Selecting a Topic and Prewriting

The topic for a process paper should be based on your personal experience or observation unless you plan to do research. The topic should be complex enough that readers won't find it obvious. You may find that narrowing the topic is essential: Even a fairly simple process paper can become surprisingly lengthy. The subject should be one you know well. To develop your thinking skills, avoid a recipe or any other process you have learned from printed instructions.

The quickest way to start is to make a scratch outline, listing the steps or stages in sequence. Leave spaces to jot in brief explanations and insert necessary precautions or warnings at the beginning and at strategic points—not at the end. *Many readers will not read the entire set of directions before they start.*

### Drafting an Introduction

An introduction to a process paper may be as short as one sentence or as long as a paragraph, depending on the purpose for writing and the assignment. Especially for directions, state the finished product or result of the process in the introduction. If you dive into the first step with no thesis statement, readers may become confused. The thesis should identify the process, make a claim, and specify the result, product, or benefit for the reader:

- White-water rafting can be an enjoyable experience for the beginner who is well prepared. (Claim/result: enjoyable experience)
- Setting up a backpacking tent correctly can net a good night's sleep. (Claim/result: good night's sleep)

The following student introductions illustrate just two of many options for an introduction.

***Generalization Followed by Restriction***   An accurate generalization may be used for the beginning of a process analysis. Patricia Jones Black opens with a generalization followed by a restriction. Safety is her key idea. Since Patricia's introduction is only two sentences long, she chooses to combine it with the first point.

### How to Process Green Beans

Home-grown green beans can be served year round when they are properly processed and stored. By following the twelve steps listed here, you can safely take green beans from the garden to the table several months later. First, pick beans that are plump and tender. Three to five pounds of beans will be needed for each quart to be processed.

***Historical Opening***   Melinda Ham selected an unusual topic that carries a hint of nostalgia. She begins by describing the slow-paced life of pioneer days (a life without television, computers, or expensive toys).

### Apple-Head Dolls: A Remnant of Yesteryear

Years ago when life was less complicated and most families lived miles away from their nearest neighbors, family entertainment was more often homespun than manufactured. Children had to invent their own games. Parents frequently made toys for their children out of natural materials because cash was scarce. One popular homemade toy was the apple-head doll. These dolls had wizened faces, like very wrinkled old people, with a variety of expressions. By following these simple instructions, you, too, can make an unusual doll for a child in your family.

***Combining Second Person with Third Person***   Note that Melinda begins the introduction by using third person. Then she skilfully switches to *second person in the middle of the final sentence* of the paragraph. This way she makes the pronoun shift smoothly.

## Developing a Process Paper

As you draft, keep a specific audience in mind so that you will know how much explanation is needed. If you are writing directions, ask yourself, What points might be difficult, unclear, or risky? Present the steps in an orderly sequence so that the reader can understand and possibly duplicate the procedure. At the beginning, specify the equipment and material necessary to complete the process. In her paper on making apple-head dolls, Melinda Ham explains the process clearly, using numerical transitions and active verbs to indicate major steps. Her transitions are italicized here.

*First*, gather the necessary materials. An apple and cotton balls are needed for the face, hair, and beard of a male doll. Or you may wish to make a pair of dolls, male and female. The apple should be large because the head will shrink later. The body consists of a fine-gauge wire coat hanger, a large paper clip, clean cotton rags (an old sheet, pillowcase, or shirt), varnish or shellac, and scraps of fabric for clothing. Other items needed are a sharp paring knife, pliers, a small bowl, a bottle of pure lemon juice, plain table salt (not iodized), and about eighteen inches of heavy thread or fine cord.

*Second*, make the face of the doll. With the paring knife, thinly peel the apple. *Then* carve out the tiny eye sockets, nose, mouth, and ears. *After the head is carved*, place it in a small bowl. Pour one-fourth cup of lemon juice over the apple. Let set for thirty seconds, *then* rotate so that all sides are covered with juice. Wait one minute. To make the eyes, press two apple seeds horizontally into the carved sockets.

Aging is the *third* step. Unbend the paper clip, leaving the smallest "hook." Push the straight end of the clip into the top of the core down through the apple. *When the wire emerges*, bend it about an inch to make a right angle to support the apple. Loop a length of heavy thread over the top hook and tie a knot. *Next* suspend the thread from a window catch, away from direct sunlight, where the apple can hang for two to four weeks. *When the desired "wrinkling" occurs*, apply a thin coat of clear shellac or varnish to prevent further deterioration. Let dry overnight.

*Fourth*, add "hair" to the head. For a male, pull apart a cotton ball to form a beard. Glue around the jawline. A narrow strip of cotton around the back will form a fringe of hair around a bald spot. For a female doll, a large cotton ball (or two) will be needed for her hair, which can be arranged as desired.

Making the body is the *fifth* step. Use pliers to twist a thin wire coat hanger into a simple stick figure. Wrap strips of rags around arms and legs to give a rounded effect. Secure the rag strips with rubber bands or adhesive tape or both.

Creating clothing is the *sixth* step. Design simple clothes for the dolls. The male doll might wear a simple dark suit with a white shirt and perhaps a cap or hat. The female doll might wear a tiny apron, shawl or cape, sunbonnet, and long dress.

*The final step is attaching the head.* Attach the apple head firmly to the neck wire. Twist the clip wire tightly around the body wire so that the apple head will remain upright. If wire shows, cover with a necktie, shawl, or scarf.

## Writing a Conclusion

An effective conclusion to a process analysis provides a sense of completion, often by referring specifically to the result of the process. If possible, end on a positive note. Even if the results of a procedure are negative, you might summarize what was learned, refer to a benefit or emotion, or add a bit of humour. Melinda ends by pointing out what makes apple-head dolls special.

> Apple-head dolls are not only easy to make, but unusual. The face and expression of each doll will vary somewhat. The clothing can vary greatly. Apple-head dolls make attractive and distinctive gifts.

## Revising a Process Paper

Clarity and completeness are the main qualities to check for as you revise your process paper. The following questions should be helpful.

> ### CHECKLIST: REVISING A PROCESS PAPER
>
> 1. Who is the audience? (*Tip:* On your outline list age, experience, and any other relevant characteristics of the audience. Refer to the list as you revise your paper.)
> 2. Does the introduction establish the purpose and point out the product or result of the process?
> 3. Have necessary precautions been included at appropriate spots?
> 4. Are reasons included at strategic points?
> 5. Do transitions clearly distinguish major steps as well as substeps?
> 6. Is each step or stage of the process discussed in sufficient detail?
> 7. Does the conclusion complete the paper in a satisfying way?

### TWO STUDENT PAPERS: PROCESS ANALYSIS

The purpose of Keith Witzel's paper was to explain how to replace a defective electrical outlet safely. He directed the paper to the average homeowner with relatively little experience in home repairs.

#### Replacing an Electrical Outlet Safely

Many people refuse to replace defective electrical connections in the home, either because of a lack of knowledge concerning the proper procedure or from fear of creating a fire hazard. By following a few simple guidelines, however, almost anyone can make minor repairs safely.

Most electrical circuits in the home are made up of general lighting circuits of either 15- or 20-amp circuits. These are the circuits used for small appliances, lamps, television, and others. These items are connected into the general lighting circuits by plugging into the wall outlet receptacles. If one of these receptacles becomes defective, it is a safe and simple process to replace it by following five main steps: First, assemble the necessary materials; second, shut off the house current; third, remove the receptacle; fourth, install the new receptacle; fifth, restore power and check the operation of the new receptacle.

First, assemble the necessary materials. These include a pair of needle-nosed pliers with a jaw approximately two inches long, tapering to a pointed end; a slotted screwdriver; a utility knife; and a new receptacle rated at 15 amps or 20 amps as required.

Second, shut off the power to the circuit that contains the defective receptacle. This is done by turning the main switch (marked on handle) to the "off" position on the circuit breaker or fuse box. Check to make certain that the electricity is off by trying to operate appliances in various locations of the house. They should not function.

Third, remove the cover plate from the defective receptacle by turning the screw in a counterclockwise direction. Remove the two screws that hold the receptacle outlet to the utility box (the small metal box mounted in the wall), and pull the receptacle from this box. There will be a white insulated wire, a black insulated wire, and possibly an uninsulated ground wire (depending on the age of the structure) attached to the receptacle. Remove these wires and discard the used receptacle.

Fourth, install the new receptacle and replace the cover. Before installation, inspect the black and white wires to ensure that each end is free of insulation for approximately five-eighths inch and the ends are formed into loops. These loops should be made in a clockwise direction. The purpose is to ensure that the wire is secured around the screw as the screw is tightened.

After that, install the wires to the new receptacle. The white wire is connected to the silver-colored side of the receptacle and the black wire to the brass-colored side. Tighten each screw firmly. Next, connect the uninsulated wire (if used) to the green screw on the bottom of the receptacle. Push the receptacle into the utility box and tighten, using the screws supplied with the new receptacle. Remount the receptacle cover, being careful not to overtighten this screw, which could cause the cover to crack.

Finally, restore power to the house and check the receptacle to see that it is functioning properly. If not, check to see that you have flipped all breaker switches.

If each of these steps is followed closely, you will have not only the satisfaction of doing the job yourself, but also the satisfaction of saving the cost of an electrician.

## Questions for Discussion

1. Is Keith's paper a set of directions for a procedure or a process description? How do you know?
2. What transition does he use to indicate the substep of step four?
3. Does he provide any precautions or warnings? Where?
4. What type of ending does he use?
5. How clear do you find Keith's analysis? Is any step or substep unclear? If so, how might it be clarified?

In the next paper, Ann Kemmerley describes a procedure used at her job to make space for new books. Embedded and signpost transitions (both are italicized) provide tight links and clarify the steps for the reader.

### How to Prepare Books for Sale at the Dorcas Carey Public Library

Many library books are read each year in the village of Carey. Some books, however, fail to be as popular as others and collect dust on the already crowded shelves. To dispose of the less popular works, the Dorcas Carey Public Library uses a *four-step process* to prepare books for sale.

"Weeding" is the term given to the *first step in this process.* Periodically, an assistant librarian looks through every book on a shelf for its last circulation date, found on the pocket inside the back cover. If this date goes back five years or more, the book is weeded from the shelf and placed in a stack beside the shelf. Often books will also be weeded if they are in poor condition because most people do not read books that are falling apart. This step of weeding is completed after the head librarian checks each book and decides whether to try the less popular work in another section or *to sell it.*

*The books selected to be sold* must then be prepared for sale. *This second step* includes ripping out the back pockets and marking out any identification. The back pocket, which holds the book's circulation card, is torn away from the page or cover where it is glued and thrown away. Any library identification, such as name and address or price, must be covered by a black marker. If this marking out is not done, a reader may confuse books bought at the book sale with those currently in circulation. An important part of this step is the saving of the circulation card, for it will be used in the *following steps.*

The removal or "pulling" of all the books' cards from the library's card catalog is the *third and lengthiest step.* In this step all cards pertaining to a book must be pulled from the drawers by tearing the lower hole. The circulation card saved in step two gives the information needed to complete this step. The circulation card's top line indicates the author, and its second line gives the title. The book's author card is pulled first. On the reverse side of this card may be a list of subjects related to the book. Each subject given is *then* found, and the cards pertaining to the book are pulled. The last card to be removed from the main card catalog is the title card. *Before step four,* it is necessary to pull another card for the book from the author file in the main office.

*The fourth and final step in preparing books for sale* is crossing them off in the accession books. The accession books list every book in a library according to an assigned number given at the time of purchase. This number is found on the circulation card's right side. The number is located in the accession book and "sold" is printed in the margin reserved for such remarks. At this time the circulation, author, subject, and title cards can be discarded, and books are ready for sale to the public.

*The four steps for preparing books for sale* are not complicated, but they do require some time. The effort put forth, however, is well worth the shelf space that can be used for new books (purchased with funds from the books sold) and the joy a reader receives from buying an inexpensive book to add to his or her own library.

## Questions for Discussion

1. Is Ann's paper a set of directions for a procedure or a process description? How do you know?

2. How clear do you find Ann's analysis of the process? Is any step or substep unclear? If so, how might it be clarified?

3. Find some instances in which Ann has taken time to explain the purpose for various steps and substeps. Do these explanations help you better understand the process? Do they ever make the process hard to follow? Explain your answer.

> ### FOR YOUR REFERENCE:
> ### PROCESS ANALYSIS ESSAYS IN THE READER
>
> - "Write Your Own Success Story," Carol Carter, page 428
> - "How Do You Know It's Good?" Marya Mannes, page 434

> ### SUMMARY
>
> - A process analysis is a logical explanation of a process, giving either directions or a description in chronological order. Numerical transitions can mark major steps; other appropriate transitions can mark minor steps.
> - When writing your process paper, keep a specific audience in mind so that you will know how much explanation is needed. Identify the topic and the result in the introduction. Develop the body with adequate details depending on how much readers already know. Include precautions and warnings if needed. Possible endings include a summary, a reference to a benefit or emotion, and humour.

## Practice

### Writing Ideas for Paragraphs

1. How to change a tire
2. How to get ready for Saturday night
3. How to make a paper airplane that will fly
4. How to tie a shoe (as explained to a five-year-old child)
5. How to prepare for your first job interview

## Ten Ideas for Process Papers

Describe or explain:

1. A natural process you have observed (butterfly hatching, erosion of a beach, aging of an oak tree, or other)
2. A procedure that you perform at work
3. How to have healthy house plants
4. How to become a good waterskier

5. How to give a shot with minimum discomfort
6. How to construct a concrete patio
7. How to make a minor household repair (such as patching plaster)
8. Painting a house the professional way
9. Burglar-proofing your home
10. Touching up paint on a car

# Illustration

## Showing with Examples

**Learning Objectives:**

After reading and applying the information in Chapter 13, you'll be able to:

• Draft, develop, and revise an essay using examples

> *Example moves the world more than doctrine.*
>
> —Henry Miller

For nearly fifty years Charles Schulz entertained Americans with the exploits of Charlie Brown, Snoopy, Lucy, Linus, and other characters in *Peanuts*. Schulz based many of his daily comic strips on examples taken from his own experience. He said, "If you were to read the strip, oh, for just a few months, you would know me because everything that I am goes into the strip." For instance, Charlie Brown's fear of rejection from the little red-haired girl originated from a refusal to a marriage proposal that Schulz once endured.*

## PURPOSE OF EXAMPLES

Giving an example is an effective way to explain, to convince, and to entice a reader to read on. An appropriate example creates an impression by evoking an image in the reader's mind. The right selection of examples will help you demonstrate your knowledge, whether in an employment application letter, a technical report, an essay exam, or a paper. Examples are valuable for explaining a concept, illustrating a problem, or supporting a reaction for papers in psychology, law enforcement, business management, literature, composition, philosophy, and other fields.

---

*Brendan I. Koerner, "Good grief! Charlie Brown says, 'So long,'" *U.S. News & World Report* 27 December 1999: 28.

Reprinted by permission of United Feature Syndicate, Inc.

In the comic strip above, Charles Schulz took an incident from his boyhood, reacted, and explained what friendship meant to him. You might say that he derived a statement of his philosophy of life.

## ELEMENTS OF ILLUSTRATION

To illustrate or to exemplify simply means to clarify through example. You include impressions, facts, statistics, or expert opinion to lend substance to your writing, according to the rhetorical situation. The key is to choose examples that count, that enable your audience to understand what you mean and to see that you know what you are talking about. On the job you might use illustration to persuade, as in a proposal or grant application. In an academic paper or a personal essay, you might use illustration to explain (see "Envy" at the end of this chapter).

## WRITING A PAPER OF ILLUSTRATION

For a paper of illustration, you have a wide range of topic choices and organizational strategies. Select a topic you can develop with interesting examples. Then arrange the examples in an order that reflects your purpose.

### Prewriting

The topic may be concrete or abstract, according to the assignment. When something is concrete, it is detectable through at least one of the five senses, often more. You can see, hear, feel, smell, or taste it. If you write about an abstract principle, you can clarify it with concrete examples familiar to the reader. You can cite a variety of examples as long as they all have a central thread.

Once you have chosen a topic, prewrite to form a pool of details. To start your creative juices flowing, write your topic at the top of a clean sheet of paper. Then jot down every idea that dives into your mind—anything that might be used as support. If you know the topic well, you will soon have a page of examples and details. To start prewriting, the following questions will be helpful:

- Why am I interested in the topic?
- What examples can I recall?
- Who is connected with the topic?
- Did he or she have a favourite saying, mannerism, or habit?
- How has he or she influenced me? Can I give an example?
- What changes have occurred; how do I feel about the changes?
- What is my main point?

Finally, draft a thesis that makes a point about your topic, ideally one that is unfamiliar to your readers.

## Organizing and Developing a Paper of Illustration

To organize and develop your paper, choose an order, select examples, and weave explanation with examples, all the while focusing on your purpose and considering your audience.

*See Chapter 4.*

**Order**   To organize a paper of illustration, select an order that suits your purpose and topic. You might organize examples chronologically or according to importance or in any other way that will advance your point. As you read the student papers in this chapter, notice the organizational strategies. Dixie O'Rourke uses chronological order, as shown in this outline:

### Envy

   I. Introduction: Example of envy at age ten (very strong).
  II. Body
     A. Age thirteen. Envy had decreased somewhat.
     B. Example: Sudden change in Dixie's perspective.
     C. Today: Envy seldom occurs.
  III. Conclusion

Other topics can be organized according to some variation in order of importance. In a paper about exotic pets, you might move from relatively familiar examples to more surprising or outrageous ones. In a paper on natural cures for common ailments, you might move from examples of cures for minor ailments to examples of cures for more life-threatening ones. Such orders have the advantage of holding readers' attention by providing examples that increase in interest.

**Relevant, Accurate, and Sufficient Examples**   Every example you include should be *relevant* to your thesis, illustrating your main point in some way. Resist the temptation to include an example just because it is odd or funny. Illustrations should illuminate a point. Irrelevant examples distract from the thesis.

Check to see that examples are *accurate*. In attempting to be humorous or to dramatize a point, writers sometimes embellish examples, but extravagance can sabotage logic. An example may be dramatic, but it should not be too far-fetched or unusual—the one-in-a-million variety. To palm off an atypical example as typical is dishonest. If you generalize from an example, it should be *typical of its class*. When researching, consider the source of your statistics. Is it reliable? Is the information up-to-date?

How many examples will be sufficient? The answer depends on the nature of your thesis and the weight of the examples. The sheer number of examples is less important than their quality. Select impressive examples that will provide strong support for your thesis. A controversial or debatable thesis will require several high-quality examples to convince a skeptical audience. As a rule, when examples are brief, you need more than when they can be developed in detail.

In a paper entitled "The Talent Within," Nicole Vanderkooi cites several brief examples in each paragraph. Each example is clearly relevant. Her third paragraph appears here:

> Possessing a natural skill can be overpowering, a constant pressure. Children with such talent have expectations already set for them. At age six, Sarah Wells was told she had a promising future in gymnastics and was enrolled in nightly classes. Despite many strained muscles, injured ankles, and missed slumber parties, she persevered and gained confidence. Yet she endured many lows as well as highs; she became critical of herself. Constant pressure from her parents and coaches and a desire to win made her dream a reality. At thirteen, Sarah began her powerful run to the vault. To keep her lead in the meet, she had to score at least a 9.5. As her hands hit the leather, she felt the adrenaline pump, and she scored a perfect 10. A spectator cheered, "That's awesome!" Sarah Wells won the meet. By now her childhood was gone, but in its place was a confidence powered by success. To some people, that is robbery; to Sarah it is a rewarding way of life.

***Weaving Examples with Explanation***   As you draft, try to find an interesting approach to your topic. You might start with a series of short examples, eye-catching details drawn from everyday life. To connect the examples to your thesis, you will need to interlace them with explanation. Bryan Vaughn weaves example with explanation as he describes his perceptions of happiness:

> During my childhood, happiness meant anything from having waffles for breakfast to being able to stay outside after the streetlights came on, catching lightning bugs and playing tag. Early in my adolescence, happiness seemed to take on another meaning. Driving fast was my new source of happiness. I discovered that a motor could be affixed to just about anything. My first few inventions were just this side of lethal. When I consider these vehicles, it's a wonder I'm still alive today. I rode go-carts, three-wheelers, snowmobiles, motorcycles—anything I could put gas in, I drove.
>
> During mid-adolescence, my perception of happiness changed again. Sports became my passion. For me, nothing could compare with the exhilaration of being part of a winning team. Our football team was the defending state champion. Our basketball team finished third in the state, and our baseball team was the conference champion. Happiness was being one of the main players on every team and having the potential to play college sports and possibly having a career in professional sports.
>
> But those dreams ended during a football game when I received a severe spinal injury. After two months in the hospital, I was sent home—handicapped, but thankful. At this time happiness took on yet a new meaning: I was just glad to be alive and able to walk. . . .

As my life began to return to normal, I saw a new source of happiness. One day I saw, parked in front of a Sunoco station, a red 1969 Pontiac GTO Judge. That same day I bought "The Judge" and spent every spare minute working on it. . . . But later an old man drove out in front of me without warning and wrecked my happiness. . . . Although I bought another car, it was not the same as the Judge.

Now that I have matured to a ripe old twenty-two, the word *happiness* means much more than ever before. . . .

## Writing a Conclusion

The conclusion to a paper of illustration, as with any essay, should provide a satisfying close. Ending on a positive note, especially after the recounting of a painful experience, is gratifying to the reader.

In a paper about a series of failures she faced, Phyllis Parks ends on an optimistic note, providing some specific examples of current successes:

Despite the failures I have experienced, all phases of my life have not been grim. My daughter from my first marriage has grown into a beautiful, healthy young lady. Fifteen months ago my new husband and I were married. I am also enrolled in college classes. Now I truly feel successful.

Sometimes writers tend to repeat their introductions in slightly different words or to summarize their body paragraphs. Try to find a more satisfying conclusion. Consider explaining a particular insight, noting an advantage, offering a suggestion, or expressing an opinion that is supported by your examples. Leave readers feeling they have learned something from the examples.

## Revising a Paper of Illustration

After your first draft has cooled a bit, go back and read through the examples carefully. Try to distance yourself from each one so that you can evaluate it impartially. As you make revisions, consider the principles you have learned so far. The following checklist will help you revise.

---

### CHECKLIST: REVISING A PAPER OF ILLUSTRATION

1. What is the main point of the paper? Is the point clear?
2. Is each example relevant, accurate, and valid?
3. Does each example add substance to my claim?
4. Do the examples create interest?
5. Are there enough examples?
6. Are examples arranged in a clear, logical order? Or could the order be improved?

TWO STUDENT PAPERS: ILLUSTRATION

In the first paper, Anita Ketcham describes her hobby in an unusual way, blending explanation with example. Her purpose was to entertain as well as inform.

### Bathtub Solitude

An avid tennis player can be found lobbing away on the court; a woodworker may enjoy crafting furniture in a workshop; a gardener may relax by tending flowerbeds. I, too, have an enjoyable hobby—one that is not only relaxing and challenging but also educational. Like tennis, woodworking, and gardening, my hobby is done in the best possible place. That is why I do crossword puzzles in the bathtub.

As a mother of four young children, I rarely find time to sit down. Any time I do take for myself is soon interrupted. Mom sitting down is like a red flag waving, signaling a parade of little feet. This is why the bathtub is the perfect place to relax while working puzzles. There I cannot answer the telephone or pour a glass of milk or dress a Barbie doll. Those tasks have to wait. For a half hour, I escape to my own private retreat. Although it's not like Hawaii or the Bahamas, yet I am totally alone with my book and my bubbles, and it seems like heaven. The toughest problem I have to face is a six-letter word for supplication.

Working crossword puzzles is challenging. My favorites are the large "challenger" puzzles because the clues are difficult, requiring considerable thought. Still, I enjoy matching wits with the puzzlemaker. Some words can have several meanings and the clues can be ambiguous. A good puzzle solver learns to look at clues from different angles. For example, a five-letter word for the clue "drop a line" could be *write* or *angle*, but the answer the puzzlemaker wanted was *erase*. "Iron clothes" could be a clue for *press*; however, *armor* was the answer. A very difficult clue can be frustrating, especially for a puzzle printed in a newspaper because answers are not available until the next day. Although I rarely complete a difficult puzzle, I always try to improve my skills in order to do better with the next one.

Working crossword puzzles is educational. By using a dictionary often, I have expanded my vocabulary. Words such as *hirsute* and *litigious* have been added to my lexicon—as well as the word *lexicon*. And where else but in crossword puzzles could one find such a plethora of insignificant information? I know that Guido's note is an *ela*, but I do not know who Guido is. I know that the answer to "Roman bronze" is *aes* and that Caesar's road is an *iter*, should anyone ask. Not all of the knowledge I have gleaned from crossword puzzles is this trivial; some I have even found useful. Knowing that Siam is the former name of Thailand and that Istanbul was once Constantinople has helped me to defeat my husband during heated games of *Jeopardy*. He thinks he is married to a genius! I will never tell him my secret.

For my soon-to-be birthday, my husband will probably give me a bottle of bubble bath, the latest copy of *Dell Championship Crosswords*, and an hour to myself. Then I can enjoy some peace and quiet, sharpen my wits, and discover words new to me. All knocks on the door will be ignored. I will come out only when my toes are too wrinkled to stay longer.

*Questions for Discussion*

1. Look at Anita's opening. What expectation does she set up with the first three brief examples?

2. What comparisons do you see in paragraph two?

3. What is the purpose of the examples in paragraphs three and four?

4. Look at Anita's ending. How do the examples function there?

Next, Dixie O'Rourke offers a series of extended personal examples to show how she learned to control her emotions.

### Envy

One evening without warning, envy crept into my young heart. The year was 1967. The place was a backyard ice rink at the home of my best friend, Sylvia. Although the time was only 5:00 p.m., dusk had already settled. Sylvia had just gone inside to eat dinner with her family in their comfortable brick home in a pleasant neighborhood.

Outside I continued to cut figure eights and spin on the ice while Sylvia ate dinner. As I paused to catch my breath, I found myself staring through the dining room window. Inside, the brightly lit room appeared warm and friendly as the family gathered around the table. Sylvia's father stood at the head, reading from the family Bible.

As I continued to window peek, I felt an overwhelming surge of envy and ill will. Suddenly, I was resentful not only of Sylvia's many possessions, but also of her intact family. I longed to live like Sylvia. This flood of painful feelings changed not only how I felt toward her, but also how I felt toward myself. The contentment of my childhood had shattered: I was ashamed of my house, my family, and myself.

Only ten years old, I was unable to deal with these new feelings of inferiority and kept them locked tightly within. I feared losing my best friend; I was afraid that if I told Sylvia how I felt, she might not like me anymore. I also feared telling my grandparents (with whom I resided); they might feel hurt and angry. So I told no one.

By junior high school, the feelings of shame and resentment had begun to diminish. Although I still felt pangs of envy when my friends flaunted their possessions, I had learned to control the envy so that it did not overwhelm me. The technique was simple—nothing new. I would count my blessings and thank God for each and every one of them. My grandparents had set a good example for me.

When I was thirteen, a sobering experience brought my perspective into a more realistic focus. During the school lunch hour, a group of students, whom I envied, gathered in front of the malt shop across from the school. This particular day the group welcomed and invited me to go with them to a carnival at a shopping center across town. The plan was to meet after school the next day and walk to the carnival. Knowing my grandfather's second job took him near the area, I offered the group a ride.

When school let out that afternoon, I ran home to plead for a ride and money for the carnival. Smiling, my grandmother lifted the lid of an old blue sugar bowl and gave me several silver coins. The next day grandpa drove his old Chevrolet, freckled with rust, to the school; and five of us piled in. When we reached a large parking lot, my friends hurried off toward the carnival without a word or backward glance to either of us.

Grandpa locked the car doors, bid me goodbye, and started toward the factory. As I watched him fade into the crowd, my eyes watered. Not one person had thanked him for the ride or waited for me. The envy I felt for that group fled. Suddenly, I felt proud of my grandfather even though he wore bib overalls and carried a lunch bucket. I felt fortunate to have both my grandparents.

Although I still feel a twinge of envy now and then, I no longer have the strong feelings of my youth. As my values have changed, I have focused my energies in a positive direction; presently, I'm working full time and attending classes for a nursing degree. Over the years, I have learned to subdue envy and to make the most of what I have.

## Questions for Discussion

1. What do you notice about Dixie's opening?

2. How does she set the scene for the reader?

3. What do you notice about Dixie's vantage point? (See the second paragraph: "outside," "inside.")

4. What incident causes a sharp shift in Dixie's perspective?

5. Examine her conclusion. What do you notice?

---

### FOR YOUR REFERENCE:
### ILLUSTRATION ESSAYS IN THE READER

- "Hooked on Plastic," Anish Majumdar, page 440
- "Lawbreakers, Armed with Paint and Paste," Kirk Sempler, page 443

---

### SUMMARY

- An illustration paper uses examples to explain, convince, or persuade, according to the rhetorical situation.
- The topic for an illustration paper may be concrete or abstract; both need concrete examples for support. The best examples are relevant, accurate, and adequate.
- Examples can be organized in various ways: chronological order, concrete-to-abstract order, and comparison are among them. Examples integrated with explanation are effective.

## Practice

### Ideas for Writing

1. A pet food company is seeking winsome cats and dogs to be featured in television commercials. Write a letter explaining why your pet should be featured. Include examples of behaviour and training.

2. You are a first-year college student, away from home for the first time. In the first few weeks of the semester, you've had to find a place to live, register for your courses, buy books, and pay for incidental fees. Freewrite on why college students are so short of money.

3. Describe a seemingly small incident such as a chance meeting or a sudden impulse that influenced your life.

4. Describe your first ride on a roller coaster.

5. Write an article for your campus newspaper using humorous examples to spoof a campus condition or a consumer product.

## Ten Ideas for Papers of Illustration

1. Optimism pays
2. How my view of work has changed
3. How my parents' divorce affected me
4. Learning from hardship
5. Aggressive drivers
6. Easy ways to save money
7. Adversity can be an asset
8. How possessions complicate our lives
9. A wonderful friend
10. Common sense is in short supply

# CHAPTER 14

# Classification

## Grouping and Dividing

---

**Learning Objectives:**

After reading and applying the information in Chapter 14, you'll be able to:

- Draft, develop, and revise a classification essay

---

*Out of clutter, find simplicity.*
—Albert Einstein

## PURPOSE OF CLASSIFICATION

Classification allows us to establish order in our lives and to function effectively. For example, our linear measurement follows the metric system. The division of distance into kilometres, metres, centimetres, and millimetres allows us to be specific. According to the Gregorian calendar, our year is divided into twelve months, each month into weeks, and each week into days. Each day is divided into hours, each hour into minutes, and each minute into seconds. That is just the beginning.

Everything on this planet can be classified in some way. The estimated five million species of life are divided into five formal classifications or kingdoms: animals, plants, fungi, bacteria, and moulds. But we also classify in other ways. Vehicles are classified as sports cars, sedans, trucks, vans, SUVs, and the like. Then they are divided into subcategories. Credit card companies and manufacturers classify consumers in order to market their wares well. You classify when you sort and store, whether documents or laundry.

## WHAT IS THE BASIS OF CLASSIFICATION?

Classification is a method of grouping and dividing items and ideas logically. To classify, you look for common features that certain elements or items have—a

157

> ### GUIDELINES: CLASSIFICATION
>
> 1. ***Classify items according to the purpose and audience.*** Have a reason.
> 2. ***Avoid overlapping parts or categories.*** Be clear-cut.
> 3. ***Make each part or category large enough to contain a significant number.*** Have a minimum of three items or details in each category.
> 4. ***Make all parts parallel.*** All items in a category should be similar, having a common principle of selection. Then they will be parallel.
> 5. ***Organize all parts or categories to fit into one logical system.*** All the parts should fit together into one organized whole.
> 6. ***Arrange in a logical order.*** See "Seven Basic Orders," page 34.

*principle of selection* that sets them off as a group. All members of the group must have this similarity. For example, lions, tigers, and house cats have enough similarity to be classified as felines (the principle of selection). Then felines can be subdivided into subcategories such as wild cats and domestic cats. Domestic cats can be subdivided further according to breed such as Manx, Persian, or Angora.

## WRITING A PAPER OF CLASSIFICATION

A paper of classification not only groups and divides but also analyzes, describes, and explains. The purpose and the topic determine the order.

### Shaping a Topic to the Purpose and Audience

Many famous writers advise selecting a subject you know and care about. Then you can shape it to your purpose and the needs of the audience. Chances are that you already have a lode of details to be mined and classified. If you are a family history buff, you might describe your dominant impression of a quirky relative by grouping traits into well-defined categories. Or perhaps you live near a scenic area with little-known features that might attract tourists. If you were to write a brochure, what features would you describe and how would you classify them?

Observing at a restaurant buffet, Patricia Rush classified the members of "Annoying Eaters of America" as "inspectors, conversationalists, and gulpers." Her purpose was to amuse, and her audience was her classmates. Here is how she described the third group:

Gulpers are the Indianapolis drivers of the table. To prepare for the race, they pile their platters high, thus cutting down on stops for refueling. They are determined to finish the meal first, even at the cost of indigestion. Stuffing their mouths and chomping, they shovel in the food and wash it down with great gulps of water. When every scrap is gone, they sometimes take a morsel of bread and swab their platters clean. Often their belches can be heard throughout the restaurant. Gulpers are usually males in ragged T-shirts and dingy jeans. For them, these garments may have more than one use; gulpers sometimes finish by wiping their hands across their chests or thighs.

## Prewriting with the "Because" Technique

With a topic in mind, you can use any of the prewriting techniques you learned in Chapter 3. Still another way of prewriting can be helpful: the "because" technique. This technique works well for topics that can be divided into advantages, benefits, or reasons. Just ask a question about the topic, then answer "because. . . ." Jot down your answer and ask "What else?" Repeat the sequence until you have enough material. After that, group the details logically into main points.

Let's assume you have a fourteen-year-old daughter, Kim, who has been invited to go riding with Brad, the sixteen-year-old next door. But you are convinced Brad is a reckless and irresponsible driver. Simply stating your belief and forbidding Kim to go may not carry much weight with her. You need evidence to support the claim and reinforce your decision. Prior to your talk, you use the "because" technique to help classify relevant facts into main points:

| *Questions* | *Answers* |
|---|---|
| 1. Why does Brad seem irresponsible? | *Because* I have seen him speed by children on bikes, run stop signs and red lights. He brakes sharply, squealing his tires. |
| 2. Are there any other reasons? | *Because* he has put several dents in his car although he's had it only three months. He backed into his mother's car last week. |
| 3. What else? | *Because* he has been cited for speeding twice. |

Your prewriting could continue until everything you know about Brad's driving has been listed. Then you could analyze the details and divide them into three categories such as: *speeding, carelessness,* and *ignoring traffic rules.*

## Organizing a Classification Paper

Perhaps the most common order for a paper of classification is some order of degree: simple to complex, least to most important, easy to difficult, and so forth. To make a case against Brad as a driver you might organize points from the least to most dangerous aspects of his driving.

**Brad is a reckless and irresponsible driver:**

1. *Because he is careless.*
   Last week he backed into his mother's car.
   His car has several dents in it after only three months.
   He does not slow down for children on bicycles.

2. *Because he speeds.*
   He has had two speeding tickets.
   He drove 80 kph on a street posted at 50 kph.
   He turns corners too fast, squealing his tires.

3. *Because he often ignores other traffic rules.*
   He turns quickly without signalling to other drivers.
   He drove through a stop sign last week.
   He sometimes drives through red lights.

## Drafting a Thesis Statement

The next step is to draft a tentative thesis. As you may recall, a thesis statement not only tells the reader the topic but also often suggests a logical order and clearly states an attitude toward the topic. In a paper of classification, the thesis statement frequently sets up an order of degree, from least important to most important. Mark Newell uses this order to arrange his three main points in his thesis:

> A good location, plenty of patience, and the right ammunition are three advantages I use to achieve successful squirrel hunting.

Not all thesis statement specify points or categories; some simply make a brief claim. For example, the parent might say, "You can't go out with Brad for three reasons."

## Developing Main Points and Embedding Transition

As you draft, develop your main points with specific details, reasons, and explanations. Each paragraph should support the claim made in the thesis. And each paragraph should have a clear link to the thesis, either through signpost or embedded transition. Subtle transition is the mark of a proficient writer.

In the next example, Mark Brady begins by stating an opinion in the first sentence. In the second sentence he gives a fact. In the third sentence, the thesis, he supports opinion with three reasons (italicized):

> Upland bird hunting in Ohio is in a sad condition. Populations of three game birds—the ring-necked pheasant, the blue grouse, and the bobwhite quail—have dwindled. Three main factors for this decline are *the kind of hunters, increased pollution,* and *clearing of woods and underbrush for farming.*

Note how Mark returns to each of the main points of his thesis in the opening sentences of his body paragraphs:

Along with the good *hunters* in the fields are a number of ignorant *hunters* who shoot every bird they can, despite the fact that they are exceeding the daily bag limit. . . .

The second reason for the dwindling bird population is the *increased pollution* in our environment. . . .

The *farmer* is probably the biggest reason for the declining bird populations. . . .

Again, in his conclusion, Mark reinforces each of his initial main points:

Frankly, most of those concerned seem to contribute to poor hunting conditions. The *nonsportsman hunter* takes home more birds than allowed. The *manufacturers who make pesticides and weed sprays* sometimes fail to adequately check the long-term effects of products upon birds and their eggs. Many *farmers* clear their land and plow in the fall, not leaving cover or grain for the game birds. Surely we must work to solve this problem before it is too late.

Mark does an excellent job of connecting his thesis to the main points of his paper, using all four kinds of embedded transition: repetition of key terms, synonyms, pronoun and antecedent, and natural relationships.

---

### FOUR KINDS OF EMBEDDED TRANSITIONS

1. **Repetition of key terms:** hunters, increased pollution
2. **Synonyms:** ignorant hunters, nonsportsman hunters
3. **Pronoun and antecedent:** hunters/they
4. **Natural relationships:** pollution/manufacturers/pesticides/sprays, nonsportsman/bag limit, farming/farmers

---

STUDENT ESSAY WITH THE MAIN POINTS IN THE THESIS

In the following essay, Michele Flahive states three main points in the thesis. She uses embedded transition to establish clear links from the thesis to body paragraphs. These links mark the path of the main idea and provide unity. Note how she repeats a key term (italicized) in the first sentence of each body paragraph:

#### Diamonds: A Girl's Summer Friend

As the batter walks up to the dusty plate on the diamond, she scans the outfield. Spying a vacancy between left and left center, she knows this is the best area to hit the ball. While the pitcher gets ready to make her move, the batter stands in position. In a slow pitch, the ball sails off into a perfect arc, dropping right where the batter wants it. With her heart pounding, she swings the aluminum bat and cracks the ball. Quickly, she runs three bases, listening to the cheers of teammates and hoping to reach home plate before the ball. For her the *challenge*, the *enjoyment*, and the *camaraderie* make softball a game worth playing.

The first game of the season seems always to pose a special *challenge*. The players often feel a bit rusty and nervous. Just walking onto the field and up to bat that first time takes strength of will. But once the umpire yells, "Play ball," the nervousness melts away and determination flows in. Enthusiasm for the game takes over.

*Enjoyment* of softball is the heart of the game. After a long day of work or school, it is a pleasure to leave the stress behind and walk out onto the diamond. Since both teammates and crowd are just out for an evening of recreation, there is no great pressure to win. The fun and action provide a refreshing reward at the end of a day.

The challenge and enjoyment would be incomplete without the *camaraderie* of teammates who share the same passion for a rousing game of softball. And when a member is feeling down for missing a ball or for striking out, words of encouragement flow from other members. Then too, there is a sense of unity as everyone plays together in the infield and outfield, backing each other up as needed.

As August slowly winds to an end, so must the summer softball season. It can be a sad time for many die-hard ball players who must leave the diamond and put away their gloves. Yet some players take heart, for not only does autumn bring bright foliage and cool evenings, but it also heralds the fall softball season!

Did you notice how Michele sets the scene and pulls the reader right into the action at the very beginning? With just a few concrete details, she creates an image of the dusty plate, batter with pounding heart, aluminum bat, sound of the bat hitting the ball, perfect arc, and cheers. This vivid description helps the reader to relive what she feels and sees as she walks up to the batter's box.

## Making Main Points Parallel

See Chapter 8.
When main points are parallel, the resulting balance strengthens transition, sentence structure, and unity. In the example below, note how Joanne M. Pohlman begins each main point with the same type of structure, a gerund phrase (italicized). Each main point in the body explains the matching point in her thesis:

**Thesis:** As a volunteer member of the National Ski Patrol, I earn the opportunity to meet many interesting people, learn challenging skills, and spend time with my family.

**Parallel points:**
1. *Joining the Central Division of the Patrol* has acquainted me with approximately eighty other patrollers. . . .
2. *Becoming a member of this national organization* takes more than being a proficient skier. My training. . . .
3. *Being able to ski with my family* is the main reason I chose to become a patroller.

## Writing a Conclusion

A conclusion should flow logically and smoothly from the main idea. As a result, the reader should gain a sense of completeness or closure. To provide a satisfying ending, writers often allude to the thesis, as Joanne Pohlman does. At the end of the paper about skiing, she repeats the name of the organization and expresses appreciation:

Finally, I feel fortunate to belong to the National Ski Patrol. Although I receive no wages, I do gain new friends, invaluable skills, and a closeness with my family that is priceless.

## Revising the Paper

A paper of classification is more complex than those discussed in earlier chapters. The checklist below should help you revise your paper successfully:

---

### CHECKLIST: REVISING CLASSIFICATION PAPERS

1. Has the topic been narrowed to one item?
2. Is the introduction focused and interesting?
3. Do the main points follow the order set up in the thesis statement?
4. Are the main points linked with the thesis?
5. Are the main points parallel?
6. Are the main points well supported with specific details and examples?
7. Does the internal order of each paragraph flow well?
8. Can clarity be improved? Is more transition needed?

---

STUDENT PAPER: CLASSIFICATION

In this paper, Nicole Vanderkooi's purpose is to inform, and her classmates are her audience. She describes three types of people a tourist might encounter on the streets of New Orleans.

### The Melting Pot of New Orleans

The sweet voice of jazz and spicy smell of Cajun cuisine capture Nicole's senses as she walks through the French Quarter of New Orleans. People from every walk of life seem to wander these cobblestone streets. On the corner of Bourbon Street sits a vagrant, playing his harmonica. In a horse-drawn carriage, a tourist reclines, listening to the clip-clop of hooves and the driver's southern drawl. In an art gallery, a sightseer from New York purchases yet another work for his loft. Carrying a briefcase, a local businessman strides past the shops, bent on another destination.

Draped with tattered overcoats and wearing tennis shoes, the homeless of this elusive city often wear weathered grins amid week-old whiskers. Their daily hours are spent collecting tips for providing the pleasure of hearing their sultry saxophones. The night brings them home to humid, stagnant alleys and alcoves. These bumbling creatures usually walk alone, attended only by their instrument and ever-faithful bottle, enclosed in a brown paper bag.

Tourists and sightseers dot the avenues of New Orleans. At daybreak they begin to roam the high-priced novelty shops and spacious old plantations surrounding the area. Often dressed in walking shorts, they sport "I survived New Orleans nightlife" T-shirts and sun visors or sunglasses. Frequently, a woman is escorted by an overburdened man and a trusty guidebook. By night, infamous nocturnal pleasures entice many to partake in Cajun feasting and boisterous drinking.

Yet another colorful feature of this Louisiana melting pot is the local business-man. Attired in a single-breasted black suit, an ivory silk shirt, and a brilliant tie, this worldly person projects professionalism and sophistication. Finding him in an art gallery or trendy coffee shop, drinking a black brew from small cups is not unusual. At night he often dines at a specialty restaurant and listens to the rhythms of jazz. His companion may be a colleague or a breathtaking, well-dressed woman.

New Orleans graciously accepts the prize for the most captivating city. There musical vagrants, inquisitive visitors, and local residents catch the eye and capture the heart.

### Questions for Discussion

1. What are Nicole's three categories? How does her way of introducing them differ from Joanne Pohlman's introduction (ski patrol)?
2. What kind of order does she use within each paragraph?
3. Where has Nicole used embedded transition to link body paragraphs to her thesis?
4. What kinds of specific details does Nicole use to describe each of her categories? Are the details comparable in each case? Why do you think so?
5. How does Nicole establish closure in her ending?
6. What else do you notice?

---

### FOR YOUR REFERENCE: CLASSIFICATION ESSAYS IN THE READER

- "It's Only a Paper World," Kathleen Fury, page 447
- "Mind over Munchies," Norman Brown, page 450

---

### SUMMARY

- Classification is the grouping and subdividing of various ideas into categories that form one system.
- To be effective, the topic should be shaped according to the purpose and audience. The "because technique" is a method of prewriting and scratch outlining.
- In a classification paper, main points and categories are often organized according to importance.
- An excellent means of connection between points is embedded transition. To support the thesis, body paragraphs should be fleshed out with facts, concrete details, and reasons.
- A reference to the thesis can establish closure at the end of a paper.

## Practice

**Collaborative Learning: Classification**

*Directions:* Select the word in each group that is not in the same category as the other three words. Then compare your selections with other group members. Discuss disagreement. You may use dictionaries.

1. tanning lotion
   shaving cream
   toothpaste
   cleansing cream

2. hickory
   walnut
   elm
   oak

3. pearl
   ruby
   diamond
   emerald

4. lace
   snowflake
   frost
   water

5. crocus
   daffodil
   zinnia
   tulip

6. wolf
   coyote
   prairie dog
   dog

7. squirrel
   rat
   woodchuck
   fox

8. lion
   hyena
   leopard
   tiger

9. daisy
   rose
   chrysanthemum
   violet

## Ten Ideas for Classification Papers

When you develop your topic, you should have a definite audience in mind. In the suggestions that follow, some possible audiences are mentioned.

1. Classify the groups you belong to and explain why each is meaningful to you. *Audience:* Your parents who want you to study more.
2. Classify small cars (or some other vehicles) and evaluate them. *Audience:* Assume you are writing for readers of *Consumer Reports.*
3. Classify families. What constitutes a family?
4. Annoying drivers
5. Students in your classes
6. Hazards in buying a used car (or anything else)
7. Classify degrees of racism. What forms can it take?
8. Commercials that irritate
9. Classification and evaluation of sports news shows
10. Friends

# Comparison and Contrast

## Explaining Likeness and Difference

**Learning Objectives:**

After reading and applying the information in Chapter 15, you'll be able to:

- Use appropriate transitions for a comparison/contrast essay
- Identify pitfalls common to the comparison/contrast essay
- Draft, develop, and revise a comparison/contrast essay

> *Happiness is like a sunbeam,*
> *which the least shadow intercepts.*
>
> —Chinese Proverb

A striking comparison can capture the essence of an idea in a single sentence. Comparing an abstract idea with a concrete image, as in the proverb above, explains the resemblance in a delightful way. We smile or sigh and think "How true." *Comparison* includes both likeness and difference, with an emphasis on likeness. A *contrast* shows or emphasizes differences.

In our personal and business lives, we use comparison and contrast to make informed choices between alternatives, weighing advantages against disadvantages, pros against cons, possibilities against difficulties. Careful choices are essential to success in business.

## PURPOSE OF COMPARISON OR CONTRAST

Every paper of comparison or contrast needs a specific purpose according to the rhetorical situation. The fact that an instructor assigns the paper is not adequate. To determine the specific purpose, you might ask yourself, "Why might the audience like to read about this topic?"

## Determining a Purpose

When a topic is unfamiliar to readers, your purpose in comparing or contrasting may be to inform them of significant distinctions between two subjects. When the topic is familiar, your purpose might still be informative; but to hold readers' attention, you should present new insights or a fresh perspective. To move beyond trite generalities, ask yourself, "How much do readers already know?"

The purpose of comparison or contrast might be to persuade. Then the strategy would be shaped to influence readers toward a certain viewpoint. For example, an employee might write a proposal comparing a present procedure to a proposed new procedure. The purpose would be to convince readers that the new procedure would save time and money. A third purpose of comparison or contrast might be to entertain by presenting the features of two subjects in an amusing way.

Comparison or contrast may have a dual purpose: to entertain and inform or to entertain and persuade or to inform and persuade. Drafting a purpose statement after you select a workable topic can help to clarify the purpose.

## Selecting a Suitable Topic

Usually, differences are more interesting than similarities, but not always. Regardless, *the subjects to be contrasted or compared should be of the same species, class, or category.* Otherwise there would be no value in comparing them. For example, there would be no practical reason to compare hockey to stock car racing, the two are not in the same class of sports. Because the topics are so greatly different, you would be unable to find opposing points to match for a logical purpose. But if you wanted to compare different kinds of race car designs or perhaps compare hockey to soccer, you could find logical points of comparison or contrast.

- **Purpose:** To inform and to entertain the reader by comparing the behaviour of the male and female praying mantis
- **Purpose:** To inform the reader of the advantages and disadvantages of Tax-Cut as opposed to Quicken
- **Purpose:** To inform and convince the reader that the way medical personnel are portrayed on television is often unrealistic

## TRANSITION IN COMPARISON OR CONTRAST PAPERS

As you move from detail to detail while comparing or contrasting, you will need special transitions to indicate shifts in meaning. Here are some transitions that point out likeness or difference:

| *Similarity* | | *Dissimilarity* | |
|---|---|---|---|
| also | too | but | yet |
| and | both | in contrast | on the other hand |
| again | similarly | however | on the contrary |
| likewise | in addition | still | although |
| besides | then too | conversely | nevertheless |

Now and then you may need a *transitional sentence* to bridge a gap in thought. For example, after discussing one horse, you might supply a sentence of transition to introduce another horse: "Whereas Big Ben looked as if he had been groomed for the Queen's Plate, Skip had the careless air of a beachcomber." Two other tips you may want to consider: (1) Place *also* or *however* within a sentence rather than at the beginning, where they may sound tacked on or out of place. (2) Substitute *too* or *then too* to avoid overuse of *also*.

## PITFALLS TO AVOID IN COMPARISON OR CONTRAST PAPERS

When selecting a topic for a comparison or contrast paper, beware of three common pitfalls: overused topics, trite expressions, and hasty generalizations. Predictable topics such as "winter versus summer" or "a bungalow versus a two-story" can cause instructors to wince. The old axiom "Don't tell readers what they already know" still applies. When you select your topic, make it fresh by putting a new spin on an ordinary idea. For example, you might contrast a husband and a wife's views of buying an antique sofa for their home.

Trite expressions often infiltrate papers of comparison or contrast. Experienced writers avoid threadbare expressions and devise original comparisons, using concrete nouns, vivid adjectives, and active verbs to make the description come alive. Few readers enjoy frayed phrases like these:

| different as day and night | a different story altogether |
|---|---|
| like two peas in a pod | are worlds apart |
| spitting image of his father | looked like twins |

Hasty generalizations—exaggerated, unsupported claims—are another frequent pitfall in comparing or contrasting. Unintentionally, writers may repeat misstatements they have heard or think are probably true yet lack evidence to substantiate. Broad, general topics in particular can lead to unsupported generalizations. For example, a student who selected the topic "city life versus country life" generalized from stereotypes. The result was a series of overstatements, such as this one: City dwellers take little time to enjoy life and nature.

To sidestep hasty generalizations, first narrow your topic. Then check each claim carefully: Do you have adequate evidence to back up your statements? To be safe, avoid pronouncements about what a majority does or does not do. Writing about your own experience decreases the likelihood of blundering into unsupported generalizations.

## ANALOGY: A SPECIAL KIND OF COMPARISON

Although the subjects of a comparison or contrast are usually of the same species, class, or category, a writer may choose to make an imaginative comparison, finding unusual likenesses in things that are of completely different categories. In "The Attic of the Brain," biologist and essayist Lewis Thomas compares the unconscious human mind with the attic of a house. In "Snapping the Leash," journalist Murray Kempton compares the darker forces of human nature to "a raging tiger" that each individual "spends [his or her] life building a cage to pen . . . in."

Such imaginative, nonliteral comparisons have much in common with the poetic devices of simile and metaphor. (See "Create a Simile or Metaphor" in Chapter 5.) When extended over the course of a paragraph or an essay, comparisons such as these become *analogies*. To be effective, an analogy should be consistent, apt, and fresh. It should also help readers see the subject in a new light. Note how the analogy of "cowboying" is used to illuminate the work of the writer:

> Both jobs—writing and cowboying—take up the whole mind and heart. . . .
> A good hand on a ranch requires vigilance, acute powers of observation, readiness
> to anticipate what might go wrong or what's coming next, a taste for recklessness,
> intuitive skills, patience, and what cowboys look for when they buy a horse: a lot
> of heart. Aspiring to those qualities as a rancher, I can only hope my writing will
> benefit as well.
>
> —**Gretel Ehrlich, "Life at Close Range"**

Analogies are often used to help explain something abstract in terms of something concrete. In this way they can play an important role in scientific and technical writing, as writers try to help readers understand ideas and concepts that are complex or difficult to grasp. Note how the next analogy illustrates the scale of geologic time:

> [G]eologists will sometimes use the calendar year as a unit to represent the time
> scale, and in such terms the Precambrian era runs from New Year's Day until well
> after Halloween. Dinosaurs appear in the middle of December and are gone the day
> after Christmas. The last ice sheet melts on December 31st at one minute before
> midnight, and the Roman Empire lasts five seconds.
>
> —**John McPhee, *Basin and Range***

In academic and professional writing, make sure that any analogies you devise have a clear explanatory purpose. Readers may not see the point of an analogy that is used primarily for decoration or entertainment.

# WRITING A PAPER OF COMPARISON OR CONTRAST

Writing a paper of comparison or contrast is similar to writing a double paper of classification. You examine relationships between elements, distinguish the similarities and differences, then organize them in a logical order that reflects your purpose.

## Gathering Information and Prewriting

If you were to compare two cars, the purpose might be to determine which one would better suit your needs and to inform an interested reader. To gather information, you might visit showrooms, talk to sales representatives, and drive the two cars. You could quote and identify the source in general terms such as "One salesperson said that. . . ." If, however, you were to read *Consumer Reports* or another publication, you would need to supply specific documentation, as explained in Chapters 24 and 25.

To save time, prewrite details in parallel lists. Simply head two columns with the selected topics, then skip a space and start listing. Each time you write in a detail for one item, add a corresponding detail for the other. Placing the details side by side will make the lists parallel.

|  | Chevrolet Lumina | Ford Taurus |
|---|---|---|
| Features: | ———— | ———— |
|  | ———— | ———— |
|  | ———— | ———— |
| Price: | ———— | ———— |
| Fuel Consumption: | ———— | ———— |
| Warranty: | ———— | ———— |
| Styling: | ———— | ———— |
| Handling: | ———— | ———— |
| Comfort: | ———— | ———— |
| Maintenance: | ———— | ———— |

Next, classify details into categories. These categories can act as main points in your paper. For example, the price, expected cost of maintenance, and cost of operation could be grouped under the category of economy.

After prewriting and grouping details, focus your paper with a thesis statement. Check to see that it (1) identifies a specific topic, (2) indicates similarity and/or difference, and (3) sets up an order of main points. Although not all thesis statements are this explicit, many instructors prefer such a clear focus, as in the following examples:

- **Thesis:** Although the Chevrolet Lumina and the Ford Taurus are similar in several respects, they vary in comfort, performance, and cost.

- **Thesis:** Whether I am in the mood for an exhilarating challenge or a leisurely ride through the woods, I have horses for each mood. (Kathy Burton)

- **Thesis:** Despite obvious differences, the two series *Earth's Children* and *The Hitchhiker's Guide to the Galaxy* have much in common. (Melissa Baker)

## Organizing a Paper of Comparison or Contrast

The *block* and *alternating* methods are two basic ways to organize parallel points of comparison or contrast. For an easily understood topic, the block method is simple and suitable. This order lists all the pertinent points about the first subject in one block of parallel details, then lists the points about the second subject in corresponding order. This balanced arrangement ensures that the details are easy to follow.

### Block Outline of Contrast

I. *Thesis statement:* Mr. Courtney and Mr. Graham, my former neighbours, contrasted greatly in appearance, demeanour, and friendliness.

II. Mr. Courtney (first subject)
- A. Appearance
  1. Meticulous. Clothes perfectly pressed.
  2. Clean-shaven. Hair neatly groomed.
  3. Short, trim, and muscular.
- B. Demeanour
  1. Solemn. Never seemed to smile. Eyes glared.
  2. Never out except to care for lawn. Swore and hurried.
  3. Children afraid of him. He scowled when greeted.
- C. Friendliness
  1. Unfriendly.
  2. Protected his privacy.

III. Mr. Graham (second subject)
- A. Appearance
  1. Clothes never hung quite right.
  2. Hint of a beard. Hair untidy.
  3. Tall and rather heavy.
- B. Demeanour
  1. Always smiling. Kind eyes.
  2. Often outside. Hummed, sang, worked in rose garden.
  3. Charmed children. Pitched ball, played hide-and-seek.
- C. Friendliness
  1. Regarded as grandparent by children.
  2. Concerned, a real neighbour.

IV. Conclusion

For a complex comparison, the alternating method is an effective way to organize. You explain comparable points paired in parallel order. In other words, you alternate the subjects. Because of frequent shifts from subject to subject, the alternating method requires more transition than the block method.

**Outline of Contrast (Alternating Subjects)**

I. Introduction

II. Appearance (first main point)
   A. Mr. Courtney
   B. Mr. Graham

III. Demeanor (second main point)
   A. Mr. Courtney
   B. Mr. Graham

IV. Friendliness (third main point)
   A. Mr. Courtney
   B. Mr. Graham

V. Conclusion

When only similarities are discussed, the pattern can be similar to one of the preceding examples of contrast. When you include both similarities and dissimilarities, the structure of the comparison becomes more complicated. Usually, similarities are discussed first, unless there is a reason for reversal.

## Drafting an Introduction

Introductions of comparison or contrast papers can set the scene for the two subjects by revealing what, where, how, and when. Chuck Chesnut gives these details as he wryly contrasts two neighbourhood animals. (His thesis is italicized.)

### The Pet and the Pest

In my neighborhood there are several animals, but none quite like "the pet" or "the pest." When I walk out my back door and see or hear the pet, as I call him, I smile. He is a friendly old basset hound that lives in the next yard behind our house. But when I walk out my front door and see or hear the pest, my hackles rise. She is the high-strung miniature poodle that resides across the street. Some days I mutter, "The dog from Hell!" or something unprintable. *These dogs vary greatly not only to the eye and the ear but also to my sense of values.*

A narrative opening is an easy and effective way to set the stage for a comparison or contrast. Terri Bloomfield uses narration by presenting a few graphic details to describe a sudden change in her life:

### My Life after Dealing with Death

As I pushed my Fiero up to sixty-five miles an hour, the possibility of being killed in an automobile accident was miles of thoughts away. Being young, I felt invincible—why should I worry about an unpleasant subject like death? In a few days, however, I had to confront that topic in an instant. On August 18, 1993, my best friend and my cousin were killed in an automobile accident. The realization of how quickly life can be snatched away changed my life, starting the moment I met death face-to-face.

## Developing a Comparison or Contrast Paper

The order in which you develop your parallel points in a comparison or contrast depends upon the purpose and the audience. One technique, level of familiarity—starting with the familiar and going to the unfamiliar—is quite effective, allowing less explanation than the reverse requires. You use analogies, anecdotes, or examples to flesh out ideas. A topic that involves physical description will need numerous concrete details to support the main points. In the next example from "My Two Neighbors," Betty Fetter's precise descriptions enable the reader to visualize two individuals:

> Mr. Courtney was a meticulous person who seemed to reflect this quality in every aspect of his life. His clothes were always perfectly pressed, his face clean-shaven, and his hair neatly groomed. His short frame was trim and muscular despite his age. He seemed always to wear a solemn expression; I never once saw him smile. His glaring eyes echoed his disgust with people and his contempt for life.
>
> Seldom did I see Mr. Courtney outdoors except to care for his lawn. Despite the swearing and hurrying to get the job done, his yard was the best tended in the neighborhood. Local children never went near his house because they knew that the slightest transgression would be met with angry retribution. Mr. Courtney was a private person, and everyone treated him and his property with the respect he so vehemently demanded.
>
> Many times a greeting to Mr. Courtney would be answered with an angry scowl. Mr. Courtney was indeed an island unto himself. Every encounter with him would remind me of another, much more gentle, man—a very dear friend who had taught me the value of friendship and the real definition of the word *neighbor.*

Note that after the first block of details, Betty smoothly introduces the second block with "would remind me of another, much more gentle, man . . . ," leading into a description of Mr. Graham:

> If judged by first appearance, Mr. Graham would not have made a very good impression. His clothes, although neatly pressed, never hung quite right on his tall, rotund body. He seemed always to have a shadow of a beard, and his hair usually looked as if he had started to comb it but had been interrupted. He was, however, always smiling; and his love for people and life was reflected in his eyes.
>
> Many times I would hear Mr. Graham singing or humming while he worked in his garden or trimmed his rosebushes. He always worked with the same patience and deliberation, nurturing and caring for each plant. With this same calm concern, he charmed the children of the neighborhood. It was common to see him pitching a ball, playing hide-and-seek, or sitting on his porch with a group of children at his feet. The children regarded him as a grandparent and treated him with great respect, as did everyone in the neighborhood. He was a real neighbor to all, friend or stranger.

## Writing a Conclusion

When the purpose of a comparison is to inform, a brief summary may be in order. In her conclusion, Betty not only summarizes but also shares insights gained from experience:

> Although Mr. Graham died a year ago, his memory will live in the hearts of the people who were lucky enough to have known him. For me, he made it easier to accept the Mr. Courtneys of the world. Mr. Graham knew the secret of happiness, and the values that he taught will remain a part of my life forever.

For a serious topic, a change of perspective can provide just the right note for ending. Terri Bloomfield concluded with this thought:

> After witnessing the death of my cousin and best friend, I cherish life much more. I know firsthand that life is precious and fragile. Now I never take today or tomorrow for granted. I feel as if I must appreciate life not only for myself, but for my cousin and my friend, too.

## Revising a Paper of Comparison or Contrast

If you keep your outline handy as you revise, this will help you to maintain the balanced order that comparison and contrast require. The checklist that follows should also be helpful.

---

**CHECKLIST: REVISING A PAPER OF COMPARISON OR CONTRAST**

1. Is the thesis clear and specific?
2. Is the order of points in the thesis the same as their order in the body?
3. Are main points and paragraph details arranged in parallel form?
4. Does every paragraph have a topic sentence?
5. Does every topic sentence have adequate support?
6. Does the conclusion seem complete?
7. Have I fulfilled the purpose of the comparison or contrast?
8. Does anything else need to be said for this audience?

---

STUDENT PAPER: COMPARISON

The following paper, by Jeff Patten, contrasts two books by the same author. Jeff's purpose is to inform. His audience consists of readers who enjoy historical fiction.

### *I, Claudius* and *Claudius the God*

In 1934 Robert Graves published a rather lengthy book of historical fiction entitled *I, Claudius.* The novel was written in such a manner as to have the reader believe it was an autobiography of the Roman Emperor Tiberius Claudius Drusus Nero Germanicus. *I, Claudius* takes the reader from the Emperor's earliest childhood remembrances up to the year 41 AD, when he became Emperor of the Roman Empire. It is there, minutes after Claudius's ascent to the throne, that the book ends.

This abrupt ending seemed to demand a sequel, and in 1935 Graves published *Claudius the God.* This second "autobiographical novel" chronicled the life of Claudius from his ascent to the throne to his murder. Although each of the novels was written about the same person, by the same author, there are few similarities. *I, Claudius* and *Claudius the God* seem similar only in the basic form in which they are written. They differ in readability, style, and entertainment value.

The two books resemble each other only in narrative autobiographical form. The reader experiences the life of ancient Rome, narrated through the thoughts and words of the Emperor Claudius. Graves has an almost mystical way of making the reader feel as if the Emperor Claudius had penned the words himself. The novels provide accounts of the seedy, scandalous lives of the ruling Caesars. Greek and Latin phrases reveal careful research. The historical accuracy makes the novels seem authentic.

There the resemblance ends. *I, Claudius* is an easily read, thoroughly engrossing book. Readers receive the impression of a smooth, flowing manuscript. They are led chronologically, with a few pauses for reflection, through the turmoil and pageantry of the Roman Empire and its rulers. *Claudius the God,* however, is a rather choppy, disjointed work. Readers are required to leap from one story line to another with little or no hint of a chronological advance. One can only speculate as to the reason. Yet one thing is certain. The readability and style of *I, Claudius* are far superior to its sequel.

Style is a significant difference between the two novels. Although both manuscripts were thoroughly researched, the historical data are presented in two very different ways. In *I, Claudius* the facts are colorful; the pompous and elegant lives of the ruling class make for fascinating reading. In contrast, the facts presented in *Claudius the God* seem dry and mundane; furthermore, the story line makes for dull reading.

The net result of these differences makes the books unequal in entertainment value. *I, Claudius,* whatever its historical worth, is a very good story. Even readers who ordinarily do not enjoy histories or autobiographies will likely enjoy this novel because it is so entertaining. The sequel, however, is a chore to read—much like reading a history textbook.

If it were not for the many weaknesses of *Claudius the God,* the set would make worthwhile reading. Robert Graves's prowess as a poet and distinguished writer shines brightly in his first novel, but fails miserably in the second.

*Questions for Discussion*

1. Why do you think Jeff spent two paragraphs on the introduction?
2. How are the two novels alike? How are they different?
3. What method of organization does Jeff use?
4. How would you characterize the tone of Jeff's essay?
5. Comment on the conclusion.

> **FOR YOUR REFERENCE:**
> **COMPARISON AND CONTRAST ESSAYS IN THE READER**
>
> - "A Nonsmoker and a Smoker," Phillip Lopate, page 455
> - "Mother Tongue," Amy Tan, page 462
> - "Gender Gap in Cyberspace," Deborah Tannen, page 459

> **SUMMARY**
>
> - Your paper of comparison or contrast should have a specific purpose. Writing a purpose statement will help you narrow the topic and focus your details.
> - Transitions that indicate similarities and differences are especially important to help readers stay on track.
> - Three common pitfalls to avoid are:
>   1) stating the obvious;
>   2) trite expressions; and
>   3) hasty generalizations.
> - Using an analogy can help readers understand a difficult concept. Prewriting details in parallel lists will save you time; after that you can classify details into main points and write a thesis.
> - The block method and alternating method are two basic organizational strategies. The block method is suitable for easily retained material; the alternating method is better for complex material.

## Practice

### Ideas for Writing

*Directions:* Select a topic from the list below (or one of your own) to contrast in a paragraph. Prewrite by making parallel lists of details.

1. Two service providers you have had
2. Two dogs (or cats) you have owned
3. Two methods of fishing
4. Two cars you have owned
5. Two brands of pizza

## *Ten Ideas for Comparison or Contrast Papers*

1. Your life and your grandmother's or grandfather's life
2. Life before attending college and after
3. A date that you enjoyed and one that you did not
4. Two athletes in the same sport
5. Two hockey teams
6. Adolescents on TV vs. in real life
7. Living in Canada compared to living in . . .
8. Two very different bosses
9. Changes in attitude, thinking, or behaviour
10. "Reality" TV vs. scripted TV dramas

# CHAPTER 16

# *Definition*

## Identifying Basic Characteristics

After reading and applying the information in Chapter 16, you'll be able to:

- Compose a formal sentence definition
- Draft, develop, and revise a paper of extended definition

> *The beginning of wisdom is the definition of terms.*
> —Socrates (470–399 BC)

## PURPOSE OF DEFINITION

Clarity is crucial to communication. Undefined terms can lead to confusion, error, and problems. Definition at the right time can dissolve misunderstanding, improve communication, and promote safety. On the job you may write simple definitions or help write complex definitions in policies or reports—defining the background, objectives, success criteria, and scope of a project.

Learning to write clear definitions will sharpen your thinking and enable you to be more precise and accurate in your word choice. In college specific, complete definitions can improve your grades. On exams an instructor may ask such questions as "Can you define *irony*?" "What is 'tool steel'?" or "What is the essence of the accounting principle of materiality?" Yet the answers beginning writers commonly supply to such questions are vague descriptions, not clear definitions.

## FORMAL SENTENCE DEFINITION

Providing a formal sentence definition on the spur of the moment is not easy. For example, a writing instructor had just explained formal sentence definition to his freshman composition class. He turned to a student who seemed half asleep and said, "Nick, will you please define *mammal* for me?"

Suddenly awake, the student stammered, "Er . . . a mammal is hairy; uh . . . it has a hard skeleton and provides milk."

With a twinkle in his eye, the instructor replied, "So far, you have not ruled out the coconut."

A formal sentence definition is a complete sentence that classifies something and then differentiates it from other members of its class. A formal sentence definition, which is more complete than a fragmentary dictionary definition, has four parts:

1. The term to be defined
2. A *be* verb—usually *is* or *are*
3. The classification (genus, class, or species)
4. The distinguishing features or characteristics

Below are two illustrations of the parts of a formal sentence definition:

| Term | Verb | Classification | Distinguishing Features |
|------|------|----------------|-------------------------|
| A pelican | is | a large, web-footed water bird | with a distensible pouch hanging from its bill for catching and storing fish. |
| A lynx | is | a species of wildcat in the Northern Hemisphere | which has a very short tail; tufted, tapering ears; and a ruff on each side of the face. |

Note the distinguishing feature of each animal. There are many water birds with webbed feet, but only the pelican has a distensible pouch hanging beneath its bill. There are several species of wildcat in the Northern Hemisphere, but only the lynx has the slender, tufted ears, unusual ruff, and very short tail.

## WRITING A FORMAL SENTENCE DEFINITION

Start with a familiar object such as an apple. Consider: Which classification does an apple belong to? How do apples differ from other members of the class, such as plums, pears, and peaches? What are the distinguishing features of apples? Write a complete sentence that includes all four parts of the formal definition:

| Term | Verb | Classification | Distinguishing Features |
|------|------|----------------|-------------------------|
| An apple | is | a/an _____ | _____ |

An apple is a fruit, of course, but you might be more precise by stating that it is an edible fruit. You might be more specific by giving its taxonomic category, the rose family. At first you may jot down features such as red and round. (Are all apples red? Round?) After you finish, see the example at the end of the chapter.

To write a formal sentence definition about any concrete term, you might find these questions helpful:

1. What distinguishing features do all items in the class have?

2. How can similar items be ruled out?

3. What purpose or function does the item serve?

Two precautions will help you to sidestep common errors when writing formal sentence definitions:

1. *Do not define a term by repeating the term or using a derivation:*

   **Avoid:**  A keystone is the key stone in an arch.

   **Instead:**  A keystone is the central wedge-shaped piece at the top of an arch that holds the other stones in place.

2. *Avoid the phrase "is when" or "is where."* This usage is ungrammatical.

   **Avoid:**  A greenbelt *is where* a band of parks, farmland, or unused land surrounds a community.

   **Instead:**  A greenbelt is a band of parks, farmland, or unused land surrounding a community.

## EXTENDED DEFINITION

The purpose of a paper of extended definition is to explain a term or concept clearly in an *original* way, drawing material primarily from your own experience. Research is generally limited to dictionaries, thesauruses, and books of quotations.

### Consulting Sources

To gather ideas, consult two or three large dictionaries to discover what they say about your topic. Be sure to consult the unabridged *Oxford English Dictionary*, a set of several volumes, which traces the history of words introduced into the English language since AD 1150. There you may find an unusual detail to serve as an attention-getter for your introduction or an example for later use in your paper. Or you might trace the history of a word whose meaning has changed during your lifetime, your parents', or your grandparents'. Or you might trace a relatively new word.

Famous quotations can be found in the library or online. *Bartlett's Familiar Quotations, The Quotable Woman*, a Bible with a concordance, and similar references are quick and easy to use. Or you might interview people of various ages to gain insights about relatively recent connotations of a word.

### Documenting Sources

See Chapters 24 and 25. If you decide to copy any material, be sure to set it off properly in your notes so that there is no confusion later. Legally, you are required to provide the following documentation:

1. Enclose short quotations with quotation marks.

2. Indent long quotations of five lines or more.

3. Specify the name of the author, the source, and the page. (Check with your instructor for the preferred format.)

## Guidelines for Using Extended Definition

Readers tend to like a quotation that is appropriate but to dislike a patchwork of quotations. They become impatient with old information unless it is a favourite story that merits retelling or a universal truth skilfully presented. Here are three guidelines for a paper of extended definition:

- **Use quotations for a purpose.** Use them to clarify and advance your discussion. Limit the number of quotations.

- **Use dictionary definitions for a logical reason.** Have a purpose, such as to clarify or to disagree.

- **Include stereotypes or overstatement only for a purpose.** Perhaps you intend to disagree with a stereotype or to overstate to provoke amusement. If so, be sure the exaggeration is so great that readers will understand its purpose.

You can freshen an old topic by presenting it from your own point of view:

**Stale:** Growing old is a fear of many people. Many people believe they are old when they turn fifty.

**Fresh:** One chilly October morning, my fiftieth birthday tiptoed in. Glancing in the bathroom mirror, I suddenly felt old.

Careless use of stereotypes not only bores the audience, but also injures a writer's credibility. Perceptive readers dismiss sweeping generalizations; they want the truth, not distortions. In the student examples below, can you spot the faulty stereotypes and other problems in logic?

- The elderly lead lonely, secluded lives, crisscrossed with financial worries.

- A mother's desired end is handling her three jobs well: housewife, mother, and career.

Both of these sentences exaggerate. Not all elderly people fit this pigeonhole. Not all mothers desire a career. Writers need to qualify generalizations—to identify opinions, perceptions, and inferences. Careless overstatement includes all-or-none claims that lack support, as in the following bloopers:

- "Friends are forever." (Question: Do all friends last a lifetime?)

- "Success is defined in as many different ways as there are people on earth." (Question: Does no one agree with anyone else?)

## WRITING A PAPER OF EXTENDED DEFINITION

To learn as much as possible from writing a definition paper, select an abstract term for the topic. What do you feel strongly about? How does this topic relate to you? How does it affect your principles and values? How much support can you provide for your thesis? You would be wise to sidestep Herculean topics such as "time," "democracy," and others that are very broad. If you choose a term you have learned in another class, do not merely summarize other people's ideas—develop your own.

### Narrowing a Topic and Prewriting

First, narrow the topic so that it can be covered adequately in the assignment. For instance, "discrimination" would be too broad. One student limited this topic to "prejudice against short men." He gave examples of how he copes with shortness through elevator shoes, hairstyles, and dress. Then he explained how these changes have improved his life and gained him respect.

See
Chapter 3.
Next, consult your dictionary notes and think about them. Then prewrite to unearth examples, anecdotes, comparisons, cause-and-effect factors, or changes in meaning. Clustering is particularly helpful for prewriting about an abstract concept.

The two sample scratch outlines below are arranged according to order of importance:

*Example I:* **Professionalism at a Golf Club**

a. Ethics = respect

b. Customer service

c. Accuracy of records

d. Dress of personnel

*Example II:* **My Procrastination**

a. Examples: Cause

b. Effects

c. How I am overcoming

### Drafting a Special Kind of Introduction

Opening with a quotation is one of the easiest ways for a beginning writer to achieve a polished introduction. A relevant quotation can set the tone and indicate the focus of the paper. The quotations that open the chapters of this book show how to format and document a quotation that precedes your main text. *Documentation:* Notice that because the quotations are indented and set apart from the text, quotation marks are not needed. The author's name appears beneath the quotation. Inclusion of the source is optional. Include dates of works written *before* the twentieth century.

***Establishing Transition***    To forge a link from an introductory quotation to the text of your paper, embed transition in your first sentence. Repeating a key term from the quotation or using a synonym or related word will establish a clear link. Try to be subtle. A direct reference, unless cleverly done, can mar the opening and stamp the work as that of an amateur. With thought, you can avoid weak transitions, such as "In this quotation . . . ," "As stated in the quotation above, . . . ," or "I think the above quotation means. . . ."

In the following example, the student writer (who prefers to remain anonymous) uses an embedded transition in her first sentence. A related word (*alcoholism*) echoes a word in the quotation (*drunkenness*). Note, too, that the first sentence here is a formal sentence definition.

### Living with an Alcoholic

*Drunkenness . . . spoils health,*
*dismounts the mind, and unmans men.*

#### —William Penn

Alcoholism is a disease caused by continual heavy drinking of alcoholic beverages. In the acute and chronic stages, alcoholism consists of symptoms ranging from the obvious to the obscure. Usually, it is not difficult to recognize a person who is inebriated; generally, staggering and slurring of speech are apparent. Accompanying neurological disorders such as tremors (shakes), hallucinations, and seizures are easily discerned. Hidden to the naked eye is the damage endured by the liver, stomach, and pancreas. Not only is excessive drinking devastating to the physical and mental health of the alcoholic, but it is also devastating to the alcoholic's family.

Living for eighteen years with my father, who was a severe alcoholic, was much like living with Dr. Jekyll and Mr. Hyde. The alcohol would turn my kindhearted, loving father into a brutal, hateful monster. Because of my father's unpredictable behavior, high anxiety and fear were normal, everyday emotions for me.

Did you notice that the first paragraph is written in *third* person? The writer gives general background information before narrowing the topic to the alcoholic's family. In the second paragraph, she shifts to *first* person because it reveals specific details about her life. See how she eases the shift from third person to first with a gerund phrase ("Living . . . with my father").

Did you note the simile in the second paragraph? The phrase "like living with Dr. Jekyll and Mr. Hyde" not only sets up a striking comparison but also establishes a natural relationship with "unmans men" in the opening quotation.

## Developing an Extended Definition

The heart of any good piece of writing is vivid imagery. Concrete details and action verbs make writing come alive. Depending on the subject and purpose, a paper of extended definition may be developed by almost any strategy or combination of strategies—description, comparison, narration, examples, or explanation, for instance. There are five basic techniques for developing an extended definition.

***Operational Definition***   To define an operation, the writer tells (a) what the object being defined does, (b) how it works, and (c) the basic principle underlying its performance. For example, a one-sentence operational definition might state that a refrigerator is a mechanized box, powered by electricity or gas, that circulates coolant to a condenser to chill food, medicines, or other items. An expanded operational definition would explain in detail how a refrigerator works. Operational definitions are often used in technical writing.

***Defining by Comparison***   Comparison is useful for explaining abstractions, such as emotions. If you can find an object to compare an idea or emotion to, then this technique will help to clarify your definition. In the following example, Marjorie Holmes begins with concrete images before going to abstract feelings:

> What feeling is so nice as a child's hand in yours? [It is] so small, so soft and warm like a kitten huddling in the shelter of your clasp. A child's hand in yours—what tenderness it arouses, what power it conjures up. You are instantly the very touchstone of wisdom and strength.

***Defining by Synonym***   In defining by synonym, a writer provides another word or phrase that has the same meaning. The synonym can be included either in parentheses or as an appositive:

- My son Daniel will play peewee (ages 11–12) hockey next year.
- At one time many people believed that human intelligence could be judged by phrenology, the study of the shape of the skull.

***Defining by Negation***   Another effective technique of definition is *negation* (denial). The writer begins by telling what the term is not. In a paper entitled "Fear of Failure," Phyllis Parks uses negation in her opening sentence:

> *Failure* is not a pretty word. The very mention of it creates images and feelings of someone who is inept and incompetent. The word itself strikes fear in my heart. Sometimes my life has seemed as though it has been one failure after another. But with time has come an appreciation for the value of failure.

In *Faith of My Fathers*, Senator John McCain begins his definition of *glory* by explaining what glory is not. Then he describes what glory means to him:

> Glory is not a conceit. It is not a decoration for valor. It is not a prize for being the most clever, the strongest, or the boldest. Glory belongs to the act of being constant to something greater than yourself, to a cause, to your principles, to the people on whom you rely, and who rely on you in return.

***Weaving Example with Explanation***   A lone example without interpretation may be of little use to readers. You cannot assume that every reader will see the connection you intend. You need to link the example to the main idea and comment appropriately. Chris Layman, a student writer, first uses negation. Then he weaves example with explanation in an extended definition of honesty:

"Do as I say, not as I do," my parents would often say as I was growing up. However, admonitions such as this often fade from the mind whereas examples form lasting impressions. As children grow they need models to follow. They need to determine how they will live their lives, what their values will be, and how they will treat other people. A father is a model that his children depend on to learn how to act within their society and to form their own set of values.

Recently, my young son and I were in a store when he noticed a $100 bill lying on the floor. I had always told my son to be honest; now I could show him what honesty meant. Together we went to the store manager and put the money in his care, hoping the rightful owner would return to claim it. This incident allowed me to act as a role model for my son, and it set an example I hope he will follow throughout his life.

## Including a Dictionary Definition

*If* a dictionary definition is *necessary* in your paper, you can easily identify the copied material by using quotation marks and by stating the source. The three examples that follow will not be suitable for every writing situation, but you can adapt them to fit your paper if appropriate.

- Although *Webster's College Dictionary* defines _____ as the "_____," this definition does not. . . .

- According to *Webster's New World Dictionary*, _____ is "_____," but that definition does not. . . .

- Meanings can change over time. The first edition of *The American Heritage Dictionary* defines _____ as "_____." The fourth edition, however, has added another meaning: "_____." We might go beyond these to say. . . .

To integrate other types of quotations into the text of your paper, see "Using Signal Phrases to Integrate Quotations into the Text," page 345.

## Writing a Conclusion

A conclusion for a paper of definition should be brief and appropriate. One way to end is with a formal sentence definition. Another is to allude to an opening quotation. A third way is to summarize changes and end on a positive note.

***Closing with a Formal Sentence Definition***   Debby Ketcham concludes her paper with a formal sentence definition. The definition is followed by a sentence of summary and another of comment:

> Finally, poise is an inner mental balance, the ability to face new situations calmly, to hold one's temper, to cope with stress, and to deal with embarrassment. All these situations require a control over emotion and the ability to present a calm, tactful, polite manner. Poise is truly a valuable trait.

***Alluding to an Opening Quotation***   A reference to the beginning creates an "echo ending" and establishes closure. Using this technique, Penny Amrine repeats parts of a quotation by Joseph Conrad in her conclusion. In the last sentence she provides a formal sentence definition:

> My loneliness did indeed wear a "mask." For months I had endured its "naked terror" without being able to identify its misleading appearance. Loneliness for me was life without intimate friends and relatives to lean on for love and companionship.

***Ending with a Personal Lesson***    Those of us who successfully survive a painful experience often extract a lesson, a bit of wisdom. The student who wrote "Living with an Alcoholic" summarized her insights:

> Over the years I have tried to educate myself on alcoholism. Counseling has helped me to understand how alcoholism victimizes the entire family. Now, at age 33, I realize that despite how it seemed at the time, my father was only a human being who was consumed by a dread disease.

The last line reveals the writer's compassion as well as her intellectual and emotional growth since those early years of torment. The implicit note of forgiveness and the gentle tone provide a positive ending to a wrenching topic.

## Revising a Paper of Extended Definitions

To revise a paper of extended definitions successfully, you need to examine its many facets. The checklist below will enable you to scrutinize individual aspects.

### CHECKLIST: REVISING EXTENDED DEFINITIONS

1. Is the topic narrow enough to be defined in a short paper?
2. Will the introduction interest the audience?
3. Have important terms been defined if they are apt to be unfamiliar to the average reader? Have terms with more than one possible meaning been explained fully?
4. Are all definitions necessary?
5. Do formal sentence definitions (if any) conform to the standard four-part format?
6. Does every detail, definition, and quotation support the thesis?
7. Are quotations worked smoothly into the text so that their point is clear in the paper? Has proper credit been given to each original source?
8. Have stereotypes and overstatement been avoided?
9. Is the organization of the paper clear?
10. Is the closing effective?

TWO STUDENT PAPERS: DEFINITION

Jeannine Caudill talked to her friends before she wrote the following paper, which is based on their experience as well as hers. Her purpose is to explain a term not found in the dictionary. Skilfully, she states several axioms (universal truths). Three questions begin her introduction.

**Mother Love**

*Love cannot be forced, love cannot be*
*coaxed and teased. It comes out of*
*Heaven, unasked and unsought.*

—Pearl Buck

What is mother love? Is it a feeling, an emotion, or the dedication of an entire lifetime? Is it bad or good, imaginary or genuine? One thing is certain; mother love is difficult to define, especially to those who have not experienced it. None of the dictionaries seem to think *mother* and *love* should be combined into the phrase *mother love*. Yet there is motherhood, mother lode, and mother-land. Could any of these words be more fitting to combine with *mother* than the word *love*?

Psychiatrists define mother love, doctors prescribe it, lawyers divide it, children bask or drown in it, and fathers observe it. Perhaps even a mother cannot define it, but some still try. Love as only a mother can feel begins for some women with the first knowledge of pregnancy. For others, it comes with beholding the charm of their own soft, sweet-smelling baby. The baby does not have to be beautiful to inspire great love. Perhaps mother love at this stage of life is a myriad of feelings: infant dependency, mother's pride of accomplishment, and primitive emotions that have been basic to the human race since its beginning. Whatever the reasons, loving a baby seems very easy.

The real growth of mother love begins later. Much of the time during a child's life, no one seems to love him or her except the mother. True mother love develops over many years and through many trials. When a toddler throws a fit in a store, shouts a loud "No," or dampens a neighbor's carpet, mother love is put to a test. But even in this stage, the child is very appealing to her. Here a new facet of love begins, pride in the child's independence.

The early school years strain the most patient mother. After the thumb-sucking, leg-hugging, insecure years come the years of grade cards, teacher conferences, show and tell, and four hundred papers to be praised and hung up.

Many older mothers say to younger mothers, "If you think things are bad now, just wait till he's a teenager!" But the young mothers often counter with "Nothing could be worse." This lack of foresight must be a tool of Mother Nature. Otherwise, only the very brave would dare to have a child.

Mother love seems never to end. It usually begins with the birth of a child and continues to encircle and entwine the mother's heart down through the years. Strangely enough, the only person who can appreciate the real meaning of mother love is a mother.

### Questions for Discussion

1. What do you notice about Jeannine's introduction?

2. Examine the first sentence of the second paragraph. What do you notice about the sentence structure?

3. Do Jeannine's examples ring true? Why or why not?

4. What does she do before she comments?

5. How would you describe the tone of the essay?

In the following paper, Ron Willetts cites a dictionary definition and parts of speech for *work* for a significant reason: He expands upon its meanings as a noun and as a verb. In the first main point, he uses narration and explanation to illustrate his early view of work. He defines later views by explanation, association, and examples.

### Changes in My View of Work

*My friend there is a Hell . . . when a man has a family to support, has his health, and is ready to work, and there is no work to do. When he stands with empty hands and sees his children going hungry, his wife without the things to do with. I hope you never have to try it.*

**—Louis L'Amour**

The *Oxford American Dictionary* defines work as a noun that means "Use of bodily or mental power in order to do or make something, especially as contrasted with play or recreation." Work is also defined as a verb: "to perform work, to be engaged in bodily or mental activity." Over the years I gradually learned to understand these concepts, but only when I became unemployed for an extended period did I understand L'Amour's definition.

When I was very young, work was not a verb, it was a noun, a place to go and a place to leave. My grandfather would come home from work in the evenings, and we would go through a ritual. As he drove his truck into the garage, I would be waiting. He would pick me up, and somewhere between the truck and the house, I would remove the hat from his head and transfer it to mine. Once inside, he would place his dinner bucket on a chair, and I would rummage through it for the leftover cookie, banana, or candy bar that was always there. At that time in my life, I did not have to worry; all my needs were taken care of.

When I became a young adult, the word *work* took on a new meaning. It was not only a noun, but suddenly a verb, a task to be performed for which one received some form of remuneration. This definition began to form when I was in the eleventh grade and began helping the janitors after school during basketball season. For sweeping the classrooms and dusting the teachers' desks, I received a modest sum and attended the home games at no cost. Thus work became associated with money. And money became closely associated with girls, cars, entertainment, and other necessities. At this time, work was a necessary evil, for it took time away from my social life.

When I became older, I found the word *work* had to be redefined once again. Along with being a place to go and an activity to perform, work became a goal. This new meaning became associated with other words such as wife, insurance, children, house, and friends. Between 1975 and 2000, work was no problem for me. If I changed jobs, the longest period of unemployment was two days. Once I quit one job on Friday and started a new one the following Monday.

In 2000, however, the story changed. Due to economic conditions, I became unemployed after working at a company for fifteen years. That company and my coworkers were as much a part of my life as my own family. I felt rejected and depressed. The severance pay ran out. The unemployment benefits were exhausted. The retirement fund vanished, and the bills began to pile up. I was no longer able to provide for my family. But then I thanked God we were living in modern times when it was acceptable for a married woman to work. Although my wife's income did not pay all the bills, it did allow us to feed the family and keep the electricity turned on.

Being unemployed for over two years creates a situation that at times is almost unbearable. Perhaps the worst part is being told that one cannot be hired because he is overqualified and undereducated. Being told that one could perform the task, but would not be satisfied with the job is enough to make a person ill. A man needs to be able to provide for his family.

Yes, my friend, there is a hell—I know, for I have been there. It is my sincere hope that I am the last person that has to define the lack of work as hell.

## Questions for Discussion

1. Discuss the use of the dictionary definition in the introduction. Would the paper have been as effective without it? Why or why not?
2. Briefly summarize the changes in Ron's viewpoint.
3. What causes are specified?
4. Discuss the effectiveness of this ending. What device does he use?

---

### FOR YOUR REFERENCE: DEFINITION ESSAYS IN THE READER

- "On Being 17," David Raymond, page 468
- "The Sweet Smell of Success Isn't All That Sweet," Laurence Shames, page 472

---

### SUMMARY

- The general purpose of any definition is to explain and clarify.
- Formal sentence definitions are one sentence with four parts: the term, a *be* verb, the classification, and features that distinguish the subject from other members of its class. Extended definitions are explanations that may include description, comparison, anecdotes, reasons, examples, or formal definitions.
- Keeping a specific audience in mind will help you avoid common problems: unnecessary definition, repeating common information unnecessarily, and using stereotypes or overstatement without a logical reason.

## Practice

### Collaborative Exercise: Discerning Genuine Definitions

*Directions:* Identify the satisfactory definitions in the list below and mark with an S. Mark the unsatisfactory with a U. Discuss why they are unsatisfactory. (You may consult a dictionary.)

1. A sprinkling can is a utensil that is not a bucket, dishpan, or bowl.
2. A cut is when you slash open the skin.
3. A book is like a little golden door to opportunity.
4. The gemsbok of southern Africa is a large antelope with long, sharp, straight horns and a tufted tail.
5. Honey is a sweet gooey substance that is delicious on breakfast cereal.
6. "Monopoly" is a table game that resembles life because you trade, buy, and sell.
7. *Morale* refers to the condition of the spirit of individuals or employees.
8. The ruffed grouse, sometimes called "partridge" or "pheasant," is a North American game bird with spotted brown feathers.
9. Gelatin is a clear quivery substance, made in various colours.
10. A dandelion is a small edible weed with fuzzy yellow flowers and saw-toothed leaves.
11. Dissatisfied means not content.
12. A suitcase has a handle and is used to carry clothing.
13. A vacation is where you tire yourself out having fun so that you are glad to go home and go to work.
14. Empathy is as refreshing as pure cold water from a spring.
15. A fruitcake is a cake that contains fruit.

### Collaborative Writing: Formal Sentence Definition

1. Appoint a recorder to jot down the comments of the group. Define one of the terms below in a formal sentence definition.

   dog    cow    cucumber    chair    couch

2. Ask each other questions to limit the term and identify the essential features. For example:
   a. How does a dog differ from a wolf or coyote?
   b. What kind of dog? Prairie dog? Wild dog? What?
   c. What is the purpose of the dog?

   (*Note:* You may want to limit the term to watchdog, police dog, Seeing Eye dog, hunting dog, or other kind of dog.)

3. Revise. Does the definition have all four parts? Does it read smoothly?
4. Repeat the procedure, using another term.

**Ideas for Formal Sentence Definition**

*Directions:* Write a formal sentence definition or a paragraph that includes a formal sentence definition. Select a concrete word from the list below or use one of your own.

oranges     ballpoint pen     drum     turnips     plums

## Possible Answer for Writing a Sentence Definition (page 179)

*An apple is an edible fruit of the rose family that can be red, yellow, green, or multi-coloured; when mature, the small seeds are encased in a core connected to a flexible stem at the top and the blossom end.*

## Ten Ideas for Papers of Definition

1. What is the "positive attitude" that employers seek?
2. Ethics for the nurse (or other professional)
3. Freedom (What kind or kinds?)
4. What does a college diploma or degree really mean?
5. Self-discipline
6. Procrastination
7. Attitude: Victim or winner?
8. A family value
9. Loyalty
10. What is an education?

# Cause and Effect

## Explaining Why

---

**Learning Objectives:**

After reading and applying the information in Chapter 17, you'll be able to:

- Conduct causal analysis
- Identify the logical principles of cause and effect
- Identify fallacies in analyzing cause and effect
- Draft, develop, and revise a cause-and-effect essay

---

*Our least deed, like the young of the land crab,*
*wends its way to the sea of cause and effect as soon*
*as born, and makes a drop there to eternity.*

—Henry David Thoreau
*Journal*, March 14, 1838

Thoreau's observation reminds us that a single decision, action, or event can cause far-reaching effects. The relationship between cause and effect can be more intricate and extensive than we may imagine. Sometimes we lack complete information and see only part of an effect. Or we may assume a connection between two events where none exists. Or we glimpse only *short-term effects* while significant *long-term effects* remain hidden for years.

All the while there is the ever-present risk of blithely underestimating the repercussions of certain acts and of making unwise decisions based on unproved assumptions and ill-founded predictions.

## PURPOSE OF CAUSAL ANALYSIS

The purpose of causal analysis is to determine whether or not a cause-and-effect relationship actually exists. If it does exist, precisely what is the connection between the cause and the effect? What happened to bring about the change?

Causal analysis allows you to reflect on an experience or event and to learn from the past. With study and practice, you can improve your ability to analyze cause-and-effect relationships. You can question doubtful information and withhold judgment until adequate proof of the final cause is available.

On the job you may analyze cause-and-effect relationships, then give input into decisions that will influence the profit or loss of your company. According to the rhetorical situation, you may write a recommendation, proposal, or report, based on your causal analysis. The greater your knowledge and insight, the more accurate the analysis will be.

---

### WORKPLACE CASE STUDY

#### THE ACCIDENT

Lisa was walking within the pedestrian lane of the large plant warehouse where she worked. The warehouse seemed even more noisy than usual. She was unaware that behind her a tow-truck driver violated company rules when he failed to sound his horn before coming around a corner. The next moment she heard the roar of a motor and glanced back. The vehicle hit her. A searing pain darted down her right leg. She crumpled and fell to the floor.

Lisa was rushed to the hospital, where a leg fracture and several deep cuts were treated. She was kept overnight. The emergency room physician said she would be unable to work for eight weeks. A witness to the accident corroborated Lisa's report, saying she was in the safety lane. The driver did not sound his horn before coming around the corner very fast. Losing temporary control of the vehicle, he swerved into the safety lane and knocked her to one side.

#### ACTIVITY:

Assume the role of the supervisor. Write a summary of the accident in your own words and recommend action. The tow-truck driver was newly hired; he has worked only three days. The plant provides no training for tow-truck drivers.

---

## WHAT IS CAUSAL ANALYSIS?

A *cause* influences or changes something or someone. The resulting change is called the *effect*. *Causal analysis* is an examination of effects that have one or more causes (conditions that may have contributed to the effect). To resolve a question of cause and effect, explore all the conditions that might have caused the effect. Since you already know the effect (by observation), start by noting its significant features. Then work backward through the chain of cause and effect. Describe the

> ## STEPS IN CAUSAL ANALYSIS
>
> 1. Specify the effects. Separate from the presumed cause.
> 2. Examine the conditions that existed.
> 3. Ask whether or not these conditions could have caused the effect(s).
> 4. Think about possible explanations: What might have happened?
> 5. Test your theories. Did the presumed causes actually produce the effect?

related condition(s). Then list possible explanations. Next, test each explanation and eliminate as many as possible. That should lead you to the cause(s). If not, keep searching.

For example, the supervisor of a department that spray-paints washing machines notices that the finish is uneven. He wonders what condition could have caused this effect. Has an atmospheric change occurred? Is there a mechanical defect? Has human error interfered? Was the batch of paint too thin? Could multiple causes exist? Only after he has ruled out all other possibilities will he be able to pinpoint the cause(s).

## A Reversed Chain of Cause and Effect

To trace a simple cause, start with the observed effect(s) and work *backward* through the chain until you find proof of the cause. In the example below, the gas hot water furnace requires electricity to operate the pump and thermostat.

*Note:* Since the pilot light cannot be lit, you assume that the gas has been shut off. Checking through old bills reveals three are unpaid. But until you check with the gas company, you do not have actual proof of the cause.

## Logical Principles of Cause-and-Effect Relationships

As you explore possible cause-and-effect connections, examine the logic of your conclusion or inference. Is it reasonable, sensible, and sound? Or has an error occurred? To be valid, a claim of causal relationship must be based on two essential standards.

- The cause is able to produce the effect.
- Other causes that might have produced the effect have been ruled out.

## Two Fallacies to Avoid in Analyzing Cause and Effect

A systems analyst says that the most frequent mistake in logic that his team makes is to assume that because one event follows another, the first caused the second—even though there is no proof. This assumption is the *post hoc* fallacy; chronology is mistaken for causation. Events in a sequence do not always have a connection.

Another fallacy of cause and effect is the *non sequitur* (meaning *a conclusion that does not logically follow from the premises*). Non sequiturs often occur in predictions. For example, it was widely believed that since a woman had never been elected Prime Minister of Canada (the premise), that a woman would never be elected Prime Minister (the erroneous conclusion). Yet Kim Campbell disproved this conclusion when she became the first female Prime Minister of Canada in 1993.

If we keep in mind that much of what we "know" is actually inference, theory, value judgment, or myth, we are more likely to pause and seek evidence before leaping to conclusions about why something happened.

## WRITING A PAPER ANALYZING CAUSE AND EFFECT

A paper of causal analysis allows for a wide range of topics to be organized and developed in various ways. Every time you inquire about *how* or *why* something happened, you begin causal analysis. To prewrite, you might sketch a reverse chain of cause and effect as shown in the earlier diagram. Keep in mind the following principle: *Complex events, conditions, or situations seldom stem from a single cause.* Therefore don't halt your search too soon. You may find more than one cause.

### Planning a Cause-and-Effect Paper

After you have sketched a cause-and-effect chain, consider how to organize details. The big question is this: "*What does the audience need to know?*" Your answer will help you decide what to include and where to start. Then set up a scratch outline in a way that seems logical. To begin, consider the following questions:

- Was there a single cause and single effect? Or were several factors involved?
- Will the major emphasis be on the specific phenomenon (cause)? Or will it be on the consequence (effect)?
- What kind of order will work best?

Chronological order is often simplest and most efficient. This way you discuss the cause before the effect. Sometimes *reverse chronological order* is used, with effect before cause. If you have multiple causes and/or multiple effects, you may need to organize your main points by order of importance. Several possible strategies are presented here. If one seems to fit your topic, adapt it as needed.

### Outline A: Single Cause with Multiple Effects (chronological order)

*Claim:* High consumption of soft drinks containing sugar and caffeine contributes to overweight, other health problems, and mild addiction.

   I. Introduction (specifies the cause): high consumption of soft drinks containing sugar and caffeine

  II. Body (order of importance)
     A. Describes/explains effect no. 1: overweight
     B. Describes/explains effect no. 2: other health problems
     C. Describes/explains effect no. 3: mild addiction

 III. Conclusion

### Outline B: Single Effect Produced by Multiple Causes (reverse chronological)

*Claim:* Many farmers are diversifying crops to increase profits.

   I. Introduction (specifies the effect): Many farmers in the South are decreasing the acreage allotted to tobacco in favour of vegetable crops. Fresh produce sold to urban markets yields more profit.

  II. Body (order of importance)
     A. Cause no. 1: Nicotine has been identified as a cause of cancer.
     B. Cause no. 2: Many people have ceased smoking because of possible health hazards.
     C. Cause no. 3: Prospects for future tobacco markets are dim.
     D. Cause no. 4: High prices of fresh produce promise lucrative returns.

 III. Conclusion

If you discuss both multiple causes and multiple effects, you will need a more complex outline. The block or alternating method might be used, depending on the rhetorical situation.

### Outline C: Multiple Causes and Multiple Effects (block method)

   I. Introduction: who, what, and where?

  II. Body: Explanation of causes and effects (why)
     A. Causes
     B. Effects

 III. Conclusion (may be recommendation)

Once in a while you may need to explain a *series* of interrelated events. To emphasize the chronology of each cause and its immediate effect, you could use an alternating method. In other words, cause and effect would alternate in pairs in chronological order.

**Outline D: Series of Events Linked to Each Other (alternating method)**

   I. Introduction: specifies nature of causal relationship

 II. Body (chronological order)

    A. Cause no. 1

    B. Effect no. 1

    C. Cause no. 2

    D. Effect no. 2 (continue as needed)

III. Conclusion

## Drafting an Introduction

The introduction may take various forms, depending on the emphasis and kind of causal relationships. For example, you might begin with a *narrative*, possibly an eyewitness account of an accident, then go on to describe the cause and effect(s). Your thesis could then link the cause with the effects you will focus on.

See Chapter 4.

Or you might open by describing a specific effect, showing why it is important or interesting to consider what caused it. You might explain the effect by classifying *examples* and presenting *illustrations*. Or you might provide an overview of the causal relationship or suggest that the causes or effects will be surprising. Watch for a hook that will make your analysis meaningful to your readers.

## Developing a Paper Analyzing Cause and Effect

Your purpose will help you to devise a suitable writing strategy to develop your paper adequately. Most topics will require a thorough explanation with specific details and examples that reflect the purpose. Usually, the primary purpose of causal analysis is to inform or to persuade. Even when the purpose is informative, the paper will still have an *argumentative edge*, or element of persuasion. It may range from a hint to much more. In short, whether *implicitly* or *explicitly*, you will argue for your claim that a cause has led or will lead to an effect. (The difference between an informative and a persuasive paper of causal analysis is a matter of degree and strategy, not necessarily of content.)

To support your claim, you need convincing proof. For example, you might contend that action should be taken to keep sixteen-year-olds from driving after midnight because of an extremely high rate of accidents for that age group. To make your claim plausible, you would have to produce valid research and possibly expert opinion to indicate that the hours after midnight are a dangerous time for sixteen-year-old drivers to be out on the roads.

## Writing a Conclusion

See
Chapter 4.

The conclusion of a cause-and-effect paper summarizes the consequence or re-sult. It may mention a repercussion, influence, benefit, or implication for the fu-ture. Or there may be an allusion to the title or opening that establishes closure, as in "Silver Lining," below. Regardless, the ending should flow from the descrip-tion of cause and effect and give a sense of completeness.

## Revising a Cause-and-Effect Paper

See "Editing,"
page 52.

As you start to revise your cause-and-effect paper, look at the larger items first. Pay particular attention to the strategy, logic, and writer's voice. After you are satisfied with these aspects, check the smaller aspects, as explained in Chapter 5. The checklist below should be helpful.

---

### CHECKLIST: REVISING A CAUSE-AND-EFFECT PAPER

1. Does the strategy emphasize the purpose?
2. Is the evidence adequate to support the claim?
3. If not, have I qualified my statements (with *seem* or *appear*, for example) to allow for chance?
4. Could another contributing cause exist?
5. Is the voice impartial and fair?
6. Is the connection clear? Have I explained enough?

---

TWO STUDENT PAPERS: CAUSE AND EFFECT

The purpose of both papers that follow is to inform classmates of the writer's per-spective on a situation. Jo Rae Sloan begins with the cause and explains the effects.

### Silver Lining

To a nineteen-year-old girl, owning her own vehicle oftentimes seems alluring. But once the dream becomes a reality, the resulting responsibilities may seem over-whelming at times. Several months ago I had an opportunity to buy a pickup truck with help from my mother. Having my own transportation is convenient, and I do take pride in my Chevy pickup; yet the upkeep and expense can be exasperating.

Before I bought a truck, I had to schedule my activities around the other family members. I had to borrow my mother's car and worry about the possibility of put-ting a dent in the fender before I returned. Now I can hop in my Chevy and go whenever I need or wish without a care. I am a cautious driver and have insurance. Although I still park in a far row of parking lots, away from other vehicles, I no longer worry about possible dents.

When I drove someone else's car, I did not really care how it looked. Once I owned my own vehicle, however, my feelings changed. I take pride in my Chevy truck. When I first purchased it, I took it to a body shop for a new paint job with stripes and for window tinting. Now I vacuum my truck every week as well as wash and wax it regularly. All this takes time and effort. The work and expense are much more than I bargained for.

In the "good old days," all of my extra cash went for clothes, cosmetics, and anything else I wanted. Not now—every cent seems to go to my truck. The expected expense is bad enough, but the unexpected expense can be heartbreaking to a full-time student with a part-time job. Insurance takes a big chunk of my earnings. Filling the gas tank is another regular expense, along with the cost of oil and periodic maintenance. The unexpected expense of a new tire, a muffler system, and other repairs has been formidable. Thank goodness, I live at home and don't have to make payments to a car dealer. My mother is willing to wait for a payment when necessary.

As a result of buying my truck, I have been forced to budget—I haven't bought any new clothes since graduation last June. Although I seldom have more than a few dollar bills and some silver lining my pockets, I have a wonderful sense of independence. My Chevy truck has transported me from adolescence to adulthood.

## Questions for Discussion

1. What is the single cause of the effects Jo Rae describes?

2. How do her expectations compare with reality?

3. How does she feel about the effects at times? What is her overall feeling?

4. Does Jo Rae use the block or the alternating method of organization?

5. What is the effect of placing advantages before disadvantages?

6. What is the effect of the title? To what old saying does it allude?

In the next paper, Mary Ann Holvick also describes a single cause that produces multiple effects. First she explains her job; then she presents the benefits:

### Why I Enjoyed Being a School Bus Driver

Often when two people are introduced, they initiate conversation by inquiring about each other's occupation. For six years my answer to that question produced raised eyebrows and caused my new acquaintances to exclaim, "You couldn't pay me enough to do that job!" Then I would explain that driving a school bus had rewards other than the usual monetary compensation: mastering a machine, enjoying nature, and participating in children's lives.

Achieving control of the school bus was an arduous task. I had to learn a maintenance routine which included checking all oil and fluid levels, inspecting all hoses and belts for signs of wear, and verifying that all lights and warning buzzers were functional. The most difficult aspect was backing the bus, thirty-eight feet long, from a narrow country road into a still narrower driveway. Yet I derived great satisfaction from knowing the children on the bus were safe because it was in top running condition, and I was confidently in control.

Nature rewarded me for my early morning hours with a spectacular array of sunrises, which fired the deep-textured woods and fence rows with iridescent colors. Although I had grown up in the country, I never tired of watching the trees, wildflowers, and farm crops grow, blossom, and display the triumphant colors of a purpose fulfilled. Under the cover of vegetation, animals and birds carried on their daily lives, unabashed by the passing of so many curious eyes. The children and I enjoyed sights such as a buck deer bounding across an open field, a skunk hunting for his insect breakfast, a flock of Canadian geese flying in formation, and a hawk carrying away his prey with victorious cries.

The children, however, were my constant source of delight. The younger ones were always eager to share their concerns with me. I became a doll fashion advisor and new clothes admirer. I sympathized with the losing Little League team and empathized with the disappointed owners of bologna sandwich lunches. I patched dozens of scraped knees and critiqued hundreds of homework papers. Grade cards were presented for approval; and, occasionally, love notes were dropped surreptitiously into my lap by red-faced little boys.

Older students generally remained aloof until desperation brought them to me, seeking advice about dating or dealing with unreasonable parents. For homecoming queens I saved newspaper pictures, and I congratulated teams for their athletic feats and scholastic achievement. And I worried over their safety each weekend when carloads of teenagers jammed the downtown square. Although I do not have any children of my own, I have loved several hundred boys and girls who made me a part of their lives.

If, like my new acquaintances, I had considered only the hard work involved in my job, then I would not have been a school bus driver. Of course, I received a monetary reward, but my real rewards were the physical discipline of driving, intimacy with nature, and the trusting love of the children.

## Questions for Discussion

1. What is the cause in Mary Ann's paper?

2. What are the effects?

3. How does Mary Ann use description to convey her feelings about her job? Which examples do you find most vivid? Why?

4. What order is used to organize details relating to children? For organizing main points?

5. How would you describe the voice of the paper?

---

### FOR YOUR REFERENCE: CAUSE-AND-EFFECT ESSAYS IN THE READER

- "Saving the Earth," David Suzuki, page 475
- "Why Marriages Fail," Anne Roiphe, page 481
- "We are tous Québécois," *The Economist*, page 485
- "Is Anybody There?" Barbara Wickens, page 488

> **SUMMARY**
>
> - Causal analysis is the study of relationships between two events or conditions, one of which is thought to have caused the other.
> - Cause-and-effect relationships can be extremely complex. We may mistakenly assume that a complex problem has a single cause, when in fact there are several causes.
> - Two basics principles of logic govern cause and effect: 1) The cause is able to produce the effect and 2) other causes that might have produced the effect have been ruled out.
> - There are two common fallacies in causal analysis: *non sequitur* and *post hoc*. As you try to determine why something happened, proceed carefully. Avoid making unfounded inferences or hasty generalizations. Proof is needed before you cite a cause. Sketching a reverse chain of cause and effect will help you distinguish the effects from the cause.

## *Practice*

### Ideas for a Cause-and-Effect Paragraph

1. Haste makes waste
2. How learning to save (or not save) has affected my life
3. Honesty is the best policy
4. How an error in judgment caused . . .
5. How learning to _____ led to . . .

### Group Exercise: Writing "If . . . Then" Statements

*Directions:* Discuss each claim and the implications that *logically* follow. Then write a series of inferences derived from each claim. (The hints will start your thinking.)

1. In 1998 a Canadian business group got a permit to export water from Lake Superior to Asia. After an outcry in Canada and the United States, Ontario cancelled the permit in 1999. Now Global Water Corp. of Vancouver, British Columbia, has secured a permit to take water from a lake near Sitka, Alaska, to sell to China. Alaskans granted the permit because they regard water as a renewable resource.

   *Claim:* Alaska should not be allowed to export water to a foreign country. (How might it affect the local supply? Water table? Might depletion affect the rate of renewal? Why?)

   - If Alaska exports water, then there will be _____ water available to _____.

   - If a _____ should occur in the lower United States, then _____.

   - If Alaska continues to export water over the years, then _____.

2. *Claim:* Exercise is good for you; therefore, you should exercise regularly. (What conditions are implicit in this statement? Think about the exceptions and fill in the blanks with logical answers.)

   - If you have no _____ [what?], then you should exercise regularly.

   - If you have _____, then you should _____ [consult whom?] before exercising.

   - If your _____ recommends _____, then you should _____ regularly.

   - If _____, then _____.

## Ten Ideas for Papers of Cause and Effect

1. The influence of my favourite teacher
2. Peer pressure in high school
3. How my thinking has changed since attending college
4. Effect of being the eldest of _____ children
5. How cancer changed my home
6. A father's example
7. Changes in my neighbourhood
8. Effects of losing a job
9. How my parents' divorce changed my life
10. Effect of college classes on my self-esteem

# CRITICAL THINKING, EVALUATION, AND ARGUMENT

## Part 4

# Problem Solving

---

**Learning Objectives:**

After reading and applying the information in Chapter 18, you'll be able to:

- Identify the six steps of Dewey's problem-solving process
- Give examples of ways to improve objectivity
- Draft, develop, and revise a problem-solving essay

---

*A problem well stated is a problem half solved.*

—Charles F. Kettering

Businesses, industries, and other organizations frequently face major problems of costs, personnel, and service. Prices of materials and wages rise. Competitors cut prices. Inventories "shrink." Equipment malfunctions. Deliveries run late. Personnel make mistakes, and customers complain. Problems of some sort occur in every workplace. How these problems are solved can mean profit or loss. Therefore job applicants with effective problem-solving skills, as well as writing skills, have an edge in interviews.

## DEWEY'S METHOD OF PROBLEM SOLVING

Since primeval times, people have been solving problems randomly, trying one plan, then another, seeking an effective solution. Over several centuries, many people have helped to formulate the basic rules of scientific research. By 1855 a basic procedure had come to be known as the "scientific method," which is still used in research.

In the early twentieth century, John Dewey, an American philosopher and educator, devised an efficient problem-solving method, based on the scientific method. Dewey, however, omitted the step of formulating a hypothesis, a step that can hinder objectivity. The researcher who formulates a hypothesis risks finding support only for the theory and overlooking evidence against it.

Dewey's systematic six-step procedure has been widely adopted and adapted by educators, business personnel, and others, according to the rhetorical situation. This basic procedure is also practical for individual use, providing an effective way to organize research papers and reports that focus on a problem. The purpose is to inform the audience of possible alternatives for solving or alleviating it. A simplified version appears here:

See Chapters 21 and 22.

1. *State the problem.* Identify it.
2. *Define the problem.* Limit its scope. Examine its history.
3. *Formulate criteria.* Devise standards to measure the problem.
4. *Propose alternatives.* Consider possible solutions.
5. *Evaluate alternatives.* Apply criteria to solution options.
6. *Recommend action.* Select best possible solution(s).

Dewey knew that a problem must be confronted and clearly identified before it can be solved. Once the problem is understood, a plan of attack can be devised. Finding practical solutions was Dewey's primary concern. His main criterion for evaluating an alternative was "Will it work?" He went to great lengths to be objective.

## HOW CAN ONE BE OBJECTIVE?

To be objective, we must be willing to relinquish old biases, to question and to seek the truth. Basically, there are two general ways to obtain information: first-hand and second-hand. Both ways can present problems in terms of objectivity. Although we observe something first-hand, we may see only part of it and yet think we saw 100 percent. Or we may misinterpret the meaning of what we observed; we may make incorrect inferences and treat them as fact. Information gained second-hand is often subject to error and distortion. So how can one be as objective as possible and minimize the chances of error?

First, *we can reserve judgment.* We can hold back our opinions until they are solidly supported. We can listen to both sides of an issue and consider all facets of a problem. By reserving judgment, we can look for facts and comprehensive coverage before making decisions.

Second, *we can try to be impartial and fair.* We can remain open to new information. The fact that one deduction fits should not lead us to ignore other possibilities or conflicting viewpoints. Often someone with a different perspective can give valuable assistance in solving a problem and in averting mistakes.

Third, *we can qualify generalizations and refrain from embellishing facts.* We can distinguish inference from fact. We can also be on the alert for clever images that carry negativity and cunning words that carry bias. To be objective, we must seek the truth.

See Chapters 6 and 20.

Fourth, *we can keep in mind that no one is immune to mistakes.* To be human means to be susceptible to error. Although we think we understand something, our information may be only partial. When we attempt to explain, we may be able

## WORKPLACE CASE STUDY

### WRITING A COMPANY POLICY

A marketing firm has recently installed software that allows executives to access and monitor electronic communication. This installation was made because several employees were playing games, gambling, job hunting, shopping, and watching porn online instead of working. (Each visit to a Web site drags along the company name.)

An attorney has advised the firm to write a policy covering email and Web use. To balance company interests and employee privacy, the attorney advised appointing a committee that includes rank-and-file employees.

### ACTIVITY

Meet with your group to draft specific guidelines for email and Web use. Consider these issues: Should employees be allowed to use email for personal messages? To trade stock during work hours? To grocery shop or engage in other leisure activities? If so, what kind of activities and for how many hours? Include penalties for policy violations. Should the number and severity of the offenses be factors?

to tell what caused something, what affects it now, and what may affect it in the future. We may even be able to discuss its apparent effect on other things. Nonetheless, our understanding is inferential, incomplete, and inconclusive at some point. This awareness should keep us not only humble, but also alert.

## WRITING A PROBLEM-SOLVING PAPER

A problem-solving paper combines various writing strategies into a basic format that is suitable not only for some short papers but also for some research papers. The outline on pages 207 and 208 is based on Dewey's method of problem solving. Although you and your peers may use the same general pattern of organization, you will make individual decisions, according to the rhetorical situation.

### Selecting a Topic and Prewriting

To find a topic for a problem-solving paper, you might begin by considering your experience, including work-related projects. Or perhaps you know of a family, a neighbourhood, a community, or a city facing a problem. The problem should be significant, yet not too technical or complex. It should have at least three alternatives. That does not mean all alternatives must be feasible. Two or more can be ruled out, but one must provide a means to alleviate or to resolve the problem. Sometimes all alternatives may be needed. If the problem cannot be alleviated, look for another topic.

As you search for details to use in a problem-solving paper, watch for changes, increases or decreases, cause and effect, side effects, risks, advantages and disadvantages. Note that changes may be negative or positive, and their effects may be simple or complicated. Advantages and disadvantages may be short-term or long-term. Asking questions will speed your search.

*Questions to Discover Details for Problem Solving*

- What exactly is the problem?
- When was it first noticed?
- What or whom does it affect?
- What are its effects? (Signs, symptoms, characteristics?)
- How far does it extend? (Scope?)
- What were the causes? (History?)
- What, if anything, has been done to alleviate the problem?
- What other alternatives exist?
- What are the advantages and disadvantages of each alternative?
- What is the best alternative? Or will a combination be needed?

See Chapter 17.

*Caution:* Beware of oversimplification. Complex problems seldom have a single cause.

## Making an Outline

Dewey's method of problem solving furnishes an easy and effective way to organize information clearly for an audience. You can adapt this method to most problems. Using the six steps, you can start your scratch outline. Steps 1 and 2 form the introduction of the paper. Steps 3, 4, and 5 form the body. Step 6 forms the conclusion as shown here.

*Introduction*

| Step 1: | Identify the problem |
| Step 2: | Define the problem |

*Body*

| Step 3: | Identify criteria |
| Step 4: | Propose alternatives |
| Step 5: | Evaluate alternatives |

*Conclusion*

| Step 6: | Recommend action |

Following the order of the six steps will simplify organizing your paper. The working outline here illustrates how you might convert the six steps into an outline.

I. Introduction
   A. Attention-getting detail
   B. Description of the problem
   C. History of the problem
   D. Identification of the cause(s)

II. Body
   A. Specific criteria stated
   B. Alternative 1 and evaluation
   C. Alternative 2 and evaluation
   D. Alternative 3 and evaluation

III. Conclusion
   A. Recommendation or best alternative
   B. Relevant comment

---

### TRANSITION IN A PROBLEM-SOLVING PAPER

A problem-solving paper requires transitions to signal cause-and-effect relationships. To direct the reader, place appropriate transitions near reasons why an event happened or a description of how it affected another event or situation:

| | | | |
|---|---|---|---|
| therefore | one difficulty | an offshoot | one part |
| thus | an outcome | a consequence | one complication |
| affected | one effect | a by-product | one influence |
| two factors | an outgrowth | as a result | one proposal |
| three aspects | influenced | contributed | changed |

---

## Drafting an Introduction

Problem-solving papers can begin in several ways. You might open with an appropriate quotation or a brief dialogue that illustrates a vital aspect of the problem. Another way is to start with a narrative that describes the problem; then you might describe cause and effect. The introduction of a problem-solving paper sets the stage for the identification of criteria and a discussion of alternatives.

## Identifying Criteria

To check decisions and to evaluate possible solutions to problems, we need to develop criteria. By identifying our own specific criteria, we can measure the existing alternatives and make more logical decisions than we might otherwise make.

***What Are Criteria?***   Instead of criteria, you may be used to talking about "guidelines," "specifications," "company policy," "diplomacy," or similar terms. All of these are criteria, used to weigh decisions and evaluate alternatives. Criteria are simply the factors that influence decision making and problem solving.

Daily life offers many opportunities to apply criteria. For instance, when planning a major purchase, you use criteria to weigh the advantages and disadvantages of comparable products. Before buying a new television set, you might consider some, or perhaps all, of the following criteria:

- screen size
- brand name
- price

- warranty
- quality of sound
- high definition

A criterion (the singular of criteria) is *one* standard, rule, principle, or test used to evaluate a decision or proposal. Dewey's first criterion—"Will it work?"—is a factor in solving any problem. Time is another important criterion to consider. Other common criteria are listed here:

- Is it cost-effective?
- Is it safe?
- Is it practical?
- Is it legal?

- Is it ethical?
- Is it fair?
- Is it appropriate?
- Is it beneficial in the short run? Long run?

***Stating Criteria***   To identify criteria, ask: "What factors will influence this decision?" Perhaps the simplest way to specify criteria is to pose each criterion as a question. In her paper Nancy Miller stated criteria as questions:

> Making our house more energy-efficient required careful consideration. When the alternatives to this problem were evaluated, three main questions were asked. First, what is the cost? Second, how energy-efficient is the alternative? Third, will the alternative raise the equity in our home?

Another example was written by a mother who had recently lost her job through a layoff. Carol Walkins specified three concerns in her job search: day shift, pay scale, and location:

> A major problem that I faced was the possibility of having to work the evening or midnight shift if I found employment in another factory. With two elementary school children, I needed to be at home in the evenings in order to spend important time with them. Since my family depends on my income, I also had to find a job

that would provide a pay scale similar to that of my former job. Location was another factor to be considered. My husband works locally, and we own our home. Therefore, moving was not an option.

For clarity in a problem-solving paper, some instructors prefer that students state criteria before alternatives. Regardless, do not confuse criteria with alternatives. Criteria are the factors or considerations that govern decisions. Alternatives are the options for action—possible solutions. In other words, criteria provide a means to weigh the benefits and risks of an alternative.

## Proposing and Evaluating Alternatives

Usually, a problem-solving paper presents at least three alternatives. Perhaps two of the choices can be eliminated, leaving one that can best solve the problem. This does not mean that every problem can be solved with one alternative. Perhaps a combination will be needed. Or perhaps the best that can be done is to alleviate the problem.

After alternatives are determined, each possibility is evaluated according to criteria. In this fifth step, advantages and disadvantages become apparent. Upon first glance, an alternative may seem to be a practical solution to a problem. After research and analysis, however, hidden disadvantages may emerge.

To evaluate alternatives for a paper, research the feasibility of each one. Do not assume there are no disadvantages. To be objective, a paper must specify disadvantages as well as advantages. (An omission of either would constitute card stacking. See Chapter 20.) Then evaluate the alternatives according to the criteria. Note that a problem may have a short-term alternative and a long-term solution. When Carol analyzed her problem of unemployment, she found both:

> My first alternative was to collect the nine months of unemployment compensation that I qualified for. I could accomplish my household tasks during the day, leaving the evenings free for my children. Collecting unemployment and saving on babysitting fees would compensate for the weekly paycheck. Although the idea of staying home was appealing, collecting an unemployment check would be temporary and not a real solution to the problem.
>
> A second alternative was to go job hunting. Although it seemed like a logical solution, I knew that a good job would be difficult to find at this time. To secure factory work with daytime hours would be almost impossible. Daytime office jobs were available, but I lacked the training needed to qualify. I realized that it was unrealistic to expect to find a suitable, well-paying job locally.
>
> A third option was available, however. Because I had lost my job due to foreign trade, I was eligible for a new federal program under the Trade Readjustment Act. This program would pay for college tuition for two years as well as books and supplies. I could attend day classes while the children were in school. The plan would also pay a small allowance for living expenses for up to one year if grade and attendance requirements were maintained. Although this option would require a drastically revised family budget, I knew I could manage.

Carol combined steps 4 and 5 of the problem-solving method: She proposed an alternative, applied criteria, and evaluated. This order enabled her to avoid undue repetition. The parallelism of her points helped to make the paper clear and easy to read. The details prepared the audience for the conclusion.

## Writing a Conclusion

The end of a problem-solving paper presents the recommendation the writer has prepared the reader to accept. In other words, the selected solution should flow logically from the discussion of alternatives. Some conclusions contain a call for action, perhaps pointing out the consequences of inaction. In a paper about the air-conditioning problem on the job, Keith Zuspan concluded by making a recommendation:

> Repairing the existing air-conditioning unit would, in fact, be the most efficient and economical method of regaining the desired environmental controls required for the complex. It is also the writer's opinion that by utilizing the in-house building mechanics to complete this project, additional money could be saved.

Other conclusions, like the ending of Nancy Miller's paper, summarize the action already taken and explain how a solution fits the criteria:

> After reviewing the three alternatives, we chose the third, which proved to be the most cost-effective as well as energy-efficient. By purchasing the siding and windows together, we received a discount. The new furnace also proved to be energy-efficient, and we saw a sizable reduction in heating expense in the first year after installation. This third option has also increased the home's equity dramatically, although part of the increase is due to inflation. In 1972 we paid just over seven thousand dollars for the house, and now, three decades later, the house is worth over sixty-five thousand dollars.

## Revising a Problem-Solving Paper

To produce your best work, allow plenty of time for revising, editing, and proof-reading your problem-solving paper. The following checklist will help to ensure that you check strategic points: See Chapter 5.

---

### CHECKLIST: REVISING A PROBLEM-SOLVING PAPER

1. Is the problem clearly defined in the introduction? Are the causes and pertinent history of the problem explained?
2. Are specific criteria for evaluating alternative solutions identified? Are these criteria reasonable and adequate?
3. Are different alternatives for solving the problem identified and described?
4. Is one alternative recommended? Is it clear why this solution is best?
5. Is the conclusion effective? Does it flow logically from the body?
6. Have transitions been used effectively?

STUDENT PAPER: PROBLEM SOLVING

In this example, Rajini Maturu proposes a solution to a problem faced in her former workplace:

### Unhappy Customers at the Bank of India

The Union Bank of India is a financial institution that has 1,000 branches all over India. In the city of Secunderabad, the Union Bank caters to the financial needs of local customers. There the branch manager has to tackle the problem of customer dissatisfaction toward the check-cashing procedure.

Presently, there are four staff members of the bank taking care of the four steps of the check-cashing routine. During the banking hours between 10 a.m. and 2:30 p.m., there are about seventy customers. The customer first presents the check to a clerk, who enters the check number and amount in a register. The clerk gives the customer a metallic coin, called a token, with a number.

Then the customer goes to another clerk, who debits the customer's account with the amount of the check. Next, an accountant verifies the customer's signature. Finally, the check is taken to the cashier, who identifies the customer by the token number and makes the payment. During this procedure each customer waits for at least thirty minutes to cash a check.

There are two important aspects to the problem of expediting the check-cashing procedure. One aspect is the cost involved in bringing about changes since the branch is allowed a budget of $2,000 dollars. The other aspect to be considered is the amount of time saved by introducing the changes.

A proposed solution is to increase the number of staff members. Three additional clerks could be appointed to handle the check cashing. The cost of this change would mean $500 per clerk. For three more clerks, the total cost would be $1,500, which is within the budget limit. The main drawback to this proposal is that the customers would still have to wait for at least fifteen minutes to cash their checks.

A second proposal is the opening of a teller counter. This would mean creation of a separate cubicle with ledgers containing customer information. The specimen signatures of the customers would be stored at the teller counter. Here the entire check-cashing procedure could be managed by one employee called the teller officer. When a check was presented for payment, the teller officer would scrutinize the customer's signature, enter the check amount in the cash register, and make payment to the customer. This proposal would cost $1,900; hence, the expenses would be within the budget. As all the operations would be managed by one employee, the check could be cashed in eight minutes. This would mean a considerable reduction in the customer's wait.

A third proposal is to computerize all the customer's records. With this method the check would be cashed in two minutes. This is the best proposal as far as the time element is concerned. The cost involved in purchasing the computers and training the clerks would be $4,000 dollars, however. The disadvantage to this proposal is that it does not meet the budget requirements.

The second proposal of creating a teller counter appears to be the most suitable action at this time. This proposal reduces the waiting period to cash a check from thirty minutes to eight minutes, and the expenses involved are within the budget specifications.

*Questions for Analysis*

1. Does the paper provide a clear description of the problem?
2. Are the criteria clear?
3. Does the order of alternatives seem appropriate?
4. Are alternatives evaluated according to the criteria?
5. Does the conclusion seem logical and complete?

---

**FOR YOUR REFERENCE:**
**PROBLEM-SOLVING ESSAYS IN THE READER**

- "How Do You Know It's Good?" Marya Mannes, page 434
- "Why Marriages Fail," Anne Roiphe, page 481

---

**SUMMARY**

- John Dewey's method of problem solving is based on the scientific method, in which objectivity is crucial.
- Dewey's six steps of problem solving provide an easy and efficient way to organize an essay:
  1) identify the problem;
  2) describe the problem;
  3) specify criteria;
  4) propose alternatives;
  5) evaluate alternatives according to the criteria; and
  6) recommend the best alternative(s).
- Criteria are standards of measurement—the factors or considerations that influence decision making. You apply criteria so that you can weigh the advantages and disadvantages of each alternative. In this way you can evaluate the practicality of possible solutions to a problem.

---

*Practice*

**Small Groups: Identifying Criteria**

The following introduction to a problem-solving paper was written by Patricia Davis. After you read it, brainstorm possible criteria that would influence the final decision. One group member should record all of these. Finally, examine your list of criteria and decide which are most important in determining a solution.

### A Pet for Aunt Emily

My aunt, although eighty-three years old and rather frail, is still able to care for herself. Aunt Emily lives alone in her own home on a limited income. Ordinarily, she is quite independent and self-sufficient, but last week she surprised me. When I dropped by, she asked for advice. Confiding that she was lonely, she explained she needed companionship and was thinking about getting a pet. But she was unsure about what sort of animal would be best for her. She asked me to help in deciding what kind of pet would be the most enjoyable and suitable.

## Small Groups: Case Problems

*Directions:* Select *one* of the authentic cases below. Steps 1 and 2 of Dewey's problem-solving method are given. Supply steps 3, 4, 5, and 6.

1. You are a member of the committee selected to plan the office Christmas party. Your instructions are to eliminate past problems or cancel! In past years, employees have bought gifts for the president of the small marketing research firm. Some buy expensive gifts and appear to be currying favours, which causes grumbling. The owner gives everyone a small rolled ham and provides a lunch of finger food and fruit punch. But someone always spikes the punch with gin. Some employees have become boisterous. Last year a few became amorous, which led to the temporary separation of one couple. Devise a plan to prevent similar problems.

2. You are a computer and software sales rep. While running a booth at a trade show, you meet a woman who asks if you still have the same sales manager, J. D. Smith. When you reply "Yes," she says, "That's too bad." Then she tells you about her boyfriend buying software out of the sales manager's home. You mull over the pros and cons of telling the owner, whom you admire and trust. You do not trust the sales manager because of his office pranks and complaints behind the owner's back. What other factors should you consider? Alternatives? What do you decide?

3. You are a clerk in a bookstore. One day you see your best friend's girlfriend. She glances around and puts a book inside her jacket. Then she walks toward the door. Store policy requires that you alert another employee, stop shoplifters after they leave the store, and retrieve the merchandise. You are to warn shoplifters that if they ever re-enter, charges will be filed. To protect your friend and yourself from an awkward situation, you are tempted to ignore the incident. What factors should be examined? Is there a third alternative? What do you decide?

4. Your husband works nights. One evening you are alone except for your three-year-old child, asleep in her room. At eleven o'clock you hear a noise in the chimney of the fireplace. Terrified, you watch a small dark creature creep out and fly across the room. It perches in one corner near the ceiling. What will you do? What are your alternatives? What factors must be considered?

5. Your neighbours often stay out until 2:30 a.m. on weekends. They leave their Doberman tied out in the backyard, where he howls—keeping you awake until they take him in. You do not know if he is hungry or lonely. The dog does not recognize you, but from a distance he seems fairly friendly. What are your alternatives? What risks are involved?

## *Ten Ideas for Problem-Solving Papers*

1. A problem on the job
2. Security for twenty-four-hour businesses
3. Automobile security from theft
4. Spotting shoplifters
5. Parking restrictions around campus
6. How can we attract more tourists?
7. Staffing athletic programs on a low budget
8. Inadequate childcare facilities for working parents
9. Registering for classes
10. Drag racing on city streets

# Shaping an Effective Argument

**Learning Objectives:**

After reading and applying the information in Chapter 19, you'll be able to:

- Identify the three classic appeals used in argument
- Recognize opposing views and overcome objections to your argument
- Draft, develop, and revise a classic argument essay

*Truth is one forever absolute, but
opinion is truth filtered through the moods,
the blood, the disposition of the spectator.*

—Wendell Phillips (1859)

Hardly a day passes without your persuading someone of something. It may be as trivial as convincing a friend to try a new restaurant or as significant as convincing an interviewer you are qualified for a position. On the job you may write a proposal, a request for new software, a grant application, or other document. In a college class you may be asked to write a persuasive essay, a reaction paper, or a paper of argument. Skill in argument and persuasion will enable you to become a more effective writer and speaker, both in college and in the workplace.

## PURPOSE OF ARGUMENT

Although there are many types of argument, the general purpose of any serious argument is to convince readers to accept a belief, adopt a policy, or enact a decision, proposal, or law. In the strictest sense, the term *argument* refers to an assertion that is based on logic and proof, a rational appeal to the intellect.

According to the rhetorical situation, however, many arguments contain not only rational appeals but also ethical and emotional appeals. This chapter explains a classic argument model that includes appeals to logic, ethics, and emotions. This model is flexible, effective, and practical. It can be adapted in various ways for general use.

## THREE CLASSIC APPEALS USED IN ARGUMENT

More than two thousand years ago, the Greek philosopher Aristotle defined three kinds of appeals that make up an argument: *logos* (logic), *ethos* (moral character or ethics), and *pathos* (emotion). Aristotle realized that logic alone is not always sufficient to persuade an audience. To be convincing, you must also gain credibility—the trust of your listeners or readers. To do so, you must be perceived as honest, fair, and responsive to moral obligations. Aristotle called this the appeal to *ethos*. In *Nicomachean Ethics*, he explains:

> Virtue then is twofold, partly intellectual and partly moral, and intellectual virtue is originated and fostered mainly by teaching; it demands therefore experience and time. Moral virtue on the other hand is the outcome of habit, and accordingly its name *éthike*, is derived by a slight variation from *éthos*, habit.

> —from *On Man and the Universe: Metaphysics, Parts of Animals, Ethics, Politics, Poetics*. Louise R. Loomis, Editor

Logical and ethical appeals are often enough to convince on some issues, but unless emotion moves an audience to act on other issues, the argument will be in vain.

You can identify the three classic appeals by the questions they raise with readers:

- **Logical appeal:** Is the claim or petition factual and reasonable? True or false? Practical or impractical?

- **Ethical appeal:** Is it just or unjust? Honest or dishonest? Right or wrong?

- **Emotional appeal:** Do the words arouse such feelings as empathy and sympathy? Do they cause the reader to care about the subject?

## The Logical Appeal

In most rhetorical situations, you will be expected to base your conclusions on sound reasoning and adequate proof. A logical argument appeals to the mind, using evidence, reasons, and examples to support a claim or proposition. Logical appeals are based on facts, sound inferences, and working theories. Reliable evidence may include established truths, primary sources, statistics, expert opinion, or personal experience.

***Established Truths***   Some evidence is so solidly grounded that no reasonable person will seriously debate it. In the examples below, the first three are *established facts*, which have been conclusively proven. The fourth example has been accepted as fact, based on the existing evidence.

- **Historical fact:** Jacques Cartier began his exploration of Canada in Newfoundland, sailing the St. Lawrence to Montréal.

### "You Got a Tiger by the Tail!"

Matthew Resome was a programmer at XYZ Company. Matt was a quiet guy with an excellent work record who got along well with other employees. For three years he had tried to work through the right channels to improve wages and working conditions. But neither had changed despite the fact that the company's sales had increased 55 percent during those years.

When Matt contacted the National Labor Relations Board (NLRB), they said that if he could secure seventy-five signatures on a petition, then they could come in and conduct a vote to unionize the plant. The company would have to provide a room with a booth where employees could come during work hours. Matt secured the required signatures, and two NLRB representatives conducted the vote at the plant. The vote failed.

The next morning J. B. Smith, the plant manager, told his assistant to fire Matt. The assistant, who had attended law school, refused. Using a *logical* appeal, he warned, "You can't do this. Federal laws prohibit discrimination against peaceful and acceptable union activities. You got a tiger by the tail! Let it go."

But four days later, the irate plant manager called Matt in and stated, "Your job has been phased out. We don't need you any more. You can clear out your desk and leave right now." Matt contacted the NLRB.

### ACTIVITY

Assume the role of the NLRB investigator. Examine Matt's work record and investigate the events preceding the firing. Summarize the situation and write a letter to J. B. Smith. Inform him that to prevent legal action, the company must reinstate and reimburse Matt for all lost wages. The company has thirty days to consider the offer.

- **Geographical fact:** Ontario borders four of the five Great Lakes.
- **Scientific fact:** When a heavy object is dropped, it falls to the ground.
- **Scientific theory regarded as fact:** The sun's gravitation attracts the planets and keeps them in their paths. Stars are held on course by the pull of heavenly bodies.

***Primary Sources***   Research that is gathered first-hand carries more credibility than that filtered through secondary researchers. If you can obtain relevant documents, letters, autobiographies, or other primary source materials, these can lend strong support to your argument. Or you may choose to gather evidence first-hand yourself. For further explanation of and suggestions for primary research, see Chapter 22, "Primary Research."

*Statistics*   Reliable statistical findings from recognized and reputable authorities can strengthen your argument. To be reliable, the findings should be based on samples that are representative and random. Yet some widely quoted findings are neither random nor representative, as explained in Chapter 22.

Another problem of reliability occurs when the researcher who is under extreme pressure, such as meeting a deadline, falsifies results. When you find unusual conclusions, check to see if the results are consistent with those of others in the field. Unless an experiment can be replicated under controlled laboratory conditions by qualified researchers, it cannot be accepted as evidence.

*Expert Opinion*   The opinion of a recognized authority in a field generally conveys credibility and enhances a argument. If you decide to use expert opinion, check out the person's qualifications first. Here the Internet is an invaluable and speedy resource for checking on well-known authorities. Interviewing can also be helpful for local issues. For instance, if you were arguing for a proposal to thwart break-ins and burglary, then the chief of police or mayor could be credible sources.

See "Watch for Credentials" Chapter 23.

*Personal Experience*   The personal stories of people who have been involved in an accident, a tragedy, or natural phenomenon such as a tornado, can be powerful. A detailed description of such an event can have a strong emotional impact and buttress a logical argument. Personal experience stories should be used to supplement logical evidence, not supplant it. The experience should be significant and have a definite, relevant point.

*Important Considerations*   When you are presenting inconclusive evidence, avoid confusing theory with fact. Be accurate and precise so as not to overstate and weaken your case. For a reference list, see "Using Tentative Words to Discuss Findings and Theories," page 335.

Inferences are often confused with fact, and generalizations are often made from an invalid sample. For a further discussion of what constitutes reliable evidence, see Chapters 6 and 20. To construct a flawless argument, you need to be able to recognize pitfalls in logic.

## The Ethical Appeal

Ethical appeals are designed to strike a responsive chord in the minds of the readers, entreating them to do what is right, good, fair, and best. Ethics can be broadly defined as a set of moral values—principles of conduct for an individual, group, profession, or society. Sound ethics are essential to a well-constructed argument.

To be ethical, an argument must respect the rights and needs of the audience. In other words, deception to obtain a selfish aim is unethical—and often illegal.

An ethical appeal requires you to first demonstrate comprehensive knowledge of your subject. *You have an ethical obligation to give the reader the whole truth*, not just proof that will make your side of the argument *seem* convincing. In other words, if there are disadvantages to your proposal, you need to be honest about them. Second, you must approach the subject in an even-handed way, presenting differing viewpoints accurately and fairly. Your written voice must sound reasonable, controlled, and concerned.

## The Emotional Appeal

Emotional appeals stir the feelings of readers with figurative language, connotation, and anecdote. Such appeals can be powerful, for they bypass the intellect. Emotional appeals work best, however, when used in moderation. They should also be ethical. Do not use an emotional appeal that gives you any misgivings or uneasiness.

Used wisely, emotion can motivate. For example, in the Workplace Case Study earlier, the assistant might have stressed his emotional appeal more. Instead of hinting with "You got a tiger by the tail!" he could have been more direct by saying, "You might lose your own job over this firing. Be careful." Perhaps the boss would have listened.

## Using the Three Appeals

The bulk of your argument paper should be a logical appeal, based on sound, logical proof. But keep in mind that credible persuasion rests on a blend of facts and ethical reasons, bonded with appropriate emotion. In other words, emotion usually plays a lesser role. To be effective, all three appeals must harmonize. An emotional appeal that conflicts with either a logical appeal or an ethical appeal is inappropriate.

---

### GUIDELINES FOR USING PERSUASIVE APPEALS

1. *Alert the audience to a problem by using suitable emotion.*

2. *Use restraint.* Do not overstate. Exaggerated appeals can backfire.

3. *Do not circumvent an issue.* Focus your argument on the issue. Answer all of the opposition's points with solid evidence and reasons.

4. *Do not oversimplify.* Guard against either/or alternatives.

5. *Avoid conflicting appeals.* Contradiction undermines arguments.

6. *Show and tell.* Use examples and anecdotes to illustrate and heighten interest.

7. *Read aloud to check for objectivity.* Evidence should be presented honestly without slanting or manipulation. The writer's voice should sound fair and trustworthy.

# UNDERSTANDING OPPOSING VIEWS
# AND OVERCOMING OBJECTIONS

Two landowners were involved in a boundary dispute that dated back to their grandfathers' time. Years before, a rail fence had been erected by one grandparent and moved by the other. At last one man consulted a lawyer. Relating the history of the argument, the client presented one view of the dispute. The lawyer assured him that the law was on his side and asked when he wanted to sue. The client replied, "Never, I just gave you the other guy's version."

Researching both views of an issue provides an opportunity not only to weigh the facts, but also to consider the priorities, values, and attitudes of readers who disagree. Sometimes readers may agree with a proposal, but not act. Then your first task is to discover the *area of resistance* and determine why they are reluctant. The second task is to prepare a persuasive strategy to overcome their objections and resistance. Once you understand the opposing view, you can decide how to shape the argument to emphasize advantages and benefits.

For example, voters may agree that more money is needed to fund local schools, but they may resist voting for a bond levy. How do you convince them that the proposed benefits justify the expense? An appeal combining logic, ethics, and emotion might be the most effective:

> Several of our school buildings are over seventy-five years old. They are drafty and expensive to heat; those big windows have single panes. The frames rattle. The electrical wiring is inadequate; there is no way to plug in computers. Plaster has fallen from some ceilings. Building now will avoid expensive renovations and save money in the long run, because construction costs continue to climb.
>
> The buildings are also overcrowded. For instance, in one building a class meets on the auditorium stage, another in the lunchroom, and two meet at the ends of halls. The children are distracted by passersby, and the acoustics are poor. The children have no place to put their coats.
>
> Our children deserve better. They deserve a place where they can concentrate and do their best. Our children are the future leaders of this country. Surely, we need to give them a chance for optimum learning. Won't you dig down in your pocket to come up with the extra dollars to make this dream come true? Vote yes for the school bond levy!

## QUESTIONS TO ANALYZE AN AUDIENCE

1. How much does the audience know about the topic?
2. How strong is their disagreement or resistance?
3. If they agree on a proposal, why are they reluctant to act?
4. What is important to them?
5. What is important to me?
6. What change can I reasonably expect?

## WRITING A CLASSIC ARGUMENT PAPER

Many times it is not enough to research the facts on an issue, for facts alone may not convince. People often act on perceptions and instincts that are not always logical. When a problem arises, you may have a practical solution and all the relevant facts; but unless you can tap into your audience's priorities and needs, chances are your proposal will be rejected. Therefore, careful audience analysis is essential to draft an effective strategy of argument. (For explanations of audience analysis, see Chapters 1 and 31.)

The strategy you select will be determined by the purpose, the topic, and the amount of resistance to the proposition. Will the audience show reluctance, firm opposition, or downright hostility? As you shape your strategy, keep in mind the three classic appeals. Consider how they can help you focus your paper.

### Selecting a Topic

The topic for an argument paper should be controversial and significant. A controversial topic has at least two points of view. To be significant, the disagreement must involve more than a definition of terms or a question of fact that could be easily checked. This means the topic would centre on more than a simple question of truth or a matter of personal preference. For instance, to argue that computers can be fun would be unsuitable. Or to argue vaguely that U2 is better than the Beatles would be futile since this judgment hinges on personal taste. But a paper that contains adequate support and criteria to evaluate the characteristics of both musical groups could yield a logical argument.

Claims of judgment involve an opinion or rating that is significant and logical, resting on facts and reasons. Aesthetic judgments evaluate the worth or value of music, art, and literature. Ethical judgments evaluate whether something is beneficial or harmful, humane or inhumane, moral or immoral, right or wrong. Functional judgments evaluate how well something or someone works. Arguments, including judgments, make five types of claims.

*Five Basic Claims Made in Arguments*

---

1. ***Claim of judgment:*** What is the writer's position on the issue? What are the criteria upon which the judgment is based?
2. ***Claim of fact:*** What is actually true? (Myth as opposed to fact or updates in scientific thinking are typical examples.)
3. ***Claim of interpretation:*** What do the facts mean?
4. ***Claim of cause:*** Why did something happen? Why is it the way it is? (A valid hypothesis provides the simplest and best explanation.)
5. ***Claim of policy:*** What should be done? What is the best alternative to solve the problem? Or are there several acceptable alternatives?

Before an argument can be resolved, the participants must agree on the *basic premise* or *proposition* upon which the argument rests. For example, two students could agree on the basic premise that a college diploma should signify competency, although they disagree about how competency should be measured. Since they agree on the underlying belief, a logical argument could be constructed.

To write effectively about a value-laden topic, you must be open-minded, fair, and alert. Topics such as abortion and religion carry emotional baggage that make them difficult to argue for three reasons: (1) rarely do the opposing views agree on a basic premise; (2) sources are often slanted toward one view; and (3) you must sift the evidence while keeping your own biases under control. Other topics for argument may have inherent hazards, too. For your consideration, some typical problems that students wade into are listed here:

*Common Hazards in Selecting Topics for Argument*

1. *The topic is too broad.* Subjects should be narrowed to a proposition that can be supported and discussed well in the allotted length.

2. *The topic is strictly informational.* A paper of argument does more than collect information. You strive to convince the reader of a proposition.

3. *The topic is hackneyed.* Sometimes students resurrect old papers or debate notes from high school. An important reason for assigning a paper of argument is to spur you to think and learn.

4. *Adequate support is unavailable.* If a topic is recent, you may find little data available. If a topic is heavily laden with emotion, you may find bias and fallacies in the sources.

Typically, instructors groan when they see old, overused topics such as capital punishment, legalizing illicit drugs, and the like. To be significant, a topic does not have to have worldwide or national implications—it may be a campus, community, or neighbourhood issue. Such topics can yield fresh material.

---

### CRITERIA FOR SELECTING AN ARGUMENT TOPIC

1. Is there disagreement about the subject or an area of resistance?
2. Is the issue significant and challenging?
3. Can I obtain enough factual information?
4. After research, will I be able to thoroughly understand the issue?
5. Can I write about the topic in a fair, objective tone?

---

## Gathering Information and Prewriting

The more knowledgeable and sophisticated your readers, the more they will insist on adequate proof of a claim. Yet a writer seldom has all the facts needed to attain a comprehensive view of a controversial topic. To be knowledgeable and objective, you need information from a variety of sources and viewpoints. In the workplace, you may talk to personnel at other companies who have resolved a similar question or problem. You may also consult journals, trade magazines, or online services.

In a college class, you may be asked to take a position on a literary work and write a paper of argument. In that case, you examine the work closely, make notes, think, and write. Or you may be required to do a research paper with text citations and a list of works cited. To focus a search for information, you might begin by posing a controlling question.

***Drafting a Controlling Question***   A controlling question narrows the search for information and establishes the focus of a paper. This question limits the topic and aids in finding suitable source materials. After you write your controlling question, check to see whether or not it performs these two vital functions:

1. Identifies the *specific* topic and scope
2. Specifies the *direction* of the research

For controversial topics, the wording of the question should receive special attention. The words should be fair and objective. Notice how a few words can change the tone of a question:

**Biased:** Should students be *forced* to take achievement tests *every year*?

**Neutral:** Should achievement tests *be given yearly*?

A neutral controlling question will help you to analyze a controversy fairly. Rereading the question from time to time will aid you in withholding judgment until key facts and implications are clear. The researcher who maintains an open mind is more likely to appraise an issue impartially than is one who leaps to a quick decision.

***Searching for Reliable Sources***   You need to gain an accurate overview of an issue, not just gather evidence to bolster one point of view. Understanding varying views is necessary in order to shape a convincing argument. To compare accounts and judge credibility, read from several sources. Not all sources are authoritative or reliable. Some may contain incorrect or outdated information, logical fallacies, or bias.

As you select books, look at the back cover, foreword, or introduction for the writer's credentials. Is he or she an authority in the field? Then scan a few pages and listen to the tone of the writing. Does it sound objective or biased? Does the coverage seem slanted? Do the significant points of the controversy seem to be covered? If you find inconsistencies or differing interpretations, jot down page numbers and authors. These discrepancies should be mentioned in your paper.

To research a local issue, you might interview the people involved and read newspaper accounts. To research a topic in a specialized field, consult journals or trade publications for technical information and opinions of authorities. Popular magazines may give brief, factual overviews of issues, but the treatment may be incomplete. (Also see "Selecting Suitable Sources" and "Evaluating Reliability of Internet Sources" in Chapter 23.)

***Note-Taking and Critical Reading***   While interviewing and reading, gather facts, statistics, expert opinion, cause and effect, reasons, and examples that constitute support for *both* sides. You will need to know the points of the opposing side so that you can refute them effectively. If you cannot answer the opposition's points by citing stronger evidence and better reasons, then your argument will not be convincing.

Take care to represent differing views fairly. That does not mean you give them equal space; you condense their main points. Try to spot anything that seems illogical, biased, or irresponsible. Write your notes in the margins of a copy or on cards. For detailed suggestions for critical reading, see Chapter 26.

***Making Con/Pro Lists***   You can simplify the task of organizing the chief points of a controversy by listing pros and cons while reading. To separate evidence against and for the proposition, just write *con* and *pro* at the top of a sheet of paper. Then as you read, list proof in two vertical columns, placing parallel points side by side. Leave plenty of white space between items to add notes. Follow each item with the name of the author and page number. This identification will save time later. The lists will resemble those below except that actual points and answers will be listed:

| *Con* | *Pro* |
|---|---|
| Main point (Barnes 140) | Agrees with facts, then disagrees about implications (Aker 39) |
| Main point (Barnes 141) | Objection and answer (Berry 149) |
| Main point (Smith 33) | Objection and answer (Conroy 12) |

## Stating a Position

After listing the significant points of disagreement for an argument, your next task is to select the viewpoint you think is sounder. Then write a proposition, indicating your position on the issue.

***Writing a Proposition***   The thesis statement of an argument is called the *proposition*. The tone of this statement is usually serious and much stronger than that of an ordinary thesis. To draft a proposition, you might start by rewriting your controlling question, then exploring its implications:

**Controlling question:** Since privacy issues are involved, should telemarketing firms be subject to restrictions?

**Possible thesis:** Telemarketing is an invasion of privacy that should not be permitted.

**Possible thesis:** Telemarketing is a legal right that should not be abridged.

***Taking a Position of Compromise***   Sometimes you may not agree wholeheartedly with either view; you see some validity in both views. If you reach an impasse, try a middle-of-the-road approach. Can you think of a way to modify your stand with a compromise that is acceptable to you? The examples below may suggest some ideas:

> **Compromise:** Telemarketing should not be permitted after 6 p.m.

> **Compromise:** Telemarketing by computerized dialing should not be allowed.

Each time you revise your thesis, check it carefully. Does it say what you mean? Could the terminology be confusing to the reader? Does it need to be revised further? Creating a focused title may also be helpful at this point.

***Writing a Focused Title***   A focused title acts like a thesis statement, clearly stating the proposition. Focused titles can be quite beneficial. You can glance back at the title from time to time to ensure that the argument is staying on course. A focused title indicates a position.

> **Focused title:** English Should Be Declared the Sole Official Language of Canada

> **Focused title:** Canada Should Keep Its Two Official Languages, English and French.

When an issue is heated, a writer may pose a question in the title to create a zone of neutrality. This zone allows the writer to present and evaluate the evidence before declaring a position in a *delayed thesis*. This *indirect approach* lowers the temperature of the argument and encourages consideration of differences. Although a neutral question title does not indicate a position, it does indicate a persuasive purpose:

> **Neutral question title:** Should English Be Declared Our Sole Official Language?

Although the neutral question title can be quite effective, your instructor may specify a focused title in order to simplify the writing of your paper. When misused, the neutral question title can lead to vague, rambling papers. Regardless of which kind of title you use, understanding the opposing view will assist in focusing your persuasive strategy.

## Planning the Shape of an Argument

There is no "one size fits all" strategy of argument. Arguments come in all shapes and sizes, depending on the rhetorical situation. Thus a writer is left to devise a strategy that will accommodate the situation in the best possible way. The structure of a logical argument consists of four basic parts: (1) making a claim (stating the purpose), (2) anticipating objections from readers, (3) countering objections by supporting the claim with solid evidence, and (4) submitting a conclusion derived from the evidence.

*Four Elements of a Logical Argument*

---

**Claim:** The specific proposition of a writer is the claim. A claim may be made directly or indirectly.

**Objections:** Knowing the main points of the opponents helps a writer answer objections effectively.

**Evidence:** A writer supports a claim with facts, interprets the facts, and explains—giving statistics, reasons, examples, or other evidence. (The most effective arguments contain an appeal designed to satisfy or benefit the reader.)

**Conclusion:** The end of an argument is often a restatement of the claim. It may be a summary of main points or a logical generalization. It may attempt to motivate the reader to act.

*Direct or Indirect Order: Early or Delayed Thesis?*   To organize an effective argument, you first consider whether to use direct or indirect order. In other words, will an early or a delayed thesis be more persuasive? How the four parts of the argument are arranged and developed depends on the implications of the topic and the probable impact on the audience. Think: How will the proposition be received by readers?

*Direct Approach*   If your readers are likely to be well informed and only mildly opposed to a proposition, you may decide to be direct and bring out the proposal early. Then the thesis can be stated in the introduction. Here is an example of a proposition that would probably meet with little resistance from employees who readily accept change:

**Early thesis:** A new system of billing will speed up the collection process and save an estimated $50,000 annually in collection costs.

*Indirect Approach*   An indirect plan, on the other hand, allows you to delay your thesis until much later in the paper. A delayed thesis allows you to consider the main points of the other side before mentioning your points. This arrangement sets the stage for a congenial discussion. Often it is wise to treat an argument as a misunderstanding or a difference in perception. This low-key approach is less likely to be perceived as threatening or combative. Any hint of antagonism, sarcasm, impatience, or superiority will undermine your stand. A reader who is patronized or derided may be offended. Negative undertones can sabotage the flawless logic of an argument.

Readers who are likely to be uninformed or hostile will require more facts and reasons than will readers who are well informed. You will need to lay extra groundwork for your recommendation. The stronger the objection, the more time you will need to prepare them to accept the proposition. As long as the path of an argument is clear, the thesis statement may be postponed until the body or conclusion.

**Delayed thesis:** Genetic engineering of food crops can be beneficial.

Sometimes, however, a thesis is implicit (unstated). Still, the argument is focused on one unmistakable conclusion. Since arguments with implicit theses require considerable skill, they are best left to experienced writers. Most instructors require an explicit thesis to aid in establishing the direction of an argument. Regardless of the type of argument you write, stress the benefits, advantages, and strengths of your proposal.

***Presenting Opposing Viewpoints***    To set the tone for a calm, courteous discussion, place the opposing view *before* your own. This method acknowledges the main points of the opposition and shows that you have considered the evidence. This arrangement is akin to listening, indicating a willingness to suspend judgment. This makes your argument stronger, because it emphasizes your answers to the opposing point of view.

When you are *for* an issue, the argument is simpler for most students to organize: *Take the pro side of the issue and place it second:*

(*Opposing view*) Opponents of gambling

(*Pro view*) Proponents of gambling

But when you are *against* an issue, setting up the terminology takes more thought. The order of the viewpoints is *reversed*. (Just remember that your view always comes second.) To prevent possible confusion in your notes, clearly label points of view and place them at the top of your lists of points:

(*Other view*) Proponents of gambling

(*Your view*) Opponents of gambling

After points of view are clearly identified, consider whether to present the argument in block or alternating (point-by-point) form. An outline is essential to keep the argument on track.

---

### FACTORS TO CONSIDER IN PLANNING AN ARGUMENT

1. What does the audience believe about the issue?
2. How does the audience feel about the issue?
3. Which order will be most effective: direct or indirect?
4. What kind of title will be most effective?
5. How much transition will be needed to make points of view clear?

***Block and Alternating Organization***    There are two basic ways to set up a controversial topic. The simplest is the block method. This way the main points of the opposing side appear in one chunk right after the introduction. One paragraph is usually adequate for this *summary of the opposing view.* Then in the next several paragraphs, you answer *all* the points raised and submit *evidence* to support your reasoning. The block method has an advantage in tone. Describing the opponent's view first not only conveys a sense of fairness but also postpones disagreement.

When an issue is complex, the alternating method is clearer than the block. The alternating pattern pairs one of the opposing points with one of yours, arguing back and forth, emphasizing your answers. (In Figure 19.1, each box represents a paragraph, although others could be added.) A possible disadvantage of alternating is that disagreement emerges earlier than in the block method. Then too, the alternating method requires extra transition.

An unanswered point poses a serious flaw in any argument. If you cannot answer a point adequately and decide to reverse your original position in the argument, it is fine to do so. It shows you have an open, logical mind.

Usually, main points are arranged in least- to most-important order so that the argument builds gradually. The best point is placed last, where it receives the most emphasis. To plan a paper on a controversy, the following questions will be helpful:

*Questions for Shaping a Controversial Topic*

1. What is at stake? Is there a hidden agenda?
2. Where is the best spot for the proposition? (Direct or indirect order?)
3. Is a definition needed?
4. How much background information will be needed?
5. Is there a common ground?
6. Can any concessions be made?
7. What are the advantages to accepting the proposition?
8. Are there disadvantages?
9. Will the block or alternating method be more suitable?
10. What is the best way to conclude the argument?

## Drafting a Neutral Introduction

The purpose of an introduction is to present a factual overview of the argument. The introduction describes the issue and its origin, cause(s), and history. The introduction tells *when, who, what, how,* and perhaps *why,* defining the area of disagreement. The appeal is primarily logical: The tone is neutral. If readers are familiar with a topic, background information may be brief. If a topic is unfamiliar, the introduction should be more detailed.

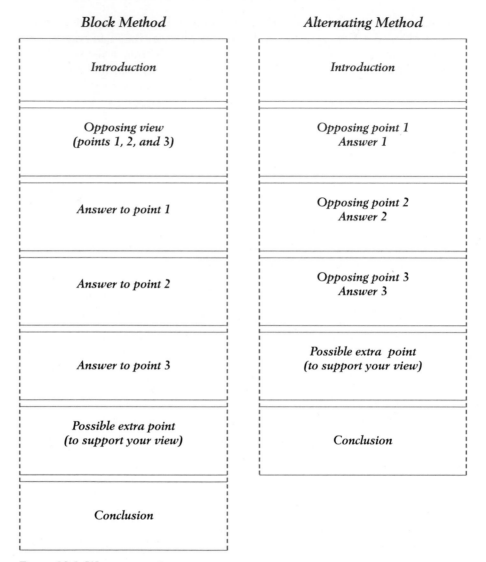

**Figure 19.1** Ways to organize an argument.

In this student introduction, Pamela J. Van Camp begins with a definition. Then she gives logical reasons why so many people are turning to alternative medical treatments. At the end of the paragraph, she introduces the element of risk.

### Alternative Medicine Has a Healthy Attraction

*Alternative medicine* is a term that describes nonconventional medical practices such as chiropractic, meditation, yoga, acupuncture, and herbal remedies. In the past two decades in the United States, more and more people are seeking alternative treatment. One reason for this growing trend is that people are looking for effective medical help without the side effects that often come with conventional medicine (Peeke 92). They are also attracted by the mind-body connection that alternative therapies claim to address for their total health (92). Many of the alternative medicine patients are well-educated people who pay for treatments out of pocket (Patel 49–50). Some are terminally ill and desperately seeking a cure even though it may carry a risk.

## Finding Common Ground

Agreement sets the scene for mutual respect. A point of agreement or *common ground* increases the chances that a proposition will receive thoughtful consideration from readers who disagree. Common ground can be a shared interest, a belief, an understanding, or a goal.

A common ground prepares the reader for a reasonable argument. In a paper about aspartame, Rita Fleming provides facts and advantages before presenting disadvantages:

> Nearly "180 times sweeter than sugar," aspartame is the most popular low-calorie sweetener available today. Each year over "100 million Americans consume carbonated beverages, iced tea, desserts, presweetened cold cereal and other products" sweetened with aspartame (Farber 52). NutraSweet has been referred to as a "dieter's dream" since it contains few calories, and many products containing aspartame have been labeled "low calorie" (*Sweeteners* 49).

To settle on a common ground, a writer not only presents facts but also listens to the connotations of words. Ill-chosen phrases can inflame feelings. But tactful words create an air of peaceful deliberation.

## Acknowledging and Clarifying Points of Agreement

While analyzing the main points of the opposing view, watch for a way to grant a point or clarify what you mean. To show agreement with the opposition's point, acknowledge it with a word or phrase such as *certainly, granted, it is true, proponents agree,* or *advocates recognize.* Then present the related pro point. The following phrases or similar ones might be used according to the purpose:

- It is true that . . . but . . .
- Proponents realize that . . . , yet they believe . . .
- Supporters recognize . . . ; still they do not acknowledge . . .
- This is not say that . . . but to . . .
- _____ argues that . . .
- _____ claims that . . .but [include evidence] reveals . . .
- In short, the opponents believe . . . because . . .

## Refuting Opposing Points

To refute means to show that the information of claim is irrelevant or just partly true or completely false. In answering opposing points, avoid any hint of disrespect or antagonism; be respectful and friendly. When you show respect for the reader's points, your chances for acceptance of the proposition will increase. To be convincing, a writer needs adequate evidence. The opinion of just one authority is inadequate; multiple sources are required. Opinion must be substantiated by facts, reasons, and examples. As a rule, the more evidence, the more convincing the argument, but do not oversell.

Select the most noteworthy points of the argument. Use quality evidence. Weak evidence will not support a claim for long. Careful readers will be apt to spot distortions, omissions, quotations taken out of context, or other problems. There must be solid proof that the proposition is logical, beneficial, and ethical. Only a sound, ethical argument will stand up under intense scrutiny.

## Dodging Fallacies

For an argument to be effective, the logic must be impeccable. A writer who misquotes, transposes statistics, misdiagnoses cause and effect, or trips over hasty generalizations may be perceived as careless, uninformed, biased, or manipulative. Although name-calling, exaggeration, or other blunders may be discounted in conversation, readers are unlikely to be so patient or forgiving. (See Chapter 20 for more on fallacies.) Let's consider two fallacies from papers:

> The most annoying thing in the world is to pick up the telephone after a long day at work and find a telemarketer at the other end of the line.
>
> A voluntary national service would solve the United States's problems.

Both claims are hasty generalizations. Certainly there are greater annoyances than a telephone interruption, and no one action could possibly solve the numerous problems faced by the United States. Another common fallacy is assuming that a complex problem results from a single cause. *Rarely does a complex problem have only one cause.* For example, presidents are often blamed for problems existing long before they took office. The truth is that many factors influence complicated problems.

A final precaution to keep in mind is that *an analogy cannot constitute proof.* Although valid analogies are useful for explanation, they prove nothing.

## Writing a Conclusion

A conclusion is the final nail in the building of an argument. The conclusion should be sound, appropriate, and complete. It should not stray into irrelevancies, fail to take a stand, or end abruptly. It should leave the reader persuaded that the reasoning is valid and worthy of consideration. If action is advocated, the tone should convey a sense of immediacy, a feeling that impels the reader to act. Rita Fleming closes with a reference to risk:

Although the FDA has allowed aspartame to remain on the market, a look at the history of this chemical raises severe doubts about its long-term safety for everyone. The risks of using this product regularly far outweigh any advantages.

To be forceful and complete, most arguments need a restatement of the thesis. Restatement redirects the reader's attention to the proposition, as in the following example. Kathy Kerchner writes:

> Finally, the use of restraints is a prime concern in geriatric facilities. Research on physical or mechanical restraint use is vague, and more is needed. For many confused residents, restraints are harmful in the long run. If a restraint not only denies freedom and dignity for the aged, but also leads to disorientation, then justification for use must outweigh possible consequences. Caregivers should exhaust all other alternatives before applying a restraint and continue to reevaluate its need from time to time.

Kathy's ending is one of compromise. She realizes that there is no one solution for all situations or all patients at all times. Still, she takes a firm stand, pointing out the dangers of long-term use of restraints.

## Revising an Argument

Reviewing your outline will help you check the organization of your paper. Could the order be improved? Would any section or subsection fit better in another spot? Reread the paper and check it with the outline as you go. Do you see any discrepancies? This method forces you to look more closely at work that has become familiar. Using a checklist will help you guard against omissions.

In summary, to build an effective argument about a controversial topic, you should (1) define the disagreement, (2) find the area of resistance or dissent, (3) respect the audience, and (4) ensure that evidence is logical and ethical.

---

### CHECKLIST: REVISING AN ARGUMENT

1. Is the issue clearly defined?
2. Does the introduction have a neutral tone?
3. Has a common ground been established?
4. Are points of view clearly identified?
5. Are main points of the opposition presented fairly?
6. Is adequate evidence presented to refute each opposing point?
7. Is the logic sound?
8. Is the language calm and rational?
9. Does the conclusion restate the position?
10. Is the organization clear to the reader?

## FOR YOUR REFERENCE: ARGUMENTATIVE ESSAYS IN THE READER

- "Why College Grads Get Jobs," Robert Sheppard, page 491
- "It's just money, honey," Irshad Manji, page 499
- "The Other Difference between Boys and Girls," Richard M. Restak, page 502
- "We Have No 'Right to Happiness,'" C. S. Lewis, page 508

## SUMMARY

- A *classic* argument combines three appeals: logical, ethical, and emotional; in order to create an effective argument, assess the rhetorical situation and combine appeals appropriately.
- An argument has a basic premise or underlying belief called the proposition. This belief is the starting point of the argument. An argument can make any of five basic claims: claims of fact, interpretation, cause, judgment, or policy.
- Before taking a definite stand, thoroughly research your topic. You might begin by writing a controlling question to direct your research. Making notes in a con/pro format will simplify your analysis of the issue.
- An effective argument has four basic parts: claim (thesis), objection, evidence, and conclusion. For cases in which there is only mild opposition, the thesis may be stated directly and early. When faced with strong opposition, however, the thesis is generally stated indirectly and is delayed. An argument on an issue can be arranged in block or alternate block order. Main points are usually placed in order from least to most important.
- In your *introduction*, describe the background to the issue and define disagreement. Include areas of agreement, if any. In the *body* of your paper, summarize opposing points if using the block method. For the alternating method, place objections and refutations in pairs. Counter each objection with logical evidence. Your *conclusion* should be suitable and complete.

## *Practice*

### Writing Exercise: Examining Opposing Points of View

*Directions:* Select a topic. Write two paragraphs from two *contrasting* points of view. Separate the paragraphs and indicate the person speaking. Be biased and emotional if the occasion calls for it.

1. *Animal Control.* Your town council is considering hiring an animal control officer because of complaints about stray cats, bats, and raccoons. You are a citizen with high property taxes who thinks the officer is unnecessary. You have varmint-proofed your home yourself and cats are not a problem. Next, write from the point of view of a citizen who has had his flowers dug up, his sleep disturbed, and a car scratched by cats. Raccoons have invaded his attic, and he is afraid they may have rabies.

2. *Deadline.* At 4:30 p.m. your boss hands you ten pages of a draft with numerous red-penciled changes. The typed project report is due at 8 a.m. tomorrow. He plans to revise the last six pages while you correct the first ten pages. You have a dinner date and know the job will take at least an hour. You normally work until 5 p.m. Write from your boss's point of view and from your point of view.

3. *Dental charge.* A busy dentist has a policy that if a patient misses an appointment without cancelling, a minimum charge of $25 is added to the bill. A woman who missed her appointment because she took her injured child (who suffered a broken arm) to the emergency room is protesting the extra charge. Write from the dentist's point of view, then from the woman's point of view.

4. *Broken window.* A ten-year-old has just batted a softball through the thermopane window of a neighbour's house. It landed on the dining room table while she was entertaining dinner guests. One guest received a nick on the face from flying glass. Write the batter's version of the event and then the neighbour's.

5. *Ball game.* Imagine you are two reporters writing accounts of the same game. One reporter favours the hometown team; the other does not.

## Workplace Issues for Discussion

1. You do not have enough money to buy your lunch. Is it all right to borrow $5 from your cash register and return the money after you get paid that evening? (You will be returning after dinner to work overtime.) Why or why not?

2. Is it all right to use your company's computer to print ten posters for a garage sale you are planning? Why or why not?

3. Is it ethical to use the company computer during work time to send several email messages to friends? To chat online? Give reasons for your answer.

4. Two office mates (one is married) are having a romance that has affected their productivity. How should the employer intervene?

5. In a foreign country where bribes are a part of the economic system, is it all right for a Canadian factory owner to offer a bribe to a purchasing agent? Why or why not?

## *Ten Ideas for Papers of Argument*

1. Should violent, "disturbed" students be permitted to attend public schools? What alternatives exist?
2. Refusal of insurance: Reasonable risk or genetic discrimination?
3. Nuclear Power: Revival or Relapse?
4. Should "nonalcoholic" beer (0.5 percent) be sold to minors?
5. Does "zero tolerance" in public schools make sense?
6. Should children under sixteen be sentenced as adults?
7. Should athletic teams be suspended for repeated poor sportsmanship leading to violence?
8. Should the legal driving age be lowered or raised?
9. Should "great books" courses be revived in high schools?
10. Should copyright protection apply to Internet content?

# CHAPTER 20

# Detecting Fallacies

**Learning Objectives:**

After reading and applying the information in Chapter 20, you'll be able to:

- Identify the eight most common logical fallacies
- Identify the seven most common emotional fallacies
- Be better able to identify and analyze fallacies in others' writing and to avoid them in your own

> *Doubt is often the beginning of wisdom.*
>
> —M. Scott Peck
> *The Road Less Traveled and Beyond*

You've probably seen dozens of stories circulating on the Internet, but how many have you questioned? An Internet search for "urban legends" demonstrates just how many specious tales are circulating. Have you heard the one about the professor who gave a one-word final exam?

Studying the chief logical and emotional fallacies will help you spot distortions in research, as well as daily life, and avoid them in your own writing. *Logical fallacies* often happen in three ways—through omission, oversimplification, or exaggeration. As we appraise an event or situation, we may overlook, ignore, or deemphasize a significant factor; or we may overemphasize another. Then we make incorrect assumptions. *Emotional fallacies* are more easily recognized by appeals to feelings. They contain a pitch designed to override logical judgment.

## LOGICAL FALLACIES

Logical fallacies are false beliefs caused by errors in reasoning. Unless you stop to think and question, the errors may seem plausible and persuasive. Logical fallacies can be found in everyday conversation, talk shows, chat rooms, political speeches, advertising, published writing, and student papers. Histories, biographies, and other works may contain distortions, misinformation, or fabrications. There are eight common logical fallacies:

*Eight Common Logical Fallacies*

1. Card stacking
2. Either/or fallacy
3. False analogy
4. Red herring
5. Begging the question/circular argument
6. Hasty generalization
7. Non sequitur
8. The post hoc fallacy

## Card Stacking

*Card stacking* (stacking the deck) is an act of slanting, distorting, or fabricating facts to suit the speaker's or writer's purpose. This fallacy involves misrepresentation, either intentional or unintentional. Although card stacking is unethical, scientific researchers have been known to fudge facts in order to support an illogical conclusion. To save time, they may take unethical shortcuts or falsify data. Or they may select only the facts that support a theory, omitting other evidence. Sooner or later such practices usually are discovered and discredited.

But what are we to make of polls and studies from reputable sources that report widely varying results? As you gather data, be aware that research methods can be flawed in various ways. The way that questions are worded can influence the answers that are given. Then, too, when respondents are asked to recall data or events, their memories may falter. The size and kind of population samples may also vary, resulting in different responses. Keep in mind that *the sample must represent the general population to produce reliable results.* (See "How Can One Be Objective?" in Chapter 18 and "Observation" in Chapter 22.)

Sometimes students unintentionally "stack the deck" while doing research for papers. They may have too few sources to provide objective coverage. Insignificant details may be exaggerated or significant details underemphasized. Important facts may be omitted through carelessness or insufficient research.

## Either/Or Fallacy

The *either/or fallacy* occurs when we assume there are only two sides to an issue or two alternatives for a problem when there are actually more. Sometimes this fallacy is called the "fallacy of false alternatives." Basically, the either/or fallacy presents the writer's view as the only correct alternative. The either/or fallacy is a simplistic judgment that may occur as a result of glancing at a problem and jumping to a conclusion. On bumper stickers you may have seen this fallacy in slogans such as "Make love, not war" and "America: Love it or leave it."

When speaking to voters, office seekers often oversimplify the country's policy-making process. For example, the either/or fallacy is apparent in this statement, voiced by a presidential candidate: "Either elect me and have a truly democratic government or elect one of my opponents and continue as we are." His either/or claim overlooks the possibility of change by other political candidates.

## False Analogy

The fallacy of *false analogy* hinges upon an invalid comparison. Just as an invalid cheque will not clear a bank's requirements, neither will a false analogy clear a test of logic. In this fallacy two cases or items are compared and assumed to be similar although they are basically different. A conclusion that is true for one is assumed to be true for the other. You may have heard someone say, "We tried this before, and it didn't work." But conditions may have changed since the first attempt, or the way the alternative was applied may have counteracted its effectiveness. Two cases are seldom the same.

A false analogy exaggerates similarity, making the comparison illogical and unsound. The fundamental problem with a false analogy is that it ignores a basic difference in the two cases. For example, a few years ago a group of citizens who lived in an earthquake-prone state argued for underground rail systems, pointing out that such systems have worked well in other states. The analogy was false, however, since the successful systems were located in states with little earthquake activity. A false analogy can be revealed by pointing out a significant difference.

## Red Herring

The fallacy called *red herring* drags in a side issue to distract the audience from the main issue. This fallacy is rather like the tactic that burglars in old movies often used, carrying steak along to throw to the watchdog before robbing the mansion. In the red herring fallacy, the writer suddenly tosses the reader a "bone," an irrelevant point, to avoid proving the original claim. In other words, the subject is abruptly changed in order to divert attention from the real issue.

Using the red herring fallacy, a speaker or writer attempts to prove a point by leapfrogging to an irrelevancy. For example, "the mayor is a man of integrity; he is a church member and a fine family man." But the discerning listener or reader knows the mayor's church membership and family status do not necessarily prove he has integrity. No real proof has been submitted.

## Begging the Question/Circular Argument

In the fallacy of *begging the question*, or *circular argument*, the argument sidesteps the issue. Here the word *question* refers not to sentence structure, but to the subject under discussion. When a question is "begged," it is not discussed. To avoid giving a direct answer, people may hide their beliefs in a thicket of words. Begging the question in this case is simply empty talk that ducks the issue.

Statements that beg the question can be short or long. They may employ phrases such as "everyone knows," "the fact is," or "obviously" when the opposite is true. An example is "Everyone knows it is not safe to swim for an hour after eating." Students sometimes beg the question when writing essay answers on tests and exams. They pile up words in an attempt to disguise the fact they lack the answer—they neglect to provide support.

When an argument avoids confronting an issue by restating a premise, we call it a *circular argument*. For example, "Football is entertaining because it is such an enjoyable sport" or "Irrelevant courses such as ancient history are a waste of time." In neither case has proof been offered. The reader is asked to agree with the first part of each statement. The argument moves in a circle by repeating the claim in different words. The issue is dodged, and the proposition is assumed to be true.

## Hasty Generalization

A *hasty generalization* is a broad general statement that lacks adequate support. The writer misstates, exaggerates, or minimizes the facts. Hasty generalizations are assumptions that occur in various ways. Three of the most common are (1) presenting inferences as fact, (2) stereotyping, (3) taking a small or atypical sample of a group and generalizing about a larger group or population.

Hasty generalization can be averted by careful, accurate word choice to reflect the facts. You can identify opinions and qualify generalizations so that they are accurate. You can avoid absolute terms unless adequate evidence is available. When conducting research, you can secure a representative sample.

See "Writing Responsibly," Chapter 6.

A hasty generalization may resemble the non sequitur (both contain inferences), but the hasty generalization does not set up a false cause and effect as the non sequitur does. Nor does the hasty generalization refer to specific instances as the non sequitur does.

## Non Sequitur

Translated from Latin, the phrase *non sequitur* simply means "it does not follow." Such fallacies contain faulty assumptions about cause-and-effect relationships. In other words, a cause is asserted for an effect, but the effect "does not follow" logically from the cause. Non sequiturs may use words such as *because*, *therefore*, and *if . . . then*, and they may be attempts to persuade someone to do something. A student may claim, for example, "I should get an A on this paper because I spent thirty hours working on it and handed it in two days early." But the quality of the paper does not necessarily follow from either of the two reasons offered for a good grade.

Non sequiturs may appear in predictions: "Because Marilyn vos Savant is listed in the *Guinness Book of World Records* as having the highest IQ on record, she would make an excellent president." The fallacy here is in assuming that the chief requirement for the presidency is stellar intelligence. Jimmy Carter, for example, was highly intelligent, but many historians consider him among the poorer presidents.

## The Post Hoc Fallacy

One evening in New York City, so the story goes, a small boy kicked a lamppost. At that moment the lights went out all over the city; a power blackout had occurred. Yet the boy thought he had caused the power failure. This kind of thinking illustrates the post hoc fallacy: Because one event follows another, the first is thought to have caused the second. But there is no evidence of a connection:

| | |
|---|---|
| **Facts:** | Event A: Boy kicked lamppost. |
| | Event B: Power blackout. |
| **Post hoc fallacy:** | A caused B. (Because event B followed event A, A is assumed to have caused B.) |

The full Latin name of this fallacy is *post hoc ergo propter hoc*, meaning "after this, therefore because of this." Although no proof is offered, this fallacy assumes that one event or condition was caused by another. The truth is that the two events or conditions only *correlate*, meaning they exist together but do not interact upon or influence one another.

We have all heard similar post hoc fallacies: Bad luck is often attributed to breaking a mirror, walking under a ladder, or stepping on a crack. And you probably know other fallacies based on superstitions. Hundreds, perhaps thousands, of years ago, these beliefs sprang up because two events happened one after the other. Perhaps someone broke a mirror and cut a foot severely. Someone else may have walked under a ladder and broken a leg soon after. In each case, the first event was blamed for causing the second.

### *The Pattern of Superstitious Thinking: A Post Hoc Fallacy*

*Part 1:* Superstition: Handling toads causes warts. (A causes B.)

*Part 2:* Because Shawn handled a toad and the following week a wart appeared on his thumb, the toad caused the wart. (Therefore, A caused B.)

A systems analyst says that his subordinates seldom have trouble with any fallacy except the post hoc. Once in a while a team member will seize on an obvious but incorrect cause for a problem. The member errs in assuming that two factors have a cause-and-effect relationship when they merely correlate.

To avoid confusing the fallacies of cause and effect, notice that post hoc involves two events that occur in sequence whereas the non sequitur has only one. If a statement contains both fallacies, label it post hoc. For your convenience, the following list summarizes the main distinctions between post hoc and non sequitur.

| *Post hoc* | *Non sequitur* |
|---|---|
| • Two sequential events or conditions. (A apparently caused B) | • Only one fact or event plus an inference. |
| • No proof that the first event caused (or will cause) the second. | • Only an opinion, often a prediction. |

## EMOTIONAL FALLACIES

We are bombarded with emotional fallacies every day. When we drive past a billboard, open a magazine, or turn on a television set, we are exposed to cleverly planned propaganda. Usually, the propaganda contains emotional fallacies designed to arouse strong feelings and impel us to buy products, donate money, or accept ideas. The propagandists know that if they can trigger strong feelings, then logic may be dethroned and emotion rule. *Emotional fallacies not only conflict with logical thinking but also interfere with fairness and objectivity.*

Understanding these fallacies can help you to both resist and detect them in your research and writing. This is not to say that all emotional appeals are to be avoided. Some emotional appeals attempt to persuade honestly and fairly.

An emotional appeal may be warranted in an argument, but the emotion should be controlled and ethical. A modicum of emotion may also be appropriate in other kinds of writing. To decide, you need an alert eye and a sensitive ear. Deceit is never acceptable.

In most emotional fallacies, *transfer* plays an important role. Transfer is a device of association that uses the connotations of words and pictures to manipulate our responses. The idea is to carry positive connotations over to products, ideas, or people. Positive transfer presents products in the most attractive way possible with appealing names and surroundings. Commercials for some products, for instance, portray endearing family scenes—perhaps of children, puppies, or kittens. On the other hand, negative transfer is often used in political campaigns to disparage opponents, as in name-calling. Eight common emotional fallacies are discussed here:

### *Seven Common Emotional Fallacies*

1. Argumentum ad hominem/straw man
2. Bandwagon
3. Status appeal
4. Scare tactics
5. Testimonial
6. Improper appeal to authority
7. Glittering generality

### Argumentum ad Hominem/Straw Man

In an *ad hominem* argument, a person's character or appearance is assaulted. Name-calling, mudslinging, and smear tactics are all forms of *argumentum ad hominem* ("against the man"). A sly variation of ad hominem uses derisive humour to discredit. A personal characteristic that is irrelevant to performance becomes the subject of joking. For example, Bill and Jill are arguing about cleaning out their closets:

**Jill:** "We should clean out the closets. They are getting a bit messy."

**Bill:** "Why, we just went through those closets last year. Do we have to clean them out every day?"

**Jill:** "I never said anything about cleaning them out every day. You just want too keep all your junk forever, which is just ridiculous." (source: *The Nizkor Project* (2005). www.nizkor.org/features/fallacies/straw-man.html)

The *straw man* fallacy, a similar assault, is as flimsy as it sounds—lacking weight or evidence. The argument attacks an opponent or a group with a trumped-up charge or issue that is easily defeated or refuted.

Both *ad hominem* and straw man fallacies are unethical and impractical. The persons who indulge in name-calling, backbiting, and false charges endanger their own credibility and careers. Students who indulge in these fallacies lose points and credibility as writers.

## Bandwagon

Another emotional fallacy urges everyone "to jump on the bandwagon," to go along with the crowd. *Bandwagon* is the fallacy of common practice—the "everyone's doing it, so you should, too," argument. Peer pressure is exerted to exploit the desire to belong to a group or to do what other people are doing. The fallacy also capitalizes on the belief that the majority knows best.

Ads and commercials using the bandwagon appeal often show large groups of happy people using the same product and enjoying the results. For example, ads for soft drink commercials feature explicit entreaties such as "Join the Pepsi Generation." In McDonald's commercials about "happy meals" for children, bandwagon is implicit. The bandwagon fallacy focuses on common ties of family, nationality, race, age, gender, job, or special interest. Thus the propagandist may call upon us to do something as Canadian citizens, Polish Canadians, men, women, baby boomers, truck drivers, or members of another group.

## Status Appeal

The old saying "keeping up with the Joneses" illustrates status appeal, or snob appeal as it is sometimes called. *Status appeal* is a pitch to better oneself by wearing stylish clothes, driving expensive cars, taking exotic vacations, or buying whatever a company sells that requires lavish spending. For example, a commercial for a well-known car uses status appeal: "It's the difference between just getting there and truly arriving." Such commercials feature attractive people, dressed in stylish attire, who purchase top-of-the-line luxuries. The implication is that the viewer can be like them by buying and using the manufacturer's product.

Status appeal is the opposite of plain folk. Whereas plain folk can arouse friendly feelings when appropriately used, status appeal may antagonize, even when used appropriately. The applications for status appeal are limited. Unless you are a marketing major who creates advertising copy or writes sales brochures or a business communications student who writes sales letters, you will probably not use the status appeal in your college writing. Nonetheless, you need to be aware of it so that you can recognize it and deal with it appropriately.

## Scare Tactics

We encounter appeals daily that use *scare tactics*. These appeals attempt to manipulate us into accepting a product, message, or person. Often the danger is exaggerated, and other alternatives do exist. For example, some insurance ads use scare tactics to sell policies. One ad showed a mother holding a young child in her arms with the caption "What will they do when you are gone?"

But scare tactics can also warn the public of possible hazards. For example, warnings about the dangers of small children drinking household cleaners or the danger of unattached safety belts are a public service. In some cases, alarming statistics are given and frightening pictures shown (such as an accident caused by a drunk driver) to motivate people to protect themselves and their families.

In research papers, scare tactics are best avoided. A calm, objective tone and a logical approach that stresses benefits is the most effective way to persuade. In a process paper, a legitimate warning may be imperative.

## Testimonial and Improper Appeal to Authority

Because Tiger Woods gives a testimonial for Titleist golf balls, a television viewer may be convinced to purchase some. Other athletes have plugged a variety of goods from shaving lotion to snuff. The *fallacy* inherent in a *testimonial* is the assumption that something is true or good just because a well-known person says so. Never forget that unless stated otherwise, the person giving the testimony has been paid by the sponsor.

Political testimonials for candidates are often given in election campaigns. Although a well-known public figure may endorse a relatively unknown candidate, we should keep in mind that endorsements are a form of patronage, an exchange of political favours. In student writing, testimonials seldom appear, but a related fallacy sometimes occurs—improper appeal to authority.

An *improper appeal to authority* is the giving of testimony by well-known persons about a particular field in which they are unqualified. The so-called authority, lacking relevant credentials, claims something is true. Some instances of this fallacy may be harmless; nonetheless, deception is inherent. For example, when physicians, researchers, or other professionals step outside their fields of expertise, their claims become meaningless. In writing papers, consider the qualifications of the researcher as well as the validity of the claim.

## Glittering Generalities

*Glittering generalities* proffer fuzzy phrases that sound good but lack substance. In other words, these vague generalizations "glitter," but have little meaning. A glittering generality contains an undefined term. If people were called upon to define the term, they might respond with different definitions.

Glittering generalities use positive words to persuade us to accept a product or proposal without thinking. Loaded with positive connotations, these statements stir emotions and cloud thinking. Propagandists often use glittering generalities to appeal to our sense of fair play, brotherhood, or love. They sprinkle their talk with virtuous words such as *liberty, loyalty, patriotism, progress, truth, honour,* or *justice.* These words suggest ideals that all "good" people believe in. Glittering generalities play on the emotions, urging us to do something without examining the facts. For example:

> Ladies and Gentlemen, it is with the greatest pleasure that I welcome you to this most auspicious of occasions. We are gathered here on the brink of a challenge to which we must all rise in concert, for not to do so would be to accept despair, which I will never do and I know you will never accept. (source: ChangingMinds.org *"GlitteringGeneralities"* http://changingminds.org/techniques/propaganda/glittering_generalities.htm)

## DEALING WITH FALLACIES

Fallacies are dishonest arguments that cheat on the facts or use an overdose of emotion to beguile an audience. Although there may be temptations to resort to fallacious persuasion, this path is unwise from both an ethical and a practical standpoint. Ethically, we have the obligation to give readers and listeners the facts. Furthermore, in the long run, deception is invariably impractical. Chances are the truth will eventually emerge, and the reputation of an unethical writer or speaker will be tarnished.

You may become fascinated by finding and categorizing fallacies, but if you find it difficult to label a particular case, don't worry. Recognizing deceit, manipulation, and misstatement is what is important, not the label. By learning about fallacies, you can develop healthy skepticism as well as thinking skills.

This chapter is much more than an intellectual exercise. The most important lesson is to *apply* your learning. Thinking skills can be applied almost anywhere. Critical thinking is valuable in writing and revising papers, in your personal life, and in the workplace. Critical thinking can improve your self-image and professional image. Critical thinking used wisely can give you *power.*

## SUMMARY

- Critical thinking requires distinguishing facts from fallacies.
- *Logical fallacies* contain errors in reasoning. Eight common logical fallacies include card stacking, either/or, false analogy, red herring, begging the question, hasty generalization, non sequitur, and post hoc; subcategories of these also exist.
- *Emotional fallacies* are appeals that are overstated and designed to manipulate; they are propaganda techniques that attempt to overrule logic with a rush of feeling. Seven common emotional fallacies include: *argumentum ad hominem,* bandwagon, status appeal, scare tactics, testimonial, improper appeal to authority, and glittering generality.

> • It is both unethical and impractical to use fallacies in your writing. Understanding fallacies can help you to avoid them and to recognize deception and manipulation.

## Test Yourself

### Fallacy Review

Identify the following descriptions as examples of: argumentum ad hominem, red herring, hasty generalization, begging the question, either/or fallacy, false analogy, bandwagon, or post hoc fallacy.

_____ 1. A comparison that has more differences than likenesses.

_____ 2. Reasoning that states or assumes only two alternatives exist when there are actually more.

_____ 3. An attack upon a person's character.

_____ 4. Circular reasoning that assumes something is true and reads as if it were true. Circumvents the issue.

_____ 5. An appeal to follow the majority and do something because "everyone else is doing it."

_____ 6. Overstatement, an inference, based on inadequate evidence.

_____ 7. (After this, because of this.) This fallacy assumes that because one event occurs after another, the first caused the second.

_____ 8. A side issue presented to distract from the main issue.

### Acceptable or Hasty Generalizations?

*Directions:* Mark A for acceptable generalization or H for hasty generalization. Then check your answers at the end of the chapter.

1. Pit bulls are killers.
2. Women tend to score higher on vocabulary tests than men.
3. Most teenage drivers today are more reckless than those of other decades.
4. Left-handed folks are better at arithmetic than right-handed.
5. Beef is a versatile and nutritious food.

### Collaborative Learning: Identify the Fallacies

*Directions:* Identify the fallacy or propaganda device in each example.

1. As a burglar entered a home, a black cat dashed across the room. He opened a wall safe, emptied it, and continued to search. Suddenly, he was confronted by two policemen with drawn guns. At that moment he realized the cat was an omen. (The safe had an alarm.)

2. Mike wrote an argument paper using information from only two sources: a paid political advertisement and three pamphlets from the National Rifle Association. Discuss any problems you see with his sources and the quality of his evidence.

3. Excerpt from a student theme: "The mature person is *continuously* open, flexible, curious, and active." (*Hint:* See a dictionary.)

4. A ninety-year-old women makes her own wine using whole grapes. Recently she had a minor stroke, but is now completely recovered. She attributes her recovery to drinking three small glasses of her homemade wine daily. Do you agree with this reasoning? Why or why not?

5. Four-year-old Jill Smythe has won twenty beauty contests. Her mother has enrolled Jill at a school of dance, because she believes that Jill will become a movie star. Discuss this path of reasoning and where it leads.

## *Test Yourself Answers*

### Fallacy Review

1. *False analogy*
2. *Either/or fallacy*
3. *Argumentum ad hominem*
4. *Begging the question*
5. *Bandwagon*
6. *Hasty generalization*
7. *Post hoc ergo propter hoc*
8. *Red herring*

### Acceptable or Hasty Generalizations?

1. *H. Three breeds of dogs are classified as pit bulls. Not all are dangerous.*
2. *A. Fact. Tend to qualifies the statement, indicating a majority.*
3. *H. Opinion, a value judgment.*
4. *H. No evidence to substantiate this statement.*
5. *A. Fact. Beef can be prepared in many ways; it contains many nutrients.*

# Research Writing

## Part 5

# Preliminary Considerations for Research

## Learning Objectives

After reading and applying the information in Chapter 21, you'll be able to:

- Collect data by means of primary and secondary research
- Produce research findings that are reliable, accurate, and objective

*Learning without thought is labour lost;*
*thought without learning is perilous.*

> —Confucius (6th century BC)
> *Analects,* 2.15, trans. James Legge

In the Information Age, learning often involves research. Professionals in business, law, engineering, medicine, and other fields gather, digest, and condense large quantities of information during the course of their working day. In your professional life, you may observe sites and situations, interview prospective employees, or survey a group to gather opinions. You may analyze annual reports, budgets, government documents, court cases, medical journals, or other records.

In your college classes, you gather information for research papers and reports. A research project can help you acquire a wide range of career skills. It can afford opportunities to develop the ability to

- Plan and schedule your time
- Observe, interview, and survey
- Locate information in the library
- Find information on the Internet
- Summarize, paraphrase, and quote
- Analyze and evaluate
- Provide proper documentation for sources
- Meet deadlines

# PRIMARY AND SECONDARY RESEARCH

You can collect information in either of two general ways—by doing primary research or secondary research—or by combining the two. Collecting data first-hand is called *primary research*. You become the researcher and go to a *primary source*, one that has not been filtered through the eyes of another researcher. Whether you observe a class, interview someone, or survey a population sample, you conduct primary research. You may make careful notes, describing what happens and your perceptions. Or you may construct a questionnaire, administer it, and tabulate the responses. The data you collect become the basis for your report or paper.

*Secondary research* is the collecting of information that has passed through someone else's hands. You use *secondary sources;* someone else has conducted the research and recorded the original data. Usually, this information has been published and printed. You may find it in a library or on the Internet.

### Basic Guidelines for Research

1. For research to be reliable, the researcher must be accurate and objective in presenting findings and interpreting results.
2. Sources must be clearly identified.
3. Primary sources are preferable to secondary sources.
4. Both primary and secondary research requires *documentation*, a listing of the source, the date, the author, and other related data. Omission of documentation can result in plagiarism. See Chapter 24

A basic concept to remember throughout your project is that for research to be reliable, the researcher must be accurate and objective in presenting findings and in interpreting results.


## The Path to Objectivity

> There are three sides to every story—yours, mine, and all that lie between.
>
> **—Jody Kern**

Recently a National Public Radio panel discussed whether or not a reporter should include opinion in a news report of an overseas conflict. Should reporters give only the facts or should they put themselves into the story as well? Traditionally, reporting and other research have constituted a quest for truth, a search for facts, not an opportunity to express a personal view.

Researchers are still expected to step back from their own beliefs and emotions—to be as objective and unbiased as possible. To maintain professional integrity and reliability, they must be observant and open to new information. They must be competent and honest, able to identify and describe data accurately, and able to understand what is occurring. They must be willing to question their own perceptions, because optical illusions and misperception can occur.

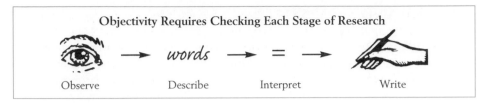

**Figure 21.1** Path to objective research.

To check for bias, researchers need to be keenly aware that observation, description, interpretation, and writing are *separate* stages of primary research (see Figure 21.1). Distortion can occur at any stage. To ensure accuracy, researchers must check their perceptions, word choice, interpretation, and final draft carefully.

## Fact or Idea?

Questioning the mental images, words, and inferences you derive through perception leads to objective writing. This doubting will help you differentiate fact from idea, which is not always easy. *Fact* is information generally accepted as real or true. But not all so-called facts are true. An *established fact* has been verified by substantial support/evidence. Some facts can be quickly verified through the five senses. Other facts are established through laboratory tests, control groups, and other measures.

In *The Modern Researcher*, fourth edition, Jacques Barzun defines an *idea* as "an image, inference, or suggestion that goes beyond the data [facts] nameable in conventional terms." This definition can guide you when the boundary between fact and idea blurs. Ask yourself if the information is entirely fact or if opinion has been injected. Is the information accepted by experts in the field as true or is it still in the realm of theory and unproven? Barzun explains, "An idea leads us on . . . . [It] suggests doubts and possibilities."

To test your alertness, consider the two sentences below. Which one is strictly fact? Which one mixes an idea with fact?

Paul Martin, a great prime minister, was elected in 2004.

Prime Minister Paul Martin was elected on June 28, 2004.

The first sentence contains the idea of greatness, which is a matter of opinion. Every word in the second sentence is factual. As you record data do not mix ideas with concrete facts. Ideas belong to a later stage, when you make inferences and derive a conclusion. Descriptions of observations should be precise and factual. Keep in mind, too, that the *image* you perceive may be incomplete or distorted, depending upon your vantage point and your knowledge of the subject. Try to ensure that you see all that happens.

Second, *choose words carefully*. Use neutral, concrete words, not emotionally charged language. Some words carry extra baggage—hidden meanings, associations, or opinions. For example, there is a big difference between "dozens of black-and-orange ladybugs have crept under my back door" (fact) and "dozens of spotted beetles have invaded my home" (idea). As you record data, avoid using words that reveal your opinion.

Third, *check interpretations and inferences*. Do they seem logical and reasonable, considering the observable facts? Do the inferences account for all the loose ends? Or are there conflicting data? If so, the conflict should be noted and discussed.

Fourth, *be tentative* in presenting interpretations and inferences. Use qualifiers such as *indicate, suggest, may, appear,* and *tend*. Remembering these precautions will help you attain objectivity.

## SCHEDULING RESEARCH TASKS

Regardless whether you do primary or secondary research, your project will require considerable time. If you interview, you will need to set up appointments, construct a list of questions, tabulate responses, and write a report of your findings. For secondary research, you will need to locate materials in the library or on the Internet. Reading, analyzing, and writing will require much time.

### Is a Schedule Really Necessary?

Procrastination may be tempting when the deadline for a research report or paper seems distant—perhaps a month or more away. But don't be lulled into complacency by believing you can draft a questionnaire or find all the books you need in an hour. Such misconceptions can lead to anxiety or even panic as your deadline looms.

A flexible schedule, tailored to your needs, can alleviate anxiety and increase efficiency. The first step is to list the tasks involved. The second step is to make a realistic estimate of the time required for each one. Keep in mind that if you are doing secondary research, you will need to locate specific information, compile source cards, read, and take notes. Writing a paper based on either primary or secondary research will require drafting, revising, editing, and proofreading. If possible, allow a little leeway here and there in your schedule.

As a safeguard, plan research tasks so that your final draft can be completed a day or two early. That way you can revise, edit, and proofread thoroughly. And should a minor emergency occur, you won't have to worry about finishing on time. Start soon so you will have the time to write a quality paper.

### Will the Internet Cut Research Time?

If you are adept at searching the Web and can find reliable and substantial information on your topic quickly, then you can save time in locating materials. But if you are a novice in cyberspace, it may take longer to locate sources on the Net than in the library. Research opportunities on the Internet are limited for several reasons:

1. Some sources on the Web are not reliable. The individual who posts the information may not be an authority or may not cite the source fully.
2. Free information on the Internet may be scant and superficial.
3. Many databases require *paid subscriptions*. They are available only at libraries or to patrons who have contracted for them.
4. Instructors often limit the number of online sources for a paper.

## TENTATIVE FIVE-WEEK SCHEDULE FOR SECONDARY RESEARCH

|  | Days Needed | Date to Complete |
|---|---|---|
| 1. Select a topic. Locate materials. Do preliminary reading. Start note cards and source cards. | 2–3 | _____ |
| 2. Limit topic, read, and write a controlling question. | 2 | _____ |
| 3. Read. Start a scratch outline. | 3 | _____ |
| 4. As you read, continue making note and source cards. | 3 | _____ |
| 5. Revise outline. Write thesis and start draft. | 3 | _____ |
| 6. Reread notes. Refine outline. Finish first draft. | 6 | _____ |
| 7. Return unneeded materials. Get more if needed. | 1 | _____ |
| 8. Read. Revise draft. Print out. | 4 | _____ |
| 9. Revise draft. Check order and format. Print. | 3 | _____ |
| 10. Alphabetize source cards. Type list of works cited. | 1 | _____ |
| 11. Revise, edit, and proofread several times. | 3 | _____ |
| 12. **Tentative deadline:** Proof again. Print final copy. | 1 | _____ |
| **Final deadline:** Submit research paper. | | _____ |

> ## SUMMARY
>
> - Collecting data yourself—gathering first-hand information—is known as doing primary research.
> - Collecting data generated by someone else—gathering second-hand information—is known as doing secondary research.
> - Research findings must be reliable, accurate, and objective.
> - A flexible schedule can alleviate stress and increase efficiency.

## *Practice*

### Drafting a Schedule

If your assignment calls for primary research, read Chapter 22, "Primary Research: Observation, Interviews, and Surveys" before drafting your schedule. For secondary research, read Chapter 23, "Secondary Research: Locating Print and Electronic Sources."

1. Choose your research topic and determine the best method or combination of methods to accomplish your purpose.
2. Prewrite: List all the tasks you will need to complete.
3. Draft: Copy your tasks in the order they will be done. At the bottom of the sheet, write *deadline*, followed by the due date.
4. If your instructor has included checkpoints, include those dates.
5. Determine the number of days until your deadline. Allot a few days to each task, making sure you do not run over the total number of days. Include a *tentative deadline* to allow for an emergency.
6. Check to see that your estimates are realistic. Revise as needed.

# *Primary Research*

## Observation, Interviews, and Surveys

---

**Learning Objectives**

After reading and applying the information in Chapter 22, you'll be able to:

- Conduct primary research through observations, interviews, surveys, or a combination of methods
- Narrow the topic and scope of research in order to create a clear and significant purpose
- Prepare questions for interviews
- Develop surveys and questionnaires
- Develop research papers and reports stating the purpose, scope, and findings

---

> *A prudent question is one-half of wisdom.*
>
> —Francis Bacon (1561–1626)

Recently a market research firm conducted focus groups of urban and suburban teens to determine which fads are in and which are out. The researchers asked questions, listened, and videotaped every word and gesture. From these observations, they predict new teen trends in various products from fast food to jeans. Corporate clients use the report to shape commercials and products to teen tastes.

## OBSERVATION

Observation can be done in other ways. In "Caterpillar Afternoon," Sue Hubbell, a naturalist, tells how she chanced upon a strange object, which appeared to be a snakeskin, lying on a dirt road. But when she knelt down, she found it was a mass of small, white, hairless caterpillars that exhibited unusual behaviour, especially when disturbed. Quite curious, she examined them and later searched through her library until she found a book that mentioned experiments with pine procession-aries by a nineteenth-century entomologist. Later, in an interview with another naturalist, Hubbell learned that such a sight was quite rare. Thus she combined primary and secondary research. (Hubbell's story is located in Part 7, The Reader.)

Observational research involves methodically watching a specimen, activity, interaction, or phenomenon and recording data. Observation can be done up close through the five senses or through cameras, tape recorders, X-ray machines, microscopes, radar, and other devices. The principal advantage of observation is that the observer sees the subject first-hand. And if strict standards are maintained, findings can be quite reliable. The principal disadvantage is that observation is limited to subjects verifiable through the senses. Observation is not a reliable method for testing attitudes or motives.

## Selecting a Site

To accurately assess specimens, situations, or behaviour, you need a certain amount of expertise. For instance, if enrolled in certain education courses, you might observe a class of school children. You could categorize their interactions with the teacher and one another, comment on patterns observed, and relate them to a course. Or, as a student who has taken several college courses, you might observe the instructional styles of several professors who teach the same course and rate their effectiveness. This would require more than your opinion; you would need to survey other students, too. Then you could compare responses.

Or you might observe the instructional styles of one instructor who teaches in two areas, perhaps composition and speech. The findings for the two areas might vary considerably. The disparity might be due to greater competency in one area, attitude of the instructor and of the students toward the subject; potential to use audiovisual aids, small groups, and humour; or other factors. Obtaining other students' opinions would make the research more valid.

## Preparing to Observe

Some research requires obtaining permission and making appointments. If you would like to tape your observation, this will require permission, which should be secured well in advance. Inquire as to when you should arrive and where you should sit so as to be unobtrusive.

Be prepared. Remember to take an extra pen and a note pad of convenient size. Devise a system to take notes, perhaps abbreviating, so that you can watch as much as possible. If you will be taping, check your supply of blank tapes and fresh batteries. Have the recorder working and ready to go with the flick of a switch. (Observing more than once will yield information to compare and verify impressions.)

## Keeping a Log

A detailed log of research data and results is essential. After you leave the site, rewrite and expand your notes as soon as possible. (The ability to recall falls off after one hour.) Flesh out the notes with precise details and examples of what happened. Your objective at this point is to record the facts, describing exactly what you saw and heard. Tell what occurred, under what conditions, the exact time of day, who was present, and other vital information. If an interaction occurred, describe it and the precise words said. Do not inject opinion.

Use quotation marks to enclose a comment or remark you include. Note nonverbal communication—gestures, frowns, smiles, touching, vocal intonations, and other nonverbal cues. Hold off on analysis and interpretation until you have the facts down on paper and have time to consider their meaning. To be as comprehensive and objective as possible, you need to look at the entire episode, not isolated fragments. The checklist below can help you expand your notes.

---

### CHECKLIST: MAINTAINING OBJECTIVITY

1. Observation
   - What do I see?
   - What do I hear?
   - What do I smell?
   - What do I taste?
   - What do I perceive by touch?
   - Is anything else significant?

2. Description
   - What are the physical features?
   - What behaviour is observable?
   - What interactions are occurring?
   - Would someone else agree?
   - Are the words neutral?

3. Interpretation
   - What might it mean?
   - What else might it mean?
   - Are the inferences logical?
   - Are the inferences unbiased?
   - Do inferences account for all events/behaviour?

4. Writing
   - Is the description neutral?
   - Is the interpretation logical?
   - Does the conclusion flow logically from observable data?
   - Is the conclusion fair?

---

Later you can analyze and look for links—common threads and patterns of behaviour. If you observed more than once, did similar or dissimilar interactions occur on different days? Describe your overall impression each time. Date each observation and record the hour. In some cases, morning or afternoon can make a difference in activities and behaviour.

# INTERVIEWS

An interview is sometimes defined as a conversation with a purpose. Employers conduct interviews to hire, appraise, debrief, and fire employees. Computer sales reps interview clients to ascertain system needs. Journalists interview politicians, seeking news and feature stories. Policemen interview witnesses and interrogate suspects. Lawyers interview clients to establish a defense. As a part of your primary research, you might conduct interviews to learn more about a community problem, the history of your city, the underground railroad, or another topic.

## Types of Interviews

Telephone interviews allow you to contact more people than face-to-face interviews do. But you usually gain less information since most people are less inclined to volunteer details to a faceless, unknown caller. Successful telephone interviews require lessening interviewees' suspicion and gaining their trust. Telephoning, however, may be a quick alternative when face-to-face interviews are cancelled and you lack time to schedule more.

Talking face-to-face takes longer than telephoning but yields more information. Face-to-face interviews require planning and persistence. You have to call ahead, request appointments, and then travel. If an appointment is suddenly cancelled, you may need to reschedule or find an alternative. Yet face-to-face interviews are worth the extra effort because you gain more details and make contacts that may prove beneficial.

***Informational Interviewing***   Informational interviews allow you to research family history, a product, or other topics. For a college research project, you might obtain pre-employment information about your career field. If you do, keep in mind that informational interviews are not a job search although they may lead to a position later. An employer is apt to be kindly disposed to someone who is motivated to conduct pre-employment research and to prepare a list of well-crafted questions. For example, you could ask about skills needed for a position, training offered, responsibilities, starting salary range, travel, chances for advancement, and related questions.

Before going to any interview, consider your choice of apparel carefully. If you are interviewing an elderly relative in her home, casual dress is appropriate. But if you are doing a pre-employment interview, dress as if you were applying for a job. Before you leave, convey your appreciation to the interviewee.

***Unstructured versus Structured Interviews***   *Unstructured* interviews are casual, with no set format. They may elicit information that would not surface in a structured interview, but they are time-consuming and difficult to compare if you are doing a series. In an unstructured interview, interviewer and interviewee often contribute equally to the conversation. Yet authorities on interviewing recommend a 30 to 70 percent ratio, with the interviewer doing the less talking, according to Charles J. Stewart and William B. Cash, Jr., in *Interviewing: Principles and Practices*. The interviewer's prime task is to listen.

The *structured* interview is based upon a list of prepared questions that is used for every interview. This approach not only saves time but also assures coverage of all planned questions. A set of questions also provides a clear basis for comparison.

## Types of Questions

Well before your interviews start, read all you can on the subject to be discussed. You need to know enough to prepare a list of quality questions that will yield the information you seek. Using a format similar to that of a questionnaire will ease tabulation. Provide checklists for answers to allow comparison of responses. Leave an extra space after each question for comments. Include some open questions to elicit unanticipated information.

*Open* questions are broad and unlimited. Their flexibility allows the interviewee to answer in several ways—for example, "Can you tell me about the duties of a bank teller?" Open questions may begin with phrases such as *what happened*, *how do you see this*, or *what experience have you*. . . . Often they are used at the beginning of interviews to decrease tension.

*Closed* questions limit an interviewee's response; they are more specific. For example, "What does a bank teller do when the day's accounts do not balance?" or "After one year what are the promotional opportunities for a teller?" These questions are so limited they have only one answer. Degrees of openness vary, as shown in the following examples:

**Open:** What types of crime have occurred in this neighbourhood?

**Less open:** What types of vandalism have occurred in this neighbourhood this year?

**Closed:** Have you had any vandalism on your property this year?

Avoid a series of closed questions that might cause defensiveness and cut off the flow of information. If questions about sensitive topics are necessary, ask them near the end of the interview. Be discreet. For example, if you ask about income or age, have the respondent indicate a range rather than a specific figure.

*Leading* questions indicate an expected answer. They yield little information and lead to dead ends. In the examples below, the tipoff word is italicized:

- Do you *dislike* filling out all those government forms?
- Do you *enjoy* flying to consulting sites?
- This seems like a progressive company. *Would you agree?*

Make several copies of your set of questions so that you have a clean sheet for each interview. During the interview, briefly note replies. Expand your notes soon afterward. With permission, you may record the interviews. Be wary of promising copies of the results unless you have the time and resources to duplicate, mail, or deliver.

## GUIDELINES FOR INTERVIEWING

1. *Call for an appointment.* Give full name and college or university. State the purpose of the call. Use courtesy words. (Reduces suspicion of unknown callers.)

2. *Arrive a few minutes early* to catch your breath and relax a bit.

3. *Shake hands.* A woman should extend her hand first so that the other person knows she is comfortable shaking hands.

4. *Do not sit until invited.*

5. *Politely decline an offer of a beverage.* Don't chance a spill.

6. *Have a typed list of questions handy.* Leave spaces to jot brief notes. Bring a clipboard or tablet for support. (Never use a corner of the person's desk.)

7. *Do not stay over the appointed time.* Ask important questions first.

8. *Thank the interviewee before you leave.*

9. *Write up your notes soon after the interview.* Expand. Include the date, place, and name of interviewee. Use quotation marks to enclose exact words.

10. *Write a thank you note to the interviewee.* Although this last tip is optional, it may be wise to cultivate some contacts for future reference.

## SURVEYS

Professional opinion polls and surveys are taken often. News organizations may survey a prime minister's popularity every week; a magazine may survey readers' preferences; manufacturers may offer free coupons to entice you to reveal personal information. A survey requires a questionnaire, skilfully designed to yield the desired information. For your research project, you might conduct a student survey on campus. You would need good questions to elicit responses that reveal views and attitudes about a concern, a problem, an issue, or other topic. After you obtain the sample responses, you tabulate and interpret the results of the research.

### Planning a Survey

An executive of ActivMedia, Inc., who designed the first marketing survey on the Internet, has valuable advice for students: "Have a *significant purpose* in mind as you draft questions. A major problem with many questionnaires is haphazard questions that yield trivial information. Another major problem with some surveys is that the samples are neither random nor representative. Make sure your sample is random; that is, that it does not overrepresent a particular segment of the population.

## Representative and Random Samples

A *representative* sample is a group that is typical of the general population in age, gender, education, socioeconomic status, and other significant characteristics. The size of a sample should be statistically significant. This means that a reasonable number of instances should be examined before any inference is made—the larger the sample, the better. Ten percent of the population is considered ideal, but few professional surveys include that many. *Still, the typicality of the sample is more important than its size.* For example, to be typical, a campus survey should include students of both genders, various age ranges and ethnic groups, all programs, and day and evening classes. In other words, the sample should represent the mix of the larger campus population.

A sample is *random* if all members of the population have an equal chance of being chosen. If not, the results do not reflect the opinion of the larger population, only the group sampled. Random sampling is not simple. Even if you were to select every thousandth name in a telephone directory, you would omit the poor, those too ill to answer, and others who do not have telephones. To obtain a random sample, consider the place, the day, the time, and any other factors that influence randomness. The checklist below will help you plan.

### CHECKLIST FOR PLANNING A SURVEY

1. *Have a significant purpose.* Find an interesting project that will supply meaningful information.

2. *Determine how the survey can be representative and random.* How large will the survey be? (Check with your instructor.) Where and how will you conduct it?

3. *How much time will the survey take?* Consider that you will need to design a questionnaire, and to duplicate, administer, tabulate, and interpret its findings in addition to writing. If you have to do research to pose questions, that takes time, too.

4. *How much will paper and copying cost?* If you research a topic for a business, supplies may be furnished. One student even received $100 for conducting a customer survey for a barber shop.

5. *Will there be an additional cost for distribution?* Some students have been dismayed to find they can easily spend $50 or more for copies, envelopes, stamps, and gas for distributing and picking up questionnaires.

Dear Student,

    Help!!! Will you please take five minutes of your valuable time to assist a fellow student? I have to conduct a survey and write a report. Will you please complete this short questionnaire and drop it in the box labelled "Survey" in the student lounge by [date]?

                                Thanks loads,
                                [Your name]

**Figure 22.1** Sample cover note for a questionnaire.

## Constructing a Questionnaire

After you determine the topic, a group to sample, and a method of distribution, draft a set of questions. They should be appropriate to the topic, situation, and audience. Try to limit your questions to one page for easy answering. Next, write a brief set of *directions* for the questionnaire. Test the directions and questions to ensure they are clear and suitable. For some topics, you might seek feedback from a half dozen classmates; or you may need the expertise of an instructor or someone in the field.

## Distributing Questionnaires

Mailing questionnaires is time-consuming and expensive. You need not only a cover letter but also a stamped, self-addressed envelope, unless you plan to pick up the questionnaires. Another disadvantage is that mailed questionnaires usually have a low rate of return. Although dropping off and picking up the questionnaires takes time, the rate of return rises considerably. Handing out a questionnaire in a store, for return later, is apt to be unsuccessful. Instead, you might have customers write on a clipboard while you wait. One student set up a card table and chairs near the front of her parents' clothing store.

For a campus survey, you might select students at random in the student lounge, but you need to spend equal time in the library and other places where students go. Otherwise, you would be unable to obtain a cross section. Or you might ask some instructors to distribute the questionnaire at the end of certain classes. If all students at your college are required to take Communications, you might get a representative sample there. If you use that method, you will need a brief note to enlist cooperation and to direct respondents to an easily found box in the same building.

## GUIDELINES FOR CONSTRUCTING QUESTIONNAIRES

1. Phrase questions clearly in *neutral* words. Be specific.
2. Ask for information that is easily recalled.
3. Keep questions *short*.
4. Ask only *one* question per sentence.
5. Provide spaces, checklists, and multiple choices for *ease in answering*.
6. Plan *equal* ranges: 1–10; 11–20; 21–30. Error: 1–10; **10**–20; **20**–30
7. Use scale items (with a key) to circle for opinion:
   SA    A    N    D    SD
   SA = strongly agree, A = agree, N = neutral, D = disagree, SD = strongly disagree
8. Arrange questions in a *logical order*.
9. Place *sensitive* questions (age, salary, and so forth) near the end. Word them carefully.
10. Place any open-ended questions at the end for additional comments.
11. Limit the questionnaire to one page if possible. (People dislike filling out long forms.)
12. If space allows, add a one-line thank you.

## WORKPLACE CASE STUDY

### CINDY SURVEYS DRESS CODES FOR BANK EMPLOYEES

Cindy is majoring in business management. For her research project, she surveyed local bank managers to determine policies on attire.

### SURVEY OF CLOTHING WORN BY LOCAL BANK EMPLOYEES

**Directions:** Please check *all* answers that apply to your bank.

1. Does the bank have a dress code?

   ☐ Dress code written in handbook or elsewhere.
   ☐ Unwritten dress code/guidelines given orally to employees.
   ☐ No dress code. Employees wear what they like.

*continued*

2. Indicate all suitable attire for employees Monday through Thursday:

☐ suit   ☐ shirt/sweater, pants   ☐ jeans
☐ jacket & slacks   ☐ women wear skirts   ☐ no expectations

3. If you have casual Fridays, please indicate all suitable attire for Friday:

☐ jacket & slacks   ☐ shorts, miniskirts
☐ shirt/sweater, jeans   ☐ T-shirt/sweatshirt

4. What is the bank's policy on jewellery and tattoos?

☐ small earrings permitted   ☐ no nose, tongue, or eye-brow piercing

☐ two per ear limit   ☐ no visible tattoos

5. Does the bank provide financial assistance to encourage professional attire?

☐ gift certificate   ☐ other _____
            (please explain)

☐ clothing bonus   ☐ no assistance

6. If an employee wears unsuitable attire, does the bank take action?

☐ sends home without pay   ☐ gives warning
☐ sends home to change   ☐ other _____
                (please explain)

7. If an employee persists in wearing unsuitable attire, does the bank take action?

☐ may fire   ☐ warns of possible firing
☐ places on probation   ☐ other _____
                (please explain)

8. Please indicate the approximate number of employees at this facility. (Do not count branch banks.)

☐ 101 or more   ☐ 61–80   ☐ 21–40
☐ 81–100   ☐ 41–60   ☐ 20 or fewer

9. Estimate the number of employees who have been notified of unsuitable attire in the past year:

☐ 21 or more   ☐ 11–15   ☐ 1–5
☐ 16–20   ☐ 6–10   ☐ none

10. Is your bank contemplating a change in the current policy on employee attire?

☐ yes   *Comment:* _____
☐ no   _____

**Thank you for your courtesy and cooperation.**

## Drawing Conclusions from a Survey and Interviews

After you tabulate the results of your survey, you draw a logical conclusion, based on the findings. This step requires interpreting the results: What do they mean and what are the implications? Then you make a reasonable generalization and possibly a prediction or recommendation, depending upon the rhetorical situation.

Let's assume Cindy's survey revealed that each of the ten banks had 21 to 40 employees. Six banks had written policies governing attire. Each bank's manager estimated five or fewer instances of improper attire in the past year. Warnings had been effective; no one was discharged.

But four banks had no policy. In follow-up interviews with the managers of these banks, Cindy learned that some employees repeatedly wore beach sandals, sheer blouses, visible tattoos, ponytails, or unusual haircuts. They were warned, which would work for a while. Three managers estimated that a dozen instances of improper dress had occurred; one manager estimated two dozen instances. Cindy concludes that written policies are more effective than unwritten policies.

## MAKING AN OUTLINE

Next, Cindy makes a working outline for her report. She follows a basic report format and lists the tabulation of each question in the original order:

I. **Introduction:** Purpose and scope of the project (list of ten banks)
II. **Method of research:** Survey of six banks and interviews with four other bank managers
III. **Body of report**
   A. Summary of results of survey (results converted to percentages)
   B. Additional findings obtained through six interviews
IV. **Conclusion:** Enforced policies with warnings and penalties do work.
V. **Recommendation:** Banks lacking a policy on proper work attire should appoint a committee composed of bank officials and employees to write one. The policy should consider not only clothing and shoes, but also jewellery, visible tattoos, body piercings, hairstyles, and hair colours.

To see a primary research paper or report, turn to the end of this chapter. The section that follows will help you organize and interpret findings for your paper or report.

## WRITING A PRIMARY RESEARCH PAPER OR REPORT

Whether you write a research paper or report, be sure you understand the assignment. Then examine your materials carefully. Do you have everything you need? If you made notes, have they been rewritten and amplified in your log so that you have all the data in front of you? If you used a set of questions, have they been tabulated? (For quick counting, use a blank copy of the questionnaire.)

If you did background reading, have you made a source card for each work (see Chapter 23)? Is a list of works cited required (Chapter 24), or can you state sources and dates in the text (see "Using Signal Phrases to Integrate Quotations into the Text," Chapter 25).

## Organizing and Interpreting Findings

Before starting to draft, consider what the findings of your research mean. Jot down your interpretation in a sentence or two. This prewriting exercise will help you focus on your thesis, the main idea of the research. Raw data are not sufficient to present in a paper or report. You must not only summarize and explain the findings but also draw a conclusion. Then the reader who is unfamiliar with the subject will understand the purpose of the project and the meaning of the results.

***Observation***    If you observe a site or subjects, you might classify the examples from your log. Classification can help you organize by importance, such as *minor to major, mild to severe*, or in another way. For example, if you observe traffic at an intersection several times (for the purpose of proving that a stoplight is needed), you might begin by classifying your observations by the type of safety infraction. Then you could organize the categories according to severity of the consequences. Which infractions led to near misses? Which led to accidents? What was the extent of damages and injuries? Was a citation issued? Anything else?

If you observed animals or people, you might classify by physical characteristics, behaviour, personality, or other traits that are relevant. For example, in a study of twins, physical characteristics and DNA results would be significant whereas these would be insignificant for some other studies. What similarities and differences might you see? What categories of behaviour would you note? Isolation? Positive interactions with others? Antisocial behaviour? What else?

Next, look for patterns, trends, or tendencies. What links and connections can you spot? What do these seem to indicate? What logical inferences can you make? What is your overall impression?

***Interviews and Surveys***    After you add the responses to each question, convert the total into a percentage. Divide each total by the number of returned questionnaires. For example, if an item received 60 *yeses* out of 80 returns, divide 60 by 80, which equals 75 percent. (Divide the smaller number by the larger one.) Next consider whether a majority is large or small. Or is opinion almost evenly split? Look for attitudes, patterns, trends. Think about implications. What reasonable inferences can you derive from these data? What can you reasonably conclude? How will you state your findings in *tentative* terms, without overstating?

To simplify the drafting of your report, make a working outline based on classification or whatever organizational strategy you select. If you used a questionnaire, you may want to follow the order set up there. (An example of an outline appears with the student report later in this chapter.)

## How Research Papers and Research Reports Differ

Research papers and reports differ considerably in format. The chief difference is that a research paper does not have internal headings. A research report is usually divided into three sections or more, each preceded by a heading.

The introduction of a research paper states the purpose and often gives an overview of the research. The methodology may be described there or in a preface or in a content note at the bottom of a page or at the end of the paper. The methodology indicates what was observed or who was interviewed or who was surveyed. For a survey the date, demographics, and size of the sample should also be provided. (For several interviews, your instructor may require a list of sources at the end of the report. See Chapter 24 for MLA or APA style.)

The first section of a report, often called the "Purpose and Scope," states the purpose and tells why the research was conducted. This section also sets forth the range (coverage of the topic) of the research and may include the methodology. Or it may be placed in a separate section. Regardless of where this essential information is placed, it should be specific. State how the observation was made and under what conditions. For an interview or survey, tell how it was conducted, the number of questionnaires given out, and rate of return.

The body of the research paper contains the findings and the discussion. There data and examples are presented; data are interpreted; patterns and trends are described. For a report, this material is also placed in the body, but in one section or more. The section may be entitled "Results of the Survey" or another suitable heading.

The conclusion of an informative research paper is a short summary of the results, the chief idea. The conclusion of a problem-solving paper recommends an alternative. In an argument, the conclusion restates the proposition. The final section of a report is often entitled "Conclusion" or "Recommendations." *Conclusion* implies a summary. *Recommendations* are suggestions for action. In student research reports, recommendations are usually those of professionals, such as physicians, engineers, environmentalists, or others.

A research paper may not be quite as concise as a report. A paper may spend more time explaining data, including definitions and examples, and may include several direct quotations—significant responses to open-ended questions. The following paper and report show two of many ways to organize and format. The structure you use will vary, depending on the assignment, the topic, and the method(s) of research.

### STUDENT PAPER BASED ON OBSERVATION

Janet Burks, a volunteer playground supervisor at her children's school, observed the situation described here. She used a problem-solving strategy to organize her paper.

#### Playground Supervision

> There was an old woman who lived in a shoe;
> She had so many children she didn't know what to do.
>
> —Mother Goose

The old lady living in a shoe and a volunteer playground supervisor have a similar problem. Both have so many children they do not know what to do. Although Mother Goose does not tell readers how many children the old woman had, the number was certainly fewer than the 120 or so children for whom the playground supervisor is responsible.

What, specifically, can be done to solve this problem? Apparently, there are three possible solutions: soliciting additional volunteers, decreasing the number of children released for recess at any one time, or presenting a tax levy to pay the salaries for full-time supervisors. But any possible solution would be governed by two major constraints: cost and feasibility.

Presently, volunteers come to the playground to supervise during the hour-long midday recess (which includes lunch time). The supervisor's responsibility is to circulate among the children and either to help them or to maintain discipline. The job is physically, emotionally, and mentally draining because the supervisor's tasks vary all the way from tying a kindergartner's shoe to helping a child who has fallen off the slide to resolving disputes. During this vigil, children may approach the volunteer frequently with problems, complaints, or accident reports. The supervisor cannot be everywhere at once. Children can be hurt before he or she even knows about a fight.

A complication arises when the supervisor must handle an extreme disciplinary situation. He or she is not allowed to administer discipline, but instead escorts unruly (and often unwilling) children to the principal's office. While the supervisor is attending to one child, 119 or so are outside without supervision.

As the volunteer program has continued, more people have been quitting because of difficulties they confront. This factor has made the playground problem even worse. One proposal is to solicit the help of more volunteers. Having more would provide two supervisors each day. Then the child-to-supervisor ratio of 120 to 1 would decrease to 60 to 1. Although this proposal has the advantage of being inexpensive, it also has the disadvantage of being unlikely. Most parents are not volunteering to help (many work) and probably will not volunteer in the future.

A second proposal is to decrease the number of children released for recess at any one time. This proposal would involve shortening the midday recess to thirty minutes and staggering recess times. Only two classes (of the usual five) would be on the playground at once, cutting the number of children to supervise to approximately 40 per session. The others would return to their rooms for quiet play with teacher supervision. But the children would probably object, and teachers would not want to assume additional duties.

The third proposal would be to present a tax levy to pay the salaries of full-time supervisors. The rate per hour would be much less than the rate required to pay teachers to supervise the playground during their lunch break. At the same time, the rate would be high enough to attract people to the job. Full-time volunteers sometimes do not come. Then, too, full-time supervisors would have standard rules, which the volunteers do not have. The main disadvantage is voter reluctance to approve higher taxes.

The writer's recommendation is a combination of the first and third proposals. First, information concerning the problem could be distributed to parents. They would know that if enough volunteers were not found, then a tax levy would be necessary. The levy would provide the necessary funds for employing full-time supervisors.

Although the old lady in the shoe did not know what to do, let it not be said that the same is true of Sycamore's parents and teachers. Let us solve this problem together.

In the student report that follows, notice that there are two sections in the body, entitled "Background Reading and Reactions" and "Self-Evaluation: Progress toward Objectives." These headings reflect the nature of the assignment and of the research.

### STUDENT REPORT BASED ON READING AND OBSERVATION

The following report by Lisa White, a nursing student, was written for an oral communications class. The project required reading one book or more, applying principles learned in class and through reading to either the student's personal or work life, and keeping a log. In their reports, students were to react to their reading, citing the most helpful ideas. Then they were to present and explain their findings as well as evaluate progress toward their objectives. Before the project, they received an outline with suggested headings for formatting the report.

No list of references was required although sources were to be provided. Lisa supplied her source information in the text of the report.

---

NONVERBAL COMMUNICATION WITH GERIATRIC PATIENTS

Prepared for Betty M. Dietsch, Prof.
CM 116 Oral Communications
Individual Goals Project

Prepared by Lisa White
February 28, 2002

---

**Nonverbal Communication with Geriatric Patients**

### I. PURPOSE AND SCOPE

Lake View Center (a pseudonym) is a geriatric care facility. The patients range from those needing postsurgical care to those needing care for Alzheimer's disease. As a nurse's aide, I daily encounter numerous situations that are taxing mentally, physically, and emotionally. Yet I lack the training to cope with them as I would like. I want to learn more about the importance of nonverbal communication and how to

---

### Outline of the Report

I. Purpose and Scope
II. Methods of Research
III. Background Reading and Reactions
    A. *How to Win Friends and Influence People,* by Dale Carnegie
    B. *Nonverbal Communication with Patients,* by Marion Nesbitt Blondis
    C. *How to Stop Worrying and Start Living,* by Dale Carnegie
    D. *How to Manage Conflict,* by William Hendricks
IV. Self-Evaluation: Progress toward Objectives
    A. Appraisal of Progress
    B. Examples of Progress
V. Conclusion

---

apply it to geriatric nursing. To become more skilled in interacting with patients and staff, I set the following objectives for this project:

1. To learn how to use nonverbal communication to enhance interactions with patients
2. To learn how to accept criticism
3. To develop ways to control anger

## II. METHODS OF RESEARCH

Four library books supplied information on nonverbal communication. Most helpful were the specific suggestions that I could apply on the job. For three weeks (January 31 to February 19), I tried out the suggestions and kept a log. Every day after work, I recorded at least one incident, telling what happened, how I felt, how the other person reacted and seemed to feel. Then I stated what I had learned. As the days passed, I began to rate my progress. The log has twenty entries.

## III. BACKGROUND READING AND REACTIONS

### A. *How to Win Friends and Influence People,* Dale Carnegie, 1981 (1964).

In this early book, Carnegie offers some fundamental techniques for dealing with people. The first is to remember that the deepest urge in human nature is the desire to be important. Sometimes we forget that other people besides us need to feel important. The second technique is to remember that everyone wants to be appreciated in one way or another. We can remember to thank in small ways by words or by a quick note.

    A third way to develop the best in another person is through encouragement. We all need to be encouraged, to know that we are heading in the right direction. Most helpful was Carnegie's reminder that other people need to feel important, too.

I tend to get so wrapped up in trying to get everything done that I forget to try to help people feel valued, especially my patients.

### B. *Nonverbal Communication with Patients,* Marion Nesbitt Blondis, 1977.

Blondis makes many excellent points about geriatric nursing. Her first suggestion is that when pausing to talk, one should speak patients' names, stand very close, look directly at them, and touch them lightly on the hand or arm. This sends a nonverbal message of "I am not too busy for you. You are important. I do care."

A second excellent point is that some elderly patients may not understand verbal communication due to hearing loss or mental impairment. But they are apt to note and understand nonverbal cues. Yet even when they understand, there is often a cultural gap of fifty or sixty years separating them from their young nurses. A word I say in one way may not be understood in the same context.

Third, patients will be more likely to judge us kindly when our nonverbal behavior is cheerful and effective. And it often seems that when one person is cheerful, the other person responds likewise. Fourth, Blondis warns that we should not confuse a patient's having a problem with the patient's being a problem. For example, some of the patients I take care of have been diagnosed as "hostile," "confused," or "senile." In reality, they may simply be unable to communicate verbally. Nevertheless, they still have thoughts and feelings.

### C. *How to Stop Worrying and Start Living,* Dale Carnegie, 1984 (1970).

In his book, Carnegie explains several ways to accept and deal with criticism. The first is to remember that when we are "kicked" and criticized, it is often done because it gives the kicker a feeling of importance. Some people seem to derive satisfaction out of denouncing others who are better educated or more successful than they are. They are envious or jealous.

A second way to alleviate the sting of criticism is to remember that unjust criticism may be a compliment in disguise. We may just need to search for the motive behind it. If we keep that idea in mind, we will be less apt to worry so much about what some people say. A third suggestion is to just do the best we know how and can do when criticized unjustly—to retain dignity.

A fourth way is to keep a log of the foolish things we do and criticize ourselves for. After that, we can ask someone we respect and trust for unbiased, helpful, constructive criticism. I think this is a great idea because it helps us to improve.

### D. *How to Manage Conflict,* William Hendricks, 1989.

Hendricks shares some practical tips on how to reduce and control anger through conflict management. His first suggestion is to have tolerance for diversity among people. We need to understand that other people's thoughts and ideas about issues may not reflect the same views we have. The second suggestion is to learn how to properly focus our anger on issues, not people. This concept is difficult to apply, at least for me. I find that venting my anger on people is much easier than focusing on the issue.

Third, Hendricks points out that repressing anger will eventually lead to an explosion. Basically what he is saying is that we need to find a healthy way to handle anger. A good way, I think, is through exercise, cleaning, crafts, or talking to a friend. This book has been very helpful because I have a quick temper.

## IV. SELF-EVALUATION: PROGRESS TOWARD OBJECTIVES

### A. Appraisal of Progress

*Objective 1.* I wanted to learn how to use nonverbal communication effectively on the job. Now when I talk to my patients, I look them in the face and smile. I speak in a cheerful tone. I also touch them on the hand to show I am not too busy for them and that I truly care. I have learned how powerful nonverbal cues can be.

*Objective 2.* I am learning to handle criticism in a calm, logical way. First, I assess the remark or comment to determine whether it is unjust or constructive criticism. If unjust, I take it as someone just being jealous or envious. If it is constructive criticism, I use it to improve myself and what I am doing. This procedure helps me to avoid taking offense.

*Objective 3.* I have been trying to focus my anger on the issue and not the person. I have also started activities to vent my emotion in a healthy manner. As soon as I get home after work, I exercise. Or if I am so angry, I cannot wait until I get home, I clean out the patients' closets. Talking to coworkers who have been in the same or a similar situation also helps.

### B. Examples of Progress

Before I started this project, I used to become upset, worry, and sometimes cry. Now I do not let anybody's unjust criticism bother me. For example, a nurse at work was criticizing what I wear. I took it as her opinion and did not become upset. In fact, I used the "sponge" method, taught in class. I told her that she was probably right and that I probably could dress differently.

Another day a nurse criticized me because I was having trouble taking patients off the bedpan and in keeping their beds dry. As a result, they were angry and complaining. I asked her if she would show me how she did it. She explained and then showed me. As a result of her constructive criticism and instruction, I learned to do the chore better and patients stopped complaining.

My log contains many other examples of progress, but two are especially significant. One evening a patient began yelling at me for not putting her to bed when she wanted. I tried using nonverbal communication in order to make her feel more important. It worked! I looked her in the eye while smiling and touching her hand. I explained it would be some time before I could put her to bed, but I would come back as soon as I could. Suddenly, she smiled and said that would be fine. Ever since then she has not given me any more problems.

The most trying incident occurred when I was trying to put a patient to bed. She slapped my face, scratched my arms, and bit me. I felt like screaming and hitting her back, but did not. Instead, I walked up and down the halls until I cooled down a bit. Then I went back and cleaned out her closet. (I cleaned out a lot of closets before the project was finished.)

## V. CONCLUSION

This project has given me the opportunity to learn more about an important part of communication and to improve my work habits. My supervisor noticed the improvement and commended me. I told her about the communication project, and she seemed quite interested. Although I am well pleased with my success, I plan to continue the project. I want to learn more about nonverbal communication and continue to gain skill in accepting criticism.

> ### SUMMARY
>
> This chapter describes how to:
> - conduct primary research through observations, interviews, surveys, or a combination of methods.
> - narrow the topic and scope of research to create a clear and significant purpose.
> - check perceptions, word choice, and inferences so that information will be unbiased and as objective as possible.
> - distinguish opinions from established facts.
> - sustain accurate record keeping, and report results in an objective way.
> - prepare questions for interviews that are open-ended in order to provide flexibility in answering.
> - develop a survey sample that is large enough to be meaningful and that is random and representative of the general population.
> - develop questionnaires that ask pertinent, clear, and easy-to-answer questions with sensitive topics placed near the end.
> - choose an effective method of distribution to improve rates of return.
> - develop a research paper and research report stating the purpose, scope, and findings using the correct method of organization for each.

## Ten Ideas for Observation, Interviewing, and Surveys

### Observation

1. Observe a neighbourhood problem such as litter control. Discuss possible alternatives and recommend action to alleviate the problem.

2. Local pollution problem: Combine observation with interviewing?

3. Preschool television: Time? Purpose? Themes? Hosts? Graphics? Value? Observe children viewing and record their responses, verbal and non-verbal.

4. Compare daily newscasts by different reporters. Divide topics: local, national, or international. Rate reporters and react (see Critical Reading in Chapter 26).

### Interviewing

5. Jobs and salaries available locally in your career field. Will you need more training to qualify?

6. How important is writing skill in your field? What documents might you write on the job? What percentage of your time might be spent writing?

7. Interview small businesses to discover the computers and software used.

*Surveys*

8.  Campus opinion poll: Survey reactions to a no-smoking, parking, or other policy.

9.  Survey student satisfaction with the bookstore. Convenience of layout, hours, service, competitive pricing, friendliness? What else?

10. Survey to determine major concerns of a community: More police? Repair of schools? New schools? Street repair? Vandalism? What?

# Secondary Research

## Locating Print and Electronic Sources

---

**Learning Objectives**

After reading and applying the information in Chapter 23, you'll be able to:

- Plan a research project
- Choose a suitable topic and limit the scope
- Record all necessary information from an electronic or hardcopy source, ensuring its retrieval for use as a reference

---

*To be conscious that you are ignorant of the facts is a great step to knowledge.*

—Benjamin Disraeli (1845)

An open mind is an asset for research. To be open does not mean you accept everything you read; it means you give new information and opposing beliefs a fair hearing. You consider unfamiliar data and dissenting views rather than hastily rejecting them because they seem strange or different. You are willing to review a claim before you evaluate it. As you examine the evidence, you try to appraise the information impartially, yet question any point that seems doubtful. *The principal goal of research is to obtain an objective assessment of the facts—to discover the unvarnished truth.*

## DETERMINING THE AIM OR PURPOSE

The first step in any research project is to determine the general aim or purpose. Your instructor may already have made this decision for you by assigning a particular kind of research paper. If not, consider whether you want to inform, investigate a problem, or persuade. All three kinds of papers require substantial reading, summary, paraphrase, quotation, and documentation of sources. As a result, the tone of research papers tends to be formal and less personal than of un-documented papers.

## Informative Research Papers

An informative research paper explores what is actually known about a topic and presents it in an objective manner. The paper ends with a logical conclusion, drawn from the research. The researcher boils down a wide range of information into a balanced summary, incorporating results of reputable studies and quoting opinions of authorities in the field, then points out the relevance to the reader.

For an informative research paper, you not only summarize and quote but also define, compare results, and paraphrase. You define terms not generally known and compare professional opinions. You report on areas of consensus or disagreement among experts. *You think about what the research means, how it can be applied, and what questions remain for future research.*

Research papers often require more than one kind of order. For example, you might use chronological order to summarize the onset of a disease and its symptoms, then use classification to list methods of treatment.

## Problem-Solving Research Papers

Many topics for research papers centre on problems. For example, you might investigate a business, medical, ethical, legal, social, or environmental problem. The problem might involve your campus, your community, your workplace, or a group to which you belong. You might do primary or secondary research or a combination of both.

See Chapters 18, 22.

Like an informative paper, a problem-solving paper reports existing data and expert opinion. But it goes a step further: You evaluate the alternatives for solving or alleviating the problem. A *recommendation* may also be included. If your paper is based on secondary research, the recommendation is based on the majority opinion of experts in the field. If you conduct primary research and are the expert, then you make the recommendation. A problem-solving paper often combines chronological order with description and classification.

## Research Papers of Argument

An argument paper is quite different from either the informative or problem-solving paper. In a paper of argument, you briefly summarize a controversy and argue in favour of a point of view, belief, or course of action. In other words, you take a stand and support it with facts, reasons, and examples. An argument may open with a chronological summary, then use illustration and classification to organize the supporting details.

The tone of the argument depends upon the purpose, the topic, and the audience. How will you approach the topic so that your argument is effective? A fair and reasonable tone, adequate and reliable evidence, and logical organization will help ensure that your argument is sound.

See Chapter 19.

## SELECTING AN APPROPRIATE TOPIC

Your research topic should be provocative, worthwhile, and challenging. This project should offer you the opportunity to learn and to draw a conclusion. Avoid a rehash of a topic you covered in high school or one well-covered in a single source. As you mull over choices, consider three important questions:

- Can you find a topic that stirs your curiosity?
- Is the topic significant?
- Can you locate conclusive support: data, studies, and expert opinion?

For example, if several of your family members have the same health problem, you might investigate the cause, the effects, and current methods of treatment. You could consult reputable medical journals or books by physicians who specialize in that area. Most of these sources, such as the *New England Journal of Medicine*, are available online. For most health conditions, you should be able to find abundant and reliable information.

To determine whether or not a topic is feasible, do a *preliminary search* of possible sources. Can you secure enough information within a few days? If a topic is new or quite old, you may find few sources. For instance, if you wanted to investigate a medication awaiting government approval, you might find only the research of the company that had developed it. Findings from that research would not constitute valid support.

Finally, your topic should be appropriate to your current level of skill. Advanced writers who are familiar with research practices may want to select topics that involve extensive research, whereas beginning writers may prefer topics that are less complex or technical. Select material you can comprehend.

## LIMITING THE TOPIC

Limiting the topic for a research paper can be intimidating—rather like picking up an octopus. The crux of the problem is this: Where and how do you grasp it? Where do you start?

### Starting Points

For some topics, you may need to acquire more general knowledge of a subject before you can limit your topic. Reading an overview in an encyclopedia, an abstract, or digest is a quick and easy way to obtain leads. This broad view will list the main aspects of the topic. You can select one and search for more information on the narrowed topic. You may find that it, too, has several aspects that require narrowing the topic again. At the ends of articles, you may find lists of related sources and topics to investigate.

## Writing a Controlling Question

After finishing your preliminary reading and deciding on a topic, you may find that it is too broad. Writing a *controlling question* will help you narrow the topic. A controlling question establishes limits. For example, the subject of breast cancer is much too broad. But you could restrict it by asking, "What are the advantages and disadvantages of various methods of treating breast cancer?" Here are more examples of controlling questions:

- How effective is solar energy for heating new homes?
- What should parents look for when selecting daycare?
- What ethical issues are at stake in fetal stem cell research?

A controlling question will help you focus your research by specifying the direction your paper will take. Formulating the question early can cut both search and writing time. Then, as you examine materials, list possible main points and start a scratch outline.

---

### CASE STUDY

#### FLORA NARROWS A VERY BROAD TOPIC

After preliminary reading on rain forests, Flora Kyle found that a number of rain forests exist around the world. She limited her topic to Amazon rain forests, but still she found too much information for the assignment of a 1500–1700-word paper. Feeling overwhelmed, she consulted her instructor, who suggested asking: How does deforestation of the Amazon rain forests affect residents of Canada? Then Flora was able to restate the question, limit her focus to three main reasons, and begin an outline:

#### SCRATCH OUTLINE

*Controlling Question:* Why should Canadians be concerned about deforestation of the Amazon rain forest?

1. Habitat of many plants and animals destroyed
2. Spread of disease from fleas and mites that leave the deforested area
3. Effect on the ozone layer by greenhouse gases produced by burning in the rain forest
4. Worldwide climate changes

> ## CHECKLIST FOR PREVIEWING SOURCES
>
> 1. *Is the material current or outdated?* Some fields need frequent updating; others do not. Material should be current and appropriate for the field.
> 2. *Is the material relevant?* Scan the table of contents, preface, and index. Read chapter titles, scan paragraphs here and there, as well as subheadings. Consider your purpose and audience.
> 3. *Is the treatment of the topic evenhanded?* Differing viewpoints should be recognized and treated with respect. Consider the tone of the article.
> 4. *Is there solid support for the conclusions reached?* Watch for inconsistencies. Are any fallacies apparent?
> 5. *Is the source primary or secondary?* Try to obtain information from primary sources whenever possible.

See Chapter 20.

See Chapter 21.

## SELECTING SUITABLE SOURCES

Not all sources are equally suitable for academic research. Although most of us are inclined to smile or shrug when headlines of supermarket publications proclaim "Man frozen in block of ice for 500 years recovers," we are less skeptical of most other printed and Internet sources. To research effectively, however, we need to question and evaluate all sources carefully. This is not so simple. Three preliminary questions will help you select suitable sources:

1. *Is the source reliable?* Beware of any materials that do not include complete documentation. The date of the research, size of study, and names of researchers should be stated. If, however, an authoritative group such as the Canadian Cancer Society publishes documents without an author, you can depend on finding accurate information. Beware, too, of books without an author, especially those that promote the views of a cult or vendor.

2. *Does the source provide comprehensive and fair coverage?* Some sources, such as popular magazines, may give a brief overview of a topic or an issue. Coverage may be superficial, with few details and omission of significant points. Even though an article may purport to give both sides of an issue, the treatment may slant toward one view. You need to ensure that your sources give full coverage of your topic.

3. *Is the source written on an appropriate level?* The source material you select should match the level of your intended audience. Reject any material that is overly simplified, directed toward adolescents, or too technical, intended for specialists in the field. For a research paper, you need solid, reliable evidence—statistics, findings, examples, and expert opinions that are clearly stated.

Once you begin gathering potential sources for your research paper, whether from a library or Web site, you will need a working bibliography to organize them.

## Making a Working Bibliography

A working bibliography is a list of possible sources for you to consult. When you go to the library, take a pack of 8 by 12 cm index cards, rather than sheets of paper, so that you can start a bibliography. Cards work well because you can easily sort and alphabetize them. These source cards or your electronic files will help you find materials and develop an outline. Similarly, if you have a computer or can work at a library computer, creating your list as a word processing file can save you time. The program will alphabetize your entries for you, and, when you are preparing your works cited or reference list, you will be able to cut and paste the sources you used from your working bibliography to your final list.

At this point, you may want to turn to Chapter 24, which shows how to document sources required for research. You may follow the MLA or APA guidelines, depending on the course and the instructor. You might mark this chapter with a paper clip so you can quickly refer to it while making your working bibliography.

***How to Begin***    To keep track of your sources, copy all information for each source onto one card, using only one side. Copy the call numbers from the catalog card or index entry onto the upper right corner of the source card. Although you won't need this information for documentation, it will help you find your source. Underneath that, copy other pertinent information such as author, title, editor (if one), year of publication, publisher, city, and province or state. Making a working bibliography will also give you a head start on your works cited or reference list.

For any reference materials, make source cards, too. For computerized listings that can be printed, printouts will suffice temporarily, but make sure the information is complete. For any item you obtain through the Internet, *write down not only the usual information but also the address (URL) and access date.* Take pains to copy the URL exactly; extra spaces may hinder retrieval.

*Making Source Notes*

1. For *books*, you need:
   a. Full name(s) of author(s)
   b. Full title (including subtitle, if any)
   c. Editor(s) or translator(s)
   d. Total volumes and specific volume number(s) you will use.
   e. City of publication (if unfamiliar, also include state), name of publisher, date of publication
2. For *periodicals*, you need:
   a. Full name(s) of author(s)
   b. Full title of article (including subtitle, if any)
   c. Name of periodical
   d. Full date of periodical (for academic journals also include the volume and issue number, if listed)

    e. Inclusive page numbers (including section letters for newspapers)

3. For *special sources*, such as nonprint material and online sources, you need to jot down various items as explained in Chapter 24. Note that nonprint sources such as tapes, compact discs, CD-ROM, television programs, and others have *no page numbers.*

---

### NEVER POSTPONE NOTING A SOURCE

When you find a promising article, document, or book, make a source card or note and check out the publication right away. If the needed article is on the Internet, print it out immediately. If you delay, the materials may be gone—borrowed by someone else or deleted from the Web site. What you find on the Internet today may not be there tomorrow. *Be sure to obtain all essential documentation and keep it until your graded paper is returned.*

---

## FINDING AND EVALUATING PRINT AND ELECTRONIC SOURCES AT THE LIBRARY

Not only do libraries have resources on the premises, they also have access to resources at other libraries and to the Internet. Unless you are doing very advanced research, your college library should provide everything you need. As you search, do not assume a source is unavailable just because you cannot locate it. There may be a second copy elsewhere, or it may have been returned but not yet checked in. Then, too, older books and newspapers may be stored on microfilm or microfiche.

Be aware, too, that your library's central catalogue may consist of one complete system or of segments, both printed and electronic. Ask at the information desk.

### Finding Your Way around the Library

Many libraries provide a map of the facility and a brochure describing available services. Look for these materials near the main entrance or at the information desk. If you don't find what you need, inquire. There may be several computer areas, each with a different function. Usually, there are indexes, CD-ROMs, and an Internet connection.

Libraries have four excellent sources for beginning a search: general references, indexes, catalogues, and bibliographies. Sources may be available in print, on microfilm or microfiche, or online. If any of these resources is new to you, do not be dismayed. Library personnel tend to be quite helpful.

### Preliminary Reading: General References

Brief preliminary reading in some general references will provide a quick overview of your topic and help you limit it. If the subject is not new, begin with short

## GUIDELINES: HOW TO MAKE A WORKING BIBLIOGRAPHY

1. ***Start with your library's database for article listings for subject ideas.*** If you don't find what you need, try a thesaurus for synonyms or an online directory.

2. ***Seek an overview.*** Read entries in dictionaries, encyclopedias, and other general references. Take brief notes.

3. ***Use indexes, printed or online.*** Indexes can help you find articles in newspapers, magazines, and journals. Make a source card for each promising title or print out relevant computer listings.

4. ***Use the electronic central catalogue or the Internet.*** To find promising book titles, type in the subject listing. If you use a search engine, add the word *books.* (See "Finding and Evaluating Internet Sources," later in this chapter.)

5. ***Make source cards or entries for your computer file.*** Double-check to ensure you have all needed information.

selections from dictionaries, encyclopedias, or abstracts. Many encyclopedias give not only an overview but also a bibliography for locating additional sources. For topics about North American subjects, *Encyclopedia Americana* is well respected. Even more comprehensive is the *Encyclopaedia Britannica,* which is more scholarly.

In addition, many encyclopedias and dictionaries are available on medical, legal, business, or other specialized topics. They range from the *Encyclopedia of Chemistry* to the *Encyclopedia of Advertising* to the *Encyclopedia of Rock, Pop, and Soul.* And, of course, some encyclopedias are available on CD-ROM and the Internet.

## Electronic Central Catalogue

After you have gained an overview of your topic, it is time to seek detailed material to flesh it out. Most libraries have transferred their old card catalogues to an *electronic central catalogue.* This allows you to use a computer terminal to locate most of the holdings housed on the premises. You can search by subject, author, title, or keyword by pressing the appropriate keys. Most systems indicate the location of a book, availability, and date of return—if it has been borrowed.

## Periodical Indexes and Abstracts

You can find recent information in newly published articles in periodicals (newspapers, magazines, journals, newsletters, and bulletins). To find these materials, consult indexes and abstracts. Indexes (printed, CD-ROM, and online) list articles alphabetically according to subject. Indexes give specific titles, authors, and publications—including magazines, newspapers, pamphlets, government publications, maps, pictures, records, tapes, films, and videos as well as books. Many specialized indexes list sources of information for science and technology, art, business, nursing, medicine, drama, education, and other areas.

Abstracts not only list subject headings but also summarize key information in a highly condensed form. For example, you might consult *Psychology Abstracts* (1927 to present) or *Historical Abstracts* (1955 to present).

***General Indexes***    General indexes list articles intended for a particular audience. For example, *The Readers' Guide to Periodical Literature* (1905 to present) lists hundreds of popular periodicals. Electronic directories list periodicals from the last decade or so, but if you want earlier articles, you will need to consult a print index.

*The Magazine Index*, often found in college libraries, is a microfilm index of hundreds of periodicals. Newspaper indexes can also guide you to articles of general interest. All these indexes include scientific, technical, and literary articles, but they are not as extensive as those found in more specialized indexes. If you use popular sources, you will need to supplement them with more scholarly sources.

***Specialized Indexes***    To find technical or scholarly research and government publications, consult specialized indexes and abstracts. For example, *The Humanities Index* (1974 to present) lists articles on archaeology, history, literature, the performing arts, philosophy, and religion. The *Social Sciences Index* (1974 to present) lists articles on economics, geography, government, law, political science, psychology, and sociology.

Prospective teachers might consult the *Education Index*. Medical technology students might search the *Cumulative Index to Nursing and Allied Health Literature*. The *Public Affairs Information Service* (PAIS) (1915 to present) carries subject listings of material by public and private agencies on economic and social concerns, international relations, and public administration.

***Government Publications***    These materials are catalogued according to a different system. Although there are indexes to these publications, the help of a librarian may be necessary.

Your library will not carry every periodical listed in every index. If you can't locate a periodical you need, ask if it can be borrowed from another library.

---

### TIP: DON'T OVERLOOK LIBRARY SOURCES ON CD-ROM

Your library may have considerable information available on CD-ROM. On CDs you can find such reference works as encyclopedias and *The Oxford English Dictionary*. You may also find back issues of magazines and other periodicals. In addition, there are interactive multimedia sources produced by the National Geographic Society and other educational publishers.

## Bibliographies

These publications are similar to catalogues and indexes, but they may be more comprehensive. *Books in Print* lists every book in print in North America, giving authors, titles, and subject area. *Paperbound Books in Print* is valuable in locating sources on recent topics. *The Bibliographic Index* is helpful for locating subjects you cannot find in other indexes.

## Finding Print Sources

To use materials that are stored on site, take your source cards or electronic catalogue listings with you to the stacks. The stacks are the rows of shelves where less recent periodicals and books are stored. To find the correct row, look up at the outside ends of the stacks. There the subject listing or the range of call letters for each row is found.

The most recent periodicals are usually displayed on shelves in a reading area. They are arranged alphabetically according to title, left to right. The shelves, on which the latest copies rest, generally lift up. Underneath are recent copies. Older periodicals in the stacks are shelved by title and date or by subject, title, and date (alphabetically by title and numerically by year). They may be stored in open containers or in binders. Still older issues may be stored on microfilm or microfiche in drawers. (Ask a librarian.)

Books are shelved in numerical order by call numbers as well as in alphabetical order by the author's last name. If books or other materials cannot be found on a shelf or in a file, consult the electronic central catalogue for availability. If materials have been loaned out, you can reserve them or perhaps borrow another copy through an interlibrary loan network (ask a librarian). For new books on recent topics, check with a bookstore.

## Skimming Sources and Evaluating Content

A brief preview in the library will save you from copying or lugging home irrelevant materials. Check the copyright date, and skim introductory pages to discover the author's credentials and what the book covers. Then read a page here and there to sample the depth and tone. To obtain a variety of viewpoints, look for materials by several authors. Although they may all cite classic research, their interpretations may differ somewhat. Each writer should also cite other research that contributes to the body of knowledge. (You may want to consult these sources, too.)

## A Precaution

Prior to taking notes at the library, refer to Chapter 25 so you know what to look for and the expected procedure. Even though you may have written a research paper before, this one may differ considerably. Chances are that your English instructor will expect a different kind of paper.

Chapter 25 offers a way to save time by taking preliminary notes, summarizing, and paraphrasing. As you make notes, *always immediately insert quotation marks around copied material to avoid confusion.* Attempting to summarize and paraphrase when rushed can lead to borrowing the author's words without being aware of it. Careful documentation will help you avoid unintentional plagiarism.

## Borrowing Materials from Other Libraries

To locate materials at other campuses and libraries, you can use a computer connected to a local or regional network. Before searching, however, narrow your topic by writing a controlling question. For a search to be fruitful, the key words should be quite specific.

*Online Catalogues*    Colleges and universities with multiple campuses and libraries may have a regional network of computers that connects all the sites. This means you can order materials from the main campus when you are on a branch campus and vice versa. Or you may be able to access a provincewide hookup of colleges and universities. You may find that you can access more than one network from the same computer terminal.

---

### GUIDELINES FOR EVALUATING SOURCES

- *When were the data collected?* Are they relevant? Scientific and technological data tend to change rapidly. Not all early sources are outdated; some are classics.

- *What is the author's professional status?* Look for a brief biography in the introduction of a book or article. What else has the author written? What are his or her professional credentials?

- *How credible is the publication?* To assess the credibility of a nontechnical book, consult *Book Review Digest.* For reviews of technical works, see *Technical Book Review Digest.* Match the copyright date of the book with the volume of the digest. You can also check the next volume after that date.

- *How much information is given about the research?* What were the characteristics of the sample or study group? Size? Was the sample representative of the general population? Have other researchers obtained similar results? If an experiment was controlled in a laboratory, have other qualified personnel been able to replicate the experiment?

- *If a topic is controversial, do sources examine various points of view?* A balance of viewpoints is necessary to give comprehensive coverage. Does the tone seem impartial or biased?

- *Are enough sources available to give comprehensive coverage?* A few articles, even well-detailed ones, are inadequate for a research paper. To understand the thinking in a field and find adequate coverage, you need numerous sources with a variety of viewpoints.

These networks allow patrons to borrow materials through an interlibrary loan system. A central catalogue for each network appears on screen, giving the site (campus, college, or university) and whether or not the materials are available.

If you plan to order items from another site and face a deadline soon, be sure to ask about delivery dates and availability. You also need to inquire about notification. Does the library notify you of arrivals, or must you check a posted list? If you are to check a list, where will it be?

## FINDING AND EVALUATING INTERNET SOURCES

The Internet is a maze of private and commercial collections in cyberspace. The World Wide Web, a part of the Internet, is an electronic Wild West because of the lack of regulation. Since almost anything can be found there, reliability and quality are concerns for researchers. This chapter discusses Internet resources that are directly related to research. You'll find tips for searching, evaluating Web sites, and judging reliability.

An Internet directory at the end of this chapter lists reliable Web sites for research. This is no guarantee you won't become sidetracked to an unreliable site. Just stay alert and apply the criteria for evaluation provided here.

---

### SEVEN TIPS FOR SEARCHING THE INTERNET

1. **Before you start, check the spelling of your topic.** Typing errors and misspellings will interfere with the search.

2. **Before using a directory or search engine, read the help information.** All these vehicles vary somewhat.

3. **Try several search engines.** There are millions of sites on the Web; it is impossible for any one search engine to cover them all.

4. **If you cannot reach a URL, try at a different time or even several days later.** Heavy traffic flow and other factors can interfere with loading.

5. **When you find a relevant Web site, check for links to similar sites.** These leads may be significant.

6. **You may be able to guess a URL.** Add the name and domain name to the standard prefix http://www. and guess at the suffix; http://www.microsoft.com.

7. **Keep searching until you find quality material from reliable sources.**

## Using Online Directories and Search Engines

Unlike most search engines, directories are organized according to *subject*. Search engines just pick out words from texts, regardless of what the words mean. Unless you are quite specific, the result is a flood of irrelevant references.

***Online Directories***   A quick way to focus a search is to write a controlling question and use an online directory, such as Yahoo. You can save time by taking the keywords from your question to activate the directory. Select at least two words to start. Connect the words with *and* (+) or enclose in quotation marks to avoid getting irrelevant pages. To narrow the search, use three to five words. *Place the most essential words first.*

Although using one keyword or a two-word phrase will take longer, it can help you narrow a topic. For example, an online directory found 110 subjects with 215 entries under the heading of "Amish." Only 8 appeared on the first screen, but one of those narrowed the topic to "Amish Social Life and Customs," which yielded 30 listings. From there, the search could be narrowed more.

***Search Engines***   Before using a search engine, narrow your topic. For some search engines, place quotation marks around the key phrase you type in the slot. All search engines are not equal. Different ones will yield different topics. Google, Looksmart, Excite, and Dogpile (a metasearch engine) are among the most popular. To locate a search engine, just preface the name with *http://www.* and then add *.com*. For example, the URL for Google is http://www.google.com.

## Evaluating Web Sites

Although the need for controls on the Internet has been in the national spotlight, to date there are relatively few. Any individual who can construct a Web page can stake out a site and post almost anything—accurate or inaccurate; legitimate or fraudulent. Thus visitors must maintain vigilance, keeping an eye out for disclaimers, errors, and doubtful information.

***Clues to Sponsors of Web Sites***   When visiting a Web site, look for the sponsor first. Sponsorship can give clues to the reliability of the posted information.

Reprinted by permission of United Feature Syndicate, Inc.

Usually, the sponsor is listed on the home page. If you arrive on some other page, look for a link to go back. The suffix at the end of the URL is a clue to the type of site. You can recognize private sites by scanning the URL. If you see a tilde (~), this indicates a personal page. If a tilde is part of an .edu URL, it usually indicates the page of a faculty member or a graduate student.

As you search, look for traditional sources. The last segment of the domain name of the URL can give you a clue. For example, in http://www.mcgrawhill.ca, the domain name www.mcgrawhill tells you it is the address of a World Wide Web page, originated by a private company, McGraw-Hill. In Canada *.com* or *.ca* is used by companies or other institutions (such as colleges and universities); *.net* by some Internet service providers; and *.org* by nonprofit groups.

Seven new domain name suffixes (TLDs), selected by the Internet Corporation for Assigned Names and Numbers (ICANN), recently went into effect: *.aero* (air-transport industry), *.biz* (businesses), *.coop* (cooperatives), *.info* (unrestricted use), *.museum* (museums), *.name* (individuals), and *.pro* (accountants, lawyers, physicians, and other professionals). For more information, see http://www .dotcom.com/news/toplevel.html and http://www.icann.org/tlds.

Additional hints for determining the source of a Web site include looking for a link that says "About This Page," "About Us," or "Home." Such links should take you to information about the sponsor. If there is no such link, try cutting the URL down to the domain name (using just the information before the first single slash).

## AVOID PLAGIARIZING ONLINE MATERIALS

**Warning**   If you stumble onto Web sites where you can view student papers or purchase professional research papers, beware. Some sites post a warning about *plagiarism;* others do not. Still, some errant students download and submit these papers to instructors, which is foolish and dangerous. Those who cheat not only rob themselves of an opportunity to learn, but they also run a high risk of detection and punishment for plagiarism. If you are tempted, consider these salient points:

- *Free student papers posted on the Internet tend to be mediocre*—replete with errors in content, sentence structure, spelling, and grammar.

- *Papers for sale tend to be poorly documented,* listing few sources. For example, one paper, "Evolution vs. Creationism," merely compares the content of two Web sites. Such methods constitute shoddy research.

- *Few students have the writing proficiency of professionals.* The differences in writing style are quite likely to be detected by experienced instructors.

- *Instructors can and do visit such Web sites.*

- *Instructors can purchase software that helps to detect plagiarism.*

***Free or for a Fee?***   Some newspapers, magazines, journals, and books offer sample articles or a chapter in order to encourage print or electronic subscription or sales. If the source is reputable (many periodicals are well-known) and the information is relevant, then use it. If you decide to purchase information by credit card, be sure that the site is secure. Why take unnecessary risks when you can obtain the same information from a library? At college and university libraries, you can access several subscription databases at no charge.

## Evaluating the Reliability of Internet Sources

Unlike library books, periodicals, and other materials that have gone through a screening process to ensure reliability and accuracy, the Internet has no screen or controls. On the Net anyone with a computer and a modem can publish anything. Researchers need to scrutinize Web sites to see if they are accurate, expert, objective, timely, comprehensive, and responsible.

***Check for a Monitor***   Traditional sites of reputable companies, institutions, organizations, and government agencies are generally monitored for accuracy. For example, *Encyclopedia Britannica* is vetted (verified) by editors. Some medical Web sites are screened by physicians. Some sites are maintained by librarians. Some news articles cite sources. But these sites are in the minority. Thus the researcher must be alert to discrepancies and wary of unreliable sites.

***Watch for Credentials***   Look for the name and qualifications of the author of the information. Reputable medical advice is available from physicians who publish the full text of articles related to their speciality. Notice that these professionals provide their names, city, province or state, and credentials at the top of the articles they publish.

***Notice the Tone***   Listen to the writer's voice. Are various theories, policies, methods, or other ideas discussed in an objective way? Or does the author seem bent on pushing an ideological or political agenda? Be suspicious if the document is filled with negativity or sensationalism. Watch out for special interests, such as informational advertisements and testimonials advocating a product. Before accepting any of these claims as fact, examine the source data. Have medicines been approved by the U.S. FDA? What side effects have occurred? If a study was done, who conducted it? Who paid for it? Companies that hire researchers may slant results to confirm their products.

***Notice Dates***   Look for dates on Web pages. Most reliable Web pages specify a date at the start or end. Lack of dates on a Web site and in the text of an article casts doubt on reliability.

***Evaluate the Coverage***   To check comprehensiveness, look for a statement of purpose. What is the intent of the Web site? How specific is the material, and is it up-to-date? Does the material seem factual? If a treatment or topic is controversial, is

## HOW TO FIND WEB PAGE DATES

If the page lacks a date, you can sometimes find it by going to "Page Info" or "Document Info" on the "View" menu.

the article well balanced, citing risks as well as advantages? Has the purpose been fulfilled? Finally, you can evaluate Internet information by comparing it to that gained from scholarly sources in a library. (See also "Guidelines: Evaluating Sources" earlier in this chapter.)

## Preserving Online Source Information

When you find a relevant and reliable article on the Internet, print it out immediately to ensure that you have all the information you need. If you wait, it may be gone when you return.

***How Much Source Data Do You Need?***   Remember to obtain as much data about each source as possible. You will need these data later to construct a works cited entry for each source. Find the author, title, date of publication, original source (if there is one), sponsor of the Web site, URL, and the date you visited. Most browsers show the URL, date, and page name as a header or footer when you print a page. (On Netscape, pull down the File menu, go to Page Setup and select Netscape Communicator to create the template for headers or footers.) You may have to hunt or follow links to find the other information.

## Balancing Library and Internet Sources

The library and the Internet each have strengths and limitations. As for which is the fastest, the time spent on research will depend on the topic, your expertise, and luck. One important asset of the library is the staff. These professionals can help you find what you need quickly. On the Internet, you are usually on your own. There it is easy to lose your way; you may have to circumvent roadblocks that consume hours.

If searching for current information, you may want to start with the Internet, then search weekly newsmagazines or professional journals in the library. If you are researching an invention, historical data, or an event of even a few years ago,

## SAVE YOUR INTERNET SOURCES AFTER TURNING IN A PAPER

Save your printed Internet source documents until after your paper is graded and returned. Your instructor may ask you to recheck a source or verify an item before a grade is placed on a paper. If you cannot provide evidence of sources, this lack may lead to embarrassing questions.

## GUIDELINES FOR EVAUATING THE RELIABILITY OF WEB SITES

### ACCURACY

- Are sources of information properly cited?
- Are there bibliographic links to check against library holdings?
- Are spelling and grammar standard usage?

### EXPERTISE

- Has the author been trained in this field?
- Is the author a member of an academic or professional organization?
- Has the document or site been reviewed by a peer or noted by a respected publication in print?
- Has the author published in print or electronic format?
- If the material is from a secondary source, are citations included for the original source?

### OBJECTIVITY

- Does the language sound professional and fair?
- Does the site contain informational advertisements, testimonials, or other commercial interests?
- If research was conducted, who paid for it? (Be wary of studies paid for by the author or sponsor.)

### TIMELINESS

- When was the site established?
- When was the material posted? Updated?
- Are there dead links on the page?

### COVERAGE

- Is the material comprehensive, covering the main aspects of the topic?
- Does it give enough specific details to serve your purpose?
- Are references, bibliographies, or links included to access other current information on the topic? (Before deciding, check out the links to other pages.)

### RESPONSIBILITY

- Is there a way to contact the author?
- Does the Web site list a Webmaster or a way to supply feedback?

the library is the best place to start. *Use of back issues of periodicals is free at the library; on the Internet you often have to pay a fee.*

If you need to read and study an entire work, the library may be the best place to obtain a novel or play. But if you need to locate a particular item, say a line, in one of Shakespeare's plays, the Internet is generally faster.

As a rule, the Internet offers a quick overview of a subject. It is not a substitute for the comprehensive sources available in the library. The Internet can supplement and enhance library research, but not replace it.

---

### SUMMARY

- The main goal of research is to discover the relevant facts.
- Plan a research project by determining your aim or purpose. Is it to inform, investigate a problem, or persuade?
- Choose a suitable topic and limit the scope.
- Complete a preliminary search for appropriate sources.
- Gain an overview of your subject by reading concise references such as encyclopedias, abstracts, dictionaries, or online directories.
- When using materials from an electronic or hard-copy source, record all necessary information to ensure its retrieval and use as a reference.

---

## *Practice*

### Preliminary Library Search

*Directions:* To become familiar with the resources available at a campus library, search the following sources. You can also start a working bibliography for your research paper. The completed search can count as a ten-point quiz.

1. *Determine which system of catalogueing the library uses.* Write it here.

2. *Find your subject.* What headings could you use in your search?

3. *Electronic Periodical Index.* Type in a subject. Select sources that might be useful. Print out a list.

4. *Electronic Central Catalogue or Network.* Select three books that might be useful. Print out (or copy) the bibliographic data. (If there is no electronic catalogue, use the card catalogue.)

5. *Encyclopedia.* Check an encyclopedia to find basic information on a topic. In three sentences, summarize the most important points. If a topic is not listed, try an almanac, atlas, or yearbook. Summarize the information in one sentence.

6. *Indexes.* Consult an index that is not computerized. Find and copy an entry that might be relevant to your research.

7–10. List four sources of information not listed on this quiz that you might consult. Specify the general area of the library where the material is located.

## *Ten Ideas for Research*

1. What career opportunities will you be qualified for after graduation? Narrow the list to two or three, then discuss the advantages and disadvantages of each.

2. Investigate potential employers you might apply to after graduation. Discuss three or fewer. Cite advantages and disadvantages of each one. Or compare two.

3. What possibilities exist for gene therapy? What risks does it pose?

4. What has happened in countries that have legalized drugs?

5. What has happened in countries that have socialized medicine?

6. Pollution of the oceans (or another element of our environment)

7. What should everyone know about heart disease?

8. Effects of noise on hearing and emotional well-being

9. How do male and female brains differ?

10. What alternatives exist for treating breast cancer?

# Documenting Sources

---

**Learning Objectives**

After reading and applying the information in Chapter 24, you'll be able to:

- Find accurate and complete documentation
- Supply information to the reader and give credit to the author using one method of documentation: MLA, APA, or Chicago Style
- Define plagiarism

---

> *Every [person] has a right to [an] opinion, but*
> *no [one] has a right to be wrong in . . . facts.*
>
> —Bernard Baruch

In the workplace, accurate and complete information is essential not only in writing cheques and invoices, but also in keeping records. Daily business and legal transactions must be preserved. Problems in safety, personnel, and other areas must be noted and investigated. Medical treatments, lab tests, and drug dosages must be logged. All this documentation constitutes proof. And proof must be provided for daily functioning as well as for complaints, disputes, or audits.

Inaccurate and inadequate documentation can result in cash imbalances, negative publicity, job loss, medical complications, and legal problems. Accurate and adequate documentation enhances credibility not only in the workplace, but also in college writing. Readers feel they can trust someone who supports a claim with substantial evidence.

## WHAT IS DOCUMENTATION?

Careful documentation is a hallmark of professionalism. When a researcher provides source information, this process is known as *documentation*. It gives credit to the author and allows readers to check facts or to search further. Legally, you may use small parts of copyrighted works (less than 10 percent of the entire work) for research if the author does not prohibit such use, and if you document clearly what you summarize, paraphrase, or quote.

## WHAT IS PLAGIARISM?

If you do not give credit to an author, the offense is *plagiarism*. Plagiarism is taking someone else's work and presenting it as your own. Whether intentional or unintentional, plagiarism is risky and impractical. Penalties for plagiarism in colleges and universities range from a failing grade to suspension. Usually, an

---

### FREQUENTLY ASKED QUESTIONS: SOURCE INFORMATION

1. Where are the publication date and the place of publication found?
   *Answer:* Near the beginning of the book, usually on the back of the title page.

2. What if there is more than one publication date?
   *Answer:* Use the most recent one.

3. What if more than one city of publication is given?
   *Answer:* Cite the first one.

4. What if the book has been published by two companies?
   *Answer:* List both publishers in the order given.

5. What if no date, page, publisher, or place of publication is given?
   *Answer:* Use n.d. to mean no date, n.pag. for no page, and n.p. for no publisher or no place.

6. What if a model for an entry is not given?
   *Answer:* Construct a model similar to the one most like it.

7. What title is used for the source page?
   *Answer:* If MLA style is used, the page is called "Works Cited." The APA style has a page called "References."

8. Are printed sources from the Internet documented in the same way as other publications?
   *Answer:* No. Construct an example according to the Internet models.

9. What extra information do sources taken from the Internet require?
   *Answer:* Web publication date (if available), date of access, URL (Web address), and other data may be required.

10. Which style of documentation should be used on the job?
    *Answer:* Some large firms have their own style manuals. If not, and if no preference is expressed, use either the MLA or APA style.

experienced instructor who is familiar with a student's writing can detect plagiarism. Each writer has his or her own individual voice and style of expression. When plagiarized material from professional writers is added to most undergraduate writing, the additions are readily apparent.

Why take this unnecessary risk when you can easily avoid it? When making source cards or note cards and drafting your paper, use the three forms of documentation listed below.

1. *Sources provided within the text.* Identify the author's name and other source information either in the text or in a parenthetical citation.
2. *Quotation marks.* Enclose copied words with quotation marks.
3. *List of sources.* Place a works cited list or a reference list (bibliographic data) at the end of a research paper to identify all sources mentioned, summarized, paraphrased, or quoted.

## WHICH DOCUMENTATION STYLE IS APPROPRIATE?

Documentation styles vary according to discipline. For disciplines and courses in the humanities, including freshman composition, the documentation style of the Modern Language Association (MLA) is widely recommended. For the social and behavioural sciences, the style of the American Psychological Association (APA) is generally used. Models for citations and entries for both styles appear in this chapter. For more detailed information, see the *MLA Handbook for Writers of Research Papers,* sixth edition, 2003, by Joseph Gibaldi, or the *Publication Manual of the American Psychological Association,* fifth edition, 2001. Both the MLA and the APA have Web sites that offer information about their documentation styles. For the MLA, visit www.mla.org, and for the APA, visit www.apastyle.org. Some colleges and universities also post MLA and APA documentation models online.

For classes in other disciplines, your instructor may ask you to use some other citation style, such as the *Chicago Manual of Style* (CMS), often used in business, history, and other similar disciplines. The Council of Science Editors (CSE), formerly the Council of Biology Editors (CBE), style is used in the life sciences and explained in *Scientific Style and Format: The CBE Manual for Authors, Editors, and Publishers,* sixth edition, 1994. The Institute of Electrical and Electronic Engineers (IEEE) style is used in computer science and other fields.

## MLA STYLE OF DOCUMENTATION

The MLA has endorsed a style of documentation that has been widely adopted for research in the humanities. The MLA style requires brief source references within the text of a research paper. The paper concludes with a list of sources entitled "Works Cited."

| CHAPTER 24 MLA STYLE DIRECTORY | |
|---|---|

## Parenthetical Citations: MLA Style

Source information placed within parentheses is called *parenthetical citation.* You will be using these citations throughout your research paper. For easy reading, keep citations brief. When feasible, insert the author's name into the text of your paper so that you can limit citations to just a page number. (Page numbers of cited material always appear in parentheses.) Key or match each of your citations to a source entry at the end of your paper. Several citations may refer to the same entry.

You may have used an earlier method of documentation that varied somewhat from the updated MLA style. As you construct MLA parenthetical citations to use in the text of your paper, keep these two guidelines in mind:

- Use a parenthetical citation *each time* a source is cited. Some paragraphs may need several citations. Rarely will you have a paragraph without a citation.
- If the source is from more than one page, cite the full range of pages (example: 19–23).

***One Author***    When you identify the author in your text, put only the page number in parentheses. When you do not mention the author's name, include the author's last name inside the parentheses, before the page number. Do *not* separate the two with a comma.

> Theodore Bernstein, assistant managing editor of the <u>New York Times</u> for seven years, points out that the word <u>bandit</u> "has a flavor of heroism." Bernstein advises: "Avoid any suggestion of glorifying outlaws" (17).

One editor has advised against the use of the word <u>bandit</u>

because its "flavor of heroism" has the effect "of glorifying

outlaws" (Bernstein 17).

Work Cited

Bernstein, Theodore M. <u>Watch Your Language</u>. Great Neck, NY:

Channel Press, 1958.

**Two or More Works by the Same Author**   To make citations for two or more works by the same author, place a comma after the author's name, followed by a condensed title and the page references: (Barrett, "Claw" 123) (Barrett, "Sickness" 103).

Works Cited

Barrett, Deirdre. "The Claw of the Panther: Dreams and the

Body." <u>The Committee of Sleep</u>. New York: Crown, 2001.

————. "Mourning Sickness." <u>The Pregnant Man</u>. New York:

Random House, 1998.

**Two or More Authors**   For works with two or more authors, include all last names; spell out *and:*

Four "aims of argument" are identified: inquiry, convincing,

persuasion, and negotiation" (Crusius and Channell 8).

Some researchers recommend "rapid-fire questioning"

during survey interviews (Kinsey, Pomeroy, and Martin 54).

For four or more authors, include only the first author's last name and the Latin abbreviation *et al.* ("and others"): (Klein et al. 53).

**Works by Two Authors with the Same Last Name**   When two authors have the same last name, give their full names in the text (preferred usage) with just the page number in each citation. If names are not given in the text, then include the first initial in the parenthetical citation: (G. Mueller 24), (A. Mueller 36).

**Entire Work**   When citing an *entire* work, not a specific page, state only the author's name in the text and, if helpful, the title. Be sure the source is on your works cited list.

H. W. Fowler's <u>Modern English Usage</u> reflects his spartan

life. Fowler believed in simplicity not only in living but also

in writing a sentence. Clarity had top priority.

***One-Page Articles***    It is not necessary to include the page number when referring to an article that is a page or less long.

> According to its secretary, Michael Heyman, "the story of the Smithsonian is also the story of its volunteers."

### Work Cited

Heyman, Michael. "Smithsonian Perspectives." <u>Smithsonian</u>
>    Apr. 1996: 16.

***Source with No Author Given***    For unsigned works, shorten long titles. Begin with the word by which the work is alphabetized in works cited: (DJIA).

### Work Cited

> "The DJIA through the Century." <u>Wall Street Journal</u> 28 May
>     1996: R29.

***Corporate Author***    Although a work by a group or an agency can be cited in parentheses, the preferred usage is to include the name in the text:

> Microsoft Corporation's 2001 annual report stated that Microsoft will continue "to work vigorously to resolve the remaining issues" of the antitrust lawsuit.

### Work Cited

Microsoft Corporation. <u>2001 Annual Report</u>. Redmond, WA:
>    Microsoft, 2001.

***Indirect Source***    When possible, use an original source rather than a second-hand one that quotes the original. If you are unable to obtain the original source and must use a secondary source, place *qtd. in* ("quoted in") before the citation for the secondary source.

> Ralph Waldo Emerson said, "Our best thoughts come from others" (qtd. in Cohen 9).

### Work Cited

Cohen, Herb. <u>You Can Negotiate Anything</u>. New York: Bantam,
>    1980.

***Quotations by Two or More Authors in One Sentence***   Follow each quotation with a separate parenthetical citation.

> Zinsser says, "The most important sentence in any article is the first one" (59), and Bernstein suggests the writer "ask . . . what it is he is writing about" to find the focus for that sentence (75).

***Two or More Sources in One Citation***   If you cite information from two or more sources, include identifying information for each source in your parenthetical citation, separated by semicolons.

> All seem to agree that good writing is hard work (Bernstein 44; Trimble 54; Zinsser 33).

***Work of More Than One Volume***   If your works cited list includes more than one volume of a multivolume work, include the volume number, separated from the page number by a colon: (Nicolson and Trautman 3: 25).

***Literary Works***   Because classic prose works may appear in different editions, include chapter (*ch.*), book (*bk.*), and part (*pt.*) in addition to page numbers. Place extra information after the page with a semicolon between.

> In the <u>Republic</u>, Plato has Socrates ask: "What do you consider to be the greatest blessing which you have reaped from your wealth?" (221; bk. 1)

Work Cited

> Plato. "Republic." <u>Five Great Dialogues</u>. Trans. B. Jowett. Ed. Louise Ropes Loomis. Roslyn, NY: Classics Club, 1942.

To cite classic verse plays, poems, and other works, leave out page numbers. Instead, give the division—canto, act, scene, book, part—and the line(s). Separate numbers by periods. For example, (*Waste Land* 1.35) refers to canto 1, line 35; (*Electra* 1.60) refers to scene 1, line 60. Note that the word *line* is spelled out in citations.

> Dickinson ends her poem "Wild Nights—Wild Nights!" with a prayer: "Might I but moor--Tonight-- / In Thee!" (lines 11-12).

> <u>Romeo and Juliet</u> provides one of Shakespeare's most quoted lines: "But soft! What light through yonder window breaks?" (2.2.2).

*Nonprint Sources*    Works taken from a Web site are cited just like printed works. If Internet sources are not marked with page numbers, paragraph or section numbers may be included. If so, include those numbers, preceded by the proper abbreviation (*par.* or *sect.*).

If a nonprint source (interview, television program, compact disc, CD-ROM, or other) lacks page numbers, you can omit a parenthetical citation if you state the author's name in the text. A works cited entry is still needed. If the author's or performer's name is not cited in the text, place it in a citation (Dave Matthews Band). For sound recordings, the medium (compact disc) is stated in the works cited entry:

Work Cited

Dave Matthews Band. "The Space Between." <u>Everyday</u>. Compact

disc. BMG/RCA, 2001.

*Long Quotations*    Quotations of five lines or more are set off, indented ten spaces. The parenthetical citation is placed one space after the final punctuation.

Charles C. Moskos summarizes the argument well:

> The principal argument raised against linking national
> service and federal educational aid is that it would
> have a regressive effect. . . . Students from wealthy
> families who do not need aid would be unaffected,
> while poor students would have to enter national
> service in order to get aid. (380)

*Punctuation*    For short quotations within the text, place a period or other punctuation *after* the parenthetical citation. For long block quotations, set off from the text, place the period one space *before* the parenthetical citation.

## Using Notes with MLA Parenthetical Citations

Content notes and bibliographic notes can be used along with parenthetical citations to provide more information. To insert a note, place a superscript Arabic number at a suitable place in the text. Then at the bottom of the same page, place a matching number before the note. Keep the notes short and informative. Content notes and bibliographic notes can be mingled and numbered in sequence.

*Content Notes*    When a secondary source is cited, a content note can provide complete publication data on the original source. Or a necessary explanation may be included, as in the example below:

Several months ago when obesity specialist Dr. Frank Greenway from UCLA revealed that a thigh reduction cream really worked, several news accounts incorrectly reported reductions of as much as 1-1/2 inches. The fact was that the most a woman's thighs shrunk was 1-1/2 <u>centimeters</u> or approximately 1/2 inch. Furthermore, the safety of the cream has been questioned.[1]

*Note*

[1] Several news sources have pointed out this misstatement.

***Bibliographic Notes***   To provide evaluative comments on sources or for references having several citations, use notes.

The <u>Wall Street Journal</u> and many other newspapers carried articles about the resignation of David Howard, head of the District Office of Public Advocate, Washington, D.C., over his use of a standard word that sounded like a taboo term.[1]

*Note*

[1] For a sample of articles taken from editorial pages, see Dooling and Parker.

Works Cited

Dooling, Richard. "What a Niggling Offense! Oops, We Mean . . ." <u>Wall Street Journal</u> 29 Jan. 1999: A14.

Parker, Kathleen. "Must We Be So Niggling about Words?" <u>Marion Star</u> 7 Feb. 1999: A6.

## PREPARING A LIST OF WORKS CITED: MLA STYLE

Use these general guidelines for the format of your works cited page.

1. Type *Works Cited,* centred, at the top of the page.
2. Alphabetize entries according to the last name of the author. When an

author's name is not known, alphabetize by the first word in the title except for *a*, *an*, or *the*.

3. Double-space the entire listing of works cited.

4. Do not indent the first line of an entry. Indent *five* spaces (or one-half inch on a word processor) for succeeding lines of the entry. This style of indention is called a "hanging indention."

5. Place a period after each subdivision of an entry and at the end of each entry.

6. Underline the title of an *entire* work, such as books, magazines, newspapers, plays, paintings, and others.

7. Place quotation marks around titles of short works that appear in longer works, such as articles, chapters, stories, poems, and songs.

8. Cite inclusive page numbers (121–28) for specific essays, articles, short stories, and so forth that appear in a book or periodical.

9. Number the works cited page using Arabic numerals, just as the other pages of the paper.

10. Use shortened forms for the names of publishers and reference sources (see Recommended Abbreviations).

## RECOMMENDED ABBREVIATIONS FOR MLA WORKS CITED ENTRIES

### PUBLISHERS' NAMES

Shorten the names of publishers, omitting *Inc.*, *Company*, and so forth, and using only the first name when there is more than one name. *University Press* is shortened to *UP* (or *U of . . . P*). In some cases, initials are used. Some examples follow:

| | |
|---|---|
| Appleton-Century-Crofts | Appleton |
| Beacon Press, Inc. | Beacon |
| Cambridge University Press | Cambridge UP |
| Henry Holt and Company | Henry Holt |
| Holt, Rinehart and Winston | Holt |
| McGraw-Hill Ryerson Ltd. | McGraw-Hill Ryerson |
| Random House Canada | Random House |

### PROVINCES

Use abbreviations without periods: ON, PEI, NB

# 1. SAMPLE MLA ENTRIES FOR BOOKS

Include the author's name as it is printed on the title page. In the works cited entry, reverse the name and place a comma between the last and first part: Bickford, Scott, Jr. Except for Jr. and Roman numerals (which are part of a name), leave out titles, affiliations, or degrees.

Underline the titles and subtitles of books. Separate the title and subtitle with a *colon* unless the main title ends with a question mark, an exclamation point, or a dash. An underline can be typed as a solid line under all the words in a title or name even when it contains a colon. Do *not* underline the period at the end of a title.

Specify the city of publication, publisher, and year of publication (or copyright date if the publication date isn't listed). You can omit the state, country, or province if there is no chance of confusion.

## 1.1. A Book by One Author

The last name of a single author comes first.

> Clarke, Arthur C. <u>The Collected Stories of Arthur C. Clarke</u>.
>
> New York: A Tom Doherty Associates Book, 2000.

## 1.2. Two or More Books by One Author

List the name once in the first entry (alphabetically by title). For the second entry, type three hyphens and a period instead of the name.

> Goldberg, Natalie. <u>Wild Mind: Living the Writer's Life</u>. New York:
>
> Bantam, 1990.
>
> ---. <u>Writing Down the Bones: Freeing the Writer Within</u>. Boston:
>
> Shambhala, 1986.

## 1.3. A Book by Two or Three Authors

When there are two or three authors, reverse only the first name. Spell out *and*. Retain the title exactly as it appears on the book.

> Musciano, Chuck, and Bill Kennedy. <u>HTML & XHTML: The</u>
>
> <u>Definitive Guide</u>. 4th ed. Sebastopol, CA: O'Reilly, 2000.

## 1.4. A Book by Four or More Authors

For a book with four or more authors, you may include only the first author and add *et al.* ("and others"), or you may state all the authors in the order given on the title page.

Lauer, Robert C., et al. <u>Social Problems and the Quality of Life</u>.

Toronto: McGraw-Hill Ryerson, 2006.

## 1.5.  Corporate Author: A Book by a Group

Boston Women's Health Book Collective. <u>Ourselves and Our</u>

<u>Children</u>. New York: Random, 1978.

## 1.6.  Second or Later Edition of a Book

Specify any edition other than the first by number (2nd ed., 3rd ed.), by name (Rev. ed.), or by year (1990 ed.).

Figler, Howard. <u>The Complete Job-Search Handbook: Everything</u>

<u>You Need to Know to Get the Job You Really Want</u>. 2nd ed.

Buffalo: Firefly Books, 1999.

## 1.7.  A Work in a Compilation, Anthology, or Collection

Enclose in quotation marks the title of an essay, a short story, a poem, or other work collected in a book. The anthology title and editor(s) follow. State the inclusive page numbers for the specific piece at the end of the entry. If you are citing a previously published scholarly article, insert *Rpt. in* ("Reprinted in"), the title of the collection, and the new publication data.

Michaels, Anne. "Hurricane." <u>The Art of Writing: Canadian</u>

<u>Essays for Composition</u>. Ed. Ronald Conrad. Toronto:

McGraw-Hill Ryerson, 2003. 98-101.

## 1.8.  A Book by an Anonymous Author

<u>Go Ask Alice</u>. New York: Prentice, 1971.

## 1.9.  A Book by an Editor or Editors

Bisset, Alex and Katherine Barber, eds. <u>Paperback Oxford</u>

<u>Canadian Dictionary</u>. Oxford: Oxford University Press

Canada, 2004.

## 1.10.  A Book with an Author and an Editor

Tolkien, J. R. R. <u>Unfinished Tales</u>. Ed. Christopher Tolkien. Boston:

Houghton, 1980.

## 1.11. A Book in Volumes

When using just one volume of a multivolume work, give that volume number before the place of publication.

> Shakespeare, William. "Cymbeline." <u>The Tragedies of</u>
>
> <u>Shakespeare</u>. Ed. Warren Chappell. Vol. 2. New York:
>
> Random, 1944.

When using two or more volumes of a work, include the total number of volumes after the title.

> Nicolson, Nigel, and Joanne Trautmann, eds. <u>The Letters of</u>
>
> <u>Virginia Woolf</u>. 5 vols. New York: Harcourt, 1977.

## 1.12. An Article from a Reference Book

The place and publisher can be omitted for encyclopedias, dictionaries, and other well-known reference books. Page numbers can also be omitted if the entries are alphabetical. If the entry is signed, lead with the author's name.

> "The Civil War." <u>Encyclopedia Americana</u>. 100th Anniversary
>
> Library Edition. 1995.

## 1.13. An Introduction, Preface, Foreword, or Afterword

Start with the author and title (if any) of the introduction, preface, foreword, or afterword, enclosing the title in quotation marks. Then name the part, using a capital letter but no underlining or quotation marks. If the book is by a different writer, place *By* before his or her name. Include inclusive page numbers.

> Hervé, de la Martinière. Preface. <u>Earth from Above</u>. By Yann
>
> Arthus-Bertrand. Trans. David Baker. New York: Harry N.
>
> Abrams, 2002. i.

## 1.14. A Translation or Edited Edition

> Dostoevsky, Fyodor. <u>The Brothers Karamazov</u>. Trans. Constance
>
> Garnett. Ed. Manuel Komroff. New York: NAL, 1957.

## 1.15. A Pamphlet

Treat a pamphlet as a book, even if very short.

> Lazear, David G. <u>Teaching for Multiple Intelligences</u>. Bloomington:
>
> Phi Delta Kappa, 1992.

## 1.16. Government Publications

When the writer is unknown, list the issuing agency as author (either federal, provincial, or municipal). If two or more works are issued by the same government agency, place three hyphens in place of the author's name (---.). Repeat if the works are by the same agency (---. ---.).

> Canada. Parliament. House of Commons. <u>Debates</u>, 35th Parliament,
> 2nd Session, 1996-1997, vol. 134, No. 141, April 8, 1997. Ottawa: Canadian Government Publishing, 1997.
>
> ---. Parliament. Senate. <u>Journals of the Senate</u>. 36th Parliament,
> 1st Session, No. 62, May 14, 1998. Ottawa: Public Works and Government Services Canada, 1998.

For additional information on how to cite government publications, please go to the text's Online Learning Centre at www.mcgrawhill.ca/college/dietsch. Many colleges and universities also offer guides on citing various government publications.

## 1.17. Sacred Writings

The article, chapter, or "book" (as in books of the Bible) is placed before the verses (if applicable). The title of the entire work follows. (Titles of sacred writings are not underlined or enclosed with quotation marks.) If the work has more than one version, the abbreviation for the version is placed last.

> Proverbs 22:1. Bible. KJV.
>
> Genesis 1:3. Torah.

## 2. SAMPLE MLA ENTRIES FOR ARTICLES

Periodicals comprise journals, magazines, newspapers, newsletters, and similar publications. Scholarly journals, which are usually published quarterly, are not aimed at a general audience. Since these articles often describe original research and give professional opinion, they are valuable sources for research papers.

Works cited entries for articles in periodicals follow the general guidelines for books except that different publication information is provided, and inclusive page numbers (for the entire article) appear. For names of publications beginning with *the*, omit the first word: *Wall Street Journal*. For a daily periodical, put the day before the month and year with no intervening punctuation. As you consult various periodicals in your research, collect the following information on your note cards. Then you will be well prepared to construct works cited entries later.

1. Name of author, editor, compiler, and translator (if given)
2. Title of article
3. Name of source (title of periodical)
4. Series (if one)
5. Volume number (scholarly journals only)
6. Issue number (if one)
7. Publication date
8. Edition (if given)
9. Inclusive page numbers of the article

## 2.1. Journal Article with Continuous Paging

Many scholarly journals use continuous paging, starting in January and continuing throughout the year. The volume number and year are sufficient; do not include the issue or month. Give the range of pages.

> Luna, Beatriz, and Mark N. Funglar. "Drug-Induced
>
> Hyperglycemia." <u>Journal of the American Medical</u>
>
> <u>Association</u> 286 (2001): 1945-48.

## 2.2. Journal Article with Each Issue Paged Separately

Include issue numbers for journals that do *not* number pages continuously. After the volume number, place a period and the issue number together with no space: 10.3 (indicating volume 10, issue 3).

> Togger, Debra A., and Phyllis S. Breaner. "Metered Dose
>
> Inhalers." <u>American Journal of Nursing</u> 101.10 (2001): 26-32.

## 2.3. Article from a Daily Newspaper

When a newspaper has different editions, specify the edition between the date and the page. If the article runs beyond one page, use a plus sign to indicate that it continues.

> Perkel, Colin. "Logging roads criss-cross Algonquin." <u>Toronto Star</u>
>
> 17 Oct. 2005, Ontario ed.: A4.

## 2.4. Article from a Monthly Magazine

Include the cover date. Abbreviate all months except May, June, and July, using the first three letters.

Perrin, Terri. "Happy in a high-rise." <u>Dogs in Canada</u> Oct. 2005:

40-43.

## 2.5. Article from a Weekly Newspaper or Weekly Magazine

Begley, Sharon, and Michael Isikuff. "Anxious about Anthrax."

<u>Newsweek</u> 22 Oct. 2001: 28-35.

## 2.6. An Anonymous Article

When the author of an article is unstated, begin with the title and alphabetize by the first significant word in the title.

"Dill Soothes an Upset Tummy." <u>Organic Gardening</u> July/

Aug. 2001:13.

## 2.7. Review

Applebaum, Herbert A. Rev. of <u>Social Anthropology of Work</u>, ed.

Sandra Wallman. <u>Current Anthropology</u> 21 (1980): 307-08.

## 2.8. Abstract and a Review

The abstract of the book appears before the abstract of the review. The periodical carrying the abstract and review is placed last. If the abstract has no review, omit *Rev. by*.

Monti, Daniel J. <u>The American City: A Social and Cultural History</u>.

Oxford, UK: Blackwell, 1999. Rev. by J. C. Schneider, <u>Journal</u>

<u>of American History</u> 87 (2001): 1537-1538. <u>Book Review</u>

<u>Digest</u> 97.6 (2001): 157.

## 2.9. An Editorial

When citing a signed editorial, start with the author's name, then the title. Next, write *Editorial* (no underlining or quotation marks). When the editorial is unsigned, start with the title.

Martin, Roger and James Milway. "Bridging Canada's fiscal

divide." Editorial. <u>Toronto Star</u> 17 Oct. 2005: A21.

## 2.10. A Letter to the Editor

Clarke, J.A. "Canadians pay too much tax." Letter. <u>Toronto Star</u>

17 Oct. 2005: A23.

## 2.11. Newsletter Article

Piwowarczyk, E. "Revisiting the Evelyn Dick Case." <u>Crime Scene:</u>

<u>A Sisters in Crime (Toronto Chapter) Publication</u> 13.3 (June

2002): 1+.

# 3. SAMPLE MLA ENTRIES FOR MISCELLANEOUS PRINT AND NONPRINT SOURCES

For broadcast, film, and recorded sources involving various personnel, you begin the entry with the name or title that is the primary subject of emphasis in your paper, as shown below:

Stouffer, Marty. "Cutthroat Trout." 2 episodes. <u>Wild America</u>. PBS.

WOSU-TV, Columbus, OH. 11 Sept. 1995-12 Sept. 1995.

"Cutthroat Trout." 2 episodes. Marty Stouffer. <u>Wild America</u>. PPS.

WOSU-TV, Columbus, OH. 11 Sept. 1995-12 Sept. 1995.

## 3.1. Television or Radio Programs

The items in a works cited entry for a television or radio program generally follow the order below. (Omit any items that are not relevant, but include relevant items such as performers, director, conductor, or number of episodes.)

1. Episode or segment title (Enclose in quotation marks. If there are two or more episodes, state the total.)
2. Author's name (in reverse order if it begins the entry)
3. Program title (underline)
4. Series title
5. Network (for example, CNN)
6. Local call letters and city (for example, WMAQ, Chicago)
7. Date of broadcast

<u>Kiss Me Kate</u>. By Sam and Bella Spewak. Music and lyrics by

Cole Porter. Perf. Nancy Anderson and Michael Berresse.

> Broadway performance. <u>Great Performances</u>. PBS. WOSU-
> TV, Columbus, OH. 26 Feb. 2003.
>
> Schama, Simon. "The Body of the Queen." 5 episodes. <u>A History
> of Britain</u>. Narr. Simon Schama. The History Channel. CNBC,
> Columbus, OH. 29 Oct. 2001.
>
> "Art of the Groove." <u>Saturday at the Pops</u>. Host and prod. Boyce
> Lancaster. WOSU-FM, Columbus, OH. 1 Mar. 2003.

If a transcript is available online, provide the information.

> Shaw, Bernard. "Clinton's Boom Era Not as Turbulent as LBJ's."
> Program segment. <u>Inside Politics</u>. CNN. 29 June 1999.
> Transcript. 1 July 1999. <http://www.cnn.com/
> TRANSCRIPTS/9906/29/ip.06.html>.

For sound recordings of television or radio programs, see 3.2. For a videotape of a performance, see 3.3. For interviews conducted on television or radio, see 3.4.

## 3.2.  Sound Recordings

If the recording is on compact disc, omit the medium. Specify audiocassette tape or LP. Also include manufacturer and date. The name you place first depends on whom you want to emphasize—composer, conductor, or performer.

> Beach Boys. <u>The Greatest Hits</u>. Capitol. 1999.
>
> Strauss, Edvard. "The Merry Widow Waltz." <u>Viennese Favorites</u>.
> LP. Cond. Arthur Fiedler. Boston Pops Orchestra.
> Audiocassette. RCA Victrola, 1983.

## 3.3.  Film or Video Recording

Include all pertinent information in an order that reflects your emphasis. For video recordings, include the original date of release as well as the date the recording was released.

### *a.  A Film Video Recording, or Performance*

> <u>Enchanted April</u>, Dir. Mike Newell. Perf. Miranda Richardson,
> Josie Lawrence, Polly Walker, and Joan Plowright.
> Screenwriter Peter Barnes. Warner Brothers, 1992.

If material is not a film, specify the medium. Some materials may include an original release date, perhaps in another form. For example, some laser discs contain films in IMAX. If material has an original release date, include that date before the medium.

### b. Videocassettes, DVD, Laser Disc, Slide Program, or Filmstrip

MacArthur Foundation, J. D. and C. T., National Science

> Foundation, and Jostens Foundation. <u>Tropical Rainforest</u>.

> 1992. Laser disc. Denver: Lumivision. 1994.

<u>Those Wonderful Dogs</u>. Narr. Richard Kiley. Writer and Prod.

> Barbara Jampel. Music by Scott Harper. National

> Geographic Society. 1989. Videocassette. Columbia Tristar,

> 1994.

## 3.4. Interviews

Published interviews are treated as excerpts from anthologies and periodicals. Broadcast interviews are treated as television or radio programs. Personal and telephone interviews are listed as such. In all cases, list the name of the person interviewed first.

MacLeish, Archibald. "Archibald MacLeish." Interview with

> Benjamin De Mott. <u>Writers at Work: The Paris Review</u>

> <u>Interviews 5</u>. Ed. George Plimpton. New York: Penguin,

> 1988. 23-48.

Senitko, Melanie. Personal interview. 27 Oct. 2001.

Witzel, Carol. Telephone interview. 29 Oct. 2001.

## 3.5. Cartoon

Schulz, Charles. "Peanuts." Cartoon. <u>Toronto Star</u> 15 June 2002:

> C13.

## 3.6. Legal References

For papers requiring several legal citations, see the most recent edition of *The Canadian Guide to Uniform Legal Citation* (Toronto: Thompson Carswell). A usual rule is neither to underline nor enclose in quotation marks any titles of laws, acts, or similar documents in the text or in the list works cited.

## 4. SAMPLE MLA ENTRIES FOR ELECTRONIC SOURCES

Entries for electronic sources begin with the author's name and title of the document, followed by print publication information (if any), electronic publication information, and access information. See the guidelines on page 315 for details about the components of an electronic source entry in MLA documentation style.

### 4.1. An Entire Online Database, Scholarly Project, Professional or Personal Site

#### a. Online Database or Scholarly Project

Cite what is given of the following information: the title of the database, encyclopedia, or project (underlined), the editor's name (preceded by "Ed."), any electronic publication information, such as version number (if not part of the title), the date of publication or latest update, and the sponsor's name. Include the date of access and URL.

> CNN.com. 2003. Cable News Network. 24 Feb. 2003 <http://www.
>
> cnn.com/>.

> Encyclopedia Britannica Online. 2002. Encyclopaedia Brittanica.
>
> 11 Nov. 2002 <http://www.britannica.com>.

> Victorian Women Writers Project. Ed. Perry Willet. 10 Dec. 2002.
>
> Indiana U. 3 Mar. 2003 <http://www.indiana.edu/~letrs/
>
> vwwp/>.

#### b. Professional or Personal Site

First give the name of the person who created the site (if given) and the title of the site (underline). If there is no title, use a description such as *Home page* (no underlining). Next give the date of the last update, or, in the case of a course home page, the dates of the course. Follow with the sponsor of the site (if applicable), the date of access, and URL.

> Hopkins Information Technology Services Home Page. Johns
>
> Hopkins University. 27 Feb. 2003 <http://www.webapps.
>
> jhu.edu/hitswebsite/>.

> Barbour, Dennis. Dennis Barbour Useful Links. 11 Apr. 2002.
>
> Online Directory. 26 Feb. 2003 <http://www.home.jhu.edu/
>
> ~dbarbour/links.html>.

## MLA STYLE: DOCUMENTING ELECTRONIC SOURCES

**Note:** When online material carries a printed source and date, cite that first, according to the MLA guidelines for books and periodicals (see 1.1 to 2.11 in the preceding discussion), before electronic information. Keep in mind that all the information below may not be available in every situation.

1. *Author(s).* Reverse the name of the first (or only) author so that it can be alphabetized. If an editor is listed instead of an author, place *ed.* after the name (see 1.9).

2. *Title of an article, a poem, short story, or similar item in a scholarly project, database, or periodical.* Enclose the title with quotation marks.

3. *Book title.* Underline both main title and subtitle.

4. *Editor, compiler, or translator.* If there is one, place *Ed., Comp.,* or *Trans.* before the name (see 1.10, 1.14 and 4.3).

5. *Edition, version, volume, or issue number.* If the version number is included in the title, do not repeat. For a journal, include the volume, issue, or any other number for identification (see 4.4).

6. *Title of the scholarly project, database, periodical, or professional or personal Web site.* Underline. If there is no title, write a description such as *Search Page* or *Home Page* (see 4.1.b).

7. *Other publication information.* Give publisher's name, place of publication, copyright date, and any other identification.

8. *Medium of publication.* If the source is on a CD-ROM, diskette, tape, DVD, or similar source, state the medium (see 4.11–4.13).

9. *Dates of information.* Include the dates of posting, electronic publication, and most recent update, if there is one.

10. *Article or work from a subscription service.* Identify the service, subscriber (often a library), and place of subscriber (see 4.14).

11. *Online posting or forum.* Supply name of list or forum (see 4.9).

12. *Range or number of pages, paragraphs, or sections.* Include if the material is numbered.

13. *Sponsor of the Web site.* Identify the individual, institution, organization, or agency sponsoring or associated with the Web site.

14. *Date of access.* Place the date you obtained the material right before the URL.

15. *URL of the source.* Place in angle brackets (< >), followed by a period. If the URL is long and complex, cite the search page URL. For a subscription service, use the home page URL. Or give the keyword of the service, preceded by *Keyword*, or give the sequence of links after the URL: *Path* and a semicolon (see 4.7).

## 4.2.  An Entire Online Book

The book below was published by Alfred A. Knopf in 1920. The online source is based on Knopf's 1922 edition.

> Mencken, H. L. <u>In Defense of Women</u>. New York: Knopf, 1920.
>
>    3 Mar. 2003 <http://209.11.144.65/eldritchpress/hlm/
>
> defense.htm>.

## 4.3.  A Poem, Short Story, or Essay within an Online Book

Begin by supplying the publication data for the print version of the work—author, title of the selection, title of the book, editor's name, place and date of publication. Then follow with electronic publication information specific to the selection, such as its URL.

> Frost, Robert. "Mending Wall." <u>Modern American Poetry</u>. Ed.
>
>    Louis Untermeyer. New York: Harcourt, 1919. 17 Mar. 2003
>
>    <http://www.bartleby.com/104/64.html>.
>
> Nesbit, E[dith]. "Many Voices." London, 1922. <u>Victorian Women</u>
>
>    <u>Writers Project</u>. Ed. Perry Willett. 31 Mar. 1999. Indiana U.
>
>    3 Mar. 2003 <http://www.indiana.edu/~letrs/vwwp/nesbit/
>
> manyvoices.html>.

## 4.4.  An Article in an Online Scholarly Journal

The online article below was printed in *American Psychologist*, volume 54, issue 10, October 1999. It had three pages. The site was accessed on March 17, 2003.

> Parott, Andy C. "Does Cigarette Smoking Cause Stress?"
>
>    <u>American Psychologist</u> 54.10 (Oct. 1999): 3 pp. 17 Mar. 2003
>
>    <http://www.apa.org/journals/html>.

## 4.5.  Article in an Online Newspaper

> Bronskill, Jim. "Quebec will have its own army, Duceppe says."
>
>    <u>Globe and Mail</u> 18 Oct. 2005. 19 Oct. 2005 <http://
>
>    www.globeandmail.com/servlet/story/RTGAM.20051018.
>
>    wquebmill018/BNStory/National>.

## 4.6.  Article in an Online Magazine

Coxe, Donald. "How to play a pandemic." <u>Macleans</u> 19 Oct. 2005.

19 Oct. 2005 <http://www.macleans.ca/switchboard/

columnists/article.jsp?content=20051024_114019_114019>.

## 4.7.  Online Abstract

The first example below shows a sequence of links after the URL.

Greene, Virginie. "How the Damoiselle d'Escalot Became a

Picture." <u>Arthuriana</u> 12.3 (Fall 2002): 31-48. Abstract. 5 Mar.

2003 <http://www.smu.edu/arthuriana/>. Path: Abstracts;

G-J.

Tavassolli, Nader T. "Spatial Memory for Chinese and English."

<u>Journal of Cross-Cultural Psychology</u> 33.4 (2002): 15-31.

Abstract. 4 Mar 2003 <http://web26.epnet.com/

citation.asp>.

## 4.8.  Article from an Online Newsletter

Justice, Rod. "Hospital Workers Forget to Wash Hands between

Patients." <u>In Touch Newsletter</u> 3.4 (2000). In Touch. 27 Feb.

2003 <http://www.intouchnews.com/sample.htm>.

## 4.9.  Posting to a Discussion Group

Osheroff, J. A. "Computers in Medicine." Editorial and online

posting. 1996-2003. American College of Physicians-

American Society of Internal Medicine. 1 Mar. 2003 <http://

www.acponline.org/computer/sgim_edit.htm>.

## 4.10.  EMail Communication

Dietsch, Betty M. "Note to Instructors." Email to Lisa Moore.

1 April 2003.

## 4.11. Periodical Published on CD-ROM

Many newspapers, magazines, journals, and other periodicals can be accessed from databases. Usually source information is provided at the beginning of the file.

> Hansen, Robert W. "Stigma, Conflict, and the Approval of AIDS
>
> Drugs." <u>Journal of Drugs</u> (Winter 1995): 129-39. CD-ROM.
>
> UMI-ProQuest. 1995.

## 4.12. Nonperiodical Publication on CD-ROM

Some nonperiodical databases are published only once with no revisions or updates. Cite nonperiodical CD-ROMs the way you would cite a book but include the publication medium. (Usually, there is a publisher but no vendor.)

> <u>1880 United States Census and National Index</u>. CD-ROM. Salt
>
> Lake City: Intellectual Reserve, 2001.
>
> "Making a Will." <u>Family Lawyer</u>. CD-ROM. Hiawatha, IA: Parsons
>
> Technology, 1995.

## 4.13. Publication on CD-ROM or Diskette

Computer programs, languages, and other software on CD-ROM or diskette may be updated from time to time. For updates, specify the edition, version (if not in the title), or other update. Separate the publication information from the title of the product with a period.

> <u>Dr. Solomon's Virex 7 for Macintosh</u>. CD-ROM. Network
>
> Associates. Santa Clara, CA: McAfee.com Corporation, 2001.
>
> Bird, Alan. "TimeOut." <u>Quickspell</u> Diskette. San Diego: Beagle
>
> Bros., 1987.

## 4.14. A Work from a Library Subscription Service

To cite material found through an online subscription service such as EBSCO, InfoTrac, and Lexis-Nexis, follow the guidelines for citing online works and add the name of the database underlined (if known), the name of the service, the name of the library, and the date of access. Include the URL of the service's home page (if known).

> Koehn, Nancy F. "Henry Heinz and Brand Creation in the Late
>
> Nineteenth Century: Making Markets for Processed Food."

> Business History Review 73.3 (1999): 349+, InfoTrac
>
> OneFile. InfoTrac. San Francisco Public Lib., 3 May 2002
>
> <http://infotrac.galegroup.com/>.

## 4.15. A Work in More Than One Publication Medium

Some stores offer bundles of software in one package. Follow the directions for a nonperiodical CD-ROM (4.12) and list the media in the package.

> Newman, John J. "Ohio." Uncle, We Are Ready! Registering
>
> America's Men 1917-1918. CD-ROM and book. North Salt,
>
> Utah: Heritage Quest, 2001.

## 4.16. Other Electronic Sources

To document online sources that are not mentioned here, find a similar model and follow the general guidelines for citing print and electronic sources. Construct your entry appropriately, making changes as needed. For example, you may need to add a label such as *map* or *interview* (no quotation marks or underlining).

## APA STYLE OF DOCUMENTATION

For research papers in the social and behavioural sciences, many instructors prefer the American Psychological Association (APA) style of documentation. The explanations and examples shown here follow the guidelines in the *Publication Manual of the American Psychological Association*, fifth edition, 2001.

---

### CHAPTER 24 APA STYLE DIRECTORY

## Parenthetical Citations: APA Style

The APA style keys parenthetical citations in a text to a list of sources. Include the author's last name, the year of publication, the abbreviation for page (*p.* or *pp.* for pages), and the page number. Ampersands (&) are used instead of *and* in a parenthetical citation. *Chapter* is abbreviated *chap.* and *section* is abbreviated *sec.* in parenthical citations.

*Single Author*   The author's name is usually mentioned in the text, followed by parentheses containing the year of publication and page. If the entire work is cited, no page numbers are needed. If the author is not listed in the text, include the author's last name in the parenthetical citation.

> Theodore Bernstein (1958, p. 17) points out that the word *bandit*
>
> "has a flavor of heroism."
>
> Research shows that experienced writers seem to have much
>
> stronger revision habits than do student writers (Sommers, 1980).

*Two or More Works by the Same Author*   Different works by one author are distinguished by their dates. For multiple references in the same year by one author, add *a*, *b*, or *c* in lowercase letters: 2002a, 2002b, and so forth.

*Two or More Authors*   For a work with two authors, cite both names every time. For three to five authors, include all names the first time, arranged alphabetically. After that, cite only the first author's name followed by *et al*. For six or more authors, cite only the first author followed by *et al.* for all occurrences.

> Rivers, Moss, and Wang (2000) claim. . . .
>
> These findings have been labelled "ridiculous, perhaps
>
> fraudulent" (King & Alberti, 2002, p. 322).

*Works by Two Authors with the Same Last Name*   Distinguish by using initials: "J. Neff (1999) and C. A. Neff (2000) also found. . . ."

*Source with No Author Name Given*   For unsigned sources, use an abbreviated version of the title. Place article titles in quotation marks, and underline or italicize book and pamphlet titles: "Timber Wolves," 2002 (*Recycling*, 1991).

*Groups as Authors*   In general, give the name of the group in full each time you cite it. If the name is long, abbreviate it in subsequent citations.

> *First reference:* (American Association of Retired People [AARP],
>
>      2002)
>
> *Later references:* (AARP, 2002)

***Secondary Source***   If you are citing an author quoted by another author, precede the secondary source with the phrase *as cited in*.

> Jameson's findings (as cited in Baure & Dinks, 2001, p. 124).

***Two or More Sources in One Citation***   List alphabetically by authors' last names, separated by semicolons: (Adams, 2000; Coates & Tan, 2001; Martiniu, 1998). If citations include two works by the same author, list the dates, separated by commas: (Wiggins, 1989, 1991).

***Personal Communications***   Email, personal interviews, letters, and the like are cited only in the text, not on the reference list.

> According to the hospital's chief administrator, the procedure is
>
> no longer performed there (J. A. Wells, personal communication,
>
> May 28, 2001).

***Long Quotations***   Quotations of forty words or more are double spaced and set off, indented five spaces. The parenthetical citation is placed one space after the final punctuation.

> Moskos (2000) summarizes the argument well:
>
> > The principal argument raised against linking national
> >
> > service and federal educational aid is that it would have a
> >
> > regressive effect. . . . Students from wealthy families who do
> >
> > not need aid would be unaffected, while poor students
> >
> > would have to enter national service in order to get aid.
> >
> > (p. 380)

## PREPARING A REFERENCE LIST: APA STYLE

Preparing a reference list is tricky, so keep the models and general guidelines below handy. Double-check the order of entries, punctuation, capitalization, parentheses, and brackets in each entry. All references cited in the text, except personal communication, belong in the reference list. Here are general guidelines for the format:

- Type *Reference List*, centred, at the top of the page.
- Double space entries.
- Alphabetize entries according to the authors' last names or, when no author is listed, the first major word of the title. Use initials and the surname. Omit suffixes such as *Jr.*

- After the author's name, enclose the date of publication (year, month, day) in parentheses, followed by a period.
- Do not indent the first line of each entry. Indent subsequent lines five spaces.
- Italicize the title of periodicals, volume numbers, and book titles. If your keyboard lacks an italicizing function, underline.
- Place nonroutine information that is necessary to identify and recover a source in brackets after the article title.
- Use Arabic numerals for volume (e.g., 4, not IV). Retain Roman numerals that are part of a title.

## A.  APA ENTRIES: PERIODICALS

Since entries for articles vary, check each item carefully after you type it, comparing it with the correct model in this section. Proofread again when you are fresh. The guidelines below will help you type your entries correctly.

- Capitalize only the first word of an article title or subtitle and proper nouns.
- Do not enclose article titles in quotation marks.
- Use an ampersand (&) instead of *and* when listing two or more authors.
- Italicize the name of the journal or magazine and the volume number. Omit *vol.*
- Spell out months.
- To list pages of newspapers, abbreviate as *p.* or *pp.*
- Place a range of pages at the end. Omit *p.* or *pp.* for references to journal and magazine articles.

## 1. Journal Article with Two Authors and Continuous Paging

Invert the names of both authors:

> Luna, B., & Funglar, M. N. (2001, October 24/31). Drug-induced
>
> hyperglycemia. *Journal of the American Medical*
>
> *Association, 286*(16), 1945-1948.

*Three to six authors:* List all the names in a series.
*More than six authors:* List six names, then *et al.,* set off by a comma.

## 2. Journal Article with Each Issue Paged Separately

Include issue numbers in parentheses after the volume number with no space between: 7(3).

> Togger, D. A., & Breaner, P. S. (2001, October). Metered dose
>
> inhalers. *American Journal of Nursing, 101*(10), 26-32.

## 3. Magazine Article

> Begley, S., & Isikuff, M. (2001, October 22). Anxious about
>
> anthrax. *Newsweek,* 28-35.

## 4. Anonymous Article

> Dill soothes an upset tummy. (2001, July/August). *Organic*
>
> *Gardening,* 13.

## 5. Daily Newspaper Article Continued to Other Pages

> Cribb, R. (2005, October 15). City tax official faces probe. *Toronto*
>
> *Star,* pp. A1, A28.

## 6. Newsletter Article

> Piwowarczyk, E. (2002, June). Revisiting the Evelyn Dick case.
>
> *Crime Scene: A Sisters in Crime (Toronto Chapter)*
>
> *Publication, 13*(3), 1, 4.

## 7. Editorial

After the article title, place nonroutine information necessary for identification in brackets.

> Maxwell, B. (2001, October 26). The messenger takes a pounding
>
> [Editorial]. *The Marion Star,* p. A6.

## 8. Letter to the Editor

> Clarke, J.A. (2005, October 17). Canadians pay too much tax
>
> [Letter to the editor]. *Toronto Star,* p. A23.

## 9. Abstract and Review from a Secondary Source (print periodical)

In scholarly research cite primary sources when possible (also see example 16). If an abstract has no review, omit *Review by*.

> Monti, Daniel, J. (1999). *The American city: A social and cultural history.* Review by J. C. Schneider (2001) in *Journal of American History, 87,* 1537-1538. Abstract and review obtained from *Book Review Digest, 2001, 97*(6), 157.

## B.  APA ENTRIES: BOOKS, BROCHURES, AND GOVERNMENT PUBLICATIONS

Entries for books include author, date, title, place of publication (city and province or state), and publisher. Use all the names in a publishing company (Simon & Schuster, not just Simon), but don't include *Publishing Company, Inc.* and other nonessential words. Retain *Books* and *Press*.

- Capitalize only the first word of the title and of the subtitle, as well as proper nouns.
- Use initials and the surname.
- Spell out the names of associations and university presses: National Audubon Society, Oxford University Press.
- Do not invert the names of editors. Identify the editor by (Ed.) after the surname.
- Italicize book titles (or underline if you lack that function). Do not enclose article or chapter titles in quotation marks.

## 10.  A Book by One Author

> Clarke, C. A. (2000). *The collected stories of Arthur C. Clarke.* New York: Tom Doherty Associates.

## 11.  Two or More Books by One Author

Books by the same author are listed according to date, from least to most recent. The author's name is repeated in each subsequent entry.

> Goldberg, N. (1986). *Writing down the bones: Freeing the writer within.* Boston: Shambhala.

Goldberg, N. (1990). *Wild mind: Living the writer's life.* New York: Random.

## 12. A Book by Two or More Authors

Musciano, C., & Kennedy, B. (2000). *HTML & XHTML: The definitive guide* (4th ed.). Sebastopol, CA: O'Reilly.

## 13. A Book by an Unknown Author

*Go Ask Alice.* (1971). New York: Prentice-Hall.

## 14. Book, Revised or Later Edition

Figler, H. (1999). *The complete job-search handbook: Everything you need to know to get the job you really want* (2nd ed.). Buffalo: Firefly Books.

## 15. Article or Chapter in a Book

Cite the inclusive pages of the article or chapter in parentheses after the book title.

Ryan, T. (2001). Such a thing as destiny. In *The prize winner of Defiance, Ohio* (pp. 283-289). New York: Simon & Schuster.

## 16. A Work in an Anthology

If you consult one book of a multivolume set, capitalize the volume number (Vol. 5) and place it after the volume title without parentheses. The example below is for a single-volume anthology:

Michaels, A. (2003). Hurricane. In R. Conrad (Ed.), *The Act of Writing: Canadian Essays for Composition* (pp. 98-101). Toronto: McGraw-Hill Ryerson.

## 17. Published Interview

Begin with the name of the person interviewed and the date of the interview, then the title (if any), and the identifying information in brackets. Complete the entry by placing information identifying the source according to the guidelines for books (or periodicals, if the interview appeared in periodically published source).

MacLeish, A. (1974, Summer). "Archibald MacLeish." [Interview with Benjamin De Mott]. In G. Plimpton (Ed.) (1988), *Writers at work: The Paris review interviews, 5* (pp. 23-48). New York: Penguin.

## 18. Review

Applebaum, H. A. (1980) Looking at work from a social anthropological perspective [Review of the book *Social anthropology of work*]. *Current Anthropology, 21,* 307-308.

## 19. Dictionary or Encyclopedia

If a major reference work has a large editorial board, you may cite only the name of the executive editor and follow it with "et al." as in the first example.

Single Volume with Several Editors

Barber, K., et al. (Eds.). (2005). *Oxford Canadian Dictionary of Current English* (1st ed.). Toronto: Oxford University Press.

No Author Given

The Civil War. (1995). In *Encyclopedia Americana* (Vol. 6, pp. 782-819), Danbury, CT: Grolier.

## 20. Chapter in a Volume in a Series

Moore, W. E. (1969). Social structure and behavior. In G. Lindzey & E. Aronson (Eds.), *The handbook of social psychology:* Vol. 4. *Group psychology and phenomena of interaction* (2nd ed., pp. 283-322). Reading, MA: Addison-Wesley.

## 21. Brochure, Corporate Author

Start with the publisher; then give the date and title. Identify the publication in brackets. List the place and author.

Personal Training Systems. (1992). *The official audio guide to Quicken for Macintosh* [Brochure]. San Jose, CA: Author.

## 22. Government Publications with a Group Author

Health Care Financing Administration. (2001). *Medicare & You 2001.* Washington, DC: U.S. Government Printing Office.

U.S. Department of Justice. (2001). *FBI National Academy*

*Directory of Graduates 2001 Edition.* Quantico, VA: FBI

Academy.

## C.  APA ENTRIES: AUDIOVISUAL MEDIA

For broadcast, film, and recorded sources, enclose in *parentheses* the contributing personnel and the date. Place the medium [Motion picture] or [Television broadcast] in *brackets.*

### 23.  Motion Pictures

Indicate the specific medium in brackets. Include the city and producing organization, if available.

Newel, M. (Director), & Barnes, P. (Screenwriter). (1992).

*Enchanted April* [Motion picture]. Burbank, CA: Warner

Brothers.

### 24.  Television Broadcasts

Identify a series of broadcasts in brackets [Television series] or give the number of episodes and transcript information, if available.

Schama, S. (Writer, narrator, & producer). (2001, October 29). The

body of the queen [Television series, 5 episodes]. *A history*

*of Britain.* Columbus, OH: The History Channel.

Shaw, B. (Reporter). (1999, July 1). Clinton's boom era not as

turbulent as LBJ's [Television broadcast, transcript]. *Inside*

*politics.* Atlanta: CNN.

### 25.  Music and Audio Recordings

When referring to specific lyrics or compositions, begin with the lyricist/composer, followed by the original copyright date. Then provide recording information, including the date, if it is different from the copyright date. Or if appropriate, begin with the performer, conductor, or title. For nonmusical recordings, start with the original writer's name (if provided) or with the title. Include the medium and the number in brackets.

Blitzstein, M. (1941). In the clear [Recorded by D. Upshaw]. On

*I wish it so* [CD]. New York: Elektra Entertainment. (1994)

> *Official audio guide to Quicken.* (1992). [Cassette recording no.
> IQU4.00M-1-A]. San Jose, CA: Personal Training Systems.

## D.  APA ENTRIES: INTERNET AND OTHER ELECTRONIC SOURCES

When an Internet entry has a printed source, cite the print information (see examples 1–24) before online information. Provide the author, date of online publication, and sponsor of the site when possible. These three guidelines will be helpful:

- Place *Retrieved from* and the date before the URL. Do not use angle brackets or add a period.
- When no date is available, use (n.d.).
- Split URLs only at slash [/] marks.

Note that many types of electronic sources can be stored on an aggregated database. This term refers to a single searchable database with many parts. Basically, the database combines words with pictures and/or numbers. Whether you access information from a database stored on a CD-ROM, loaded onto a college or library server, or available on the Internet, you need to attach a retrieval statement to your entry.

First, identify the work, using the appropriate format. Then indicate where the source was *Retrieved from*, the date it was retrieved, and the name of the database. If there is an item or access number, place it at the end of the entry in parentheses. If you access the database online, also provide a URL that links to its main search page.

### Internet Articles Based on a Print Source

If the print version has been unchanged on the Internet, no retrieval statement is necessary. Just add [Electronic version] after the article title. If page numbers are not given or if the format differs from the print version, add a retrieval statement with the date and URL.

### Periodicals on the Internet

### 26.  Article in a Journal

> Parrott, A. C. (1999, October). Does cigarette smoking cause
> stress? [Electronic version] *American Psychologist, 54,*
> 817-820.

## 27. Article in a Magazine

Morse, J. (2001, July 27). Congress tries to tell the bad schools from the mediocre. *Time.* Retrieved November 3 from http://www.time.com/time/columnist/morse/article/ 0,9565,169152,00 htm

## 28. Article in a Newspaper

Bronskill, J. (2005, October 18). Quebec will have its own army, Duceppe says. *Globe and Mail.* Retrieved October 19, 2005, from http://www.theglobeandmail.com/servlet/story/ RTGAM.20051018.wquebmill018/BNStory/National

## 29. Article in an Internet-Only Newsletter

Justice, R. (n.d.) Hospital workers forget to wash hands between patients. *In Touch Newsletter.* Retrieved October 26, 2001, from http://www.intouchnews.com/sample.htm

## 30. Abstract

Glenn, M. J., & Mumby, D. G. (1998). Place memory is intact in rats with perirhinal cortex lesions. *Behavioral Neuroscience, 112,* 1353-1365. Abstract retrieved February 26, 1999, from http://www.apa.org/journals/bne/1298ab.html#6

## Nonperiodical Documents on the Internet

## 31. Chapter or Section in an Internet Document

The book below was originally published in 1878. The online source is based on Harper's 1892 edition.

James, Henry. (1878) Part I. *Daisy Miller.* New York: Harper (1892). Retrieved November 1, 2001, from http:// www.newpaltz.edu/~hathaway/daisyO.html

## 32. Online Anthology

Frost, R. (n.d.) "Mending Wall." *Modern American Poetry.*
C. Nelson (Ed.). Retrieved November 2, 2001, from Oxford
University Press Web site http://www.english.uluc.edu/
maps/poets/a_f/frost/wall.htm

## 33. Collection of Short Stories from a Book

Sawyer, R. J. Gators. (1997). In J. Sherman, & K. R. DiCandido
(Eds.) *Urban Nightmares.* Bronx: Baen. Retrieved
November 2, 2001, from http://www.sfwriter.com/
stgator.htm

## 34. Document Available on University Program or Department Web Site

Ward, H. (1999, May 18). The Story of Bessie Costrell. (1895). In
P. Willett (Ed.) *Victorian Women Writers Project.* Retrieved
June 11, 1999, from Indiana University Web site http://
www.indiana.edu/~letrs/vwwp/ward/bessie.html

## 35. Online Encyclopedia

Wild rice. (2001). *The Columbia electronic encyclopedia* (6th ed.).
Retrieved October 25, 2001, from http://
www.encyclopedia.com

## 36. Professional or Personal Site

*Hopkins Information Technology Services.* Home page. Retrieved
October 26, 2001, from Johns Hopkins University Web site
http://webapps.jhu.edu/hitswebsite/

Barbour, D. (2001, January 7) *Dennis Barbour useful links.* Online
directory. Retrieved October 26, 2001, from http://
www.hme.jhu.edu/~dbarbour/links.html

## 37. Message posted to an Online Forum or Discussion Group

Kasworm, E. (2000, October 15). A totally implantable artificial

heart. Message posted to http://www.med.utah.edu/ethics/

## 38. EMail

Online correspondence between individuals is cited as *personal communication* in the text of your paper only, as shown below. List the initials of the sender and the exact date.

(C. M. Smith, personal communication, May 1, 2002)

## Nonperiodical Publications on CD-ROM

Cite nonperiodical CD-ROMs the way you would cite a book title and author. Include the publisher and disc or item number (if there is one).

## 39. CD-ROMs

The example below refers to one disc of a set of CD-ROMs that is available at many public libraries. Since the sets are stored on the premises, there is no URL.

*1880 United States Census and National Index.* (2001). Retrieved

November 1, 2001, from Family Search Family History

Resource File [CD-ROM]. Salt Lake City, UT: Intellectual

Reserve.

## 40. Daily Newspaper Article, Electronic Version Available by Search

Harlin, Kevin. (n.d.). Students develop 'smart parking' system.

*New York Times.* Retrieved November 4, 2001, from http://

www.nytimes.com

## 41. Material from an Electronic Database

Koehn, Nancy F. (1999). Henry Heinz and brand creation in the

late nineteenth century: Making markets for processed

food. *Business History Review 73*(3), 349+. Retrieved May 3, 2002, from *InfoTrac OneFile* database.

## 42.  Computer Software and Computer Programs

Schulman, R., Schrader, J., & Jacobs, J. (1999). *Quicken Deluxe 99* [Computer software]. Menlo Park, CA: Intuit.

---

### SUMMARY

- Accurate and complete documentation is essential both in the workplace and in college.
- The primary purpose of documentation is to supply information to the reader and to give credit to the author.
- When material is borrowed without providing documentation, the offence is plagiarism.
- Different styles of documentation are used for research papers such as MLA, APA, or Chicago Style.

---

## *Practice*

### Recognizing Items That Need to Be Documented

*Directions:* Go to a library or use some of your own materials to create examples of entries for an MLA style list of works cited or an APA style reference list. Follow the textbook models carefully, checking format and punctuation.

1. Book by two or three authors
2. Book with an editor or editors
3. A work in an anthology by several authors
4. Book with several volumes
5. Article from a daily newspaper
6. Article from a monthly magazine
7. Article from a journal with continuous paging
8. Videotape
9. One author quoting another author
10. Internet source: published newspaper, magazine, or journal article
11. Internet source: article from a professional Web site

# CHAPTER 25

# *Using Sources and Writing a Research Paper*

## Learning Objectives

After reading and applying the information in Chapter 25, you'll be able to:

- Research effectively
- Report research findings
- Summarize, paraphrase, and quote all required documentation
- State a clear thesis
- Use clear transitional language when integrating summaries, paraphrases, and quotations in the essay
- Develop citations and a list of references

*I have lived in this world just long enough to look carefully the second time into things that I am the most certain of the first time.*

—Josh Billings (1818–1885)
(Henry Wheeler Shaw)

Research can be scientific investigation, as in primary research, or scholarly inquiry, as in secondary research. Both kinds require a fair and thorough consideration of existing facts before reaching a conclusion. When doing any research, be open to new evidence even if it conflicts with what you believe. Withhold judgment until you have examined the facts, noted inferences, and labelled theories. Otherwise, expensive mistakes may be made.

See Chapter 21.

See "The Logical Appeal," page 217.

## RESEARCH READING

Reading for research, if you are absorbed in your topic, can be just as engrossing as the latest best-seller. By reading widely, you can gain not only a comprehensive view of your topic but also knowledge of the latest discoveries in a field. Research reading, however, requires an organized, analytical approach that reflects your purpose. At some points you need to be critical.

## WORKPLACE CASE STUDY

### TRACKING THE TRUTH

As an employee was leaving a plant, security guards stopped him to search his briefcase. They found a $35 telephone. Assuming he had stolen the phone, the company fired him. Notices were placed on eleven bulletin boards and the electronic mail system, saying the phone was company property and the employee had violated work rule number 12 about theft. The employee filed suit against the company for libel.

At the trial a coworker testified to going with the defendant to a mall where he had purchased the phone. The defendant explained that his company phone had been damaged by a flood. But he had lost the sales slip for the new phone. His boss had said to just keep the phone. After the firing, the man had applied for a hundred jobs, but was rejected each time it was learned why he had been fired. The jury awarded the defendant $1.3 million in damages. The moral of this story is that an open mind is a prerequisite to tracking the truth.

## Examining Dates and Credentials

As new knowledge is discovered, previous knowledge may become dated. As you read, examine the dates of surveys, studies, and other research as well as the credentials of the writers and researchers. To find this background information, check the home page of a Web site and the preface, introduction, or any footnotes of printed materials.

## CHECKLIST FOR EXAMINING SOURCES AND CREDENTIALS

1. Is the source primary or secondary? Is enough documentation provided?

2. Does the author/researcher have advanced degrees, licences or certification, and a good reputation in the field?

3. When was the study, poll, or other research conducted? Where? What was the size of the sample?

4. Does the interpretation of results seem logical? Does the language seem objective? Or does the writer seem to have a hidden agenda? For example, a nutritionist on a radio talk show recommended a vitamin preparation that he had invented.

5. Has other research reported similar or conflicting results? What do authorities in the field generally accept?

## Using Tentative Words to Discuss Findings and Theories

The rhetorical situation of a research paper requires more precision in word choice than that of a less formal paper. As you read reputable accounts of polls, experiments, and studies, notice the tentative, or provisional, words that qualify discussions of results. These *uncertain* words indicate that evidence is *not* conclusive even though a growing body of research may indicate a conclusion or theory is probably true. Look at how the journal *Science* uses tentative words (italicized here) to discuss results of several studies about the cause of perfect pitch:

> A research team from Düsseldorf, Germany, *may* have located the physical basis of one exceptional form of mental performance: perfect pitch—the ability to identify any musical note without comparison to a reference note. . . .
>
> A team led by neurologists Gottfried Schlaug and Helmuth Steinmetz of Düsseldorf's Heinrich Heine University *reports* that the planum temporale, a region of the brain cortex that processes sound signals, is far larger on the left side than on the right in professional musicians—and especially in those who have perfect pitch.

Overstatement undermines the credibility of research. Yet beginning writers sometimes assume that because a study or experiment *suggests* that something is true, it is, indeed, true. By the time they summarize their research notes, they have catapulted theory into the realm of fact. Often one word, *prove*, is what launches this assault upon truth. To discuss uncertain research findings competently, qualify your statements with tentative words. Use accurate terminology; examples are listed in the box.

### TENTATIVE WORDS COMMONLY USED IN RESEARCH

| Verbs | Nouns | Phrases |
|---|---|---|
| indicates | indication | probable cause |
| found | findings | possible influence |
| may | possibility | apparently is |
| reported | report | is often a sign of |
| suggest | suggestion | could indicate |
| influence | influence | suggests that |
| theorize | theory | |
| imply | implication | |
| seems | symptoms | |
| appears | appearance | |

## Recognizing Information
## That Must Be Acknowledged

The rhetorical situation of a secondary research paper requires that the majority of what you write be based on outside sources. Careless noting of sources can result in unintentional plagiarism. Perhaps knowing that the Latin *plagiarius* means "kidnapper" will remind you not to kidnap absentmindedly any original words. The penalties for this offence can be severe (See Chapter 24). Take care in gathering all of the source information needed for parenthetical citations and works cited entries.

***Restating Common Knowledge***   Factual information that is familiar to the general public is considered common knowledge. For example, it is common knowledge that orange juice is high in vitamin C, that Thomas A. Edison perfected the incandescent lightbulb, and that Alfred Hitchcock directed suspense films. So if you come across such facts in your research, you will not be expected to acknowledge the source for them—*unless you decide to quote the source directly*. If you copy an author's words, you need to enclose them in quotation marks and cite the source. In your early efforts at research, it is best to cite the source of any piece of information that you were unaware of before your reading.

***Acknowledging Everything Else***   Practically all other information gathered in research requires documentation. Here is a list of items to watch for so that you can make a source card for each item:

- Historical information that is not commonly known
- Current information based on a writer's direct observation or reporting
- Statistics
- Surveys and opinion poll results. Give the researcher, date, place, size of sample, and any other pertinent information in the text of the paper if possible.
- Research results and interpretations. Give names of researchers, date.
- Expert opinion, estimates, predictions
- Theories. Identify the person who originated the theory, if possible.
- Artistic interpretations or criticisms
- Tables, charts, graphs, and other visual material
- Any statement that is subject to debate
- Footnote from printed material

***Stating Your Own Ideas and Conclusions***   If you combine primary research with secondary research, describe your findings in detail. Offer a logical interpretation of the evidence, taking into consideration the opinions of authorities. To

---

### TIPS FOR COMPILING A LIST OF SOURCES

- Start making source cards early. Note the author, publication, date, page numbers, or other source information.
- To make entries, find the correct model in Chapter 24. Check the order and punctuation of each entry you construct.
- As you add more parenthetical citations to your paper, make a new source entry for each citation unless the source already has an entry.
- *Alphabetize* source cards before typing your list of sources.
- Double-space entries when typing your list of sources for your paper.

See Chapters 22 and 24.

---

start thinking, you might ask yourself, *"Why are the findings significant? What does it all mean? What are the implications?"* As a rule, informative secondary research papers by first-year students do not include personal opinion or reactions. If you are unclear on this point, be sure to ask your instructor.

A paper based on observation or a survey alone does not require a list of sources, but a series of interviews would need a list of sources. When primary and secondary research are both used, the source entries can be combined into one list.

## NOTE-TAKING, SUMMARIZING, PARAPHRASING, AND QUOTING

Take care to preserve the meaning of the original passage as you take notes, summarize, paraphrase, and quote. Distinguish fact from opinion. Transcribe numbers and other figures correctly. With thought and care, you can avoid four common problems in student research papers:

- pulling ideas out of context
- omitting significant information
- overuse of quotations
- inadequate documentation

An informative first-year research paper is usually expected to consist mainly of summary. Paraphrase appears at times, and short direct quotations are sprinkled at appropriate intervals. One or more long direct quotations may be used, depending on the assignment and the material. An example of an informative research paper appears at the end of this chapter. To see researched arguments, turn to Chapter 19.

## Note-Taking and Critical Reading

The most important requirement as you take notes, either in the margins of photocopies or on note cards, is to *insert quotation marks around any material that you intend to copy into your research paper or report*. This chapter explains how to integrate quotations into a paper as well as use ellipsis, brackets, and explanatory notes. For extensive help with note-taking, commenting, and reacting to ideas, see "Critical Reading" in Chapter 26. The handbook provides grammar rules and examples, pages H-18 to H-33.

For sentence
patterns, see
Chapter 8.

## Summarizing

A summary condenses and restates. To summarize, you extract the main ideas of a passage and *convert them into your own words and sentence patterns*. You reduce the passage—perhaps several paragraphs or even several pages—by 50 to 75 percent. To focus on the main ideas of an original, reword the topic sentences. Use synonyms to replace major words (nouns, verbs, adjectives, and adverbs) and combine lesser ideas. Restructure sentences, retaining only the gist of the material.

Minor words such as articles (*a, an, the*), prepositions, and conjunctions may be repeated from the original if necessary to preserve the meaning. A thesaurus and dictionary can help you quickly find synonyms to replace the author's words. Examples of summary, paraphrase, and quotation follow. The original example is a story that has become a classic, involving a horse thought to have the ability to communicate with people.

### Original

Herr von Osten purchased a horse in Berlin, Germany, in 1900. When von Osten began training his horse, Hans, to count by tapping his front hoof, he had no idea that Hans was soon to become one of the most celebrated horses in history. Hans was a rapid learner and soon progressed from counting to addition, multiplication, division, subtraction, and eventually the solution of problems involving factors and fractions. As if this were not enough, von Osten exhibited Hans to public audiences where he counted the number in the audience or simply the number of people wearing eyeglasses. Still responding only with taps, Hans could tell time, use a calendar, display an ability to recall musical pitch, and perform numerous other seemingly fantastic feats. After von Osten taught Hans an alphabet which could be coded into hoof beats, the horse could answer virtually any question—oral or written. It seemed that Hans, a common horse, had complete comprehension of the German language, the ability to produce the equivalent of words and numerals, and an intelligence beyond that of many human beings.

**Mark L. Knapp**
*—Nonverbal Communication in Human Interaction*

### Summary

Mark L. Knapp tells an amazing story of a horse owned by Herr von Osten of Germany in the early 1900s. His owner taught Hans to do arithmetic, drummed out with a front hoof. Then von Osten began showing the horse in public, where Hans computed the total of persons with spectacles and did other tricks. He seemed to have learned the alphabet, for he could tap out a response to most queries. Many people were convinced Hans knew German well. In fact, he appeared brighter than many people (1).

The summary, less than half as long as the original, makes essentially the same points. Note that the source is clearly identified in the first sentence of the summary. At the end, the page number of Knapp's passage is placed in parentheses *before* the period. Synonyms replace major words that are not *generic* (the name of a category). Generic words such as *horse, musical pitch*, and *alphabet* have no close synonyms. Therefore they are included without quotation marks. (Don't assume that a word is generic; check in a dictionary. For example, Kleenex is not generic; *facial tissue* is generic.)

In the example of plagiarism below, major words have been copied when they should not have been. In addition, variations of major words have been used. For instance, Knapp writes "began training," and the unacceptable example uses "trained." The plagiarized portions are underlined.

### Plagiarized Summary

According to Mark L. Knapp, in 1900 in Berlin, Germany, Herr von Osten *purchased a horse. When von Osten trained* the horse to *count* by rapping his hoof, he did not know that Hans would *become one of* the most famous horses *in history*. Hans was a *rapid learner and soon* could do arithmetic and other tricks. *After Herr von Osten taught Hans a coded alphabet, it seemed* Hans, a horse, understood German well and knew more than many people (1).

## Paraphrasing

Paraphrase, which is longer than summary, is the restatement of an original passage. To paraphrase, *reword and use different sentence patterns*. Retain the meaning of the original; do not distort. Look up words that you do not know. As you paraphrase, take care to select accurate synonyms, not variations of the original words. For example, if an author uses *defend*, do not write *defending*. Find another word such as *protect*. Use paraphrase for the following reasons:

See Chapter 8.

- **To emphasize important ideas.** Use paraphrase for significant points that will support your rhetorical purpose.
- **To clarify a difficult passage.** Reword and make ideas clearer.
- **To combine details.** You may want to condense lesser ideas.

If a passage seems impossible to paraphrase, you can include a few brief quotations, as in the following example, which might have been awkward to paraphrase. Note that even if you do not use a quotation, you still need to give the page number and make a works cited entry.

**Paraphrase**

To explain how animals "read" nonverbal signals, Mark L. Knapp tells a strange story of a horse bought by Herr von Osten in Berlin, Germany. While teaching the horse, Hans, to rap out numbers with a fore hoof, von Osten did not suspect that the animal would ever become famous. But Hans learned so fast that he could soon do arithmetic. When von Osten showed Hans in public, the horse "counted the number of people wearing eyeglasses." He could even "tell time," read a calendar, remember musical pitch, and do other tricks. When von Osten drilled the horse in the alphabet, tapped out with a hoof, Hans responded to almost any query. He appeared not only to understand German well, but also to know more than many people (1).

## Using Quotations

Quotation is a respected practice that is used by educators, researchers, and other writers. Appropriate quotation in a research paper indicates responsible writing. Below are five reasons you might include quotations. (The examples are from *The Writer*, January 2001.)

1. **To present technical words for which there is no accurate paraphrase.** Quoting the exact words prevents misunderstanding. In "Selling Your Work Online," Emily Vander Veer points out a new term:

   Stephen King single-handedly catapulted the term "e-publishing" into the mainstream last March when over half a million readers logged onto their computer and downloaded electronic copies of his novella *Riding the Bullet*.

---

### GUIDELINES: WRITING SUMMARIES AND PARAPHRASES

1. Read the entire original carefully several times so that you are sure you understand it completely. If you can mark the original, underline the topic sentences and key points for ease of reference.

2. Rewrite, retaining the order of the original. Changes in order may distort meaning.

3. Reread the original. Check to see that you have not changed the order or unwittingly copied material that should be paraphrased.

4. If you are unable to paraphrase difficult phrases, copy and enclose in quotation marks.

5. For a summary, reduce material by 50 percent or more. Paraphrase topic sentences, quoting key terms as needed. Restate major points. Combine and condense related ideas. Omit examples and minor details.

6. Cite source and pages.

7. Checkpoint. Is the summary or paraphrase clear? Has all important information been included? Are all spellings correct?

2. **To allay any doubt about the accuracy of a surprising statement or evidence.** By giving the exact words, you avert the reader's suspicion. In "Take the Reader Along," Martha Sutro quotes a paradoxical truism to illustrate the risks that authors take in pitching their work to editors:

> Throughout the process, I remembered a helpful adage: "You have to increase your rate of failure in order to increase your rate of success." You have to be willing to put yourself out there.

3. **To capture the flavour of the original.** Paraphrase will often not do justice to a passage that is vivid and unusual. Aly Colón opens "Avoid the Pitfalls of Plagiarism" by quoting a distinctive phrase:

> Plagiarism is the "unoriginal sin," writes writing coach Roy Peter Clark, a senior scholar at the Poynter Institute, in an article first published in the March 1983 issue of *Washington Journalism Review*. And it seems to be a very common sin.

4. **To avoid an awkward or wordy paraphrase.** Do not abuse this privilege, however. Keep such quotations brief. Here Colón quotes a list of criteria rather than attempting to paraphrase it. Because the material is identified and indented, no quotation marks are required. It is treated as a long quotation:

   - Was there intent? Did the writer intend to pass the work off as his or her own?
   - If there was no intent, did the writer's work habits and methods lead to unintended replication?

5. **To enhance your credibility as a writer.** By including quotations appropriately, you demonstrate professionalism.

Use quotations for a purpose. Keep most quotations brief, according to your assignment and the difficulty of the material. Technical material may require more quotation than usual.

## Making Changes in Quotations

Your readers expect that what you enclose in quotation marks will be the exact words of the original source. Yet some quotations may be lengthy and wordy. To shorten a quotation, you may omit unnecessary words and replace them with an ellipsis as long as the meaning is not changed.

*Ellipsis*   An ellipsis (a set of three spaced dots) can replace wordy or irrelevant material you wish to omit at the beginning, middle, or end of a sentence. The result should still be a complete sentence. The example below, an excerpt from a *Wall Street Journal* article entitled "Chemicals Bad for Ozone Are Declining," by Amal Kumar Naj, shows an ellipsis:

> "Dr. Montzka said the measurements . . . make it possible to predict when the ozone layer will recover. He said the rate of recovery will depend on stratospheric temperature and chemical emissions from volcanoes" (B4).

To omit an entire sentence or more, use four dots. (The fourth dot is the period.) If you omit material and use an ellipsis, take care not to distort the meaning. (The example above shows the traditional MLA recommendations. If, however, your instructor wishes you to follow the latest MLA style, see the Handbook section of this text.)

***Brackets***    If you need to add something to a quotation for clarity or logic, you can insert the explanatory words within brackets [ ]. Originally, the paragraph below used *he*, which has been replaced with the name of the researcher:

> "Barring unusual changes in temperature and emissions, [Dr. Montzka] esti-mated that it will take 50 to 60 years before the Earth's ozone layer is restored to the levels before 1970."

When the verb tense of a quotation differs from the text of your paper, you can resolve this inconsistency by substituting another tense in brackets. In the example below, the original was written in the present tense. For the sake of logic, two changes to the past tense (in brackets) replace the original wording.

> Farley Mowat describes the clothes of the Ihalmiut, a tribe that became extinct in the 1950s, as "two suits of fur, worn one over the other. . . . The inner suit [was] worn with the hair of the hides facing inward and touching the skin while the outer suit [had] its hair turned out to the weather" (422).

Once in a while, you may find an error in grammar or spelling in one of your sources. To indicate that you are reproducing the original error rather than creating one of your own, you may insert the Latin word *sic* ("thus") in brackets after the error, as shown after this grammatical mishap:

> An example of the radical nature of the organization is this advice from a pamphlet it published: "Thieves should be punished by having there [*sic*] hands cut off."

Keep in mind, however, that some words have two or more correct spellings. It is always a good idea to check two dictionaries to be sure a word is actually misspelled or misused.

***Quotation within a Quotation***    When your source contains a quotation, change the double quotation marks in the original to single marks (' '). Then enclose the full quotation in double quotation marks, as shown below:

> In *Strictly Speaking* Edwin Newman writes: "Most conversation these days is as pleasing to the ear as a Flash-Frozen Dinner is to the palate, consisting largely of 'You've got to be kidding,' 'It's a bad scene,' 'How does that grab you?' 'Just for openers . . .'" (16).

## MAKING A WORKING OUTLINE

Once you have completed the bulk of your research and note-taking, you can use your note cards to start a working outline. A simple way to start is to classify your

> ### QUESTIONS FOR DEVELOPING A THESIS AND AN OUTLINE
>
> 1. *What is the purpose of the paper?* How can I make the purpose clear?
> 2. *What are the main points of my research?*
> 3. *What thesis can serve as an umbrella for all the main points?* Do I have irrelevant material? Do I need to narrow the topic?
> 4. *Is chronological order apparent anywhere?* Are there historical items to place in chronological order? Might they make an interesting introduction or should they come later? Will the overall order be chronological or just the introduction?
> 5. *How should the body of the paper be organized?* Should main points be arranged according to importance? Or should they go from concrete to abstract? Or would some other order, possibly problem solving, work best?
> 6. *Does the material seem comprehensive?* Are there significant gaps? Do I need more information to be complete?

note cards. Sort through the cards according to subject and place related items in piles. Then examine each pile and label it with a category under which all items will fit. After that, organize the categories into a possible order. If you become puzzled, ask yourself questions as you draft your outline.

When you are comfortable with a tentative order, number your note cards and copy the categories and subcategories into outline form. Leave spaces for adding items. By the end of the writing process, your working outline will have become a formal outline, ready for submission along with your paper, if required. (An example of an outline submitted with a student paper appears near the end of this chapter.)

## DRAFTING A RESEARCH PAPER

As you begin to draft, keep in mind that your working outline is subject to change. In the course of getting your thoughts on paper, you may make slight changes or even find a different organization emerging. If so, take the time to rethink your working outline before continuing to draft.

### Drafting a Thesis and Introduction

The sooner you can state a clear thesis, the sooner you can begin to organize and draft your research paper. If you are uncertain, reexamine your controlling question and rewrite it as a thesis statement. Or you might prefer to draft the introduction as a whole unit rather than in pieces. You may even find that your thesis has mushroomed out over several sentences as in Wilma Dunnington's introduction. Although her purpose is clearly informative, there is no one thesis sentence:

### The Genome Project

Possible effects

Probably few readers can imagine a time when genetic profiles would be used as a basis for marriage or divorce, a time when genetic testing would be required by employers to screen applicants. It is easier to envision a world where children "diagnosed with cystic fibrosis would be spared their fate by a gene transplant," a world where cancers would be revealed and treated before a single cancer cell could grow (Bishop and Waldholz 22). These are the "threats and promises" of what could be the "most ambitious scientific research project ever undertaken" (22). The Human Genome Project is an effort to identify all of the genes in the human body.

Definition

Main goal

In *Principles of Anatomy and Physiology*, Tortora and Anagnostakos report that the Human Genome Project will take an estimated fifteen years and cost three billion dollars. The overriding goal of the project is to "conquer genetic disease" (953). Marwick points out that in the human body are more than 100 thousand genes. Occasionally, a gene is injured, resulting in "abnormal features or disorders." Sometimes an embryo will not grow; other times children are born with defects. Some conditions caused by a damaged gene may not be apparent until a person becomes aged (3247).

Explanation

Another way to begin an introduction is with a definition of a special term, followed by a brief history and explanation. Note, too, that Kathy Rummer includes a statement of purpose.

### Dr. Nightingale: Nurse Practitioners in Primary Medical Care

Definition

The role of the nurse practitioner has evolved over several decades in response to a shortage of physicians and physician's assistants, escalating costs, and a shortage of affordable health care. A nurse practitioner (NP) is a registered nurse who has completed an "accredited two-year program of study and clinical practice," earned a master's degree in nursing, and passed a national exam ("Nurse Practitioners" 4). In California, for example, NPs are certified to provide basic medical care, prenatal care, and family planning assistance. They must pass a course in pharmacology and work for six months in an internship, receiving intense supervised training, before they can write prescriptions ("Need a" 4).

Example

History

The nurse practitioner program has evolved as a result of the short supply of physician's assistants (PAs). In 1965 the physician's assistant program was created to relieve the shortage of physicians. Using a physician's assistant for routine medical care freed physicians to concentrate on more complex medical problems (Sidel and Sidel 203, 204). But for some reason the program attracted relatively few medical students. In 1970 the American Medical Association asked the American Nurses Association (ANA) to supply nurses to be trained as physician's assistants. Instead of complying with the request, the ANA created its own alternative to the physician's assistant—the nurse practitioner (Sidel and Sidel 204).

Purpose

The intent of the American Nurses Association was that this new health care professional's "training and philosophy [would reflect] nursing and not medicine" (Sidel and Sidel 204). Dock and Stewart point out that this philosophy is based on the "Nightingale concept" of nursing in which there is "neither independence nor subordination but interdependence and cooperation." According to the Nightingale philosophy, nursing is not a "subcaste of medicine." A nurse is not a "handmaid," but a "helpmate and partner" (367).

For other kinds of openings, see Chapter 4.

## Using Signal Phrases to Integrate Quotations into the Text

Every quotation you use requires transition to weave it into your text. Usually, a *signal* phrase precedes the quotation. This introductory phrase signals the reader that a direct quotation will be presented. To keep your signal phrases strong and responsible, give the full name of the researcher, team, organization, study, or poll whenever possible. To identify a person, give degrees, position, or other credentials. The examples below illustrate signal phrases for introducing quotations:

- According to Dr. Sheila S. Smith, a psychologist at Simon Fraser University,
- A study by a University of Western Ontario medical team found ". . . ."
- In March 2005, the Canadian Medical Association reported:
- James A. Bell, a scientist at Jones Laboratories of New York City, stated:
- Others, like Dr. I. R. Smythe, believe that ". . . ."

More examples of signal phrases can be viewed in student examples throughout the chapter as well as in the research paper at the end of the chapter.

***Weak Phrases***   Some popular magazines and newspapers omit vital source information. Instead, they substitute vague transitional phrases and the word *it*. All of the following examples are evasive and *inappropriate* for research papers and reports:

| | |
|---|---|
| A study revealed . . . | (What study? Who conducted it?) |
| Experts/researchers/authorities say . . . | (Who? All?) |
| It is believed . . . | (Who believes?) |
| It is estimated . . . | (Who estimated?) |
| It is predicted . . . | (Who predicted?) |
| "In my opinion" or "I feel" | (So what?) |

***Short Quotations***   Quotations of four lines or fewer (three for poetry) are considered short. You can use short quotations to identify special terms or include vivid words and difficult-to-paraphrase segments. Short quotations, too, require transition to link them to the text.

Sometimes you may lack the name of a researcher to use as a transition to a quotation. Popular magazines often summarize research, giving only a minimum of details about several studies. When April Rausch was confronted with this problem, she presented the vital information that was available, using two short quotations:

In 1991, as reported by *USA Today*, thirty-seven babies in the United States died "while sleeping in bean-bag infant cushions." Although some of the babies were thought to have died of Sudden Infant Death Syndrome, others apparently smothered. After a research team headed by James S. Kemp and Bradley T. Thach tested bean-bag cushions from two makers, using rabbits, the Consumer Product Safety Commission cited the cushions as a potential "asphyxiation hazard." In late 1991 infant bean-bag cushions were removed from the market (*USA Today* 5).

***Block Quotations***    A block quotation is a long quotation of five lines or more (four for poetry). For a research paper (MLA style), double-space and indent block quotations *ten* spaces on the left margin, none on the right. Do *not* use quotation marks for a block quotation because the indentation and parenthetical citation alert the reader that the material has been borrowed. Careful writers use long quotations for a valid reason; overuse signals a hastily written paper. In the example below notice that (1) the source and author are identified in the text of the paper *before* the long quotation, (2) a *colon* is placed after the verb, (3) the period appears one space *before* the citation.

> In <u>The Managerial Woman</u>, management consultants Margaret
> Hennig and Anne Jardim state:
>
>> Studies of women who enroll in continuing college
>>
>> education programs show that many of the women
>>
>> who fail in these programs . . . have never discussed
>>
>> their goals with their husbands. The husbands never
>>
>> really understood why their wives had gone back to

---

**VERBS IN SIGNAL PHRASES**

The verb in a signal phrase should indicate the intent of the writer or speaker. Usually the verb is in the present tense unless the context requires the past tense (found, reported, stated). The reference list of verbs below are all in the present tense:

| | | | | |
|---|---|---|---|---|
| admits | concedes | discloses | holds | observes |
| agrees | concludes | disputes | highlights | refuses |
| argues | concurs | emphasizes | insists | refutes |
| believes | denies | finds | maintains | reveals |
| claims | disagrees | grants | notes | stresses |

> school, and the wives on their own had attempted to
> maintain the same level of housework they had been
> accustomed to. (212)

## Inserting Explanatory Notes

Once in a great while you may have material that is useful in discussing your subject but that seems to interrupt the text. In such cases you have the option of including the information in an explanatory note. To do so, insert a superscript numeral at an appropriate point in your text. Then you can place the note either at the bottom of the same page or on a separate page, headed "Note" or "Notes." Begin the note with a matching superscript number (see "Content Notes" in Chapter 24).

## Writing a Conclusion

The conclusion of a research paper may be longer than those of the other papers you have been writing. A graceful ending of three to five (or more) sentences is usually expected. Although new information is not introduced in the conclusion, a writer may leave the reader with a new thought. A brief summary or reference to the future may be appropriate. Peggy Bean combines these three techniques in her closing:

> Although the fetal alcohol syndrome is a tragic disorder, it is also a preventable one. Therefore, it is important that the general public become aware of the risks ethanol poses to the developing fetus, especially to the fetus of a chronic alcoholic. Once families know the cause of this disorder, they can assist the alcoholic mother-to-be in securing professional help.

Bonnie L. Rice ends her research paper with a reference to the future and to what a reader might do to help in a similar situation:

> Efforts toward education, intervention, and prevention of adolescent suicide are being made. They must continue and expand. But can the individual do something to help? Yes, the greatest problem for the unhappy adolescent is isolation from close relationships; one person can be that caring friend who is missing from someone's lonely life.

Sometimes beginning writers tack on a quotation at the end without transition. Although the quotation may be appropriate, the gap between the body and the quotation halts the smooth flow of thought. To link a quotation to a conclusion, use a transitional segment, as italicized in the following example:

> *Child abuse is an ancient problem, but it is an occurrence that concerns us all, a problem that needs to be solved. For as James Agee wrote,* "In every child who is born, under no matter what circumstances, and of no matter what parents, the potentiality of the human race is born again; and in him, too once more, and of each of us, our terrific responsibility towards human life. . . ."

## REVISING, EDITING, AND FORMATTING

When you finish the rough draft of your research paper, heave a sigh of relief, and take a break if possible. If not, perhaps you might alphabetize the entry cards for your works cited list and start typing that or do some other related chore. Before you start to revise your paper, however, you need to gain distance so that you can come back and examine it objectively.

### Revising

See Chapter 5. Persistence, time, and care are the keys to successful revision and proofreading. Yet you may be so preoccupied with content that order, documentation, and mechanics receive low priority. Several revisions spaced over several days will catch more errors than one intensive session the night before a deadline. The checklist below will prove helpful in assisting a tired brain to focus during this all-important stage.

### Checking Documentation

Every source you use in your research paper must be acknowledged according to a standard documentation style. Two of the most common—Modern Language Association (MLA) style and American Psychological Association (APA) style—are described in detail in Chapter 24. Both use parenthetical citations within the text that are keyed to a complete bibliographical list.

---

### CHECKLIST: REVISING SOURCE-BASED PAPERS

1. Compare your outline and paper. Is the order the same? Is it sound?
2. Now read the paper aloud. Is the introduction interesting and complete?
3. Are the main ideas clear?
4. Is there sufficient transition? Is each quotation linked to the text?
5. Are there too many direct quotations? Should some be paraphrased or summarized instead?
6. Could the order of details within paragraphs be improved?
7. Is the conclusion logical and complete?

In the course of drafting and revising, even the most conscientious writer may omit, misplace, or lose a text citation while rearranging sentences or paragraphs. If a problem occurs, don't panic! Remember you have your earlier drafts and note cards. Also check to see that every paragraph in your research paper has at least one text citation unless there is a reason for not including one. Remember, too, that if you split a paragraph you will probably have to make another citation.

## Editing and Proofreading

To catch errors in a research paper, proofread when you are alert. Go over your paper several times—one sitting is seldom enough. For example, watch to see that you have the correct spelling of prefixes, as in words beginning with per- and pre- . To attain the high grades that most students desire, revise and proofread several times. If you follow the editing guidelines outlined in Chapter 5 and provide the necessary effort, your paper should be a success.

See
Chapter 5.

## Using an Appropriate Format

Some instructors may give few or no instructions for formatting a research paper; others may give precise instructions. Most expect good quality white, 21.5 cm by 28 cm paper. If you plan to use erasable paper or to submit a photocopy, check with your instructor first. A title (cover) page may or may not be required. Some instructors like the title page format commonly used in the workplace (see the research paper at the end of this chapter). The MLA style does not require a title page whereas the APA style does. Both styles require that you double-space the entire manuscript, including quotations and list of sources. Some instructors also prefer that you staple or use a paper clip rather than a binder to keep pages together.

***Margins and Indentation***   Standard specifications for research papers call for one-inch margins (top, bottom, and sides). Page numbers are placed one-half inch from the top right and flush with the right margin. Indent the first line of paragraphs 1.25 cm (five spaces on a typewriter). For long quotations, the MLA style indents 2.5 cm (*ten* spaces) from the left margin. The APA style, however, indents long quotations 1.25 cm (*five* spaces).

***MLA Style Heading, Title, and Page Numbering***   If you decide not to have a title page, MLA style advises starting the first page of the manuscript with your name, your instructor's name, the course number, and the date on consecutive lines 2.5 cm from the top left margin. Next, centre the title. Capitalize the first and last words and major words of the title. Do not italicize any words unless you mention a book title or use a foreign phrase or other wording that requires italicizing. (Never italicize your own title.) Page numbers, in the upper right corner, are preceded by the writer's last name. The top of the first page of a research paper, MLA style, looks like this:

Bellows 1

Susan N. Bellows

Professor Raintree

English Composition 112

May 15, 2006

New Sources of Antibiotics from Land and Sea

Many of the wonder drugs of former decades are losing their effectiveness as bacteria acquire immunity to certain antibiotics. Thus there is a never-ending search for new medicines to replace older ones that have become obsolete.

***APA Style Headings, Title, and Page Numbering***   The APA style requires a title page with a "running head" (abbreviated title) of the first two or three words of the title, the full title, and the byline. The full title should summarize the main idea of the manuscript briefly and simply. The byline contains the writer's name and the institutional affiliation (college, university, or other site). In the byline use no extra words such as *by* or *from*. The preferred form of an author's name is first name, middle initial, and last name.

First, type the running head (the first two or three words of the title) and the page number 1.25 cm from the top right margin in upper and lowercase. Skip down about one-third of the page and type the full title, centred in lowercase with capitals (if needed, on two lines, double-spaced). Double-space, then centre the writer's name. Double-space again and centre the name of the institution. The top of a title page, APA style, looks like this:

New Sources of Antibiotics        1

New Sources of Antibiotics from Land and Sea

Susan N. Bellows

Professor Raintree

English Composition 112

May 15, 2006

Page numbers in APA style are preceded by the running head from the title page on succeeding pages. This means that the first two or three words are taken from the title. Note that the page number appears five spaces after the head.

## SUMMARY

- Effective research requires an open mind and thorough consideration of available evidence.
- In reporting research findings and commenting on implications, use provisional words, such as *suggests* and *indicates*.
- While taking notes use language that summarizes most of the time; when copying, enclose the material copied in quotation marks.
- Summaries, paraphrasing, and quotations all require documentation.
- Use sorted note cards to develop a working outline when completing the first draft of an essay.
- State a clear thesis.
- Use clear transitional language when integrating summaries, paraphrases, and quotations in the essay.
- For every parenthetical citation, make a corresponding citation and/or a list of references, providing full bibliographical data.

## Test Yourself

### What Are the Facts about Documentation?

*Directions:* Fill in the blank with true (T) or false (F). To check your answers, turn to the end of this chapter.

_____ 1. Minor words such as *a, an, the, but, of, on* may be copied without documentation.

_____ 2. Plagiarism may be unethical, but it is legal.

_____ 3. Plagiarism refers only to copying from published works.

_____ 4. A general word that has no accurate synonym can be copied without documentation.

_____ 5. If an author's unique idea is used but not his or her words, the source must be identified.

_____ 6. All special terms should be set off with quotation marks or italics the first time they are used.

_____ 7. A selection from an author's work may be copied if placed in quotation marks and if the source is identified.

_____ 8. If even a few of an author's major words are copied, they must have both quotation marks and a citation.

_____ 9. Quotation marks and documentation are both needed for copied material that is not indented.

_____ 10. If only statistics are copied, quotation marks are not used, but a source is supplied.

## Practice

### Transitional Phrases to Introduce Quotations

*Directions:* For the following items, write a transitional phrase to introduce the quotation. For help, see "Using Signal Words to Integrate Quotations into the Text," in Chapter 25. (*Source for this exercise:* Siebert, Al. *The Survivor Personality.* New York: Berkley, 1996. Both quotations appear on page 64 of Siebert's book.)

1. Quotation: "The most direct access to the subconscious mind is through dreams. When we fall asleep, our rational, logical thinking relaxes."

2. Quotation: "Our dreams contain information about what is happening in our lives, our bodies, and the world around us."

### Writing a Summary

*Directions:* Write a summary following "Guidelines for Writing Summaries and Paraphrases" in this chapter. Your tasks are as listed:

1. Find a one- or two-page article (three pages if much space is taken by pictures) in a popular magazine. Or if you prefer, select a short article from a journal to be used for your research paper.

2. Photocopy the article. This copy will be turned in to the instructor along with the summary.

3. Reread the article. Underline each topic sentence and essential supporting data. Number each topic sentence for convenience in writing your summary.

4. To begin your summary, write an introductory sentence that gives the author's name and the source. (Turn back to "Using Signal Words to Integrate Quotations into the Text.")

5. Make one entry for a works cited list. Place at the bottom of your paper.

6. Staple the copy of the article to your completed summary.

## Test Yourself Answers

1. *true*
2. *false*
3. *false*
4. *true*
5. *true*
6. *true*
7. *true*
8. *true*
9. *true*
10. *true*

# READING AND WRITING ABOUT ESSAYS

## Part 6

# Reading and Responding to Essays

After reading and applying the information in Chapter 26, you'll be able to:

- Read critically in order to respond to essays
- Employ strategies used in critical reading
- Write a reaction paper
- Write and respond to essay exam questions

> . . . *the unexamined life is not worth living.*
>
> —Socrates
> (in Plato, *Apology*)

You may read essays in magazines, on editorial pages of newspapers, or in literature and other classes. In college or university classes, essays may be referred to as readings. There you not only read but also respond in discussions, reaction papers, or essay exams. To assist you, this chapter presents an overview of essays and suggests strategies for critical reading. The chapter also explains how to write a paper of reaction and long essay exam answers.

## WHAT TO EXPECT IN ESSAYS

An essay is a short literary composition that focuses on one major idea. Essays range all the way from lighthearted spoof to political commentary to serious argument. Essayists reflect, reminisce, discuss incidents, or argue about daily life, trends, justice, values, and other subjects. Their words may echo nostalgia or disgust, cheeriness or sadness, cheekiness or humility. Often the ideas in essays are universal and timeless. An essayist may marvel at nature's beauty or decry its despoilment, explore humane acts or condemn inhumane acts, search for a purpose in life or wonder if there is one.

Essays are usually nonfiction. They often appear in op-ed columns, meditations, memoirs, diaries, journals, and letters. But some essays are fiction. They may appear in such forms as fables, parodies, or satire. For example, in 1729 after three years of drought and poor crops, Jonathan Swift wrote a satire entitled "A Modest Proposal." The essay raised quite a stir because many people took it seriously. The offending segment follows:

> I have been assured by a very knowing American of my acquaintance in London, that a young healthy child well nursed is at a year old a most delicious, nourishing, and wholesome food, whether stewed, roasted, baked, or boiled; and I make no doubt that it will equally serve in a fricassee or a ragout.

Although the general populace did not understand Swift's bitter irony, "A Modest Proposal" became famous. It is still widely read today as a classic example of satire.

Like fictional works, essays may contain figurative language and symbolism. Sometimes these devices are so cleverly used, the essay may seem like a short story. So how can you distinguish the two? First, check to see how the piece is categorized. In a magazine or book, turn to the table of contents or introduction. Consider that essays tend to be self-expressive and idea-centred. They often express an opinion about a significant topic. Stories, however, have a theme, which is invariably implicit. Rarely is there a direct attempt to share an opinion, as in an essay.

## Purpose of Essays

The chief purpose of an essay is to explore an idea and reflect upon it. Sometimes an essayist may simply seek a means of fresh expression, not necessarily agreement. Other essayists seek to inform or entertain. Others attempt to persuade the reader to agree with a position on an issue.

*Personal* (informal) essays often expose a human frailty or condition and attempt to elicit empathy or sympathy from the reader. Some essayists go against popular opinion in an attempt to surprise, shock, or arouse public indignation. Some writers use humour not only to entertain but also to make a point.

*Formal* essays invariably have an earnest, intent purpose. The writer seeks to stimulate thought and persuade the reader to agree or at least consider a point of view. Holman and Harmon's *A Handbook to Literature* describes the formal (impersonal) essay as having "seriousness of purpose, dignity, logical organization, length. . . . The technique of the formal essay is now practically identical with that of all factual or theoretical prose writing in which literary effect is secondary to serious purpose."

## Characteristics of Personal Essays

Personal essays often appear to be spontaneous as they meander in and through a subject or circle it, coming closer and closer to the heart of the discussion. Others move along a time line, narrating an incident. You can identify personal essays by their conversational tone, self-disclosure, humour, freshness, and casual structure. They tend to be subjective and honest, inspiring trust in the reader.

The personal essay is essentially self-revelation. The writer, like a friend, shares personal details, opinions, and biases. In *The Art of the Personal Essay*, editor Phillip Lopate explains:

> The hallmark of the personal essay is its intimacy. The writer seems to be speaking directly into your ear, confiding everything from gossip to wisdom. . . . At the core . . . is the supposition that there is a certain unity to human experience.

***Characteristics of Formal Essays***   Despite the apparent spontaneity of many essays, the words are carefully chosen for a purpose. Typically, the language of a formal essay is restrained. Cynthia Ozick, in "Portrait of the Essay as a Warm Body" (*Atlantic Monthly*, Sept. 1998), describes a "genuine" essay as a "fireside [chat], not a conflagration or a safari." Ozick says these essays have power, derived from an alluring use of language. She explains, "I may not be persuaded by Emersonianism as an ideology, but Emerson—his voice, his language, his music—persuades me."

## Point of View and Voice

The perspective of the writer usually permeates an essay, although other viewpoints may be present. The way the topic is viewed affects the voice you hear from the printed page. This written voice may sound informal or formal, humble or arrogant, friendly or cantankerous, cheerful or cranky—just as the human voice reflects a range of emotion. Once in a great while, an essayist will assume a *persona*, a fictitious narrator, to tell a story. To determine how the words should be taken, seriously or in jest, you need to listen carefully to the written voice.

### *Questions to Analyze Point of View and Voice*

1. Whose perspective is presented?
2. How friendly does the speaker sound?
3. How is the subject treated? Seriously? Sympathetically? Ironically? With sly ridicule? How?
4. How does the speaker seem to feel about the subject?
5. Does the voice seem overly biased? Reasonably objective? How so?

In "A Ride through Spain," a descriptive essay by Truman Capote, the reader hears a light, conversational voice like that of a friend. Capote writes from the point of view of a passenger on the train. His written voice reveals enjoyment of the experience. The opening and ending of this informal essay appear here:

### A Ride through Spain

Certainly the train was old. The seats sagged like the jowls of a bulldog, windows were out and strips of adhesive held together those that were left; in the corridor a prowling cat appeared to be hunting mice, and it was not unreasonable to assume his search would be rewarded.

Slowly, as though the engine were harnessed to elderly coolies, we crept out of Granada. The southern sky was as white and burning as a desert; there was one cloud, and it drifted like a traveling oasis. . . .

**Ending** It was like a party, and we all drifted back to the train as though each of us wished to be the last to leave. The old man, with my shirt like a grand turban on his head, was put into a first-class carriage. . . .

The train moved away so slowly butterflies blew in and out the windows.

## Figurative Language

Comparison in the form of metaphor, simile, and analogy is often used in essays and other nonfiction writing. In the excerpt from "A Ride through Spain," Capote uses concrete images and figurative language, which enable the reader to share the train ride vicariously. Frequent similes ("sagged like the jowls of a bull dog") and other images enable the reader to visualize the trip and to sense the camaraderie of fellow travellers.

Assonance and other devices of sound contribute to the imagery and movement. An example of assonance appears in the last sentence. Here the sounds of the words reflect the movement of the train: The long *o* in *so* and *slowly* slows the rate of speech as do the three syllables of *butterflies* and the phrase *in and out the windows*. In fact, the language is rather like that of a lyric poem.

## The Power of Plain Words

Many essays are more direct and plainspoken than Capote's "A Ride through Spain." In fact, the words of some may seem stark and unadorned. Nonetheless, the essays attain power as significant details accrue. The secret of that power resides in the telling—the skill of the essayist, not the method.

# CRITICAL READING

When you curl up with a novel or other leisure reading, you read primarily for pleasure. You may skim long descriptive passages and slow down to savour others. Rarely, if ever, do you take notes. *Critical reading* for college or university classes and the workplace, however, has other purposes that are much more demanding. Critical reading requires you to analyze and evaluate—to think about ideas and ponder their meaning.

Critical reading can be divided into three stages: prereading, rereading, and prewriting. Often the stages overlap. You can use prewriting notes to clarify and to question as you reread. They can provide the starting point for your draft. Prewriting is an integral part of critical reading.

## Evaluating What You Read

Critical reading requires you not only to examine and weigh ideas but also to consider their implications. With a skeptical eye, you contemplate the writer's analysis, interpretation, or argument—while waiting to form an opinion. Give the author a fair hearing; hold off making a judgment until all evidence has been carefully reviewed.

With an open mind, scrutinize inferences, data, results of studies, claims, reasons, examples, or whatever the author offers. Try to determine the *reliability* of any quoted sources. Ask questions such as "Who did the study? When? Was the sample representative? Are the entire results presented or has something been pulled out of context?" Question and puzzle over any inconsistencies. Compare various accounts and interpretations of the same information.

See "The
Logical
Appeal,"
page 217.

Emotion can colour the perceptions of a writer as well as a reader. When discussing an issue, the writer may not give an opposing belief a fair hearing. The critical reader's task, then, is to spot bias, illogic, and inaccuracy. This task requires knowledge, objectivity, and awareness of common fallacies and methods of propaganda.

See
Chapter 20.

## A Strategy for Critical Reading

Some essays are relatively simple and easy to understand; others are complex and difficult. A methodical approach to critical reading can simplify the task and yield more insights than a haphazard approach. A good place to start is with a brief background of the author.

1. **Read a biographical sketch.** Reading a synopsis of an author's background can give you a sense of the culture and the era that influenced the essay. Sometimes background material appears just before or after the piece. Books of essays by the same author usually print biographical information in the introduction or preface. Encyclopedias also contain biographical sketches of well-known authors. Examine, too, the writer's credentials. Is he or she an authority in the field?

2. **Look for the date of the essay.** A biographical sketch may yield the year an essay was written. Some essays may refer to events, which can help to determine the year. Then ask yourself whether or not the message is timely or dated. Some essays, regardless of age, remain timeless and universal. They continue to have relevance down through the centuries.

3. **Consider the title and other clues.** Often essay titles not only identify the topic but also suggest an attitude or point of view. Sometimes a title is deliberately misleading, however. It may indicate a literal meaning when a significant symbolic meaning also exists. Watch for clues that point to double meanings and layers of meaning.

   As you read the body of an essay, think how it fits with the title. If you find an odd description or an apparent meandering, ask yourself how this relates to the main idea. An analogy or other bit of symbolism may be hiding there.

4. **Preread to gain an overview.** Previewing can improve your comprehension and retention. Read quickly to gain an impression of the piece. Note

headings or subheadings or italicized phrases. Notice ideas and names that are repeated.

5. **Consider tone and point of view.** Before you form an opinion, try to view the subject through the author's eyes. Read the entire piece before making a judgment. Consider how the written voice sounds. Is the author serious, joking, or ironic? Does the point of view seem sensible and logical? What values underlie the piece? For example, how does the author regard responsibility? Sanctity of human life? Other universal concerns?

6. **Reread to examine and understand.** Read the essay slowly the second time. Look for the thesis. If it is elusive, look in the first and the last paragraphs. Once in a while, a thesis is unstated and implied—with just a hint in the title or elsewhere.

7. **Start your prewriting notes.** Underline the thesis and mark any clues to it. Look for key points and underline them. Then ask yourself, "What is this essay about?" Keep in mind that the first idea may merely introduce the topic. The main idea may come later. Finally, summarize the main point of the essay in one sentence. That sentence will clarify the focus.

   Star any definitions or copy them onto note cards. Circle unfamiliar words and look them up. Question any information that omits significant details or raises doubt. Write your questions in the margins or on cards. You can also check to see if the author answers the questions you raise. These notes will help you understand connections in the text and form a starting point for your draft.

   If you spot doubtful information, an apparent fallacy, or a contradiction, place a question mark beside it. Watch to see if the author provides sources for any information not generally known or accepted. If a claim differs from the general thinking of experts in the field, does the writer provide sufficient support to be convincing? Finally, ask yourself, "What is my overall impression of what the author is saying?" Jot down your perception in three sentences or less.

8. **Look for the premise of an argument.** Where is the starting point or basis of the discussion? On what vital point does the argument hinge? For example, the *premise* of an animal rights proposal might be the belief that animals have a right to enjoy their lives. From this premise, the proponents might argue that animals should not be eaten.

   But opponents might argue that this view conflicts with the traditional belief that humans should rule over animals and eat certain ones. If opposing factions cannot agree on a premise, they will be unable to convince the other side.

9. **Write a synopsis or make an outline.** In your own words, summarize the content of the essay in a paragraph or two. Scan each topic sentence so that all key ideas are included. Or if you prefer, make a brief outline. Either technique will help to clarify your understanding.

10. **Check out new or doubtful ideas further.** If a reading topic is unfamiliar, find out what other authors have written about it. Or set up telephone or face-to-face interviews with officials of local agencies or businesses who would know. To make an informed judgment, you need to gather sufficient evidence and weigh it impartially.

## WRITING A PAPER OF REACTION OR ESSAY EXAM ANSWERS

In psychology, literature, philosophy, history, or other college or university courses, you may write short papers and essay exam answers that *react to ideas* in essays, short stories, histories, or other literature. In one or two pages, you are expected to respond to content, not structure. A paper of reaction and some examination questions require you to analyze the central idea of a reading and contribute an *informed opinion*. That opinion should be based on facts and reasons, not emotion. A written reaction is expected to be logical, focused, clear, and complete.

### Two Types of Reactions

A reaction paper or an exam answer is a thoughtful response to a writer's ideas. The purpose is to present a point of view and persuade the audience that the response is sound and reasonable. This assignment allows considerable leeway in responding to a topic. Usually, a reaction is either a commentary or an argument, although the two are sometimes blended, depending on the rhetorical situation.

*A Commentary*   A reaction may be a *commentary* that considers *how* the reading presents the main idea. For example, you might discuss the originality of the piece, insights of the author, and the humour, then give your response. On weightier matters, you would consider the facts and possible consequences or implications of the main idea. For example, you might discuss the implications for your field of study.

When appropriate, you can allude to historical figures or literary characters or cite quotations. You might compare or contrast, discuss cause and effect, give real-life examples, or organize in any way that is effective. There is no special way to organize a reaction.

*An Argument*   A reaction is often an argument. It examines, interprets, evaluates, and states an opinion. To be effective, an argument requires specific facts and reasons to defend and support a stand on an issue. Although a reaction paper or an exam answer may not be a full-fledged argument, an element of persuasion is inherent in many assignments. When an assignment is not explained, you may have to interpret it.

## TASKS IN RESPONDING TO READINGS

- **Summarize:** To condense, giving only the chief points. The purpose of a summary is to show that you understand the main ideas and relationships between ideas of a work (see page 338).

- **Paraphrase:** To restate in your own words. The purpose of paraphrasing is generally to report or to clarify (see page 339).

- **Quote:** To copy someone's work and to give credit to the author. Requires quotation marks and source identification (see Chapter 25).

- **Analyze:** To examine the parts of a whole. Analysis goes beyond a summary. You have to look closely at a work and think about what is happening. The purpose is to understand how the author achieves the effect (result). For example, you may be asked to analyze elements of structure or style.

- **Evaluate:** To rate, appraise, or judge. The purpose is to attach an opinion of value or worth to something. For example, problem solving and argument require evaluation.

## Prewriting and Outlining

To expand your prewriting notes, look at your questions in the margins. Did the author answer them? If not, you might raise them in your draft. Did any of the author's statements seem doubtful or inconsistent? How might you check these? Were you impressed by any descriptions or insights? Can you think of further comments to make? Asking yourself more questions will help you to expand your prewriting notes and start drafting.

### Questions for Prewriting

1. What is the main point of the essay?
2. Is the support convincing? Why or why not?
3. Has the writer omitted any significant facts? Are there implications or possible side effects that should be discussed?
4. What is especially interesting or challenging?
5. Is there any aspect I particularly like or dislike?
6. How does the author's voice sound?
7. How do I feel about the values underlying the essay? Why?
8. Might the ideas in the essay be applied to my field of study?

To make your draft go quickly, expand your working outline. If you haven't started an outline yet, just copy your thesis at the top of a clean sheet. Underneath, list your main points. Leave spaces between the points to add subpoints later. If a definition is required, write it on the outline. This framework will establish the direction of the paper. Although reactions are often responses to essays, they can also be responses to a piece of fiction.

## Drafting

There is no one way to start a draft, but it helps to know where you are going. Look over your working outline. Will you be writing a commentary, argument, or combination? What order is indicated? Revise your outline so that it clearly reflects a suitable order.

*Writing a Commentary*    To begin a commentary, you might identify the author and title of the work, then add a statement about the piece. (*Tip:* In your prewriting notes, find the one-sentence summary of the author's main point.) When you agree with an author, you might comment on a significant point or statement, the

---

### WORKING OUTLINE FOR A PAPER OF REACTION

**Question:** Define *poetic justice* and explain how it functions in the "The Lady and the Tiger." What outcome would you predict?* Why? [In this short story by Frank Stockton, the main character has a chance to live and marry a lovely woman if he opens the right door. Behind one of the three doors lurks a tiger.]

**WORKING OUTLINE:**

Definition  1. Poetic justice—goodness is rewarded and evil is punished, often ironically.

Thesis  2. I think the tiger will come out the opened door.

Reasons  3. Why do I think so?
    a. Hints about "poetic justice." (Give examples)
    b. You can't believe the king—or his daughter? (Example)
    c. The princess is "semi-barbaric." (Explain)
    d. Nothing indicates she loves him so much she'll give him to another woman. She is jealous. (Give example)

Ending  4. Allude to "Nor hell a fury like a woman scorned." William Congreve, *The Mourning Bride* (1697) [Give the original source, regardless of where you find the line.]

*The word *predict* implies a reaction. The question calls for an opinion that will provide a logical outcome to the story.

research, or an example. Or you might discuss the implications for you and your future career. The ending of a reaction paper can be brief, just a few well-stated sentences that give a sense of closure.

***Planning an Argument*** If you disagree with an author, then you need to construct a reasonable argument and provide adequate support. Before plunging into the fray, list pros and cons on your outline. In the first paragraph, identify the author and title and summarize the issue or controversy. The tone of this description should be neutral. Next, briefly summarize the author's position, taking care to be fair. After that, give your rebuttal, answering the main points of the other side. Cite facts and other logical support. Use a summary ending, restating your thesis.

A paper of reaction rarely requires research. Usually, you are expected to study only one reading and draw from your own experience. If you do consult outside sources, however, proper documentation is always required.

## Revision and Editing

Before you revise and edit a paper of reaction, it is often helpful to reread the directions for the assignment. Then as you revise, check to see you have fulfilled every one of them. Examine the organization, development, and logic of your paper. Would any sentence be more effective if moved elsewhere? Does more need to be said at any point? Is there needless repetition? Are the words clear?

Read your paper aloud to hear how your written voice sounds. Is the tone consistent with your purpose? Do you sound objective and knowledgeable? Can you find a better way to express an idea? Use a dictionary and a thesaurus to help you refine words so that you say what you intend in a suitable tone.

---

### CHECKLIST FOR REVISING A REACTION PAPER

1. Is the thesis clear?
2. Is the order clear and logical?
3. Do I go beyond a summary and actually contribute to the discussion? Does my opinion sound informed?
4. If I am disagreeing, have I responded to all the writer's points?
5. Is my defence well supported?
6. Are facts correctly stated?
7. Are inferences logical and identifiable?
8. If there are allusions to other writers' works, have I given credit? If I consulted outside sources, are they properly documented?
9. Is my written voice appropriate?
10. Is there anything else that should be said?

Edit each sentence with care. Even though you may have run a computer check for spelling, grammar, or punctuation, *proofread your paper carefully*. Software will not pick up all errors, and some packages may disagree with the rules your instructor advocates. Don't guess about spelling corrections—take a few seconds to open an up-to-date dictionary.

## STUDENT PAPER: REACTION

A college philosophy class was assigned a short paper of reaction with topics drawn from readings discussed in the classroom. One of the topics was to react to the philosophy of Martin Buber and to give practical applications. Scott Allen discusses the implication of Buber's beliefs for classroom teachers. He presents impressions, draws comparisons, and points out applications.

### A Reaction to Martin Buber's Philosophy

#### SUMMARY/COMPARISON

Martin Buber's philosophy, as set forth in *Between Man and Man*, seems similar to Plato's in many respects. Although the philosophers disagree about the source of goodness, they both believe that goodness is an absolute, quite distinct from people. They believe we strive to attain goodness by making wise choices. Buber's philosophy has important applications for teachers.

Buber feels that the formal teaching of values is worthless. Nonetheless, he believes that the teacher presents a selection from the real world and acts as a model to the pupil (indirect teaching). Buber develops the concept of "inclusiveness," which is the complete realization of the submissive person (i.e., the student).

To develop the mental powers to make good choices, Plato suggests the [direct] study of mathematics, philosophy, and other disciplines. Plato attempts to outline an ideal society where everyone can live peacefully and develop to the fullest capacity.

#### REACTION AND IMPLICATIONS

In the educational situation, this inclusiveness means that educators must beware of the dangers of such a relationship. They must refrain from arbitrariness and must exercise responsibility in interpreting the real world to the pupil. I agree: Teachers should consider the needs and rights of their pupils and try to respond in a way that will benefit them. This goal requires not only responsibility in the selection of classroom material but also fairness in grading, settling disputes, and other situations which arise. I concur with Buber's theory about the teaching of values: values are caught, not taught. A teacher should be of good character and should act as a role model for students.

How can educators accomplish this responsibility? Buber says they can do it by conscious and willed selection. In other words, educators should know what they want to achieve and select the proper means to achieve it. They should examine their basic principles and understand what is happening—not merely what they think they are doing. They must be objective as well as responsible.

Finally, Buber believes that "Life lived in freedom is personal responsibility or it is a pathetic farce" ("Education," Section III). Rousseau, in a similar vein, says that pupils are obliged to develop their intellectual powers to learn a vocation and provide for themselves. Like Buber, Rousseau is greatly concerned about the educator's responsibility of keeping evil away from pupils. This idea of personal responsibility involves intellectual self-discipline as well as physical self-discipline, but it helps us to gain self-respect and stature in the eyes of others. It helps us to find a purpose beyond ourselves—and perhaps that is what life is really all about.

CONCLUSION

In short, although Buber's traditional Judeo-Christian philosophy will not appeal to Ayn Rand fans or existentialists with leanings toward Nietzsche or Sartre, I believe it provides an excellent set of principles for undergirding education.

---

## SUMMARY

- Essays are short literary compositions, usually non-fiction, on a single topic.
- Essays employ points of view on a single subject that ranges from formal to informal, and serious to humorous.
- Critical reading has three stages: pre-reading, rereading, and prewriting.
- Strategies used in critical thinking can simplify the task.
- Reaction papers require careful reading of the original source that develops an analysis of the facts and their implications.
- A reaction paper presents a perspective based on logical reasoning and informed opinion—a commentary, not simply a summary.

---

## *Practice*

### One-Minute Reactions

*Directions:* Select one of the following topics or another and write until your instructor tells you to stop.

1. Are you satisfied or dissatisfied with your province's highways? Why?
2. What is the most annoying problem in your neighbourhood or city?
3. What is your favourite make of automobile? Why?
4. How would you describe a politician? Why?
5. Did you ever get into mischief in school? How did you react?

## *Ten Ideas for Reaction Papers*

All of the essays mentioned below are located in Part 7: The Reader. Or you may prefer to react to another of your choice.

1. React to "Mind over Munchies" and Brown's treatment of the topic.

2. React to Phillip Lopate's "A Nonsmoker with a Smoker." How do you feel about banning smoking? Why?

3. Respond to "Mother Tongue," by Amy Tan. Summarize her conclusions. Do you think her experience was unique or does it have widespread implications? Why?

4. React to "The Sweet Smell of Success Isn't All that Sweet," by Laurence Shames. Do you agree or disagree with his thesis? What would you add?

5. React to "We Have No 'Right to Happiness.'" What is C. S. Lewis's real point? Do you agree or disagree? Why?

### Other Suggestions

6. Listen to a television or radio talk show and react to a view about a significant issue.

7. Scan newspapers, magazines, or Web sites for positions on political or educational issues, and react to one.

8. Turn to the opinion page of a newspaper. Read the columns and letters there. Then write a reaction to one.

9. React to an incident that seemed trivial but had unexpected results.

10. React to a favourite saying of someone who was significant in your life. How were you influenced?

# Essay Exam Writing and Oral Presentations

## Part 7

# *Writing Effective Essay Exams*

**Learning Objectives:**

After reading and applying the information in Chapter 27, you'll be able to:

- Review and study for exams strategically
- Analyze and respond effectively to essay exam questions

*Procrastination is the thief of time.*

—Edward Young
   *Night Thoughts* (1742–46) 1.393.

Many students procrastinate when preparing for examinations. They wait until the night before and drink cola or coffee by the bucket to stay awake while they study. During the exam they are so exhausted they can barely keep their eyes open, much less focus scattered thoughts to write complete essay answers. Pulling an all-nighter is not an effective way to study for any exam, particularly essay exams, which often require analytical thinking and synthesis of ideas. To write effective essay answers, you need to prepare well throughout the term.

## PREPARING FOR EXAMS

Excellent preparation is probably the best way to decrease anxiety before an exam. Good study habits not only decrease stress but also yield better grades than cramming. The rule of thumb for college study is "two hours out of class for every hour in." This means if you're taking sixteen hours of classes per week, you should study thirty-two hours per week. About ten days before final exams, start allowing extra time for review every day. Allotting this much time for study requires skilful planning.

## Reviewing for Essay Exams

If you have studied regularly throughout the term, attended classes, taken good notes (and perhaps typed them each evening), then a week or so of review should be enough. Cramming should be unnecessary. The suggestions that follow can help you organize your review time.

1.  *Plan the review.* To start your review, first scan the table of contents of your textbook. There you can gain an *overview* of material assigned during the term. Note how the chapters are divided into major and minor categories. Second, *mark HP (High Priority) by the categories (or chapters) that will need extensive review.* Mark others either MP (Medium Priority) or LP (Low Priority). Then review the high-priority sections first, the medium-priority next, and the low-priority (material you know well) last. That way if you run out of time, you will have reviewed the most difficult chapters.

2.  *Think and question.* As you review, think about the major ideas and how they are related. Since you will not have time to reread all the assigned material, pay close attention to textbook headings. *Turn the headings into questions* and try to answer orally. If you can't answer a question, scan the section for the answer. Better yet, make up several essay questions and write out the answers. This will force you to examine and synthesize ideas in your own words as you strive for complete answers.

    As you review your notes, highlight major points the instructor has emphasized. In a history, sociology, psychology, art, philosophy, literature, or other course, consider *causes, influences,* and *trends. How have they affected the culture?* Consider how people and events are linked. What changes have occurred? Making a diagram or outline can help you visualize and retain this information.

3.  Use *memory aids.* In science, geography, composition, and other courses, you may review processes and memorize information. Then it is important to know the steps of the process and to understand how the steps influence the result. A course may require you to memorize statistics, definitions, rules, principles, or other information.

    Any way that you can think of to divide material into smaller recognizable units will make it easier to retain. Some students make *flashcards* (from index cards) to review definitions, dates, and rules, putting a few on each card. Some use *colour coding* to group items in a list. For example, one student divided a list of twelve items into two columns. Then she tinted the first three items red, the second group green, the third yellow, and the fourth group orange. The colours helped her visualize the list.

    Making acronyms can also help you remember. For example, if you have four items, such as communication skills, to learn, memorize the first letter of each one as a reminder: **RSRR**

      • Restatement/paraphrasing

- **S**ummarizing
- **R**esponding to nonverbal cues
- **R**esponding to feelings

A traditional method of review that works well for many students is recitation. You say answers aloud to yourself or to someone else. Recitation can be combined with flashcards and colour coding. Just say the answer before you look at the cards or coloured lists.

Some students prefer to type an outline of their notes, particularly of difficult material. For them, an outline condenses and makes remembering easier. It also saves time in reviewing. You may find that certain methods work better for certain types of material. Try to discover a combination that works well for you.

4. *Encourage yourself.* If you have followed your study schedule well and completed your high- and medium-priority tasks this term, commend yourself! These achievements take self-discipline, which is not easy. If you haven't done so well, resolve to turn over a new leaf and begin now!

As you review each lesson, *give yourself positive feedback and encouragement*. Visualize yourself completing the exam successfully. Refuse to succumb to negative thoughts and the "what if" syndrome. ("What if I can't remember the answer? What if I fail?") Negative thinking is a dead end. It sabotages your time and ability to concentrate. From time to time, reward yourself with brief breaks. A glass of ice water and a bit of exercise will help you think more clearly.

## Predicting Essay Exam Questions

Attending class regularly, particularly the sessions before exams, is advisable. Many instructors share study hints and sample questions during classes before an exam. Have a pen poised, ready to record even the casual remarks an instructor makes about an exam. Listen carefully for hints that may be disguised by a joking manner—for example, "Memorize the headings!" Translated, this usually means you need to study the major ideas of the textbook. If in doubt ask, "Do you mean word for word?"

Or an instructor may smile and say, "Just remember *everything* I've covered in the lectures!" This means you can depend heavily on your notes—if they are complete. If not, try to secure a good copy from someone else. Beware, however, of letting your own notes out of your sight unless you have them on a computer disk in a safe place. There is the danger of notes not being returned or of their being lost or stolen.

Some instructors may prepare a short study guide. Others may volunteer only the time of the exam and vague suggestions for study. In either case, feel free to ask reasonable questions: Will dictionaries, spelling checkers, or thesauruses be allowed? Will the exam be on paper or computer? Will the exam contain essay questions only?

***Open Book Exams***   Be forewarned that a question about open book exams may evoke laughter. To the uninitiated, an open book exam sounds as if it would not require much study. But the truth is that you have to prepare just as much or even more! Although textbooks are permitted during an open book exam, the odds are stacked against your having time to use them.

Open book exams tend to be so long that spending time searching for answers will make finishing the exam impossible. Once I saw three students come in to an exam with textbooks loaded with coloured slips of paper and topical references. During the exam they rapidly flipped pages, hunting for answers. None of the three completed the exam. There is no substitute for well-planned study and review.

## Two Types of Essay Questions

Exam questions may be broad or narrowly focused. Broad questions allow leeway in answering. They may ask you to *trace or state* influences, developments, or history. Such questions require listing a series of significant events or changes in *chronological* order and explaining their evolution, as in the question below:

- Trace the development of computers from the first practical model to the present.

Or you may be asked to *analyze, discuss, explain, comment on,* or *account for* influences, changes, or trends, as in this question:

- Analyze the influence of World War II on women's lives from 1941 to 1950.

Narrowly focused questions are more specific. Sometimes they use some of the same words but narrow the scope of the answer. They may ask you to *identify, cite, compare, contrast, list, argue, defend, justify, support, evaluate,* and so on. These questions may be stated in one sentence or in more than one, as in the following examples:

- Discuss the relationship between the Canadian and American economies, referring specifically to the effect of the Dow Jones's performance in 2002.
- Compare the use of camera imagery in any two of Margaret Atwood's poems.

## Taking Essay Exams

To perform at your best level, get a full night's rest before an exam. Eat lightly on exam day, but avoid meal skipping. Going without food can lower the blood sugar, which can result in fatigue and inability to concentrate. Daily exercise, even walking a few blocks before the exam, contributes to a sense of well-being and helps to control *test anxiety.* Deep breathing and drinking cold water can also help you feel more alert and less anxious. Rested and energized, you will be able to think more clearly.

---

### TIPS FOR WRITING ESSAY ANSWERS

1. **Preview the test.** Scan the entire test. If you have a choice of questions, say five of seven, mark out the two you will not answer. *Do not spend time on extra questions for which you will receive no credit.*

2. **Plan your time according to the worth of the questions.** If all questions are weighted equally, allot equal time. If a question is worth more than the others, allot more time there.

3. **Start with the easiest question.** Answering one completely will boost your confidence.

4. **When stalled for an answer, move on to another question or take a quick break.** Walk down the hall, breathe deeply. You may think of the answer. If not, move on and do your best.

5. **Keep your exam until the last possible moment.** Do not leave early. Instead, go back and check your answers. If you see any omissions or think of significant details, add them.

6. **If you see you are running out of time, start outlining your answers.** It is better to earn partial points than to leave a question blank and earn none.

---

Arrive about five minutes early with all your supplies on exam day. If you arrive too early, you may find yourself listening to someone wail about the upcoming exam. Take two pens (one may run dry), plenty of paper (the instructor may not supply it), a dictionary, and anything else you need. If the exam is on computer, some supplies may seem unnecessary but may still be useful.

*Check the chalkboard for messages.* Sometimes an instructor has been detained, or the exam has been moved to another room. Yet some students sit and chat, not thinking to glance at the board.

*Avoid bringing coffee, soft drinks, or food to class.* If you are nervous or someone bumps you, drinks may spill. Crumbs and smears may stick to exams. Then too, food wrappings can be noisy and distracting to other students who are trying to concentrate.

## WRITING COMPLETE ESSAY EXAM ANSWERS

Before writing an exam answer, read the entire question. Two major causes of low grades on essay exams are that students omit parts or misread the question. Hurrying through instructions is a path to disaster. Be sure that you understand what is required. A minute spent reading and considering a question can make the difference between an incomplete answer and a complete one.

To answer essay questions completely, you need to follow directions, organize, and provide adequate support. You may need to supply a definition or example, compare or contrast, classify, formulate a persuasive argument, or apply some other writing strategy. Instructors expect you to cite significant points and explain connections clearly without becoming entangled in trivial details. Clear, concise answers are better than long, rambling, padded ones. Strive for quality, not quantity.

## Understanding the Question

To answer essay questions completely, you need to know the precise meanings of certain verbs commonly used on exams. These words contain clues to the writing strategy that will best organize an essay answer. Listed below are definitions of verbs frequently found on essay exams:

### Definitions of Common Verbs in Essay Questions

*Account for:* to explain, as a cause and its effect; to justify

*Analyze:* to examine the parts of and determine their connections

*Clarify:* to explain; to present details, reasons, or examples

*Defend, justify, support:* to give reasons for; to offer evidence

*Define:* to give the meaning; to describe basic characteristics

*Discuss:* to examine and consider; to present details and reasons

*Evaluate:* to examine advantages and disadvantages; rate or judge

*Explain:* to make clear; to define or offer reasons

*Identify:* to define; to give the characteristics of

*Trace:* to track or explain in chronological order

Every word of an essay question should be read carefully. Then think about the meaning. Even if you draw a blank, do not panic. Reread the question. Mark key words and phrases so that you can quickly refer to them when needed. These words will direct your answer and indicate the strategy of writing you need to organize your answer.

## Drafting Complete Essay Answers

As soon as you are clear about what a question requires, begin prewriting in the margins or on the back of the exam. Then identify your main points and number them. This start can serve as a working outline. Write your first draft on the exam paper or in the exam booklet; rarely is there enough time to recopy. Instead, use any extra time to check and edit your answers. Instructors are more concerned with accuracy, completeness, and correctness than with neatness.

**Paragraph Essays**   Usually, the instructor gives out a sheet with half a dozen essay questions or else writes them on the chalkboard. From the list, select one or more, as directed. To begin an essay paragraph, write a clear topic sentence. To organize support sentences, refer to your working outline.

As you draft, keep in mind the *basic pattern of claim and evidence.* In other

## WRITING STRATEGIES SUGGESTED BY KEY PHRASES

| *Key Phrases* | *Writing Strategies* |
|---|---|
| *Trace, give the history of* | Narration |
| *Provide details, describe* | Description |
| *Explain, list, provide examples of* | Illustration |
| *Discuss or analyze the parts of* | Division-classification |
| *Analyze, explain how, show how* | Process analysis |
| *Discuss advantages/disadvantages* | Comparison-contrast |
| *Show similarities/differences* | Comparison-contrast |
| *Account for, analyze the results of* | Cause-effect |
| *Discuss or explain reasons for* | Cause-effect |
| *Identify, clarify, explain the term* | Definition |
| *Defend, evaluate, justify, support* | Argument-persuasion |

words, every detail and example in the paragraph should support the claim of the topic sentence. Use complete sentences. Fragments can lead to confusion and a loss of points. At the end of your answer, leave a few lines in case you think of more information later.

When you are faced with writing several essay exam answers, focus on one question at a time. If you should think of information for another question before you finish the first, jot down the idea and put it aside. Continue this way, using your prewriting and outlining to organize each answer. The precautions that follow will also help you write complete essay answers.

SAMPLE PARAGRAPH ESSAY

The three-part essay question below calls for definition, contrast, and division. The one-paragraph answer opens with a definition before the topic sentence. The support sentences follow.

**Question:** Define *information interview*. How does it differ from an employment interview? State three specific advantages of this interview.

**Answer:** An information interview is a meeting with an employer for the direct purpose of gaining information about a career field, not to get a job. The information interview has three distinct advantages. It provides firsthand information about a position you hope to be working in some day. It allows you an inside look at a company to see whether or not you would enjoy working there. It allows access to employers whom you might not be able to contact otherwise. You may even be asked to bring your résumé or to come in for an employment interview. In fact, that is what happened to me last week. Tomorrow I start my new job as a medical transcriptionist. The

*[margin labels:]* Definition · Contrast · Topic Sentence · Support · Example

> ## PRECAUTIONS FOR WRITING COMPLETE ESSAY ANSWERS
>
> 1. *Heed directions:* Listen to oral instructions. Check the blackboard for any corrections. Read exam questions twice.
> 2. *Highlight* or *underline* key terms.
> 3. *Number the parts* of multifaceted questions.
> 4. *Check off numbers* of parts after you answer each one.
> 5. *When finished with the exam,* check the answers you are least sure of. If you think of more information, add. Proofread.

*Summary*        information interview is truly an excellent technique for uncovering the "hidden jobs" that are never advertised.

***Long Exam Essays***    Instead of several paragraph essays, you may be asked to write an in-class paper. Always state your thesis early.

Some essay questions call for a *reaction.* A written reaction goes a step further than an analysis. A paper of reaction includes an opinion based on facts. If you are asked to react to a reading, respond to the main *idea* and add your well-reasoned opinion (see Chapter 26).

> ## SUMMARY
>
> - Regular study throughout the term is the best way to decrease test anxiety and earn good grades. Cultivating a positive attitude also can alleviate anxiety and improve your study habits.
> - Understanding and predicting types of essay questions can help you write complete responses; be sure to read each question carefully. Prewrite before you start drafting your answer.

## *Practice*

### Make Your Own Study Questions

To master the suggested study techniques for essay exams, make up your own study questions based on the headings in this chapter. Leave spaces for your answers. After you have finished, check your answers with the text to see that you have included all significant points.

### Draft an Essay Exam Answer

*Sample Exam Question:* Identify the chief obstacles you face when preparing for an essay exam. Which suggestions in this chapter might you adopt to alleviate these concerns and improve your study habits? Write a well-developed paragraph, citing specific details, reasons for your answer, and a plan for effective study.

# Oral Presentations

---

**Learning Objectives:**

After reading and applying the information in Chapter 28, you'll be able to:

- Analyze your audience and choose an appropriate topic for an oral presentation
- Develop and organize an oral presentation according to occasion and purpose
- Develop effective introductions and conclusions for an oral presentation
- Deliver an oral presentation effectively

---

*It's not who you are that holds you back, it's who you think you're not.*

—Author Unknown

A survey of 480 companies asked what qualities were considered most important when hiring. The most frequent response was "communication skills." Employers want applicants who can write well and speak effectively. To help meet this need, more and more colleges and universities are incorporating speaking skills, including oral presentations, into courses across the curriculum. But many students quake at the thought of standing before a group and making a presentation.

## WHETHER SPEAKING TO SIX OR TO SIXTY . . .

If your heart does a rapid tango and your face pales at the thought of giving an oral presentation, you will be glad to know that these responses are both common and surmountable. And the fundamentals of speaking are easy to learn. In fact, many students discover they are better speakers than writers.

Whether facing six classmates or coworkers, or sixty participants at a training seminar, you can learn to speak with confidence. The first key is to get your fear under control. By giving yourself a pep talk and applying the many guidelines in this chapter, you can ease the task of giving an oral presentation. The second key is to practise enough but not too much. We'll talk more about this point later.

The third key is to think of the audience as friends with whom you will share some interesting information. If you are enthusiastic, they will sit up and listen. Finally, the chances are good that your college classmates will be an empathic audience because they will be presenting, too. They are apt to encourage you by listening attentively, providing the kind of support they will want when they are speaking. Now are you ready to start?

## HOW DO WRITING AND SPEAKING DIFFER?

See Chapter 1.

If you are asked to present a paper orally to the class, rest assured that you have already accomplished a big chunk of the work. With a little tweaking, you can adapt the paper for presentation to a live audience. To start, you need to consider how your role as writer changes to that of speaker. For both rhetorical situations, the purpose and topic remain the same, but three other factors—occasion, audience, and voice—change dramatically.

### Writing and Speaking: Comparing Two Types of Rhetorical Situations

Three basic elements differ in the rhetorical situations of writing and speaking: the occasion, audience, and voice. These differences influence how an effective presenter prepares and how an audience receives the message.

| Occasion | Purpose | Topic | Audience | Voice |
|---|---|---|---|---|
| Writing | To inform first-semester students of the counselling services available at their college | Counselling Services: We're here to help you | Readers *see* words | *Writer's* voice |
| Speaking | Same | Same | Listeners *see* actions and *hear* words | *Speaker's* voice |

In a paper the content, punctuation, and spelling are important. *In an oral presentation, however, the content and delivery are important.* Thus this chapter contains an overview of revising a paper for presentation as well as guidance for delivering the presentation. You will see examples of purpose statements, thesis statements, introductions, conclusions, and a sample student speech. Specific tips for preparing notes and audiovisuals; practising; and improving eye contact, articulation, and vocal variety are also provided.

## PREPARING A PAPER FOR ORAL PRESENTATION

If you are asked to present a paper orally, don't panic! No radical changes are required. Here is an overview of the necessary steps. Tips and examples appear later in the chapter.

1. **Mark up your paper as you simplify and condense.** Most papers, especially research-based papers, will need to be simplified and condensed. Working on a printed copy of your paper, highlight the thesis, and sharpen it further (see "Define the Purpose" on page 383). Highlight statistics and brief anecdotes that lend support to your main point. Delete minor details and less relevant examples. Put brackets around extended discussions or complicated points, and jot summaries in the margins. Watch for an unusual fact or arresting quotation. Divide long sentences into shorter ones.

2. **Perk up the introduction.** To make your opening attention-getting, start with a catchy quotation or example. Emphasize a vital link to tie the topic to the listeners. Build your introduction around the ways your audience will be able to use the information.

3. **Include transition to your main points.** Prepare a link from your thesis to each main point, using numerical or embedded transition according to your purpose (see pages 74 and 139).

4. **Plan an effective and memorable conclusion.** Summarize the main idea, and then give your audience something extra that's memorable. You might add a bit of wisdom, a provocative thought, or a look toward the future.

5. **Prepare an outline.** Using note cards, sheets of paper, or the notes pages tool of presentation software, work from your marked-up paper and written plans to prepare notes. Outline your main points and significant subpoints.

6. **Prepare audiovisual aids.** People like to see as well as hear. If you are talking about coaching bantam hockey, wear your jersey and bring a stick and gloves. If you have access to PowerPoint or another presentation software program you may want to use it to support your thesis (see "Creating Effective Audiovisual Aids").

7. **Time the presentation.** Pause briefly between sentences. If allowed four to six minutes, aim for five. The extra minute will give you time to pause for emphasis (or laughs). If needed, cut or condense points.

8. **Practise but do not overpractise.** Practise enough times so that you're comfortable but not so many that you memorize every word. Your presentation will seem fresh and spontaneous.

9. **Revise troublesome phrases.** Mark any words that cause stumbling. Use a thesaurus to find synonyms, so you can recast and shorten awkward or confusing sentences. Find words you can use comfortably and pronounce easily.

10. **Check arrangements and arrive early.** Have your notes and audiovisual aids in order. Test projection and computer equipment to make sure it's hooked up and working properly. Good preparation will ease your mind.

## Presenting versus Reading

Any effective presentation requires that the speaker exude the energy, enthusiasm, and vocal variety found in animated conversation. Eye contact, facial expression, gestures, and tone of voice can make words come alive. A compelling speaker can make a message vibrant and persuasive in a way that differs radically from the mechanical reading of the same message.

Yet students who lack training in oral communication are often unsure of what is expected. Some assume they can just stand up and read their paper aloud. At a Society of Technical Communication conference in Chicago, a scientist made this mistake. After five minutes of his droning, people began to leave. As he continued in a monotone, bowed head with no eye contact, more and more left. By the end of the hour, two-thirds of the audience had gone.

By applying the guidelines in this chapter, you will be spared the embarrassment this man endured. As you gain experience in presenting, you will appear more confident and knowledgeable during job interviews. If asked to introduce yourself, report on a team project, give a sales presentation, or summarize a research paper or project, you will be able to smile, control the butterflies, and do a creditable job.

## FOUR TYPES OF ORAL PRESENTATIONS

A speaker can choose from four types of oral presentations: *manuscript, memorized,* and *impromptu.* Successful reading of a manuscript takes skill, training, and charisma. Memorized presentations are hazardous because they often lack spontaneity. Then too, nervousness can cause forgetfulness.

The most effective type of prepared presentation appears extemporaneous. The secret of success for this type of presentation is sufficient preparation and speaking in a *conversational* manner. Although the presenter may glance at notes, the tone is informal and friendly. An impromptu speech is a spur-of-the-moment talk, given without preparation. For example, you speak impromptu when introducing yourself to the class, when escorting visitors around your workplace, or when filling in for a master of ceremonies who is late or unexpectedly unable to attend an event. As you develop skill in making oral presentations, your ease in impromptu speaking will increase.

## PLANNING AN ORAL PRESENTATION

The first step toward an effective oral presentation is to analyze the rhetorical situation. The setting may impose limitations that can be circumvented, but if the presentation is inappropriate to the occasion and the audience, it has little chance for success.

### Preview the Setting

To begin planning any presentation, find out where it will be held and the nature of the space. How large is the room? How will the seating be arranged? Is there a lectern for notes? Will you be using a microphone? Can projectors or any other necessary equipment be reserved? Is an Internet connection available? Are electrical outlets near the lectern, or are extension cords available? Is the lighting satisfactory?

The closer you can be to the audience, the more intimate and informal the setting. A semicircle is ideal because it allows you to establish eye contact with everyone. For very large audiences, a centre aisle is desirable so that you can actually walk into the audience and involve individuals, particularly if there is a question-and-answer session.

If you will be using a microphone, try to practise at least a few minutes beforehand. Familiarizing yourself with the room and the equipment will not only diminish the fear of the unknown but also allow you to plan around any deficiencies and tailor the presentation to the setting.

### Assess the Audience

Before definitely settling on a topic, consider the attitudes, beliefs, and values of the people to whom you will speak. Find out as much as you can about their demographics—age range, gender, ethnicity, occupation, education, or other relevant cultural factors. Then estimate how the audience will be likely to react to your topic. To analyze the audience, you might start with the familiar pattern of *who, what, why, where, when,* and *how:*

- Who will be attending? How many? (All men? All women? Mixed group?)

- What special interests or concerns do they have? (Consider age, education, culture.)
- Why will I be making the presentation? (What do they expect and want?)
- How much does the audience *already know* about the topic?
- How do they *feel* about the topic? (Is the topic charged with emotion?)
- When will the presentation occur? How will the time of day, current events, or even upcoming holidays affect it?

The answers to these questions will guide you in planning your approach—thinking about how you can stimulate their interest. If you lack a topic or decide to switch to another, see "Ten Ideas for Oral Presentations" at the end of the chapter.

---

**CASE STUDY**

### MURPHY'S LAW IN ACTION

Skipping audience analysis can invoke Murphy's law: "If anything can go wrong, it will." One student who skipped this step asked in a strong confident voice, "How many of you have tried to quit smoking?" Only two of twenty-five classmates raised their hands. When the presenter realized that almost all of her audience were nonsmokers, her face paled and her voice wavered. Her enthusiasm fled. The response of the audience was polite but lukewarm. With an audience of smokers, the presentation had the potential to earn an A; as it was, it earned a C.

---

## Consider the Occasion

When and why a presentation is given influences the length, approach to the topic, and organization. In the classroom, oral presentations will be much shorter than those generally given at work, to clients or prospective customers, or in the community. For a class you might give a one- to three-minute practice speech or a lab report. A graded presentation might run from four to eight minutes, depending on the time available and the size of the class. The purpose and audience will influence how you shape and organize the material for the presentation.

## Define the Purpose

The *general* purpose of an oral presentation may be to inform, persuade, inspire, dedicate, celebrate, entertain, express appreciation, or a combination of these purposes. The general purpose indicates the type of presentation. The *specific purpose statement* has three parts: purpose, topic, and desired result. Once you define your specific purpose, you can write a clear thesis statement reflecting that purpose. The thesis statement is the central idea you want to convey.

*Specific Purpose Statements*

---

                [purpose]                       [topic]

- The purpose is to *inform* the audience about *common spiders* and

  [desired result]

  *show how to determine friend from foe.*

                [purpose]                     [topic]

- The purpose is to *persuade* the audience that since *most spiders are*

                          [desired result]

  *harmless and beneficial, they should not be killed.*

*Thesis Statements*

---

- Common spiders are harmless and easily distinguished from several poisonous varieties. (Informative)
- We should not kill beneficial and harmless spiders. (Persuasive)

Notice that the examples above illustrate how the same subject can be approached in different ways, according to your general purpose. Before starting your outline or notes, write a specific purpose statement. It will clarify your intent and help you stay on track. Your thesis can be written later.

## Select an Appropriate Topic

For a successful classroom presentation, the topic should be suitable to both you and the audience. Never speak on a subject that causes you to feel uneasy; discomfort blunts enthusiasm and dulls a presentation. Select a topic you can discuss rationally without excessive emotion—one that offers an opportunity for listeners to learn as well as to enjoy. Opinions about issues such as gun control, abortion, religion, and politics tend to be deeply ingrained and highly charged. There is little chance of changing anyone's mind; in fact, a shouting match may erupt and distract from your presentation.

Chances are that if you have already prepared a paper for another class, and it has been graded, then the topic is suitable for an oral presentation. If in doubt, ask your instructor. The following tips will help you adapt the paper or select an entirely new topic.

***Get off the Beaten Path***   Topics that have been highly publicized tend to make boring presentations. For example, most people already know quite a bit about cancer, AIDS, illegal drugs, and various kinds of abuse. Unless you can provide additional information that is fresh and interesting, the audience will be unlikely to listen closely. You may need to research your topic further (see Chapter 23).

Sometimes you can freshen an old topic by researching the latest discoveries, such as advances in medicine. Or if you decide to look for another topic, you might share an area of personal expertise that would interest the audience, such as desktop publishing, genealogical research, or building a musical instrument.

***Link the Topic to the Audience*** During the introduction, effective presenters establish a link between the audience and the topic. To include listeners, use personal pronouns *(you, your, we, us)*. State an advantage, benefit, or reason for them to listen. To search for a connection, you might ask yourself:

- Why should the audience listen to me?
- What benefit can they derive? (Learn, improve, enjoy, or what?)
- How can I make them eager to listen? (Look for the unusual or amusing.)

***Role-Playing*** You might ask the class to assume a role. A bank manager wanted to practise a presentation she would be giving at work. Before the presentation, she asked the class to pretend they were managers of local branch banks who were attending a training seminar. This role-playing heightened their interest, and their attentive feedback enabled her to give an excellent presentation.

---

### CASE STUDY

#### FINDING A LINK TO THE AUDIENCE

A student who collected antique glass wanted to share his hobby but doubted that the men in the audience would be interested. When he sought help in finding a link, his instructor asked, "What are men generally interested in?"

The student thought a moment, smiled, and replied, "Money?"

"Right! You could present antique glass not only as fun but also as an investment. Have you ever made a profit this way?"

"Yes, just last week," he replied. "I was driving through a village and spotted a general store. On a dusty bargain table I found a lovely old glass bowl that was hand signed. It cost just $5, but a catalog lists it for $100!" That anecdote became the opening for his presentation.

---

## Audience Analysis: Make a Brief Written Plan

Writing down a plan or an overview of the rhetorical situation for your presentation will help to clarify the steps of preparation. In fact, your instructor may require that a plan be handed in. Below is a sample format for such a plan or overview.

### Presentation Plan/Rhetorical Situation Overview

1. General purpose: to _____
   Specific purpose: to _____
2. Demographics of audience:
   Estimated age range: _____ to _____ Gender: _____
   Relevant cultural factors: _____

3. What does the audience know about the topic? _____

4. What else can you tell them? _____

5. How does the audience *feel* about the topic? _____
   Any touchy aspects? If so, what? _____

6. What are the implications of your audience analysis for this presentation?
   _____

7. *If* you use an argument format, how will you establish common ground?
   (See Chapter 19.)
   _____

8. What audiovisual aids will you use? _____ When and how will
   you use them? _____

9. What factors influence your credibility? _____

10. What will be your biggest challenge? Why? _____
    _____

## CREDIBILITY, ORGANIZATION, AND DEVELOPMENT

The aim of an oral presentation is to talk *with* an audience in a forthright manner, not *at* them. This requires showing respect for their integrity, intelligence, and values. To gain the trust of the audience and establish credibility, you need to show regard for accuracy, for ethics, and for the listeners. A knowledgeable presenter who is poised, prepared, and considerate will earn respect. Preparation includes not only collecting reliable information, planning, organizing, and practising but also giving attention to other factors that influence credibility.

See Chapter 25.

### Considering Credibility

Your *credibility* (estimate of trustworthiness by the audience) is based upon the quality of the information you present and the way you present it. To gain trust and respect, you need to sound as if you know and believe what you say. That means you must collect reliable information, identify sources, and radiate sincerity.

Your credibility emanates not only from thorough preparation and reliable information but also from professional demeanour and energy level. A clear confident voice, proper pronunciation, and correct grammar promote respect. Appropriate attire and a neat appearance also contribute to credibility. Look professional, not flashy. To feel tip-top and maintain your energy level, get a full night's rest and eat breakfast. To decrease anxiety, do some form of exercise.

### Organizing an Informative Presentation

Clarity, logical reasoning, and flexibility are the chief factors to keep in mind as you organize an oral presentation. Depending upon the rhetorical situation, an informative presentation can be organized in various ways. For example, to explain a training procedure, use chronological order just as you would in a process paper.

See Chapter 12.

If you are explaining something by giving three reasons, characteristics, or other categories, you could arrange them according to importance. To describe the layout and features of a historical park, you could use spatial order or a combination of orders. As you practise a presentation, revise the order as needed.

See "The Seven Basic Orders," Chapter 4.

## Organizing a Persuasive Presentation

A low-key argument is generally more effective than direct confrontation. The wise presenter downplays disagreement by starting with a neutral overview of an issue. A wise strategy is to follow with a point that both sides agree on. This *common ground* sets the stage for discussion. Next, state the points of the opposition *fairly* before presenting your points.

See Chapter 19.

Treating an issue as a problem to be resolved will establish an air of objectivity and fairness. Try to find a common goal. Use the pronoun *we* whenever possible: "*We* all want Children's Services to keep on serving needy children in this area. The question is, How do *we* continue services after the present funding runs out?" This attitude will foster respect for the other side and keep tempers banked. To elicit cooperation, *ask* questions such as "What are the alternatives?" "What are the advantages and disadvantages of each alternative?" "What is the best overall solution?"

To shape an effective argument, determine the *area of resistance* and find a way around it. Why does the other side reject a proposal? Often the area of resistance is cost. You might point out "The operating levy on the ballot is a renewal. It will not increase your taxes." List the benefits and conclude with a summation such as "Anything worthwhile is going to cost money. Let's not be penny-wise and pound foolish. Let's plan for the future."

## Considering Ethics, Logic, and Emotion

An important factor in any presentation is the blending of logic, ethics, and emotion. Yet there is no quick formula. First of all, appeals should be ethical. Second, most classroom presentations will require that logic predominate and emotion remain subordinate. Refer to Chapter 19 for more information on logical and ethical appeals. Appeals to emotion should be subtle and suitable, used to reinforce the central point. The emphasis should be on facts, data, details, reasons, and examples.

## Choosing the Right Words

When considering words, select a level of formality that is appropriate to the topic and the audience. This guideline rules out nonstandard English for classroom presentations. Informal Standard English is generally suitable for these presentations. Contractions will lend a conversational tone. If you need a technical term that the audience may not know, define it and perhaps give a brief example.

See Chapter 2.

See
Chapter 9.

Sometimes you can make a presentation come alive with a vivid comparison—a simile, metaphor, or analogy.

Shy away from buzz words, slang, and clichés that may not be understood by some generations or ethnic groups. Avoid stereotypes and any language that might offend.

## Improving Transition

To track the main idea, listeners need guide words even more than readers do. When there is a shift in meaning, place a transitional word or phrase at the head of the sentence. For example, "*But* the proponents believe that . . ." If you use chronological order or an order of importance, begin with numerical transition (*first, second, third*). For other situations involving time, you can insert transitions of time: *fifty years ago, today,* or *in the future.* If you speak of different places, begin with phrases such as *in Europe* or *at Madiera Beach.* (For lists of transitions, see the index.)

# OPTIONS FOR INTRODUCTIONS AND CONCLUSIONS

Unless you plan carefully, the closing of your presentation may be the only part that an audience remembers. Unless you hook their attention early, some may daydream throughout the entire presentation. The attention of others may fade in and out like a weak radio signal. A successful introduction has three key ingredients:

1. **Attention-getter.** It must relate to the topic.
2. **Topic.** State the topic and the thesis unless there is a logical reason for delaying the thesis.
3. **Link the topic to the audience.** Whet their curiosity and interest.

## Introductions

An attention-getter hooks listeners and stimulates interest, perhaps through a reference to the occasion, an anecdote or example, unfamiliar facts or fragments of history, a startling statistic or opinion, an intriguing question, an apt quotation, or original humour—something that happened to you.

***Refer to the Occasion***   Does the day of the presentation have historical significance? Is the occasion special for the audience or just for you? A reference to the occasion can provide an effective entry into the main idea. On July 1, 2004, Adrienne Clarkson, the governor general of Canada, made a speech in honour of Canada Day, an excerpt of which follows:

> Happy Canada Day to you all—from Alert Bay, off the tip of Vancouver Island, to Cape Spear in Newfoundland, from Grise Fjord to Point Pelee. We all wanted to be

part of this celebration on Parliament Hill, the symbol of everything that makes us the country that we are—a peace tower and buildings which symbolize our freedom.[1]

***Offer an Anecdote or Example***   A personal story that illustrates the main point allows you to ease into the topic. For example, if your purpose is to inspire and pay tribute, you might begin, "My uncle would have scoffed if someone had said he had great courage. He would have replied, 'I just did what needed to be done.'" Then the story or example would follow.

***Provide an Unfamiliar Fact or Bit of History***   Little-known information about a famous person, event, or place can provide an interesting opening. For example, an article from the *Wall Street Journal* (16 October 1998) could serve as an opening for a persuasive presentation:

> Our Congressional Cemetery, 191 years old and located near Capitol Hill, has sunk into obscurity and decay. In fact, this cemetery—where John Philip Sousa, Mathew Brady, and other noted persons lie—was cited in 1997 as "one of the nation's 11 most endangered historic places." That fall volunteers worked for two days cutting shrubbery and sprucing up the grounds. Retired FBI agents placed a bench and fence on J. Edgar Hoover's plot, but major improvements are needed.

***Give a Surprising Statistic or Opinion***   To capture attention, begin with an unexpected fact or statement. This opening is handy if the topic is familiar to the audience. To interest them, you need something different, a fresh angle or an unusual comment to make them sit up and listen. Consider the following example:

> Friends, before his passing, the Canadian journalist, Peter Gzowski, used to say of our province, "Saskatchewan is the heartland of Canada, the most Canadian of all provinces." In many ways, Peter Gzowski was correct. You know, we are the most representative of Canadian peoples, the most multicultural of all provinces; we are the only province in Canada where neither official language grouping is in the majority. [2]

***Ask a Question***   Asking a *rhetorical question*, one you will answer in the presentation, can stimulate curiosity about the topic. For instance, if you were going to talk on beekeeping, you might ask, "Did you know that worker bees have to put the queen on a diet before she can fly and start a new hive? Normally, she is too heavy. They have to keep her from eating until she is light enough to fly."

Or you might ask a question and take an answer from the audience. If you take individual responses, limit to three. Call on people who are unlikely to toss in a joke or hog the stage. The safest way is to ask a direct question of the entire

---

1 "Her Excellency the Right Honourable Adrienne Clarkson: Speech on the Occasion of the Canada Day Celebration" http://www.gg.ca/media/doc.asp?lang=c&DocID=4235

2 Calvert, Lorne. Premier's Speech, Special Olympics Fundraising Dinner. Prince Albert, Saskatchewan. 19 April, 2002.

audience, one that requires a brief yes or no, such as "How many of you have bought a lovely house plant only to have it die within a short time?" Then raise your own hand to indicate a show of hands.

***Find an Apt Quotation***   The right quotation at the beginning can lend a professional touch. In the first line of the introduction, repeat a key word or phrase from the quotation.

> Helen Keller said "life is either a daring adventure or nothing." My wish for you is that your life in every aspect continues or becomes a daring adventure.  Gloria Steinham via her writing and her public speaking has encouraged people to commit one outrageous act a day. Now if you are a graduate in the nursing program, social work, or gerontology, that outrageous act may not necessarily be wisely executed amongst your patients. Although, on occasion, follow your instincts if a patient needs a hug, some extra human contact, versus a "totally" professional approach. If you are in the visual merchandising arts, that one outrageous act might be very appropriate as you step out of the colour palates of the day and make a bold statement in a pitch to one of your clients.  One of my outrageous acts, in celebration of surviving cancer for over a year, was to go sky diving a couple of months prior to my 50th birthday.[3]

This repetition provides a direct lead to the main idea. If you cannot create a link, find a quotation that is relevant.

***Use Humour***   Using humour is like lighting a fire—you need to know what you are doing, or you may be burned. Original humour is best, especially brisk one-liners that bring you quickly to the main idea. Do not tell irrelevant jokes just because they are funny. Keep anecdotes and jokes short. A long-winded tale can create a top-heavy presentation. If you direct good-natured humour toward someone, choose a close friend or the head of the company—a self-confident person who will not take

---

### GUIDELINES FOR USING HUMOUR

Inappropriate humour can blast a speaker's credibility. If you intend to use humour in a presentation, appraise it carefully, and follow these guidelines:

1. **Be original and relevant.** Relate humour closely to the main idea.
2. **Use humour like salt—sparingly.** Keep jokes and stories brief.
3. **Be kind.** Avoid remarks that might offend individuals or groups.
4. **Practise your timing.** If people do not laugh, go right on.
5. **Practise your punch line.** Pause before the punch line. Then say it clearly. Do not rush. Emphasize the important words.

---

3 Mulvale, Ann.  Convocation Speech.  Sheridan College, Oakville. 12 June, 2003.

offence. Or better yet, tell jokes on yourself. The audience will love it, and it will keep you humble. Avoid ethnic, sexist, and off-colour jokes. Be professional.

## Conclusions

In a serious presentation, the conclusion has two prime functions: to summarize and to provide closure. For most informative and persuasive presentations, the ending should *restate the main idea*. As you restate the thesis, allude to the importance of the topic to the audience. Be concise. Three guidelines can help you avoid common problems:

- Do not end abruptly.
- Do not introduce new points.
- Do not ramble.

To devise an effective closing, think about the impression you want to leave. What do you want listeners to remember? Six common endings are listed here. They can be combined in various ways, depending upon the presentation.

***Summarize***   For emphasis in a serious presentation, remind listeners of the thesis, either directly or by allusion. When you repeat the main idea, listeners are more apt to remember it. Or summarize your main points if appropriate. To spice up a summary ending, combine it with another type of closing.

***End with a Quotation***   A relevant quotation can provide a thoughtful conclusion. Do not quote an entire poem—use only a few lines that apply to the central idea of the presentation. If you began with a quotation, do not end with another. Chances are the two will conflict and detract from the presentation.

***Loop to the Introduction***   Allude to the opening in some way for closure. If you began with a rhetorical question, you might answer it briefly in the conclusion. If you began with a quotation, you might repeat a key phrase. Or if you began with a story, you might quickly finish it.

***Pose a Challenge or Question***   A challenge or provocative question can motivate an audience. This ending is often used to persuade. For example, a presentation that reports the progress on a volunteer playground project might end with appreciation, a summary, and a question (note the emotional appeal):

> We appreciate your generosity. You have opened your pocketbooks and lent your hands. The job is almost complete. Will you come once more to help rake the site and spread mulch this Saturday or Sunday? Seeing the delight on the children's faces when they can use this playground will make you glad you did.

***Call for Action***   A persuasive presentation requires a restatement of the proposition. Often a call for action is also included to motivate the audience. For example, "Tonight set your alarm ten minutes early. Then stop by the voting booth on your way to class or to work. You owe it to yourself and your country."

*Refer to the Future*   Mentioning the future can lend an optimistic note. In "I Have a Dream," Martin Luther King combined three techniques in his ending: he summarized the main idea, alluded to the future, and quoted from an old song. Note, too, the use of *we* to unite listeners:

> When we let freedom ring, when we let it ring from every village and every hamlet, from every state and every city, we will be able to speed up that day when all of God's children, black men and white men, Jews and Gentiles, Protestants and Catholics, will be able to join hands and sing in the words of the old Negro spiritual, "Free at last! free at last! Thank God almighty, we are free at last!"

## PREPARING NOTES AND AUDIOVISUAL AIDS

Preparing careful notes and effective audiovisual aids can enhance your presentation. Although some experienced speakers manage without notes, most carry them as insurance. Even professional presenters are not immune to sudden memory loss. Confidently, one presenter strode up to the lectern without his notes because he had practised well. But when he looked out over a sea of 500 faces, his mind went blank. While the audience waited, he walked back to his chair for the notes. That was a humbling experience.

### Notes on Paper or Cards?

By now you should be convinced that notes are essential, even if your instructor does not require them. The one remaining question is whether to put the notes on paper or file cards. If you ever present a seminar, you might decide to type your outline on paper, double spaced in large type. If you're using presentation software, the program will include options for preparing notes.

A few sheets of paper are simpler to handle than a dozen note cards unless there is air blowing near you. (Overhead projectors, for instance, can scatter pages.) Number the sheets in the upper right corner. Place them in a neat pile on one side of the lectern before you begin. As you finish covering the points on each page, *slide the page to the other side of the lectern while looking at your audience.* Continue in this way, and the audience will be unlikely to notice your notes. This method takes more skill and practice than using a few note cards.

For classroom presentations, carefully prepared note cards are easy to use. Just lay out the cards and leave them alone during the presentation. Six large cards will usually fit neatly on a lectern. Although six may seem like quite a few, beware of crowding words. *You need to be able to scan the cards quickly without picking them up or bending over.* Note cards should be legible from three feet away (unless you are very short).

### Creating Effective Audiovisual Aids

Chances are that you will have a software program such as PowerPoint at your disposal for use in a presentation. Or you might use an overhead projector, a flip chart, a VCR, a tape player, or other audiovisual aid. (A chalkboard is not recommended because it lacks novelty and requires turning your back while the audience waits.)

## TIPS FOR MAKING NOTE CARDS

1. **Use large 12.5 cm by 20 cm cards.** For easy reading, avoid crowding.
2. **Number the cards in the upper right corner.** Avoid mixups.
3. **Use an outline format.** Leave blank space to add key phrases later.
4. **Print neatly with black ink in large letters.** Use broad strokes.
5. **Use numbers or bullets to list points.** Enhance visibility.
6. **Use only one side of each card.** Turning cards over diverts attention.

The purpose of an audiovisual aid is to enhance a presentation, not overpower it. Avoid clutter. As you plan graphics, check to see that each frame or sheet conveys a single idea. If you have several statistics or other complex items, prepare a handout to distribute before you begin. *Do not interrupt your presentation to pass out materials.* Less relevant information can be left near the door to be picked up later.

## GUIDELINES FOR PLANNING AUDIOVISUAL AIDS (AVA)

1. **Make sure an AVA will not harm the audience or make them squirm.** No snakes, guns, explosives, volatile liquids, or other dangerous items.
2. **Predict the effect of the AVA and test it.** Be sure there are no trouble spots. *Run unusual ideas past your instructor.*
3. **Limit the number of AVAs and keep them fairly simple.** Otherwise, you may feel like a juggler with too many balls in the air.
4. **Limit tapes and videos to one minute in a five- to seven-minute presentation.**
5. **Make graphics neat and attractive.** Plan layouts so they are clear, uncluttered, and pleasing to the eye. Limit to one idea each.
6. **Use colour for a purpose.** Human eyes, like those of bees, are attracted to red and black. Use red for emphasis and dark colours for lettering.
7. **Check to see that visuals are clear to persons seated in the back row.** If you are discussing a small object, show an enlargement.
8. **Retain the element of surprise.** Keep visuals hidden until you use them. For example, reverse posters until you are ready to show them.

# PRACTISING A PRESENTATION

Planning and practice are essential for an effective presentation. Last-minute attention to equipment and materials, hurrying, and dropping or misplacing items can give the impression of carelessness and incompetence. Careful preparation will boost your confidence and help fend off mishaps.

Practise your presentation several times, using your note cards and audiovisual aids, but do not overpractise or it may sound memorized. To lend a natural, conversational tone, you might imagine you are talking to friends. *Act as if you feel calm, even if you don't.* If you have the opportunity to videotape a practice session, do so. Then you can critique your eye contact, posture, gestures, vocal variety, and use of notes and audiovisual aids.

## Using Audiovisual Aids

Plan how and when to use audiovisual aids so that the audience does not have to wait. Can you set up and adjust PowerPoint, the VCR, or any projectors before class? How will you prop up the antique doll? Can you get an easel so that the poster will not flop over? Other questions to consider are when to bring out objects and how long to leave them out.

As you speak, *look at the audience, not the visuals.* When using an overhead projector, use a pencil to point on the transparency. When slides or other visuals are projected onto a screen behind you, use a longer object to point to areas of the screen. That way you can glance at it and look at the audience, not the screen. If you are describing an unfamiliar object or craft, such as punched tin, bring it out early. If the object will not distract, leave it out the entire time. Or some objects are more effective shown only at the end.

One student, who had won several trophies showing her horse, did not want to appear to be bragging, so she decided to display just one trophy. First she described the fun of displaying the horse in the ring; then she explained the unglamorous work behind the scenes. At the end she held up a large trophy and said, "But all the hard work was worthwhile, because I won first prize!" By then she had charmed the audience, and they were glad her efforts had been rewarded.

## Revising Note Cards

As you practise your presentation, highlight key points on your notes with a coloured marker. If you quote someone, highlight the quote. If certain terms are difficult to recall, print them in red. Reword any phrases or sentences that cause stumbling. Write the revision on your note card. Star the spots where audiovisual aids will come. On the final card or page, write out the last sentence you want to say as a safety blanket. If your notes become messy from revision, recopy them as necessary for easy reading.

## Improving Eye Contact, Posture, and Gestures

Before you open your lips, you send silent messages that enhance or diminish your credibility. Your eye contact, posture, and gestures greatly affect your presentation.

Do you look at the audience—or do you stare at a point on the back wall? Do you stand erect or slumped? Do you have notes in hand ready to lay out, or do you fumble through a briefcase, backpack, or handbag?

*Eye Contact*   Smile and establish eye contact immediately before you say a word. During the presentation, look at one person for several seconds before moving on. Look at various people in different parts of the room, not just the front row. Avoid eye dart. You may *glance* at your note cards from time to time, but do not linger. Their purpose is merely to remind you of the next idea.

*Gestures*   Like your words, your gestures should appear spontaneous and natural. You might rest one hand on the lectern, but do not clutch it with both hands. The purpose of a lectern is to hold notes, not to lean on or hide behind. Once in a while you may want to walk out from behind the lectern, but beware of purposeless movement and repetitive gestures. Consider, too, that some gestures may have negative or humourous connotations. Three common stances have been identified as detrimental for speakers:

- **The Fig Leaf** Avoid standing with hands clasped in front.
- **Parade Rest** Avoid standing with hands clasped behind the back like a general reviewing the troops.
- **Closed Mind** Avoid crossed arms on the chest. This posture may suggest coldness and a reluctance to admit new information.

While you speak, let you arms hang loosely at your sides so that you can use them naturally. Avoid nervous habits that dispel the illusion of spontaneity and distract. Common habits include scratching the nose, twisting long hair or beard, fidgeting with earrings, jingling coins, taking glasses on and off, or waving a note card around.

## Improving Vocal Variety

The human voice is an instrument that conveys distinctive speech sounds that vary in volume, rate, and pitch. When we are relaxed and happy, the sounds are more pleasing than when we are tired or upset. Fear, anxiety, and anger tighten the vocal cords, producing a higher, thinner pitch than normal. With practice you can gain greater control of your voice. Volume and rate are easier to control than pitch, but all can be improved to some extent. Taping an entire presentation allows you not only to time it but also to hear how you sound.

*Volume*   A presenter's voice should be loud enough to be heard by everyone in the room, unless a microphone is available. Volume is seldom a problem for male voices, but some female voices are barely audible. Women often need to speak louder than normal. To project your voice to the back row, you need plenty of air in the lungs. Shallow breathing interferes with vocal variety and quality. Try varying your volume according to the effect you wish to create. Emphasize important words. Be careful that your voice does not trail off at the ends of sentences, making them inaudible.

***Rate***   "Mallspeak" or immature speech patterns may be a concern for some readers. In "Taking Aim at Student Incoherence" (*Chronicle of Higher Education* 26 March 1999), Alison Schneider cites this sample, delivered breathlessly: "Okay. Today I'm going to be talking to you guys about malaria." During the presentation the student fidgeted and giggled, ending with "So, in conclusion, I'd just like to say, malaria, you know, is the most prevalent of all tropical diseases."

Speaking too fast, fidgeting, and giggling may be due to nervousness or feelings of inadequacy, intensified by habit. If you have any of these concerns, give yourself a little pep talk. Reassure yourself that these minutes are yours and you have an interesting topic to share. The audience is alert and waiting. You don't have to race to the finish line. Don't be afraid to pause at the right places, including a slight pause after periods. Pausing after an important point gives emphasis and allows the audience time to absorb the idea. Knowing that it is all right to pause naturally may help you delete unintentional fillers such as *uh, um, okay,* or *you know*.

***Articulation***   Practice and pausing can alleviate slurring (running words together) or other problems in articulation. The lips, the tongue, and the teeth form speech sounds—they articulate the words. At the same time, the mouth has to open wide enough to let the words out or mumbling occurs. And *it must be empty*—chewing gum, candy, or cough drops interfere with clear delivery.

Common concerns are slurring and addition of or omission of syllables. Tape yourself and then check a dictionary for problem words. Listed here are common mispronunciations and the correct pronunciations:

| *Incorrect* | *Correct* |
|---|---|
| acrost | a-cross' |
| ath-*a*-lete | ath'lete |
| fishin' | fish'ing |
| gonna | go'ing to |
| pitchur | pic'ture |
| wanna | want to |

***Pitch***   Pitch refers to the lowness or highness of the voice. We all have a natural pitch that varies according to our emotions and health. Other factors also influence pitch. For example, if we ask a question, our voice goes up at the end of the sentence. At the end of a declarative sentence, the voice goes down. Most speakers, when relaxed, vary their pitch naturally. Those who speak in a monotone can add expression to their words through vocal exercise and practice (see the exercises at the end of the chapter).

## GIVING A PRESENTATION

*Enthusiasm* and *sincerity* are two keys to an effective presentation. Enthusiastic speakers know and care about their topics. They vary their volume, rate, and pitch just as they would in casual conversation. Chances are that if you like your topic and prepare well, your enthusiasm will radiate from your face and your voice. And if you truly believe what you are saying, your sincerity will be apparent.

## Arrive Early

Go early to the room where you will speak. Erase the chalkboard if necessary. Check to see that the equipment you need is in working order. (One mortified student forgot to plug in the VCR.) If you are supposed to sign equipment out somewhere else, go get it.

## Take a Deep Breath . . .

When introduced, take a deep breath and approach the lectern. Put down your notes or, if you're using note cards, lay them out in sequence. Then look out over the audience and smile. Chances are that some people will smile back. If you come across as a friendly person, listeners will be more apt to give you their undivided attention. For some topics, smiling may be inappropriate.

On the job or in a community setting, extend an appropriate greeting, such as "Good Morning" or "Welcome." You may want to thank someone who has assisted or the group for inviting you. In the classroom these little courtesies are not expected.

## Don't Apologize Unnecessarily

Even if you feel unprepared, rushed, or nervous, don't apologize or toss in unnecessary comments. Just ignore your feelings and begin with your planned opening. Once you get past that and the audience responds, speaking will become easier. If you should mispronounce a word, just correct yourself and go on. Avoid weak, *ineffective* remarks such as these:

- Uh, I guess I'm a little nervous.
- I didn't have as much time to prepare as I would have liked.
- I regret I am not an expert on this topic (false modesty).

## Adapt to the Audience

Watching the audience will take your mind off yourself. Are they listening attentively? Or do they slump in their seats, gaze at the ceiling, or fidget? To regain lost attention, you can move out from behind the lectern, use more gestures, increase volume, or lower your voice to a whisper.

Handle unexpected incidents with poise. If a transparency falls, let it lie unless you need it. If the bulb in an overhead projector burns out, flip the switch for the spare bulb. If there is none, continue anyway. If computer equipment malfunctions, take a moment to resolve the problem, and if the problem can't be fixed quickly, go on without your computerized audiovisual aids. Seldom is there cause to interrupt a presentation. In the unlikely event of a power outage, sonic boom, fire alarm, or a storm alert, stop and wait. Then when you resume the presentation, you might toss in a quick joke. The audience will admire your calm, professional demeanour and ability to function under duress.

## End Purposefully and Gracefully

The last few words of a presentation tend to linger in the minds of the audience. Once in a while, an inexperienced presenter will skid to an abrupt stop with "That's it" or "that's all." Some go to the other extreme—tacking on afterthoughts, irrelevant jokes, or stories. Such tactics throw a presentation off balance and weaken its impact. Know when to stop.

## Be Prepared for Questions

After a presentation, you may have the opportunity to say, "Are there any questions?" If so, listen carefully to the entire question before responding. Maintain eye contact. If the question is unclear, restate it as a question. If you don't know the answer, ask for a phone number or an email address so that you can get back to the person.

STUDENT SAMPLE: A PERSUASIVE PRESENTATION

Carol Witzel gave the following oral presentation. She had outlined it on note cards but wrote out the draft later, when requested.

### Give It More Respect!

Do you know what the hottest part of your body is? Do you know what part is the most dangerous if it becomes infected? The answer to both questions is your mouth, specifically your gums and teeth. Are you surprised? Like Rodney Dangerfield, your mouth and its contents get little respect. After you hear of my unfortunate experience, you should accord this part of your body much, much more respect.

During a regular checkup two years ago, my physician said that he did not like the looks of my gums and that I should have a dentist take a look at them. Immediately, I made an appointment with my regular dentist. I told him my mouth had a metallic taste, and my teeth seemed to hurt often. During the exam the dentist told me not to worry, everything was fine. He did not bother to take x-rays.

One year passed and the symptoms worsened. By then my gums were bleeding when I brushed my teeth. When I opened my mouth in cold air, my face and teeth hurt. I decided it was time to consult a different dentist. The second dentist did a quick exam—the results were dismal. Several teeth had advanced decay. Worst of all, my gums were in an advanced stage of periodontal disease or gingivitis. Gingivitis is inflammation and infection of the gingiva or gums. There are five stages of the disease, and I was in stage four.

What I needed was minor surgery on the gums to clear away the infection. Then he put in seven crowns to correct the problems with decayed teeth. After that came bridge work, which involved three additional crowns and two pontics (false teeth). The bridge was made to cover the loss of two teeth due to poor care. Correcting all these problems cost nearly $7000.

Today you cannot tell my natural teeth from the crowns or bridgework. My teeth no longer hurt when I drink hot or cold liquids. I can actually breathe through my mouth without severe pain emitting from teeth to all points on my face.

Now you are probably wondering how you can prevent some of the problems I've experienced. The first step is to have regular dental checkups with a responsible dentist. Second, take good daily care of your teeth and mouth. Third, watch for any of these five symptoms:

1. **Bleeding in the mouth.** Have it checked just as you would if some other part of your body was bleeding regularly.

2. **A metallic taste.** If you already have fillings, this could mean you have decay under the filling, and the old filling is leaking.

3. **Extreme sensitivity** to hot and cold temperatures.

4. **Chronic bad breath.**

5. **Chronic tiredness, headaches, or white spots on the gums** could indicate infection. Those who use tobacco should watch these signs closely because of the risk of cancer in the mouth.

If your dentist does not stress good gum care, maybe you should consider finding another dentist. Just remember that your mouth is the gateway to your body. To have good health, respect and maintain your mouth, gums, and teeth. You will be glad you did!

*Questions for Discussion*

1. How does Carol involve the audience in her opening?

2. What common order does she use to present information?

3. What signpost transitions indicate this order?

4. Can you find the transitional sentence that she uses to go from talking about herself to explaining about good dental care?

5. What do you notice about her ending?

---

### SUMMARY

- Writing and speaking differ greatly in their treatment of occasion, audience, and voice; these elements influence the preparation and delivery of an effective presentation.
- When developing your oral presentation, check out the setting as well as the audience so that you can tailor your approach to the topic. Define your topic and make sure to use reliable sources when conducting research.
- In the opening of your presentation, link your topic to the audience. During the delivery of your presentation, use simple audiovisual aids. Be sure to practise your presentation several times, but don't memorize.
- Be aware of the way you deliver your presentation: Good eye contact, erect posture, appropriate gestures, and a neat appearance add to a presenter's credibility. Vocal variety and clear articulation add interest and clarity. Behave professionally, avoiding apologies and unnecessary remarks. Restate the main idea at the end of your presentation for emphasis.

## Practice

### Exercise: Articulation

To improve your articulation, say the alphabet aloud. Exaggerate each letter and say it distinctly. Listen and think about the position of your tongue and lips. They must be in the right position for a letter to be clear. To form an *l*, the tip of the tongue touches the roof of the mouth, and the mouth opens slightly. The *r* sound rumbles deep in the throat as the tongue is held up slightly and the mouth curls down, slightly open.

If dropping of *g*'s is a problem for you, practise words ending with *-ing* and think about the position of your tongue and mouth as you say them correctly, emphasizing *-ing*. As you attain greater self-awareness, your vocal variety will improve.

### Ungraded Presentations

The chief purpose of an ungraded presentation is to alleviate speech fright. A one- or two-minute practice speech can use the basic claim-and-evidence order (opinion and support). For example, you might disagree with a news item, magazine article, political decision, or movie review. Give reasons. Close with a complete sentence, such as "See *Clint Rides Again* only if you want to be bored stiff." Or you might use one of the ideas below or one of your own.

1. Funny, exciting, or embarrassing moment
2. An unusual ancestor, neighbour, or boss
3. An incident: How your spouse proposed, prank at summer camp, et cetera
4. Description: Your best teacher, first job, first car
5. Anecdote: a lost pet, special birthday, or disastrous first date

## Ten Ideas for Oral Presentations

### Informative Topics

1. Present a research-based paper or project to the class (condense and simplify).
2. Present tips for improving something.
3. Suggest three interesting one-day trips to lesser-known spots.
4. Describe factors to consider when buying a new computer, car, camping equipment, or other item.
5. Describe your hobby.

### Persuasive Topics

6. Research a timely issue and take a position.
7. Voting is a responsibility.

8. Cut your sugar intake.
9. Take steps to prevent fires in your home.
10. Prevent skin cancer.

# THE READER

Part 8

*Reader Contents*

## ALTERNATE CONTENTS: THE READINGS BY THEME

# Introduction to the Reader

The twenty-six essays in this reader have been carefully selected not only for quality but also for interest. They cover unusual topics, ranging from geographic profiling to philosophical issues such as "Do we have a right to happiness?" All of the readings should stimulate thinking and questioning; they open windows on different eras, cultures, personalities, problems, and points of view.

## WHAT IS AN ESSAY?

An essay is a short literary composition that focuses on a single idea. Usually, the author's opinion is present. For example, the author may speculate about the meaning of an event or a course of action and possible consequences. An essay of argument may question one viewpoint and offer another. Essays tend to be direct, with the thesis clearly stated. They are organized in various ways, depending on the purpose and the subject.

## CRITICAL READING

As you examine and discuss these readings, you will learn much about the craft of writing. You'll notice how writers use openings to set the stage for an idea and endings to conclude gracefully. You'll gain skill in scrutinizing logic. In short, you will learn to read critically—analyzing and evaluating not only content but also structure. A strategy for critical reading is explained in Chapter 26. This strategy outlines three stages of critical reading—prereading, rereading, and prewriting—and gives helpful steps to apply as you read.

As you read, think, and discuss, take note of a significant distinction: The *writer's purpose* and the *writer's intent* are not the same. The writer's purpose is usually *stated* in an essay. You can find the purpose in the thesis statement, if there is one. A good thesis statement makes it clear whether the purpose of a piece is to entertain, inform, define, persuade, or combine some of these functions. When the purpose is stated, then it is possible to evaluate whether the writer has achieved what he or she set out to do.

On the other hand, we seldom know what a writer has intended, for *intent is rarely stated*. Unless an author spells out his or her intentions, we cannot be sure of what they are. They may, in fact, be quite different from the stated purpose.

## SECOND GUESSING

Sound critical reading does not second guess an author's intent. A writing may be richer and deeper than a writer consciously intends. It is not unusual for authors to admit they were unaware of certain symbols or themes in their works until someone pointed them out. All we can logically evaluate is what the writer has *achieved*.

The more experience readers gain, the more they will notice. Perhaps the best piece of advice is to read quickly for enjoyment the first time. Then go back, reread, and ponder the piece. The better you understand the effect of a work, the more you will enjoy and appreciate its artistry.

# Narration

## Recounting Events

### *Rosetta Disk Is Foundation's Gift to Future Linguists*

David Bank

---

*The Rosetta Stone is the key to ancient languages used in Egypt. This black granite slab was found in 1799, half-buried in the mud at the mouth of the Nile delta, by a French officer in Napoleon's army. In 1801 it was taken by the British and later placed in the British Museum. Upon the Rosetta Stone are three identical texts, carved in Egyptian hieroglyphics, Greek, and Demotic—the popular language of Egypt during the reign of Ptolemy Epiphanes IV from 203 to 181 B.C. His son, Ptolemy V, began to rule at age thirteen; during his reign, a council of priests inscribed a decree on the stone about 196 B.C. A French scholar, Jean François Champollion, first translated the Greek portion. Then gradually he decoded the rest, publishing the results in 1822.*

    *Linguists now estimate that one language is lost every ten days worldwide. To offset this loss, the Rosetta Project, a global collaboration, is creating an archive of 1000 languages on a three-inch nickel disk, encased in a glass ball. In the future, when our digital computers become obsolete, the disk will provide a key to the languages of the twenty-first century. David Bank, the author of this article, is a staff reporter for the* Wall Street Journal. *He has also published* Breaking Windows: How Bill Gates Fumbled the Future of Microsoft *(2001).*

---

Around 196 B.C., a council of ancient Egyptian priests inscribed a decree on a    1
granite slab affirming the rule of 13-year-old Ptolemy V and providing three translations, including one in a form of ancient Greek. After Napoleon's troops in Egypt recovered the slab, the Rosetta Stone, in 1799, linguists used the Greek to unlock the Egyptian hieroglyphics, whose meaning had been lost for centuries.

    Now, a small San Francisco foundation is leading an effort to create a modern Rosetta Stone, a collection of 1,000 translations of the first three chapters of the book of Genesis into languages from Abkhaz to Zulu. The foundation's far-thinking backers hope the project will help decoders in the distant future recover languages of our own day, many of which will certainly be lost.

"If it's good with three, why not with 1,000?" asks Stewart Brand, best known as the founder of the Whole Earth Catalog and now a board member of the Long Now Foundation, which is coordinating the Rosetta Project. "In the fullness of time, civilizations come and go. It would be good to have better re-start capabilities."

When the collection is completed next year, roughly 30,000 pages of linguistic submissions will be inscribed by ion beams in tiny text onto three-inch nickel disks and encased in glass balls. The technology provider, Norsam Technologies, of Hillsboro, Ore., says tests show the disks will last at least 1,000 years, withstanding salt water, sunlight and nuclear radiation using the technology, developed at the Los Alamos nuclear labs. The foundation will distribute 1,000 disks to libraries and museums, and sell them to individuals around the world, all under the archival principle, "*Lots of Copies Keep Stuff Safe.*"

The hope is that at least some of the disks will survive and prove useful to future archaeologists. The glass balls encasing the disks are rudimentary magnifying glasses. Larger text in eight languages spirals around the edge of the disk as a kind of hint to discoverers to magnify the disks further. The Rosetta Project backers assume future generations will at least have a 1,000-power microscope to enlarge the tiny type. They won't need what will surely be long-lost technology: the personal computer, a Windows operating system or even electricity. The information will be presented in plain text, not digital bits.

Linguistic experts say by 2100, up to 90 percent of the world's 6,000 to 7,000 languages are in danger of becoming moribund, or even extinct, as industrialization and globalization reach every corner of the globe. Most of the world's recent losses come in once language-rich regions of the world, such as Papua New Guinea, Indonesia and Nigeria. One language becomes moribund every 10 days, on average, experts say, meaning that children no longer learn it and speak it.

With modest funding—$165,000 over two years from the Lazy Eight Foundation, of Denver, Colo.—the project is attracting submissions by linguists from around the world. No single expert could possibly check every submission, so the Rosetta Project relies on a network of linguists to correct each others' work.

Mr. Mason began by collecting nearly 1,000 translations of the world's most widely translated text, Genesis, mainly from Bible societies. The decision to use a biblical text generated a heated debate within the foundation over its religious associations, but Mr. Mason says the availability of translations made it the only practical choice. The next most-translated text, the Universal Declaration of Human Rights, has been translated into about 300 languages.

The project's Web site, www.rosettaproject.org, is becoming one of the broadest collections of language information on the Internet. Jim Mason, the anthropologist directing the project, calls it "the Linux of linguistics," referring to the open-source operating system developed collaboratively over the Internet. "A large collection of languages is way too complex for one person, or even one group of people to tackle," Mr. Mason says. "The only way to do it is create a global collaboration."

5

In technology terms, Mr. Mason describes the Rosetta Project as a "platform"    10
able to support a wide variety of activities. It includes a range of material in each
language, including indigenous creation stories, terms for colors, the so-called
Swadesh list of the 100 words that occur in almost every language and "orthog-
raphies" describing writing and speaking styles.

The project began as a demonstration of possibilities for long-term data preservation. The record of the digital age—dependent on ever-changing computer
platforms and formats—promises to be startlingly impermanent. Older media
aren't much better. Newspapers and videotapes have a life expectancy of less than
30 years. Acid-free paper and some types of microform can last up to 500 years
but are susceptible to heat, humidity, scratching and sunlight. History has shown
that libraries burn down, museums are neglected and time capsules are forgotten.

"We're building amnesia into our civilization, which is probably a non-robust
thing to do," remarks Mr. Brand.

The Long Now Foundation's focus on the far distant future is meant to
stretch the time-horizon of planners, executives and leaders by 100 or 500 years,
if not by 10,000. (It's already working on the deca-millenium bug, referring to the
current year as 02001.) Its most well-known project is a "10,000-year clock" currently in several prototype forms, including one at the National Museum of Science and Industry in London. It ticks once a year, has a century hand that advances
every 100 years and tolls every 1,000 years.

The Rosetta Project is a kind of complement. "It's very hard to send information into the future," says Kevin Kelly, a foundation board member and former executive editor of Wired magazine. "It's even harder to send values, or any kind of
information that's embedded in a culture."

Other board members include musician Brian Eno, futurist Paul Saffo, Stan-    15
ford University Librarian Roger Kennedy, and old-timers Danny Hillis, a pioneer
in supercomputing, Mitch Kapor, a founder of Lotus Development Corp., pundit
Esther Dyson and Doug Carlston, the co-founder of Broderbund Software.

The first and so far only completed submission is for Degema, spoken by
about 22,000 people in two communities in Nigeria. A Nigerian linguist studying
in Japan, Ethelbert Kari, prepared a detailed description of the language, pronunciation and common words. There were originally three dialects of Degema, but
one became extinct when its speakers adopted Kalabari, the language of the
Abonnema people.

"If one is a native speaker of a language, one will soon realize how sad and
hopeless it is not to be able to speak or think in that language again," Mr. Kari said
in an e-mail exchange. "Indeed, this pain is hanging upon the faces of many speakers who have lost their languages."

There is no complete survey of the world's languages, says Doug Whalen, vice
president of research at Yale University's Haskins Laboratories and the founder of
the Endangered Language Fund. The fund has distributed about $60,000 to help
in such projects as recording elderly speakers of Dakota and a video drama in
Choctaw, both Native American languages, but it has resources to capture
no more than a handful of languages. The Rosetta Project is useful in focusing

attention on the long-term preservation of keys to unlocking language fragments that might survive into the future.

"I'm happy preserving samples for 100 years, but thinking about what we'd like to leave for 10,000 years, that's a different picture," Dr. Haskins says. "If this was all that remained of these languages, it's really not enough to preserve them. It doesn't stop the extinction, but it's better than nothing."

## Reflecting and Interpreting

1. Consider that the first paragraph could have been omitted. What valuable functions does it perform?

2. Which text will be inscribed in 1000 languages on the Rosetta Disk? Despite the controversy, why was it finally selected?

3. What other material will be included?

4. In creating the disk, what two assumptions have linguists made?

5. How many languages do linguists estimate exist? In what areas of the world are languages rapidly becoming "moribund"?

6. Which group of languages in the United States is disappearing? Which two of these are mentioned in the article?

7. What five problems commonly interfere with long-term data preservation? Which medium will last up to 500 years under optimum conditions?

8. What five languages do you think will be predominant 50 years from now? Why? What methods of data preservation can you envision for the future?

9. Jim Mason, the anthropologist directing the project, calls it "the Linux of linguistics." What literary device is this?

10. Examine the rhetorical structure of Bank's article. Which method of organization does he use to open? What other rhetorical strategies does he combine?

## A Writer's Response

Make a list of the documents in your family that you would like to see preserved for at least one hundred years. Since most paper will disintegrate much sooner than that, how can you easily and inexpensively make copies on acid-free paper (available at most office supply stores)? If you don't have the equipment, do you know someone who does?

# *Home for Christmas*

Carson McCullers

*Nestled among Carson McCullers's memories was one drawn from her childhood in Georgia. Through twelve-year-old eyes, she described her family's preparations for the Christmas season, a season so special that she and her siblings sang carols in August to break the monotony of summer. This anecdote, first printed in her autobiography, reveals how she began to ponder the mystery of time. McCullers (1917–67) was also the author of several acclaimed works of fiction, including* The Heart Is a Lonely Hunter *(1940),* Reflections in a Golden Eye *(1941),* A Member of the Wedding *(1946), and* The Ballad of the Sad Cafe *(1951).*

Sometimes in August, weary of the vacant, broiling afternoon, my younger    1
brother and sister and I would gather in the dense shade under the oak tree in the
back yard and talk of Christmas and sing carols. Once after such a conclave, when
the tunes of the carols still lingered in the heat-shimmered air, I remember climb-
ing up into the tree house and sitting there alone for a long time.

Brother called up: "What are you doing?"

"Thinking," I answered.

"What are you thinking about?"

"I don't know."

"Well, how can you be thinking when you don't know what you are thinking    5
about?"

I did not want to talk with my brother. I was experiencing the first wonder
about the mystery of Time. Here I was, on this August afternoon, in the tree-
house, in the burnt, jaded yard, sick and tired of all our summer ways. (I had read
*Little Women* for the second time, *Hans Brinker and the Silver Skates, Little Men,*
and *Twenty Thousand Leagues under the Sea.* I had read movie magazines and even
tried to read love stories in the *Woman's Home Companion*—I was so sick of everything.) How could it be that I was I and now was now when in four months
it would be Christmas, wintertime, cold weather, twilight and the glory of the
Christmas tree? I puzzled about the *now* and *later* and rubbed the inside of my
elbow until there was a little roll of dirt between my forefinger and thumb. Would
the *now I* of the tree-house and the August afternoon be the same *I* of winter, firelight and the Christmas tree? I wondered.

My brother repeated: "You say you are thinking but you don't know what you
are thinking about. What are you really doing up there? Have you got some secret
candy?"

September came, and my mother opened the cedar chest and we tried on
winter coats and last year's sweaters to see if they would do again. She took the
three of us downtown and bought us new shoes and school clothes.

Christmas was nearer on the September Sunday that Daddy rounded us up    10
in the car and drove us out on dusty country roads to pick elderberry blooms.
Daddy made wine from elderberry blossoms—it was a yellow-white wine, the
color of weak winter sun. The wine was dry to the wry side—indeed, some years
it turned to vinegar. The wine was served at Christmastime with slices of fruitcake
when company came. On November Sundays we went to the woods with
a big basket of fried chicken dinner, thermos jug and coffee-pot. We hunted partridge berries in the pine woods near our town. These scarlet berries grew hidden
underneath the glossy brown pine needles that lay in a slick carpet beneath the
tall wind-singing trees. The bright berries were a Christmas decoration, lasting in
water through the whole season.

In December the windows downtown were filled with toys, and my brother
and sister and I were given two dollars apiece to buy our Christmas presents.
We patronized the ten-cent stores, choosing between jackstones, pencil boxes, water colors and satin handkerchief holders. We would each buy a nickel's
worth of lump milk chocolate at the candy counter to mouth as we trudged from
counter to counter, choice to choice. It was exacting and final—taking several
afternoons—for the dime stores would not take back or exchange.

Mother made fruitcakes, and for weeks ahead the family picked out the nut
meats of pecans and walnuts, careful of the bitter layer of the pecans that lined
your mouth with nasty fur. At the last I was allowed to blanch the almonds, pinch-
ing the scalded nuts so that they sometimes hit the ceiling or bounced across the
room. Mother cut slices of citron and crystallized pineapple, figs and dates, and
candied cherries were added whole. We cut rounds of brown paper to line
the pans. Usually the cakes were mixed and put into the oven when we were in
school. Late in the afternoon the cakes would be finished, wrapped in white
napkins on the breakfast-room table. Later they would be soaked in brandy. These
fruitcakes were famous in our town, and Mother gave them often as Christmas
gifts. When company came thin slices of fruitcake, wine and coffee were always
served. When you held a slice of fruitcake to the window or the firelight the slice
was translucent, pale citron green and yellow and red, with the glow and richness
of our church windows.

Daddy was a jeweler, and his store was kept open until midnight all Christmas week. I, as the eldest child, was allowed to stay up late with Mother until
Daddy came home. Mother was always nervous without a "man in the house."
(On those rare occasions when Daddy had to stay overnight on business in Atlanta, the children were armed with a hammer, saw and a monkey wrench. When
pressed about her anxieties Mother claimed she was afraid of "escaped convicts or
crazy people." I never saw an escaped convict, but once a "crazy" person did come
to see us. She was an old, old lady dressed in elegant black taffeta, my mother's
second cousin once removed, and came on a tranquil Sunday morning and an-
nounced that she had always liked our house and she intended to stay with us until she died. Her sons and daughters and grandchildren gathered around to plead
with her as she sat rocking in our front porch rocking chair and she left
not unwillingly when they promised a car ride and ice cream.) Nothing ever hap-

pened on those evenings in Christmas week, but I felt grown, aged suddenly by trust and dignity. Mother confided in secrecy what the younger children were getting from Santa Claus. I knew where the Santa Claus things were hidden, and was appointed to see that my brother and sister did not go into the back-room closet or the wardrobe in our parents' room.

Christmas Eve was the longest day, but it was lined with the glory of tomorrow. The sitting-room smelled of floor wax and the clean, cold odor of the spruce tree. The Christmas tree stood in a corner of the front room, tall as the ceiling, majestic, undecorated. It was our family custom that the tree was not decorated until after we children were in bed on Christmas Eve night. We went to bed very early, as soon as it was winter dark. I lay in bed beside my sister and tried to keep her awake.

"You want to guess again about your Santa Claus?"

"We've already done that so much," she said.                                              15

My sister slept. And there again was another puzzle. How could it be that when she opened her eyes it would be Christmas while I lay awake in the dark for hours and hours? The time was the same for both of us, and yet not at all the same. What was it? How? I thought of Bethlehem and cherry candy, Jesus and skyrockets. It was dark when I awoke. We were allowed to get up on Christmas at five o'-clock. Later I found out that Daddy juggled the clock Christmas Eve so that five o'clock was actually six. Anyway it was always still dark when we rushed in to dress by the kitchen stove. The rule was that we dress and eat breakfast before we could go in to the Christmas tree. On Christmas morning we always had fish roe, bacon and grits for breakfast. I grudged every mouthful—for who wanted to fill up on breakfast when there in the sitting-room was candy, at least three whole boxes? After breakfast we lined up, and carols were started. Our voices rose naked and mysterious as we filed through the door to the sitting-room. The carol, unfinished, ended in raw yells of joy.

The Christmas tree glittered in the glorious, candlelit room. There were bicycles and bundles wrapped in tissue paper. Our stockings hanging from the mantle-piece bulged with oranges, nuts and smaller presents. The next hours were paradise. The blue dawn at the window brightened, and the candles were blown out. By nine o'clock we had ridden the wheel presents and dressed in the clothes gifts. We visited the neighborhood children and were visited in turn. Our cousins came and grown relatives from distant neighborhoods. All through the morning we ate chocolates. At two or three o'clock the Christmas dinner was served. The dining-room table had been let out with extra leaves and the very best linen was laid—satin damask with a rose design. Daddy asked the blessing, then stood up to carve the turkey. Dressing, rice and giblet gravy were served. There were cut-glass dishes of sparkling jellies and stateliness of festal wine. For dessert there was always sillabub or charlotte and fruitcake. The afternoon was almost over when dinner was done.

At twilight I sat on the front steps, jaded by too much pleasure, sick at the stomach and worn out. The boy next door skated down the street in his new Indian suit. A girl spun around on a crackling son-of-a-gun. My brother waved sparklers. Christmas was over. I thought of the monotony of Time ahead, unsolaced by the distant glow of paler festivals, the year that stretched before another Christmas—eternity.

## Reflecting and Interpreting

1. What do you notice about McCullers's first sentence? How do the length and punctuation affect the pace? Is the pace of the second sentence similar or different? How do the two sentences set the scene?

2. What do you notice about the next six lines? Describe their effect.

3. What do you learn about the narrator in paragraph 7? Does she seem to be an average twelve-year-old? How would you describe her?

4. What seems to be the essence of Christmas for the author?

5. The episodes that McCullers recounts occurred in 1929. Consider paragraphs 10 to 14. What strikes you as unusual or interesting? What do you learn?

6. Beginning in September, the entire family helped to prepare for the Christmas season. List the steps that the author describes.

7. What privileges did Carson enjoy as the eldest child? How did these privileges affect her?

8. The mystery of time is referred to again in paragraph 17. What is this mystery? How does her perception of time on Christmas Eve differ from her sister's?

9. The author uses sensory language to create vivid scenes. Which scene particularly stands out in your mind? What words help to create the image?

10. Examine the last paragraph. What does McCullers mean by "paler festivals"? How does she feel about these days as compared to Christmas? Why?

## A Writer's Response

1. Does one particular holiday celebration stand out in your collection of memories? Write a description of a particular scene, using active verbs and specific adjectives as McCullers does.

2. With your group, discuss the factors that influence our perception of time. Have you ever gone through periods in your life when time seemed to slow drastically? How does a vacation affect the passing of time for you? What inferences can you draw from this discussion in regard to happiness, well-being, and the use of time?

# Description

## Conveying Impressions

## Caterpillar Afternoon

Sue Hubbell

*Sue Hubbell is a naturalist, a commercial beekeeper, who lives in the Ozark Mountains. She is the author of seven books, including* A Book of Bees *(1988),* On This Hilltop *(1991),* Waiting for Aphrodite *(2000), and* Shrinking the Cat *(2001). One day as Hubbell was walking down a dusty country road, she spied what appeared to be a snake skin lying in the road. Curious, she bent down and saw, instead, a strange procession of maggoty-like caterpillars.* "Caterpillar Afternoon," *from* A Country Year *(1999), illustrates one way primary and secondary research can be combined.*

A year ago, on an afternoon late in springtime, I was walking on the dirt road that   1
cuts across the field to the beehives. I noticed a light-colored, brownish dappled something-or-other stretched across the roadway ahead of me, and decided that it was a snakeskin. I often find them, crumpled husks shed by snakes as they grow. They are fragile and delicate, perfect but empty replicas of the snakes that once inhabited them. I started to turn it over with the toe of my boot, but stopped suddenly, toe in air, for the flecked, crumpled-looking empty snakeskin was moving.

It gave me quite a start and I was amused at my own reaction, remembering that Ronald Firbank wrote somewhere that the essence of evil was the ordinary become unnatural, the stone in the garden path that suddenly begins to move.

I squatted down to see what queer thing I had here, and found that my supposed snake skin was a mass of maggoty-like caterpillars, each one no more than half an inch long. They were hairless, with creamy white smooth skin, black heads and brown stripes along their backs. They were piled thickly in the center, with fewer caterpillars at the head and rear end of the line, which was perhaps eighteen inches long. They moved slowly, each caterpillar in smooth synchrony with its fellows, so that a wave of motion undulated down the entire length of the line.

They seemed so intensely social that I wondered what they would do on their own. I gently picked up half a dozen or so, and isolated them a few inches from the column. Their smooth, easy movements changed to frantic, rapid ones, and they wriggled along the ground quickly until they rejoined the group. They certainly were good followers. How did they ever decide where to go? The single caterpillar in the lead twisted the forepart of his body from side to side as though taking his bearings; he appeared to be the only one in the lot capable of going in a new direction, of making a decision to avoid a tuft of grass here, of turning there. Was he some special, super-caterpillar? I removed him from the lead position and put him off to the side, where he became as frantic as had the others, wriggling to rejoin the group somewhere in the middle, where he was soon lost to view, having turned into just another follower. At the head, the next caterpillar in line had simply assumed leadership duties and was bending his body from side to side, making the decision about the direction the column was to take. I removed three leaders in a row with the same result: each time, the next caterpillar in line made an instant switch from loyal and will-less follower to leader.

What were they doing? Were they looking for food? If so, what kind? What 5 manner of creature were they? The beework that I had set out to do could wait no longer, so I went back to the hives. When I returned along the road, the caterpillars, if that is what they were, had disappeared.

Back in my cabin, none of the books on my shelves were much help explaining what I had seen, except one by Henri Fabre, the nineteenth-century French entomologist who had conducted one of his famous experiments with pine processionaries, one of the Thaumatopoeidae. Fabre's caterpillars were *Thaumatopoea processionea*, "the wonder maker that parades"; eventually they become rather undistinguished-looking moths.

The pine processionaries are a European species, but their behavior was similar to that of my caterpillars, although not identical. Pine processionaries travel to feed in single file, not massed and bunched, but they do touch head to rear and have only one leader at a time. Fabre found them so sheeplike that he wondered what they would do if he could somehow manage to make them leaderless. In a brilliant experiment, he arranged them on the upper rim of a large vase a yard and a half in circumference, and waited until the head end of the procession joined the tail end, so that the entire group was without a leader. All were followers. For seven days, the caterpillars paraded around the rim of the vase in a circle. Their pace slowed after a while, for they were weary and had not been able to feed, but they continued to circle, each caterpillar unquestioningly taking his direction from the rear of the one in front, until they dropped from exhaustion. However, even Fabre never discovered what it was that could turn one caterpillar into a leader as soon as he was at the head of the line.

It was not until several months later, when I was talking to Asher, that I was able to find out anything about the caterpillars I had found in the roadway. He said that I probably had seen one species or another of sawfly larvae. They are gregarious, he told me, and some are whitish with brown stripes. Sure identification could only be made by counting the pairs of their prolegs, and of course I had not known enough to look at them that closely. Asher said that they were a rare sight and that I would probably never see them again, but if I did I should gather up a few and put them in a solution of 70 percent alcohol; then he would help me identify them. He had read about Fabre's experiment too, but knew nothing more about their behavior.

He added, "If you ever find out what makes processionary caterpillars pro-sesh, please enlighten me. Maybe it's the same thing that makes people drive in Sunday traffic or watch TV or vote Republican."

It is springtime again. I would like to count the caterpillars' prolegs and am     10 prepared to pickle a few to satisfy my curiosity, but mostly I should just like to watch them again. This time I should let the beework go. I should like to know where these caterpillars go, and what it is they are looking for. I wonder if I could divide them up into several small columns that would move along independently, side by side. I have more questions about them than when I first saw them.

This spring I often walk along, eyes to the ground, looking for them. There may have been nobler quests—white whales and Holy Grails—and although the Ahabs and Percivals of my acquaintance are some of my most entertaining friends, I am cut of other stuff and amuse myself in other ways. The search for what may or may not be sawfly larvae seems quite a good one this springtime.

## Reflecting and Interpreting

1. What two strategies of exposition does Hubbell use to explain her research?
2. Note the distinctive way that Hubbell describes the caterpillars. What device does she use in the third sentence?
3. What was unusual about the physical appearance of the caterpillars?
4. What spur-of-the moment experiments did Hubbell conduct? How did the individual caterpillars react?
5. What paragraph presents the questions that Hubbell wants to research?
6. What transition shifts the reader to the next scene, where Hubbell continues her research?
7. How and when did Hubbell gain more specific information about the kind of caterpillars she had seen? By what name are they tagged?
8. What had Henri Fabre discovered in the nineteenth century about a similar caterpillar?
9. What experiment does Hubbell plan to do if she ever finds more of these strange caterpillars?
10. Do you see any similarities between the behavior of the caterpillars and some people? What kinds of events can cause people to suddenly become leaders?

## A Writer's Response

1. Have you ever been thrust into a circumstance in which you suddenly had to assume a leadership role? If so, write an essay describing your experience.
2. *Small Groups:* Have you ever seen something that appeared to be something

else at first? What does this reveal about the process of perception? Can you list a few precautions to promote objectivity? (After the group is finished, turn to "Checklist: Maintaining Objectivity" in Chapter 22.)

# One Writer's Beginnings

Eudora Welty

*Eudora Welty (1909–2001) published her first short story in 1936. After writing short fiction for ten years, she published a novel,* Delta Wedding, *in 1946. In all she wrote twenty-six books, receiving a Pulitzer Prize in 1971. In 1980 she received the National Medal for Literature and the Presidential Medal of Freedom. In this excerpt from* One Writer's Beginnings *(1984), she explores the connection between reality and the imagination in an attempt to trace her origin as a writer.*

I had the window seat. Beside me, my father checked the progress of our train by moving his finger down the timetable and springing open his pocket watch. He explained to me what the position of the arms of the semaphore meant; before we were to pass through a switch we would watch the signal lights change. Along our track, the mileposts could be read; he read them. Right on time by Daddy's watch, the next town sprang into view, and just as quickly was gone.    1

Side by side and separately, we each lost ourselves in the experience of not missing anything, of seeing everything, of knowing each time what the blows of the whistle meant. But of course it was not the same experience: what was new to me, not older than ten, was a landmark to him. My father knew our way mile by mile; by day or by night, he knew where we were. Everything that changed under our eyes, in the flying countryside, was the known world to him, the imagination to me. Each in our own way, we hungered for all of this: my father and I were in no other respect or situation so congenial.

In Daddy's leather grip was his traveler's drinking cup, collapsible; a lid to fit over it had a ring to carry it by; it traveled in a round leather box. This treasure would be brought out at my request, for me to bear to the water cooler at the end of the Pullman car, fill to the brim, and bear back to my seat, to drink water over its smooth lip. The taste of silver could almost be relied on to shock your teeth.

After dinner in the sparkling dining car, my father and I walked back to the open-air observation platform at the end of the train and sat on the folding chairs placed at the railing. We watched the sparks we made fly behind us into the night. Fast as our speed was, it gave us time enough to see the rose-red cinders turn to ash, each one, and disappear from sight. Sometimes a house far back in the empty hills showed a light no bigger than a star. The sleeping countryside seemed itself to open a way through for our passage, then close again behind us.

The swaying porter would be making ready our berths for the night, pulling    5
the shade down just so, drawing the green fishnet hammock across the window so the clothes you took off could ride along beside you, turning down the tight-made bed, standing up the two snowy pillows as high as they were wide, switching on the eye of the reading lamp, starting the tiny electric fan—you suddenly saw its

blades turn into gauze and heard its insect murmur; and drawing across it all the pair of thick green theaterlike curtains—billowing, smelling of cigar smoke—between which you would crawl or dive headfirst to button them together with yourself inside, to be seen no more that night.

When you lay enclosed and enwrapped, your head on a pillow parallel to the track, the rhythm of the rail clicks pressed closer to your body as if it might be your heart beating, but the sound of the engine seemed to come from farther away than when it carried you in daylight. The whistle was almost too far away to be heard, its sound wavering back from the engine over the roofs of the cars. What you listened for was the different sound that ran under you when your own car crossed on a trestle, then another sound on an iron bridge; a low or a high bridge—each had its pitch, or drumbeat, for your car.

Riding in the sleeper rhythmically lulled me and waked me. From time to time, waked suddenly, I raised my window shade and looked out at my own strip of the night. Sometimes there was unexpected moonlight out there. Sometimes the perfect shadow of our train, with our car, with me invisibly included, ran deep below, crossing a river with us by the light of the moon. Sometimes the encroaching walls of mountains woke me by clapping at my ears. The tunnels made the train's passage resound like the "loud" pedal of a piano, a roar that seemed to last as long as a giant's temper tantrum.

But my father put it all into the frame of regularity, predictability, that was his fatherly gift in the course of our journey. I saw it going by, the outside world, in a flash. I dreamed over what I could see as it passed, as well as over what I couldn't. Part of the dream was what lay beyond, where the path wandered off through the pasture, the red clay road climbed and went over the hill or made a turn and was hidden in trees, or toward a river whose bridge I could see but whose name I'd never know. A house back at its distance at night showing a light from an open doorway, the morning faces of the children who stopped still in what they were doing, perhaps picking blackberries or wild plums, and watched us go by— I never saw with the thought of their continuing to be there just the same after we were out of sight. For now, and for a long while to come, I was proceeding in fantasy.

## Reflecting and Interpreting

1. What do we learn about Welty and her father in the first and second paragraphs? Do they seem similar or different? How?

2. As Welty attempts to trace her origins as a writer, why does this train trip seem significant?

3. How do Welty's childhood dreams differ from the reality of the train?

4. The description of the porter making up the berths is filled with similes and metaphors. Which ones do you especially like?

5. Welty spends a paragraph describing the sounds of the engine, rails, whistle, and structures that vary the "pitch, or drumbeat, for your car." What device is used here? What do these details reveal about her, even as a child?

6. Note the alternating of images when she describes riding in the sleeper. How do these images and sounds reflect the rhythm of the train?

7. Is the essay written, for the most part, from the point of view of a ten-year-old or from an adult in retrospect? Where does a shift occur? What was "his fatherly gift"? Why does Welty seem to need that?

8. Images that connote safety and seclusion while experiencing the world from a distance appear throughout this essay. Which ones do you notice?

9. Welty was interested in photography. How is this excerpt of her writing like a series of photos?

10. What might the author mean at the end when she says, "For now, and for a long while to come, I was proceeding in fantasy"?

## A Writer's Response

1. Describe a trip you took as a child that was memorable. Use vivid images and sensory language to recapture the experience and your feelings at the time.

2. Welty opens with "I had the window seat." Later she says, "I saw it going by, the outside world, in a flash." You might say we all have a window seat from which we view life as it flashes by. Select one vivid "flash" from your window on life to describe in an essay.

# *Dawn Watch*

## John Ciardi

*A renowned poet, essayist, and translator, John Ciardi (1916–86) wrote over fifty books. He received the Prix de Rome of the American Academy of Arts and Letters, the Harriet Monroe Memorial Award, and the NCTE Award for Children's Poetry. He first published a book of poems entitled* Homeward to America *(1940). Two years later he enlisted in the Army Air Force and served with distinction as an aerial tail gunner during World War II. He taught at Harvard and Rutgers; spent twenty years as poetry editor for the* Saturday Review *magazine; wrote children's books, poetry textbooks, and others; and translated* The Divine Comedy *and other classic works. Some of his well-known works are* Mid-Century American Poets *(1950),* How Does a Poem Mean *(1959),* Selected Poems *(1984),* Saipan: The War Diary of John Ciardi *(1988),* The Birds of Pompeii *(1988), and* The Selected Letters of John Ciardi *(1991), some of which were published posthumously. In this essay from* Manner of Speaking *(1972), Ciardi praises a magical time of day.*

Unless a man is up for the dawn and for the half hour or so of first light, he has    1
missed the best of the day.

The traffic has just started, not yet a roar and a stink. One car at a time goes by, the tires humming almost like the sound of a brook a half mile down in the crease of a mountain I know—a sound that carries not because it is loud but because everything else is still.

It isn't exactly a mist that hangs in the thickets but more nearly the ghost of a mist—a phenomenon like side vision. Look hard and it isn't there, but glance without focusing and something registers, an exhalation that will be gone three minutes after the sun comes over the treetops.

The lawns shine with a dew not exactly dew. There is a rabbit bobbing about on the lawn and then freezing. If it were truly a dew, his tracks would shine black on the grass, and he leaves no visible track. Yet, there is something on the grass that makes it glow a depth of green it will not show again all day. Or is that something in the dawn air?

Our cardinals know what time it is. They drop pure tones from the hemlock    5
tops. The gang of grackles that makes a slum of the pin oak also knows the time but can only grate at it. They sound like a convention of broken universal joints grating uphill. The grackles creak and squeak, and the cardinals form tones that only occasionally sound through the noise. I scatter sunflower seeds by the birdbaths for the cardinals and hope the grackles won't find them.

My neighbor's tomcat comes across the lawn, probably on his way home from passion, or only acting as if he had had a big night. I suspect him of being one of those poolroom braggarts who can't get next to a girl but who likes to let on that he is a hot stud. This one is too can-fed and too lazy to hunt for anything. Here he comes now, ignoring the rabbit. And there he goes.

As soon as he has hopped the fence, I let my dog out. The dog charges the rabbit, watches it jump the fence, shakes himself in a self-satisfied way, then trots dutifully into the thicket for his morning service, stopping to sniff everything on the way back.

There is an old mountain laurel on the island of the driveway turnaround. From somewhere on the wind a white morning-glory rooted next to it and has climbed it. Now the laurel is woven full of white bells tinged pink by the first rays through the not quite mist. Only in earliest morning can they be seen. Come out two hours from now and there will be no morning-glories.

Dawn, too, is the hour of a weed I know only as day flower—a bright blue button that closes in full sunlight. I have weeded bales of it out of my flower beds, its one daytime virtue being the shallowness of its root system that allows it to be pulled out effortlessly in great handfuls. Yet, now it shines. Had it a few more hours of such shining in its cycle, I would cultivate it as a ground cover, but dawn is its one hour, and a garden is for whole days.

There is another blue morning weed whose name I do not know. This one    10
grows from a bulb to pulpy stems and a bedraggled daytime sprawl. Only a shovel will dig it out. Try weeding it by hand and the stems will break off to be replaced by new ones and to sprawl over the chosen plants in the flower bed. Yet, now and for another hour it outshines its betters, its flowers about the size of a quarter and paler than those of the day flower but somehow more brilliant, perhaps because of the contrast of its paler foliage.

And now the sun is slanting in full. It is bright enough to make the leaves of the Japanese red maple seem a transparent red bronze when the tree is between me and the light. There must be others, but this is the only tree I know whose leaves let the sun through in this way—except, that is, when the fall colors start. Aspen leaves, when they first yellow and before they dry, are transparent in this way. I tell myself it must have something to do with the red-yellow range of the spectrum. Green takes sunlight and holds it, but red and yellow let it through.

The damned crabgrass is wrestling with the zinnias, and I stop to weed it out. The stuff weaves too close to the zinnias to make the iron claw usable. And it won't do to pull at the stalks. Crabgrass (at least in a mulched bed) can be weeded only with dirty fingers. Thumb and forefinger have to pincer into the dirt and grab the root-center. Weeding, of course, is an illusion of hope. Pulling out the root only stirs the soil and brings new crabgrass seeds into germinating position. Take a walk around the block and a new clump will have sprouted by the time you get back. But I am not ready to walk around the block. I fill a small basket with the plucked clumps, and for the instant I look at them, the zinnias are weedless.

Don't look back. I dump the weeds in the thicket where they will be smothered by the grass clippings I will pile on at the next cutting. On the way back I see the cardinals come down for the sunflower seeds, and the jays join them, and then the grackles start ganging in, gatecrashing the buffet and clattering all over it. The dog stops chewing his rawhide and makes a dash into the puddle of birds, which splashes away from him.

I hear a brake-squeak I have been waiting for and know the paper has arrived. As usual, the news turns out to be another disaster count. The function of the wire services is to bring us tragedies faster than we can pity. In the end we shall all be inured, numb, and ready for emotionless programming. I sit on the patio and read until the sun grows too bright on the page. The cardinals have stopped singing, and the grackles have flown off. It's the end of birdsong again.

Then suddenly—better than song for its instant—a hummingbird the color of    15
green crushed velvet hovers in the throat of my favorite lily, a lovely high-bloomer I got the bulbs for but not the name. The lily is a crest of white horns with red dots and red velvet tongues along the insides of the petals and with an odor that drowns the patio. The hummingbird darts in and out of each horn in turn, then hovers an instant, and disappears.

Even without the sun, I have had enough of the paper. I'll take that hummingbird as my news for this dawn. It is over now. I smoke one more cigarette too many and decide that, if I go to bed now, no one in the family need know I have stayed up for it again. Why do they insist on shaking their heads when they find me still up for breakfast, after having scribbled through the dark hours? They always do. They seem compelled to express pity for an old loony who can't find his own way to bed. Why won't they understand that this is the one hour of any day that must not be missed, as it is the one hour I couldn't imagine getting up for, though I can still get to it by staying up? It makes sense to me. There comes a time when the windows lighten and the twittering starts. I look up and know it's time to leave the papers in their mess. I could slip quietly into bed and avoid the family's headshakes, but this stroll-around first hour is too good to miss. Even my dog, still sniffing and circling, knows what hour this is.

Come on, boy. It's time to go in. The rabbit won't come back till tomorrow, and the birds have work to do. The dawn's over. It's time to call it a day.

## Reflecting and Interpreting

1. Ciardi's essay has an argumentative edge that is apparent in his thesis statement. Where is it?

2. What is the dominant impression of "Dawn Watch"?

3. Can you find similes?

4. Can you find an example of personification?

5. Throughout the essay, Ciardi's carefully chosen words create sensory descriptions that convey an essence of the scene. How many types of appeals to the senses can you find?

6. What is the primary order used to organize details?

7. Ciardi alternates subjectivity with objectivity at times in his description. Can you find examples of each?

8. Instead of presenting only beautiful images of the morning, Ciardi pairs negative images with positive ones and presents other unusual contrasts. What are the effects?

9. Does Ciardi make his reversed schedule seem logical? Has he supplied enough support for his claim to be convincing? Give reasons for your answer.

10. Describe the voice of the writer. Where does he seem to be poking fun at himself?

*A Writer's Response*

1. Whether you agree or disagree with Ciardi's belief that early morning is the best time of all may depend upon whether you are a "lark" or "night owl." What time of day do you like best? Why?

2. List favourite spots where you can be alone. Focus on one and freewrite about the atmosphere there, incorporating as many sights, sounds, and other sensory images as possible. Next add a chronological structure, similar to Ciardi's, describing the "events" of a typical visit from beginning to end. How does the passing of time affect what happens there? What time of day is best? Rewrite your draft into a revised essay.

# Process Analysis

## Explaining How

## *Write Your Own Success Story*

Carol Carter

---

*Coasting through high school, seldom studying, seventeen-year-old Carol Carter was yanked from a career disaster by a conversation with her brother. This vivid essay from* Majoring in the Rest of Your Life: Career Secrets for College Students *(1999) relates how she suddenly changed direction, "determined to learn all she could." Since graduating from the University of Arizona, Carter has also written* Student Planner *(1998) and* Keys to Success *(2000). She has coauthored and collaborated on more than a dozen other books designed to help students increase their effectiveness.*

Who am I to talk to high school graduates and college freshmen about planning?    1
As a high school student in Tucson, Arizona, I never planned. I just coasted along
letting things happen to me. Sure, I was spontaneous. I spent weeknights talking
on the phone and studied only when I felt like it—i.e., seldom. On weekends my
friends and I roamed shopping malls and partied in the mountains. The typical irresponsible high school student.

And then BOOM. The ax fell. The ax was not some accident, scandal, or divine intervention. It was simply a conversation with my older brother Craig during the first week of my senior year in high school. Our talk changed the course
of my life.

At seventeen, I was intimidated by my four older brothers. I saw them as
bright, motivated, and respected achievers—the opposite of me. Whenever one of
them asked me about what I was doing or thinking, I'd answer with a one-liner
and hope he'd soon leave me alone.

This conversation with Craig was different. He didn't give up after five minutes despite my curt, vague responses.

"Carol, what are you interested in?"    5

"I dunno."

"What do you think about all day?"

"I dunno."

"What do you want to do with your life?"

"I'll just let things happen."                                                                    10

Craig persisted. His voice grew indignant. He criticized me for talking on the phone, for spending too much time at pep rallies and rock concerts, for not studying, for not challenging myself. He pointed out that I hadn't read an unassigned book in three years. He asked if I intended to approach college the way I'd approached high school—as one continuous party. If so, he warned, I'd better start thinking of a career flipping burgers at the local hamburger stand because no respectable employer would ever take me seriously. He asked me if that was what I wanted to do with my life. He cautioned that out of laziness and lack of planning I would limit my options so narrowly that I would never be able to get a real job. I had wasted three years of high school, he said. College was a new start, since employers and graduate schools seldom check as far back as high school for records. So he advised me to quit making excuses, decide what I wanted and plan how to achieve it. My only limitations would be self-imposed.

Craig then left my room—sermon completed. I didn't speak to him before he flew back to New York that afternoon to finish his senior year at Columbia. I hated him for interfering in my life. He made me dissatisfied with myself. I was scared he was right. For the first time, I realized that "typical" was not necessarily what I wanted to be.

The next day, still outraged but determined to do something, I went to the library and checked out six classics: *Pride and Prejudice* by Jane Austen; *The Great Gatsby* by F. Scott Fitzgerald; *A Farewell to Arms* and *For Whom the Bell Tolls* by Ernest Hemingway; *A Portrait of the Artist as a Young Man* by James Joyce; and *Sister Carrie* by Theodore Dreiser. Then I wrote down in a notebook a few goals that I wanted to accomplish. They all seemed boldly unattainable: earn straight A's (previously I had made B's and C's), study every week including one weekend night, keep reading classics on my own. If I couldn't make it in my senior year of high school, why should I waste time and money in college? I'd beat fate to the door and begin my career at the hamburger stand directly.

Three weeks later I got a letter from Craig. He knew how angry I was with him. He told me our conversation wasn't easy for him either but if he hadn't cared, he wouldn't have bothered to say anything. He was right. I needed that sermon. If I didn't come to terms with my problems, I could never have moved from making excuses to making things happen.

I worked hard and got results. The second semester of my senior year I made     15
all A's (except for a B in physics). I finished the six classics and others as well. I started reading newspapers and magazines. I had to move the *Vogue* on my nightstand to make room for *Time, Harper's,* and *Fortune.* I found that I could set goals and attain them, and I started to realize that I wasn't so different from my brothers after all.

To my utter astonishment, I discovered that for the first time I enjoyed learning. My world seemed to open up just because I knew more about different kinds of people, ways of thinking and ways of interpreting what I had previously assumed to be black-and-white. (If you are a shy person, joining a club and getting to know—and actually like—a few people whom you originally perceived as unfriendly or uninteresting may astonish you as much as my newfound appreciation for learning astonished me.)

The summer before college, I thought about what I wanted to do with my life, but couldn't decide on a direction. I had no notion of what I wanted to major in. What to do . . . what to do?

I turned to Craig, a phone call away in New York City. He told me not to worry in my first year of college about what I wanted to do. The main priority: learn as much as I could. College, he told me, was my golden opportunity to investigate all kinds of things—biology, psychology, accounting, philosophy. He told me I'd become good at writing and critical thinking techniques—skills that would help me learn any job after graduation. And though I could continue to expand my educational horizons throughout life, college was the best opportunity to expose myself to the greatest minds and movements of our civilization.

Craig also warned me that being a scholar, though important, wouldn't be enough. (He had just graduated from Columbia as a Phi Beta Kappa, but since he hadn't gained any real-world experience in college, it took him several months to find his first job.) To maximize options upon graduation, I would have to do three things:

1. Learn as much as possible from classes, books, professors, and other people

2. Participate in extracurricular activities

3. Get REAL-WORLD experience by working part-time and landing summer internships

If I did these three things reasonably well, Craig assured me, I could choose    20
from a number of career opportunities at the end of my senior year. And even if I only did two of the three full-force and one half-speed, I'd be in good shape. The effort in each area, and a modest outcome, was an attainable goal. That way I could balance my college experience and open options for the future.

Craig advised me that I should look ahead and develop a plan of action for each of my four years of college. He told me that foresight—the ability to consider the bigger picture beyond short-term challenges and intermittent goals—is invaluable in most jobs; it distinguishes outstanding people from the rest of the pack. . . . Most important, you'll learn that everyone—including YOU—has his or her own set of skills, abilities, passions and talents to tap. Finding the career and lifestyle that allows you to cultivate and nurture them is one of the most important success secrets.

## So Take Action!

A good way to start is to assess your shortcomings and strengths. As I've already told you, one of my shortcomings in high school was not learning all I could from my classes and teachers. Your shortcoming may have been that you focused entirely on your studies without developing many outside interests. Someone else may feel that he concentrated so much on an outside activity—such as training for a particular sport—that he had no time for studies or friends. What was your major shortcoming in high school?

Now think about three things:

1. What pleased you in high school?
2. What could you have done better?
3. What do you want to improve upon in the future?

Identifying these areas will help you strike a good balance during college.    25
Once you get in the habit of analyzing past experiences, you will have a clearer
notion of what you do and don't want in the future. That's important.

As a high school senior, a college freshman, or a college senior, the next thing
you must do is decide to take action. Don't worry if you don't know what you
want to do. Just commit yourself to the process. If you do, you'll eventually find
out which careers might be best for you and how you could best prepare for them.

RECAP: The priorities

1. Gain knowledge
2. Participate in activities
3. Get REAL-WORLD experience

## Making It Happen

"Luck is the residue of design," said Branch Rickey, known as the baseball
mahatma for his strategic methods for playing and organizing baseball. He developed the farm system on which the minor leagues were formed. His PLANS OF
ACTION took a handful of disjointed teams in faraway cities and banded them
into an organization which has left its mark on American culture.

Nothing happens magically. If you want to be a success, you are going to have
to take personal responsibility for your life. Why do some graduates get twenty
job offers and others receive none?

While successful people may appear lucky, they, in fact, illustrate the maxim    30
that "luck favors the prepared mind."

Joe Cirulli agrees. He is the owner of the successful Gainesville Health and
Fitness Center in Florida. Early on in his life, exercise was a priority, an essential
part of his day. So he followed his interests and put his talents to work to start
his own health club. While many other clubs have folded around him, he has
experienced enormous success—his membership continues to grow, and he is able
to keep his club filled with the best equipment and the most knowledgeable professionals.

When Joe was twenty, he worked as an assistant manager and a sales representative for a health club. One of his responsibilities was to train new sales representatives for the club. He worked hard to prepare them for their jobs only to
have to compete with them once they were trained.

He remembers talking with the vice president of the company about his frustration. The vice president, a person Joe respected, advised him to keep on putting
his best efforts into his work. "Right now you may not see the benefit of your hard
work, but one day you will."

Joe followed his advice. Less than five years later his skill at training people in the health club industry paid off—he was able to put his expertise to work for his own health club. "Knowing how to motivate employees to do their best, to care about the quality of their work, and to care about our customers has had an enormous impact on the success of my own company."

Joe believes the secret to his success is giving 100 percent of himself in everything he does. "Success is the culmination of all your efforts. There are thousands of opportunities for people who give their all." 35

How do you arrange to have the most options when you leave college? Plan, develop foresight, and take charge of your life, and you will become one of the lucky ones. Most important, decide that you want to succed—and believe it.

Charles Garfield a clinical psychologist who has spent his career studying what motivates people to superior effort, says that the drive to excel comes primarily from within. Can "peak performances" be learned? Yes, says Garfield. High achievers are not extraordinarily gifted superhumans. What they have in common is the ability to cultivate what the German writer Johann Wolfgang von Goethe termed "the genius, power, and magic" that exists in all of us. These doers increase the odds in their favor through simple techniques which anyone can cultivate:

1. Envision a mission
2. Be result-oriented
3. Tap your internal resources
4. Enlist team spirit
5. Treat setbacks as stepping stones

## First Things First

The first thing to keep in mind when planning: accept the world the way it is. Your plans should be based on a realistic assessment of how things are, not some starry-eyed vision of how they should be. You can dream, but there's a happy medium between cold reality and pie in the sky. That's why you must be open to opportunity. Indeed, you must create it. Although you can't change the hand you were dealt, you can play it as wisely as possible.

So start today. Start now.

The more questions you ask now, the better prepared you'll be in four years. 40 You don't want to be stuck in a boring job or wondering why you can't find work.

Are you going to make mistakes? I hope so, unless you're not of the human species. Making mistakes is the process by which we learn. And whenever we're disappointed by the outcome, we have to maintain a positive attitude, log the information, and keep going. The key is to learn from mistakes without letting them slow us down.

### Reflecting and Interpreting

1. What rhetorical strategy does Carter use in the first sentence? What is the effect?

2. How did Carol's careless attitude in high school affect her self-image?

3. What three main points did Craig make in his criticism?

4. How did Carol react to her brother's advice? Why? What did she do the next day?

5. What three things did Carol discover about herself?

6. When Craig pointed out that high grades alone were not enough to land a job, what three actions did he recommend?

7. What four actions does Carol recommend readers take to "have the most options when you leave college"?

8. Does the author seem convincing? Why or why not?

9. What type of support does she provide other than personal experience?

10. What is appealing about her writing style?

## A Writer's Response

What is the most significant point that you derived from this essay? Did you learn anything that can help you be more successful in school? On the job? What do you plan to do differently to improve your grades and chances for success? Write an essay that responds to these questions and any other points Carter raised.

# How Do You Know It's Good?

## Marya Mannes

*What makes writing, art, music, or theatre good? One popular approach denies the existence of any valid criteria to measure the quality of a work. This approach claims that decisions about value are merely a matter of personal taste. But Marya Mannes disagrees, saying there are standards to determine value. She says that the prime function of art is "to create order out of chaos—again, not the order of neatness or rigidity or convention or artifice, but the order of clarity. . . ." There is room for "incredible diversity of forms" within a universal pattern and rhythm. Mannes (1904–90) was born into a family of prominent musicians and chemists. She was a columnist, editor, and television commentator for PBS. She wrote two novels,* Message from a Stranger *(1948) and* They *(1968), as well as an autobiography,* Out of My Time *(1971). Best known was her collection of essays,* But Will It Sell? *(1964), in which "How Do You Know It's Good?" was first published.*

Suppose there were no critics to tell us how to react to a picture, a play, or a new    1
composition of music. Suppose we wandered innocent as the dawn into an art exhibition of unsigned paintings. By what standards, by what values would we decide whether they were good or bad, talented or untalented, successes or failures? How can we ever know that what we think is right?

For the last fifteen or twenty years the fashion in criticism or appreciation of the arts has been to deny the existence of any valid criteria and to make the words "good" or "bad" irrelevant, immaterial, and inapplicable. There is no such thing, we are told, as a set of standards, first acquired through experience and knowledge and later imposed on the subject under discussion. This has been a popular approach, for it relieves the critic of the responsibility of judgment and the public of the necessity of knowledge. It pleases those resentful of disciplines, it flatters the empty-minded by calling them open-minded, it comforts the confused. Under the banner of democracy and the kind of equality which our forefathers did *not* mean, it says, in effect, "Who are you to tell us what is good or bad?" This is the same cry used so long and so effectively by the producers of mass media who insist that it is the public, not they, who decides what it wants to hear and see, and that for a critic to say that *this* program is bad and this program is good is purely a reflection of personal taste. Nobody recently has expressed this philosophy more succinctly than Dr. Frank Stanton, the highly intelligent president of CBS television. At a hearing before the Federal Communications Commission, this phrase escaped him under questioning: "One man's mediocrity is another man's good program."

There is no better way of saying "No values are absolute." There is another important aspect to this philosophy of *laissez faire:* It is the fear, in all observers of all forms of art, of guessing wrong. This fear is well come by, for who has not heard of the contemporary outcries against artists who later were called great? Every age has its arbiters who do not grow with their times, who cannot tell evolution from revolution or the difference between frivolous faddism, amateurish experimentation, and profound and necessary change. Who wants to be caught *flagrante delicto* with an error of judgment as serious as this? It is far safer, and certainly easier, to look at a picture or a play or a poem and to say "This is hard to understand, but it may be good," or simply to welcome it as a new form. The word "new"—in our country especially—has magical connotations. What is new must be good; what is old is probably bad, and if a critic can describe the new in language that nobody can understand, he's safer still. If he has mastered the art of saying nothing with exquisite complexity, nobody can quote him later as saying anything.

But all these, I maintain, are forms of abdication from the responsibility of judgment. In creating, the artist commits himself; in appreciating, you have a commitment of your own. For after all, it is the audience which makes the arts. A climate of appreciation is essential to its flowering, and the higher the expectations of the public, the better the performance of the artist. Conversely, only a public ill-served by its critics could have accepted as art and literature so much in these last years that has been neither. If anything goes, everything goes; and at the bottom of the junkpile lie the discarded standards too.

But what are these standards? How do you get them? How do you know 5 they're the right ones? How can you make a clear pattern out of so many intangibles, including that greatest one, the very private I?

Well for one thing, it's fairly obvious that the more you read and see and hear, the more equipped you'll be to practice that art of association which is at the basis of all understanding and judgment. The more you live and the more you look, the more aware you are of a consistent pattern—as universal as the stars, as the tides, as breathing, as night and day—underlying everything. I would call this pattern and this rhythm an order. Not order—an order. Within it exists an incredible diversity of forms. Without it lies chaos. I would further call this order—this incredible diversity held within one pattern—health. And I would call chaos—the wild cells of destruction—sickness. It is in the end up to you to distinguish between the diversity that is health and the chaos that is sickness, and you can't do this without a process of association that can link a bar of Mozart with the corner of a Vermeer painting, or a Stravinsky score with a Picasso abstraction; or that can relate an aggressive act with a Franz Kline painting and a fit of coughing with a John Cage composition.

There is no accident in the fact that certain expressions of art live for all time and that others die with the moment, and although you may not always define the reasons, you can ask the questions. What does an artist say that is timeless; how does he say it? How much is fashion, how much is merely reflection? Why is Sir Walter Scott so hard to read now, and Jane Austen not? Why is baroque right for one age and too effulgent for another?

Can a standard of craftsmanship apply to art of all ages, or does each have its own, and different, definitions? You may have been aware, inadvertently, that craftsmanship has become a dirty word these years because, again, it implies standard—something done well or done badly. The result of this convenient avoidance is a plenitude of actors who can't project their voices, singers who can't phrase their songs, poets who can't communicate emotion, and writers who have no vocabulary—not to speak of painters who can't draw. The dogma now is that craftsmanship gets in the way of expression. You can do better if you don't know *how* you do it, let alone *what* you're doing.

I think it is time you helped reverse this trend by trying to rediscover craft: the command of the chosen instrument, whether it is a brush, a word, or a voice. When you begin to detect the difference between freedom and sloppiness, between serious experimentation and ego-therapy, between skill and slickness, between strength and violence, you are on your way to separating the sheep from the goats, a form of segregation denied us for quite a while. All you need to restore it is a small bundle of standards and a Geiger counter that detects fraud, and we might begin our tour of the arts in an area where both are urgently needed: contemporary painting.

I don't know what's worse: to have to look at acres of bad art to find the little good, or to read what the critics say about it all. In no other field of expression has so much double-talk flourished, so much confusion prevailed, and so much nonsense been circulated: further evidence of the close interdependence between the arts and the critical climate they inhabit. It will be my pleasure to share with you some of this double-talk so typical of our times.

Item one: preface for a catalogue of an abstract painter:

"Time-bound meditation experiencing a life; sincere with plastic piety at the threshold of hallowed arcana; a striving for pure ideation giving shape to inner drive; formalized patterns where neural balances reach a fiction." End of quote. Know what this artist paints like now?

Item two: a review in the *Art News:*

". . . a weird and disparate assortment of material, but the monstrosity which bloomed into his most recent cancer of aggregations is present in some form everywhere. . . ." Then, later, "A gluttony of things and processes terminated by a glorious constipation."

Item three, same magazine, review of an artist who welds automobile fragments into abstract shapes:

"Each fragment . . . is made an extreme of human exasperation, torn at and fought all the way, and has its rightness of form as if by accident. *Any technique that requires order or discipline would just be the human ego.* No, these must be ego-less, uncontrolled, undesigned and different enough to give you a bang—fifty miles an hour around a telephone pole. . . ."

"Any technique that requires order or discipline would just be the human ego." What does he mean—"just be"? What are they really talking about? Is this journalism? Is it criticism? Or is it that other convenient abdication from standards of performance and judgment practiced by so many artists and critics that they, like certain writers who deal only in sickness and depravity, "reflect the chaos about them . . ."? Again, whose chaos? Whose depravity?

I had always thought that the prime function of art was to create order *out* of chaos—again, not the order of neatness or rigidity or convention or artifice, but the order of clarity by which one will and one vision could draw the essential truth out of apparent confusion. I still do. It is not enough to use parts of a car to convey the brutality of the machine. This is as slavishly representative, and just as easy, as arranging dried flowers under glass to convey nature.

Speaking of which, i.e., the use of real materials (burlap, old gloves, bottle-tops) in lieu of pigment, this is what one critic had to say about an exhibition of Assemblage at the Museum of Modern Art last year:

> Spotted throughout the show are indisputable works of art, accounting for a quarter     20
> or even half of the total display. But the remainder are works of non-art, anti-art, and
> art substitutes that are the aesthetic counterparts of the social deficiencies that land
> people in the clink on charges of vagrancy. These aesthetic bankrupts . . . have no le-
> gitimate ideological roof over their heads and not the price of a square intellectual
> meal, much less a spiritual sandwich, in their pockets.

I quote these words of John Canaday of *The New York Times* as an example of the kind of criticism which puts responsibility to an intelligent public above popularity with an intellectual coterie. Canaday has the courage to say what he thinks and the capacity to say it clearly: two qualities notably absent from his profession.

Next to art, I would say that appreciation and evaluation in the field of music is the most difficult. For it is rarely possible to judge a new composition at one hearing only. What seems confusing or fragmented at first might well become clear and organic a third time. Or it might not. The only salvation here for the listener is, again, an instinct born of experience and association which allows him to separate intent from accident, design from experimentation, and pretense from conviction. Much of contemporary music is, like its sister art, merely a reflection of the composer's own fragmentation: an absorption in self and symbols at the expense of communication with others. The artist, in short, says to the public: If you don't understand this, it's because you're dumb. I maintain that you are not. You may have to go part way or even halfway to meet the artist, but if you must go the whole way, it's his fault, not yours. Hold fast to that. And remember it too when you read new poetry, that estranged sister of music.

> A multitude of causes, unknown to former times, are now acting with a combined
> force to blunt the discriminating powers of the mind, and, unfitting it for all voluntary
> exertion, to reduce it to a state of almost savage torpor. The most effective of these
> causes are the great national events which are daily taking place and the increasing ac-
> cumulation of men in cities, where the uniformity of their occupations produces a
> craving for extraordinary incident, which the rapid communication of intelligence
> hourly gratifies. To this tendency of life and manners, the literature and theatrical ex-
> hibitions of the country have conformed themselves.

This startingly applicable comment was written in the year 1800 by William Wordsworth in the preface to his "Lyrical Ballads"; and it has been cited by

Edwin Muir in his recently published book, *The Estate of Poetry*. Muir states that poetry's effective range and influence have diminished alarmingly in the modern world. He believes in the inherent and indestructible qualities of the human mind and the great and permanent objects that act upon it, and suggests that the audience will increase when "poetry loses what obscurity is left in it by attempting greater themes, for great themes have to be stated clearly." If you keep that firmly in mind and resist, in Muir's words, "the vast dissemination of secondary objects that isolate us from the natural world," you have gone a long way toward equipping yourself for the examination of any work of art.

When you come to theatre, in this extremely hasty tour of the arts, you can     25
approach it on two different levels. You can bring to it anticipation and innocence, giving yourself up, as it were, to the life on the stage and reacting to it emotionally, if the play is good, or listlessly, if the play is boring; a part of the audience organism that expresses its favor by silence or laughter and its disfavor by coughing and rustling. Or you can bring to it certain critical faculties that may heighten, rather than diminish, your enjoyment.

You can ask yourselves whether the actors are truly in their parts or merely projecting themselves; whether the scenery helps or hurts the mood; whether the playwright is honest with himself, the characters, and you. Somewhere along the line you can learn to distinguish between the true creative act and the false arbitrary gesture; between fresh observation and stale cliché; between the avant-garde play that is pretentious drivel and the avant-garde play that finds new ways to say old truths.

Purpose and craftsmanship—end and means—these are the keys to your judgment in all the arts. What is this painter trying to say when he slashed a broad band of black across a white canvas and lets the edges dribble down? Is it a statement of violence? Is it a self-portrait? If it is *one* of these, has he made you believe it? Or is this a gesture of the ego or a form of therapy? If it shocks you, what does it shock you into?

And what of this tight little painting of bright flowers in a vase? Is the painter saying anything new about flowers? Is it different from a million other canvases of flowers? Has it any life, any meaning, beyond its statement? Is there any pleasure in its forms or texture? The question is not whether a thing is abstract or representational, whether it is "modern" or conventional. The question, inexorably, is whether it is good. And this is a decision which only you, on the basis of instinct, experience, and association, can make for yourself. It takes independence and courage. It involves, moreover, the risk of wrong decision and the humility, after the passage of time, of recognizing it as such. As we grow and change and learn, our attitudes can change too, and what we once thought obscure or "difficult" can later emerge as coherent and illuminating. Entrenched prejudices, obdurate opinions are as sterile as no opinions at all.

Yet standards there are, timeless as the universe itself. And when you have committed yourself to them, you have acquired a passport to that elusive but immutable realm of truth. Keep it with you in the forest of bewilderment. And never be afraid to speak up.

### Reflecting and Interpreting

1. Where is the thesis statement located?

2. Mannes says a denial of the existence of criteria to evaluate the arts has been popular for several reasons. What are they?

3. What is the general fear of observers of all forms of art? Yet what danger lies in accepting a critic's verdict of "exquisite complexity" without evaluation?

4. Mannes says that appreciation is necessary for the arts to flower. How do the expectations of the public influence art? Are there any other factors that Mannes does not mention?

5. What two basic criteria can be used to judge any piece of art? (Hint: See paragraphs 6 and 7.)

6. What does Mannes mean when she says, "The dogma now is that craftsmanship gets in the way of expression."

7. How does Mannes define *craft*? She says that an audience needs to be able to distinguish what from what?

8. Mannes gives a final piece of advice. What is it?

9. Mannes suggests we ask, "What does an artist say that is timeless; how does he (*sic*) say it?" Using these guidelines, how would you explain Jane Austen's popularity?

10. What four steps does Mannes suggest the reader take to acquire the standards needed to distinguish good art from bad?

### Small Group Discussion

With your group explore the criteria you use to rate a film as good or bad—one that you would or would not recommend to friends. Have a recorder jot down the proceedings and tabulate the votes for each criterion. After the discussion, the recorder should read the results.

# Illustration

## Showing with Examples

## *Hooked on Plastic*

Anish Majumdar

*Credit card offers abound at college and university; indeed, many students acquire their first credit card at college or university. What are the risks? In this article, Anish Majumdar, a freelance writer in Montreal, explores the lure of not-so-easy money.*

It's the first of the month. Montreal teems with the sounds of industry, a pounding cacophony of labourers earning cash, saving cash, spending cash. Yet in the midst of all this, I am a ghost. An anxious non-entity. A credit card addict.    1

The latest StatsCan figures reveal that the average single Canadian under 25, if he has any assets or debts at all, is $11,000 in debt. However, within this demographic is a constituency prone to fiscal extremes, one which regards this figure as merely a starting point. Sooner or later, those of us in the latter group begin a monthly ritual of frantic calls to the customer service numbers provided on the back of the cards. The scenario usually goes something like this: after an eternity on hold, the droning muzak segues into the chirpy voice of a call-centre operator reciting the company's greeting script. Desperation overriding courtesy, I cut her off mid-spiel: "I'm interested in getting a credit-line increase?"

"Well sir, I can certainly look into that for you. Do you mind if I put you on hold for moment?"

"Not at all." My heart's beating like a jackhammer, my palms are sweaty and I'm hunched over with tension inside a decrepit telephone booth. This soul-sick moment is the difference between making the rent and an abyss of dissolution.

"Hello, sir?"    5

"Yes?"

"We've checked our files and, according to them, we'd have to check with the credit bureau to see if you qualify."

I hand up—why bother? They'd inquire about my financial background, I'd lie about imaginary assets, and three weeks later a letter would appear in my mailbox ever-so-politely declining my request. For now, it's a nauseating trip to the pawn shop to hawk a luxury like my DVD player or Xbox, and a stunned question: "How did it come to this?"

I entered college in the fall of 2000 equipped with a $500-limit "starter" MasterCard, grateful to have a piece of plastic to help make dorm life seem a little less spartan. An overreliance on the card, however, combined with a lusty freshman appetite for Happy Hour specials, lead to a crisis point midway through the semester, when I found myself unable to pay the bills and eat simultaneously. In a fit of desperation, I called up MasterCard, searching for way to delay the month's payment. Imagine my shock when the cheerful person on the line offered me, not a reprieve, but a credit-limit increase: "How much were you looking for?"

What a question! Is there truly a proper amount adequate for someone rationing out ramen noodles and walking marathon distances to avoid subway fares? I responded with complete honesty: "As much as you can, please."     10

This was how, in less time than it takes to apply for a part-time job on campus, I sauntered away with more funds than I would have earned working for it for the next four months. A lifetime of staid parental dictums on fiscal responsibility was instantly wiped out: dead broke to flush in an instant. I was hooked.

Two years later, I've learned my lessons well. I'm out of school, now with four credit cards covering the cost of living. This life of trust-fund-like ease allows me to spend my days in one of two ways: freelance writing for magazines without the fiscal nail-biting inherent in the profession; and in the leisurely pursuit of late night revels and languid brunches. Is this decadence in any way warranted? Absolutely not. An accountant reviewing my obscene debt load and nonexistent savings would conclude that getting a real job is not only the right option, but an urgent one.

By why should I? Just 24, I have the Good Life spread out before me. All I have to do is keep on spinning the lie, keep taking cash advances on one card to make the minimum payments on the others. Sure, lurking somewhere unacknowledged is the truth of just how precarious this balance act is. But even my increasing anxiety isn't enough to make me want to give up my freedom.

As the balances on my cards soared ever upward, the amount being offered in credit-line increases lowered. Getting new cards to cover this shortfall provided stopgaps of a few thousand, yet at the cost of a lowered credit rating, crippling the possibility of future loans. My freedom was, of course, illusory, and even the desperate moves no long worked. My reckoning came in a musty pawn shop. I was hawking my prized 27-inch television, once the centrepiece of a dazzlingly chic bachelor pad, for the ignoble sum of $50. I was being given the once-over by the greasy shop owner who coyly asked if the set was stolen before finally peeling two $20s and a $10 from a damp wad of bills—knowing full well that any offer would be accepted. As I stuffed the money in my pocket just so I could eat that day, I had an epiphany. I was done.

It was time to join the rat race. You want fries with that?     15

## Reflecting and Interpreting

1. What reason does Majumdar give for being a credit-card addict?
2. What language does Majumdar use to show that he is an addict?
3. What are some of the implications of continually requesting an increase in your credit limit?
4. At the height of his addiction, how did Majumdar pay his credit card bills every month?
5. An increasingly heavy debt load was not enough for Majumdar to give up his freedom; what, ultimately, was the last straw?

## A Writer's Response

1. Do you think younger generations are more susceptible to such addictions? Why or why not?
2. Consider some other modern-day addictions, such as gambling or video-games. Write an essay about one such addiction, giving specific examples.

# Lawbreakers, Armed with Paint and Paste

Kirk Semple

*Street art or vandalism?* Graffitti, *as it was once known, has come a long way since the days of furtive spray painting. What are your views on street art? Here Kirk Semple, a* New York Times *reporter, explores the art form.*

Swoon frontloads her days with caffeine and works on her art late into the night.    1
It can take her two weeks to produce a series of the large, intricate paper cutouts and hand-pulled block prints that have gained her considerable renown in one particular sector of the art world. When she is done—her arms aching and her clothes and skin speckled with paint and ink—she takes her pieces outside, slaps them up on old walls around the city, then disappears on her bike.

That is when her work, now left to the mercy of the elements and public taste, comes alive. "You know, it's weird, but I love it," she said. "I don't feel they need to be kept in a vault as precious art."

Swoon, 26, is a luminary in a movement known, at least among many of its proponents, as street art. Two decades after the heyday of graffiti, the spray can has given way to posters, stickers, stencils and construction tools, and the streets of New York and other cities around the world vibrate more than ever with the work—some say the destruction—of guerilla artists like her. (Swoon is a nom de peinture; like many other artists interviewed for this article, she asked that her real name not be used for fear of prosecution because unauthorized graffiti is illegal.)

The movement is sustained and driven by Web sites, magazines, word of mouth and its practitioners' self-righteousness.

At one end of the spectrum are doodles, icons and designs, often drawn or    5
printed on stickers, a medium that allows for pre-strike preparation at home and quick, furtive execution in public.

Others are using more complicated art techniques, such as the meticulous printing and paperwork preferred by Swoon, ceramics, lithography, silk screening, painting, leathersmithing and woodworking. Some have even used welding torches, notably the once-ubiquitous New York graffiti writer known as Revs, who has installed three-dimensional versions of his stylized name, or "tag," around the city. Darius (also known by his graffiti tag, Verbs) and Downey, a Brooklyn tandem now living in London, turn old street signs into sculptures or small billboards for provocative messages and reinstall them, often in the plain light of day. "We're using the city against itself," Downey, 23, said in a recent interview.

Any surface goes; the more visible and the less frequently buffed the better: walls, doors, the backs of stop signs, the base of light poles, utility boxes, trash bins, sidewalks, rooftops, the frames of subway car advertisements.

In New York, the streets of the Lower East Side and SoHo, Dumbo and Williamsburg are filled with fresh work. Even in the most closely policed neighborhoods, rare is the city block where some visual mischief has not been unleashed.

"Size is not what it's about," said Marc Schiller, 40, a New York marketing executive who, as a hobby, runs the Wooster Collective, a curatorial Web site for street art around the world. "It's about being clever. It's about being unique." (One unknown artist has arrayed 18 luggage locks, each decorated with a baby's picture, on a fence on Crosby Street in SoHo. Periodically the artist will rearrange the locks to make a new design.)

And while much of the work seems to be art for art's sake—or at least humor's sake—street art occasionally resonates with overt social and political commentary. In one arresting series that recently appeared (and just as quickly disappeared) in Lower Manhattan, an artist replaced the silhouetted dancers in the current iPod advertisement with silhouettes of Abu Ghraib torture victims. The tag line "10,000 songs in your pocket, Mac or PC" became "10,000 volts in your pocket, guilty or innocent." 10

Like any artistic movement, the origins of street art are nebulous, through it is clearly an outgrowth of the stylized graffiti writing that began in New York in the 1960's and became emblematic of hip-hop culture. According to Tristan Manco, a graphic designer in Bristol, England, and author of the street art compendium "Street Logos," the term "street art" was first used in the 1980's in reference to urban guerrilla art that was not hip-hop graffiti, and described the pioneering work of New York painters like Keith Haring and Kenny Scharf, and Parisian stencil artists like Blek and Nemo.

Street art has since spread around the world, from the East End of London to Tokyo, Moscow to Johannesburg, Melbourne, Australia, to São Paulo, Brazil. And in spite of the movement's underground nature, the work of today's most prominent street artists if increasingly sought by galleries and collectors around the world, though the pieces are not yet fetching the sums attached to the art of New York's graffiti pioneers. (Mr. Haring's chalk drawings on black subway-advertisement placeholders command thousands of dollars at auction.)

Ask street artists to talk about why they do what they do, and brace for a torrent of rationalization. Shepard Fairey, a 34-year-old artist who is famous for his global "Obey Giant" sticker campaign featuring the glowering mug of the late World Wrestling Federation star Andre the Giant, has even published a manifesto in which he calls his work "an experiment in Phenomenology," the first aim of which, he says, "is to reawaken a sense of wonder about one's environment."

Artists and their supporters say they are simply responding to what they regard as a visual assault by corporations and commercial interests. "Why is the ad I see in the Gap more acceptable than any art that I hang on a public lamppost?" Mr. Schiller asks. "Let's balance the scales a bit. We're talking about anybody having the right to express themselves." (If Mr. Schiller's message seems incongruous with his profession—marketing—he says he hopes his passion for street art has made him better at his job by making him more sensitive to the negative effects of advertising.)

But may street artists will admit to a less noble motivation: the urge to go out    15
and break the law. The waft of fresh wheat paste, it seems, can inspire a night of vandalism. "That's something that people really love about it: getting over on the man," said Kelly Burns, 38, the author of the book "INY," a photographic exploration of New York street art.

The law does not make a distinction between a tag scratched on a sticker or Swoon's cutouts. It is all vandalism. (The New York Police Department turned down a request for an interview.)

Swoon, who has never been arrested, says she is "fully in touch with the ambiguity" of what she does—by which she means the illegality. So she picks her spots carefully, exploring what she calls "third spaces"—not really public, maybe private, undoubtedly neglected. Her backdrops include abandoned buildings, run-down warehouses, and broken walls. "There are so many spaces that don't really need to be brown," she said.

Swoon first took her art to the street five years ago while she was a fine-arts student at Pratt Institute in Brooklyn. She was compelled to take her work outside after suffering what she calls "the quiet, boring preciousness" of the gallery world.

"I wanted to jump out of my skin," she said. But the streets were free and open to a wider range of expression. "Because it's kind of an outlaw thing, you don't have to go through official channels," she explained. "It's trying to create a visual commons out of the derelict walls of the city." (She has since returned to the gallery scene, as the star of her own shows in Berlin, Miami and Cincinnati. "I need to make a living," she shrugged.)

On a recent afternoon, Swoon, a fit, enthusiastic woman with wavy, straw-    20
berry blond hair and a small silver nose ring, interrupted her work on her most recent project, which was a day or two away from completion, to give a brief bicycle tour of some of the pieces that have survived in Boerum Hill and Prospect Heights. Her recent and most famous work involves life-size cutouts and block prints of people with which, she says, she is "populating the city."

She stopped in front of the trash-strewn loading dock of an old warehouse on Bergen Street near Flatbush Avenue, across the street from a police station in Prospect Heights. A worn silhouette of a hooded, hunched man lurked on the wall. "It's a good place for him to hang out," she said warmly. "I want them to become part of their space, to interact in a human way. A sticker can't do that."

Swoon avoids sentimentality and regards her distribution method as a game of evolutionary fate. "I'm getting them out there and seeing which ones survive, like baby sea turtles," she explained Even her preferred paper—newsprint, a highly fragile material—limits the life expectancy of her work. But she loves how the paper curls and rots, giving the art character and a voice where there might otherwise be silence.

*Reflecting and Interpreting*

1. According to the article, how has street art evolved over the past 20 years?
2. Why do artists engage in street art? Give three reasons why street art holds such allure for its practitioners.
3. Find one specific example of street art for each reason given above.
4. What is another term for graffiti/street art?
5. This article provides numerous examples of street art and the names of its artists. How does the article provide closure?

*A Writer's Response*

Street art: vandalism or fresh artistic vision? Write an essay defending your position.

# Classification

## Grouping and Dividing

## *It's Only a Paper World*

Kathleen Fury

---

*Even if you have never worked in an office, you will appreciate Kathleen Fury's spoof of the innovations people use to channel the never-ending flow of paper. She is a native New Yorker (born 1941) who graduated from Purdue University. She has worked as a writer and editor for* Redbook, Savvy, *and* Ladies Home Journal. *She has published* Dear 60 Minutes *(1985);* Forever Young, A Guide to Life After 50 *(1996); and contributed to* Death, then what? *(online anthology). She has also written for* TV Guide, Cat Quotes, New Woman, *and other magazines. For years she contributed regular columns to* Working Woman, *one of which appears here.*

Many experts claimed that the computer age heralded the advent of the paper-less office. Clearly, this is not to be. If anything, offices are overwhelmed by even more paper, much of it now with sprocket holes. 1

Humankind is adapting, fortunately. According to the dictates of our varied individual natures, we have developed ways of copying with our changing ecosystem.

The beaver uses paper to build. It may not be exactly clear to observers just what she's building, but deep in her genetic code she knows.

On one side of the typical beaver's desk leans a foot-high stack of papers. Close by is a vertical file stuffed with bulging folders, some waving in the air, unable to touch bottom. In between, the beaver constructs a clever "dam" to prevent the entire structure from falling over: Her two-tier In/Out box supports the pile and allows movement of papers from one place to another.

Incredibly, to nonbeaver observers, the beaver has an uncanny ability to locate 5 a two-month-old report buried within the pile. With deft precision, she can move her hand four millimeters down the pile and extract what she's looking for, confident that the dam will hold.

In this way, the beaver has evolved a protective mechanism that makes her invaluable within the organization, for nobody else, including her secretary, can find anything on her desk. When the beaver goes away on vacation, her department simply ceases work until she returns. She is thus assured that the cliché "nobody's indispensable" doesn't apply to her.

The squirrel's desk, by contrast, is barren. Throughout the year, in all kinds of weather, the squirrel energetically stores away what her brain tells her she may need someday. In her many file cabinets, drawers and book-cases she neatly stores memos, letters, printouts and receipts she believes will nourish her in the months and years to come.

Unlike her co-worker the beaver, the squirrel does not always know exactly where she has hidden a particular item. She knows she *has* it but is not skilled at remembering the exact location.

Like the maple tree, which produces enough seeds to reforest a continent, the squirrel illustrates nature's method of "overkill." By saving and storing everything, she increases her chance of retrieving something.

Of necessity, squirrels have developed the ability to move through a wide ter- 10 ritorial range. When a squirrel moves on to another job, as she tends to do rather often due to lack of space, management must hire a special team of search-and-destroy experts to go through her files.

Nature's scavengers, her "clean-up crew," crows are regarded with wary admiration by squirrels and beavers, who recognize their contribution to keeping the corporate ecosystem tidy.

Crows are responsible for such paper-management advice as "Act on it—or throw it away." They are deeply drawn to paper shredders, trash compactors and outsized waste receptacles and will buy them if they happen to work in purchasing.

Crows belie the common epithet "birdbrained," for it has taken centuries of evolution to create a mind disciplined enough to know with certainty that it is OK to throw the CEO's Statement of Corporate Policy in the wastebasket after a glance.

Other species, who must adapt to the corporate food chain, quickly learn not to address any crow with a sentence that begins, "Do you have a copy of . . . ?"

The clever bees are among the wonders of the corporate world. A bee neither 15 hoards nor destroys paper; she redistributes it, moving from office to office as if between flowers.

Her methods are various and unpredictable, but there is no madness in them. Sometimes she arrives in an office with paper in hand and, distracting a colleague with conversation, simply leaves the paper inconspicuously on his desk. Sometimes she moves paper through seemingly legitimate channels, sending it through interoffice mail with ingenious notes like "Please look into this when you get a chance." More often, she employs the clever notation invented by bees, "FYI."

Whatever her method, she ensures that paper floats outward and does not return to her. Students of human behavior have come to call this crosspollination "delegation," though to the bee it is simply a genetic imperative.

While others of the species hoard, distribute and destroy paper, the possum follows the evolutionary dictates of all marsupials and carries it with her.

Instead of a pouch, the office possum has a briefcase—in some cases, several. It is large and soft sided to accommodate her needs. Some possums, as an auxiliary system, carry handbags large enough to hold legal-size files. When a possum needs to retrieve paper, she goes not to a file cabinet or an In box but to her bags. She protects her paper by carrying it with her at all times—to her home, to the health club, to lunch.

Though she has no natural predators, the possum's habits create special risks.    20
She must spend considerable time at the lost-and-found department of theaters and restaurants and knows by heart the telephone number of the taxi commissioner. One of her arms is longer than the other.

But in nature, all things serve a purpose. And if the office burned down, the lowly possum would be the sole possessor of the paper that is the raison d'être of all the other animals.

## Reflecting and Interpreting

1. Can you find an example of foreshadowing?
2. How does paragraph 2 function? What is the analogy that is introduced here?
3. How can you identify a "beaver"? What special ability does she have? Why is she indispensable?
4. Why is the squirrel's desk bare? How efficient is the squirrel?
5. Why do other office workers never ask a "crow" for anything?
6. What are some clues that can help you spot a "possum"?
7. Notice the references to genetics and evolution throughout the essay. How do these function?
8. What literary device is the basis for Fury's classifications?
9. Can you find instances of irony in the essay?
10. Why is the last paragraph effective?

## A Writer's Response

Can you think of another type of office worker, unnamed by the author? If so, write a paragraph describing this creature. Give the advantages and disadvantages of his or her method of managing the flow of paper.

# *Mind over Munchies*

Norman Brown

---

*"Food cravings are like fingerprints," or so Norman Brown has decided. We all have individual food cravings that surface, perhaps at a particular time of day or under certain conditions. He presents research about "comfort foods," "mood foods," and "happy foods" but with no definitive results. Although researchers do not agree about what causes food cravings, they do agree that excessive cravings of certain foods and nonfoods are a good reason to consult a physician. "Mind over Munchies" was first published in* Northwest Airlines *(June 1992) and later in* The Thoughtful Reader *(1994).*

Got any favorite foods? They can reveal a lot about your personality, say    1
experts who have been digging into our "edible complex" ever since Cleopatra's
milk baths and fig outs. Not surprisingly, those gastronomical urges are also the
subject of considerable debate.

Some researchers believe there are strong physiological links to food cravings.
But others feel that our urges are not that deep-rooted or overwhelming. How
much is scientific fact—and should we be that concerned about "mood foods"
which are supposed to make us happier, smarter or sexier?

Current research lends support to both sides. Scientists now believe that food
cravings are a smorgasbord of biological and psychological events that help the
body regulate its intake of nutrients. The notion, though controversial, has obvious appeal. Whether you crave a pizza or nachos, it's comforting to think the
body is getting a desired carbohydrate fix—or quick salt injection.

Food cravings are like fingerprints. In those sluggish hours when there's nothing better to do than imagine the perfect entrée, our choices are as varied as they
are precise: McDonald's fries, subgum chow mein, or chocolate chip cookies.

### Necessary Comforts

"Comfort foods are really an individual thing," says Dr. Kelly Brownell, professor    5
of nutrition at Yale University in New Haven. He compares cravings to a wave in
the ocean—starting small, building to a peak, then rapidly subsiding. If you track
where you are in the cycle, or if the urge strikes at the same time each day, you
can ward it off by taking a brisk walk.

Brownell admits he's not sure whether cravings are in the head or stomach.
"It's possible that there's nothing physiological about them," he says. "Even if you
buy that argument, our protein intake is amazingly steady. What varies wildly is
fat and sugar consumption—and which foods you choose depends on habit."

In a survey for the *Wall Street Journal*, half of all respondents said they did
seek solace in food when depressed. First choice: ice cream or chocolate bars (with

34 percent of the vote). Pizza, beer, soft drinks, hot soup, peanut butter and burgers completed the list of comforting edibles.

Other scientists agree that what we eat (or don't eat) is often rooted in the nurturing, warmth and security we felt in childhood. "Some cravers want a little taste of what Mom gave them to feel better," explains Dr. Tom Castonguay, associate professor of nutrition at the University of Maryland. "Others use food to be bad."

The very word "craving" conjures up an addiction, but that's not the kind of thing a person with a sweet tooth is experiencing. "Cravings are not that deep-rooted or overwhelming," says Castonguay. "But people are making money talking about them in that way."

### Eat for Success?

Every fad diet for "cravers" that hits the bookstores claims to rely on scientific    10
proof and it all has to do with those elusive brain chemicals that can send you to the sack—or to the refrigerator. Among the strongest proponents of "mood foods" is Dr. Judith Wurtman, nutritional biochemist at the Massachusetts Institute of Technology.

Her research over the past several years seems to indicate that irrational desires for certain foods may indeed be biologically based. Carbohydrate cravers, she says, feel calmer—and less tired and depressed—after satisfying their need.

Wurtman notes that dietary needs vary from person to person, but suggests that carbohydrate craving may be linked to the activity of serotonin, a chemical produced in the brain when sugar or starch is ingested. When cravers were given a substance that increases serotonin, she says, "the cravings went down to nothing."

Her books and advice have become immensely popular, but she's quick to point out that food is not a panacea for all our ills. "There are myths to confront," says Wurtman. One is that sugar causes anxiety. Her research has shown that sugar or starch actually has a calming effect and may be an unconscious attempt at self-medication.

She advises stress-plagued executives to cut down on "dumb" foods and eat smart: low-fat carbohydrates like bananas and crackers to chase away tension, or high-protein snacks (peanut butter or cottage cheese) for the alertness chemicals dopamine and norepinephrine.

### Happy Foods

Campbell Soup Co. is also investigating how food may affect people's moods, and    15
is doing research projects with Tufts University School of Medicine. "We feel mood is going to be really big in the 90s and that positioning foods as making one smarter or happier could be a gold mine," says Tony Adams, marketing research chief.

The company is studying carbohydrates, caffeine and other components of food. "But the research puts some folks at Campbell in a nervous mood. "People here worry about making claims," says Adams. "We'll have to be careful to separate fact from witch doctoring."

Other researchers think carbohydrate cravers may be deluding themselves. What they really yearn for are those fat-sugar mixtures, says Dr. Adam Drewnowski, nutrition professor at the University of Michigan School of Public Health.

"Hardly anyone craves pure carbohydrates such as macaroni or cabbage," he says. "But almost everybody can identify with an uncontrollable desire for a Snickers bar or piece of cheesecake." He has demonstrated that such food cravings can be blocked by the drug naloxone, which is also given to addicts to ease opiate cravings.

Other scientists are studying a hormone (cholecystokinin) that may hold the key to why we pig out. They believe that the hormone, secreted during digestion, sends signals to the brain that cause the can't-eat-another-bite sensation. The trick in stopping binges is to make this reaction happen sooner—not later.

And behaviorists argue that we *learn* our food fixations. "Taste may be more    20 addictive than calories or nutrients," says Dr. Stephen Chang, food science professor at Rutgers University. The brain is more interested in what's happening on the tongue than in the stomach. "If the tongue is happy, then the brain will be happy," he says.

## Brain Chemicals

Drewnowski and others speculate that in some people, food cravings increase the output of endorphins, mood-altering brain chemicals with potent effects similar to narcotics. Not only do endorphins soothe headaches and calm frazzled nerves, they can sweep us into euphoria—or kindle destructive behavior such as excruciating workouts or compulsive gambling.

Childbirth would be unbearable without the easing effects of these natural opiates, which increase four or five times during labor. After the baby is born, endorphins return to their former levels. Not surprisingly, people with chronic pain have only half the endorphins of a healthy person.

It's not that cravings are significantly more common during pregnancy. Rather, women are more likely to satisfy them at that time, explains Dr. Judith Rodin, professor of psychology at Yale. Pregnant women do require the extra salt and calories that pickles and ice cream provide as fetal development begins.

Aversions, the flip side of cravings, are particularly strong during the first trimester. Since that's when the fetus is most vulnerable, aversions to coffee or alcohol are very protective, says Rodin.

When food cravings (or aversions) have an obsessional quality, or are persistent,    25 it may indicate a more serious eating disorder such as bulimia or anorexia, she says. For most of us, cravings are either short-lived or the result of temporary stress.

Food intolerances also can cause anxiety, food cravings and obesity. Additives, irritants and toxins are common culprits. But there may be an acquired biochemical defect, such as the inability to digest milk sugar (lactase deficiency). Finding *healthy* ways to boost our moods through endorphins and other brain chemicals could even keep us from falling into dangerous addictions.

## Mood Medicine

Food cravings can be the undoing of even the most conscientious eaters. So, how do we deal with them? "You can't control the fact that cravings occur," says Dr.

Harvey Ross, psychiatrist and author of *The Mood Control Diet* (Prentice Hall, 1990). "But you can control how you react to them."

His research shows that certain foods, or substances concentrated from them, can be used in the same way as drugs to improve your sleep or the way you handle stress. Avoiding "trigger" foods can be effective in treating disorders as varied as depression and yeast infections.

The most controversial aspect of food cravings or intolerances is the claim that they are often the underlying causes of such disorders as hypoglycemia (low blood sugar), allergies, anemia, and chronic fatigue. Most allergists dispute such claims, but additional studies may eventually bear out many of them.

If you find yourself craving inordinate amounts of the following, consult your   30
physician to rule out any serious medical condition:

*Salt.* Excessive cravings can be a sign of adrenal insufficiency in which tissues and blood are depleted of saltwater, and blood pressure plummets.

*Water.* Constant thirst may signal juvenile or adult-onset diabetes. Weight loss may also occur despite constant hunger or voracious eating.

*Sugar.* Severe cravings may be a symptom of reactive hyperglycemia and the body's inability to maintain adequate levels of blood sugar (glucose).

*Ice.* Persistent need can be a sign of anemia (sore mouth or tongue) or chronic kidney disease due to disturbances in blood chemistry.

*Nonfoods.* Abnormal cravings for items such as laundry starch by pregnant   35
women and paint chips by children is known as pica. Fetal risk and lead poisoning are possible effects.

### *Reflecting and Interpreting*

---

1. What rhetorical device does Brown use in the first and second paragraphs?

2. Dr. Judith Wurtman advises eating certain foods to alleviate stress and increase alertness. What are they? What four examples does she give?

3. Dr. Wurtman claims that sugar has a calming effect. Do you agree or disagree? Is it possible that different people react differently to sugar?

4. What hormone is thought to "hold the key to why we pig out"? Yet what do behaviorists argue as being more "addictive than calories and nutrients"?

5. Researchers speculate that in some people, food cravings increase the output of endorphins, mood-altering brain chemicals. How can endorphins affect us?

6. What is the most controversial aspect of food cravings or intolerances?

7. The author cites five kinds of cravings that deserve the attention of a physician. What are they?

8. You may have to hunt to find Brown's thesis. What is the main idea of this essay? How would you state it in your own words?

9. Although the author cites research, this is not a technical article. How does he achieve the light tone?

10. How would you rate Brown's objectivity in presenting this research?

## A Writer's Response

1. Before your group begins, appoint someone to chart categories of individual food cravings and the times they occur. Then share experiences. What factors seem to affect your cravings? Do you attempt to control them? What seems to work best? After the discussion, tally the responses and read them to the group.

2. What are your favourite foods? Do you experience cravings at particular times? Do you think they reveal anything about your personality? Write a short essay analyzing and classifying your eating habits.

# Comparison–Contrast

## Exploring Likeness and Difference

## *A Nonsmoker with a Smoker*

Phillip Lopate

*Phillip Lopate, a well-known essayist, is the author of* Against Joie de Vivre: Personal Essays *(1989), from which this essay is taken. Lopate, a nonsmoker, ponders his thoughts on smoking, contrasting the feelings and views of smokers and nonsmokers. He creates a kaleidoscope of images which cause us to feel—not merely see—first one side of smoking and then the other. The result? A remarkably balanced viewpoint. Lopate is also a poet, fiction writer, literary and film critic, as well as editor of several anthologies of essays. He has published several books, including* The Ordering Mirror: Readers and Contexts *(1993), Totally, Tenderly, Tragically: Essays and Criticism from a Lifelong Love Affair with the Movies *(1998), and* John Koch: Painting a New York Life *(2001).*

Last Saturday night my girlfriend, Helen, and I went to a dinner party in the    1 Houston suburbs. We did not know our hosts, but were invited on account of Helen's chum Barry, whose birthday party it was. We had barely stepped into the house and met the other guests, seated on a U-shaped couch under an A-framed ceiling, when Helen lit a cigarette. The hostess froze. "Uh, could you please not smoke in here? If you have to, we'd appreciate your using the terrace. We're both sort of allergic."

Helen smiled understandingly and moved toward the glass doors leading to the backyard in a typically ladylike way, as though merely wanting to get a better look at the garden. But I knew from that gracious "Southern" smile of hers that she was miffed.

As soon as Helen had stepped outside, the hostess explained that they had just moved into this house, and that it had taken weeks to air out because of the previous owner's tenacious cigar smoke. A paradigmatically awkward conversation about tobacco ensued: like testifying sinners, two people came forward with confessions about kicking the nasty weed; our scientist-host cited a recent study of indoor air pollution levels; a woman lawyer brought up the latest California legislation protecting nonsmokers; a roly-poly real estate agent admitted that, though he had given up smokes, he still sat in the smoking section of airplanes because "you meet a more interesting type of person there"—a remark his wife did not find amusing. Helen's friend Barry gallantly joined her outside. I did not, as I should have; I felt paralyzed.

For one thing, I wasn't sure which side I was on. I have never been a smoker. My parents both chain-smoked, so I grew up accustomed to cloudy interiors and ever since have been tolerant of other people's nicotine urges. To be perfectly honest, I'm not crazy about inhaling smoke, particularly when I've got a cold, but that irritating inconvenience pales beside the damage that would be done to my pluralistic worldview if I did not defend smokers' rights.

On the other hand, a part of me wished Helen *would* stop smoking. That part   5
seemed to get a satisfaction out of the group's "banishing" her: they were doing the dirty work of expressing my disapproval.

As soon as I realized this, I joined her in the garden. Presently a second guest strolled out to share a forbidden toke, then a third. Our hostess ultimately had to collect the mutineers with an announcement that dinner was served.

At the table, Helen appeared to be having such a good time, joking with our hosts and everyone else, that I was unprepared for the change that came over her as soon as we were alone in the car afterward. "I will never go back to that house!" she declared. "Those people have no concept of manners or hospitality, humiliating me the moment I stepped in the door. And that phony line about 'sort of allergic'!"

Normally, Helen is forbearance personified. Say anything that touches her about smoking, however, and you touch the rawest of nerves. I remembered the last time I foolishly suggested that she "think seriously" about stopping. I had just read one of those newspaper articles about the increased possibility of heart attacks, lung cancer, and birth deformities among women smokers, and I was worried for her. My concern must have been maladroitly expressed, because she burst into tears.

"Can't we even talk about this without your getting so sensitive?" I had asked.

"You don't understand. Nonsmokers never understand that it's a real addic-   10
tion. I've tried quitting, and it was hell. Do you want me to go around for months mean and cranky outside and angry inside? You're right, I'm sensitive, because I'm threatened with having taken away from me the thing that gives me the most pleasure in life, day in, day out," she said. I shot her a look: careful, now. "Well, practically the most pleasure. You know what I mean." I didn't. But I knew enough to drop it.

I love Helen, and if she wants to smoke, knowing the risks involved, that remains her choice. Besides, she wouldn't quit just because I wanted her to; she's not that docile, and that's part of what I love about her. Sometimes I wonder why I even keep thinking about her quitting. What's it to me personally? Certainly I feel protective of her health, but I also have selfish motives. I don't like the way her lips taste when she's smoked a lot. I associate her smoking with nervousness, and when she lights up several cigarettes in a row, I get jittery watching her. Crazy as this may sound, I also find myself becoming jealous of her cigarettes. Occasionally, when I go to her house and we're sitting on the couch together, if I see Helen eyeing the pack I make her kiss me first, so that my lips can engage hers (still fresh) before the competition's. It's almost as though there were another lover in the room—a lover who was around long before I entered the picture, and who pleases her in mysterious ways I cannot.

A lit cigarette puts a distance between us: it's like a weapon in her hand, awakening in me a primitive fear of being burnt. The memory is not so primitive, actually. My father used to smoke absentmindedly, letting the ash grow like a caterpillar eating every leaf in its path, until gravity finally toppled it. Once, when I was about nine, my father and I were standing in line at a bakery, and he accidentally dropped a lit ash down my back. Ever since, I've inwardly winced and been on guard around these little waving torches, which epitomize to me the dangers of intimacy.

I've worked hard to understand from the outside the satisfaction of smoking. I've even smoked "sympathetic" cigarettes, just to see what the other person was experiencing. But it's not the same as being hooked. How can I really empathize with the frightened but stubborn look Helen gets in her eyes when, despite the fact we're a little late going somewhere, she turns to me in the car and says, "I need to buy a pack of cigarettes first"? I feel a wave of pity for her. We are both embarrassed by this forced recognition of her frailty—the "indignity," as she herself puts it, of being controlled by something outside her will.

I try to imagine myself in that position, but a certain smugness keeps getting in the way (I don't have that problem and *am I glad*). We pay a price for our smugness. So often it flip-flops into envy: the outsiders wish to be included in the sufferings and highs of others, as if to say that only by relinquishing control and surrendering to some dangerous habit, some vice or dependency, would one be able to experience "real life."

Over the years I have become a sucker for cigarette romanticism. Few Hollywood gestures move me as much as the one in *Now Voyager*, when Paul Henreid lights two cigarettes, one for himself, the other for Bette Davis: these form a beautiful fatalistic bridge between them, a complicitous understanding like the realization that their love is based on the inevitability of separation. I am all the more admiring of this worldly cigarette gallantry because its experiential basis escapes me.

The same sort of fascination occurs when I come across a literary description of nicotine addiction, like this passage in Mailer's *Tough Guys Don't Dance:* "Over and over again I gave them up, a hundred times over the years, but I always went back. For in my dreams, sooner or later, I struck a match, brought flame to the tip, then took in all my hunger for existence with the first puff. I felt impaled on desire itself—those fiends trapped in my chest and screaming for one drag."

"Impaled on desire itself"! Such writing evokes a longing in me for the centering of self that tobacco seems to bestow on its faithful. Clearly, there is something attractive about having this umbilical relation to the universe—this curling pillar, this spiral staircase, this prayer of smoke that mediates between the smoker's inner substance and the alien ether. Inwardness of the nicotine trance, sad

15

wisdom ("every pleasure has its price"), beauty of ritual, squandered health—all those romantic meanings we read into the famous photographic icons of fifties saints, Albert Camus or James Agee or James Dean or Carson McCullers puffing away, in a sense they're true. Like all people who return from a brush with death, smokers have gained a certain power. They know their "coffin nails." With Helen, each cigarette is a measuring of the perishable, an enactment of her mortality, from filter to end-tip in fewer than five minutes. I could not stand to be reminded of my own death so often.

### Reflecting and Interpreting

1. What is the effect of the anecdote as an opening to the essay?
2. How does Lopate feel about an issue on which most people have clear-cut opinions? Describe the tone.
3. What happens after Helen leaves the room?
4. Comment on the contrast between Helen's behaviour and her feelings.
5. Lopate admits that he has selfish reasons for wanting Helen to quit smoking. What are they? Comment on the image near the end of paragraph 11.
6. Can you find two vivid similes that dramatize Lopate's deep feelings about *tobacco*?
7. What is the "cigarette romanticism" that he mentions? Do you think it is still prevalent? Why or why not?
8. Despite Lopate's attraction to a smoker and smoking, he does not smoke. Why?
9. After reading the essay, how do you feel about the author? How does he sound?
10. For Lopate, cigarettes have also acquired a deadly symbolism: "an enactment of . . . mortality." Where does he explain this?

### A Writer's Response

1. Using some of Lopate's techniques, compare and contrast two views in an essay. For example, you might discuss a habit you disapprove of but, nonetheless, tolerate in someone you love.
2. *Small Groups:* Summarize the viewpoint of the host and hostess, listing their reasons. Then summarize the view of smokers. Now analyze. Which reasons are based on fact? On emotion? What about etiquette? Who was being rude?

# Gender Gap in Cyberspace

Deborah Tannen

*Are gender differences reflected in the world of electronic communication? Deborah Tannen is a professor of linguistics at Georgetown University and has published 19 books. This article was originally published in* Newsweek.

I was a computer pioneer, but I'm still something of a novice. That paradox is    1
telling.

I was the second person on my block to get a computer. The first was my colleague Ralph. It was 1980. Ralph got a Radio Shack TRS-80; I got a used Apple II+. He helped me get started and went on to become a maven, reading computer magazines, hungering for the new technology he read about, and buying and mastering it as quickly as he could afford. I hung on to old equipment far too long because I dislike giving up what I'm used to, fear making the wrong decision about what to buy and resent the time it takes to install and learn a new system.

My first Apple came with videogames; I gave them away. Playing games on the computer didn't interest me. If I had free time I'd spend it talking on the telephone to friends.

Ralph got hooked. His wife was often annoyed by the hours he spent at his computer and the money he spent upgrading it. My marriage had no such strains—until I discovered e-mail. Then I got hooked. E-mail draws me the same way the phone does: it's a souped-up conversation.

E-mail deepened my friendship with Ralph. Though his office was next to    5
mine, we rarely had extended conversations because he is shy. Face to face he mumbled so, I could barely tell he was speaking. But when we both go on e-mail, I started receiving long, self-revealing messages; we poured our hearts out to each other. A friend discovered that e-mail opened up that kind of communication with her father. He would never talk much on the phone (as her mother would), but they have become close since they both got on line.

Why, I wondered, would some men find it easier to open up on e-mail? It's a combination of the technology (which they enjoy) and the obliqueness of the written word, just as many men will reveal feelings in dribs and drabs while riding in the car or doing something, which they'd never talk about sitting face to face. It's too intense, too bearing-down on them, and once you start you have to keep going. With a computer in between, it's safer.

It was on e-mail, in fact, that I described to Ralph how boys in groups often struggle to get the upper hand whereas girls tend to maintain an appearance of cooperation. And he pointed out that this explained why boys are more likely to be captivated by computers than girls are. Boys are typically motivated by a social structure that says if you don't dominate you will be dominated. Computers, by their nature, balk: you type a perfectly appropriate command and it refuses to do what it should. Many boys and men are incited by this defiance: "I'm going to whip this into line and teach it who's boss! I'll get it to do what I say!" (and if they work hard enough, they always can). Girls and women are more likely to respond, "This thing won't cooperate. Get it away from me!"

Although no one wants to think of herself as "typical"—how much nicer to be sui generis—my relationship to my computer is—gulp—fairly typical for a woman. Most women (with plenty of exceptions) aren't excited by tinkering with the technology, grappling with the challenge of eliminating bugs or getting the biggest and best computer. These dynamics appeal to many men's interest in making sure they're on the top side of the inevitable who's-up-who's-down struggle that life is for them. E-mail appeals to my view of like as a contest for connections to others. When I see that I have 15 messages I feel loved.

I once posted a technical question on a computer network for linguists and was flooded with long dispositions (*sic*), some pages long. I was staggered by the generosity and the expertise, but wondered where these guys found the time—and why all the answers I got were from men.

Like coed classrooms and meetings, discussions on e-mail networks tend to be dominated by male voices, unless they're specifically women-only, like single-sex schools. On line, women don't have to worry about getting the floor (you just send a message when you feel like it), but, according to linquists Susan Herring and Laurel Sutton, who have studied this, they have the usual problems of having their messages ignored or attacked. The anonymity of public networks frees a small number of men to send long, vituperative, sarcastic messages that many other men either can tolerate or actually enjoy, but turn most women off.    10

The anonymity of networks leads to another sad part of the e-mail story; there are men who deluge women with questions about their appearance and invitations to sex. On college campuses, as soon as women students log on, they are bombarded by references to sex, like going to work and finding pornographic posters adorning the walls.

Taking time: Most women want one thing from a computer—to work. This is significant counterevidence to the claim that men want to focus on information while women are interested in rapport. That claim I found was often true in casual conversation, in which there is no particular information to be conveyed. But with computers, it is often women who are more focused on information, because they don't respond to the challenge of getting equipment to submit.

One I had learned the basics, my interest in computers waned. I use it to write books (though I never mastered having it do bibliographies or tables of contents) and write checks (but not balance my checkbook). Much as I'd like to use it to do more, I begrudge the time it would take to learn.

Ralph's computer expertise costs him a lot of time. Chivalry requires that he rescue novices in need, and he is called upon by damsel novices far more often than knaves. More men would rather study the instruction booklet than ask directions, as it were, from another person. "When I do help men," Ralph wrote (on e-mail, of course), "they want to be more involved. I once installed a hard drive for a guy, and he wanted to be there with me, wielding the screwdriver and giving his own advice where he could." Women, he finds, usually are not interested in what he's doing; they just want him to get the computer to the point where they can do what they want.

Which pretty much explains how I managed to be a pioneer without becoming an expert.                   15

### Reflecting and Interpreting

1. How does the author engage the reader at the beginning of the article (refer to Chapter 4 for more information).

2. Does the article use the block or alternating form of organization?

3. How do men's and women's approaches to computers reflect male and female group dynamics?

4. According to the article, how has technology enabled men to communicate more openly?

5. What does Tannen mean by "I managed to be a pioneer without becoming an expert"? How does this statement tie in to the beginning of the article?

### A Writer's Response

1. Consider your approach to computers. Can you relate to either of the approaches mentioned in the article?

2. Consider another form of communications technology (i.e., PDAs, text messaging, etc.). Write an essay comparing or contrasting two approaches to it.

# *Mother Tongue*

## Amy Tan

---

*Born and raised in California, Amy Tan (1952–) graduated from high school in Montreux, Switzerland. She earned a master's degree in linguistics from San Jose State University. Her first novel,* The Joy Luck Club *(1988), brought her international acclaim. Her other works include* The Kitchen God's Wife *(1991),* The Hundred Secret Senses *(1995),* The Bonesetter's Daughter *(2001), and two children's books—*The Moon Lady *and* The Chinese Siamese Cat. *Tan's books have been translated into twenty languages. This essay first appeared in* Threepenny Review *(1989).*

I am not a scholar of English or literature. I cannot give you much more than personal opinions on the English language and its variations in this country or others. [1]

I am a writer. And by that definition, I am someone who has always loved language. I am fascinated by language in daily life. I spend a great deal of my time thinking about the power of language—the way it can evoke an emotion, a visual image, a complex idea, or a simple truth. Language is the tool of my trade. And I use them all—all the Englishes I grew up with.

Recently, I was made keenly aware of the different Englishes I do use. I was giving a talk to a large group of people, the same talk I had already given to half a dozen other groups. The nature of the talk was about my writing, my life, and my book, *The Joy Luck Club.* The talk was going along well enough, until I remembered one major difference that made the whole talk sound wrong. My mother was in the room. And it was perhaps the first time she had heard me give a lengthy speech, using the kind of English I have never used with her. I was saying things like, "The intersection of memory upon imagination" and "There is an aspect of my fiction that relates to thus-and-thus"—a speech filled with carefully wrought grammatical phrases, burdened, it suddenly seemed to me, with nominalized forms, past perfect tenses, conditional phrases, all the forms of standard English that I had learned in school and through books, the forms of English I did not use at home with my mother.

Just last week, I was walking down the street with my mother, and I again found myself conscious of the English I was using, the English I do use with her. We were talking about the price of new and used furniture and I heard myself saying this: "Not waste money that way." My husband was with us as well, and he didn't notice any switch in my English. And then I realized why. It's because over the twenty years we've been together I've often used that same kind of English with him, and sometimes he even uses it with me. It has become our language of intimacy, a different sort of English that relates to family talk, the language I grew up with.

So you'll have some idea of what this family talk I heard sounds like, I'll quote     5
what my mother said during a recent conversation which I videotaped and then
transcribed. During this conversation, my mother was talking about a political
gangster in Shanghai who had the same last name as her family's, Du, and how
the gangster in his early years wanted to be adopted by her family, which was rich
by comparison. Later, the gangster became more powerful, far richer than my
mother's family, and one day showed up at my mother's wedding to pay his respects. Here's what she said in part:

"Du Yusong having business like fruit stand. Like off the street kind. He is
Du like Du Zong—but not Tsung-ming Island people. The local people call pu-
tong, the river east side, he belong to that side local people. That man want to
ask Du Zong father take him in like become own family. Du Zong father wasn't
look down on him, but didn't take seriously, until that man big like become a
mafia. Now important person, very hard to inviting him. Chinese way, came only
to show respect, don't stay for dinner. Respect for making big celebration, he
shows up. Mean gives lots of respect. Chinese custom. Chinese social life that way.
If too important won't have to stay too long. He come to my wedding. I
didn't see, I heard it. I gone to boy's side, they have YMCA dinner. Chinese age I
was nineteen."

You should know that my mother's expressive command of English belies
how much she actually understands. She reads the *Forbes* report, listens to *Wall
Street Week*, converses daily with her stockbroker, reads all of Shirley MacLaine's
books with ease—all kinds of things I can't begin to understand. Yet some of my
friends tell me they understand 50 percent of what my mother says. Some say
they understand 80 to 90 percent. Some say they understand none of it, as if she
were speaking pure Chinese. But to me, my mother's English is perfectly clear,
perfectly natural. It's my mother tongue. Her language, as I hear it, is vivid, direct,
full of observation and imagery. That was the language that helped shape the way
I saw things, expressed things, made sense of the world.

Lately, I've been giving more thought to the kind of English my mother
speaks. Like others, I have described it to people as "broken" or "fractured" English. But I wince when I say that. It has always bothered me that I can think of no
way to describe it other than "broken," as if it were damaged and needed to be
fixed, as if it lacked a certain wholeness and soundness. I've heard other terms
used, "limited English," for example. But they seem just as bad, as if everything is
limited, including people's perceptions of the limited English speaker.

I know this for a fact, because when I was growing up, my mother's "limited"
English limited *my* perception of her. I was ashamed of her English. I believed that
her English reflected the quality of what she had to say. That is, because she expressed them imperfectly her thoughts were imperfect. And I had plenty of em-
pirical evidence to support me: the fact that people in department stores, at banks,
and at restaurants did not take her seriously, did not give her good service, pre-
tended not to understand her, or even acted as if they did not hear her.

My mother has long realized the limitations of her English as well. When I    10
was fifteen, she used to have me call people on the phone to pretend I was she. In
this guise, I was forced to ask for information or even to complain and yell at people who had been rude to her. One time it was a call to her stockbroker in New
York. She had cashed out her small portfolio and it just so happened we were going to go to New York the next week, our very first trip outside California. I had
to get on the phone and say in an adolescent voice that was not very convincing,
"This is Mrs. Tan."

And my mother was standing in the back whispering loudly, "Why he don't
send me check, already two weeks late. So mad he lie to me, losing me money."

And then I said in perfect English, "Yes, I'm getting rather concerned. You had
agreed to send the check two weeks ago, but it hasn't arrived."

Then she began to talk more loudly. "What he want, I come to New York tell
him front of his boss, you cheating me?" And I was trying to calm her down, make
her be quiet, while telling the stockbroker, "I can't tolerate any more excuses. If I
don't receive the check immediately, I am going to have to speak to your manager
when I'm in New York next week." And sure enough, the following week there
we were in front of this astonished stockbroker, and I was sitting there redfaced
and quiet, and my mother, the real Mrs. Tan, was shouting at his boss in her impeccable broken English.

We used a similar routine just five days ago, for a situation that was far less
humorous. My mother had gone to the hospital for an appointment, to find out
about a benign brain tumor a CAT scan had revealed a month ago. She said she
had spoken very good English, her best English, no mistakes. Still, she said, the
hospital did not apologize when they said they had lost the CAT scan and she had
come for nothing. She said they did not seem to have any sympathy when she told
them she was anxious to know the exact diagnosis, since her husband and son had
both died of brain tumors. She said they would not give her any more information until the next time and she would have to make another appointment for
that. So she said she would not leave until the doctor called her daughter. She
wouldn't budge. And when the doctor finally called her daughter, me, who spoke
in perfect English—lo and behold—we had assurances the CAT scan would be
found, promise that a conference call on Monday would be held, and apologies
for any suffering my mother had gone through for a most regrettable mistake.

I think my mother's English almost had an effect on limiting my possibilities    15
in life as well. Sociologists and linguists probably will tell you that a person's developing language skills are more influenced by peers. But I do think that the language spoken in the family, especially in immigrant families which are more in-
sular, plays a large role in shaping the language of the child. And I believe that it
affected my results on achievement tests, IQ tests, and the SAT. While my English
skills were never judged as poor, compared to math, English could not be considered my strong suit. In grade school I did moderately well, getting perhaps B's,
sometimes B-pluses, in English and scoring perhaps in the sixtieth or seventieth
percentile on achievement tests. But those scores were not good enough to over-

ride the opinion that my true abilities lay in math and science, because in those areas I achieved A's and scored in the ninetieth percentile or higher.

This was understandable. Math is precise; there is only one correct answer. Whereas, for me at least, the answers on English tests were always a judgment call, a matter of opinion and personal experience. Those tests were constructed around items like fill-in-the-blank sentence completion, such as, "Even though Tom was _____, Mary thought he was _____." And the correct answer always seemed to be the most bland combinations of thoughts, for example, "Even though Tom was shy, Mary thought he was charming," with the grammatical structure "even though" limiting the correct answer to some sort of semantic opposites, so you wouldn't get answers like, "Even though Tom was foolish, Mary thought he was ridiculous." Well, according to my mother, there were very few limitations as to what Tom could have been and what Mary might have thought of him. So I never did well on tests like that.

The same was true with word analogies, pairs of words in which you were supposed to find some sort of logical, semantic relationship—for example, "*Sunset* is to *nightfall* as _____ is to _____." And here you would be presented with a list of four possible pairs, one of which showed the same kind of relationship: *red* is to *stoplight, bus* is to *arrival, chills* is to *fever, yawn* is to *boring.* Well, I could never think that way. I knew what the tests were asking, but I could not block out of my mind the images already created by the first pair, "*sunset* is to *nightfall*"—and I would see a burst of color against a darkening sky, the moon rising, the lowering of a curtain of stars. And all the other pairs of words—red, bus, stoplight, boring— just threw up a mass of confusing images, making it impossible for me to sort out something as logical as saying: "A sunset precedes nightfall" is the same as "a chill precedes a fever." The only way I would have gotten that answer right would have been to imagine an associative situation, for example, by being disobedient and staying out past sunset, catching a chill at night which turns into feverish pneumonia as punishment, which indeed did happen to me.

I have been thinking about all this lately, about my mother's English, about achievement tests. Because lately I've been asked, as a writer, why there are not more Asian Americans represented in American literature. Why are there few Asian Americans enrolled in creative writing programs? Why do so many Chinese students go into engineering? Well, these are broad sociological questions I can't begin to answer. But I have noticed in surveys—in fact, just last week—that Asian students, as a whole, always do significantly better on math achievement tests than in English. And this makes me think that there are other Asian-American students whose English spoken in the home might also be described as "broken" or "limited." And perhaps they also have teachers who are steering them away from writing and into math and science, which is what happened to me.

Fortunately, I happen to be rebellious in nature and enjoy the challenge of disproving assumptions made about me. I became an English major my first year in college, after being enrolled as pre-med. I started writing nonfiction as a freelancer the week after I was told by my former boss that writing was my worst skill and I should hone my talents toward account management.

But it wasn't until 1985 that I finally began to write fiction. And at first I    20
wrote using what I thought to be wittily crafted sentences, sentences that would finally prove I had mastery over the English language. Here's an example from the first draft of a story that later made its way into *The Joy Luck Club*, but without this line: "That was my mental quandary in its nascent state." A terrible line, which I can hardly pronounce.

Fortunately, for reasons I won't get into today, I later decided I should envision a reader for the stories I would write. And the reader I decided upon was my mother, because these were stories about mothers. So with this reader in mind— and in fact she did read my early drafts—I began to write stories using all the Englishes I grew up with: the English I spoke to my mother, which for lack of a better term might be described as "simple"; the English she used with me, which for lack of a better term might be described as "broken"; my translation of her Chinese, which could certainly be described as "watered down"; and what I imagine to be her translation of her Chinese if she could speak in perfect English, her internal language, and for that I sought to preserve the essence, but neither an English nor a Chinese structure. I wanted to capture what language ability tests can never reveal: her intent, her passion, her imagery, the rhythms of her speech and the nature of her thoughts.

Apart from what any critic had to say about my writing, I knew I had succeeded where it counted when my mother finished reading my book and gave me her verdict: "So easy to read."

## Reflecting and Interpreting

1. Note how the author opens the first two paragraphs. What parallel pattern does she use to precede the definition? ("I am not . . . I am.") What technique is this?

2. How does Amy Tan define *writer*?

3. How did her mother's English influence Amy?

4. Amy Tan and her husband sometimes use her "mother's tongue" to communicate when they are alone. Why?

5. Does Amy's mother's English reflect the depth of her understanding of the language? How do you know?

6. How do the public and hospital employees react to Mrs. Tan's broken English?

7. What does Amy Tan notice about math and English test scores of Asian students? How does this affect course scheduling in high schools?

8. How does Amy Tan react to disillusionment?

9. What advantages does Standard English have over broken English?

10. If this essay had been written in third person by a biographer, how would that change have affected the essay?

## *A Writer's Response*

1. Have you ever turned disillusionment or failure into something positive? Write an essay describing how you achieved this feat.

2. *Small Groups:* How many tips for good writing can you glean from this essay?

# Definition

## Identifying Basic Characteristics

## On Being 17, Bright, and Unable to Read

David Raymond

*Someone who has experienced a disability can give an insider's view, providing insights that increase an outsider's understanding in a way that a technical definition cannot. David Raymond was still in high school when his essay on dyslexia was published in the* New York Times. *Dyslexics think in pictures and experience problems in perceiving letters or numbers. Words may appear jumbled, upside down, backwards, or in other ways that hinder reading. Symptoms vary in range and intensity. Special programs are now available to help dyslexics.*

One day a substitute teacher picked me to read aloud from the textbook. When    1
I told her "No, thank you," she came unhinged. She thought I was acting smart, and told me so. I kept calm, and that got her madder and madder. We must have spent 10 minutes trying to solve the problem, and finally she got so red in the face I thought she'd blow up. She told me she'd see me after class.

Maybe someone like me was a new thing for that teacher. But she wasn't new to me. I've been through scenes like that all my life. You see, even though I'm 17 and a junior in high school, I can't read because I have dyslexia. I'm told I read "at a fourth-grade level," but from where I sit, that's not reading. You can't know what that means unless you've been there. It's not easy to tell how it feels when you can't read your homework assignments or the newspaper or a menu in a restaurant or even notes from your own friends.

My family began to suspect I was having problems almost from the first day I started school. My father says my early years in school were the worst years of his life. They weren't so good for me, either. As I look back on it now, I can't find the words to express how bad it really was. I wanted to die. I'd come home from school screaming, "I'm dumb. I'm dumb—I wish I were dead!"

I guess I couldn't read anything at all then—not even my own name—and they tell me I didn't talk as good as other kids. But what I remember about those days is that I couldn't throw a ball where it was supposed to go, I couldn't learn to swim, and I wouldn't learn to ride a bike, because no matter what anyone told me, I knew I'd fail.

Sometimes my teachers would try to be encouraging. When I couldn't read     5
the words on the board they'd say, "Come on, David, you know that word." Only I didn't. And it was embarrassing. I just felt dumb. And dumb was how the kids treated me. They'd make fun of me every chance they got, asking me to spell "cat" or something like that. Even if I knew how to spell it, I wouldn't; they'd only give me another word. Anyway, it was awful, because more than anything I wanted friends. On my birthday when I blew out the candles I didn't wish I could learn to read; what I wished for was that the kids would like me.

With the bad reports coming from school, and with me moaning about wanting to die and how everybody hated me, my parents began looking for help. That's when the testing started. The school tested me, the child-guidance center tested me, private psychiatrists tested me. Everybody knew something was wrong—especially me.

It didn't help much when they stuck a fancy name onto it. I couldn't pronounce it then—I was only in second grade—and I was ashamed to talk about it. Now it rolls off my tongue, because I've been living with it for a lot of years— dyslexia.

All through elementary school it wasn't easy. I was always having to do things that were "different," things the other kids didn't have to do. I had to go to a child psychiatrist, for instance.

One summer my family forced me to go to a camp for children with reading problems. I hated the idea, but the camp turned out pretty good, and I had a good time. I met a lot of kids who couldn't read and somehow that helped. The director of the camp said I had a higher I.Q. than 90 percent of the population. I didn't believe him.

About the worst thing I had to do in fifth and sixth grade was go to a special     10
education class in another school in our town. A bus picked me up, and I didn't like that at all. The bus also picked up emotionally disturbed kids and retarded kids. It was like going to a school for the retarded. I always worried that someone I knew would see me on that bus. It was a relief to go to the regular junior high school.

Life began to change a little for me then, because I began to feel better about myself. I found the teachers cared; they had meetings about me and I worked harder for them for a while. I began to work on the potter's wheel, making vases and pots that the teachers said were pretty good. Also, I got a letter for being on the track team. I could always run pretty fast.

At high school the teachers are good and everyone is trying to help me. I've gotten honors some marking periods and I've won a letter on the cross-country team. Next quarter I think the school might hold a show of my pottery. I've got some friends. But there are still some embarrassing times. For instance, every time there is writing in the class, I get up and go to the special education room. Kids ask me where I go all the time. Sometimes I say, "to Mars."

Homework is a real problem. During free periods in school I go into the special ed room and staff members read assignments to me. When I get home my mother reads to me. Sometimes she reads an assignment into a tape recorder, and then I go into my room and listen to it. If we have a novel or something like that to read, she reads it out loud to me. Then I sit down with her and we do the assignment. She'll write, while I talk my answers to her. Lately I've taken to dictating into a tape recorder, and then someone—my father, a private tutor or my mother—types up what I've dictated. Whatever homework I do takes someone else's time, too. That makes me feel bad.

We had a big meeting in school the other day—eight of us, four from the guidance department, my private tutor, my parents and me. The subject was me. I said I wanted to go to college, and they told me about colleges that have facilities and staff to handle people like me. That's nice to hear.

As for what happens after college, I don't know and I'm worried about that.    15
How can I make a living if I can't read? Who will hire me? How will I fill out the application form? The only thing that gives me any courage is the fact that I've learned about well-known people who couldn't read or had other problems and still made it. Like Albert Einstein, who didn't talk until he was 4 and flunked math. Like Leonardo da Vinci, who everyone seems to think had dyslexia.

I've told this story because maybe some teacher will read it and go easy on a kid in the classroom who has what I've got. Or, maybe some parent will stop nagging his kid, and stop calling him lazy. Maybe he's not lazy or dumb. Maybe he just can't read and doesn't know what's wrong. Maybe he's scared, like I was.

## Reflecting and Interpreting

1. Rather than calling on one person to read, what might the teacher have done?
2. At no point does the author give the technical definition of dyslexia. Should he? What is the effect of this omission?
3. What is dyslexia? Does it vary in the way it affects people?
4. What experience was a turning point for David? How did it help?
5. What changes occurred in David's life during junior high school?
6. Why is he confident that he can graduate from college? What does he fear?
7. Why does he mention Albert Einstein and Leonardo da Vinci?
8. David includes many colloquialisms in the essay. How do "blow up" and "didn't talk as good as other kids" affect the tone?
9. What is the author's purpose in writing the essay?
10. What factor do you think is most influential in David's or anyone's success?

*A Writer's Response*

Have you had a long, difficult experience that makes you somewhat of an expert? Write an essay that gives an insider's view. If you haven't, perhaps a close family member has. How did the problem affect you and other family members?

# The Sweet Smell of Success Isn't All That Sweet

Laurence Shames

*Dozens of definitions of "success" reverberate across our culture, influencing our values and choice of careers. In this essay, Laurence Shames mentions several current definitions of that illusive concept, but he believes that a "noble failure" is better. Shames, a graduate of New York University, is best known for his eight mystery novels, of which* Mangrove Squeeze *(1998),* Welcome to Paradise *(1999), and* The Naked Detective *(2001) are the latest. He has also written nonfiction for* McCall's, Saturday Review, Vanity Fair, The New York Times, *and others. His two nonfiction works,* The Big Time: The Harvard Business School's Most Successful Class and How It Shaped America *(1986) and* The Hunger for More: Searching for Values in an Age of Greed *(1991) reveal his concern with values.*

John Milton was a failure. In writing "Paradise Lost," his stated aim was to "justify      1
the ways of God to men." Inevitably, he fell short of accomplishing that and only wrote a monumental poem. Beethoven, whose music was conceived to transcend Fate, was a failure, as was Socrates, whose ambition was to make people happy by making them reasonable and just. The inescapable conclusion seems to be that the surest, noblest way to fail is to set one's own standards titanically high.

The flip-side of that proposition also seems true, and it provides the safe but dreary logic by which most of us live: The surest way to succeed is to keep one's strivings low—or at least to direct them along already charted paths. Don't set yourself the probably thankless task of making the legal system better; just shoot at becoming a partner in the firm. Don't agonize over questions about where your talents and proclivities might most fulfillingly lead you; just do a heads-up job of determining where the educational or business opportunities seem most secure.

After all, if "success" itself—rather than the substance of the achievements that make for success—is the criterion by which we measure ourselves and from which we derive our self-esteem, why make things more difficult by reaching for the stars?

What is this contemporary version of success really all about?

According to certain beer commercials, it consists in moving up to a premium      5
brand that costs a dime or so more per bottle. Credit-card companies would have you believe success inheres in owning their particular piece of plastic.

If these examples sound petty, they are. But take those petty privileges, weave them into a fabric that passes for a value system and what you've got is a national mood that has vast motivating power that can shape at least the near future of the entire country.

Under the flag of success, modern-style, liberal arts colleges are withering while business schools are burgeoning—and yet even business schools are having an increasingly hard time finding faculty members, because teaching isn't considered "successful" enough. Amid a broad consensus that there is a glut of lawyers and an epidemic of strangling litigation, record numbers of young people continue to flock to law school because, for the individual practitioner, a law degree is still considered a safe ticket.

The most sobering thought of all is that today's M.B.A.'s and lawyers are tomorrow's M.B.A.'s and lawyers: Having invested so much time and money in their training, only a tiny percentage of them will ever opt out of their early chosen fields. Decisions made in accordance with today's hothouse notions of ambition are locking people into careers that will define and also limit their activities and yearnings for virtually the rest of their lives.

Many, by external standards, will be "successes." They will own homes, eat in better restaurants, dress well and, in some instances, perform socially useful work. Yet there is a deadening and dangerous flaw in their philosophy: It has little room, little sympathy and less respect for the noble failure, for the person who ventures past the limits, who aims gloriously high and falls unashamedly short.

That sort of ambition doesn't have much place in a world where success is    10 proved by worldly reward rather than by accomplishment itself. That sort of ambition is increasingly thought of as the domain of irredeemable eccentrics, of people who haven't quite caught on—and there is great social pressure not to be one of them.

The result is that fewer people are drawn to the cutting edge of noncommercial scientific research. Fewer are taking on the sublime, unwinnable challenges of the arts. Fewer are asking questions that matter—the ones that can't be answered. Fewer are putting themselves on the line, making as much of their minds and talents as they might.

The irony is that today's success-chasers seem obsessed with the idea of *not settling.* They take advanced degrees in business because they won't settle for just a so-so job. They compete for slots at law firms and investment houses because they won't settle for any but the fastest track. They seem to regard it as axiomatic that "success" and "settling" are opposites.

Yet in doggedly pursuing the rather brittle species of success now in fashion, they are restricting themselves to a chokingly narrow swath of turf along the entire range of human possibilities. Does it ever occur to them that, frequently, success is what people settle for when they can't think of something noble enough to be worth failing at?

## Reflecting and Interpreting

1. Consider the way the three examples in the first paragraph are presented. How would you describe the writer's voice?

2. What kind of success is described in the second paragraph?

3. How is success related to self-esteem? Is one's perception of oneself and one's success always realistic? Why?

4. What does Shames mean by "noble failure"? What assumptions does he make?

5. He points out a "great social pressure" to be a success in the eyes of the world. Do you see a greater pressure that influences you and your friends?

6. How do you reconcile his example of "reaching for the stars" by "making the legal system better" (paragraph 2) with his apparent disdain in paragraph 9, where he includes "perform socially useful tasks"?

7. Examine paragraph 11. What factors influence people to take on the challenge that he speaks of?

8. What strategies of exposition are used in this essay?

9. How would you summarize Shames's definition of success?

10. His definition of success seems limited to an either/or proposition. Do you agree or disagree? Why?

## A Writer's Response

Write an essay defining your vision of success. How do you measure success? What internal and external rewards are included in your definition?

# Cause and Effect

## Explaining Why

## *Saving the Earth*

David Suzuki

*David Suzuki is Canada's best-known science broadcaster, working in radio, print, and on television. He has been described as "one of the world's most effective popularizers of science, alongside Carl Sagan and Jacques Cousteau." In this article, David Suzuki argues that the earth cannot possibly sustain our consumer lifestyles, and suggests how we might re-evaluate our priorities.*

*An award-winning scientist and broadcaster, David Suzuki has become a living symbol to Canadians of concern for the environment. Based in Vancouver, he has for almost 30 years explained life on earth as host of such programs as the long-running CBC-TV series The Nature of Things and his CBC Radio series, From Naked Ape to Superspecies. In this essay, he delivers a passionate warning to people that the earth cannot sustain their consumption-driven lifestyles, and a plea to focus on real values.*     1

In recent years, if you've been able to look beyond the media obsession with celebrity, violence and sex, you may have begun to realize that the planet is undergoing cataclysmic and unprecedented change. Ironically, in 1992, the year the largest gathering of heads of state in human history met at the Earth Summit in Rio de Janeiro to take concrete steps towards a sustainable future, the Canadian government was forced to acknowledge the unthinkable: the vast shoals of northern cod that had supported people for hundreds of years had all but disappeared. Since then, record floods have hit Quebec and Manitoba, flash fires spread across Alberta, and an ice storm ravaged parts of Ontario and Quebec, knocking out electricity for weeks. Rates of breast and testicular cancer, asthma and lymphoma have reached epidemic levels and continue to rise. Hurricane Mitch wiped out thousands of people in Central America while heat waves killed 700 people in Chicago and thousands in India. Insurance companies have paid in the 1990s close to four times the weather-related claims in the entire decade of the 1980s. Can we continue to believe these are all just random, isolated events?

But the media have been mesmerized by the spectacular rise in Dow Jones averages, megamergers and record profits, as well as the catastrophic disintegration of economies from Japan to Brazil. Rachel Carson's seminal 1962 book *Silent Spring* created an enormous wave of awareness and concern about the environment that grew to a peak in Rio in 1992. But since then, the economy has become our dominant preoccupation. We are bludgeoned by the relentless mantra of buzzwords like globalization and free trade, debt and deficit, competitiveness, profitability, inflation and interest rates. So where are we heading? As we approach the end of a millennium, the only way we can gain an intimation of where we are going is by reflecting on where we have come from.

I was born in 1936, when the human population of the entire planet was around 2 billion. In my lifetime, the number of human beings has tripled. In the year of my birth, the population of Vancouver was 253,000, of Calgary 83,000, and Toronto 645,000. Back then, more than 95 percent of the world's forests were still intact and pristine while vast areas of Africa, the Amazon and Papua New Guinea were yet to be penetrated by people from the industrialized world. As a child in British Columbia, I hiked through virgin forests, drank from any creek without a second thought and ate raw food pulled directly from the soil or off a tree.

My family moved to London, Ont., in 1949 when the city had a population    5 of 70,000. We had been impoverished by the war and I spent a lot of time fishing in the Thames River to help feed the family. For me, it wasn't work. Walking the banks of the Thames, I had some of my most memorable experiences with nature. My grandparents owned a farm just outside the city where I spent many happy days hunting freshwater clams or turtles in their creek or watching foxes and pheasants in the fields. Often, I would stop off at a nearby swamp where I would find salamander eggs, catch frogs or collect insects. Those were magical times, imprinting an indelible love of nature that let to a career in biology.

Today, I return to a very different London, a rapidly growing, vibrant city that boasts more than 300,000 inhabitants. But the Thames River is so polluted, people recoil in horror at the notion of eating a fish from it. The only things my grandparents' farm now grows are highrise apartments, while the creek runs invisibly through underground culverts. The magical swamp that captivated me as a boy is covered over with an enormous shopping centre and large parking lot. So where do London's youth find their inspiration today? From grazing through malls filled with consumer items, playing Nintendo games or surfing the Net? The world of young people now is a human-created one that celebrates the inventiveness and productivity of human beings. But there is no way that human ingenuity can match the incredible wonder, magnificence and inspiration of the natural world four billion years in the making. That is not a put-down of our species; it is simply a recognition of the complexity and interconnectedness in nature that we barely comprehend.

Human beings are a remarkable species. We emerged along the Rift Valley in Africa a mere quarter of a million years ago. In evolutionary terms, we are an infant species gifted with a complex brain that is our major survival attribute. That brain conferred curiosity, memory and inventiveness, which more than compensated for our lack of speed, strength or sensory acuity. Today, we have become the most numerous and ubiquitous mammal on the planet.

In this century, our species has undergone explosive change. Not only are we adding a quarter of a million people to our numbers every day, we have vastly amplified our technological muscle power. When I was born, there were no computers, televisions, jet planes, oral contraceptives, transoceanic phone calls, satellites, transistors or xerography, just to mention a few. Children today look at typewriters, vinyl records and black-and-white televisions as ancient curiosities. Taken together, this technology has dramatically increased the impact of each human being on earth.

In the second part of this century, one of the great insights from biology resulted from the application of molecular techniques to examine specific genes within individuals. To our amazement, when a creature such as a fruit fly was studied, genes were found to exist in many different forms. Even though such species were highly evolved to occupy specific environmental niches, they did not become homogeneous; instead, they maintained a wide array of gene forms. The phenomenon is known as genetic polymorphism, and we now understand that this is the key to a species' resilience. Over the broad sweep of evolutionary time, the environment is constantly changing. A genetic combination that might be well-suited for one environment might not do as well when conditions change, while other, less favourable gene forms might flourish under the altered conditions. So long as the species as a whole carries diverse genes, combinations better suited to the new circumstances can be selected out when conditions change.

In the same way, it is thought that species diversity within ecosystems, and 10 ecosystem diversity around the world, help to explain life's incredible tenacity under different conditions and volatile surroundings. Planetary conditions have changed tremendously over the four billion years that life has existed—the sun is 25 per cent hotter, poles have reversed and then changed back, continents have moved and smashed together, ice ages have come and gone—yet species have not only survived, they have flourished, and much of that is due to diversity. The converse of genetic polymorphism is monoculture; that is, the spreading of a single genetic stock or species over a broad area. We have learned expensively in fisheries, forestry and agriculture that monoculture creates vulnerability to new infections, disease or altered environmental conditions.

Human beings have added another level of diversity, namely culture, to the equation of adaptability. It is diverse cultures that have enabled our species to survive in so many ecosystems, from the Arctic to the equator. In this wonderful array of cultures, there were many different notions of wealth, purpose in life and cosmic meaning. Today, that has changed dramatically: one kind of economics is hailed as the source of all wealth and material well-being. This notion is based on perceiving the entire planet as the source of resources while all people in the world form a potential market. But if we live in a finite world, then all resources have limits and prudence demands that we recognize the existence and extent of those limits.

No one person, company or government sets out to deliberately trash our surroundings, yet the collective effect of human numbers, technology and consumption is corroding the life-support systems of the planet. That pronouncement is not the rant of an eco-catastrophist; it is the conclusion reached by leading members of the scientific profession. In November, 1992, more than half of all living Nobel Prize winners signed a document called "World Scientists' Warning to Humanity" that began wit this stark statement:

> Human beings and the natural world are on a collision course. Human activities inflict harsh and often irreversible damage on the environment and on critical resources. If not checked, many of our current practices put at serious risk the future we wish for human society.

Scientists are extremely cautious when making pronouncements to the general public, so this was a most unusual alarm call. The warning went on to list the areas where the crises exist and the measures needed to avoid a catastrophe. The document then grew more ominous and urgent: "No more than one or a few decades remain before the chance to avert the threats we now confront will be lost and the prospects for humanity immeasurably diminished." It is puzzling to me that we seem frantic to know the most intimate details about O.J. Simpson, Diana, Princess of Wales, or Monica Lewinsky and consume pronouncements by Bill Gates, Larry King or Oprah Winfrey as if they are gospel. But when more than half of the Nobel laureates warn of an impending but avoidable disaster, we are too busy to take notice.

Humanity has repeatedly demonstrated a capacity to respond heroically and    15 immediately to a crisis. Hurricanes, floods, fire or earthquakes elicit remarkable responses. After Pearl Harbor, there was only one choice in North America, to respond and win. There was no debate about whether we could afford an all-out war effort or what the results of not responding might be. In biological terms, the globe is experiencing an eco-holocaust, as more than 50,000 species vanish annually and air, water and soil are poisoned with civilization's effluents. The great challenge of the millenium is recognizing the reality of impending ecological collapse, and the urgent need to get on with taking the steps to avoid it.

But our obsession with economics has become an impediment to taking appropriate action. I have often been told, "Listen, Suzuki, we have to pay for all those parks and environmental cleanups. We can't afford to protect the environment if we don't have a strong, growing economy," or words to that effect. That sentiment flows from a belief that the economy provides us with all of our products, from food to oil to manufactured goods. This is nonsense, of course. Everything that we depend on, whether it is cars, popcorn or computers, comes from the earth and will eventually end up going back to it. It is the biosphere, that thin layer of air, water and soil within which life exists, that creates the earth's productivity and abundance that, in turn, make economies and our lives possible.

But now, ignoring evolution's priceless lesson about the value of diversity, we are monoculturing the planet with a single notion of progress and development that is embodied in the globalized economy. As all nations rush to carve out a place in this construct, we tie our entire future to it. But what if, as many believe, it's based on mistaken notions or assumptions? What will we have to fall back on?

It is widely believed that trade enables human beings to exceed the ability of a certain region to support its inhabitants. Thus, Canadians can acquire Panamanian bananas, Turkish rugs or Japanese electronic products by trading for them with resources or products that are plentiful in Canada. But the reality is that we still require the earth to generate our food, clothing and shelter and to absorb and detoxify our wastes. Trade enables us to co-opt someone else's land to provide goods for us. Adding up the total amount of land (and ocean) required to provide our annual needs, ecologist Bill Rees of the University of British Columbia has calculated that every Canadian (and inhabitant of an industrialized country) now requires the production from seven to eight hectares. If every human being on the planet aspired to a comparable level of prosperity, it would take between five and six more planets! Even if we ignore the entire developing world, we in the wealthy nations already consume more than the earth can provide sustainably. We are blinded from seeing the alternate ecological imperative that demands that we pull back and slow down.

I suggest the following thought exercise can help to get our priorities in order. Imagine that you have lived a full and rich life and are now on your deathbed. As you reflect back on life, what memories fill you with happiness, pride and satisfaction? I suspect it will not be the latest designer clothing, a huge house, a sport utility vehicle or a Sony entertainment centre. In fact, what makes life worthwhile and joyful is not "stuff" that can be bought with money. The most important things are family, friends, community and the sharing, caring and co-operating together that enhances the quality of all of our lives.

There are several reasons we are failing to see the urgency of what is happening. A few of them are:          20

1)  Most people alive today were born after 1950 and thus have lived all their lives during a period of spectacular, unprecedented and unsustainable growth and change. But for most of us, this is all we've ever known and it seems normal. Rapid change also brings rapid collective forgetfulness, and memories of what the world once was quickly fade.

2)  Most people now live in the human-created environment of big cities where it's easy to believe the illusion that we have escaped our biological dependence on the natural world.

3)  The explosive increase in information shatters the world into fragments devoid of the history or context that might explain their relevance, importance or significance. In order to attract attention, stories or reports become shorter and increasingly shrill, sensational or violent.

4)  Political "vision" is focused on re-election and fulfilling the special demands of campaign funders. Political promises are contradicted with little fear or reprisal amid the cacaphony of immediate crises and short-term electoral memory.

5)  In a global economy freed from the constraints of national boundaries or regulations, the search for maximal profit in minimal time has little allowance for long-term sustainability of local communities.

6) The great public faith that "they"—scientists and technologists—will resolve our problems is simply unwarranted. While technology can be impressive, our knowledge of the complexity and interconnectivity in the real world is so limited, our "solutions" have little hope of long-term success. For example, we have no idea how to replace or mitigate thousands of species now extinct, substitute for pollination once done by insects killed by pesticides, or repair the ozone layer.

We can't carry on with business as usual if we wish to avoid an increasingly uncertain and volatile world. The signs are everywhere. But if "experts" lack credibility, try talking to any elder about what fish, birds or woods were like when they were young. Then extrapolate ahead from the changes they have lived through to the kind of world our children and grandchildren will have if we continue along the same path.

What are our real basic needs in order to live rich and fulfilling lives? I believe there is no dichotomy between environmental and social needs. Hungry people will not care if their actions endanger an edible species or an important habitat. Unemployment, injustice or insecurity lead to desperation and the need to survive at all costs. To protect an environment for future generations, we have to build a society on a foundation of clean air, water, soil and energy and rich biodiversity to fulfil our biological needs; we have to ensure full employment, justice and security for all communities to serve our social needs; and we have to retain sacred places, a sense of belonging and connectedness with nature and a knowledge that there are cosmic forces beyond our comprehension or control, to satisfy our spiritual requirements. Then, we can work on the best kind of economy to construct from there. Right now, we seem to be trying to shoehorn everything into the constraints dictated by the economy without establishing the fundamental bottom line.

## Reflecting and Interpreting

1. What is the purpose of the opening paragraph?

2. According to Suzuki, what is human beings' "major survival attribute"?

3. Suzuki argues that diversity is essential to survival; what, then, would be the implications of globalization of the world's economies?

4. What, according to Suzuki, is unsustainable about global trade?

5. Do you agree with Suzuki's claim that we are more concerned with celebrities' statements than with those of Nobel scientists? What would Suzuki claim is the cause of this?

## A Writer's Response

Suzuki compares his childhood haunts with those children can find today. Consider your childhood, and write an essay about how your childhood experiences affect your perception of nature today.

# Why Marriages Fail

## Anne Roiphe

*Born in New York City, Anne Roiphe graduated from Sarah Lawrence College with a BA degree. In the past four decades, she has published a dozen fiction and nonfiction books, as well as collaborated on several others. Her latest works include* If You Knew Me *(1995),* Lovingkindness *(1997),* Fruitful: Living the Contradictions: A Memoir of Modern Motherhood *(1997),* For Rabbit, with Love and Squalor: An American Read *(2000), and* 1185 Park Avenue: a Memoir *(2000). In this essay, which first appeared in* Family Weekly *(27 Feb. 1983), she analyzes the factors that lead to divorce.*

These days so many marriages end in divorce that our most sacred vows no longer     1
ring with truth. "Happily ever after" and "Till death do us part" are expressions that
seem on the way to becoming obsolete. Why has it become so hard for couples to
stay together? What goes wrong? What has happened to us that close to one-half
of all marriages are destined for the divorce courts? How could we have created
a society in which 42 percent of our children will grow up in single parent homes?
If statistics could only measure loneliness, regret, pain, loss of self-confidence and
fear of the future, the numbers would be beyond quantifying.

Even though each broken marriage is unique, we can still find the common
perils, the common causes for marital despair. Each marriage has crisis points and
each marriage tests endurance, the capacity for both intimacy and change. Outside pressures such as job loss, illness, infertility, trouble with a child, care of aging parents and all the other plagues of life hit marriage the way hurricanes blast
our shores. Some marriages survive these storms and others don't. Marriages fail,
however, not simply because of the outside weather but because the inner climate
becomes too hot or too cold, too turbulent or too stupefying.

When we look at how we choose our partners and what expectations exist at
the tender beginnings of romance, some of the reasons for disaster become quite
clear. We all select with unconscious accuracy a mate who will recreate with us
the emotional patterns of our first homes. Dr. Carl A. Whitaker, a marital thera-
pist and emeritus professor of psychiatry at the University of Wisconsin explains,
"From early childhood on, each of us carried models for marriage, femininity, masculinity, motherhood, fatherhood and all the other family roles." Each of us falls
in love with a mate who has qualities of our parents, who will help us rediscover
both the psychological happiness and miseries of our past lives. We may think we
have found a man unlike Dad, but then he turns to drink or drugs, or loses his job
over and over again or sits silently in front of the T.V. just the way Dad did. A man
may choose a woman who doesn't like kids just like his mother or who gambles
away the family savings just like his mother. Or he may choose a slender wife who

seems unlike his obese mother but then turns out to have other addictions that destroy their mutual happiness.

A man and a woman bring to their marriage bed a blended concoction of conscious and unconscious memories of their parents' lives together. The human way is to compulsively repeat and recreate the patterns of the past. Sigmund Freud so well described the unhappy design that many of us get trapped in: the unmet needs of childhood, the angry feelings left over from frustrations of long ago, the limits of trust and the recurrence of old fears. Once an individual senses this entrapment, there may follow a yearning to escape, and the result could be a broken, splintered marriage.

Of course people can overcome the habits and attitudes that developed in     5
childhood. We all have hidden strengths and amazing capacities for growth and creative change. Change, however, requires work—observing your part in a rotten pattern, bringing difficulties out into the open—and work runs counter to the basic myth of marriage: "When I wed this person all my problems will be over. I will have achieved success and I will become the center of life for this other person and this person will be my center, and we will mean everything to each other forever." This myth, which every marriage relies on, is soon exposed. The coming of children, the pulls and tugs of their demands on affection and time, place a considerable strain on that basic myth of meaning everything to each other, of merging together and solving all of life's problems.

Concern and tension about money take each partner away from the other. Obligations to demanding parents or still-depended-upon parents create further strain. Couples today must also deal with all the cultural changes brought on in recent years by the women's movement and the sexual revolution. The altering of roles and the shifting of responsibilities have been extremely trying for many marriages.

These and other realities of life erode the visions of marital bliss the way sandstorms eat at rock and the ocean nibbles away at the dunes. Those euphoric, grand feelings that accompany romantic love are really self-delusions, self-hypnotic dreams that enable us to forge a relationship. Real life, failure at work, disappointments, exhaustion, bad smells, bad colds and hard times all puncture the dream and leave us stranded with our mate, with our childhood patterns pushing us this way and that, with our unfulfilled expectations.

The struggle to survive in marriage requires adaptability, flexibility, genuine love and kindness and an imagination strong enough to feel what the other is feeling. Many marriages fall apart because either partner cannot imagine what the other wants or cannot communicate what he or she needs or feels. Anger builds until it erupts into a volcanic burst that buries the marriage in ash.

It is not hard to see, therefore, how essential communication is for a good marriage. A man and a woman must be able to tell each other how they feel and why they feel the way they do; otherwise they will impose on each other roles and actions that lead to further unhappiness. In some cases, the communication patterns of childhood—of not talking, of talking too much, of not listening, of distrust and anger, of withdrawal—spill into the marriage and prevent a healthy exchange of thoughts and feelings. The answer is to set up new patterns of communication and intimacy.

At the same time, however, we must see each other as individuals. "To achieve     10
a balance between separateness and closeness is one of the major psychological tasks of all human beings at every stage of life," says Dr. Stuart Bartle, a psychiatrist at the New York University Medical Center.

If we sense from our mate a need for too much intimacy, we tend to push him or her away, fearing that we may lose our identities in the merging of marriage. One partner may suffocate the other partner in a childlike dependency.

A good marriage means growing as a couple but also growing as individuals. This isn't easy. Richard gives up his interest in carpentry because his wife, Helen, is jealous of the time he spends away from her. Karen quits her choir group because her husband dislikes the friends she makes there. Each pair clings to each other and are angry with each other as life closes in on them. This kind of marital balance is easily thrown as one or the other pulls away and divorce follows.

Sometimes people pretend that a new partner will solve the old problems. Most often extramarital sex destroys a marriage because it allows an artificial split between the good and the bad—the good is projected on the new partner and the bad is dumped on the head of the old. Dishonesty, hiding and cheating create walls between men and women. Infidelity is just a symptom of trouble. It is a symbolic complaint, a weapon of revenge, as well as an unraveler of closeness. Infidelity is often that proverbial last straw that sinks that camel to the ground.

All right—marriage has always been difficult. Why then are we seeing so many divorces at this time? Yes, our modern social fabric is thin, and yes the permissiveness of society has created unrealistic expectations and thrown the family into chaos. But divorce is so common because people today are unwilling to exercise the self-discipline that marriage requires. They expect easy joy, like the entertainment on TV, the thrill of a good party.

Marriage takes some kind of sacrifice, not dreadful self-sacrifice of the soul,     15
but some level of compromise. Some of one's fantasies, some of one's legitimate desires have to be given up for the value of the marriage itself. "While all marital partners feel shackled at times, it is they who really choose to make the marital ties into confining chains or supporting bonds," says Dr. Whitaker. Marriage requires sexual, financial and emotional discipline. A man and a woman cannot follow every impulse, cannot allow themselves to stop growing or changing.

Divorce is not an evil act. Sometimes it provides salvation for people who have grown hopelessly apart or were frozen in patterns of pain or mutual unhappiness. Divorce can be, despite its initial devastation, like the first cut of the surgeon's knife, a step toward new health and a good life. One the other hand, if the partners can stay past the breaking up of the romantic myths into the development of real love and intimacy, they have achieved a work as amazing as the greatest cathedrals of the world. Marriages that do not fail but improve, that persist despite imperfections, are not only rare these days but offer a wondrous shelter in which the face of our mutual humanity can safely show itself.

## Reflecting and Interpreting

1. Reread the first paragraph. What rhetorical strategy is used here? How does it function?

2. In paragraph 3, Roiphe cites expert opinion. Why?

3. Do you agree or disagree with Dr. Whitaker's theory? Why?

4. What is the basic marriage myth that Roiphe wrote about two decades ago? Do you think the myth still exists? Why or why not?

5. What five qualities does Roiphe identify that are essential for a marriage to endure? Can you think of any others?

6. What pretense does a partner often use to "solve old problems"? How effective is it? What are the risks? (Think about the opening sentence.)

7. What are some of the factors that have created more tension in modern marriages than those of a century ago?

8. Roiphe says that divorce is common for one chief reason. What is it? What can couples do to evade divorce? Can you think of ways that she does not name?

9. What is the basic question that couples must resolve in order for a marriage to succeed?

10. What advantages does a successful marriage offer a family? Consider effects on children, education, health, and others.

## A Writer's Response

1. If you are married, analyze the growth that you have attained since your wedding vows. Write an essay analyzing the cause and effects. If you are single, describe the kind of marriage you would like to have some day. Then analyze the responsibilities you will need to assume and the changes you will need to make.

2. *Small Groups:* Roiphe points out that growth must take place for a marriage to succeed. What kind of growth does she mean? How do changes in perception and perspective figure in? Can you give some examples?

# We Are Tous Québécois: English Quebeckers Learn to Live and Love in French

*The Economist*

*Has the relationship between French- and English-speaking Quebeckers changed since the days of the FLQ crisis of the 1970s? Apparently so. According to this article, most Anglophones now also can speak French, and the province has seen a corresponding increase in Francophone–Anglophone unions. "We are tous Québécois" originally appeared in the January 8, 2005 edition of* The Economist.

Traditionally, the English-speaking minority in Quebec kept itself pretty much to     1
itself, in the leafy western suburbs of Montreal or the farming towns to its south. The Anglos had little interest in mixing with the province's French-speaking majority and little ability to do so: most spoke French poorly and infrequently, if at all. So goes the stereotype of the Anglo-Quebecker in the province's (French-language) literature, film and television.

If this was once accurate, it is no longer so. Now more than two-thirds of Quebec's 750,000 English-speakers can also speak French—double the proportion of the 1970s. Even in those rich ghettos in western Montreal, French is spoken almost as much as English. "The stereotype has evolved from a real man to a straw man," jokes Jack Jedwab of Montreal's Association for Canadian Studies and the author of a recent government report on Quebec's English-speakers. The report noted other signs of integration. As Anglos learn to speak French younger and better, frequently choosing to study in French schools, there has been a surge in marriage (or at least coupling) outside the community. Now, 40% of them have non-anglophone partners, and a quarter have paired with French-speakers.

Closer contact has eased tensions between what were once known as "the two solitudes" who share Quebec. Even the most militant English-speakers—dubbed the "angryphones"—seem less outraged by the provincial government's efforts to promote French. However, several court challenges to Law 101, the province's strict language law, remain pending.

Passed in 1977, this law has made French the first language of government, business and education. Only children who have a parent who was educated in English in Canada can attend an English-speaking public school; all others, including immigrants from Britain, must study in French—or in private schools. Law 101 has in turn created an economic incentive to learn French. Without it, a young anglophone is twice as likely to be unemployed; if he has a job, he can expect to earn only 65% as much as a bilingual colleague.

The result: many of the province's traditional English institutions are declin-    5
ing, and some are dying. Since the 1970s, enrolment in English-speaking schools
has fallen by 60%. Dozens have closed their doors, or switched to French. Six
more in the Montreal area are due to close in September. Quebec's only English-
language daily newspaper, Montreal's Gazette, is in similar straits. In the early
1980s, its Saturday edition sold 280,000 copies; now it sells 163,000. English universities are faring better, because they face no language restrictions. They are re-
cruiting French-Canadians keen to study in English.

All of this has implications for Quebec's politics. Since its rise in the 1960s,
the fortunes of the secessionist movement in the province have risen and fallen in
unison with tensions over language. When the separatist Parti Québécois (PQ)
was first elected to the provincial government in the 1970s, English was still the
language of power and public conversation—even though French-speakers out-
numbered those of English by six to one. One of the PQ's first acts was to push
through Law 101. Within five years, 100,000 English-speakers and many businesses left the province. Many of those who stayed have learnt French. They have
been joined by English-speaking migrants from Asian countries and the
Caribbean, whose children now speak French, if compulsorily.

With linguistic tension much reduced, the sovereignty movement will need a
new cause around which to rally, says Deirdre Meintel, an anthropologist at the
University of Montreal who specialises in minorities. Quebec provides her with
rich material: both English- and French-speakers are both a majority and a minority depending on whether the reference point is Canada, North America or
just the province. Perhaps that explains why most francophone Quebeckers still
feel French is threatened in the province and English secure, while anglophones
say the opposite. Even so, according to Ms Meintel, Anglophone openness to
French is reciprocated in less "francophone chauvinism" and a more inclusive society. "You can be Québécois now without having spoken French all your life," she
says. "You can still have an accent." So the language issue itself is now neither grave
nor acute.

## Reflecting and Interpreting

1. Consider the title of the article: "We Are Tous Québécois." What does it imply, if anything?
2. Consider the effects of Law 101 as outlined in the article. Would you say that
   Law 101 has been a success? Why or why not?
3. Can you see any further effects of closer contact between the "two solitudes"?
4. What are the implications of the decline of traditional institutions in Quebec? Are they worth saving, given the increase in French-speaking residents?
5. Do you think the linguistic tension in Quebec will ever disappear, given
   Deirdre Meintel's position on English and French speakers' reference points?
   Why or why not?

## A Writer's Response

Do some research on the phrase "the two solitudes," attributed to Hugh MacLennan, a Canadian novelist. Do you think these "two solitudes" still exist? Write an essay outlining the causes of their continued existence, or the causes of their dissolution.

# Is Anybody There?

Barbara Wickens

*Barbara Wickens explores the nature of friendship in the modern age: How does the hectic pace of life affect our ability to make friends? Wickens is a senior editor at* Macleans.

Like many woman I know, I vowed when I was younger that I'd never be like my mother. And like many of those women, I can see my mother looking back when I look in the mirror. There's a hairline that's high at the temples, a chronic case of the fidgets, you name it. But there's one crucial difference—in middle age I suddenly find myself wanting, needing even, to make some new friends.

Three years ago, we threw an 85th birthday party for my dad. It was a small gathering, but in some ways an extraordinary one: eight couples, all married for 50-odd years, all friends for nearly as long. They had a shared history of good times, bad jokes, and tolerating one another's foibles. Sure, there were shifting allegiances over the years, one foursome being closer for awhile, then another. But there was always that core group, and that night there was a sense in the room of just how special it was. It would be the last time they were together like that. In the early spring of 2002, my parents died just four weeks apart. They were mourned by these wonderful friends they'd known virtually their entire adult lives.

Maybe I'll be so lucky—if I live into my hundreds. But right now I'm dangerously close to becoming a hermit. Oh, I have people with whom I can go to a move or hiking or some such. But as my friend Ruth puts it, you have friends for a reason, a season, or a lifetime. You expect those first two types to come and go, but the last group? One was transferred to Vancouver, another has a new man in her life, as well as a new job and a new house out in the suburbs, and might as well be in Vancouver. A third, a former six-figure-a-year Bay Street lawyer, is no less busy now that she's a full-time soccer mom. A fourth friend's husband is gravely ill and it is only natural that I've dropped low on her list of priorities. Email and bargain long-distance phone rates make it easy to stay in touch with all of them. But there is no substitute for a téte-â-téte, for just picking up the phone and saying, "Hey, let's go grab a coffee."

Again, I can't help but think about my parents' disappearing world. After spending the first few years of their married life in Vancouver, they moved to Brantford, Ont., my mother's hometown—and there they stayed for the next 55 years. They even kept the same phone number all that time (I pity whoever got it after it was recycled). While I've lived in Toronto for some time now, I'm not from here and neither are most of the people I know. And how long any of us will be here is anyone's guess. The simple act of getting together has become an elaborate ritual, preceded by emails planning when we'll talk on the phone to make our plans. We set up a lunch date three months away, only to change it several times so that it's actually more like five months before we ever get together. My parents never had Day-timers, never needed them.

I'm hardly alone in my aloneness. According to a study presented in June at    5 the International Housing Conference in Toronto, Canadians spent 34 per cent of their spare time by themselves at home in 1998, a five-per-cent increase from 1986. In that same period, they spent slightly more time socializing with friends and family in such places as cafés and restaurants, but this did not make up for the overall decline in social contact. Still, knowing that major social and demographic forces are at play hasn't made writing this any easier. I feel as it I've place a giant L on my forehead—Lonely or Loser, take your pick.

Part of that stems from the exalted position friends hold in our lives today. With family members sometimes thousands of miles away, nearly 40 per cent of marriages ending in divorce and individuals who live by themselves constituting the fastest growing type of household in Canada, friends for many people are de facto family. Popular culture reflects that change. Early sitcoms like Leave It to Beaver and Father Knows Best were all about family life. On The Dick Van Dyke Show in the '60s, the star goofed around on the job with his co-workers, but his family remained central. A decade later, the actor who played his wife would star in her own program, The Mary Tyler Moore Show. Now she was a single career woman whose co-workers stood in for friends and family. By the time Friends came along in the '90s, well, the title pretty much says it all.

The flip side is it's almost impossible to find positive images of solo individuals. The Lone Ranger, for one thing, isn't "lone"—he has Tonto. Spider-Man is about as good as it gets—and that Peter Parker is one conflicted guy. No, the natural instinct is to be suspicious of the friendless, to loathe them even. Dr. Frankenstein's creature is one of a kind—a freak. Quick, storm the castle! The character generally regarded as the first anti-hero in literature—not counting the Devil—is Raskolnikov in Dostoevsky's *Crime and Punishment*, a loner. And of course, real life is worse. The Unabomber. Jeffrey Dahmer. Now there are some guys without friends.

I know that couples can feel isolated as well, especially when the only adults they talk to besides each other are co-workers or the parents of their kids' friends. Still, being single pretty much cuts me off from that world of coupledom. In fact, it's hard to shake the notion that if I'm feeling abandoned, it's because that's what I deserve. We're talking the long, dark tea time of the soul. After all, there are all those sins of omission: the phone calls I let slide, the help offered too late to be genuinely useful. Not to mention the sins of commission, even if offence was given where none was intended.

Still, blame, even where deserved, is not productive. Better to move ahead, to make new friends. This is not just about wanting more to look forward to on Friday night than the latest DVD (though, of course, that's part of it). Studies have repeatedly shown that those who are socially isolated have greater health problems and even die younger than those who are surrounded by friends and family.

10          The question is how, in practical terms, does one go about making new friends? There are muscles that have been allowed to atrophy over the years. When you're little, you can play all day with a kid whose name you never learn. Later, school and even first jobs provide natural breeding grounds for friendships—they offer a shared experience to a group of people at relatively the same stage in their lives. Much beyond that, though, and obligations and preoccupations are established. People hardly have time for the friends they do have, let alone new ones.

There's little help to be found on the bookshelves. Mainly, there are self-help tomes for the lovelorn and much of their advice boils down to, "do something you enjoy and even if you don't meet someone special, you'll make new friends and maybe they will have a sibling or cousin they can introduce you to." Making friends, it seems, is the means, not the end, no explanation necessary.

Any extroverts are probably wondering just what the problem is. But fellow introverts know just how hard it can be to be outgoing, to be friendly and relaxed in unfamiliar situations. I could draw on one of the skills I've acquired as a reporter, actually asking the sorts of questions that draw people out—but that would make it feel too much like work.

For some, the holidays can be the loneliest time of the year. I'm fortunate that I do have family, however small, and that far-flung friends returned home. There was a busyness to the season that was distracting. But now January is here, and I should make the effort to make new friends as if my life depended on it—because, in a way, it does.

## Reflecting and Interpreting

1. Given the ease and efficiency of modern communications, can you find any irony in the essay?
2. How does the author's life compare to that of her parents?
3. How do popular TV shows reflect the state of a generation's relationships?
4. What are some of the effects of leading increasingly isolated lives?
5. According to the author, how are "solo individuals" generally regarded in literature and popular culture?

## A Writer's Response

What communications tools do you use—email, text messaging, cell phones, PDAs, etc.? Write an essay on the effects such tools have had on your daily life and/or relationships.

# Shaping an Effective Argument

## Why College Grads Get Jobs
Robert Sheppard

*The question of university vs. college has been one that many high-school students have had to face over the years. Recently, however, the decision has been more difficult to make. Job-readiness is a draw for many students who opt for college. Robert Sheppard is a writer for Macleans.*

When the Kanitz twins completed high school in 1988, they went their separate ways. Kristi, the brainer, headed to the University of Western Ontario in London as far from their King City home, north of Toronto, as her scholarship money would take her. Her brother Justin enrolled in auto mechanics at Centennial, a college of applied arts and technology in Toronto. For Kristi Kanitz-Woolsey, the penny dropped when she completed her BA in 1992 and both she and her brother applied to teachers' college at the University of Toronto. Justin was accepted. Kristi was not. "It was a blow to my ego," she says, laughing about it now. "I was supposed to be the academic in the family." Indeed, first in her geography class at Western, she retreated to a two-year master's program where she became increasingly disillusioned with the prospect of getting a job in her field. Today, Kristi, 28 and the new mother of twins, is the contented manager of small Waterloo manufacturer of U-bolts—an unusual fit for someone with an MA in international relations—and Justin teaches in the tech shop of a Toronto high school. Says Kristi: "My father used to say, 'You go to university if you want a challenge, you go to community college to prepare yourself for real life.' And after going to university for six years, I tend to agree with him."

So do an increasing number of today's young people. To a generation scarred by recession and reared on consumer choice, the exalted university degree is fast losing its traditional allure to the more prosaic college diploma. One reason is cost: the typical diploma carries a tuition of $1,500 to $2,200 a year, while the university equivalent is in the $3,300 range and rising. The second reason is the

1

rush for jobs, for security in an insecure world, that is reshaping social attitudes and the postsecondary universe in its wake. This summer, when management consultant Ernst & Young asked pollster Angus Reid to explore how Ontarians felt about jobs and education, 35 per cent of the respondents said a college diploma in a technical occupation was the most valuable type of education they could envision. Only half as many believed a university degree in science would do the trick; only three per cent had faith in a BA. The mood has been changing since at least 1993, when Environics Research Group Ltd. began asking whether people would direct a high-school graduate to a trade school or univrsity, and subsequent polls showed a widening gap in favor of the former. Parents with university degrees were still keen to see their children follow in their footsteps. But for almost everyone else, including the pollster's top category of professionals, senior administrators and business owners, the job-focused college came out on top.

But never mind what adults think. The real trend in the postsecondary ranks is that many of the larger colleges report that up to 30 per cent of their students already have a unversity degree—a phenomenon that has been growing right across the country for several years. That trend has  colleges crowing and universities rethinking their roles as students question the value of investing six or seven years to get the right mix of the theoretical and the practical. Stephen Quinlan, president of Toronto's Seneca College, the largest in the country, runs what he calls "the grad school of choice" for nearby York University. At Winnipeg's Red River College, 15 of the 20 students seeking an advanced diploma in geographic information systems technology have a university background.

Meanwhile, Thomas Wood, president of Mount Royal College in Calgary, reports that the huge growth in their student body has largely been due to transfer students, meaning those moving back and forth between a college and a university campus. A notable, some say advanced, feature in the western provinces, the transfer system has been growing in small steps across the country and is designed to allow students to find their way at a local college before transferring on, credits intact, to a univeristy. But in the West at least, the transfer system may be working more to the advantage of the college partner. "Right now," says Wood, "we are receiving more students transferring in than transferring out."

For a sign of the times, consider the case of Joe Albert, 34, a project manager    5
with the Stentor Alliance of telephone companies in Ottawa. Four years ago, when the brokerage firm he was working for in Yarmouth, N.S., went under, he had a decision to make: whether to finish up the university degree he had started in his 20s, or pursue a three-year computer network technician course at the Nova Scotia Community College. He chose the latter. "The irony is I went from a business background to acquire a technical degree, only to go back to the business solutions and management side," says Albert. "But that was my game plan when I went back to school and it worked out almost precisely."

Then there is Bryan Thompson, 26, currently taking a machinist course at Durham College in Oshawa, Ont. Thompson already has two degrees under his belt: a bachelor of commerce and a bachelor of arts, specializing in labor relations, from McMaster University in Hamilton. "I was steered in the direction of university because my grades were really good," says Thompson. "I kind of resent that because what I am doing now I should have been doing six years ago." His buddies who went to Durham after high school now have houses of their own and are starting families. Thompson is living in an apartment with his girlfriend and paying off the remaining portion of a $65,000 university bill. "In my day, colleges were for people who couldn't make the grade in high school, who couldn't do their OACs, which is just wrong."

Universities are alert to the trend. Says York University president Lorna Marsden: "We are certainly becoming much more aware of what's really going on by virtue of students' feet." York is one of those at the forefront of those, at least in Ontario, trying to shorten the learning experience for students by negotiating program-specific arrangements with certain colleges—"without giving up our brand name," says Marsden. But will that be enough? After 30 years of being the junior partners in the country's postsecondary system, Canada's colleges are starting to show what Seneca's Quinlan likes to call "upstart tendencies." Seneca's most recent exploit—a 24,300 square-metre building of its own smack in the middle of the York University campus—is a case in point. The high-tech outpost, scheduled to open in the spring, will house 4,000 college students and whatever university ones come around seeking technical skills. Interest is such that work has already begun on an expansionary second phase. A modest 1,100 square metres is being set aside in case York wants to set up any high-tech labs itself.

Nimble as ants, Canada's colleges have become so flush with their ability to place students in real jobs—most boast a success rate in the range of 90 per cent—that nothing seems to daunt them. Colleges are in the business of producing not only welders and machinists, but world-class chefs, a new generation of multidisciplinary health-care workers—and whiz-kid animators for Nelvana and Disney. Need more computer technicians? Seneca says it can produce as many as any university can, and at half the cost. But this may be comparing apples and oranges. Colleges produce more of the well-paid workers in information technology, the ones who set up and monitor a company's computer networks. Universities tend to provide the more analytical programmers.

In Alberta and Quebec, colleges have taken responsibility for some technical and managerial training for the armed forces. Quebec's CEGEPs, with a 30-year tradition as mandatory feeder schools for the province's universities, are also showing signs of branching out, developing speciality programs that are attracting out-of-province students. But the big push is coming in the field of apprenticeship training. Federal cutbacks in funding for trade programs, and a growing dearth of senior journeymen to train apprentices, have persuaded some provinces to pass a larger proportion of the job into the hands of colleges, wresting it from the unions. Wayne Samuelson, president of the Ontario Federation of Labour, sees a danger in college-run courses that could become too localized, too industry-specific. Universities are routinely chastised these days for becoming too close to their corporate donors. But if anything, community colleges are closer still, almost joined at the hip. In Oshawa, in the heart of General Motors country, Durham College president Gary Polonsky, a bright, engaging man, talks about his student streams as "product lines" and says he personally had to take a GM-approved total quality management course before the automaker would let Durham bid on any training contracts. And the first sentence out of any college president's mouth is generally about the number of business partnerships he or she has struck in recent months.

The pilot project at St. Clair College in Windsor, Ont., provides a clue to the    10 future of apprenticing. Started in January, in conjunction with Chrysler Canada and the Canadian Auto Workers union, the program replaces the traditional five years of apprentice work—often preceded by a brief pre-apprenticing course—with a four-year electronics engineering diploma. Students spend three days a week in class, and two at Chrysler earing $16 to $18 an hour. Thirty-five students have enrolled in the project and in a historical twist, Daimler-Benz has been studying the venture, with an eye to exporting the system back to Germany.

For all their industry connections, colleges are not beating universities in enrolment numbers—yet. But in many parts of the country, university enrolment has been flat or declining throughout the 1990s, with part-time enrolment plunging dramatically, while the number of full-time college students has been steadily on the rise. What is more, college registrars say they are being swamped by a wave of high-school graduates with top marks—and a keen eye on the debt-load for university students. Student debt has been rising sharply since 1990 and now averages $25,000 for an undergraduate degree, according to the Canadian Federation of Students.

Many business leaders—and many universities—argue that a degree is worth more in the job market and offers better protection against an economic downturn. It may. But with the recent movement between universities and colleges, the value of a simple undergraduate degree is becoming harder to measure. What is unassailable is the penalty for stopping at high school: between 1990 and 1996, the number of jobs for those without a degree or college diploma fell by 910,000, while employment for those with a postsecondary credential increased by more than 1.4 million.

But scratch the surface and it is more than just the old political slogan—"Jobs, jobs, jobs"—that is driving the college option. Eighteen-year-old Tammy Walsh from Cold Lake, Alta., had her choice of universities and was thinking only along those lines when she completed high school last year. But her armed forces family was moving to Calgary, and she followed her guidance counsellor's advice, enrolling in Calgary's Mount Royal College in a two-year program aimed at helping people with disabilities. Walsh believes she will "most likely" go on to university—Alberta's transfer system enables her to apply her college credits towards a university degree—but this year is opening her eyes to other options, including colleges in the United States. "We are such a close-knit group here—small classes, my teachers know me by name," says Walsh. "I know people who went to Mount Royal first and then to university and didn't like it. I'll have to see."

Raised in Kentville, N.S., 19-year-old Christine Delbridge has her sights set on an engineering degree at the University of New Brunswick. But first she is going to complete a two-year surveying course at an offshoot of the Nova Scotia Community College. "I want to get a skill to support myself during university," says

Delbridge. "I don't want to come out of university owing a lot of money." Money was also a concern for 21-year-old Carrie Bannon, completing a two-year program in developmental services at Fanshawe College in London, Ont. But it was not the overriding one: "A lot of my friends are going to university and they have no real direction. I thought college would give me more direction and it has."

"This is a tough generation," says Durham's Polonsky. "They are more like    10
their grandparents' generation than their parents'. People in their early 20s have lived much of their life in a recession, and they will always be wary of economic cycles." Indeed, today's college student, with an average age of 26, is slightly older than his or her university counterparts and has spent more time in the workforce, often being buffeted from job to job. At Durham, Polonsky estimates that about 1,000 of the 4,500 full-time students have children and many are single parents juggling jobs and kids.

For many, college is not a place to find yourself, but it still can be a destination for those who want to change the world. At the Michener Institute for Applied Health Sciences in downtown Toronto, 40 students ranging in age from 19 to their mid-40s are paying $8,500 a year for a four-year program in acupuncture and Oriental medicine. "When I tell my friends what I am doing, they always ask two things," says Elizabeth Aubry. "'Can you try it on me?' and 'You're paying how much?'"

Like the animation program at Sheridan College in Oakville, Ont., which has a similar tuition and is being copied across the country, Michener's acupuncture program is one of those godsends for college administrators: a high-end earner that helps offset progressive years of government cutbacks. Tuition is five times the cost of a normal college program, nearly three times that of a bachelor's degree. But for the students involved, it is something else as well. "We are the pioneers," says Aubry, 31. "We should be in tremendous demand." Indeed, nearby Mount Sinai Hospital has just signed an agreement with Michener to use the graduates in a new acupuncture clinic to treat cancer patients and others whose pain cannot be controlled well by conventional drugs. Adds fellow student Steven Josephs, 25: "This is not something strictly for the Oriental community. We are going to be the bridge to Western society."

In an age of perilous government support, even the slightest shift in student preference can disrupt the postsecondary universe. The current demand for cheaper, more relevant education is not lost on the universities. When colleges such as Humber in west-end Toronto moved to offer a variety of one-year certificates for those with university degrees or advanced standing, several universities followed suit with similar add-ons of their own. In the past several years, a wide range of creative partnerships have taken shape, from the dedicated university buildings springing up on college campuses to joint ownership of facilities where common programs are taught.

The most creative partnerships have taken place in the West—particularly in British Columbia, but also in Alberta, Saskatchewan and Manitoba—and at the University College of Cape Breton in Nova Scotia. With some restrictions, students can take advantage of credit transfers between colleges, universities, and in

British Columbia's case, the new hybrid university colleges, institutions that grant both diplomas and degrees. Half those studying for an undergraduate degree in British Columbia today are not doing so at a traditional university.

Student-rich Ontario has experimented with some limited transfer arrangements between universities and colleges, negotiated by individual institutions. "It's the wave of the future," says University of Western Ontario president Paul Davenport. "But the western model does not work here. We have more than enough degree-granting institutions." Ontario universities have been especially unwilling to allow community colleges to grant that most sacred of parchment—the applied or associate degree. "Look," says Harvey Weingarten, provost at Mc-Master University, "it's a jungle out there. The fact is, we need the tuition revenue. In Ontario, we have 17 universities beating each other's brains out, and competing with community colleges as well." There is much colleges and universities can do together, he says, "but there is a distinction in philosophy between universities and colleges, and that should be reflected in the credential that is given."

20

That objection sticks in many colleges' craw. "Anything that takes away from our focus on jobs is dumb," says Polonsky. "But in the 30 years we've been around, our programs have become just as sophisticated as the universities'. We focus on application. They focus on analysis. But whoever said application is less rigorous?" The global credential is the degree, says Polonsky, not the diploma or the course certificate. Not having a degree is limiting college graduates from working or furthering their studies abroad. Indeed, he says, he knows of one Durham grad working as a consultant who was stopped at the border while on a job because U.S. customs officials would not accept his diploma as a professional credential.

Ontario universities and colleges struck a committee at the beginning of the year to examine the issue. But so far, its work seems hung up on the objections of some of the larger universities who are unwilling to compromise. "We are not asking for parity," says Polonsky. "All we want is for our engineering tech grads, with good marks, to be granted standing at universities so they can get a degree in two years if they want."

Unlike universities, hampered by governing senates and hundreds of years of tradition, colleges are much more free to spin on a dime and offer courses on the latest computer or health-services technique—whatever the market will bear. "I spend my days talking to business people, trying to find what they want," says Seneca's Quinlan. His tactic for not being bamboozled by half-baked ideas: he asks companies for a commitment to hire Seneca grads three years down the line if he sets up a program, or to loan him that $100,000 piece of new equipment for training. College presidents say they can zap a new program in place in anywhere from six months to a year, depending on the availability of the training materials and instructors. "It's tough to do," says Michener president Renate Krakauer. "But otherwise, the world passes you by."

The result, though, is that these programs continue to shift and change focus—and are often cut back if the jobs do not materialize. Now, as much as half of a college's budget can come from "earned income," which includes such high-tuition speciality programs as animation or acupuncture, and tailor-made training for GM or the local furniture maker. The quick stops and starts saddled 12 of Ontario's 25 community colleges with $29 million in debt at the end of 1997. Preliminary figures suggest they are climbing out of that hole, but are doing so in part by opening their doors to students with non-academic credentials: between 1994 and 1996, the number of those entering college on the basis of job-related experience—and short interviews—jumped from 741 to 2,767 in Ontario alone.

When they were created in the 1960s, products of social and educational up-    25
heaval, colleges were designed in large measure to deal with the fallout from the baby boom, to cushion the entrance to the job market of a growing number of young people. Since then, they have evolved on many fronts—skills merchants, career reshapers, credentialists for everyone from journalists to funeral-services workers. Now, they are approaching the final frontier, international respectability.

Developing countries are tired of sending their best and brightest to become doctors or engineers at North American universities, only to see them stay. With Canadian colleges bringing their computer or health-care technician courses right to Chile or Trinidad, these countries are now able to envision building their own infrastructure. Toronto's Seneca earned $10 million last year, 20 per cent of its revenue, on international ventures mostly in developing countries. Together, the country's colleges have been involved in at least 300 educational development projects in 70 countries. Red River College in Winnipeg and Camosun in Victoria have joined forces to develop a program on child care standards at the University of Danang in Vietnam; Grant MacEwan Community College in Edmonton recently established an office in northern Russia to maintain contact with the graduates of its health-care administration program. On the Team Canada trade mission to Latin America earlier this year, colleges turned out to be the big draw at breakfast business meetings, surprising many who wondered why they were along in the first place.

The irony is that colleges can sell abroad what many of them cannot sell at home—a coherent system of flexible postsecondary education. "The advantage of the community college is its tremendous sense of place," observes Ray Ivany, head of Nova Scotia Community College, a single administered body with 13 campuses. "You cannot imperil in any way that primary connection to the communities they serve." But at the same time, he says, "that old dichotomy between 'education' and 'training' is rapidly falling away. Students are moving back and forth between college and university. They pop in, they pop out of the workforce. What this province needs, what Canada needs, is greater clarity in the roles of colleges and universities and a seamless transition so the debt-load of students can be reduced." How easy it will be, given their years of mutual mistrust and competition, for the institutions of higher education to muster that sort of clarity is anybody's guess. But for this generation of students, with a tight grip on their education dollars, the assault on the old barriers and attitudes has already begun.

## *Reflecting and Interpreting*

1. What purpose does the first paragraph of the article serve?
2. What is the thesis statement of the article?
3. Why is a college education becoming more appealing to today's students?
4. How are universities responding to this loss of students?
5. Why are Ontario universities reluctant to offer the university–college transfer agreements so popular in Western Canada?

## *A Writer's Response*

1. Have you ever had to decide between college and university? What helped you make your decision? Write an essay defending your choice.
2. Imagine you are a parent (if you're not one already). Would you advise your child to attend college, university, or both? Write an essay supporting your choice.

# It's Just Money, Honey

## Irshad Manji

*Irshad Manji, author of the bestseller* The Trouble with Islam: A Wake-Up Call for Honesty and Change *and host of TVOntario's "Big Ideas," writes here about the relationship between our financial and emotional health.*

"Net worth does not equal self-worth." How many times have we uttered that          1
phrase to ourselves and wished society would drum it into our daughters?

But maybe there's a good reason that society doesn't convey it. Maybe the reason is: our net worth does reflect our self-worth.

Consider the story of Oseola McCarty, a Mississippi washerwoman who died in 1999 with a net worth of $250,000. She earned it over 75 years of doing other people's laundry. McCarty could have burned the cash on a gas-guzzling car that would have taken her well beyond the grocery store and church, to which she walked every week. Instead, she saved.

At 87, McCarty bequeathed $150,000 to a scholarship fund for African Americans of limited means at the University of Southern Mississippi. Her donation encouraged more contributions so that, with her principal compounding as others added to it, the Oseola McCarty Endowed Scholarship Fund accumulated $330,000 when she died four years later.

McCarty enjoyed the means to do good precisely because she afforded her-          5
self the dignity of discipline. As she observed in the 1996 book, *Simple Wisdom for Rich Living*, "It's not the ones that make the big money, but the ones who know how to save, who get ahead."

With this statement, she showed that what often distinguishes those with a high net worth from those with a power paycheque is whether they value themselves. Do they have the faith in themselves to believe they're responsible for their choices? Are they self-assured enough to avoid the reckless spending involved in keeping up with the Joneses? Do they know the difference between their needs and their wants? In short, can they appreciate that the immediacy of their self-worth shapes the eventuality of their net worth?

Those questions become more relevant as several realities converge. First, because women are outliving men, women have to generate more retirement income. Second, mutual funds are making investment accessible to everyone (indeed, they emerged in the 1960s to bust the elite's grip on the stock market). Third, the Internet is driving a do-it-yourself ethic by posting previously private information and delivering real-time data. Finally, all of these factors are giving rise to discount brokerage that further undermine the "you-gotta-have-money-to-make-money" assumption.

Translation: Investing is now up to us, gals. Beauty is, we can achieve the kind of personal consciousness-raising through capital-raising that evenings of feminist theory once offered (and, to be sure, still do for some).

For instance, if you diversify your portfolio too much, that could mean you don't know what you want for yourself, thus shedding light on why you're never happy in your relationships.

On the other hand, you might delude yourself that you're balanced by virtue       10
of maximizing your RRSPs through mutual funds, then dabbling in the stock market with whatever remains. But if you dive into a speculative stock, get whooped, get out, yet suddenly find yourself getting back in for the next "opportunity," you could be addicted to saga. This, in turn, might help explain why you're always looking for something to argue about with loved ones. (A purely hypothetical example, I assure my partner.)

Now suppose you hang on to that plunging stock, rationalizing that it's in the central sector of our decade—wireless communications—and will therefore bounce back. Months later, suppose it's even stinkier, yet you continue to hold because you've come this far with it and why cut your losses if there's a remote possibility of the share price skyrocketing?

Are you an unabashed optimist who makes the best of a complicated world? Or does your romanticism signal a deep personal tendency to be charmed, manipulated by fear and finally exploited until you have nothing left to give? (The hypothesis continues . . . she writes nervously.)

Above all, if you put most of your money into bonds, will you learn anything from the guaranteed gains? Without volatility, how will you toughen your coating to withstand the uncertainties of life in this non-linear age? And will you regret having taken the ultimate risk—namely, confusing safety with security?

Money is emotional. What a lucrative substitute for therapy. I say "lucrative" because for anyone with the luxury of a long-term horizon—young women, listen up—investing will almost certainly pay off well.

The magical math of compound interest is so inescapable that even those       15
who lost 80 per cent of their holdings in the stock market crash of 1929 walked away winners by 1955 as long as they didn't sell.

The next several months could put my hope to a very harsh test. The Bush power revival in the U.S. might inflame Middle East tensions and, with them, oil prices. A recession may hit. Company profit warnings could slash stock valuations to a fraction of the fraction that they already are.

But that would make investing an even better bargain. At this point, you really won't need to be rich to get rich. Like Oseola McCarty, you'll just need to accept that you're worth it.

### Reflecting and Interpreting

1. What purpose does the example of Oseola McCarty serve? Why does Manji place it near the beginning of the article?

2. What kind of tone do you sense in the article?

3. According to the article, how are financial investments and personal relationships connected?

4. What examples does Manji use to support her argument?

5. In your own words, explain what Manji means when she states that money is "a lucrative substitute for therapy."

## A Writer's Response

Consider what money represents to you. Write an essay agreeing or disagreeing with Manji's statement, "Money is emotional."

# The Other Difference between Boys and Girls

Richard M. Restak

*A practising neurologist in Washington, DC, Richard Martin Restak is interested in the philosophical aspects of scientific research. He is a consultant to the Council for Science and Society (London) and a visiting lecturer for numerous colleges, universities, the Central Intelligence Agency, NASA, and other organizations. He is the author of ten books, including* Premeditated Man *(1975),* The Infant Mind *(1980),* The Self Seekers *(1982),* The Brain Has a Mind of Its Own *(1991),* The Modular Brain *(1994),* Brainscapes *(1995), and* Older and Wiser *(1997), as well as coauthor of* Brainmakers *(1994), and* The Longevity Strategy: How to Live to 100 Using the Brain-Body Connection *(1998). In the following article, first printed in the* Washington Post, *Restak recommends social and educational changes because men and women do not think alike.*

Boys think differently from girls. Recent research on brain behavior makes that    1
conclusion inescapable, and it is unrealistic to keep denying it.

I know how offensive that will sound to feminists and others committed to overcoming sexual stereotypes. As the father of three daughters, I am well aware of the discrimination girls suffer. But social equality for men and women really depends on recognizing these differences in brain behavior.

At present, schooling and testing discriminate against both boys and girls in different ways, ignoring differences that have been observed by parents and educators for years. Boys suffer in elementary school classrooms, which are ideally suited to the way girls think. Girls suffer later on, in crucial ways, taking scholarship tests that are geared for male performance.

Anyone who has spent time with children in a playground or school setting is aware of differences in the way boys and girls respond to similar situations. Think of the last time you supervised a birthday party attended by five-year-olds. It's not usually the girls who pull hair, throw punches or smear each other with food.

Usually such differences are explained on a cultural basis. Boys are expected    5
to be more aggressive and play rough games, while girls are presumably encouraged to be gentle, nonassertive and passive. After several years of exposure to such expectations, the theory goes, men and women wind up with widely varying behavioral and intellectual repertoires. As a corollary to this, many people believe that if child-rearing practices could be equalized and sexual stereotypes eliminated, most of these differences would eventually disappear. As often happens, however, the true state of affairs is not that simple.

Undoubtedly, many of the differences traditionally believed to exist between the sexes are based on stereotypes. But despite this, evidence from recent brain research indicates that many behavioral differences between men and women are based on differences in brain functioning that are biologically inherent and unlikely to be modified by cultural factors alone.

The first clue to brain differences between the sexes came from observations of male and female infants. From birth, female infants are more sensitive to sounds, particularly to their mother's voice. In a laboratory, if the sound of the mother's voice is displaced to another part of the room, female babies will react while male babies usually seem oblivious to the displacement. Female babies are also more easily startled by loud noises. In fact, their enhanced hearing performance persists throughout life, with females experiencing a fall-off in hearing much later than males.

Tests involving girls old enough to cooperate show increased skin sensitivity, particularly in the fingertips, which have a lower threshold for touch identification. Females are also more proficient at fine motor performance. Rapid tapping movements are carried out quickly and more efficiently by girls than by boys.

In addition, there are differences in what attracts a girl's attention. Generally, females are more attentive to social contexts—faces, speech patterns and subtle vocal cues. By four months of age, a female infant is socially aware enough to distinguish photographs of familiar people, a task rarely performed well by boys of that age. Also at four months, girls will babble to a mother's face, seemingly recognizing her as a person, while boys fail to distinguish between a face and a dangling toy, babbling equally to both.

Female infants also speak sooner, have larger vocabularies and rarely demonstrate speech defects. Stuttering, for instance, occurs almost exclusively among boys.          10

Girls can also sing in tune at an earlier age. In fact, if we think of the muscles of the throat as muscles of fine control—those in which girls excel—then it should come as no surprise that girls exceed boys in language abilities. This early linguistic bias often prevails throughout life. Girls read sooner, learn foreign languages more easily and, as a result, are more likely to enter occupations involving language mastery.

Boys, in contrast, show an early visual superiority. They are also clumsier, performing poorly at something like arranging a row of beads, but excel at other activities calling on total body coordination. Their attentional mechanisms are also different. A boy will react to an inanimate object as quickly as he will to a person. A male baby will often ignore the mother and babble to a blinking light, fixate on a geometric figure and, at a later point, manipulate it and attempt to take it apart.

A study of nursery preschool children carried out by psychologist Diane McGuinness of Stanford University found boys more curious, especially in regard to exploring their environment. McGuinness' studies also confirmed that males are better at manipulating three-dimensional space. When boys and girls are asked to mentally rotate or fold an object, boys overwhelmingly outperform girls. "I folded it in my mind" is a typical male response. Girls, when explaining how they perform the same task, are likely to produce elaborate verbal descriptions which, because they are less appropriate to the task, result in frequent errors.

In an attempt to understand the sex differences in spatial ability, electroencephalogram (EEG) measurements have recently been made of the accompanying electrical events going on within the brain.

Ordinarily, the two brain hemispheres produce a similar electrical back-    10
ground that can be measured by an EEG. When a person is involved in a mental task—say, subtracting 73 from 102—the hemisphere that is activated will demonstrate a change in its electrical background. When boys are involved in tasks employing spatial concepts, such as figuring out mentally which of three folded shapes can be made from a flat, irregular piece of paper, the right hemisphere is activated consistently. Girls, in contrast, are more likely to activate both hemispheres, indicating that spatial ability is more widely dispersed in the female brain.

When it comes to psychological measurements of brain functioning between the sexes, unmistakable differences emerge. In 11 subtests of the most widely used test of general intelligence, only two subtests reveal similar mean scores for males and females. These sex differences have been substantiated across cultures and are so consistent that the standard battery of this intelligence test now contains a masculinity-femininity index.

Further support for sex differences in brain functioning comes from experience with subtests that eventually had to be omitted from the original test battery. A cube-analysis test, for example, was excluded because, after testing thousands of subjects, a large sex bias appeared to favor males. In all, over 30 tests eventually had to be eliminated because they discriminated in favor of one or the other sex. One test, involving mentally working oneself through a maze, favored boys so overwhelmingly that, for a while, some psychologists speculated that girls were totally lacking in a "spatial factor."

Most thought-provoking of all is a series of findings by Eleanor Maccoby and Carol Nagly Jacklin of Stanford on personality traits and intellectual achievement. They found that girls whose intellectual achievement is greatest tend to be unusually active, independent, competitive and free of fear or anxiety, while intellectually outstanding boys are often timid, anxious, not overtly aggressive and less active.

In essence, Maccoby and Jacklin's findings suggest that intellectual performance is incompatible with our stereotype of femininity in girls or masculinity in boys.

Research evidence within the last six months indicates that many of these    20
brain sex differences persist over a person's lifetime. In a study at the University Hospital in Ontario that compared verbal and spatial abilities of men and women after a stroke, the women did better than men in key categories tested. After the stroke, women tended to be less disabled and recovered more quickly.

Research at the National Institute of Mental Health is even uncovering biochemical differences in the brains of men and women. Women's brains, it seems, are more sensitive to experimentally administered lights and sounds. The investigator in charge of this research, Dr. Monte Buchsbaum, speculates that the enhanced response of the female brain depends on the effect of sex hormones on the formation of a key brain chemical. This increased sensibility to stimuli by the female brain may explain why women more often than men respond to loss and stress by developing depression.

It's important to remember that we're not talking about one sex being generally superior or inferior to another. Rather, psychobiological research is turning up important functional differences between male and female brains. The discoveries might possibly contribute to further resentments and divisions in our society. But must they? Why are sex differences in brain functioning disturbing to so many people? And why do women react so vehemently to findings that, if anything, indicate enhanced capabilities in the female brain?

It seems to me that we can make two responses to these findings on brain-sex differences. First, we can use them to help bring about true social equity. One way of doing this might be to change such practices as nationwide competitive examinations. If boys, for instance, truly do excel in right-hemisphere tasks, then tests such as the National Merit Scholarship Examination should be radically redesigned to assure that both sexes have an equal chance. As things now stand, the tests are heavily weighted with items that virtually guarantee superior male performance.

Attitude changes are also needed in our approach to "hyperactive" or "learning disabled" children. The evidence for sex differences here is staggering: More than 95 percent of hyperactives are males. And why should this be surprising in light of the sex differences in brain function that we've just discussed?

The male brain learns by manipulating its environment, yet the typical student is forced to sit still for long hours in the classroom. The male brain is primarily visual, while classroom instruction demands attentive listening. Boys are clumsy in fine hand coordination, yet are forced at an early age to express themselves in writing. Finally, there is little opportunity in most schools, other than during recess, for gross motor movements or rapid muscular responses. In essence, the classrooms in most of our nation's primary grades are geared to skills that come naturally to girls but develop very slowly in boys. The results shouldn't be surprising: a "learning disabled" child who is also frequently "hyperactive."

"He can't sit still, can't write legibly, is always trying to take things apart, won't follow instructions, is loud, and, oh yes, terribly clumsy," is a typical teacher description of male hyperactivity. We now have the opportunity, based on emerging evidence of sex differences in brain functioning, to restructure elementary grades so that boys find their initial educational contacts less stressful.

At more advanced levels of instruction, efforts must be made to develop teaching methods that incorporate verbal and linguistic approaches to physics, engineering and architecture (to mention only three fields where women are conspicuously underrepresented and, on competitive aptitude tests, score well below males).

The second alternative is, of course, to do nothing about brain differences and perhaps even deny them altogether. Certainly there is something to be said for

25

this approach too. In the recent past, enhanced social benefit has usually resulted from stressing the similarities between people rather than their differences. We ignore brain-sex differences, however, at the risk of confusing biology with sociology, and wishful thinking with scientific facts.

The question is not, "Are there brain-sex differences?" but rather, "What is going to be our response to these differences?" Psychobiological research is slowly but surely inching toward scientific proof of a premise first articulated by the psychologist David Wechsler more than 20 years ago:

> The findings suggest that women seemingly call upon different resources     30
> or different degrees of like abilities in exercising whatever it is we call in-
> telligence. For the moment, one need not be concerned as to which ap-
> proach is better or "superior." But our findings do confirm what poets and
> novelists have often asserted, and the average layman long believed,
> namely, that men not only behave, but "think" differently from women.

## Reflecting and Interpreting

1. What is Restak's thesis? What does he say is the reason for basic differences between boys and girls?

2. How does the second paragraph contribute to Restak's credibility?

3. How does paragraph 4 function? Why is it included?

4. What sexual differences have been observed in tests with newborns and infants?

5. Restak says that schooling and testing discriminate against both boys and girls in different ways. What does he mean?

6. What differences in spatial reasoning between the sexes have been found?

7. Although girls have superior fine motor skills, boys tend to be much more interested in computer games than girls. What does Restak say that would explain this difference?

8. What biochemical differences have been found between men's and women's brains?

9. What caution does Restak give?

10. What are two alternative ways of responding to these findings? Which does he advocate?

## A Writer's Response

1. Have you ever been unable to do something that most other children (or adults) can do? Write a paragraph describing this situation and how you coped with it. Did it affect your later life? If so, how? Or perhaps you have had a family member or friend who underwent such an experience. Can you describe it?

2. *Small Groups:* Consider the pros and cons of Restak's recommendations for changes in education (paragraphs 23 through 27). Do they seem advisable to you? Why or why not?

# We Have No *"Right to Happiness"*
C. S. Lewis

*What exactly is the "pursuit of happiness," which we claim as a right? Does it have limits? In this essay C[livel] S[taples] Lewis (1898–1963) raises questions of morality that are even more pertinent today than four decades ago. A writer of world renown, Lewis also taught literature courses at Oxford and Cambridge Universities. His work includes adult fiction, children's books, poetry, and numerous books and essays on Christianity. Some of his best known works are* The Allegory of Love: A study in Medieval Tradition *(1936),* The Screwtape Letters *(1942),* Mere Christianity *(1943),* Miracles: A Preliminary Study *(1947), and the seven* Chronicles of Narnia *(1950–1956).*

"After all," said Clare, "they had a right to happiness." 1

We were discussing something that once happened in our own neighborhood. Mr. A. had deserted Mrs. A. and got his divorce in order to marry Mrs. B., who had likewise got her divorce in order to marry Mr. A. And there was certainly no doubt that Mr. A. and Mrs. B. were very much in love with one another. If they continued to be in love, and if nothing went wrong with their health or their income, they might reasonably expect to be very happy.

It was equally clear that they were not happy with their old partners. Mrs. B. had adored her husband at the outset. But then he got smashed up in the war. It was thought he had lost his virility, and it was known that he had lost his job. Life with him was no longer what Mrs. B. had bargained for. Poor Mrs. A., too. She had lost her looks—and all her liveliness. It might be true, as some said, that she consumed herself by bearing his children and nursing him through the long illness that overshadowed their earlier married life.

You mustn't, by the way, imagine that A. was the sort of man who nonchalantly threw a wife away like the peel of an orange he'd sucked dry. Her suicide was a terrible shock to him. We all knew this, for he told us so himself. "But what could I do?" he said. "A man has a right to happiness. I had to take my one chance when it came."

I went away thinking about the concept of a "right to happiness." 5

At first this sounds to me as odd as a right to good luck. For I believe—whatever one school of moralists may say—that we depend for a very great deal of our happiness or misery on circumstances outside all human control. A right to happiness doesn't, for me, make much more sense than a right to be six feet tall, or to have a millionaire for your father, or to get good weather whenever you want to have a picnic.

I can understand a right as a freedom guaranteed me by the laws of the society I live in. Thus, I have a right to travel along the public roads because society gives me that freedom; that's what we mean by calling the roads "public." I can also understand a right as a claim guaranteed me by the laws, and correlative to an obligation on someone else's part. If I have a right to receive £100 from you, this is another way of saying that you have a duty to pay me £100. If the laws allow Mr. A. to desert his wife and seduce his neighbor's wife, then, by definition, Mr. A. has a legal right to do so, and we need bring in no talk about "happiness."

But of course that was not what Clare meant. She meant that he had not only a legal but a moral right to act as he did. In other words, Clare is—or would be if she thought it out—a classical moralist after the style of Thomas Aquinas, Grotius, Hooker and Locke. She believes that behind the laws of the state there is a Natural Law.

I agree with her. I hold this conception to be basic to all civilization. Without it, the actual laws of the state become an absolute, as in Hegel. They cannot be criticized because there is no norm against which they should be judged.

The ancestry of Clare's maxim, "They have a right to happiness," is august. In    10 words that are cherished by all civilized men, but especially by Americans, it has been laid down that one of the rights of man is a right to "the pursuit of happiness." And now we get to the real point.

What did the writers of that august declaration mean?

It is quite certain what they did not mean. They did not mean that man was entitled to pursue happiness by any and every means—including, say, murder, rape, robbery, treason and fraud. No society could be built on such a basis.

They meant "to pursue happiness by all lawful means"; that is, by all means which the Law of Nature eternally sanctions and which the laws of the nation shall sanction.

Admittedly this seems at first to reduce their maxim to the tautology that men (in pursuit of happiness) have a right to do whatever they have a right to do. But tautologies, seen against their proper historical context, are not always barren tautologies. The declaration is primarily a denial of the political principles which long governed Europe: a challenge flung down to the Austrian and Russian empires, to England before the Reform Bills, to Bourbon France. It demands that whatever means of pursuing happiness are lawful for any should be lawful for all; that "man," not men of some particular caste, class, status or religion, should be free to use them. In a century when this is being unsaid by nation after nation and party after party, let us not call it a barren tautology.

But the question as to what means are "lawful"—what methods of pursuing    15 happiness are either morally permissible by the Law of Nature or should be declared legally permissible by the legislature of a particular nation—remains exactly where it did. And on that question I disagree with Clare. I don't think it is obvious that people have the unlimited "right to happiness" which she suggests.

For one thing, I believe that Clare, when she says "happiness," means simply and solely "sexual happiness." Partly because women like Clare never use the word "happiness" in any other sense. But also because I never heard Clare talk about the "right" to any other kind. She was rather leftist in her politics, and would have been scandalized if anyone had defended the actions of a ruthless man-eating tycoon on the ground that his happiness consisted in making money and he was pursuing his happiness. She was also a rabid teetotaler; I never heard her excuse an alcoholic because he was happy when he was drunk.

A good many of Clare's friends, and especially her female friends, often felt—I've heard them say so—that their own happiness would be perceptibly increased by boxing her ears. I very much doubt if this would have brought her theory of a right to happiness into play.

Clare, in fact, is doing what the whole western world seems to me to have been doing for the last forty-odd years. When I was a youngster, all the progressive people were saying, "Why all this prudery? Let us treat sex just as we treat all our other impulses." I was simple-minded enough to believe they meant what they said. I have since discovered that they meant exactly the opposite. They meant that sex was to be treated as no other impulse in our nature has ever been treated by civilized people. All the others, we admit, have to be bridled. Absolute obedience to your instinct for self-preservation is what we call cowardice; to your acquisitive impulse, avarice. Even sleep must be resisted if you're a sentry. But every unkindness and breach of faith seems to be condoned provided that the object aimed at is "four bare legs in a bed."

It is like having a morality in which stealing fruit is considered wrong—unless you steal nectarines.

20      And if you protest against this view you are usually met with chatter about the legitimacy and beauty and sanctity of "sex" and accused of harboring some Puritan prejudice against it as something disreputable or shameful. I deny the charge. Foam-born Venus . . . golden Aphrodite . . . Our Lady of Cyprus . . . I never breathed a word against you. If I object to boys who steal my nectarines, must I be supposed to disapprove of nectarines in general? Or even of boys in general? It might, you know, be stealing that I disapproved of.

The real situation is skillfully concealed by saying that the question of Mr. A.'s "right" to desert his wife is one of "sexual morality." Robbing an orchard is not an offense against some special morality called "fruit morality." It is an offense against honesty. Mr. A.'s action is an offense against good faith (to solemn promises), against gratitude (toward one to whom he was deeply indebted) and against common humanity.

Our sexual impulses are thus being put in a position of preposterous privilege. The sexual motive is taken to condone all sorts of behavior which, if it had any other end in view, would be condemned as merciless, treacherous and unjust.

Now though I see no good reason for giving sex this privilege, I think I see a strong cause. It is this.

It is part of the nature of a strong erotic passion—as distinct from a transient fit of appetite—that it makes more towering promises than any other emotion. No doubt all our desires make promises, but not so impressively. To be in love involves the almost irresistible conviction that one will go on being in love until one dies, and that possession of the beloved will confer, not merely frequent ecstasies, but settled, fruitful, deep-rooted, lifelong happiness. Hence *all* seems to be at stake. If we miss this chance we shall have lived in vain. At the very thought of such a doom we sink into fathomless depths of self-pity.

Unfortunately these promises are found often to be quite untrue. Every experienced adult knows this to be so as regards all erotic passions (except the one he himself is feeling at the moment). We discount the world-without-end pretensions of our friends' amours easily enough. We know that such things sometimes last—and sometimes don't. And when they do last, this is not because they promised at the outset to do so. When two people achieve lasting happiness, this is not solely because they are great lovers but because they are also—I must put it crudely—good people; controlled, loyal, fairminded, mutually adaptable people.

25

If we establish a "right to (sexual) happiness" which supersedes all the ordinary rules of behavior, we do so not because of what our passion shows itself to be in experience but because of what it professes to be while we are in the grip of it. Hence, while the bad behavior is real and works miseries and degradations, the happiness which was the object of the behavior turns out again and again to be illusory. Everyone (except Mr. A. and Mrs. B.) knows that Mr. A. in a year or so may have the same reason for deserting his new wife as for deserting his old. He will feel again that all is at stake. He will see himself again as the great lover, and his pity for himself will exclude all pity for the woman.

Two further points remain.

One is this. A society in which conjugal infidelity is tolerated must always be in the long run a society adverse to women. Women, whatever a few male songs and satires may say to the contrary, are more naturally monogamous than men; it is a biological necessity. Where promiscuity prevails, they will therefore always be more often the victims than the culprits. Also, domestic happiness is more necessary to them than to us. And the quality by which they most easily hold a man, their beauty, decreases every year after they have come to maturity, but this does not happen to those qualities of personality—women don't really care twopence about our *looks*—by which we hold women. Thus in the ruthless war of promiscuity women are at a double disadvantage. They play for higher stakes and are also more likely to lose. I have no sympathy with moralists who frown at the increasing crudity of female provocativeness. These signs of desperate competition fill me with pity.

Secondly, though the "right to happiness" is chiefly claimed for the sexual impulse, it seems to me impossible that the matter should stay there. The fatal principle, once allowed in that department, must sooner or later seep through our whole lives. We thus advance toward a state of society in which not only each man but every impulse in each man claims *carte blanche*. And then, though our technological skill may help us survive a little longer, our civilization will have died at heart, and will—one dare not even add "unfortunately"—be swept away.

### *Reflecting and Interpreting*

1. Examine paragraph 3. What irony do you see?
2. What implicit question is the central idea of this essay? (Look at the first sentence and the title.)

3. Can you find an example of negation, a technique of definition?

4. Is there a difference between a right to happiness and the right to pursue happiness? If so, what is it?

5. Clare believes that "behind the laws of the state there is a Natural Law." Does Lewis agree or disagree? Why?

6. In paragraph 10 Lewis begins to trace the history of Clare's belief and where it leads. What is the pivotal question on which he disagrees?

7. How does Lewis view the marrige vow?

8. What kind of happiness does Lewis believe Clare means? Why does this kind raise moral questions?

9. What does Lewis say is necessary for two people to achieve lasting happiness?

10. What six rhetorical patterns does Lewis combine to organize his complex argument?

## A Writer's Response

Lewis says that "women are more naturally monogamous than men; it is a biological necessity." Write an essay agreeing or disagreeing with his position. Cite facts and examples to support your claim.

# THE HANDBOOK

## Part 9
## A Brief Guide to
## Grammar, Punctuation,
## Mechanics, and Usage

## HANDBOOK DIRECTORY

INTRODUCTION

# INTRODUCTION

This brief, concise handbook is a handy guide to frequently asked questions about standard written English. Here you can quickly find established rules, conventions, and examples that will help you to write correct and effective sentences. Whether you write essays, papers, letters, reports, or other documents, you can find answers to most of your writing questions either in this reference section or in related parts of the textbook.

## WHAT IS THE BEST WAY TO USE THIS HANDBOOK?

To find quick answers to usage questions, first turn to the Handbook Directory, which appears on the opposite page. Next, scan the headings to locate the section you need and the page number, such as H-2. Then turn to that page and skim the rules until you find the appropriate information. Or you may wish to brush up on all of the rules in a particular section. If you desire more help, look for cross-references in the handbook that direct you to other sections of the text where you'll find related information.

Another way to locate related discussions in various chapters is to consult this book's subject index. For example, cross-references and the index indicate that Chapter 25 provides extra help with ellipsis, brackets, and quotation marks. Chapter 8 explains voice of verbs, *be* verbs, sentence structure, adverb and adjective clauses, commas, and editing. For more help with word choice, you could turn to Chapters 6 and 9, and for an overview of revising, editing, and proofreading, Chapter 5.

## SHOULD A WRITER EVER BREAK A RULE?

If you deliberately break a stylistic rule, it should be done for a purpose that promotes effective writing. To estimate how effective the writing will be, consider the rhetorical situation (Chapter 1). You might ask yourself two key questions: What do readers expect? Is the writing appropriate for the occasion? If readers expect standard written English and you punctuate creatively, they may think you are uneducated. As a result, your ideas may not receive the attention they deserve.

When in doubt about questions of grammar, mechanics, punctuation, and usage, consult this book, your instructor, the campus writing centre, or an online writing lab (OWL). For example, you might visit the one hosted by Purdue University at http://owl.english.purdue.edu.

# 1. PUNCTUATION

## 1a. COMMA (,)

The primary task of the comma is to clarify by indicating sentence structure. Commas should be used for a reason. (The old general rule to insert a comma for a pause does not always work.) In fact, many comma errors are due to unnecessary commas. To guide you, here are three don'ts:

- ▶ Do not place a comma before a parenthesis.
- ▶ Do not place a comma between a verb and a direct object.
- ▶ Do not insert a comma if you lack a reason.

1. **Use a comma to separate coordinate words, phrases, or clauses in a series.**

   - ▶ The Delany children were named *Lemuel, Sarah, Elizabeth, Julia, Henry, Lucius, Manross, Hubert, Laura,* and *Samuel.* [a series of nouns]
   - ▶ A 1994 book by Sadie and Bessie Delany *made the best-selling nonfiction list, ran as a successful play,* and *won several awards.* [a series of verb phrases]
   - ▶ Sarah "Sadie" Delany, *by completing high school, graduating from Columbia University's Teachers College,* and *circumventing prejudice,* gained a teaching position in an all-white New York City school during the Depression. [a series of participial phrases]
   - ▶ *If Sadie had accepted the stereotypes of the time, if she had succumbed to the racial barriers, if she had rejected the long hours of work and study,* she would have remained in the South, uneducated and unknown. [a series of adverb clauses]

   (For more information on coordination, see "Parallelism with Items in a Series," Chapter 8.)

2. **Use a comma to separate addresses, dates, and titles.**

   - ▶ In the late 1890s Henry and Nanny Delany lived with their ten children in a small house on the campus of *Saint Augustine's School, Raleigh, North Carolina.*
   - ▶ Elizabeth "Bessie" Delany was born on *September 3, 1891.*
   - ▶ In 1918 Henry Beard Delany, *Jr.,* encouraged his sister to become a dentist, too.
   - ▶ Bessie Delany, *D.D.S.,* became the second black woman licensed in New York City to practise dentistry.

3. **Place a comma before a coordinating conjunction that joins independent clauses (clauses that could be complete sentences).**

The coordinating conjunctions are *for, and, nor, but, or, yet, so*. (See Chapter 8 for more on joining independent clauses.)

▶ In 1869 the territory of Wyoming granted women the right to vote, *but* Amendment 19 to the Constitution did not become law until August 1920.

4. **Use a comma to separate an introductory subordinate clause from the main part of the sentence.**

When the introductory clause is short and will not be misread, the comma may be omitted. (See Chapter 8 for more on subordinate clauses.)

▶ *After Victoria Claflin Woodhull became one of the first two female stockbrokers in the United States,* she became, in 1872, the first woman to run for the presidency.

5. **Use a comma after an introductory participial phrase or infinitive phrase.**

▶ *Living in Tasmania and southern Australia,* wombats are marsupials that feed on roots, leaves, and vegetables.

▶ *To see a wombat,* you must look at night.

6. **Use a comma after two or more introductory prepositional phrases or a long introductory prepositional phrase (a good rule of thumb is four words or more).**

▶ *In the icy waters of the North Atlantic,* the savage wolf fish grows up to one metre long. *Along the sea bottom,* the sea robin walks on its breast fin rays, looking for food.

7. **Use commas to set off transitional expressions and conjunctive adverbs.**

Transitional expressions include phrases such as *in fact* and *for example*. Conjunctive adverbs include words such as *however, consequently,* and *therefore*.

▶ *Finally,* the flood waters receded after ten days of rain.

▶ It was, *in fact,* the worst flooding on record in the region.

▶ Flooding is common in the area; *consequently,* people are being discouraged from rebuilding homes there.

8. **Use commas to set off nonessential (nonrestrictive) elements.**

Use a comma to set off tag words such as *well, yes,* and *isn't it* at the beginning or end of a sentence.

▶ *Yes,* you really did win a new Lexus.

▶ You are a very lucky fellow, *aren't you?*

Use a pair of commas to set off nonessential phrases that interrupt the flow of a sentence.

▶ One department head, *working late*, inadvertently erased the weekly sales report.

▶ Ricardo Alvarez, *a business owner*, joined our Toastmasters' Club last week.

▶ Our students, *who come from surrounding counties*, usually commute daily.

9. **Use a comma to set off a contrasting expression.**

▶ My billfold is lying on the dresser, *not the chair*.

10. **Use a comma to prevent misreading.**

Sometimes a comma is needed for clarity.

▶ Inside, the stereo was going full blast.

▶ Outside, the children were roaring around the house on their motorbikes.

11. **Use commas to set off a speaker tag or source tag from a direct quotation.**

A speaker tag or source tag identifies the speaker or writer and includes a verb of saying, such as *said, called, asked,* or *wrote*.

▶ *Derek yelled*, "Get out! The rear tire is on fire!"

▶ "The law must be stable," *wrote Roscoe Pound*, "but it must not stand still."

Note that when the speaker tag follows a quotation or part of a quotation, the comma preceding it is placed inside the quotation marks.

## 1b.  SEMICOLON (;)

Basically, the semicolon has only two uses. If you understand the rules governing it, you should be able to use the semicolon with confidence. Remember that the semicolon is a stronger mark of punctuation than the comma and that it is used for the *larger* divisions within a sentence.

1. **Use a semicolon to connect two closely related independent clauses not joined by a comma and a coordinating conjunction (*and, but, or, nor, for, so,* and *yet*).**

▶ Hundreds of members attended the conference; many could not find a place to stay.

2. Use a semicolon between two independent clauses joined by a conjunctive adverb or other transitional expression.

> ▶ Sue is an accounting major; *however,* she plans to switch to data processing.

> ▶ Kevin was not feeling well; *nonetheless,* he went to the dance.

3. Replace commas with semicolons for clarity when items in a series contain commas.

> ▶ Here is our new slate of officers: *Jean Henson, president; Mike Henry, vice president; Scott Trainor, treasurer; and Mary Wiley, secretary.*

4. If there are commas within the independent clauses of a sentence, use a semicolon rather than a comma before the coordinating conjunction.

> ▶ The Harvest House, a new restaurant on Centre Street, features ethnic foods; and the crowds, surprisingly large for a small town, flock in.

## 1c. COLON (:)

A colon is used after an independent clause to signal that something will follow.

1. Use a colon to precede a list or series that does not fit smoothly into a sentence.

> ▶ Sue ordered the following items: *one pair of scissors, two yards of denim, one thimble, and one tape measure.*

> ▶ Nanette will need these tools: *needle-nose pliers, a monkey wrench, a claw hammer, and a hacksaw.*

However, do not use a colon after a verb or preposition.

*Incorrect*

> ▼ My grocery list included: zucchini, papaya, mangoes, and sunflower seeds. [The colon is not needed.]

2. Use a colon to formally introduce a quotation.

> ▶ My point can be summarized in the words of Sir Winston Churchill: "All great things are simple, and many can be expressed in single words: freedom, justice, honour, duty, mercy, hope."

3. Use a colon between independent clauses when the second explains the first.

> ▶ Jim has a real problem: his hair started falling out last month.

► "Let the world slip: we shall ne'er be younger." (William Shakespeare, *The Taming of the Shrew*)

4.  **Use a colon in biblical references, expressions of time, and after salutations in business letters.**

Use a colon between chapter and verse numbers of the Bible.

► Psalm 27:3

Use a colon between the hour and the minute in referring to time.

► 6:05 p.m.

Use a colon after the salutation of a business letter.

► Dear Ms. Brown:

## 1d. APOSTROPHE (')

The apostrophe has three basic uses: to form possessives, to form a few plurals, and to indicate omissions.

1.  **Use an apostrophe with *s* to form the possessive of singular nouns and irregular plural nouns not ending in *s*.**

    ► today's fashions    ► my mother's life    ► the city's attractions
    ► men's clothing    ► children's toys    ► mice's lifespans

    Note that when adding *s* to form the possessive sounds awkward in speech, some writers add only an apostrophe in writing: *Mr. Rogers' neighbourhood, Charles' sons*. But it is never incorrect to add both an apostrophe and *s* for such words. Whichever practice you adopt, be consistent.

2.  **Add only an apostrophe to form the possessive of a plural noun ending in *s*.**

    ► boys' jeans    ► horses' manes    ► butterflies' wings

3.  **Indefinite pronouns (*anyone, everyone, everybody, nobody, one*) in the possessive case are treated as singular nouns and require an apostrophe before *s*.**

    ► Everyone's invitation was mailed.    ► Each one's jacket was labelled.
    ► Anybody's guess is as good as mine.    ► No one's car was ticketed.

4.  **To show joint possession and to show possession with hyphenated terms and names of organizations, make only the last word possessive.**

- ▶ Bill and Thad's boat
- ▶ father-in-law's car
- ▶ Cutter and Holt's Welding Company

5. **To show individual possession, use an apostrophe with each name.**

- ▶ Sue's and Joan's essays are late.

6. **Use an apostrophe to form the possessive of words referring to time or to amounts of money.**

| | | |
|---|---|---|
| ▶ a minute's rest | ▶ a week's wages | ▶ one cent's worth |
| ▶ two hours' work | ▶ one month's rent | ▶ two cents' worth |
| ▶ three days' pay | ▶ two years' time | ▶ a dime's worth |

7. **Use an apostrophe to form the plurals of numbers, letters, symbols, and words referred to as words. (Sometimes the apostrophe is omitted if there is no problem of clarity.)**

- ▶ My house number is simply three 7's, or 777.
- ▶ *Occasionally* is spelled with two *c*'s and one *s*.
- ▶ How many ='s should there be in this equation?
- ▶ Ashley had three *and*'s in one sentence.

8. **Use an apostrophe to replace omitted letters or numbers in a contraction.**

- ▶ They don't know when they'll be called back to work. [*do not; they will*]
- ▶ Terry can't go until tomorrow. [*cannot*]
- ▶ It's his turn. [*It is*]
- ▶ The class of '89 is planning a reunion. [*1989*]

*NOTE:* Do not confuse *it's* with the possessive pronoun *its*, which does not require an apostrophe: "The cat lost its catnip mouse." (*Its*, like *his* and *hers*, is in the possessive case.)

## 1e.  DASH (—)

Dashes, parentheses, and brackets share a basic function: to set off information from the rest of the sentence. But these marks of punctuation differ in effect. Dashes emphasize material whereas parentheses de-emphasize. Brackets are generally used to enclose clarifying information in direct quotations.

The dash is informal punctuation that indicates an interruption of a sentence. A dash can signal a break in thought or provide special emphasis. Often used in pairs, dashes are bold and dramatic—as long as they are used sparingly. (When using word-processing software, use two hyphens without spacing to make a dash.)

1.  **Use a dash or a pair of dashes to emphasize an appositive or other explanatory material.**

    ▶ "Soon members of the PMAC—referred to as the Derg—were dispatching their 'enemies' without trials."

    ▶ "There was not—and never had been—a Communist Party in Ethiopia: the country was linked to the West and dependent on free-world aid."

    ▶ "Soon he realized that his one hope was to make contact with two notorious smugglers who might guide him out—an idea fraught with risk."

    ▶ "He had to do this—regardless of the consequences."

    ─────────

    *Note:* The preceding examples of dashes are taken from "Escape from Ethiopia," by Trevor Armbrister.

2.  **For clarity, use a dash or a pair of dashes to set off nonrestrictive (nonessential) elements containing commas.**

    ▶ The Kincaid triplets—Jane, Janice, and Jeanette—enrolled in Miss Hickman's grade one class.

3.  **Use a dash or a pair of dashes to set off interrupters or to indicate a pause.**

    ▶ Sarah has twenty—yes, twenty—Angora cats!

    ▶ He's a nuisance—just a big, fat freeloader.

## 1f.  PARENTHESES ( )

For a discussion of the basic functions and different effects of parentheses and dashes, see the first paragraph of section 1.e. in this handbook.

1.  **Use parentheses to enclose (and de-emphasize) nonessential material.**

    ▶ The first Canadian postage stamp (issued in 1851) is on display at the Canadian Postal Museum in Ottawa.

2.  **Use parentheses to enclose explanations or definitions.**

    ▶ Six metropolitan daily newspapers have joined in a WWW (World Wide Web) site called CareerPath, featuring employment advertisements.

    ▶ Since the World Wide Web has no central organization, you need a "search engine" (a special site that locates other sites) to surf the Web.

    ▶ Semicolons have two basic uses (see section 1b.).

## 1g. BRACKETS [ ]

1.  **Use brackets to insert explanatory material in quotations.**

    (For more information on using brackets in quoted material, see Chapter 25.)

    ▶ "In a Pullman berth [a curtained bunk on a sleeping car of a train], a man can truly be alone with himself. . . ."

2.  **For clarity, use brackets instead of parentheses to enclose material already within parentheses.**

    ▶ We should be sure to give Emanuel Foose (and his brother Emilio [1812–1882] as well) credit for his role in founding the institute.

## 1h. HYPHEN (-)

1.  **Use a hyphen to divide a word at the end of a line.**

    At least one syllable of three or more letters should be before the division: *con-se-quently.*

2.  **Use a hyphen in spelled-out compound numbers from twenty-one through ninety-nine.**

3.  **Use a hyphen in spelled-out fractions.**

    ▶ one-fourth        ▶ five-eighths
    ▶ two-thirds        ▶ four and one-third

4.  **Use a hyphen between two or more words used together as a modifier before a noun (unless the first word ends in *ly*).**

    ▶ thought-provoking speech    ▶ all-out effort
    ▶ problem-solving quiz        ▶ on-the-job training
    ▶ rosy-cheeked baby           ▶ up-to-date data
    ▶ lightly salted peanuts      ▶ highly rated programs

    However, do not hyphenate such modifiers when they do not precede the noun they modify.

    ▶ The quiz was on problem solving.
    ▶ The baby was rosy cheeked.
    ▶ Training was conducted on the job.
    ▶ The data were up to date.

5. **Use a hyphen with certain prefixes.**

These include *ex-* and *self-* with the exceptions of *selfless, selfsame*. There is no hard-and-fast rule about other prefixes such as *anti-, co-, pre-, pro-, re-,* and *well-*. Check an up-to-date dictionary, and, if given a choice, be consistent.

▶ anti-intellectual        ▶ pre-election

▶ co-owner                 ▶ self-denial

▶ ex-president             ▶ well-being

*NOTE:* Always use a hyphen when the word to be prefixed begins with a capital as in *pro-American, non-British,* or *mid-July.*

6. **Use a hyphen to avoid doubling a letter and to avoid confusion.**

▶ semi-invalid [avoids *semiinvalid*]

▶ re-enlist [avoids *reenlist*]

▶ re-form [avoids confusion with *reform*]

# 1i.  QUOTATION MARKS (" ")

Although quotation marks have more than one use, they usually indicate the beginning and end of someone's exact words. Dialogue requires quotation marks. Citations require quotation marks (see Chapter 25). Quotation marks may also be used to indicate words used in special ways. Titles of short written works or parts of works are enclosed with quotation marks.

1. **Use quotation marks in dialogue to enclose the exact words of a speaker.**

▶ Phoebe called, "Sparky, bring that shoe back here!"

▶ "Come on, Sparky," she cajoled, "bring the shoe back, and I'll give you some Teeny Bits."

2. **Use quotation marks to enclose short direct quotations.**

*Short* is defined differently in different documentation styles. The most commonly used style in English, that of the Modern Language Association (MLA), defines *short* as four lines or less. Long quotations are indented.

▶ In *The Conduct of Life,* Emerson wrote as follows: "The art of conversation, or the qualification for a good companion, is a certain self-control, which now holds the subject, now lets it go, with a respect for the emergencies of the moment."

3. **Use quotation marks to enclose the titles of parts of books and periodicals.**

Because this rule is often confused, here is an informal guideline that will help you remember the principle: Underline (italicize) the title or name of a whole item;

use quotation marks around the title of a part. The lists below indicate how the guideline applies:

| *Underline "Whole" Items* | *Use Quotation Marks for "Parts"* |
|---|---|
| book title | chapter or story title |
| songbook title | song title |
| poetry book title | poem title |
| title of a very long poem [e.g., *Paradise Lost*] | |
| name of a newspaper | comic, article, or feature title |
| name of a magazine | article, feature, or story title |
| pamphlet title | speech, short report |
| name of a plane, ship, or train | |
| title of a film, painting, record album, television or radio program | title of an episode of a radio or television series |

4. **Use single quotation marks to enclose a quotation within a quotation.**

If a quotation occurs within a quotation already marked with double quotation marks, enclosed the inside quotation in single quotation marks. This will sometimes result in three quotation marks at the end of the quotation.

▶ "You must have read Eiseley's 'The Real Secret of Piltdown,'" Bill's friend observed.

*NOTE:* In ordinary American usage, the only exceptions to the use of double quotation marks for main, or outside, quotations are long quotations (block quotations), which are not placed within quotation marks because they are indented.

5. **Traditionally, quotation marks were used to enclose words discussed as words. However, many writers now prefer italics for this purpose.**

▶ "Computer" is derived from the Latin verb *computare*.

6. **Use quotation marks to enclose words used in a special or ironic sense.**

▶ What chain of events caused the sinking of an "unsinkable" ship such as the *Titanic?*

7. **Use other punctuation with quotation marks correctly.**

Commas and periods always go *inside* closing quotation marks (except in one documentation situation). Colons and semicolons always go *outside* closing quotation marks. The rule for all other punctuation is that if the punctuation is part of the quotation, it goes inside, and if it is not part of the quotation, it goes outside.

▶ "Reading *Space Technology* gives me the insider's view," he says, adding, "It's like having all the top officials sitting in my office for a discussion."

▶ He said, "I will pay the full amount"; this certainly surprised us.

▶ She has two favourite "sports": eating and sleeping.

## 1j.  *ITALICS* (<u>UNDERLINING</u>)

Italics is a typeface that slants to the right, e.g., *Moby Dick*. Italics can indicate foreign words; special names of vehicles, vessels, or artworks; words used as words; and titles of long works. Since many foreign words have been adopted into English, check a dictionary to see whether or not they should be italicized. Direct quotations in another language are not italicized.

1    **Use italics (underlining) for titles of long works.**

For a discussion of when to use italics and when to use quotation marks in titles, see section 1j.3 of this handbook. The treatment of titles differs from one documentation style to another. Listed here are the most common kinds of works with italicized titles:

**books:** *A Tale of Two Cities*

***Exception:*** Do not use italics (or underlining) for the names of sacred books: the Bible (or the Holy Bible), the New Testament, the Koran, and so forth.

**long poems:** *Paradise Lost*, *The Iliad*, *The Wasteland*

**newspapers and magazines:** the *New York Times*; *National Geographic*

**pamphlets:** *Letters from an American Farmer*

**vessels (planes, trains, ships, spacecraft):** the *Titanic*; the *Burlington Zephyr*; *Challenger*

**plays:** *Hamlet*; *The Music Man*

**comic strips:** *Doonesbury*

**films and television and radio programs:** *Aladdin*; *The X-Files*; *A Prairie Home Companion*

**albums and long musical works:** *Thriller*; Mahler's *Symphony No. 9*

**paintings and sculpture:** da Vinci's *Mona Lisa*; Michelangelo's *David*

**software:** *Windows 98*; *PageMaker 6.5*

2.    **For clarity, use italics for words discussed as words, particularly when quotation marks are used in the same sentence for another purpose.**

▶ The word *boudoir* comes from an Old French verb, meaning "to pout or sulk."

3.　Use italics for emphasis, but do so sparingly.

▶ Trust me—take Route 315, *not* Route 23.

▶ What is the *evidence* for that position?

## 1k.　PERIOD (.)

1.　Use a period at the end of statements, mild commands, and indirect questions.

▶ The temperature in the cave is a constant 15 degrees.

▶ As you tour the cave, please stay on the marked trail.

▶ Many people have asked how the cave was first discovered.

2.　Use a period (or periods) with some abbreviations.

If an abbreviation comes at the end of a sentence, use only one period.

3.　Use a period as a decimal in numbers.

▶ 1.06　　　　▶ 0.910　　　　▶ $149.95

## 1l.　QUESTION MARK (?)

1.　Use a question mark at the end of a direct question or request.

▶ Will you please pick up a book of stamps on your way?

▶ A group of citizens discussed the question, "Does our town need a city manager instead of a mayor?"

2.　Use a question mark after each elliptical question in a series.

▶ Should obscenity be controlled on the Internet? If so, by whom? How?

3.　Use a question mark in parentheses after an item that is of doubtful accuracy.

▶ The tunnel from his cell, disguised by a huge poster, was started in 2001(?) but was discovered only after he had fled.

## 1m.  EXCLAMATION POINT (!)

An exclamation point indicates strong emotion: pain, fear, surprise, indignation, or excitement. An exclamation point cannot bolster a weak statement nor make an argument more convincing. Use exclamation points sparingly; otherwise, they lose their power.

1. **Use an exclamation point to add force to a command or expression of emotion.**

   ▶ "Ouch!"
   ▶ "Help!" Jimmy screamed. "The horse is standing on my foot."
   ▶ WATCH OUT! Deer Crossing

# 2. CAPITALIZATION

If you become lost in the thicket of capitalization, first consult an up-to-date dictionary. If you should find more than one way to capitalize, let your audience be your guide. In other words, when you are writing for an employer, follow conventional business and technical usage. When writing a college research paper, follow the style manual your instructor recommends.

You may be surprised at certain variations in capitalization. One of the most striking differences concerns the names of software. Business and technical personnel generally follow the spelling of the manufacturer, even if it means placing a capital in the middle of a brand or trade name: for example, *InfoTrac*. Fortunately, the capitalization of most words is standard and can usually be found in a good desk dictionary.

Once you master the following standard rules of capitalization, you will be able to capitalize most words without consulting other sources.

1. **Capitalize the first word of a sentence.**

   ▶ The sentence above is an example; so is this one.

2. **Capitalize proper nouns and trade names.**

Capitalize the names of people; places; political, racial, and religious groups; institutions and organizations; sacred writings; brand and trade names; ships, planes, and trains; monuments; awards; and specific academic degrees and courses.

   ▶ Karen O'Neill          ▶ University of Alberta
   ▶ the Dead Sea Scrolls    ▶ Catholic, Protestant, Jewish
   ▶ the Bible (or the Holy Bible)  ▶ the Koran
   ▶ Yonge Street           ▶ the Bluenose

▶ Yukon River
▶ the South
▶ Calculus 101

▶ Purina Cat Chow
▶ League of Women Voters
▶ Master's of English Education

*EXCEPTIONS:* Do not capitalize directions, ideologies, or philosophies (unless derived from the name of an individual—Marxism, for example).

▶ After Ken left Kenora, he drove *south*.
▶ Shelly is an *idealist*.
▶ Many Russians feel they were better off under *communism*.

3. **Capitalize proper adjectives and abbreviations.**

Capitalize adjectives and abbreviations derived from proper nouns.

▶ the French language
▶ Cooper's hawk
▶ Japanese maple
▶ CSIS

▶ Palestinian soldiers
▶ Appalachian quilt
▶ Boston terrier
▶ CD-ROM

4. **Capitalize official and personal titles.**

Capitalize a title (or rank) immediately before the name of a person.

▶ Dr. Stephanie Winters
▶ Justice Sandra Day O'Connor
▶ General James Wolfe
▶ Mr. Jacob Turner

▶ Professor Celia Kincaid
▶ Prime Minister Trudeau
▶ Reverend Jamison
▶ Ms. Shannon Maguire

*EXCEPTION:* When no name is given, do *not* capitalize a title.

▶ The professor encouraged the class to share their opinions.
▶ The prime minister of India visited flood victims.

5. **Capitalize titles of literary and other artistic works.**

Ordinarily, capitalize the first and last words as well as all major words in the title of a literary or artistic work.

▶ Last week Jack read the biography of Malcolm Lowry, *Malcolm Lowry: Vancouver Days*.
▶ At the Louvre, we saw Leonardo Da Vinci's *The Mona Lisa*.

6. **Capitalize calendar items and historical periods.**

Capitalize months, special weeks, days, holidays, and historical periods.

▶ April
▶ Tuesday

▶ New Year's Day
▶ Right-to-Read Week

- ▶ Easter
- ▶ the Renaissance

- ▶ Middle Ages
- ▶ the Great Depression

*EXCEPTIONS:* Do not capitalize seasons or centuries.

- ▶ our spring break     ▶ the twentieth century     ▶ in the winter

7. **Capitalize events and documents.**

Capitalize wars, treaties, constitutions, and other important events and documents.

- ▶ World War II
- ▶ World Series
- ▶ Rose Bowl game

- ▶ Treaty of Versailles
- ▶ Magna Carta
- ▶ War of 1812

*EXCEPTIONS:* Do not capitalize laws, theories, or hypotheses:

- ▶ nature's laws
- ▶ code of Hammurabi

- ▶ theory of relativity
- ▶ Mendelian principles

# 3. ABBREVIATIONS

When writing, avoid unnecessary abbreviations and use them appropriately. Use only conventional abbreviations that can be easily understood. In desk dictionaries and many other reference sources, you will find a key to the abbreviations used, either in the front or back of the publication.

## 3a. GUIDELINES FOR USING ABBREVIATIONS

Abbreviation styles may differ significantly from one dictionary to another or from one documentation style to another. If you are writing a research paper and following a particular style, check the appropriate guidelines. *Generally, use abbreviations in a table and a list of works cited, but not in the text of a research paper.* If you do use an abbreviation in the text, be sure to define it. The examples that follow are based upon the *MLA Handbook for Writers of Research Papers,* 5th ed., by Joseph Gibaldi.

1. **Use no periods or spaces between abbreviations of most letters that are capitalized.**

| | | | |
|---|---|---|---|
| FBI | IBM | MD | BA |
| PSAT | PhD | RN | AD |
| IRS | EST | DNA | BC |

*Some exceptions:*

| | |
|---|---|
| Scott Felder, Jr. | Mr. Daley |
| N.P. | S.S. |
| J. R. Smith | Ms. Jones |

2. **Use a period after each lowercase letter of most abbreviations that represent a word.**

| | | |
|---|---|---|
| p.m. | ed. | s.t. |
| a.m. | r.s.v.p. | e.g. |
| n.p. | p.p.a. | |

*There are many exceptions:*

| | | |
|---|---|---|
| 2nd | km | rpm |

3. **Use a period after most abbreviations that end with lowercase letters:**

| | | | | |
|---|---|---|---|---|
| govt. | Eng. | wk. | Wed. | assn. |
| dept. | mkt. | mo. | Mar. | biog. |
| Mar. | obs. | yr. | fig. | introd. |
| adj. | arch. | ed. | def. | cont. |

## 3b. COMMON ABBREVIATIONS AND REFERENCE TERMS

| | |
|---|---|
| AD | *anno Domini* (in the year of the Lord). Precedes numerals (AD 16). Follows centuries (eighth century AD). |
| arch. | archaic |
| BC | before Christ. Follows numerals (23 BC) |
| c., ca. | *circa:* "about"; used with approximate dates |
| comp., comps. | compiled by, compiler(s) |
| e.g. | *exempli gratia:* "for example" |
| et al. | *et alii:* "and others" |
| ex., exs. | example(s) |
| DA, DSI | Dissertation Abstracts, Dissertation Abstracts International |
| diss. | dissertation |
| doc. | document |
| ibid. | *ibidem:* "in the same place" |
| i.e. | *id est:* "that is" (set off by commas) |
| ms., mss. | manuscript(s) |

| par. | paragraph |
| pref. | preface, preface by |
| pt. | part |
| rept., repts. | reported by, report(s) |
| rpt. | reprint, reprinted by |
| sec., sect. | section |
| *sic* | thus in the source (place in square brackets as an editorial note, otherwise in parentheses) |
| var. | variant |

# 4.  GRAMMAR AND USAGE

## 4a.  SENTENCE FRAGMENTS

Traditionally, sentence fragments have been frowned on and complete sentences advocated except in dialogue, conversation, and other informal situations. In formal writing, fragments are avoided in all but a few special circumstances.

**Definition:** A fragment is a portion of a sentence that is punctuated as if it were an entire sentence. Lacking a subject, a verb, or both, a fragment is an incomplete thought. A fragment may be a word, a phrase, a dependent clause, or any combination of words that deviate from the basic subject-verb (or verb-subject) sentence pattern.

**Usage:** A general guideline for using fragments is to consider the rhetorical situation and use a fragment only for a purpose. The most important special uses of the fragment are answers to questions, exclamations, and requests, or commands.

▶ When is the next meeting? Next Thursday at 2:30 p.m. [fragment answer to question]

▶ What a shame!          ▶ No! Not really! [exclamations]

▶ No smoking.            ▶ Ready, get set, go! [requests or command.]

If you decide to use a fragment, be sure (1) your reader will approve, (2) you know how to avoid unintentional fragments, (3) the fragment is appropriate in the context. To be effective, a fragment should have a purpose.

1.  **Avoid using *-ing* words or infinitives as main verbs, thus creating a fragment.**

    *Incorrect*

    ▼ *Driving* 160 km a day to and from classes, *doing* complex assignments, and *raising* a family. I found that my undergraduate days were exhausting. [The first group of words is a fragment.]

▼ Jim and Shane stayed home last night. The reason *being* that they were broke. [The second group of words is a fragment.]

▼ First, the proper equipment *to get* out on the lake or pond. A canoe with a paddle or chest waders will do the job. [The first group of words is a fragment.]

*Correct*

▶ *Driving* 160 km a day to and from classes, *doing* complex assignments, and *raising* a family, I found that my undergraduate days were exhausting. [Join the fragment to the sentence with a comma.]

▶ Jim and Shane stayed home last night *because* they had no money. [The fragment and the sentence could be joined with a comma, but the result would be wordy.]

▶ First, *gather* the proper equipment to get out on the lake or pond. Either a canoe with a paddle or chest waders will do the job. [Add a verb to the first word group; the subject is understood to be *you*, meaning "you gather."]

2. **Avoid treating phrases that merely add additional details as complete sentences.**

*Incorrect*

▼ Then there is the high-speed driver. *A real maniac.*

▼ Kevin called his father collect last night. *To ask for a loan.*

▼ The company refused to honour the warranty. *Even though I purchased the lawn mower only six months ago.*

*Correct*

▶ Then there is the high-speed driver, a real maniac.

▶ Kevin called his father collect last night to ask for a loan.

▶ The company refused to honour the warranty even though I purchased the lawn mower only six months ago.

3. **Avoid treating dependent clauses as complete sentences.**

*Incorrect*

▼ *After I learned the market price for comparable antique tables.* I decided to rescue mine from the attic and refinish it.

*Correct*

▶ After I learned the market price for comparable antique tables, I decided to rescue mine from the attic and refinish it. [The introductory adverb clause is made a part of the sentence with a comma.]

## 4b.  COMMA SPLICES AND FUSED (RUN-ON) SENTENCES

Beginning writers sometimes omit punctuation between clauses in a compound sentence. (See Chapter 8 for more on compound sentences.) This error results in a *fused sentence*, sometimes called a *run-on sentence*. A related error is the *comma splice*, which occurs when two clauses are joined (spliced) with a comma. Never use the comma alone to punctuate a long compound sentence. If you use a comma, you must also have a coordinating conjunction. Note also that a semicolon is required before a conjunctive adverb such as *however* or *therefore*. The examples below will help to clarify punctuation of compound sentences:

1.  **Punctuate sentences correctly to avoid comma splices.**

    *Incorrect*

    ▼ Terrariums are costly at a flower shop, they are inexpensive to make at home.

    ▼ Terrariums are costly at a flower shop, however, they are inexpensive to make at home.

    *Correct*

    ▶ Terrariums are costly at a flower shop, *but* they are inexpensive to make at home. [Coordinating conjunction and a comma]

    ▶ Terrariums are costly at a flower shop; however, they are inexpensive to make at home. [A semicolon replaces the coordinating conjunction and comma.]

2.  **Punctuate sentences correctly to avoid fused (run-on) sentences.**

    *Incorrect*

    ▼ The ordinance won wide support it was passed by a two-thirds vote.

    *Correct*

    ▶ The ordinance won wide support; it was passed by a two-thirds vote. [semicolon added]

## 4c.  PRONOUNS

Pronouns have different uses and therefore have different forms. A pronoun that is a subject is in the *subjective* case; a pronoun that shows ownership is in the *possessive* case; and a pronoun that acts as an object is in the *objective* case.

Pronouns also show person. *First person* refers to the individual who is speaking: *I (We)* will leave soon. *Second person* refers to the individual spoken to: *You* are very thoughtful. *Third person* refers to the people or things spoken about: *She (He, It, They)* will arrive soon. The following table will help you review the uses of pronouns.

**Case of Pronouns**

|  | *Subjective* | *Possessive* | *Objective* |
|---|---|---|---|
| **Singular** | | | |
| *First person* | I | my, mine | me |
| *Second person* | you | your, yours | you |
| *Third person* | he, she, it | his, her, hers, its | him, her, it |
| **Plural** | | | |
| *First person* | we | our, ours | us |
| *Second person* | you | your, yours | you |
| *Third person* | they | their, theirs | them |

1. **Use the correct case of pronouns.**

   ***Subjective case. Use the subjective case for the following:***

   *Subjects of main or subordinate clauses*
   - ▶ *I* will act as chairman during Brad's absence.
   - ▶ Jane's party was the best *I* have ever attended.

   *Appositives identifying words in the subjective case*
   - ▶ Only two people—*Ray and I*—decided to go.

   *Subject complements following linking verbs*
   - ▶ The winners were *he* and Joan.

   ***Possessive case. Use the possessive case for the following:***

   *To designate ownership*
   - ▶ That hat is *hers*.
   - ▶ The committee was late in finishing *its* report.

   *Before a gerund (a verb form used as a noun)*
   - ▶ *Your* not writing upset Mother.
   - ▶ *Her* drum playing angers the neighbours.

*Objective case. Use the objective case for the following:*

*Direct objects, indirect objects, and objects of prepositions*

▶ Bradley hit *it* over third base. [direct object]

▶ Jack sent *her* flowers. [indirect object]

▶ The letter was addressed to *me*. [object of preposition]

*Appositives identifying objects*

▶ The club elected two new members, Erin and *her*.

*NOTE:* After *than* or *as*, use the pronoun case that correctly completes your meaning.

▶ My mother understands my sister better than *I*. ("than I do")

▶ My mother understands my sister better than *me*. ("than she understands me")

Notice that *we* or *us* before a noun takes the same case it would if you dropped the noun.

▶ *We* students have complained to the administration about this problem before.

▶ It is difficult for *us* new mothers to get enough sleep.

**2.  Make sure that what each pronoun refers to is clear.**

Since a pronoun is a substitute for a noun or a noun phrase, a pronoun's meaning is apparent only when the reader or listener knows to what the pronoun refers. In other words, a pronoun should have a clear antecedent.

*Unclear*

▼ The law firm of Creager and Colvin failed after *he* withdrew the operating capital and fled to Switzerland.

▼ Teresa proofread my paper, but she didn't find a single *one*.

▼ He believes in reincarnation, but he does not believe that *they* appear to the living.

▼ *It* said in the newspaper that the election would be close.

*Clear*

▶ The law firm of Creager and Colvin failed after *Colvin* withdrew the operating capital and fled to Switzerland.

▶ Teresa proofread my paper, but she didn't find a single *error*.

▶ He believes in reincarnation, but he does not believe that *the dead* appear to the living.

▶ The newspaper reported that the election would be close.

### 3.   Make pronouns and their antecedents agree in gender, person, and number.

Pronouns must have the same gender, person, and number as the word or phrase they refer to. Because gender and person seldom pose problems with pronouns (but see section 4c.4 on sexist usage), the discussion here is limited to agreement in number. The rule is simple: Use plural pronouns to refer to plural antecedents. Use singular pronouns to refer to singular antecedents.

*Indefinite pronouns*

Most indefinite pronouns indicate number. The plural forms seldom pose problems, but the singular forms are confusing, sometimes violating logic. For example, the word *everyone* means all, but *everyone* is singular and *all* is plural. An easy way to recall these eccentricities of usage is to remember that any pronoun containing *one* or *body* is singular. Listed below are the most common singular pronouns:

| | | |
|---|---|---|
| anyone | everybody | somebody |
| anybody | everyone | one |
| either | someone | each |
| neither | no one | |

If you have trouble with *either, neither,* or *each,* then mentally add *one* and think: *either one, neither one, each one.* Likewise, in a word that has the suffix *body,* substitute *one*: for *anybody,* think *anyone*; for *somebody,* think *someone.*

*Compound antecedents*

In general, use a plural pronoun to refer to compound antecedents linked by *and*:

▶ George and Martha are taking *their* time.

However, when a compound antecedent is preceded by *each* or *every*, use a singular pronoun:

▶ Every cafe and restaurant in town has seen *its* business suffer.

Use a singular pronoun to refer to singular antecedents linked by *or* and *nor.* Use a plural pronoun to refer to plural antecedents linked by *neither* and *nor*:

▶ A dog or a cat has *its* special needs during warm summer months.
▶ Neither friends nor family members gave *their* approval to the marriage.

### 4.   Avoid sexist use of pronouns.

Use *he or she* and *his or her* sparingly. One *he or she* or one *his or her* will not disrupt the flow of a sentence, but the repeated use of these terms can distract the reader. Instead, rewrite sentences to avoid male and female pronouns. You can omit the third-person pronoun, repeat the noun, or make the entire sentence plural. Consider the following correct examples:

► If a person is insincere, chances are that *his or her* insincerity will be detected.

► If a person is insincere, chances are that *the* insincerity will be detected. [preferable]

► If *people* are insincere, chances are that *their* insincerity will be detected. [preferable]

As a way of avoiding sexist usage, people sometimes use the plural *their* when a singular personal pronoun such as *his* or *her* is called for. This colloquial usage is heard in sentences such as "*Everyone* should remember to take *their* ground cloth and tent." But for most writing, this sentence would be considered incorrect. Standard usage would be as follows:

► *Everyone* should remember to take a ground cloth and tent.

► *All* should remember to pack *their* rain gear.

► Not *one* of the runners felt *she* had run *her* best. [All the runners are women.]

► Not *one* of the alumni remembered to wear *his* old football jersey.

### 5.    Use relative pronouns correctly.

There are only six relative pronouns, easily memorized because five begin with *w*: *who, whom, whose, which,* and *what.* The other one is *that. Which, what,* and *that* have the same form for all three cases. *Who* is in the subjective case, *whose* is in the possessive case, and *whom* is in the objective case.

► *Who* is calling? [subject]

► *Whose* gerbil is that? [possessive]

► To *whom* it may concern: [object of preposition]

Relative pronouns are used to introduce adjective clauses. Sometimes these pronouns cause problems in punctuation and usage. In the first example that follows, the adjective clause (italicized) is nonessential—unimportant to the main idea of the sentence; *which* is used and the phrase is set off by commas. In the second sentence, the adjective clause is necessary for the sentence to be clear and complete; *that* is used and no commas are needed.

► A dog, *which had no collar,* followed me home. [nonessential clause]

► The dog *that is wearing the collar* is mine. [essential clause]

*NOTE: Who* and *whom* generally refer only to people. *Which* and *that* refer to animals, places, or things. Sometimes *who* is used to refer to animals with names, but such usage is unusual.

6. **Avoid inappropriate shifts of person.**

A careless shift in person can confuse your reader. Maintain a consistent point of view by writing in the same person: first person (*I, we*), second person (*you*), or third person (*he, she, it, they*).

*Inappropriate*

▼ *I* always spend the morning hours on work that requires mental effort, for *your* mind is freshest in the morning.

*Revised*

▶ *I* always spend the morning hours on work that requires mental effort, for *my* mind is freshest in the morning.

## 4d. VERBS

All verbs have four basic forms. These principal parts are *the infinitive, present participle, past,* and *past participle.* These basic forms can be varied by the addition of helping verbs (*is, are, was, were, be, been, has, have, had,* etc.) or the preposition *to. To* indicates the infinitive, which is in the present tense.

**Four Principal Parts**

| Infinitive | Present Participle | Past | Past Participle |
|---|---|---|---|
| (to) live | (is) liv*ing* | liv*ed* | (has, have, or had) liv*ed* |

**Six Troublesome Verbs**

| Present tense | Past tense | Past participle |
|---|---|---|
| lie (to recline) | lay | (has, had) lain |
| lay (to place an object) | laid | laid |
| sit (to take a seat) | sat | sat |
| set (to place an object) | set | set |
| rise (to get up) | rose | risen |
| raise (to lift) | raised | raised |

1. **Use verb forms correctly.**

Try to be consistent in using verb forms. If you have a question, consult a dictionary. Once in awhile, you may find that two or more forms are considered acceptable. Since verbs are the most complex part of speech in the English language, a full treatment of the topic is impossible here. Only commonly misused forms are discussed.

### The "troublesome six" verbs

Six verbs, sometimes called "the troublesome six," are outlined in the preceding table. Use the correct form of these verbs. Remember that *lay, set,* and *raise*—when used in the active voice—all require direct objects and that *lie, sit,* and *rise* do not take objects. This guideline should help prevent confusion. In the examples below, the direct objects are italicized.

| *Direct Objects* | *No Direct Objects* |
|---|---|
| Please lay the *book* there. | Lie down, Rover. |
| Sharon laid her *coat* on the bed. | Sue has lain in the sun two hours. |
| Barry set his *briefcase* on my desk. | Harry sat there. |
| Jim raised the *blind.* | The sun rises at 6:30 a.m. |

### Four more verbs requiring caution

Try to be consistent in your choice of tense. Four verbs—*can, may, will,* and *shall*—are frequently misused because people mix tenses improperly. But if you understand the principal parts of verbs and remember the groupings listed below, you should be able to use these verbs correctly.

| *Present tense* | *Past tense* |
|---|---|
| can | could |
| may | might |
| will | would |
| shall | should |

If you have a question about the tense of a verb, consult your dictionary. Be aware that two or more forms are sometimes considered acceptable.

### Principal parts of irregular verbs

The following list of irregular verbs and their principal parts is based on the *American Heritage Dictionary*, 3rd edition. The verbs are used with helping verbs (such as *is, are, was, were, have, has, have been*) to form tenses.

| *Present* | *Present Participle* | *Past* | *Past Participle* |
|---|---|---|---|
| bear | (is, are) bearing | bore | (has, have, had) borne |
| beat | beating | beat | beaten |
| become | becoming | became | become |
| begin | beginning | began | begun |
| bite | biting | bit | bitten |

| Present | Present Participle | Past | Past Participle |
|---|---|---|---|
| blow | blowing | blew | blown |
| break | breaking | broke | broken |
| bring | bringing | brought | brought |
| burst | bursting | burst | burst |
| buy | buying | bought | bought |
| catch | catching | caught | caught |
| choose | choosing | chose | chosen |
| come | coming | came | come |
| cut | cutting | cut | cut |
| creep | creeping | crept | crept |
| dive | diving | dived | dived, dove |
| do | doing | did | done |
| draw | drawing | drew | drawn |
| drink | drinking | drank | drunk |
| drive | driving | drove | driven |
| eat | eating | ate | eaten |
| fall | falling | fell | fallen |
| find | finding | found | found |
| fling | flinging | flung | flung |
| fly | flying | flew | flown |
| forget | forgetting | forgot | forgot, forgotten |
| freeze | freezing | froze | frozen |
| get | getting | got | gotten, got |
| give | giving | gave | given |
| go | going | went | gone |
| grow | growing | grew | grown |
| hang (suspend) | hanging | hung | hung |
| hang (execute) | (is being) hanged | hanged | hanged |
| hit | hitting | hit | hit |
| hurt | hurting | hurt | hurt |
| keep | keeping | kept | kept |
| know | (is) known | knew | known |
| lead | leading | led | led |
| leave | leaving | left | left |
| lend | lending | lent | lent |

| Present | Present Participle | Past | Past Participle |
|---------|-------------------|------|-----------------|
| let | letting | let | let |
| pay | paying | paid | paid |
| lose | losing | lost | lost |
| ride | riding | rode | ridden |
| ring | ringing | rang | rung |
| rise | rising | rose | risen |
| run | running | ran | run |
| say | saying | said | said |
| see | seeing | saw | seen |
| shake | shaking | shook | shaken |
| shine (the sun) | shining | shone | shone |
| shine (to polish) | shining | shined | shined |
| sing | singing | sang or sung | sung |
| sink | sinking | sank or sunk | sunk |
| speak | speaking | spoke | spoken |
| spring | springing | sprang, sprung | sprung |
| stand | standing | stood | stood |
| steal | stealing | stole | stolen |
| sting | stinging | stung | stung |
| strike | striking | struck | struck |
| swear | swearing | swore | sworn |
| swim | swimming | swam | swum |
| swing | swinging | swung | swung |
| take | taking | took | taken |
| teach | teaching | taught | taught |
| tear | tearing | tore | torn |
| tell | telling | told | told |
| throw | throwing | threw | thrown |
| wear | wearing | wore | worn |
| write | writing | wrote | written |

## 2. Use *be* correctly.

The verb *be* should not be used as if it were a complete verb. Except in a few special instances (see the discussion of the subjunctive mood in section 4d.6), some other form of *be* or a helping verb such as *will* is required.

*Nonstandard*

I *be* a college student.

I *be* going there.

Mrs. Beck, you *be* leaving soon?

*Standard*

I *am* a college student.

I *am* going there.

Mrs. Beck, *will* you *be* leaving soon?

3.  **Make subjects and verbs agree in number.**

Use singular verbs with singular subjects; use plural verbs with plural subjects. Verb agreement is sometimes a problem, particularly for international students. But if you remember—when using the third person—that adding an *s* to a verb makes it singular, this principle should help. (Adding an *s* to a noun makes it plural.) Here are some third-person examples:

| *Singular* | *Plural* |
|---|---|
| is | are |
| was | were |
| has | have |
| skates | skate |

*Words between the subject and verb*

Words and phrases that appear between the subject and the verb sometimes mislead. In the following sentences, the verbs are plural to agree with the plural subjects:

▶ The letters, along with the package, *were* mailed today.

The word *package* is not the subject. But because *package* comes immediately before the verb, it may seem natural to use *was*. This is not correct. In the following sentence *were* is correct:

▶ The letters and the package *were* mailed this morning.

▶ The package and the letters *were* mailed this morning. [preferable]

*Compound subject linked with or or nor*

Another troublemaker is the sentence that has a singular and a plural subject without *and*. Then the subject nearest the verb determines the agreement of the verb:

▶ Neither the cookies nor the fruitcake *was* fresh.

▶ Neither the fruitcake nor the cookies *were* fresh.

### Inverted word order

In questions and in statements beginning with *there,* the subject usually follows the verb. Be careful that the verb agrees with the subject.

▶ *Are* the photocopies ready to be picked up? (photocopies *are*)

▶ There *is* only one clerk at work today. (clerk *is*)

### Relative pronoun subjects

In a clause beginning with a relative pronoun—*who, which,* or *that*—look for the pronoun's antecedent to decide whether the verb is singular or plural.

▶ People who *litter* should be fined heavily. (people *litter*)

▶ This house, which *needs* some work, could be a bargain. (house *needs*)

4. **Use the active voice of verbs unless there is a good reason for using the passive voice. (See Chapter 8.)**

Use the active voice in most sentences. The active voice occurs when the subject is the doer of the action expressed by the verb. The passive voice occurs when the subject is not the doer of the action expressed by the verb.

▶ Sergei Grinkov *won* an Olympic gold medal twice. [active voice]

▶ Twice an Olympic gold medal *was won* by Sergei Grinkov. [passive voice]

5. **Avoid inappropriate shifts of tense, voice, or mood.**

Inappropriate shifts in the tense, voice, or mood of verbs can be distracting and even confusing to the reader.

*Inappropriate*

▼ Before he *went* to class, he *drinks* three cups of coffee. [needless shift from past to present tense]

▼ A cocoon was sighted on a liatris plant, and in the spring a beautiful moth crept out. [needless shift from active to passive voice]

▼ *Go* to school, and *you should* take an umbrella. [needless shift from imperative to indicative mood]

*Appropriate*

▶ Before he goes to class, he *drinks* three cups of coffee. [both verbs in present tense]

▶ On a liatris plant, I *found* a cocoon; and in the spring a beautiful moth *crept* out. [both verbs in past tense and active voice]

▶ *Go* to school and *take* an umbrella. [both verbs in imperative mood]

### 6. Use the subjunctive mood correctly.

The subjunctive mood is the form of a verb used to express doubt, desire, probability, a condition contrary to fact, or a hypothetical situation. The subjunctive appears in three ways: (1) in *if* clauses indicating unreal conditions; (2) in *that* clauses after verbs expressing requests, suggestions, wishes, or commands; and (3) in a few idioms.

*Unreal conditions*

▶ My husband acted as though he *were* an expert at ironing until he scorched a shirt.

▶ In Chicago's traffic jams, I felt as if I *were* having a bad dream.

▶ Terry could fix that leak if he *were* here.

*That* clauses after verbs expressing requests, suggestions, wishes, or orders

▶ Her boss asked that she *remain* in the building during her coffee break.

▶ The company requires that I *be* on duty at 8:00 a.m.

▶ The committee agreed that Jane *be* given released time to complete the project.

▶ Henry moved that the meeting *be* adjourned.

*A few idioms*

▶ If this *be* true    ▶ Far *be* it from me

▶ *Come* what may    ▶ Long *wave* the stars and stripes!

# 4e MODIFIERS

### 1. Avoid misplaced modifiers.

Misplaced modifiers are simply modifying words or phrases (adjective or adverb) that are out of place. They sneak into places where they do not belong. Consider some examples:

*Misplaced*

▼ "Who says kids *only* like junk food?" [an ad for spaghetti]

▼ "If *only* your feet could talk." [an ad for a podiatrist]

▼ "If you *only* inspect your draft sentence by sentence, you can easily overlook how its parts work together." [a textbook]

*Revised*

▶ Who says kids like *only* junk food?

▶ If your feet could *only* talk.

▶ If you inspect your draft *only* sentence by sentence, you can easily overlook how its parts work together.

The adverbs *almost* and *even* are other frequent offenders. Like *only*, they should be placed exactly before the word they modify.

*Misplaced*

▼ She *almost* used the entire bottle of bath oil for one bath.

▼ I *even* felt worse after I took the medicine.

*Revised*

▶ She used *almost* the entire bottle of bath oil for one bath.

▶ I felt *even* worse after I took the medicine.

Clauses and phrases may also be misplaced in sentences, often leading to unintentionally humorous misreadings:

*Misplaced*

▼ Jane wore a flower in her hair *that was pink*. [What was pink?]

▼ Dick kept an odd-shaped piece of jade in his jacket pocket, *which he considered lucky*. [What was lucky?]

▼ A spider dropped off the piano bench as I opened the door *into a large web*. [Did the spider web have a door?]

▼ I easily spotted the rare bird *using high-powered binoculars*. [Was the bird using binoculars?]

*Revised*

▶ In her hair Jane wore a flower that was pink. [Or: In her hair Jane wore a pink flower.]

▶ Dick kept an odd-shaped piece of jade, which he considered lucky, in his jacket pocket.

▶ As I opened the door, a spider dropped off the piano bench into a large web.

▶ Using high-powered binoculars, I easily spotted the rare bird.

2. **Avoid dangling modifiers.**

Dangling modifiers are phrases that lack a referent: The noun or pronoun needed to make the phrase clear and logical has been omitted. Usually, dangling modifiers cling precariously at the beginning of a sentence. Here are two examples from student papers:

*Dangling*

▼ When only a youngster in grade school, *my father* instructed me in the art of boxing. [Who was in grade school?]

▼ After standing up well under the two-year exposure test, the *manufacturers* were convinced that the paint was sufficiently durable. [The manufacturers stood up well?]

*Revised (referent added)*

▶ When *I was* only a youngster in grade school, my father instructed me in the art of boxing.

▶ After *the paint* stood up well under the two-year exposure test, the manufacturers were convinced that it was sufficiently durable.

*NOTE:* Whenever you include an *-ing* phrase (participial phrase) at the beginning of a sentence, check to see that the word it modifies immediately follows it. If not, rewrite the sentence to make that word the subject of the first clause. Probably the best way to find tangled syntax is to read your writing aloud and listen carefully. Does each sentence make sense? Beware of answering in the affirmative too quickly. Writers know what they mean. *The question is whether each sentence will be clear and logical to readers.*

# 5. SPELLING

## 5a. SPELLING TIPS

The mystery of poor spelling has not been completely solved. But we do know that incorrect pronunciation sometimes leads to incorrect spelling. Students who mispronounce words frequently misspell those same words. The left list below contains some words that are commonly misspelled due to mispronunciation:

| *Incorrect* | *Correct* |
| --- | --- |
| Artic | Arctic |
| congradulations | congratulations |
| discribe | describe |
| goverment | government |
| enviroment | environment |
| secratary | secretary |
| wreck havoc | wreak havoc |
| then (used in comparison) | than |

If you are unsure of the spelling or pronunciation of a word, look it up in a dictionary. Then practise writing and saying the word correctly.

The best spellers are those who can visualize words. During spelling bees, students can write words on scraps of paper, in the air, or on a corner of the blackboard to see how the words look. Remembering the appearance of a word can help in recalling the correct letters.

If you can strengthen your mental images of any problem words, you can improve your spelling. One way is to keep a list of words that you misspell frequently and practise writing them. (Chances are there will be fewer than a dozen.) After you look up the correct spelling of each word on your list, write each one at least a dozen times.

## 5b.  OTHER SPELLING AIDS

▶ Only one English word ends in *sede: supersede.* Only three words end in *ceed: exceed, proceed, succeed.* All other words of similar sound end in *cede: precede, recede,* and so forth.

▶ Drop the final *e* in most words when the suffix you are adding begins with a vowel: *chang(e)ing, hop(e)ing, purchas(e)able.* (In a few instances, however, the final *e* is kept: *changeable, knowledgeable, peaceable.* And some words can be spelled either way: *salable, saleable; livable, liveable.*) Usually the final *e* is kept when the suffix begins with a consonant: *hopeful, vengeful, homeless.*

▶ *Pre* means "before." *Per* means "through, to, for, by each," or "by means of." *Pro* means "in favour of" or "acting as."

*preschool:* before school

*perceive:* to become aware of directly through the senses

*procapitalism:* in favour of capitalism

▶ Plurals of words ending in *y* are formed as follows: When a consonant precedes the final *y*, change the *y* to *i* and add *es: company, companies; lady, ladies; cherry, cherries.* Exception: plurals of proper names, for instance *the Kelleys.* When a vowel precedes the *y*, keep the *y* and add *s: monkeys, attorneys, byways.*

▶ To form the plural of nouns ending in *ch, s, sh, x,* and *z,* add *es: matches, gases, bushes, taxes, buzzes.* This rule also applies to the singular forms of verbs ending in these letters.

▶ When adding a suffix that begins with a vowel, double a final consonant if the word meets all of these criteria: (1) It is one syllable or is stressed on the final syllable; (2) there is only one vowel in the word or in the final syllable; (3) the word or syllable ends in a single consonant. The following words meet all these criteria: *rap, rapped, rapping; occur, occurred, occurrence; fit, fitter, fittest; repel, repelling, repellent.* Note that for words ending in *e,* the *e* is dropped but the remaining consonant is never doubled: *write, writing* (not *writting*).

▶ A modification of this rule applies when the pronunciation of the word changes after the suffix is added. For example, *infer* becomes *inferring* (doubled final consonant) because the stress remains on the final syllable; but it becomes *inference* (no double consonant) because here the stress shifts to the first syllable. A related modification is seen in words such as *offer, offered, offering* and *order, ordered, ordering.* The stress is always on the first syllable, and thus the consonant is not doubled.

## 5c. SIX WAYS TO IMPROVE SPELLING

Probably the biggest factor in any improvement is motivation. If you resolve to refine your spelling skill and follow a plan, you will become a better speller. Here are six techniques to aid you:

1.  **Use a dictionary to check words if you are unsure of their spelling.** Carry a spelling checker or pocket dictionary and keep a desk dictionary in a convenient place at home. But remember that computer spelling checkers are limited in their helpfulness. (see "Glossary of Usage" pages H-36–H-41—for similar words that are commonly confused.)

2.  **Pronounce words correctly.** If you leave out letters or syllables in pronunciation, you may leave them out when writing the word.

3.  **Compile your own spelling list.** Review this daily for a few weeks. Look at each word. Then shut your eyes and see if you can spell it correctly.

4.  **Write misspelled words correctly several times so that you can visualize their correct spelling in your mind.**

5.  **Familiarize yourself with the memory association aids.** Then devise some aids of your own.

6.  As a last resort, if you cannot recognize misspelled words, ask someone to mark them. Then get out the dictionary and correct the spellings yourself. With practice, your spelling ability will improve, and you will be able to catch more of your errors.

# 6.  GLOSSARY OF USAGE

Some words in the English language are commonly confused because they look or sound alike. Other words used in conversation are sometimes mistaken for standard usage. This glossary will help you select the appropriate word for your college and business writing. The recommendations here are based on usage listed in current dictionaries. For clarity, misspellings and other unaccepted variations are listed after the standard word.

**a, an**  Use *a* before words starting with a consonant sound. Use *an* before words starting with a vowel sound.

- a bristlecone pine, a history, a quail, a sinkhole
- an aardvark, an egg, an infant, an honourable man

**accept, except**  *Accept* means "to believe," "to approve," or "to take" (as take an offered gift). *Except* means "without" or "excluding."

- Can he *accept* constructive criticism?
- All the children *except* Jane are here.

**access, excess**  The noun *access* is the "ability or right to enter, to use, or to approach." The verb *access* is used in a technological sense, as "to locate data." *Excess* means "too much" or "exceeding that which is normal and sufficient."

- It is impossible to gain direct *access* to the freeway from here.
- Lucinda can *access* those files easily.
- She stored the *excess* bread dough in the refrigerator.

**adapt, adept, adopt**  *Adapt* means "to make suitable for a specific situation." *Adept* means "very skilled; proficient." *Adopt* means "to take up and use as one's own," as an idea, word, or the like. *Adopt* also refers to the process of child adoption.

- Do you think you can *adapt* the part to make it fit?
- Jeff is *adept* at programming.
- When customers complain, Sarah *adopts* the tactic of "A soft answer turneth away wrath."

**adverse, averse**  *Adverse* means "harmful or unfavourable." *Averse* means "unwilling" or "disinclined."

- William has surmounted *adverse* circumstances before.
- Mike is *averse* to risk taking.

**advice, advise**  *Advice* is a noun that means "a view, opinion, or judgment." *Advise* is a verb that means "to counsel," "to inform" or "to recommend."

- His *advice* was to look for another job.
- I really don't know what to *advise*.

**affect, effect**  *Affect* is a verb meaning "to change or to influence." *Effect* is usually used as a noun to mean "result." As a verb *effect* means "to make" or "to implement."

- How will that *affect* your decision?
- What will be the *effect* of that decision?
- Can you *effect* an improvement in that procedure?

**all ready, already**  *Already* refers to time, meaning "previously." *All ready* means "prepared" or "available for action."

- Did you *already* clock out?
- Are you *all ready* to leave?

**all right**  *All right* means "satisfactory" or "proper." *Alright* is a common misspelling.

- It is *all right* to go in the kitchen; the floor is dry.

**all together, altogether**  *All together* means "in a group." *Altogether* means "completely."

- The birds huddled *all together* to keep warm.
- Joe's answer was not *altogether* right.

**allusion, delusion, illusion** An *allusion* is "a reference" (often to a literary work). A *delusion* is a "mistaken idea." An *illusion* is "an erroneous perception of reality."

- He made an *allusion* to Hamlet.
- He suffers from the *delusion* that he is immortal.
- The ghost was an *illusion*, created with special lighting.

**allot, a lot** *Allot* means "to parcel out" or "to give a certain portion." *A lot*, used to mean "a large extent, amount, or number," is informal. *Alot* is a common misspelling.

- The government *allots* only one per family.
- He has *a lot* of confidence.
- Jill's grandmother is *a lot* better.

**among, between** Use *among* when referring to three or more units or people. Use *between* when referring to only two.

- Let's keep this secret *among* our family members.
- *Between* you and me, I like his beard.

**amount, number** *Amount* refers to a quantity or weight. *Number* refers to a numeral, unit, or indefinite quantity of items or individuals.

- The recipe called for a small *amount* of black pepper.
- The crowd *numbers* in the thousands.

**an, a** See *a, an.*

**any, any other** *Any* means "one, some, every, or all." *Any other* is used in a comparison. Do not substitute *any* (by itself), which in the following example would mean that Brian was faster than himself.

- Brian was faster than *any other* runner in his age group.
- You may select *any* of the top prizes.

**anyone, any one** *Anyone* is a pronoun that means "any person" or in some instances, "everyone." *Any one* means "whichever one (just one) of a group." *Any one* can refer to a person or a thing.

- *Anyone* may come, not just members.
- *Any one* of the band members can carry the flag.

**appraise, apprise** *Appraise* means "to evaluate or estimate the value." *Apprise* means "to give notice to or inform."

- Will you *appraise* this emerald ring for me?
- Did you *apprise* the prisoner of his rights?

**assure, ensure, insure** *Assure* means "to inform positively." *Ensure* means "to make sure or certain." *Insure* means "to cover with insurance." *Insure* also means "to make certain, especially by taking precautions."

- I *assure* you that every precaution will be taken.
- Checking the map beforehand will *ensure* that you find the right road.
- Did you *insure* the contents of your house?

**averse** See *adverse, averse.*

**awhile, a while** *Awhile* is an adverb that means "a short time." *A while*, which consists of an article and a noun, means "a period of time." (The preposition *for* may be used with *a while.*)

- He stopped *awhile* to rest. (not *for awhile*)
- Don't rush off—stay for *a while*.

**beside, besides** *Beside* means "next to." *Besides* means "also."

- The scissors are lying *beside* my sewing basket.
- *Besides* my fishing equipment, I'm taking a picnic lunch.

**between** See *among, between.*

**breath, breathe** *Breath* is a noun; *breathe* is a verb. Both refer to inhalation and exhalation.

- The speech instructor advised taking a deep *breath* before starting to speak.
- *Breathe* deeply as you work out.

**capital, capitol** *Capital* refers to the "official place or city of government" or an "amount of money." *Capitol* refers to the "building that houses the official government offices."

- Whitehorse is the *capital* of Yukon Territory.
- We need more *capital* to fund the project.
- Sue visited the *capitol* building during her trip to the state *capital*.

**censor, censure** *Censor* is "to examine books, films, or other materials to remove or suppress what is considered objectionable." *Censure* is "to criticize severely or blame."

- The school board plans to *censor* books purchased for the school.
- The editorial *censured* a city council member for his failure to attend meetings regularly.

**cite, sight, site** *Cite* means "to quote." *Sight* refers to the ability to see or view. *Site* refers to location, as a building site.

- Can you *cite* his exact words?
- Can you *sight* Venus above the evening horizon?
- They selected a lovely wooded *site* for their new home.

**complement, compliment** *Complement* means "to complete or bring to perfection." *Compliment* means "to express praise."

- That floral arrangement *complements* your table setting.
- Brad *complimented* Cindy on her new shoes.

**conscience, conscious** *Conscience* is "the awareness of a moral or ethical aspect of one's conduct" and the desire "to prefer right over wrong." *Conscious* refers to "awareness of one's environment and existence."

- Jeannette returned the wallet to its owner to relieve her *conscience*.
- Is the patient *conscious* yet?

**continual, continuous** *Continual* means "recurring regularly or often." *Continuous* means "uninterrupted."

- Uncle Jake's *continual* complaining made our visit unpleasant.
- The flow of fresh air throughout the building is *continuous*.

**council, counsel** *Council* refers to a group of people who are delegated "to serve in an administrative, legislative, or advisory capacity." *Counsel*, as noun or verb, refers to advice.

- Anthony is a member of the town *council*.
- The admissions office *counsels* students.
- Lawyers charge for their *counsel*.

**criteria, criterion** A *criterion* is a "standard, rule, or test upon which a judgment or decision can be based." *Criteria* is the plural of *criterion*.

- She gave only one *criterion* for the job: a strong back.
- He stated six *criteria* for the upcoming performance evaluation.

**delusion** See *allusion, delusion, illusion.*

**effect, affect** See *affect, effect.*

**emigrate, immigrate** When people *emigrate*, they leave their homeland to reside elsewhere. When they *immigrate*, they enter a different country to reside.

- My paternal ancestors, five brothers, *emigrated* from Wales in the late 1700s.
- They *immigrated* to the United States and travelled to the territory that later became Ohio.

**eminent, imminent** *Eminent* means "of high rank, station, or quality." *Imminent* means "about to occur, impending."

- Today is the birthday of that *eminent* inventor Thomas A. Edison.
- Skating on thin ice poses an *imminent* danger.

**enthusiastic** *Enthusiastic*, meaning to have great excitement or interest, is standard usage. Enthused is used only colloquially.

- Cody was *enthusiastic* about traveling to the Rocky Mountains.

**except** See *accept, except.*

**excess** See *access, excess.*

**explicit, implicit** *Explicit* means fully and clearly expressed; leaving nothing implied." *Implicit* means "implied or understood though not directly expressed."
- The doctor's directions were *explicit:* "Take one tablet with a full glass of water after meals."
- The company president has *implicit* trust in Sheila's judgment.

**farther, further** *Farther* refers to "physical distance" and *further* to a nonphysical dimension such as distance in time.
- We drove *farther* than usual the second day of our trip.
- If we go *further* back a few generations, we find other family members who also suffered from breast cancer.

**fewer, less** *Fewer* is used in comparisons to refer to "individual units, things that can be counted." *Less* is used in comparisons to mean a smaller amount or "a mass of measurable extent."
- *Fewer* people attended the state fair this year than last year.
- Opals cost much *less* than diamonds of the same size.

**flaunt, flout** *Flaunt* means "to parade or display ostentatiously." *Flout* means "to show contempt for" or "to scorn."
- Lorrie *flaunted* her new engagement ring.
- Timothy *flouted* the dress code.

**further** See *farther, further.*

**get** *Get* means "to receive" or "to bring." Avoid the many colloquial uses of *get* in college and business writing. (See a dictionary for other examples of colloquial usage.)
- Standard: Will you *get* a bag of milk when you go out?

- Colloquial: I hope the frost doesn't *get* our garden.
- Colloquial: That really *gets* to me!

**good, well** *Good* is an adjective meaning "positive or desirable." *Well* is often used as an adverb to mean "satisfactorily or sufficiently" or "skilfully or proficiently." *Well* is also used as an adjective to mean "a satisfactory condition; right or proper."
- Jerry received *good* news this morning.
- Jeremy did *well* on his calculus exam.
- Henry is *well;* he has completely recovered from pneumonia.
- The project is going *well.*

**hanged, hung** People are *hanged.* Objects are *hung.*
- The convicted murderer was *hanged.*
- Derek *hung* the painting over the fireplace.

**idea, ideal** An *idea* is "a thought." An *ideal* is "a principle" or "a conception or model of something in its absolute perfection."
- Suddenly he had a delightful *idea.*
- Her *ideal* husband would be a wonderful father.
- Always be true to your *ideals.*

**illusion** See *allusion, delusion, illusion.*

**implicit** See *explicit, implicit.*

**its, it's** *Its* is the possessive form of *it. It's* is a contraction of *it is.*
- The dog has lost *its* collar.
- *It's* over 100 km to the next town.

**leave, let** *Leave* means "to go out or away from." *Let* means "to permit or allow."
- Will you *leave* Jiffy at the kennel when you go to the lake?
- Please *let* me help you with those packages.

**less** See *fewer, less.*

**let** See *leave, let.*

**loose, lose** *Lose* is a verb meaning "to mislay." *Loose* is an adjective meaning "not tight" or "unconfined."
- Did you *lose* an earring?
- My watchband is too *loose*.
- An orangutan was *loose* in the park.

**medium, media** *Medium* is (1) an "intermediate course," the midpoint between two extremes; (2) a way that something is "transmitted or carried"; (3) "an agency by which something is accomplished or conveyed or transferred." *Media* is the plural of *medium* and takes a plural verb.
- The Internet is a *medium* that relays daily stock market reports.
- The *media* frequently refer to the escapades of the royal family.

**moral, morale** *Moral* is an adjective that refers to "judgment of the goodness or badness of human action and character." *Morale* is a noun that means "the state of the spirits of a person or group."
- The *moral* code of society seems to be changing.
- Employee *morale* is high at XYZ Company.

**number** See *amount, number.*

**passed, past** *Passed* is a verb that means "having moved on; proceeded." *Past* as an adverb means "beyond" and as a noun or adjective refers to time that is over. Do not write "*past* history" because all history is past.
- Jerry *passed* the bakery without stopping.
- Jerry drove *past* the bakery without stopping.
- Let's forget the *past* and look to the future.

**patience, patients** *Patience* is the ability to "bear pain, provocation, or annoyance with calmness." *Patients* refers to people who "receive medical attention, care, or treatment."

- *Patience* is a quality that is learned.
- The physician saw thirty-seven *patients* yesterday.

**personal, personnel** *Personal* refers to the private matters of an individual. *Personnel* refers to a group of people who work for an organization. (Note that *personnel* has two *n*'s.)
- Please don't ask *personal* questions.
- Their *personnel* are very courteous.

**precede, proceed** *Precede* means "to go before." *Proceed* means "to go" or "to continue."
- The semifinal matches *precede* the final match.
- Let's *proceed* with the meeting.

**principal, principle** (see "Association Aids to Improve Spelling," page H-34.)

**quiet, quite** *Quiet* means "free of noise." *Quite* means "very; entirely."
- Our dorm is rarely *quiet*.
- Your homemade apple pie is *quite* tasty.
- It is *quite* all right to park there.

**quotation, quote** *Quote* is a verb that means "to repeat or copy the words of (another)," usually citing the source. *Quotation* is a noun meaning "the act of quoting" or "a passage quoted."
- Do you plan to *quote* Nelson Mandela in your speech?
- A *quotation* from Winston Churchill might make an effective introduction.

**real, really** *Real* is an adjective meaning "genuine or authentic," "free of pretense or falsehood." (Avoid using *real* to mean "very.") *Really* is an adverb meaning "truly; genuinely."
- Her diamond is *real*.
- *Really*, I can't go with you.

**regardless** *Regardless* means "in spite of everything; anyway." Irregardless is redundant and nonstandard.
- Many people neglect to buckle their seat belts, *regardless* of the danger.

**sight**  See *cite, sight, site.*

**sometime, some time, sometimes** *Sometime* means "an indefinite or unstated time." *Some time* refers to an amount of time. *Sometimes* means "occasionally."

- Stop in *sometime*.
- I haven't seen him for *some time*.
- *Sometimes* I feed the elephants at the city zoo.

**stationary, stationery** *Stationary* means "not moving" or "not capable of being moved." *Stationery* refers to writing materials.

- The tables in that restaurant are *stationary*.
- Would you like some monogrammed *stationery* for Christmas?

**than, then** *Than* is a conjunction indicating a comparison. *Then* is an adverb indicating time.

- Harrison likes pistachio ice cream better *than* chocolate.
- I will meet you *then*.

**their, there, they're** *Their* is the possessive form of *they*. *There* is an adverb that refers to place. (*There* can also be used in several other ways.) *They're* is a contraction of *they are*.

- *Their* cars are parked on the street.
- Do you see that ten-dollar bill lying *there* in the grass?
- *They're* the third couple from the left.

**to, too, two** *To* is a preposition meaning "toward," "in contact with," "in front of," or "constituting"; or it can be the sign of an infinitive. *Too* means "also" or "more than enough." *Two* is the whole number following *one*; a couple.

- I walked *to* the town square.
- *To* ensure you arrive safely, check the cable that is towing your glider.
- May I go, *too*?
- *Two* robins built a nest.

**try to** *Try to* means "to attempt." Try and is not generally accepted usage.

- *Try to* pull up the cap of the bottle after the arrows meet.

**two**  See *to, too, two.*

**which, who** Use *which* when referring to an object or an animal. Use *who* when referring to a person. (For more information about usage, see section 4c. on pronouns.)

- The black horse, *which* is near the barn, belongs to Stanley.
- *Who* did you say is calling?

**who, whom** *Who* is in the subjective case, *whom* in the objective case.

- These are the men *who* you thought were responsible. [*who* were responsible]
- These are the men *whom* you chose for the job. [you chose *whom*]

**who's, whose** *Who's* is a contraction of *who is* or *who has*. *Whose* is the possessive form of *who*.

- *Who's* the best candidate for the position?
- *Whose* dalmatian is that?

**your, you're** *Your* is the possessive form of *you*. *You're* is the contraction of *you are*.

- Will you take *your* car?
- *You're* the winner of a trip to Tahiti.

# Credits

# Author-Title Index

Student writers and works are indicated by an asterisk.

# Subject Index